Winged Shield, Winged Sword

A History
of the
United States
Air Force

Winged Shield, Winged Sword

A History
of the
United States
Air Force

Volume I
1907–1950

Bernard C. Nalty
General Editor

Air Force History and Museums Program
United States Air Force
Washington, D.C. 1997

Foreword

The History of the United States Air Force is more than a tribute to the men and women responsible for the advancement of military aviation. Individual heroes do emerge, air battles are recounted, and record-setting flights described, but the book also deals with the ideas and decisions that have made the U.S. Air Force the professional military organization it is. Activity in the lecture hall and on the flight line, in the corridors of government and in aeronautical research facilities, and in both peacetime and during wars have helped shape the institution, influence its conduct, and fix its goals.

The Air Force continues to serve the country effectively and efficiently because its men and women understand that experience provides the foundation for progress. More than any other military organization, the U.S. Air Force searches out and listens to the experience history offers. Few problems arise from a void or occur without precedent; and while every challenge possesses its unique aspects, the perspective of time and the careful consideration of what already has succeeded or failed inevitably improves the effectiveness of today's decisions and the quality of planning for the future.

History is therefore important to the Air Force; the recorded past is a foundation for doctrine, policy, strategy, tactics, equipment development, organization, force structure, and virtually every other element of air power. This volume, published in commemoration of the fiftieth anniversary of the Air Force as an independent service, is especially valuable. Not only should it both inspire and enlighten the members of the Air Force, it should also serve as a convenient source of information for those outside the service who are interested in the origin, growth, evolution and application of American air power.

RICHARD P. HALLION
Air Force Historian

Preface

Throughout its first century, military aviation helped advance the interests of the United States. From a curiosity, fragile and of uncertain value, the warplane has become a devastating weapon. Moreover, ballistic missiles and surveillance satellites have joined aircraft in this aerial array. In these volumes, we try to describe and analyze, in the context of national policy and international rivalries, the evolution of land-based air power since the United States Army in 1907 established an Aeronautical Division responsible to the Chief Signal Officer. This work, in addition to commemorating the Air Force's fiftieth anniversary, also commemorates almost one hundred years of progress in the design and use of aerial weaponry. By placing airmen and their machines in an appropriate context, it provides a clearer understanding of the central role of the Air Force in current American defense policy.

Early in the conceptualization of this work, we decided that a collaborative effort would make the best use of whatever special skills or knowledge each of us might possess. We knew, however, that successful collaboration requires a plan, and the blueprint was the work of Warren A. Trest, then the chief of the Histories Division, Office of Air Force History. He devised a basic outline for the book, and after his transfer elsewhere in the Air Force history program, Bernard C. Nalty saw the design through to its completion. Under the general guidance of these two, we wrote, reviewed, and revised each chapter. A panel of historians and military officers reviewed the manuscript, which then underwent the final revisions that these distinguished individuals suggested.

The history is divided into two volumes. Volume I, containing the first 12 chapters, begins with balloons and the earliest heavier-than-air machines. It carries the story through World War II to the establishment of the United States Air Force as a service separate from, but equal to, the Army and the Navy. Volume II picks up the narrative at the Korean War, takes it through the War in Southeast Asia, the Gulf War, to the drawdown following the end of the Cold War.

A number of men and women helped produce the volume. Capt. Susan Cober, USAF, and her successor as office librarian, Capt. Lucinda M. Hackman, USAF, obtained needed books from libraries throughout the Washington area. RitaVictoria Gomez provided information on the role of women in military aviation, and Eduard M. Mark shared the results of his research on aerial interdiction during World War II, the Korean conflict, and the Vietnam War. The late Marcelle Size Knaack made available the information she had collected for her research on Air Force transport aircraft. Paul Stillwell of the United States Naval Institute generously gave access to certain oral histories done for his organization. The Air Force command historians, present and former, who commented on drafts of the chapters were Gerald T. Cantwell, Herbert P. Carlin, John H. Cloe, Charles J. Gross, Bob W. Rush, David W. Shircliffe, Robert J. Smith, Thomas S. Snyder, and Bernard J. Termena. The typists, word processing specialists, and computer operators who struggled with the seemingly endless succession of drafts and disks included Elaine Ahearn, Fontella D. Worthington, SSgt. John Wyche, Sgt. James A. Branham, Sgt. Glenn B. Reynolds, SrA. Rosalyn L. Culbertson, Amn. Terry R. Nance, and Debra A. Moss.

Contents

Part I: The Early and Interwar Years, 1907–1939

Part II: World War II, 1939–1945

Part III: Building the Air Force, 1945–1950

History of the United States Air Force

Part I

The Early and Interwar Years, 1907-1939

Chapter 1

The Roots of U.S. Military Aviation

Alfred F. Hurley
William C. Heimdahl

When military aviation had its first stirrings in the United States, the balloon was the only practical tool of military aviation. In 1783, after helping negotiate the Treaty of Paris that brought the American War for Independence to a successful conclusion, Benjamin Franklin had observed the hydrogen or hot air balloons that frequently ascended from the French city and predicted that invading armies would someday use such craft to cross enemy-dominated seas. Later, other American visionaries urged unsuccessfully that balloons be sent aloft at night so that observers could locate Indian campfires during campaigns against the Seminole tribes of Florida in the 1830s and 1840s and that balloons be employed to bomb the fortifications of Vera Cruz in 1847 during the war with Mexico. Although the United States failed to act, two European nations attempted practical use of the balloon in war. France employed observation balloons at Maubeuge near the border with Belgium in 1794, and in 1849 Austrian forces tried unsuccessfully to attack Venice with unmanned balloons loaded with explosives.

Not until the Civil War, however, did a suitable combination of factors come together to introduce military ballooning into the United States. The struggle

3

was so titanic and the stakes so high—nothing less than survival as a nation—that both the federal government and the rebellious Confederate States of America eagerly accepted any innovation that might provide an advantage in battle. In addition, a cadre of civilian balloonists, whether mere enthusiasts or professionals paid to make ascents before excited crowds, stood ready to offer their services to the rival governments.

The most experienced of the balloonists remained loyal to the United States. As a result, the Confederacy was able to construct just three balloons that were used for reconnaissance principally in defense of Richmond, Virginia, and Charleston, South Carolina. The first was made of cotton and kept aloft by the heat of pine knots burned by the aeronaut in a furnace within the basket. The other two were inflated with gas and made of varicolored silk. A legend arose that belles of the Confederacy had donated silk dresses to fashion the envelopes; in fact, the builders had purchased bolts of that scarce material intended for sale to dressmakers. The result was a pair of gaudy balloons that seemed more appropriate for a carnival than for a war.

Because of their fame and long experience, the two most prominent aeronauts in the North, John La Mountain and Thaddeus S. C. Lowe, became bitter rivals for an appointment as chief of the Union Army's balloon corps. Lowe prevailed, taking charge of the organization's eight aeronauts and seven balloons, but he was denied the military rank that he thought should go with the office. Indeed, all the balloonists who served the Union cause remained civilians paid by the day, and their influence depended on the receptiveness of the general to whom they were attached. Despite their anomalous status, the aeronauts proved they could gather important information when the battle lines were stable or changing slowly.

The first Union general to employ a balloonist for systematic reconnaissance was Benjamin F. Butler of Massachusetts, before the war an investor and politician but now exercising an independent command in Virginia, who relied on John La Mountain to help maintain surveillance over the approaches to Fortress Monroe, which served as Butler's headquarters. When Butler left for another assignment, his successor saw no need for balloons. La Mountain therefore took his equipment to Washington and conducted reconnaissance of the Confederate positions in nearby northern Virginia.

During an unsuccessful advance on Richmond in 1862, Lowe and his assistants stirred the enthusiasm of Generals George B. McClellan and Fitz-John Porter, so much so that Porter ascended for a personal look at rebel dispositions near Yorktown, Virginia, a flight that almost resulted in his capture. On that occasion, with the general alone in the basket, the tether broke, and Porter drifted over Confederate lines until he chanced on winds that carried him to safety. Another officer who ventured aloft, though he insisted on the company of a trained aeronaut, was a future general, George Armstrong Custer, then a lieutenant of cavalry.

Civil War balloon filling from hydrogen-generating equipment on left.

Despite its popularity with some commanders, the balloon had grave disadvantages. When ascending or descending, it attracted hostile fire, and it required horses and road-bound wagons for transport, gas generators in which sulfuric acid was poured over iron filings to produce hydrogen, ropes for tethering, and trained men for operation and maintenance. The cost of operation and the likelihood of arousing the wrath of enemy gunners could have been endured, but the lack of mobility proved an insurmountable handicap when the conflict became a war of movement. Because the balloon corps dealt with the transmittal of information, along with intelligence and map making, it was transferred in the summer of 1863 to the signal officer of the Army of the Potomac, Col. Albert J. Myer. Although the aeronauts had concentrated on observation, the code they devised for transmitting the information they gathered was cumbersome and not especially useful, a failing that caught the attention of an officer who specialized in communication. No wonder that Myer, who would become Chief Signal Officer of the postwar Army, decided to disband the balloon organization, after about two years of service, on the grounds that, as the war became more mobile, aerial reconnaissance could produce little useful intelligence and would cost more than it was worth.

After the war, the Signal Corps remained in contact with several balloonists, prevailing on them to record meteorological observations during their ascents, for at the time the Corps operated the nation's weather service. Merely accepting a record of wind currents and temperatures from civilian aeronauts or sending a soldier along as a passenger to record the data did not satisfy the new Chief Signal Officer, Adolphus W. Greely, who took over the corps in 1887. A friend of many of the leading scientists of the day, he was convinced that aeronautics had a place in the Signal Corps. His goal was to convert the balloon into a dependable vehicle for gathering and transmitting battlefield intelligence by combining it with the telegraph to ensure the rapid transmission of information from the fighting front to a headquarters some miles in the rear. General Greely's efforts resulted in the purchase of a balloon manufactured in Paris and ironically christened *General Myer* after the officer who, while a colonel, had disbanded the aeronautical unit during the Civil War.

The officer who had purchased the *General Myer*, 1st Lt. William A. Glassford, recruited Sgt. Ivy Baldwin to care for the craft. Born William Ivy, the sergeant had been a circus aerialist when he met "Captain" Thomas S. Baldwin, who ran a show that featured balloon ascensions and parachute jumps. Advancing from the ranks of the parachutists and trapeze performers, Ivy learned the art of ballooning from his employer, whom he so admired that he changed his name to Ivy Baldwin. The sergeant took charge of the *General Myer* in 1894, two years after it entered service, trained ground crews, and supervised maintenance, but not even his skill could prevent deterioration of the balloon, which had to be stored in an improvised shed at Camp Logan, Colorado. In 1896 the envelope burst while being inflated at the Colorado installation.

Since funds were not available for a new balloon, Glassford purchased silk, from which Sergeant Baldwin and his wife fashioned a new envelope. The replacement was ready when the United States and Spain went to war in 1898. As a result, the expedition dispatched to liberate Cuba, a Spanish colony, included the handmade observation balloon, for the occasion christened the *Santiago*. The vehicle, which bobbed about on its tether above the troops advancing on the defenses of Santiago de Cuba, proved better at attracting than directing fire. Before shell fragments punctured the envelope and the balloon settled to earth, it had served as a handy point of reference for Spanish gunners aiming at the American column on the road below. The casualties suffered by American troops in the vicinity of the *Santiago* obscured the fact that it had produced useful intelligence on the local road network during the time that Sergeant Baldwin and his men managed to keep it aloft. The craft had been valuable enough to inspire the Signal Corps to retain its aeronautical component, which by December 1899 totaled four spherical balloons and one sausage-shaped kite balloon. Despite this expansion of the program, Ivy Baldwin would soon decide against reenlisting and briefly revive his high-wire act before returning to an aeronautical career.

Meanwhile, spurred by work like that of the British pioneer Sir George Cayley, interest was growing in the development of a heavier-than-air flying machine sturdier than the balloon and not subject to the vagaries of the wind. By 1896, not yet fifty years after Cayley's experiments in gliding, one of General

Greely's friends, Samuel P. Langley, the Secretary of the Smithsonian Institution, seemed on the verge of perfecting just such an invention. Progress toward this goal had been rapid during the last half of the nineteenth century, as Cayley and others converted the ancient kite into the wing and planned to use the windmill as the model for a propeller to drive the craft through the sky. Designs for airplanes appeared in some profusion during the period. As many as three steam-driven prototypes lunged briefly into the air, either rising directly from the ground or employing an inclined ramp, but none was capable of sustained or controlled flight. The various inventors lacked a lightweight powerplant, and until one became available, the glider remained the best vehicle for their experiments. Langley, however, seemed likely to obtain such an engine, bringing the objective of sustained and controlled flight within his reach.

As the ascent of a hydrogen-filled balloon had moved Benjamin Franklin to think in terms of military tactics, the sight of a steam-powered model of Langley's invention inspired Alexander Graham Bell, the inventor of the telephone and a friend of both Greely and Langley, to predict that the new device would make armies "an impertinence" and "our $4,000,000 battleships so much junk." The Spanish-American War had begun before Secretary of War Russell A. Alger accepted the favorable report of an investigating committee, which included Bell, and arranged a $50,000 grant in return for rights to Langley's so-called *Aerodrome*.

To the embarrassment of the War Department, the investment failed to produce a workable flying machine. In October 1903, during an experiment on the Potomac River near Washington, D.C., the full-scale *Aerodrome* became entangled in the launching mechanism on board a houseboat and toppled into the water. A second attempt at powered flight, on December 8 of that year, saw the *Aerodrome* begin breaking up as it left the catapult, and it again crashed into the river.

On December 17, 1903, just nine days after the second crash of the *Aerodrome*, Orville and Wilbur Wright made four successful flights in a biplane powered by a gasoline engine. The scene of their triumph was Kill Devil Hill, near the village of Kitty Hawk on the outer banks of North Carolina. Over the previous four years, they had built a series of experimental gliders, developed a method of control, and finally perfected the lightweight engine needed to power the Wright Flyer. Their work was based on whatever theoretical data they could obtain from current literature, including reports issued by the Smithsonian Institution. Of great value were the ideas of Octave Chanute, an American aeronautical experimenter. Since 1875, Chanute had been gathering and circulating data concerning flight, information that he incorporated in the gliders he designed and built during the 1890s.

Langley's failure, exposed as it was to public view, stirred the press to criticize and even ridicule both the inventor and the War Department that sponsored him. In contrast, the success of the Wright brothers on the isolated outer banks

Langley's *Aerodrome* breaking up as it leaves the houseboat catapult.

of North Carolina passed almost unnoticed in the newspapers, a result of the remote location, the reticence of the two men, and the fact that the collapse of the
Aerodrome had conditioned the press to expect failure. Stung by the treatment
of Langley's efforts in the newspapers, the War Department was reluctant to approach the Wrights, fearing yet another failure after the two crashes of
Langley's machine. Finally, the Wright brothers decided to market the invention
themselves. In 1905, after concluding that, except for wealthy sportsmen, the
Army would be the only major user of their airplane, they tried to persuade the
War Department to buy it. Despite help from their congressman, they could not
gain the endorsement of the Board of Ordnance and Fortification, the agency
that evaluated new weapons for the Army. To be fair, difficulties existed on both
sides. The Wrights were apprehensive about revealing their secrets before they
had obtained patents, which were granted in 1906. Indeed the Wright brothers
were so secretive about their achievement that the board may never have realized that the two men had flown repeatedly in perfecting their airplane during
1904 and 1905. Unaware of the true measure of their accomplishment, the board
kept reminding the brothers of its policy, adopted after the failure of the Langley
Aerodrome, to invest only in a proven machine.

   While the two inventors and the War Department tried in vain to reach an understanding, Europeans were demonstrating a renewed interest in lighter-than-
air craft. In the hands of Count Ferdinand von Zeppelin, the dirigible had be-

come a practical aerial vehicle, and his success inspired imitators elsewhere. In 1904 Thomas Baldwin, who had inspired William Ivy to become Ivy Baldwin and had advised the Signal Corps on many balloon projects, introduced the first practical dirigible into the United States with his *California Arrow*, which had a rigid keel slung beneath an envelope with a volume of 6,000 cubic feet. The keel accommodated two crewmen, one of whom manipulated the control surfaces while the other tended an engine built by Glenn Curtiss, who was in the process of abandoning motorcycle racing for a career in aviation.

At this time of rapid advances in aeronautics, the Signal Corps lost its most persistent advocate of experimentation with aerial flight when Adolphus Greely retired after nineteen years as Chief Signal Officer. Offsetting this loss was the organization, only a few months before his retirement, of the Aero Club of America, made up of industrialists, businessmen, and sportsmen interested in promoting aviation. In quest of its stated objective, "the promotion and development of the science of aerial navigation," the club functioned as the American representative of the *Federation Aeronautique Internationale*, which licensed balloon pilots and (as it does today) certified records for such things as distance and altitude. Under its sponsorship, balloon racing gained popularity as a new sport in which the Army actively participated.

Among the pilots who represented the Aero Club in balloon competition was 1st Lt. Frank Lahm, a 1903 graduate of West Point and a cavalryman. In September 1906, he became the first American to win an international balloon competition when he triumphed in the first James Gordon Bennett race, a distance event that Bennett, the publisher of the New York *Herald*, sponsored and named for himself. Lahm, during an earlier visit to France, had taken up the sport under the instruction of his father and replaced him in the race as one of the representatives of the Aero Club of America. Lahm and his copilot, Henry B. Hersey, flew 400 miles from Paris to the vicinity of Hull in the British Isles. Although ballooning attracted civilian sportsmen, the James Gordon Bennett competition of 1906 had definite military overtones, for officers were pilots or observers on most of the sixteen balloons from the seven participating countries.

The Aero Club also influenced two others in the small group of enthusiasts who promoted aeronautics within the Signal Corps. Maj. Samuel Reber and Capt. Charles deForest Chandler were guests on another Aero Club balloon flight in Massachusetts, a month after Lahm's success. Reber had supervised a Signal Corps balloon during maneuvers in the summer of 1902. Chandler, a volunteer Signal Corps officer during the war with Spain, had written a promotion thesis on methods of generating gas for balloons and, while on leave of absence in 1905, had studied the balloon organization at Farnborough, England, the center for lighter-than-air development in Britain. Reber and Chandler's report to the War Department about their Aero Club of America flight prompted the Signal Corps to order its largest balloon ever, a 76,000-cubic-foot vehicle manufactured in France and intended for training aeronauts.

Brig. Gen. James Allen,
Chief Signal Officer,
August 1907–February 1913.

While Lahm, Reber, and Chandler engaged in active ballooning, Maj. George O. Squier directed the theoretical study of aeronautics at Fort Leavenworth, Kansas, where he commanded the newly relocated Signal School. Squier, an 1887 West Point graduate, was the only Ph.D. in the Army. After completing his doctorate in physics at Johns Hopkins in 1893, he earned an international reputation in the fields of electrical engineering and radio. Through his contacts with the scientific community, he was able to lecture at the school on the performance characteristics of the Wright machine at least a year before the War Department entered into serious negotiations for the purchase of one.

Among Squier's assistant instructors was Capt. William "Billy" Mitchell who joined the Volunteer Signal Corps in 1898 and became a regular officer when the Army expanded in 1901. Mitchell lectured on the uses of the balloon and dirigible in reconnaissance and bombardment. Like Squier, he lacked practical experience, but he had studied aeronautical theory at Fort Myer in the old Signal School and again while preparing for the examination that qualified him for promotion to captain. Years later when he had become one of the proponents of American air power, he would recall that it was General Greely who made him and all his colleagues conscious of aeronautics.

In July 1907, Major Squier went to Washington as executive officer to Brig. Gen. James Allen, Greely's successor as Chief Signal Officer. Squier had barely settled into his new duties when he convinced Allen to put Chandler and two enlisted men into a separate division. On August 1, the new Aeronautical Division took "charge of all matters pertaining to military ballooning, air machines, and all kindred subjects,"[1] thus becoming the progenitor of today's United States Air Force. The creation of this office satisfied, without undue expense, those civilians, many of them members of the Aero Club, who were urging that the War Department become more actively involved in aviation.

As the chief of the new section, Chandler directed the instruction of his expanding group of enlisted men in the techniques of lighter-than-air flight so that they could conduct exercises with the balloon recently purchased in France. Even as the captain drilled his balloon unit, General Allen and Major Squier began noticing the success of dirigibles in Europe, notably the German Zeppelin. This craft, named after the aerial pioneer who had perfected it, consisted of one or more gasbags enclosed within a fabric-covered, lightweight metal frame. Engines powered the vehicle, which could be maneuvered by means of control surfaces at the stern. While Squier pressed military intelligence for the latest information on German airships, General Allen requested Lahm, victor in the 1906 James Gordon Bennett race, to make a study of European dirigibles.

Although the early negotiations with the Wright brothers proved fruitless, the Army remained interested in heavier-than-air flight. Indeed, a recent graduate of the Military Academy, 1st Lt. Thomas E. Selfridge, had obtained permission to participate in the work of the Aerial Experimentation Association, headed by Alexander Graham Bell. The group, which included Glenn Curtiss, conducted its first experiments at Bell's estate in Nova Scotia. Like the Wrights, Bell and his associates combed the existing literature and took a scientific approach to the problem of mechanical flight, with Selfridge participating in the work. Initially, Bell had hoped to proceed from the man-lifting kite to the powered airplane, much as the Wright brothers had advanced by means of the glider. Selfridge earned the honor of piloting a cellular kite towed aloft from the surface of a lake, but the craft, which resembled a huge honeycomb, crashed when the wind suddenly shifted. As a result, Selfridge recommended abandoning manned kites and following the example of the Wrights—start with a glider based on Chanute's research, devise a control system, and finally install an engine. During the early summer of 1908 Selfridge learned to fly two of the series of powered biplanes developed by Bell's group, thus becoming the first Army officer to pilot a heavier-than-air machine.

While Bell and his colleagues were conducting their experiments in Nova Scotia and later at Hammondsport, New York, the Aero Club mounted a campaign to persuade the War Department to invest in the Wright airplane. The president of the organization, the wealthy aviation enthusiast Cortlandt F. Bishop, asked his brother-in-law, Congressman Herbert Parsons, to intercede with the Army on behalf of the Wright brothers. Parsons, a New York Republican, went to President Theodore Roosevelt, who set the acquisition machinery in motion. Negotiations between the Wrights and the Army got under way by mail, with the two brothers holding out for $100,000 from the War Department and behaving as though time were on their side. Their confidence stemmed from a belief, erroneous as Curtiss would demonstrate in 1909 at the controls of his own airplane, that they were five years ahead of any other aircraft designer.

Even as the War Department dickered with the Wright brothers, General Allen and the new Aeronautical Division continued to recommend research into the military uses of the dirigible. As late as 1907, Allen and Chandler were ar-

Baldwin's airship at Ft. Myer, July 1908.

guing that the dirigible, with its greater range and lifting power, could carry out reconnaissance and bombardment better than an airplane; and they persuaded the Army to spend up to $25,000 to purchase one of the new airships. War Department specifications for the craft called for a nonrigid dirigible with a metal or wooden keel, with webbing rather than a lattice framework attaching the keel to the gas bag. The new airship had to carry two persons, fuel, and ballast—a total load of 450 pounds—and attain a speed of 20 miles per hour. The winning bidder was also required to teach two Army men how to fly the dirigible. Since the proposed craft closely resembled the *California Arrow*, Thomas Baldwin submitted an unrealistically low bid of $6,750, for he was willing to lose money on what he hoped would be the first of several sales either to the government or to private citizens.

As confident of their aircraft as Baldwin was of his, the Wright brothers agreed to accept a basic payment of $25,000 if their airplane satisfied the requirements established by the War Department. A successful machine had to carry two persons with a combined weight of 350 pounds and fuel enough to fly 125 miles. The desired speed was 40 miles per hour, with a minimum requirement of at least 36 miles per hour. The builder would incur penalties for each mile-per-hour below 40 and win a bonus for every one above that goal. The desirable characteristics included easy disassembly for transport by wagon and the ability "to ascend in any country which may be encountered in field service."[2] In short, the Army's airplane had to be faster than the dirigible and more easily portable, though it could carry slightly less. In July 1908, before the Wright brothers were ready to demonstrate their airplane, Baldwin delivered a satisfactory dirigible. The veteran balloonist and his engine builder, Glenn Curtiss,

12

formed a crew that met every specification except one, for their speed was a fraction short of the required 20 miles per hour.

During August, Baldwin trained three officers to fly the new dirigible, one more than the contract stipulated. The three pilots—Lahm, Selfridge, and 1st Lt. Benjamin D. Foulois—had different aeronautical experience. Lahm had demonstrated his skill as a balloonist in the James Gordon Bennett race; Selfridge had flown Bell's airplanes, his longest flight lasting ninety seconds and reaching an altitude of seventy-five feet; and Foulois was an infantryman recently detailed to the Signal Corps. He had run away from his job as a steam fitter's and plumber's apprentice to enlist in the Army when the war with Spain began. He received a commission as a result of the Army's expansion of 1901; and in 1906 and 1907 he attended the Signal School, where he encountered the recently instituted course on the theory of military aeronautics. For his graduation thesis he chose to write on "the tactical and strategic value of the aerodynamical flying machine."[3] He came to believe that his assignment to learn to fly the dirigible was a result of his choice of a topic, along with his weight of just 126 pounds in a field where weight was an important consideration.

The group of dirigible pilots—Lahm, Selfridge, and Foulois—began breaking up almost as soon as it was formed. President Roosevelt agreed to send the new airship to St. Joseph, Missouri, where just two of the pilots would stage exhibition flights at a state fair. Foulois supervised the dismantling of the dirigible and with a detachment of enlisted men departed for Missouri, where Selfridge was to join him.

By this time, the Wright machine was ready. Selfridge, who had flown both a dirigible and an airplane, obtained an appointment as an official observer at the tests, which were scheduled for September 1908 at Fort Myer, located across the Potomac River from Washington, D. C., and named for the officer who had disbanded the balloon contingent as the Civil War drew to an end. Only Orville Wright was on hand to demonstrate the airplane, for Wilbur was in France, flying exhibitions with a similar machine. Frank Lahm, a friend of the Wrights, flew first, and Squier, chairman of the acceptance committee, went later. Several test flights lasted close to an hour, and on September 13, Orville and a passenger remained in the air for seventy minutes.

On September 17, since the time was approaching for Selfridge to depart for St. Joseph, the Army lieutenant asked to go aloft before his scheduled turn. When one of the two official Navy observers, Lieutenant George Sweet, gave up his place, Wright agreed. A few minutes into the flight, one of the new propellers installed for that day's flying came loose, struck a wire brace, and threw the machine into a dive from which Orville Wright was only beginning to recover when the airplane hit the ground. Selfridge died that night from head injuries suffered in the crash; thus ended the career of one of the few officers of his time to combine theoretical research with practical experience in designing and flying aircraft. Wright's injuries, although not fatal, hospitalized him for several months. Despite the accident, the impressive performance of the airplane persuaded the War Department to postpone the trials until another Wright aircraft was available.

In June 1909 the Wrights brought an improved aircraft to Fort Myer, spent a month assembling and tuning it, and resumed the flights begun the previous year. Both Lahm, who had replaced Selfridge at the Missouri fair, and Foulois served as observers. On July 27, Orville Wright, with Lahm again as passenger, fulfilled the requirement to stay aloft more than an hour and established a world's record for a flight with a passenger on board. Three days later an excited crowd, which included President William Howard Taft, watched the plane return from a ten-mile cross-country speed trial between Fort Myer and Alexandria, Virginia. Accompanied by Foulois, Orville Wright averaged 42.5 miles per hour, enough to win a bonus of $5,000 above the contract price of $25,000. The Army accepted the Wright airplane on August 2.

Now that it had an airplane, the Signal Corps needed pilots. The agreement for purchase of the airplane required that the Wrights instruct two officers to operate the machine, just as Baldwin had trained crewmen for his dirigible. In October 1909, using an airfield at College Park, Maryland, near the present site of the state university, Wilbur Wright taught Lahm and 2d Lt. Frederic E. Humphreys to fly, the latter a last-minute replacement for Foulois, who received orders to attend an aviation congress in Europe. Lahm and Humphreys completed some three hours of instruction and soloed on October 26; Foulois had time for part of the training but not enough to solo. On November 5, Lahm and Humphreys, seated side by side as pilot and passenger at the forward edge of the lower wing, crashed the Army's only airplane. Neither was hurt, but the Signal Corps lost them both shortly afterward when they returned to their normal assignments. Lahm went back to the cavalry, a victim of the so-called Manchu Law, which restricted line officers to four consecutive years of detached duty. This policy was part of the unsuccessful battle within the Army to prevent the creation of a true general staff, which would have required the long-term services of officers detached from the branches in which they held commissions. Humphreys rejoined the engineers; in 1910 he left the service, but returned to the Army and to aviation during World War I. Foulois, though not fully trained, became the Army's only pilot. His first task after returning to the United States was to repair the damaged Wright machine at College Park; then, in January 1910, the Chief Signal Officer sent him and a few enlisted men to display the airplane at an exposition in Chicago.

Meanwhile, the Army's lighter-than-air program withered away at Fort Omaha, Nebraska, despite General Allen's abiding interest in balloons and dirigibles. Lahm was to some extent responsible for this atrophy, since he had returned from Europe prior to the first test of the Wright military airplane with reports of the difficulties that airmen and ground crews experienced in handling dirigibles in high wind. The innate weakness of the fabric-covered gasbag was an even more serious failing; as if to prove this, the Baldwin dirigible gradually fell apart because of the corrosive effects of weather and hydrogen gas. By 1911, the dirigible's envelope had become so porous that it could lift no more than one individual at a time; the following year the Baldwin airship was condemned and sold at auction. Although dirigible technology continued to improve in Europe, the Signal Corps embarked on no more lighter-than-air projects until the revival of interest in tethered observation balloons just before the United States entered World War I.

With the coming of winter at College Park, the focus of the Army's heavier-than-air activity shifted early in 1910 to Fort Sam Houston, Texas. When Foulois completed his assignment at Chicago, he boarded a train for the Texas post where he and his detachment erected a hangar on the drill ground in the northwestern part of the reservation. The men then overhauled the Wright biplane; and on March 2, 1910, Foulois made the first flight in the state of Texas. He described it as his "first solo, landing, takeoff, and crash."[4] Other flights followed, but wind gusts, an underpowered engine, the awkward landing skids, and his lack of experience produced crashes and extensive repair work. Foulois escaped injury, but to keep the plane flying, he had to spend his own money for spare parts after the funds allotted for that purpose ran out. Using ingenuity rather than cash, he improved the aircraft by salvaging some wheels from a farm cultivator for a tricycle landing gear and obtaining a cinch strap from the saddlery to fashion a safety belt. Also, on advice from the Wright brothers, he removed the two elevator surfaces from the front, moving one to the rear, correcting the airplane's tendency to buck when headed into gusty winds.

As the spartan conditions at Fort Sam Houston and the deterioration of the balloon at Fort Omaha demonstrated, the Signal Corps had neither the money nor the manpower to maintain its aviation program. Congress did provide funds for other military and naval projects; but only those that gave real protection, like a battle fleet, or those, like infantrymen and engineers, that helped maintain order or improve living conditions in the recently acquired Philippines. Flying machines could neither rival the warship as a weapon nor help administer a new American empire. Even in the best of times, therefore, aeronautics occupied a place far down in budgetary priorities, and times were bad. The financial panic of 1907 and resulting depression reduced federal revenues and imperiled many military and naval projects of greater immediate value than Army aviation.

Military aviation in the United States had been blessed by its intimate connection with the creators of the first practical aircraft, the Wright brothers, and its home in a populous, technically ingenious, industrialized and resource-rich country. During its first decade, however, the Army air arm's progress was excruciatingly slow, plagued by miserly funding, an indifferent Army, contentious manufacturers, and no serious threat to national security to spur development. The first direct appropriation for military aviation did not come until 1911. With the economic horizon brightening, James Mann, a congressman from Illinois,

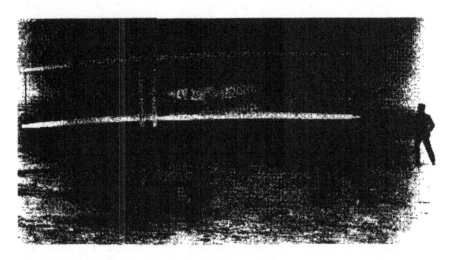

In 1903, the Wright brothers' plane flew at Kitty Hawk (top), but they learned to fly in gliders (right). A 1911 test of a reconfigured aircraft (below), shows wing warping. At the bottom, a Wright aircraft sits on the rail before launch.

The Wright machine moves to the field at Ft. Myer in a cart in 1908 (top left). Lt. Selfridge and Orville wait for takeoff (top right), a flight that ended in disaster (left). In 1909, Orville and Lt. Lahm wait for the launch of the endurance flight (below), and the aircraft banks into a turn during a successful flight (bottom left).

backed by the Smithsonian Institution, the Aero Club, and other components of a rapidly forming aviation lobby, attached a rider to an Army appropriations bill covering the fiscal year beginning in July 1911 that was being hurriedly debated in an end-of-session rush to adjourn. Despite the tendency of Congress to approve legislation with a minimum of change as adjournment nears, his original proposal for $250,000 was cut in half, an indication of both the lowly status of military aviation and the weakness of the aviation lobby.

Meanwhile, Foulois was facing a more practical problem in the spring of 1911—how to make his much modified Wright Flyer, already earmarked to become an exhibit at the Smithsonian, serve as the eyes of the maneuver division, a unit formed by massing in Texas almost the entire Regular Army. This unusual concentration of force, the largest body of troops incorporated in a single command since the War with Spain, was a warning to revolution-torn Mexico that the United States would, if necessary, intervene to protect American lives or property. Although intervention did not prove necessary, Foulois flew some aerial reconnaissance missions, though not in his obsolete airplane, which was in such poor condition that the Signal Corps had to use a newer Wright biplane rented for one dollar from Robert F. Collier, owner of *Collier's Weekly* magazine. During their first surveillance flight, from Eagle Pass to Laredo, Texas, Foulois and Phil Parmalee, a civilian pilot for the Wright company, could detect no sign of hostile activity. On their second mission, the engine was inadvertently cut off, and the airplane glided to a crash landing in the Rio Grande, temporarily depriving the maneuver division of its rented air support.

Although the Wrights sought an interpretation of their patents to humble him, a rival had appeared to challenge their dominance of American aviation. Glenn Curtiss, formerly an associate of Bell, Selfridge, and Thomas Baldwin, was offering strong competition in the construction of aircraft and the training of pilots. In January 1911, before Foulois reported to the maneuver division, Curtiss invited the Army and Navy to enroll students in his new flying school at San Diego, California. He had already worked with the Army, supplying a pilot and airplane in August of the previous year when 2d Lt. Jacob E. Fickel fired a rifle from the air, placing two of four bullets in a three-foot by five-foot target.

When seeking trainees for the new Curtiss school in California, the Adjutant General of the Army established the principle that only volunteers would enter flight training. His instruction to commanders specified that only those who desired such duty would be selected. During 1911 three volunteers learned to fly at San Diego—1st Lt. Paul W. Beck and 2d Lts. John C. Walker, Jr., and George M. Kelly. Before beginning his instruction, Beck had experimented with a bombsight and 1st Lt. Myron Crissy, an artillery officer stationed in California, had developed an aerial bomb that was released by hand; but bomb and bombsight were never used together by Curtiss or his students.

Unlike the Wright machine, in which pilot and student sat side by side, the Curtiss airplane of 1911 had a single seat, which meant that the fledgling pilot

18

Lt. Fickel tests firing a rifle from an aircraft, Sheepshead Bay, August 1910.

had to fly it by himself, learning by the "grass cutting" or "short hop" method. First he learned to operate the controls. Next, with the foot throttle tied back to limit the speed to fifteen miles per hour, too slow to become airborne, the student began taxiing in as straight a line as he could. When he reached the edge of the airfield, he got out of the airplane, picked up the front end, swung it around, and taxied in the opposite direction. The first flight, to an altitude of about ten feet, had to be solo as did all subsequent ones.

After receiving introductory training from the Curtiss instructors at San Diego, Beck, Walker, and Kelly joined the aviation detachment at Fort Sam Houston, which had just received a new Curtiss biplane to replace the Wright machine that Foulois had been flying for more than a year. When a new Wright Flyer arrived shortly afterward, the aviators formed two different sections, each flying only one type of airplane because of the distinctive control techniques involved. The Curtiss had a control wheel to activate the elevator and rudder, as well as a shoulder harness that enabled the pilot to operate the ailerons, which controlled rolling movements, simply by leaning in the desired direction. In contrast, the pilot of a Wright product sat between two levers, one of which controlled the elevator and the other the rudder and a system of cables that warped the wings, increasing camber and lift on the right or left and causing the aircraft to tilt in the opposite direction. (By 1917 the Army had adopted a standard method of control in which the pilot rotated a control stick or a control wheel mounted on a movable column with his hands, thus manipulating both the elevator and ailerons, and used his feet to move a bar that controlled the rudder.)

Lieutenant Beck assumed command of the flying unit; and Foulois, now the most experienced of the airmen, wrote "Provisional Aeroplane Regulations" and "Flying Safety Rules," general guides to help standardize maintenance and flight techniques. Unfortunately, no manual could take all the risk out of flying. On one occasion Walker landed a Curtiss so hard that he refused to fly again. In May 1911, Kelly's machine dived suddenly during a tight turn at low altitude, and he died in the resulting crash. Following Kelly's death, the commander of the maneuver division banned further flying at Fort Sam Houston, and the Provisional Aero Company moved from Texas to the newly reopened aviation school at College Park, Maryland, where Wilbur Wright had instructed Lahm and Humphreys and, briefly, Foulois.

With Captain Chandler serving as commander (and for a second time as head of the Aeronautical Division), the school officially opened on July 3, 1911. Chandler sent two of the prospective pilots, 2d Lts. Thomas DeWitt Milling and Henry H. "Hap" Arnold, to Dayton, Ohio, to learn to fly at the Wright factory, after which they became instructors at College Park. Their first pupils were Chandler and 1st Lt. Roy S. Kirtland, the adjutant of the school and the officer in charge of its construction. Chandler, a veteran balloonist and qualified dirigible pilot, received a brief indoctrination from Arnold and then went to Dayton where, during further training, he demonstrated a maturity and soundness of judgment that impressed the Wright brothers. Although Arnold, set free from the infantry, introduced Chandler to the intricacies of the Wright airplane, Milling was considered the most skillful of the Army's aviators and was the only one of this group to master the differing control systems of the Curtiss and Wright machines. Milling, who enjoyed serving in the cavalry as much as Arnold had detested the infantry, received an invitation from Capt. Arthur S. Cowan to apply for aeronautical training in the Signal Corps. Arnold had impressed Cowan in the jungles of Luzon, and Milling had demonstrated a flair for horsemanship at Fort Leavenworth, Kansas, that, in Cowan's opinion, revealed the kind of reflexes required of a pilot. Impressed by the sight of Lieutenant Lahm flying the Army dirigible and of a Curtiss biplane in action, Milling decided that aviation meant excitement, applied for detail to the Signal Corps, and was accepted.

The students at College Park included 2d Lts. Leighton W. Hazelhurst, Jr., William C. Sherman, and Harry Graham, and Capt. Frederick B. Hennessy. The first National Guardsman to undergo pilot training at College Park (and the second pilot in the National Guard of any state) was Lt. Col. Charles B. Winder, who used the instruction to embark on a career as an exhibition pilot. Beckwith Havens, a member of the Curtiss exhibition team, had enlisted as a private in the

Airfield at College Park, Maryland, with two Wright and two Curtiss aircraft.

New York National Guard before Winder completed his training and edged out Winder as the first aviator in the National Guard. The Signal Corps tried to recruit ten to twenty volunteers from the other branches of the service, but a shortage of officers forced the War Department to set a limit of just ten. Nor were commanders in the other branches at all eager to help, for they could not expect replacements for any of their officers who volunteered for pilot training.

The purpose of the course at College Park was to qualify the pilot trainees for a license issued by the *Federation Aeronautique Internationale*, which set the standards for pilots of heavier-than-air machines as well as for balloonists. As the representative of the Aero Club of America, Chandler administered the test, requiring the candidate to make three different, closed-circuit flights of about three miles at an unspecified altitude. After each flight, the trainee had to stop the engine and glide to a landing within 150 feet of a designated point.

Once airplanes and engines became more dependable, the Signal Corps began demanding greater skill from its pilots than was required by the aviation federation. Eventually, the federation's test became only the first step in a logical progression to the ratings of Junior Military Aviator and Military Aviator. By the fall of 1912, the Signal Corps began to send pilot trainees to factory schools to qualify for the basic license and then to College Park for the additional instruction needed to meet War Department standards. Besides introducing the pilot to the techniques of flight, the factory schools afforded better instruction in the maintenance and repair of engines and airframes than was available at College Park.

As pilot instruction became systematized, so too did maintenance procedures. In 1911, while training at Dayton, Arnold prepared the first set of detailed instructions on how to care for the airplane. In addition, while training at the Wright factory, he and Milling photographed all the components of the Wright airplane, labeling each one to simplify the instruction of mechanics and the stocking and ordering of new parts.

The airmen stationed at College Park believed that the airplane could do more than serve as a vehicle for aerial reconnaissance. With the approval of their superiors in the Signal Corps, they conducted a variety of experiments to define the uses of military aircraft. Foulois, who was assigned to nonflying duty with the Militia Bureau, occasionally appeared at the airfield, for instance, taking part in the test of an airborne radio that could send but not receive Morse code. Riley Scott, a former Army officer, worked briefly on his experimental bomb-sight, with which he could drop an 18-pound missile accurately from an altitude of 400 feet. Since the Air Corps did not want the sight, Scott sold the French an improved model that could attain fair accuracy from 2,000 feet. Isaac W. Lewis evoked considerable interest in his machinegun, which was light and compact enough to be fired from the observer's seat on the lower wing of the Wright bi-plane, but the Army Ordnance Department decided against large-scale procure-ment because it already had a standard machinegun, the Benet-Mercier. Unfortunately, this weapon, fed from the side by a long clip, proved too bulky for use in the airplane, in contrast to the Lewis, which served for years as a stan-dard weapon of British airmen.

The Chief Signal Officer, General Allen, who had retained direct control over the College Park facility, hoped to conduct training there year-round. During the early months of 1912, however, unusually heavy snowfall, followed by flood-ing as the snow melted, put the College Park airport out of action. The general therefore obtained permission from the War Department to move the College Park program in the winter months to a more favorable climate. With the help of

Wireless telegraph installed in a Wright aircraft in 1911.

Riley Scott using his mechanical bombsight to drop bombs from a Wright aircraft, 1911.

the Weather Bureau (which had given assurance of light snows at College Park), Chandler found a strip of countryside extending through South Carolina and Georgia where winds tended to be gentle. He inspected five locations, four in South Carolina, but finally recommended Augusta, Georgia. Despite the careful study of meteorological data, the region experienced winter weather almost as bad as that encountered in Maryland, and operations suffered accordingly in the first season at Augusta. Only the Wright machines and pilots returned to Augusta for one final winter (1912–13); the Curtiss machines and pilots went to San Diego. Volunteers who happened to be stationed in the Philippines and Hawaii that winter also received some instruction, and another detachment briefly conducted training at Palm Beach, Florida.

History of the United States Air Force

Lieutenant Frank Lahm opened a flying school at Fort William McKinley near Manila, on the Philippine island of Luzon, in March 1912. One of his first students was Cpl. Vernon Burge, a mechanic, who became the first enlisted pilot in the Signal Corps. During the next two years, Lahm used Wright airplanes to train several pilots, including 2d Lt. Herbert A. Dargue, destined to become a prominent military aviator in the 1920s and 1930s. The school at Fort Kameha-meha, Hawaii, established in the summer of 1913 under 1st Lt. Harold Geiger, lasted little more than a year because of primitive facilities and tides that played hob with the seaplanes used for training.

While flight training flourished, albeit briefly, in the overseas possessions, the search continued for a site in the United States that was usable throughout the year. The owners of the College Park airfield owners asked $400,000 for their land, far more than Secretary of War Henry L. Stimson was willing to pay. After the owners failed to muster congressional pressure to override the cabi-net officer, the War Department looked elsewhere. Pilots urged the selection of North Island at San Diego, which boasted consistently good weather, could ac-commodate land planes or seaplanes, and was available for the immediate fu-ture at no cost to the government. Unfortunately, the owners of the North Island site refused to sign a long-term agreement with the War Department. Despite the attitude of the owners, the Signal Corps in 1913 designated North Island as its aviation school and abandoned the airport at College Park. In late December, twenty officers were on aviation duty at San Diego, administering or undergo-ing training that included time in the classroom as well as at the controls. Distinguished scientists like Albert F. Zahm of the Smithsonian, William F. Durand of Stanford University, and William J. Humphreys of the United States Weather Bureau helped design the curriculum.

Although flight training absorbed much attention, the Signal Corps and its Aeronautical Division also sought to procure aircraft durable enough to ac-company Army forces in the field. Unfortunately, the principal American air-craft manufacturers of the time—the Wright corporation, Curtiss, and a Wright licensee, the Burgess company—could not provide airplanes with the necessary ruggedness, simplicity, and dependability. When Chandler asked the builders why Europeans were forging ahead in aircraft development, Orville Wright pointed out that the governments of Europe subsidized the construction of ex-perimental prototypes, usually by purchasing the product whether fully satis-factory or not. If Army aviators were to fly airplanes comparable to the most ad-vanced European models, the American government would have to underwrite the inevitable failures that would litter the path to success. The alternative, said the manufacturers, was unthinkable—to do as Squier was now suggesting and allow the Signal Corps to buy aircraft in France.

Congress, however, approved neither the purchase of foreign airplanes (though the Signal Corps was able to buy engines overseas) nor subsidies for ex-perimental types built in the United States. Army aeronautics received only

24

$100,000 for fiscal 1913, $25,000 less than the amount Representative Mann had obtained for the previous fiscal year. In fact, Congressman James Hay of Virginia, a Democrat who served as chairman of the House Military Affairs Committee, tried to hold the new appropriation to $75,000. An important consideration in the congressional debate was the criticism that, six months into fiscal 1912, the Signal Corps had used only a third of its aviation appropriation for that year. Actually, this reluctance to spend served only to demonstrate the difficulty in obtaining suitable airplanes.

Army airmen had definite ideas about the kinds of aircraft they wanted. While still at College Park, the aviators had worked with the Chief Signal Officer, General Allen, on the first set of aircraft specifications issued since the acceptance of the Wright machine in 1909. Because the Signal Corps, beginning in the era of the tethered balloon, had used aircraft for the gathering and dissemination of information, its airplanes would engage primarily in reconnaissance. Allen and his aviators sought two distinct types: a fast, short-range model to locate and report mounted troop movements and a slower aircraft with longer range to obtain information on the enemy when opposing forces neared each other. Since both were to serve with Army forces in the field, they had to be capable of operating even from plowed fields.

The Wright Type C, designed as a "speed scout," proved especially dangerous to fly. At College Park, one crashed, killing both the civilian test pilot, A. L. Welch, who had been Arnold's instructor at Dayton, and Lieutenant Hazelhurst. Arnold barely escaped death at Fort Riley, Kansas, while locating targets for artillery in a Wright scout. On November 5, 1912, from an altitude of 400 feet, the aircraft carrying Arnold and an observer suddenly made a full circle and plunged downward, falling to within 20 feet of the ground before Arnold could regain control. On the day following this brush with death, a thoroughly shaken Arnold wrote Chandler that "my nervous system is in such a condition that I will not get in my machine."[5] So bad was the reputation of this particular aircraft that Milling refused to fly it by himself to Fort Leavenworth, a distance slightly less than a hundred miles. Although he had not seen the incident that almost claimed Arnold's life, Orville Wright believed that the airplane had stalled. As had happened in Kelly's fatal crash, the velocity of the air over the upper surface of the wings had slowed and the current of air had separated from the airfoil, causing a loss of lift and sending the plane plummeting earthward. Arnold realized that he had been lucky indeed. He now weighed his desire to fly against the memory of his terrifying fall and the soaring number of aviation fatalities. Selfridge had died in 1908 and Kelly three years later; in 1912, however, three Army aviators and a civilian instructor were killed. A further complication was the fact that Arnold planned to marry, and aviation was becoming far too dangerous an occupation for a married man. As a result, he gave up flying, served briefly as an aide to Brig. Gen. George P. Scriven, Allen's replacement as Chief Signal Officer, and reported for duty as an infantry offi-

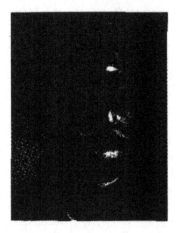

Brig. Gen. George P. Scriven,
Chief Signal Officer,
February 1913–July 1917.

cer in the Philippines. Arnold remained interested in aviation, as indicated by his unsuccessful application to study aeronautical engineering at the Massachusetts Institute of Technology, but not until 1916 did he overcome the memory of his near crash and return to flying.

Arnold was not alone in abandoning flying, for five officers left the cockpit in 1913 out of the fourteen on duty when the year began. More than enough officers chose aviation and completed training to compensate for that year's deaths and transfers, so that the number engaged in flying actually increased to eighteen when 1914 began. Transfers continued, however, and those who left in 1914 included Lewis H. Brereton, prompted by two crashes at North Island. He would return, eventually become a general, and command air units in both world wars. Another future general, Frank M. Andrews, whose career ended in a fatal airplane crash during World War II, postponed his entry into military aeronautics because he planned to marry.

The hazards and uncertainties of aviation made it imperative that the Army compensate for the risks taken by airmen, and to encourage more volunteers Congress considered giving flyers extra pay and accelerated promotion. Although the Army had routinely granted extra pay for overseas service or as a result of temporary promotion for special assignments, flight pay did not become a reality until 1913. That same year Congress tied promotion to proficiency in the air by authorizing qualified aviators to advance to the next higher grade. Flight pay, along with various forms of temporary promotion, would remain a source of controversy until well after World War II.

Congress approved flight pay in 1913, but did not seriously consider a vast expansion of military aviation, a recommendation prepared by the Signal Corps during the previous year in response to a congressional request. The proposal, more a dream than a plan, called for an aviation component consisting of 285 officers, 720 enlisted men, and 120 airplanes divided into 15 squadrons. In terms of manpower, aviation would contain only about one percent of the

Army. The basic aviation unit, the squadron, was to consist of eight airplanes, 19 officers, and 48 enlisted men; to keep pace with the ground forces, each squadron would have trucks for transporting its men and equipment. Three of the squadrons would support a projected field army, one unit being assigned to each of two divisions and the third serving with army headquarters. Four squadrons would help defend American overseas possessions, and the remaining eight were to participate in the coastal defense of the United States. The plan also called for the establishment of five aviation centers across the nation, supplemented by auxiliary centers in each state, to train pilots and mechanics for both the Regular Army and the National Guard. In addition, the aviation centers would provide instruction in meteorology, wireless telegraphy, and the use of small arms and machineguns as aerial armament. Such were the dreams of Army aviators only nine years after the Wright brothers flew for the first time.

Although the Signal Corps emphasized reconnaissance in its response to Congress, the airplane, fragile though it was, had already demonstrated that it could inflict damage on an enemy in addition to gathering information about his movements. On November 1, 1911, an Italian airman, Giulio Gavotti, tossed small spherical bombs, a little bigger than hand grenades, into hostile encampments at Ain Zara and Taguira in Turkish-controlled Libya. The Italian press described the bombing as an "unexpected celestial assault," but the sudden explosions caused more confusion than actual harm.

Neither the air raids in Libya, whatever their potential for the future, nor the detailed study offered by the Signal Corps could inspire Congress to approve a major expansion of military aviation. The military appropriations bill for fiscal 1914, drafted in March 1913, authorized the detailing of up to thirty officers to aviation duty for indefinite periods, fourteen fewer than the Signal Corps wanted. Like most such legislation, the new appropriations act was a patchwork of authorizations, some mutually incompatible, as indicated by the fact that the officer corps could not expand to compensate the other branches for those individuals lost to the Signal Corps and Army aeronautics. Commanders who permitted their officers to enter aviation still could not expect replacements.

Many of the difficulties encountered by Army aeronautics, among them the reliance on officers borrowed from other branches, stemmed from the lack of a clearly defined status and function for aviation within the service. Aviation was becoming a costly military experiment in terms of manpower, materiel, and facilities; and the Signal Corps found it increasingly difficult to support the fledgling air arm while carrying out other assigned duties. At least one flyer, Lieutenant Beck, concluded that military aviation would never make satisfactory progress unless it received independence from the Signal Corps and a manpower authorization fixed by law. Inspired by Beck, Representative Hay introduced a bill that called for removing aviation from the Signal Corps and establishing it as a separate branch of the Army.

History of the United States Air Force

The legislation, proposed in 1913, got nowhere, even though Hay, its chief proponent, was chairman of the House Military Affairs Committee. The War Department was not yet ready for such a step, and Beck was so unpopular among his fellow airmen that anything he championed was likely to arouse their opposition. His subordinates believed he was insensitive to their safety, not deserving of command, and an incompetent pilot. He had, in fact, survived two crashes, a frequency of accidents that was not unusual for the time. Given the technology of the period, not even Beck himself could devise a reasoned doctrine for the employment of an aerial branch, should it achieve parity with the infantry or coast artillery. At most, he hoped for his air service to conduct reconnaissance and the kind of bomb-dropping that Gavotti had done in Libya during the Italo-Turkish War. Ironically, one of those who opposed the separation of aviation from the Signal Corps was Billy Mitchell, who later would campaign for an air arm independent of the Army.

While the bill inspired by Beck and sponsored by Hay failed to pass, Congress nevertheless enhanced the prestige of military aeronautics. A law enacted on July 18, 1914, created within the Signal Corps an Aviation Section, which had greater permanence and stature than the division it replaced, and transferred to it the $250,000 appropriated for military aviation for fiscal year 1915. The new law authorized 60 officers and 260 enlisted men to serve in the section, adding these to the number already approved for the Signal Corps as a whole. Even so, aeronautics accounted for less than 0.4 percent of an Army of 98,544 officers and men. Moreover, most officers would be volunteers from branches other than the Signal Corps, who would serve four years in aviation before returning to their units.

The premature move to break away from the Signal Corps and the creation of the Aviation Section occurred after General Scriven had replaced General Allen as Chief Signal Officer. An 1878 graduate of the Military Academy, Scriven joined the Signal Corps in 1890 and ten years later made his mark as communications officer for the American component of the international force that broke the siege of Peking, China, during the Boxer Rebellion. After taking office early in 1913, he had to begin preparing to deal with a possible crisis closer to home.

Chaos in Mexico had prompted the massing of most of the Army's combat troops in Texas during 1911 to form the maneuver division. The pattern of violence in Mexico and military preparation north of the border persisted into 1913, when Victoriano Huerta seized power. Once again the possibility surfaced of armed intervention in Mexican territory to protect the lives and property of Americans. The Signal Corps sent a detachment of eight pilots and nine airplanes to Texas, and this organization began training at an accelerated pace to serve in the event of war as the eyes of the ground forces that had gathered in the state. Based at Texas City, the provisional First Aero Squadron had just three pilots who were fully qualified; the other five had completed only the first

Wright aircraft at Texas City, Texas, in 1913 as
part of the provisional First Aero Squadron.

phase of their training. As a result, the senior instructor, Lieutenant Milling, ran
the organization on behalf of the nominal commander, Captain Chandler.
Because the tension between the United States and Mexico relaxed, the
squadron did not face the test of combat before moving on to the new base at
North Island, but the pilots spent a great deal of time in the air, especially on
cross-country flights.

Even though engaged only in training, the Army aviators complained loudly
about their old and unsafe craft. The press dramatized the issue of safety, and
when the reports originating in Texas newspapers reached Washington, General
Scriven headed for the Southwest to investigate the grievances firsthand. The
flyers expressed a lack of confidence in Chandler, their commander at Texas
City, whom they blamed for the collection of obsolete aircraft they were flying,
and insisted that they have a greater voice in running the aviation program. Soon
afterward, Chandler left for an assignment in the Philippines; and when he returned, he assumed command of the observation balloon program, rather than
a heavier-than-air organization.

In addition to expressing dissatisfaction with Chandler, many pilots in military aeronautics were growing impatient with the nonpilots commanding them.
A consensus was emerging among the aviators that the commander who flew
rarely or not at all could not understand the structural limits of the airplane, the
importance of maintenance, or the other considerations affecting flight safety.
The selection of Captain Cowan, a nonflyer, to replace Chandler did nothing to
satisfy the objections of the flyers, even though the captain had been instrumental in recruiting early aviators like Arnold and Milling and in nurturing the

29

growth of military aviation. Within a year, Cowan's subordinates in Texas were maneuvering to depose him, allegedly because he played favorites and ignored safety. Actually the root of his departure from the air arm was the mutual misunderstanding between pilots, understandably concerned with safety, and a non-flying manager determined to get the most efficient use from the obsolescent machines entrusted to him.

In April 1914, the Army airmen returned briefly to Texas, again because of a crisis in Mexico, and again they saw no fighting. Mexican officials at Tampico briefly detained some sailors from an American warship and refused to apologize for what the United States government chose to interpret as an outrage, triggering an eight-month American occupation of Vera Cruz, the port of entry for ships carrying armaments destined for Huerta's army. A few naval aviators participated in the Vera Cruz operation, becoming the first American flyers to see combat overseas. The intervention achieved its purpose; Huerta, perceived by the United States government as an obstacle to peace in Mexico, resigned in midsummer. In April 1915, with trouble still brewing in Mexico, an aviation detachment moved by train from San Diego to Brownsville, Texas, to help the ground forces gathered in the area should any Mexican irregulars attack the United States. One of the revolutionaries competing for power in Mexico, Francisco "Pancho" Villa, seemed reckless enough to cross the border and raid towns or ranches to obtain arms, food, and money. Incursions into American territory might also rally behind him those Mexicans who resented the recent occupation of Vera Cruz. On this occasion, Villa did not strike, but in March 1916, he raided Columbus, New Mexico.

The administration of President Woodrow Wilson ordered Brig. Gen. John J. Pershing, Commanding General of the Punitive Expedition, to avenge the March 1916 attack. Pershing pursued Villa into Mexico with a force that included the 1st Aero Squadron, no longer a provisional unit, which was commanded by Foulois, now a captain. The aviation unit was to fly communication and observation missions for Pershing's expedition, supplementing the efforts of cavalry patrols to bring Villa to bay. Although the first attempt at aerial reconnaissance, flown by Capt. Townsend F. Dodd with Foulois as his observer, went well enough, the squadron faced problems that defied solution. Foulois and the other pilots soon discovered that they could neither coax their ninety-horsepower Curtiss JN–3s over the towering Sierra Madres nor buck the whirlwinds and downdrafts encountered in the mountain passes. Pershing soon realized that the airplanes lacked the power to do what he wanted of them, and although he praised the airmen for their courage and willingness he dismissed their aircraft as useless either for reconnaissance or for maintaining liaison with the advance elements of his punitive expedition.

Scarcely had the squadron entered Mexico when Foulois asked for better airplanes. His pleas were justified, for after a month only two of his original eight JN–3s survived, and they were unsafe for further field service. Congress realized that the Army needed new aircraft and in March 1916 approved an emergency appropriation of $500,000, twice what the Aviation Section received during the previous fiscal year. Without going through the formality of competitive bidding, the Signal Corps hurriedly bought and shipped to Mexico four Curtiss N–8s, improved models, but very much like the JN–3s. The squadron evaluated the N–8s, but found them to be inadequate, and they were shipped to San Diego for use as trainers.

When these aircraft proved little better than their predecessors, aviators, Congress, and the press joined in criticizing the War Department. In Washington, Billy Mitchell, acting head of the Aviation Section, took the full force of this verbal barrage; but he stood firm, insisting that no better planes were being produced in the United States. Ironically (in view of his tactics during the 1920s) Mitchell complained that the flyers were leaking information to reporters. He believed that such data ought to flow through channels rather than the press.

Actually, Mitchell had done his best to equip the squadron in Mexico. The Curtiss corporation had even diverted planes ordered by Great Britain, now a combatant in World War I, but the British intended to use the aircraft for training rather than reconnaissance. Foulois and the others were discovering that a good trainer, operating under difficult conditions in the field, would not necessarily perform adequately as a reconnaissance craft. Overlooking the possibility that they might have expected too much from the Curtiss product, Army aviators blamed American manufacturers in general for the Mexican debacle. Sensitive to the criticism and the publicity it generated, the Signal Corps had already created a Technical Advisory and Inspection Board to recommend equipment, inspect factories, and evaluate aircraft.

Milling, now a captain, was in charge of the new agency; serving with him were 1st Lt. Byron Q. Jones and Capt. Virginius E. Clark, two flyers who had recently attended the Massachusetts Institute of Technology. The board also drew on the talents of various civilians, including Donald Douglas, whose aircraft would prove so important during World War II. The first major recommendation of the board was that the Army equip a reconnaissance squadron with 12 Curtiss R–2s, aircraft powered by 160-horsepower engines, and send the unit to Mexico. By the time the new airplanes arrived, however, an uneasy truce prevailed between Pershing's men and the Mexican army, but even routine operations revealed that the new aircraft were, at best, only a slight improvement over the ones they replaced. For example, the laminated wood of the propellers tended to come apart in flight because of the dry climate of northern Mexico. The American aviation industry could not on short notice provide serviceable propellers, and the squadron remained a flawed military instrument. At most, Foulois had managed to provide for a time an aerial messenger service between Pershing's field headquarters and his main base at Columbus, New Mexico.

Although the squadron, in a tactical sense, failed to live up to the hopes of either Pershing or Foulois, it did provide a means for testing ideas and equipment.

Curtiss aircraft at Columbus, New Mexico, in 1916.
The tents in the background are hangars.

Because the airmen operated under only the most tenuous control by the Signal Corps, they could experiment with weapons that might make airplanes useful beyond reconnaissance for the ground forces. For example, while Foulois waited for the N–8s, he asked the Aviation Section in May 1916 for bombsights, flechettes (steel darts), and both explosive and incendiary bombs. Bombsights were unavailable because the War Department had decided against developing them, and flechettes had proved ineffective on the battlefields of Europe. The only available bombs were hand-held types, like the ones that Gavotti had used in Libya, and these soon demonstrated their inherent lack of accuracy. The Ordnance Corps sent Lewis machineguns to the 1st Aero Squadron, but for want of adequate mounts, the airmen had to use them as shoulder weapons, hardly a satisfactory method of firing from a maneuvering airplane. Despite efforts of this sort, the squadron was barely able to conduct sustained reconnaissance, let alone attack an enemy with bombs or gunfire.

By the time the Wilson administration withdrew the American forces from Mexico in January 1917, Foulois and his fellow Army officers had learned some painful lessons about conducting a lengthy campaign. The punitive expedition failed to catch Villa but it did provide realistic training for the Regulars who launched the pursuit and for the National Guard units mobilized during the operation. The flyers, though handicapped by shoddy equipment, won Pershing's respect for their bravery and persistence. Even as he praised the airmen, however, the general blamed the Signal Corps for not supporting the aviators properly. Basing his judgment largely on the potential for reconnaissance and courier duty, he predicted that an army without aviation would be defeated by an army that possessed it.

The National Defense Act of 1916, adopted in June of that year, contained the promise that the Aviation Section would soon be able to provide the reconnaissance and courier functions that Pershing had thus identified. The new law increased the number of officers from 60 to 148 (or from slightly more than one percent of the officer corps to almost three percent), enabled the President to fix the enlisted strength as he deemed appropriate, and approved the creation of a reserve that included both officers and enlisted men. The possibility of American involvement in the European war, which had begun in the summer of 1914, inspired both this legislation and the appropriations act of August 29, 1916, which allocated slightly more than $13 million for military aeronautics in the Signal Corps and National Guard and for the acquisition of land for airfields.

Although the foray into Mexico aroused Pershing's interest in aviation, it also demonstrated how far the American aircraft industry had fallen behind manufacturers in France, Great Britain, Germany, and Italy. The nation that invented the airplane had adapted it to military uses but had allowed it to remain an appendix to the Army. Despite Pershing's recognition of its potential for gathering and disseminating information, the airplane did not yet have a truly vital function. Far different were conditions in the skies over the battlefields of Europe, where fast, highly maneuverable aircraft were dogfighting, while other specialized types carried out bombardment and reconnaissance. Not only did the foreign machines outfly the slow Curtiss types that Foulois and his squadron had used in Mexico, European pursuit planes mounted machineguns synchronized to fire through the propeller's arc, a far cry from the few hand-held Lewis guns tested by the airmen in Pershing's expedition. American factories were not turning out pursuit planes or bombers, and by European standards, the best American reconnaissance craft were little more than trainers.

A variety of factors contributed to the lethargy that benumbed the American aircraft industry. The Wright brothers, once they had conquered the air, concentrated on protecting their patents instead of perfecting their invention. In January 1914, nineteen months after Wilbur's death from typhoid fever, a federal court decided that the Wright patent covering wing warping applied to the aileron and any other mechanism that controlled the rolling motion of an airplane. The resulting struggle over licenses and royalties absorbed the energies of American builders at a time when European manufacturers were making spectacular progress, spurred by the demands of World War I. Not until the United States entered the conflict and the government arranged licensing procedures did the American aircraft industry turn from quarreling over profits from past accomplishments to resume the task of advancing aeronautical science.

Whether in building and employing airplanes or in raising and equipping armies, the embattled nations of Europe had moved far ahead of the United States. To deal with the latest crisis in Mexico, almost the entire Regular Army and National Guard had been mobilized in the American Southwest. In contrast

33

to this effort, which produced about 150,000 officers and men, France had mobilized almost four million men at the onset of war in 1914 and Germany two million. In Europe, machineguns by the thousands were slaughtering advancing infantry along a battle line that stretched from Switzerland through Belgium; although the American Army used these weapons in Mexico, they remained a novelty, with no more than four in an infantry regiment. The absence of conscription laws needed to generate national armies and the inability to appreciate such military innovations as the airplane and machinegun demonstrated that the American Army had not yet completed the transition from a lightly armed but highly mobile constabulary designed to deal with marauding Indians or Filipino insurgents to a heavily armed, thoroughly modern force capable of the kind of sustained combat being fought in Europe.

Chapter 2

The Air Service in the Great War

Daniel R. Mortensen

W hen Europe went to war in the summer of 1914, the belligerents tended to believe that swift and certain victory awaited the side that deployed its forces first, in the greatest strength, and at the decisive point. General staffs throughout the continent had drawn up mobilization plans long before a Serbian-trained terrorist murdered an Austrian archduke and set in motion the terms of a system of alliance and counteralliance that triggered a world war. As tensions heightened, conscripts trained in peacetime mustered for war, and Germany invoked a complex plan, much modified and ultimately bungled, that called for a sweeping envelopment through neutral Belgium to turn the flanks of the French armies and isolate them from Paris, the capital city. Once France had been beaten, the victorious German forces would redeploy eastward and defeat Russia, an ally of the French. By the end of the first week of August 1914, the Allies—principally Great Britain, Belgium, France, and Russia—arrayed themselves against the Central Powers, consisting of Germany and the dual monarchy of Austria-Hungary. Turkey joined the Central Powers later in 1914; Japan and Italy sided with the Allies in 1914 and 1915, respectively.[1]

History of the United States Air Force

Except for the British, who believed in sea power and the strangling effect of naval blockade, the European combatants relied primarily on land armies. Military aviation served mainly in a reconnaissance role for troops on the ground, although the dirigible in particular, and the airplane to a lesser degree, seemed useful for dropping bombs. The earliest attempts at aerial bombardment from dirigibles proved disappointing, however. Hoping, perhaps, for a decisive psychological effect, the German forces attacking the stubbornly held Belgian fortifications at Liege used an airship to drop modified artillery shells on the defenses. The dirigible not only caused no damage, but at an altitude of 4,700 feet, it proved mortally vulnerable to fire from the ground. Leaking hydrogen from its punctured gas cells, the damaged craft staggered away and crashlanded in a forest near Bonn, Germany. During a raid on Antwerp, another dirigible escaped damage but dropped its bombs in a residential neighborhood, killing civilians and contributing to the list of German atrocities against the Belgian people that was being compiled and publicized by Allied propagandists.[2]

The airplane, from which less was expected, proved an equally feeble offensive weapon during the early months of the war. For several days, frail German Taube monoplanes appeared over Paris and dropped small bombs, but the attacks were a nuisance at most. The British had somewhat better success when they responded to the initial airship raids by sending airplanes to attack the dirigible sheds at Cologne, Dusseldorf, Cuxhaven, and Friedrichshafen. Four attacks resulted in the destruction of one airship, and the most dangerous mission—a 250-mile flight from Belfort, France, to Friedrichshafen and back—inflicted superficial damage, at the cost of one of the three Avro 504 biplanes that reached the target.[3]

Unlike bombardment, aerial observation proved invaluable to the contending armies, even though German observers failed to recognize a British encampment in France and did not provide warning that an expeditionary force had arrived from the United Kingdom. British airmen proved more successful, however, detecting the advancing Germans who, as a result, encountered entrenched British infantry at Mons in Belgium and had to fight yard by yard through the town. Similarly, French aviators discovered that the enemy's right wing would swing eastward short of Paris. The information led to a counterattack that disrupted totally the already modified German plan of conquest. The aerial observers used wireless telegraphy to adjust artillery fire. German airmen employed this technique during the battle at Mons, as did the British when they frustrated the enemy's final attempts to turn the Allied left flank. Once that flank rested securely against the Belgian coast, trench warfare began along a line that stretched all the way to neutral Switzerland.

Military aviation played a larger and more complex role four years later in the great battles that broke the stalemate. In contrast to the 200-odd airplanes available to the French and British when the war began, some 1,400 Allied airplanes took part in a single battle, the St. Mihiel offensive, in the fall of 1918.

Moreover, the aircraft of 1918 performed specialized functions—pursuit, observation, day bombardment, and long-range night bombardment—that required distinctive attributes in the machines being used. Although the same kind of aircraft employed for observation might double as a daytime bomber, each category usually had a single function. The fast, highly maneuverable pursuit plane or fighter normally fought against hostile aircraft of the same type, trying to drive them from the sky to protect friendly day bombers and observation craft and prey on those of the enemy. Multiengine night bombers attacked distant targets, in the case of the Germans, assuming this mission from dirigibles. Considered a promising bombardment vehicle in 1914, airships enjoyed some success against lightly defended cities before encountering the incendiary bullet that demonstrated the explosive vulnerability of the hydrogen gas keeping the huge craft aloft. Tethered balloons, however, had become a normal instrument of warfare, supplementing the work of observation planes close to the battle front. As missions became increasingly specific, unique types of aircraft and specialized tactics evolved to carry them out; four years of fighting revolutionized the equipment and tactics of aerial combat and magnified its importance.[4]

The United States entered World War I late, more than two and a half years after the war began. The other belligerents had all made tremendous advances in their military power and employment of it, particularly in aviation. Before the war, the country remained largely in its somnolent peacetime state, but in a year and a half of wartime effort, the military made extraordinary strides. Although its relative contribution to the war might have been small, by the end of the war, the size, technological capability, and proficiency of the U.S. military approached those of the European powers. Likewise, the Army's air arm, in a scant eight months, reoriented, equipped, and trained hundreds of thousands of men; procured thousands of aircraft; organized and reorganized itself; and undertook some of the largest combat air operations of the war.

The United States joined the Allied ranks because of a German gamble, taken early in 1917, that unrestricted submarine warfare would starve Great Britain into submission before the United States, a champion of neutral rights and freedom of the seas, could intervene on the battlefields of Europe. During 1916, the United States had almost severed diplomatic relations with Germany because of the loss of American lives in the torpedoing of British passenger liners and merchantmen. When German submarines began sinking ships flying the American flag, the United States could not remain a bystander. Submarine warfare and a German attempt to entice Mexico into becoming an ally in the event of war with the United States—an overture contained in a message that was intercepted, decoded, and released by British intelligence—combined to bring America into the European conflict. On April 6, 1917, Congress approved President Woodrow Wilson's call for a declaration of war.

Until the United States became a belligerent, its Army had contributed nothing to the wartime development of military aircraft and aerial tactics. As the per-

Curtiss JN–4 at Memphis Aviation School in 1917.

formance of the Curtiss scouts during the pursuit of Pancho Villa clearly showed, the great advances in aircraft design since 1914 came from Europe. For example, by the time the United States declared war, a third generation of wartime fighters—aircraft with speeds surpassing 100 miles per hour and engines developing 160 horsepower—was entering service in Europe. The timing mechanism that enabled a pilot to fire a machinegun through the propeller arc without striking the whirling blades was the product of European engineers. Whereas the airplanes assigned to Pershing in Mexico could barely struggle through the mountain passes, multiengine German bombers of 1917 could fly so high that crew members had to suck oxygen through pipestem tubes. Only two American aircraft found favor among the European Allies, the Curtiss JN–4 Jenny, though as a trainer rather than a combat aircraft, and the Curtiss America flying boat. Ironically, engineers trained in Britain had helped design both aircraft—B. Douglas Thomas, the Jenny, and John C. Porte, the seaplane.[5]

Although a few American volunteers flew for the Allies, they lacked the rank to influence the employment of military aviation. Instead, they helped devise the tactics that enabled the individual pilot to make the deadliest use of his machine. These men became skilled aviators, learning the watchfulness, disciplined marksmanship, and precise maneuvering that won aerial victories. They were combat pilots who fought for the sky, rather than planners who determined how an air force should be used or exactly what it should accomplish.

When the United States entered the war, the mission of the pursuit plane, or fighter, was to gain control of the skies by driving off hostile aircraft and preventing the enemy from locating or attacking friendly troops, supply lines, depots, or airfields. Although the Germans, French, and British all grouped their fighters into squadrons, the combatants differed on how best to employ these units. The British and French preferred to send pursuits to look for a fight deep

38

in enemy territory, but the Germans tended to remain on the defensive, intercepting the Allied aerial incursions. German fighters might patrol the front lines or remain on alert at airfields nearby, but they habitually allowed the British and French to retain the initiative. The Germans did, however, establish a warning network of observers at the front linked by telephone to a central headquarters that was in communication with the airfields.

The greatest proponent of the offensive use of fighters was Maj. Gen. Hugh M. Trenchard, who, while commander of the Royal Flying Corps in France, insisted that his pursuit pilots maintain unceasing pressure on the enemy even when the Germans had markedly superior fighters. He demonstrated his willingness in 1915 and 1916 to allow the slow and poorly protected observation planes of that era to plod unescorted across the front lines while his own pursuits were elsewhere, challenging the Germans to come up and fight. Only when the odds against the completion of vital reconnaissance missions seemed prohibitive, did Trenchard relent and assign as many as three fighters to escort a single observation craft. French aviation commanders tended to heed Trenchard's example and hurl their pursuit squadrons against German fighters, but at times they, too, had to yield to requests by observation or bomber squadrons for fighter escort.[6]

Shortly after the United States entered the war, but not quite a year before American squadrons saw their first action in France, Allied airmen realized that the new and more powerful pursuit planes entering service could attack troops on the ground as well as aircraft. In May 1917, British fighters strafed German troops massing for a counterattack and, also for the first time, systematically machine-gunned enemy emplacements in the path of advancing infantry. This tactical innovation was an inevitable result of improvements in military aircraft—greater speed and power, synchronized machineguns mounted on the engine cowling and easily aimed by the pilot, and a more durable airframe. Although the skeleton of the aircraft could survive the aerodynamic stress of high speeds and treetop altitudes, the fuel tanks, the engines, and the pilots in unarmored cockpits were vulnerable to fire from rifles and machineguns on the ground. Consequently, pursuit pilots disliked strafing missions, considering them more dangerous than dogfights, a justifiable belief given the fate of Maj. Edward "Mick" Mannock. This British pilot, who shot down seventy-three Germans in aerial combat, died when a rifle bullet, fired as he passed low over the battlefront, punctured his fuel tank and the hot engine ignited the leaking gasoline.[7]

The tactics and equipment used in aerial reconnaissance also changed drastically under the pressure of war. In 1914, the observer treated the pilot as his aerial chauffeur; furthermore, British observers did not have true military maps, for these were needed by the traditional combat arms and none could be spared for an untested organization like military aviation. At best, the British observer might be able to refer to a Michelin map, intended for sightseers, as he searched with binoculars or the unaided eye for signs of the enemy in an area assigned him by a ground commander. Although the corps or division commander continued to specify the areas to be searched and the kind of information to be brought back, by 1918 the pilot was in command of his airplane, with the observer doubling as aerial gunner. The reconnaissance crew no longer passed information by dropping messages attached to weights or by landing to make oral reports; wireless telegraphy put the airmen in immediate contact with headquarters, and the aerial camera recorded what they saw from the sky. Instead of scrounging for travel maps as his predecessor did in 1914, the aerial observer of 1918 had easy access to up-to-date military maps and aerial photographs.

By the time the United States entered the war in April 1917, day bombers—in some instances observation craft fitted with bomb racks—were carrying loads of explosives and flying distances barely dreamed of in the fall of 1914. Early in the war, when three unarmed Avro 504s droned 125 miles from Belfort to Friedrichshafen to attack the dirigible base, each could carry no more than four 20-pound bombs. A typical day bomber of 1917 mounted two machineguns on the cowling, synchronized to fire through the propeller arc, and one or two others on a swivel mount in the rear cockpit; it could carry almost a quarter-ton of bombs more than 100 miles, drop them using an optical sight, and return to base. Its usual targets were railyards, road junctions, airfields, and towns or villages that sheltered or supplied the enemy. When the day bombers attacked troop concentrations on or just beyond the battlefield, they experienced the same danger from rifle and machinegun fire that strafing fighter pilots rightly feared. To reduce vulnerability, two German aircraft designers, Hugo Junkers and Otto Reuter, in 1917 introduced a biplane designed for trench strafing, or close air support, with armor five millimeters thick protecting the engine, the fuel tanks, and the two-man crew. This aircraft and an all-metal Junkers monoplane introduced the following year were the only armored attack aircraft that appeared during the war.[8]

When the German right wing wheeled through Belgium in 1914, only the dirigible seemed to have the combination of endurance and lifting power necessary for long-range aerial bombardment. During that campaign, however, army airships proved suicidally vulnerable because they could not operate at altitudes beyond the range of Belgian gunners. In contrast, the hydrogen-filled dirigibles of the Imperial German Navy soon demonstrated that they could soar beyond the reach of the existing antiaircraft guns, outclimb the British airplanes of the day, and drop perhaps four 660-pound high-explosive bombs or as many as 40 smaller incendiaries weighing between 25 and 128 pounds. In January 1915, navy dirigibles made their first attack on a British city, launching a campaign that continued until August 1918 and included raids on London. Although German schoolchildren sang songs about Zeppelins destroying England with fire, the airships were too few and their bombing too inaccurate for that kind of damage. Operating mainly at night, they dropped 196 tons of bombs, killed 557 persons, injured 1,358, and caused millions of dollars in property damage. By 1917, heavier antiaircraft guns were in action, along with new fighters that fired incendiary bullets capable of igniting the hydrogen on board the airships. The improved defenses forced the Germans to develop "height climber" dirigibles, but the need to operate at higher altitudes restricted bomb capacity, since so much weight had to be invested in fuel and ballast, and further reduced bombing accuracy. Nevertheless, German airships remained in combat long after British defenses demonstrated their vulnerability, and accidents or hostile action killed the equivalent of 40 percent of the dirigible crews trained by the German Navy during the course of the war.[9]

Because the dirigible was so vulnerable, it gave way to the multiengine airplane as the principal instrument of long-range aerial destruction. In the summer of 1917, German Gotha biplanes, later joined by the much larger Giants, launched a bombing campaign of their own. The first raid occurred in May, some six weeks after the United States went to war, and the last a year later. The bombers killed 836 persons, injured 1,982, and inflicted property damage comparable to that caused by the airships. Because the raids occurred within the space of one year, the bombing had a greater impact on civilian morale than the less concentrated attacks by dirigibles. Workers, for example, proved reluctant to report to factories, like the Woolwich arsenal, in areas that had just been bombed. The effect on morale of the attacks by Gothas and Giants lent urgency to the move to create a British Air Ministry and an air arm independent of the army and navy. The Air Ministry became a part of the cabinet on January 2, 1918; and the Royal Air Force, equal in status to the older services, came into being on April 1. One of the first tasks facing the Royal Air Force was to retaliate against Germany for the raids on London and other British cities. To accomplish this, it reorganized the bombardment units already in France and acquired new and more powerful bombers.[10]

Other nations besides Germany and Great Britain developed and used long-range, multiengine bombers. Imperial Russia had been first, in December 1914 grouping into a single striking force several huge biplanes designed by Igor Sikorsky and sending them against targets as far as 150 miles beyond German lines. In three years of service, Russian bombers flew some 350 attack or reconnaissance missions before their operational careers came to an end. In March 1918 the new communist government, which had taken over after the abdication of the Czar a year earlier and the subsequent collapse of a provisional regime, accepted peace terms dictated by Germany. Italy, too, employed big bombers. Aircraft designed by Gianni Caproni attacked Austrian war industries at Trieste, airfields, and seaports. Whether German, British, Russian, or Italian, these aircraft were marvels of engineering but weapons of limited value. At the mercy of the weather, ultimately forced by fighter opposition to fly by night, fitted with primitive navigational equipment and crude bomb sights, the huge bombers lacked the destructive might to cripple the industry or commerce of a

British Handley Page O–400

hostile power. Their impact was almost exclusively on civilian morale, undermining it to some degree in the enemy's cities while restoring confidence at home. That so many of the combatants could develop these massive aircraft and use them even to marginal effect demonstrated the progress made by European aviation during the war.[11]

With the exception of Glenn Curtiss, whose flying boats were built under license in Great Britain, American aircraft manufacturers exerted no influence as European firms turned out a succession of improved designs. The nations of Europe were quick to recognize the need to give governmental encouragement to aeronautical research, whether in universities or in institutes operated by the government. Not until 1915, however, did the United States establish the National Advisory Committee for Aeronautics, which slowly took shape under the temporary chairmanship of Brig. Gen. George P. Scriven, the Chief Signal Officer. Fortunately, the U.S. Army followed the progress of military aviation in Europe, relying on the reports of military attaches or observers, among them Lt. Col. George C. Squier, who visited Europe in 1914 and 1915 and talked with the leaders of the Royal Flying Corps, and Capt. Charles deF. Chandler, who concentrated on the tactical use of observation balloons. Chandler was a former chief of the Aeronautical Division; Squier had been the head of the Aviation Section and was the Chief Signal Officer when the United States entered the conflict. Considerations of Allied military security affected the content of the reports, although Squier was able to describe in general such topics as the development of aircraft engines, training, and organization for operations.[12]

The Allies wanted several things from the United States, which had only tenuous contact with wartime military developments. French and British ground commanders sought men, fresh troops to be fed into the battleline as replacements for the massive losses suffered since 1914. This expectation went unful-filled, however, for the American Expeditionary Forces retained its separate identity throughout the fighting. Allied airmen wanted both men and machines; they encouraged the United States to adapt its genius for mass production—em-bodied in Henry Ford, who was turning out automobiles by the thousands—to produce aircraft suitable for combat and to train men to operate them.

Among the first to propose that the United States create an aerial armada was Alexandre Ribot, until September 1917 the premier of France. The United States had been a belligerent for less than a month when he sent a cable to the French ambassador in Washington proposing that the newest of the Allies cre-ate an air force of 4,500 planes. To maintain that strength, Ribot continued, would require a production rate of 2,000 aircraft per month. He made no men-tion of specific types and imposed no deadline for reaching the goal, although someone in the embassy altered the text to request the 4,500 airplanes and the men to operate them in time for a summer campaign in 1918.

Vague as it was, the Ribot message reflected an equally ill-defined interest in military aviation within the French high command. Among the officers who were enthusiastic about aeronautics was Gen. Philippe Petain, who predicted that it would prove a decisive force. However, Petain's judgment may have re-flected wishful thinking rather than confidence, since he was trying to ease the pressure on an army demoralized by an April 1917 offensive that had promised victory but had produced only casualties. Like the German Navy, which turned to the airship at a time when its battle fleet seemed no match for the Royal Navy, Petain may have embraced aviation as a means of buying time to rebuild his forces and ultimately reinforce them with American soldiers.[13]

Billy Mitchell, a major when the United States entered the war, but destined to become a brigadier general before the fighting ended, claimed to have con-tributed to one of the French staff studies that inspired the Ribot cable. Mitchell had entered military aeronautics as a nonflying officer after a tour of duty on the general staff convinced him, and his superiors, that he was better suited to an as-signment in the field, possibly in aviation, than to remain a staff officer else-where in the Signal Corps, the usual duty of an officer of his rank and experi-ence. Once involved in aeronautics, he became an enthusiastic advocate of the specialty and an aspiring pilot. In 1916, at his own expense, he enrolled with a private instructor and began a frequently interrupted course of training that would result in his receiving the badge of a junior military aviator in the fall of the following year. Sent to France as a personal observer for General Squier, Mitchell arrived in Paris just four days after the United States declared war on Germany. He promptly organized an unauthorized headquarters made up of un-paid volunteers, both French citizens and Americans living in Paris, and plunged into the task of discovering all he could about military aircraft and their uses. He talked with senior Allied airmen, including Trenchard, who grumbled that he could not postpone official business to answer questions for any visitor.

Billy Mitchell in his Spad XVI.

Mitchell. with a diplomacy rarely displayed in his later years, replied that the business of the Royal Flying Corps in France was no doubt so well organized that it could continue unattended for a few hours. Trenchard succumbed to Mitchell's flattery, and the American embraced Trenchard's ideas, coming away from the discussion convinced of the overriding importance of seizing control of the air and using military aviation for offensive action.[14]

Although Mitchell's role in its preparation could at best have been minor, the Ribot cable became the basis for an American production plan designed to ensure that the desired force of 4,500 planes would be available in time for the projected offensive in the summer of 1918; the objective would be met by building a total force of 12,000 combat aircraft—6,000 pursuit planes, more than 4,000 observation craft, and the rest bombers. The Joint Army-Navy Technical Board, with Maj. Benjamin Foulois an Army representative, endorsed the scheme on May 29, 1917. The War Department General Staff, however, questioned the wisdom of tying up industrial resources and raw materials on so ambitious a scale. George Squier, now a brigadier general and the Chief Signal Officer, favored the plan so wholeheartedly that he circumvented the General Staff, appealing directly to Secretary of War Newton D. Baker. Secretary Baker promptly endorsed the proposal and sent it to Congress, which approved some $640 million to carry it out, an amount more than 45 times the appropriation voted for military aviation in the fiscal year just ending.[15]

Military aviation now had a goal and the money to achieve it. What remained was to obtain the desired aircraft, decide how to employ them, and fashion and train an organization to use them effectively. All these tasks, moreover, were interrelated and had to be addressed simultaneously. Preparing for war posed a truly formidable challenge to an air arm that a year earlier had been hard pressed to operate a handful of reconnaissance craft in Mexico.

American airplane builders seemed unlikely to be able to help, for they lagged far behind their European counterparts. If anything, their lack of accomplishment reinforced the tendency of the Wilson administration to centralize wartime production in the hands of proven managers. In this instance, because no aircraft firm had achieved a large volume of production, the President tapped the automobile industry, which was turning out a standardized product in impressive numbers. He chose Howard E. Coffin of the Hudson Motor Car Corporation, a former president of the Society of Automotive Engineers and a proponent of industrial mobilization, to lead the Aircraft Production Board, and other automobile executives became involved as either civilians or wartime reserve officers in the manufacture of airplanes. For a year, Coffin's Aircraft Board, as it was redesignated in October 1917, retained responsibility for production, while the Army handled development and employment.[16]

As if the unavoidable confusion attendant on rapid expansion were not enough, the aircraft industry suffered from an improvised administrative structure borrowed from a different industry, from an emphasis on production to the detriment of aeronautical engineering, and from friction between men used to aircraft construction and those familiar with making automobiles. When he took office, Coffin exuded optimism, for he was, after all, an expert in the manufacture of automobiles. Unfortunately, he did not understand either the process of building an airplane or the expendable nature of aircraft in combat. He believed not only that a flying machine could be assembled easily from mass-produced parts, like a car with wings, but also that mechanics at a frontline airfield could give it the kind of tender care lavished on the family automobile.

Hap Arnold, who had reentered aviation after leaving five years earlier to get married, received a wartime promotion to colonel and was working with the Aircraft Board, later described Coffin's attitude. In one of his expansive moods, the chief of production had boasted to Arnold that 40,000 aircraft would be completed by June 1918. When the officer asked how many spare parts were on order, Coffin replied that he had not seen the need for any. Although Coffin may have been joking, the quantity of spare parts proved so inadequate that some of the planes listed in the production totals had to be cannibalized and, as a result, never left the ground.

Coffin and the other veterans of the auto industry found that aircraft production was ill-suited to the techniques that could assemble as many as 10,000 identical Model T Fords in a single year. Instead of an easily assembled box consisting of a wooden floor and roof, shaped pieces of metal, and panels of glass like the automobile, the typical airplane resembled a hooded bird cage, its frame made of spruce longerons and frames, spars and ribs, joined by hundreds of individual fittings, then covered by cloth that was treated with a special paint—called dope—to shrink the fabric and make it waterproof. Furthermore, skilled craftsmen had to adjust the tension in the wires that held the wings in place, balance the control surfaces, and rig the control cables to respond to the pilot's touch. About all the auto and airplane had in common was a gasoline engine.

Some time could be saved by standardizing designs and settling on one type of aircraft for each major category and by manufacturing the major components—wings, engine, fuselage, tail surfaces—separately, then assembling them, instead of treating each airplane as a single unit from wingtip to wingtip and propeller to tail skid. Even so, aircraft manufacture required skills in shaping wood, cutting and sewing fabric, and rigging the finished product, skills that were alien to the automobile factory. The problem proved especially acute when laminated wood began to replace doped cloth, for that material required the techniques of the trained cabinetmaker.[17]

While Coffin and his colleagues concentrated on production, aeronautical engineers exercised their initiative to improve existing designs and, to a lesser extent, devise new ones. Since the facilities proposed for the National Advisory Committee for Aeronautics had yet to be built, aeronautical research and testing, which that organization might have conducted, had to be done elsewhere. The site chosen was McCook Field at Dayton, Ohio, an industrial city with a large work force and ties not only to the Wright brothers, but also to the corporation that held their patents. Because the prewar Aviation Section had done little in the way of aerodynamic research or aircraft development—except to send an occasional officer to graduate training in aeronautical engineering—the engineers who served at McCook Field were a mix of civilians, Regular officers,

De Havilland DH–4 over McCook Field, Dayton, Ohio.

and wartime reservists. There were professional military men like Virginius Clark, sent by the Army to the Massachusetts Institute of Technology and now a wartime lieutenant colonel; talented civilians like Alfred Verville; and the ubiquitous automobile manufacturers in uniform, among them Jesse G. Vincent of the Packard Motor Car Company. Although the engineers made useful contributions in such fields as weapons, instruments, and aerodynamics, their efforts remained subordinate to the work of the production specialists. As a result, Vincent, an automobile builder with the reserve rank of lieutenant colonel, commanded the entire operation at McCook Field with Clark as his assistant.

Despite the emphasis on production, aircraft manufacturing responded sluggishly to the management techniques of the automobile executives, even though these men were experts in their own field. Once aircraft types were chosen for mass production, drawings had to be made, factory space leased or built, wood and fabric stockpiled, and workers trained in operations more complicated and less suited to standardization than work on the automobile assembly line. As time passed, the shortage of workers eased as women entered the factories and men transferred from jobs not directly related to the war effort. In addition, special programs relieved shortages of raw materials. A Spruce Production Division, for instance, employed 10,000 soldiers to locate, cut, transport, and process spruce and fir for airframes. Researchers developed a long-fiber cotton cloth for aircraft covering to replace the linen normally imported from Europe. Also, the Department of Agriculture encouraged the planting of 100,000 acres of castor beans to produce a lubricant used in the rotary engines that powered many types of Allied airplanes. The petroleum industry developed a Liberty Aero Oil especially for the new Liberty engine that would power the war planes built in the United States.[18]

Hard work and improvisation did not result in miracles of production. During the war, American firms turned out roughly 7,000 aircraft, only half of them combat types. Most of the rest were trainers patterned after the Curtiss products used in chasing Pancho Villa. Not until February 1918 did the first American-built combat aircraft emerge from the factory. During that month, American workers produced nine examples of a British-designed aircraft that doubled as a day bomber and an observation craft. The production rate increased rapidly to 15 in April and to almost 1,100 per month in October and November. At the time of the armistice, November 11, 1918, on the basis of the current output of all types of aircraft, the nation's manufacturers claimed an annual production rate of 13,500 airplanes. The fact remained, however, that only 1,200 combat aircraft had reached France when the fighting ended.

Even if production had attained the volume described in Premier Ribot's cable, the U.S. Army's air arm would have had to fly aircraft developed by the European Allies, for in April 1917 its entire inventory consisted of trainers, and American designers had nothing on the drawing board that could be built, tested, and put into mass production in time for a summer offensive in 1918. The question in the spring of 1917 was not whether American factories should build

European aircraft, but which types to manufacture and in what proportion. Ribot had not mentioned specific categories of aircraft; and when Billy Mitchell sought to correct this oversight with numbers and types that French officers had mentioned to him, his comments went astray in the confusion that attended mobilization. It remained for a special technical mission to try to elaborate on Ribot's request.

At the recommendation of the National Advisory Committee for Aeronautics, General Squier sent a mission to Europe to determine what types of aircraft the United States should build and also to survey the obviously successful manufacturing techniques used in France, Great Britain, and Italy. At the head of the mission was Maj. Raynal C. Bolling, in civil life an executive of the United States Steel Corporation, who had learned to fly while a member of the New York National Guard. His six colleagues were Captains Edgar S. Gorrell and Virginius Clark, who had both recently completed courses in aeronautical engineering at the Massachusetts Institute of Technology; two civilian executives from the automobile industry; and two naval officers. Accompanying the seven-member mission were a hundred American technicians—engine and airframe mechanics, draftsmen, and aircraft riggers—who were to fan out among the various factories and see firsthand how European firms built airplanes.

During their investigation, completed late in July 1917, the Army members of the commission—Gorrell, Clark, and Bolling—became fascinated by the prospect of a force of long-range bombers that could be used against Germany and German-occupied territory, much as the Italians were using their Caproni bombers against Austrian ports, airfields, and occasionally industries. With roughly fifty of the bombers, Italy's airmen could not seriously hamper Austria-Hungary's ability to wage war, but the raids did inspire a volatile Italian officer, Giulio Douhet, to think out a concept of strategic air warfare. He would present his ideas publicly in 1921 in *Command of the Air*, which envisioned aerial attacks capable of destroying the factories, cities, and other vital centers that enabled a nation to fight. The potential striking power of Caproni's aircraft inspired the commission to recommend that the designer's trimotor bombers be built in the United States. Caproni presented a tentative theory of strategic bombing that impressed the airmen on the mission, but the impact may have come more from the Italian's personality than from his logic. The members of the mission had trouble making converts among officers never exposed to Caproni's enthusiasm. Indeed, the high command of the U.S. Army continued to believe that aviation should gain control of the air over the battlefield and assist the ground forces by strafing, bombing, and observation. When the War Department General Staff in October 1917 addressed the subject of the composition of the wartime air arm, it established a ratio among pursuit, observation, and bombardment aircraft of 5:3:1. Gorrell, largely on the basis of Caproni's arguments, would have preferred a ratio of 5:3:6, but Pershing insisted on 6:4:3 for the aerial component of his expeditionary forces.

While the air arm was oriented toward ground support, the Caproni bomber encountered unexpected competition from a new twin-engine Handley Page biplane designed in the United Kingdom. The tardy delivery of detailed drawings and the difficulty in reconciling Italian and American methods of production slowed the Caproni project and led to a decision to manufacture parts for the Handley Page in the United States and ship them to Great Britain for assembly and the installation of American-built engines. Only one Caproni bomber rolled from the factory before the war ended, and not a single American-built Handley Page was put together in Britain, although the components for 101 of the craft were shipped across the Atlantic. Largely as a publicity stunt to stimulate the war effort, one of the Pages was assembled in the United States during the summer of 1918.[19]

Even more doleful were the attempts to build pursuit aircraft. The French Spad chosen by the Bolling mission could not be modified to accept the standard American-built engine that was to power all combat aircraft made in the United States. Two British products were substituted for the Spad: the single-seat SE–5, designed at the Royal Aircraft Factory, and the two-place Bristol fighter. When fitted with an American engine in place of the usual Rolls-Royce, the Bristol proved to be overweight and dangerously nose heavy. The American version of the SE–5 would have performed satisfactorily as a trainer, but it appeared too late for the war.

Of the aircraft chosen by the Bolling mission, only the DH–4, originally designed by Geoffrey de Havilland for Britain's Aircraft Manufacturing Company, lent itself to American production methods and performed satisfactorily in combat when fitted with an American engine. About 1,200 of the 3,400 DH–4s built in the United States during the war were shipped to France, where British-built models already were serving in the air arm of the American Expeditionary Forces. Army airmen used the plane mainly for observation, but Marine Corps airmen and some Army flyers found that it performed acceptably as a day bomber.

All of the combat aircraft manufactured in the United States were powered by the American-built Liberty engine, a successful product of the automobile industry. In May and June 1917, before the Bolling mission had arrived in Europe and begun selecting aircraft, Jesse Vincent and Elbert J. Hall drew on their years of experience with auto manufacturers like the Packard and Hudson companies and designed a new engine. A standard powerplant with interchangeable parts, the Liberty could be built with four, six, eight, and twelve cylinders. The largest model was the most widely used, accounting for some 13,500 of the 15,000 engines mass-produced by the American automobile industry during the war. The factories turned out roughly four engines for every completed airframe with a Liberty engine installed.

By the spring of 1918, when the first Liberty-powered DH–4s were taking to the air, it had become obvious that the ambitious production schedule inspired by the Ribot cable and shaped by the Bolling mission was in danger of collapse. The Wilson administration decided to shake up the bureaucratic structure of military aviation. At the heart of this decision was the belief, certainly justified, that General Squier was overburdened by the task of directing military aeronautics and, at the same time, carrying out his responsibilities for such other Signal Corps functions as photography, cryptography, and radio. As a result, the President approved the concentration of all matters relating to Army aviation in the Division of Military Aeronautics, directly responsible to Secretary of War Newton D. Baker instead of to the Chief Signal Officer. In May 1918, Brig. Gen. William L. Kenly, a nonflyer who had served as Pershing's chief of aviation in France, became the first Director of Military Aeronautics and assumed responsibility for personnel matters, administration, training, and the establishment of military requirements for aircraft—in short, for everything but production. Assigned to Kenly's division was Hap Arnold, who functioned as the director's principal assistant until going overseas in the fall of 1918. The same bureaucratic reform that created Kenly's office abolished the old Aircraft Board, shunted its chief executive, Coffin, into an advisory job, and appointed John D. Ryan, the former president of Anaconda Copper, as director of a Bureau of Aircraft Production, responsible to the Secretary of War.

Maj. Arnold with 12-cylinder Liberty engine.

For three months, the Division of Military Aeronautics and the Bureau of Aircraft Production operated almost independently of each other. True, both General Kenly and Mr. Ryan reported directly to Secretary Baker, but the Secretary of War was, if anything, more overworked than the Chief Signal Officer had been and did not have the time to resolve differences between the two agencies. Therefore, President Wilson late in August elevated Ryan to the rank of Second Assistant Secretary of War and made him Director of the Air Service of the U.S. Army, which embraced both the Bureau of Aircraft Production and the Division of Military Aeronautics. The war ended before the new organization could be evaluated, but Ryan's brief tenure did establish a precedent for having a civilian assistant within the Office of the Secretary of War represent the views and interests of military aviation. When Ryan resigned, however, the post of second assistant secretary was left vacant, and a major general took over the Air Service.

In retrospect, wartime aircraft production resembled the cliché about olives coming easily from the narrow-necked bottle after the first one is removed, but in this instance prying loose the first airplane took almost a year. If contrasted to the newspaper headlines predicting that fleets of American-built aircraft would darken the skies over Germany, the record of the nation's manufacturers seemed dismal indeed. More than any other factor, sluggish growth in the volume of aircraft production had led to the removal of military aviation from the Signal Corps and the establishment late in August 1918 of the Army Air Service. The difficulties with production also triggered an investigation of charges of profiteering and inefficiency resulting from a rampant conflict of interest among business executives in uniform and the firms that had employed them. Chosen by President Wilson to investigate aircraft production was Charles Evans Hughes, a former Justice of the Supreme Court and Wilson's unsuccessful opponent in the 1916 election. An investigation completed in October 1918 convinced Hughes that there had been technical violations of federal law, but he recommended prosecuting only one person because, in his opinion, most of the illegalities occurred when individuals bent the rules to help win the war. A sharp increase in production during the autumn and the armistice that ended the fighting in November may have helped turn aside the wrath of politicians and the public; ultimately, no one was prosecuted, not even the person Hughes had singled out.

Although aircraft production was a source of embarrassment, the Army and the nation could take pride in the recruitment, training, and deployment overseas of an air arm comparable in skill and effectiveness to those fighting in Europe. Between the American declaration of war on April 6, 1917, and the end of hostilities on November 11, 1918, the Army air arm increased from a mere 1,200 officers and men to a force of almost 200,000, with 25 percent serving overseas. During the early months of American participation in the conflict, some 38,000 volunteers sought to become flyers and enter the romantic and highly publicized realm of men like Roland Garros of France and Max

Immelmann of Germany. Garros, before the war the first person to fly across the Mediterranean, fitted steel deflector plates to his propeller so that a machinegun fixed to the fuselage could fire through the arc of the rotating propeller. In this fashion he introduced the fighter plane. Immelmann was credited, perhaps erroneously, with inventing the climbing turn that bears his name. Many of the fledglings hoped to join the company of aces, the aviators who had destroyed five or more enemy aircraft, but for some, the opportunity to fly was goal enough. Douglas Campbell, who became an ace, had looked forward to the excitement of flying, which seemed to him the hobby of millionaires until the war offered him the chance to become an aviator. Another ace, Reed Chambers, had been fascinated from childhood with the idea of flying. He read all he could about the Wright brothers, saw the Wright demonstration team in action, and even tried unsuccessfully to enter pilot training through the National Guard before he was able to join the Signal Corps Reserve and become a military aviator. More complex were the motives of Harold M. Bixby, who became a pioneer in commercial aviation; he was terrified of being maimed in the war, returning without an arm or leg, and he felt that as an aviator he would come back in one piece or not at all. Bixby's application went astray, however, and when the fighting ended he was a sailor learning to operate dirigibles.

Like the rest of the Army, the air arm turned to reserve officers to increase its wartime strength. Since there no longer was time for the personal instruction of prewar schools, the eyes of American planners turned to Canada, where pilots already were being trained en masse. A fact-finding mission to Canada, which included Foulois, returned with a plan that divided training into ground, primary, and advanced phases. So impressive were the results of the Canadian methods that the Signal Corps promptly adopted them. Chosen to take charge of the American version of Canada's training program was Hiram Bingham, an explorer and history professor at Yale University, who learned to fly at the age of 41. Commissioned a major in the reserve, Bingham set to work establishing ground training units at educational institutions, as had been done in Canada. The eight American universities that participated in the program accepted almost 23,000 cadets. Of these, more than 17,000 successfully completed a course lasting from eight to twelve weeks that included theory of flight, radio and aerial photography, and engine and airframe maintenance.

Next came primary training, usually lasting six to eight weeks, when the cadet encountered his first aircraft, the Curtiss JN–4 or JN–6 Jenny (or its substitute, the Standard J–1). During this phase, the cadet learned to control an aircraft in flight by using a swiveling stick that moved the ailerons and elevator and a bar under his feet that turned the rudder. To complete primary training, become a Reserve Military Aviator, and qualify for a commission, the cadet had to pass a test that included flying cross-country, reading a map, and using a compass. More than half the 15,000 cadets who entered primary training in the United States emerged as pilots and officers.

To sustain the ambitious program of primary training, the Army increased the number of flying fields from three in the spring of 1917 to twenty-seven in November 1918. With some exceptions, among them Selfridge Field, Mount Clemens, Michigan, most of the new bases were built in the South or Southwest to take advantage of the milder flying weather. The climate also figured in a trade with the government of Canada. Canadian instructors taught Americans to fly at airfields in Canada during the summer of 1917 while the first of the new airfields were being built in the United States, and beginning that winter, Canadians were trained in Texas by Americans. A few British instructors taught in the United States, among them Vernon Castle, a dancer on Broadway who abandoned his stage career to fly for Great Britain but was killed in a midair collision over Texas.

Rare was the trainee in the United States who learned flying from a combat veteran like Castle, for few Americans had flown in the war and only a comparative handful of British veterans could be spared as instructors. Nor were there enough civilian instructors for the number of cadets arriving at the American training bases. As a result, some graduates of primary training had to teach subsequent classes to fly, receiving additional instruction either informally or in a course established for that purpose.

The original scheme of instruction assumed that those who finished primary training in the United States or Canada would receive advanced training in France, for the United States had neither suitable aircraft nor adequate numbers of skilled instructors to teach combat tactics. Time inevitably was lost in acquiring primary trainers, building airfields in the United States, and converting student pilots into instructors. As a result, General Pershing in July 1917 requested that the Army begin sending cadets to Europe, where manned and fully equipped instructional facilities already existed for both primary and advanced instruction. The War Department complied, ordering cadets to train in France, Great Britain, and Italy, as well as in Canada and the United States. The group that went to Italy included Fiorello La Guardia, a member of the House of Representatives from New York, who had already received some flight instruction as a civilian. The congressman and most of the other American graduates of a flying school at Foggia stayed in Italy to fly Caproni bombers against the Austrians.

During the war, about 1,600 fully trained pilots graduated from schools in France, Great Britain, and Italy. Sometimes new arrivals from the United States underwent primary training alongside members of American ground units already in France who had volunteered for military aviation. British instruction resembled American, though the Farman or Avro trainer was normally used instead of the Jenny. Cadets taught in France started in aircraft with clipped wings that were incapable of flight, learning to manipulate the throttle and taxi in a straight line before moving on to the Nieuport trainer. For their advanced training, the Americans flew operational types, some of them recently judged obsolete, like the British Sopwith Pup, while others were first-line aircraft.

Field number 4 at Issoudun.

Some of the European-trained airmen became celebrated aces. Field Kindley, for example, learned to fly in Britain, flew for a time with a British combat squadron and downed his first German, then joined an American unit and scored eleven more aerial victories. Edward V. Rickenbacker, a race driver and the leading American ace of World War I, went overseas as a sergeant in the aviation section of General Pershing's headquarters, occasionally was Billy Mitchell's chauffeur, learned to fly at Issoudun in France, and served there as an instructor before entering combat.

Issoudun was the largest American training base in France. Unfortunately, the installation was built on clay that turned to sticky mud when saturated by the winter rains. According to one student aviator, life there was characterized by cold, bad food, broken bones, and influenza. Mud thrown from the wheels of the airplanes broke propellers as fast as they could be put on. The trainees, in their misery, joked that the Prussians ran the place, for besides Rickenbacker, the staff included men with names of Weidenbach, Tittel, and Spegal, as well as Carl A. Spatz, who changed his last name to Spaatz in 1937; ten years later he became the first Chief of Staff of the U.S. Air Force. During the war Weidenbach changed his name, presumably because it sounded too German when Germany was the enemy; as Charles A. Willoughby he served as General Douglas MacArthur's intelligence officer during World War II and the Korean War.

The burgeoning air service needed mechanics and riggers to care for the airplanes expected from American factories. At first, the War Department simply issued a call for volunteers, without considering the likely effect on American industry; in response, many skilled workers abandoned their jobs and rushed to enlist. Although some workers were assigned as riggers or mechanics in aviation units, too few experienced men were available for the rapidly expanding air arm; consequently, the Army tested soldiers to determine their aptitude for dealing with machinery, teaching the most promising to become mechanics. After trying unsuccessfully to train small groups at several aircraft or engine factories, the War Department opened formal schools to produce aviation mechanics. The initial sites were air bases in the northern states—Selfridge Field and Chanute Field in Illinois—that could be used during the winter months when weather interfered with flight training. Handicapped at the outset by a shortage of qualified instructors, Kelly Field, Texas, eventually became the center where soldiers could learn to maintain and repair engines and airframes. Despite the establishment of service schools, trade and technical schools under contract to the Army remained the main source of wartime mechanics and craftsmen. Institutions of this sort turned out more than 5,000 graduates, about half the total that completed instruction by the summer of 1918. Some training took place in Europe, especially in Britain, where mechanics might sharpen their skills before moving on to operational units.[20]

Besides pilots and airframe or engine mechanics, the Army had to train officers or enlisted men in a myriad of specialties, including aerial observation, aircraft engineering and armament, radio operation and repair, aerial photography and photo analysis, and even carpentry and bricklaying. These last skills were needed for construction projects at airfields. In some instances, civilian institutions provided the necessary training: the Massachusetts Institute of Technology conducted a course in aircraft engineering; Columbia University taught military cinematography, a subject that included the making of still photographs as well as motion pictures; and several schools gave instruction in radio telegraphy. Cornell University joined forces with the Eastman Kodak company to teach aerial photography. Most of the other skills, however, were learned from uniformed instructors at military bases.

While it was training men for heavier-than-air units, the Army at the same time invested money, effort, and manpower in observation balloon companies. These organizations operated the sausage-shaped, hydrogen-filled vehicles tethered near the front and used for adjusting artillery fire. By the armistice, almost 17,500 officers and men, a few assigned temporarily from the field artillery, were serving as aerial observers, administrators, communications specialists, and balloon handlers. Almost 7,000 had gone overseas before the war ended and were performing dangerous and important work for the expeditionary forces.

Tethered observation balloons, essential for accurate artillery fire, contained highly combustible hydrogen gas and presented a tempting target for German fighters. To protect the balloons, antiaircraft weapons ringed the launching sites, and ground crews learned to reel in the cable quickly and get the balloons out of harm's way. More important, the comparatively spacious observation basket enabled an observer to carry the cumbersome parachute of that era. One observer, a lieutenant named McDevitt, parachuted four times within a month, twice on the same day, to escape attacking pursuit planes. Another lieutenant, C. J. Ross, had no such luck, dying during his first jump when the burning hydrogen in the collapsing envelope ignited his parachute canopy.

However useful the observation balloon was at this time, flying an airplane, particularly a pursuit, caught the fancy of the public and attracted many an adventurous young man eager to serve his country. The press compared the pursuit pilots to the knights of old, meeting in individual combat, but by 1918 an air battle was a twisting, turning melee in which a tense and tired pilot, aiming through goggles fogged by oil and powder smoke, might fire on several wildly maneuvering enemy planes before scoring a kill or breaking off the action to avoid being shot down himself. Unlike the trenches below, the skies were devoid of mud, mustard gas, rats, and decomposing flesh, but airplanes usually burned when hit, and until the Germans adopted them late in the war, fighter pilots were not issued parachutes because policymakers feared that this means of escape could undermine aggressiveness. The prospect of gliding 10,000 feet while being charred by flames from burning fuel and fabric caused not a few pilots to carry a pistol to put an end to the agony. Yet, dangerous though it was, aviation seemed a nobler, more individualistic, and cleaner form of service than warfare in the trenches.

Before the United States entered the war, a few Americans had been fighting in the skies over France, most as members of the Lafayette Escadrille, the aviation division of the French Foreign Legion. Among the 267 Americans who volunteered for duty in French aviation, 180 completed the training and served at the front; they downed 199 German aircraft at the cost of 51 killed, 19 wounded, and 15 taken prisoner. Some of the pilots were former infantrymen in the Legion, a few had come to France to drive ambulances, and others had come directly from the United States to train as enlisted pilots in the school of military aviation at Avord near Tours. Some members of the escadrille believed their unit represented the better class of Americans. They were soldiers of fortune who went to France for a variety of reasons, but all shared the love of adventure. They were characterized as university men who, as a rule, were rather irresponsible, but cool-headed enough to put up a good fight when necessary in combat situations.

One of the Americans who trained at Avord was a legionnaire, though not a member of the Lafayette Escadrille. Far from being a member of the better classes, Eugene Jacques Bullard was the descendant of slaves, a professional boxer, who had found in France the social acceptance refused him in the United States, where racial segregation prevailed. Bullard became the first black pilot to score a verified aerial victory, shooting down a Fokker triplane in November 1917. Unlike most of the other Americans flying for France, he was not accepted by Pershing's air service; he never received an explanation, but at the time the U.S. Army was accepting no blacks for duty in aviation, neither as officers nor enlisted men.

This burning hydrogen-filled observation balloon was downed by an airplane.

Of the veterans of the Lafayette Escadrille, ninety-three transferred to the Air Service of the American Expeditionary Forces and provided a leaven of combat experience for the organization's new squadrons, while another twenty-six entered naval aviation. The need for skilled leaders induced examining physicians to waive medical standards, even for a partially deaf flyer, who had poor vision in one eye and suffered from an injured knee. This aviator, William Thaw, one of the few Americans to attain commissioned status while in the service of France, became a major in the American air service and took command of the 103d Aero Squadron, formed largely of survivors of the escadrille. The new unit remained under French control until the summer of 1918, when it joined the American 3d Pursuit Group, over which Thaw, now a lieutenant colonel, took command.

Although Thaw immediately assumed command of a combat unit, another veteran of the Lafayette Escadrille, Raoul Lufbery, who had shot down seventeen German aircraft, found himself trapped behind a desk at Issoudun after entering the American air service with the rank of major. He succeeded in return-

Alan Winslow (above) and Douglas Campbell (opposite page), respectively
the first and second U.S. flyers to down German aircraft in World War I.

ing to the cockpit, however, instructing the fledgling pilots of the 94th and 95th
Aero Squadrons in combat tactics. During May 1918, when attacking a German
reconnaissance craft, Lufbery's French-built Nieuport pursuit burst into flames,
apparently struck by machinegun fire from the observer-gunner in the enemy
airplane. Like other Allied pilots of that era, Lufbery had no parachute. He
stayed with the fighter as it staggered downward, then leapt or fell toward a
stream below. Already terribly burned, he died as a result of the fall.

Another veteran of the escadrille, James Norman Hall, barely escaped death
while a flight leader in the 94th Aero Squadron. As he dived on a German fighter, the fabric covering the upper wing of his Nieuport split along the leading
edge, a failing common to that model of aircraft, although any fighter could easily be overstressed in a dogfight. Moments later a dud antiaircraft shell disabled
the engine, but the fuel lines remained intact and there was no fire. Hall managed a crash landing beyond enemy lines and became a prisoner of war for the
duration of the conflict.

On April 14, 1918, 2d Lt. Alan F. Winslow, formerly a sergeant in the
Lafayette Escadrille, became by a matter of minutes the first U.S. Army aviator to shoot down a German plane, destroying it within sight of the airdrome
at Toul, where the 94th Aero Squadron was based. Scarcely had Winslow's vic-

tim crashlanded, when Douglas Campbell, a reserve officer who had recently completed training at Issoudun, brought down a second plane. On July 31, 1918, after an explosive bullet shattered his arm, Winslow crashlanded behind enemy lines; a surgeon at a German hospital amputated the arm above the elbow.[21]

An American army air arm had been recruited, trained, equipped (although largely with European aircraft), sent to the battlefront, and strengthened by the infusion of men like Thaw, Lufbery, Hall, and Winslow, who fought as volunteers under the flag of France. Pershing, the American commander in chief in France, initially chose Maj. Townsend K. Dodd, a veteran of the punitive expedition into Mexico, as his air officer; but when Pershing and his staff arrived in France, Billy Mitchell, a colonel, already was there. Since he outranked Dodd, Mitchell took over and presented Pershing with a plan for the employment of military aviation that was based on recent conversations with British and French airmen. He proposed the creation of special strategic forces to operate against enemy aircraft and material some distance beyond the battleline. For the benefit of Pershing, a former cavalryman, he described his aviation units, albeit vaguely, as a cavalry of the sky, not only driving the enemy from the air over the battlefield but also harrying his lines of communication and supply well beyond the range of the heaviest Allied artillery. Pershing, however, was not ready to give an airman the kind of freedom that cavalry generals had exercised as recently as the American Civil War; there would be no aerial equivalent of

Sheridan's campaign in the Shenandoah Valley or Stuart's ride around the Union Army before Richmond. As the American air units arrived in France, they were incorporated in the Air Service of the American Expeditionary Forces, reflecting Pershing's views on the use of military aviation. In the American Expeditionary Forces, aviation would remain responsible to the army and corps commanders and occasionally, in the case of some observation squadrons, to division commanders.

For administrative purposes, Pershing divided his Air Service, as he had the American Expeditionary Forces as a whole, into a Zone of Interior, responsible for logistics and related matters, and a Zone of Advance that dealt with combat operations. Because of this division of labor, Bolling took charge of aviation matters in the Zone of Interior, such as production of French aircraft for American use and the training of American airmen in France, while Mitchell retained responsibility for air operations in the Zone of Advance. To ensure cooperation between the rear areas and the forward units, Pershing appointed as Chief of the Air Service, American Expeditionary Forces, Brig. Gen. William L. Kenly, an artilleryman who later became the first Director of Military Aeronautics.

As the number of American troops and aviators multiplied, titles changed, new officers arrived, and the number of assignments for senior airmen increased. Foulois, now a brigadier general, arrived from Washington in the autumn of 1917 with a staff chosen at Signal Corps headquarters and replaced Kenly, but Mitchell resented serving under the newcomer. Conceding that Foulois "meant well and had some experience in aviation," Mitchell considered the recent arrivals "an incompetent lot" out of touch with the realities of war; he compared them to a cavalry troop with "200 men who had never seen a horse, 200 horses who had never seen a man, and 25 officers who had never seen either."[22]

In part to bring harmony to the headquarters, but also because he resented having the commander of his air service chosen at Washington without being consulted, Pershing appointed an engineer and classmate from West Point, Brig. Gen. Mason L. Patrick, as Chief of the Air Service, moving Foulois to the First Army, and abolished the Zone of Advance, assigning Mitchell to I Corps, where he could devote full attention to operational matters while Foulois dealt mainly with administration at the higher headquarters. Then, in July 1918, when the possibility arose of massing aviation units for an entire army, Foulois did something that, Mitchell later confessed, amazed and surprised him. Realizing that Mitchell had studied the war on the Western Front and developed a grasp of aerial tactics unique among American airmen, Foulois persuaded General Patrick to change the assignments of the two officers. Mitchell took over at First Army headquarters as an operational commander, and Foulois became an assistant to Patrick, an assignment that used his talents as a supply officer and administrator. In the meantime, Bolling had given up his assignment in the Zone of Interior (redesignated the Service of Supply). The former National Guard officer, now

Secretary of War Newton D. Baker, left, Brig. Gen. Foulois, second from left, and Gen. Pershing, far right, with a group of Allied observers at Issoudun.

holding a commission in the reserve, died in March 1918, during a tour of the front lines, when his staff car came under fire from German troops that had broken through French positions.

Despite the dominant role of Mitchell, who in October 1918 took command of aviation for an army group made up of three American armies, and the prominence of Bolling and Foulois, other air officers helped determine the role of military aviation in France. Charles deF. Chandler—a veteran of the detachments at College Park, Augusta, San Diego, and Texas City—had become a colonel and served as the officer in charge of balloon, radio, and photography for the Air Service of the American Expeditionary Forces. Lt. Col. John A. Paegelow commanded the balloon units operating at the front; Col. Thomas DeW. Milling replaced Mitchell at First Army when Mitchell moved to the army group headquarters; Col. Frank Lahm was air officer of the Second Army; and when a Third Army was formed immediately before the armistice, Townsend Dodd, now a colonel, took command of its aviation component. Training in France was the responsibility of Col. Walter G. Kilner, who had flown in Mexico with Foulois.[23]

In employing the various components of Pershing's Air Service, Mitchell and his fellow airmen had to heed the demands of the ground war, using Allied tactics and equipment, whether in pursuit aviation, observation, or bombardment. For example, the first of six day bomber units to serve in France, the 96th Aero Squadron, entered combat on June 12, 1918, flying Breguet biplanes provided by the French. From the vast grass airfield at Amanty in France, six Breguets took off simultaneously, maintained a V formation on the way to the target so the rear-seat gunners could provide mutual protection, and dropped almost 2,000 pounds of bombs on the railroad yards at a town called Dommary-Baroncourt, France, leaving a path of craters across the tracks and scoring a hit on a warehouse. The usual targets during most of the summer were the railroad centers through which trains passed carrying ore from the German-held Briey iron deposits, along with munitions dumps, command posts, and transshipment points for troops and military cargo.

Besides antiaircraft fire and German pursuit planes, weather posed a continuing threat to the American airmen. On July 10, for example, after six Breguets took off to harry rail traffic, a thick layer of cloud formed and clung to the ground, rain began falling, and the wind changed velocity and direction. Blown off course and with only the compass for orientation, the formation groped about until the commander found what appeared to be a French airfield and led the group to a landing. Unfortunately, the airstrip lay within German lines and the two dozen crewmen became prisoners of war. Despite the mitigating circumstances, this error in the unfamiliar art of navigation infuriated Billy Mitchell, for it caused a three-week delay in the squadron's operations until the aircraft could be replaced.

The results of the daylight bombing raids carried out during the summer of 1918 proved hard to calculate. Crews reported seeing explosions, often on target as during the first raid in June, and subsequent aerial photographs sometimes disclosed work crews making repairs, an indication that damage had been done. Seldom, however, was there the kind of positive confirmation that came on August 21 when French intelligence cited eyewitness reports that a recent attack on the railroad facilities at Conflans, France, had killed fifty persons and destroyed forty crated aircraft.

Plans called for American crews to participate in long-range night bombardment with the Independent Force, established by the Royal Air Force to carry the war into Germany, but only a few officers, flying missions that would qualify them to become instructors, had seen action with the British when the fighting ended. Under the leadership of Trenchard, who was responsible to the Air Min-

A camera is loaded into an observation plane (left) for a reconnaissance
mission. Photos are joined together to make a ground map (right).

istry in London rather than to the British commander in chief in France, the
Independent Force dropped 543 tons of bombs on Germany, but only 60 percent
of the total hit urban targets. The rest fell on enemy airfields, for German fighters
proved dangerous enough, even at night, to justify attacks on their bases.

To the army, corps, or division commander, aerial observation was always more
important than night bombardment and usually more valuable than the daylight
raids beyond the battlelines. Observers not only provided essential information on
enemy activity, but also enabled a general to determine whether his organization
was successfully concealing its preparations for an attack, a relief, or any other tactical movement. In all, eighteen U.S. observation squadrons saw combat service
in France, the last arriving thirteen days before the armistice. These units normally supported the headquarters of an army or a corps. At the army level, the usual activities were mapping and aerial photography and locating targets for artillery or
aircraft. Within the corps, the major component of an army, observation squadrons
performed the same basic functions, tailoring their work to the needs of the combat divisions within the corps and the supporting artillery. The squadrons serving
an army commander usually flew the two-place, French-built Salmson 2, whereas
those assigned to a corps might use either that type or another two-place aircraft
like the French Spad XI scout or the British DH–4 day bomber.

Although aerial observation had little of the glamour of pursuit aviation or
even bombardment, a pilot and an observer from the 50th Aero Squadron, a
corps observation unit, earned the Medal of Honor for aiding American troops
isolated behind German lines. First Lieutenant Harold E. Goettler, the pilot, and
2d Lt. Erwin R. Bleckley, the observer, braved machinegun fire to fly at treetop
height over tortuous ravines in an attempt to locate the men, soldiers of the
308th Infantry, 77th Division. Both pilot and observer suffered fatal wounds,

but Goettler made a successful forced landing near a French outpost before he died. Notes made by the dying Bleckley narrowed the area where the unit might be found, but it was one of the trapped soldiers who worked his way through the German encirclement and brought help back to the so-called lost battalion.

The most celebrated of airmen were the pursuit pilots, especially the aces; the pursuit squadrons (totaling twenty, including two that served with the British) were the most numerous units in the Air Service, American Expeditionary Forces. The fame of the individual pilots and the number of units reflected the fact that the pursuit plane was the cutting edge of the aerial weapon from 1915 until the end of the war. Of all the American pursuit pilots, the most famous was Eddie Rickenbacker. Despite the reluctance of Carl Spaatz to see him reassigned from Issoudun, Rickenbacker obtained a transfer to the 94th Aero Squadron. There, Major Lufbery took a special interest in the newcomer, whose coordination, a consequence of his profitable career in automobile racing, and mature judgment (he was twenty-seven) enabled him to absorb and apply the advice the veteran airman was offering. Rickenbacker scored his first victory on April 29, 1918, sharing with Hall in the destruction of a Pfalz pursuit. According to the rules then in effect, both men received full credit for the kill; by the time of the armistice, Rickenbacker had destroyed twenty-six aircraft, four of them balloons.

If Rickenbacker represented caution and precision, America's second ranking ace, Frank Luke, was a daredevil, always impulsive and alternately boastful and sullen. Teamed with 1st Lt. Joseph F. Wehner, Luke specialized in low-altitude attacks on enemy observation balloons, always heavily defended because they were so important in adjusting artillery fire. Braving the fire of weapons that ranged from rifles to 77-mm antiaircraft guns and risking collision with trees or hillsides in the gathering dusk, Luke preferred to strike in the shadows of late afternoon, when his dark-colored Spad was all but invisible to fighters patrolling above. During his forays, Luke shot down fourteen balloons and four airplanes, and Wehner destroyed six balloons and two fighters. On September 18, 1918, Luke roared through the gathering twilight to set fire to two balloons, but as the second settled burning to earth, a pair of German Fokker D VII fighters jumped him and his wingman. Luke destroyed both enemy pursuits, but not before one of them shot down Wehner, who died in the crash. Eleven days later, Luke met his death after single-handedly attacking three observation balloons in succession. According to eyewitnesses, he survived the crash of his damaged fighter and, although wounded, exchanged shots with a German patrol until a rifle bullet killed him.

The importance of pursuit aviation had been clearly demonstrated by the time Mitchell began planning the great campaigns that helped defeat Germany in the fall of 1918. Like Trenchard, he believed firmly in taking the offensive, driving the enemy from the sky, and then attacking his ground forces. His principal concern was that he might have to succumb to pressures to protect

Eddie Rickenbacker (left) and Frank Luke (right), the two leading U.S. aces.

American forces by patrolling with pursuit planes all along the battleline as the Germans tended to do. In his opinion, which Trenchard had helped shape, he could best protect the infantry by attacking the enemy, forcing the German aircraft to do battle, and destroying them. As used by the Germans, aviation formed a thin defensive veneer, easily penetrated; in Mitchell's hands it became a club with which to batter the enemy.[24]

When the American Expeditionary Forces joined in the Aisne-Marne offensive in July 1918, the American 1st Pursuit Group found itself overmatched; its pilots were inexperienced compared to the German veterans, and its aircraft were Nieuports, which lacked the firepower and durability of the enemy's Fokker D VII. Furthermore, American observation squadrons on important aerial photography missions pleaded with Mitchell for fighter escort. Determined to employ the pursuit group on offensive thrusts into enemy territory rather than defensively, Mitchell followed Trenchard's principles and insisted that observation craft, in effect, escort themselves. On a typical mission, a three-aircraft formation would cover the assigned area, the observer in one taking photographs while the rear-seat gunners in the other two provided protection. Although the pursuit group suffered most of the month's twenty-three casualties during the two-week battle, the survivors became excellent pilots, and they began receiving the new Spad XIII, a vast improvement over the fragile Nieuport.[25]

By the time the First Army of Pershing's American Expeditionary Forces attacked the German-held St. Mihiel salient on September 12, 1918, Mitchell had enough aircraft to maintain pressure on the enemy by day and night, over the battlefield and beyond. As the First Army's air officer, he had direct control over or could rely on the assistance of 1,481 aircraft—701 pursuit, 366 observation, 323 day bombers, and 91 night bombers—although less than half were flown by Americans. Most of the others were French, predominantly pursuit units with some day bombers and observation planes, a total of 58 squadrons. Of the 91 night bombers available for the offensive, Mitchell had control only of those supplied by the Italians, about 25 percent of the total; the single-engine British night bombers remained a part of the Independent Force, but Trenchard promised to use them against targets that would affect the outcome of the St. Mihiel fighting.

When the campaign began, the Germans were outnumbered ten to one in pursuits, with the squadrons nearest the St. Mihiel salient at an even greater disadvantage because the pilots were learning to fly the new Fokker D VII. Despite rapid reinforcement by the enemy, Mitchell never lost control of the air. He could depend on the day bombers and observation planes to attract German pursuits, which then became the prey of Allied fighters. Offensive penetrations of German air space by Mitchell's pursuits neutralized the deadly Fokkers, even engaging the enemy over his own airfields. The observation craft still had to defend themselves, however, as did the day bombers, which at times adopted a 12-plane formation to mass their defensive fire. During the St. Mihiel offensive, American airmen fired 30,000 rounds of machinegun ammunition, dropped 75 tons of bombs, and claimed the destruction of 12 balloons and 60 aircraft. Besides patrolling in search of enemy fighters and balloons, American pursuit pilots strafed and even bombed enemy road traffic, while day bombers attacked towns that served as road or rail junctions and joined the fighters in hitting targets on the battlefield. Mitchell's aviation units might have done even more except for the weather. The wheels of heavily laden aircraft churned rain-soaked grass airfields into mud, and cloud cover at times prevented American airmen from locating targets on the ground or intercepting the Fokkers in the air. Since the Germans were conducting a fighting withdrawal from the salient, yielding territory in return for the opportunity to inflict casualties, roads leading to the rear were crowded with troops, but low-hanging clouds frequently screened these and other targets. Despite the difficult flying conditions, Mitchell's aviators contributed to a clear-cut victory on the ground.[26]

During the Meuse-Argonne campaign, a succession of battles that lasted from September 26 until the end of October and left 110,000 American dead or wounded, Mitchell followed the tactics of the St. Mihiel fighting but made better use of his aircraft. In seizing and exploiting control of the air, he benefited from generally good weather, although banks of clouds at times interfered with observation and bombardment and provided concealment for hostile pursuit pilots. From the outset, Mitchell sent entire pursuit groups of about 100 planes beyond the battleline, where they attacked enemy observation balloons, strafed troops and supply convoys, and challenged the outnumbered German fighter force. When enemy bombers began attacking by night, American pursuit pilots tried to intercept, harassing the raiders but failing to down any.

Allied day bombers proved especially effective, whether defending themselves, attracting enemy fighters that escorting pursuit planes could engage, or

The French Spad XIII (above) and the German Fokker D VII (below) may
have been the best pursuit aircraft of the opposing forces. The Allies
thought so highly of the Fokker that it was named as war material
to be handed over to the victors in the terms of the Armistice.

causing casualties among German ground forces. Self-defense improved because of the insistence on larger formations that enabled gunners to mass their
fire. Using the day bombers as bait, American pursuit pilots intervened with
deadly effect; on October 4, for example, they shot down 11 Fokker and Pfalz
biplanes that were attacking a formation of three squadrons. The largest day-

time raid took place on October 9, when Mitchell dispatched some 200 American bombers and 100 fighters against German troop concentrations. The deadliest attack, according to intelligence reports, struck the town of Bayonville on October 18, when de Havillands and Breguets, flown by American airmen, received credit for killing 250 enemy soldiers and wounding three times that number.[27]

The American victory on the battlefields of the Meuse-Argonne was but one aspect of an Allied general offensive against a German nation on the verge of starvation after four years of naval blockade and bled to exhaustion by the unceasing slaughter on the Western Front. Even as Germany's military and political leaders realized that the war was lost, American military men were considering how to unleash new weapons against an already battered enemy. Hap Arnold, having spent more than two years dealing with aircraft production and the administration of the new Army Air Service, was having his first contact with weapons development. He arrived in France in November 1918 to arrange for the testing of a pilotless flying bomb devised by Charles Kettering, an automobile engineer, and powered by an engine built by Henry Ford, the auto manufacturer. A gyroscope held the "Bug" on course and an aneroid barometer kept it at a prescribed altitude until the propeller shaft had turned a specified number of revolutions. Then the craft shed its wings, plunged to earth, and detonated the 300 pounds of high explosive in its nose. Neither the Kettering Bug nor a similar weapon devised by Lawrence Sperry for the Navy was perfected in time to see combat.

Also too late for wartime use was another weapon whose impact on warfare could not yet be guessed. The Aircraft Armament Section of the Army's Ordnance Department had arranged to test in November 1918 a new projectile developed by a young physicist named Robert H. Goddard. Goddard successfully demonstrated his new weapon—a solid-fuel rocket, four inches in diameter, that could be launched from an aircraft with absolutely no recoil—within days of the armistice. The return of peace, however, signaled an end to the Army's interest in the prototype for the aerial rockets of World War II and the distant progenitor of more massive weapons, yet undreamed of, with intercontinental range.

By the time the armistice went into effect at 11:00 a.m., November 11, 1918, military aviation had proved its importance to the battle on the ground. By massing his aircraft to achieve local superiority, the aviation officer had driven the enemy from the skies over the battlefield, strafed and bombed hostile forces and supply lines, and obtained accurate and timely information for his commanding general as the battle unfolded. The airplane, however, remained basically a battlefield weapon, for it lacked the range and striking power and was not available in sufficient numbers to carry the war far beyond the trenches and demoralize the enemy or cripple his ability to fight. Great Britain had survived bombardment by airship and airplane, and, aside from an occasional break in civilian morale, the greatest effect of the bombing was to arouse demands for re-

Armistice Day, 1918, San Diego California.

venge. The vengeance attacks had little impact, however, for German authorities ignored those war-weary citizens bold enough to demand protection from the bombers of Trenchard's Independent Force.

Using the conventional aircraft of the time, few of them American-built, the Air Service of the American Expeditionary Forces destroyed 776 enemy planes and 72 balloons, dropped 138 tons of bombs in 150 raids, and took 18,000 individual photographs of German positions. This was an impressive record for an air arm that just two years before could muster only 55 airplanes and some 1,200 officers and men. The price of success was 569 airmen killed or wounded, 654 dead because of illness or accidents, and the loss of 290 planes and 37 balloons.

In the nineteen months from April 6, 1917, to November 11, 1918, the Army air arm absorbed the lessons of individual tactics, employment, training, and organization that European airmen had been learning since the war broke out in 1914. Pilots like Rickenbacker and Luke proved as good as Europe's best, and Mitchell demonstrated his competence in employing large numbers of squadrons from different nations. In training and organization, the U.S. Army in general copied the Allies, but the concept of an independent air force or a tactical striking force responsible to the chief of that service rather than to a ground commander was as yet too radical for acceptance by the American high command. Indeed, the future of the Royal Air Force as the peer of Great Britain's army and navy was far from assured when the war ended.

At the time of the armistice, American manufacturers were beginning to produce respectable numbers of aircraft, including slightly more than a thousand DH–4s in the months of October and November 1918. The DH–4 provided useful, if not spectacular, service during the war and after; the SE–5 was somewhat successful as a trainer; and the postwar Army found some use for its eight Handley Pages (seven assembled from American-made parts after the armistice) and its five Capronis (four finished after the fighting ended). Of the standard types manufactured in the United States, only the Liberty-powered Bristol fighter was an utter failure.

Moreover, a research and development establishment began to take shape at McCook Field, where the Army had conducted its wartime aeronautical engineering activity, rather than at the facilities of the National Advisory Committee for Aeronautics at Hampton, Virginia, where a suitable laboratory had not been completed. Even during the war, the engineers at McCook Field had worked on a number of important development projects. For example, Alfred Verville, a civilian engineer employed there, designed a courier aircraft, produced as the Sperry Messenger, and at the time of the armistice was working on a pursuit. While assigned to McCook Field, a member of the wartime French military mission to the United States, Capt. G. Le Pere, designed a two-place fighter, two examples of which were shipped to France for further testing. Army contracts let during the conflict encouraged the work of American airplane builders like the Glenn L. Martin Company, which developed the twin-engine MB–2, a successful postwar bomber, and the Thomas-Morse Aircraft Corporation, which produced a single-seat pursuit used by the wartime air arm as a trainer. In terms of fostering development, as well as building aircraft and using them in combat, the U.S. Army and the American aviation industry had responded to the spur of war and caught up with the nations of Europe.[28]

Chapter 3

From Air Service to Air Corps: The Era of Billy Mitchell

John F. Shiner

When Col. Henry H. "Hap" Arnold returned from France after World War I, he found himself something of an outsider. The leadership of the postwar Air Service seemed to rest firmly in the hands of those airmen who had commanded aviation units in France, officers like William L. "Billy" Mitchell and Benjamin D. Foulois, both wartime brigadier generals, or Thomas DeW. Milling and Frank P. Lahm, who had received wartime promotions to colonel. Those who had remained in Washington, overseeing the hectic expansion of both military aeronautics and the aviation industry, now had to make way for the officers who had directed the Air Service of the American Expeditionary Forces. Arnold received orders to take command at Rockwell Field, San Diego, California, where he encountered two officers whose futures would be interwoven with his own. One of them, Maj. Carl Spaatz, who had shot down three German planes, was Arnold's executive officer. The other, Ira Eaker, a young first lieutenant recently transferred to aviation from the infantry, became post adjutant.

When Arnold assumed command in 1919, some 8,000 enlisted men, 375 officers, and hundreds of aircraft were based at Rockwell Field. His job, however, was not to forge the men and machines into a fighting unit but to process the departure of the draftees and reserve officers who had entered the Air Service to fight Germany and to inspect the assigned airplanes, cull those not needed by the Air Service, and get rid of the surplus. The excess aircraft judged usable were sold to civilians, many to barnstormers who flew from town to town selling brief flights for a few dollars. Those airplanes that could not be flown safely were junked. Once again, the United States built a formidable military machine to fight a war and then proceeded to disband it when the sound of firing died away. But, and this, too, had become a pattern, the postwar Army would be larger than the prewar force.

While Arnold tended to the demobilization of a part of the wartime air arm, Mitchell returned from France with the understanding that he would take over the Army Air Service, replacing the civilian, John D. Ryan, who had directed the organization from August 1918 until his resignation shortly after the armistice. When Mitchell arrived at Washington in 1919, he found that an officer senior to him, Maj. Gen. Charles T. Menoher, had received the assignment he thought was his. The selection of Menoher, who had distinguished himself in command of an infantry division in France but had no practical experience in aviation, dramatized the War Department's attitude toward military aeronautics. Instead of Mitchell, clearly the most competent of aviation planners, an infantryman had taken charge of the air arm. That Mitchell became Menoher's principal assistant served only to underscore the belief on the part of the Army's leadership that aviation was subordinate to operations on the ground, a view that Mitchell and others were beginning to challenge. On the basis of his experience in France, Mitchell had concluded that neither land nor sea campaigns could succeed without control of the air.

In the years from 1918 to 1925, the Army Air Service's experience was somewhat paradoxical. On the one hand, it experienced sharply reduced manning and budgets, a diminishing inventory of obsolescent and deteriorating aircraft, and considerable indifference to its plight on the part of its Army masters. On the other hand, one can find in this period the seeds of far greater prosperity. Manning and budgets, although short of the Air Service's desires, far exceeded prewar levels. New, technically advanced aircraft types, although not procured in numbers, were developed. More important, perhaps, American airmen kept trying to push performance limits outward through their pursuit of various speed, endurance, and altitude records. A vigorous debate developed over the desirability of an independent air force, and, maybe most important of all, Army airmen began developing a coherent theory of air power.

In France Mitchell had used aviation to help Pershing attack at St. Mihiel and the Meuse-Argonne; indeed, given the available equipment and the organization of the American Expeditionary Forces, he could not have conducted operations except in support of troops on the ground. By the time he returned to Washington, however, he was trying to predict how the lessons of the recent past

From Air Service to Air Corps: The Era of Billy Mitchell

Brig. Gen. Billy Mitchell

would be applied in a shadowy future when military aeronautics included aircraft carriers, with which the British had been experimenting, and ocean-spanning dirigibles, as well as pursuit, observation, and bombardment aircraft that were vastly improved over those used in France. Since he had exercised control over the massed aircraft of different nations in the last months of the war, he now proposed the centralized control of all American aviation—lighter-than-air and heavier-than-air, land-based and sea-based, including air mail and the commercial operations that were just beginning. He advocated the creation of a department of aviation to provide land-based squadrons for the field armies, aircraft carriers to accompany naval expeditions, and bombers and pursuit planes to defend the coasts of the United States against seaborne invasion or attack by hostile airships. A cabinet officer equal in status to the Secretary of War and Secretary of the Navy would head the new department. In addition, this proposed cabinet office would encourage through purchases and outright subsidies an American aviation industry that, since the return of peace, could no longer depend on sales to the military.[1]

Articulate, bemedaled, handsome in his personally designed uniform, Mitchell took center stage, but he was not yet the most outspoken champion of an air arm independent of the Army. Whereas Mitchell insisted throughout 1919 that his campaign be handled "on a broad basis and a high plane," Foulois attacked head-on, protesting in testimony for a congressional committee that, since the establishment of the Aeronautical Division of the Signal Corps in 1907, the War Department had proved through its indifference that it had "no right or title or claim to further control over aviation or the aviation industry of the United States." As time passed, however, each man adopted the tactics of the other. Mitchell grew increasingly strident in his demands for an independent air force, at first in a department of aviation and later in a department of national defense, and Foulois became effective in working within the framework of the War Department.

History of the United States Air Force

A few American politicians were receptive to the idea of an independent air arm modeled after the British Royal Air Force, and a number of bills to accomplish this were introduced in Congress shortly after the war. For a time, one sponsored by Senator Harry S. New, a Republican from Indiana, to create a federal department of aeronautics seemed to enjoy strong support, but once the political battleline had been drawn, Congress shrank from challenging an institution—the U.S. Army—that had so recently proved itself in war. The arguments of those who favored independence faded before the opposition of the men who had defeated Germany—spokesmen for the War Department like John J. Pershing, Mason Patrick (who had returned to the Corps of Engineers after commanding military aviation in France), and Secretary of War Newton D. Baker.

Pershing's view of aviation reflected the findings of studies prepared by officers of the American Expeditionary Forces after the fighting ended. He conceded that aviation was an important auxiliary but insisted that it remain a part of the Army, which needed its unique contributions, instead of becoming independent. As he saw it, aviation could not be the equal of the Army and Navy because of the disparity in what each could accomplish. Armies had demonstrated their ability to destroy an enemy's ground forces, invade his territory, and force his surrender; fleets could blockade a hostile state and starve it into submission. Only when aeronautics could similarly prevail would the air arm deserve to become a separate service equal with the Army and Navy.

In opposing an independent air force like Britain's Royal Air Force, General Patrick questioned the motives of those who advocated the change. The quarrels between the Foulois group and Mitchell's followers in 1917 and 1918 may have persuaded Patrick that prestige meant as much to airmen as results. Whatever the reason, he concluded that the Army aviators seeking independence were interested mainly in their own advancement; and, in fact, promotions were a consideration. With a few exceptions—Mitchell and Charles deF. Chandler, both lieutenant colonels; Foulois, a major; and a handful of other majors (including Spaatz) promoted permanently for service in France—Army airmen had been flying only since 1916 and held the permanent rank of captain or lieutenant. These junior officers were understandably concerned that unless a system of temporary peacetime promotion was adopted (a reform that did not appear until 1935), senior officers from nonflying branches of the Army would be able to transfer into the Air Service at the upper reaches of the Army's single promotion list, which already was clogged near the bottom with officers commissioned during the war. Since seniority was the sole criterion for promotion, and retirement was not mandatory, advancement within the Army would be painfully slow for the recently commissioned airman. In contrast, a separate service would have its own promotion list and would be commanded by officers experienced in military aviation rather than by recent transfers from components outside aviation. Once he realized the nature of the problem, Patrick would relent on the question of promotion, although he continued to believe that a solution was possible within the existing military establishment.

For the present, Secretary of War Baker expressed his satisfaction with the organizational status of the postwar Army Air Service, thus disregarding the findings of a commission he sent to Europe in 1919 to study wartime developments in aviation. Assistant Secretary of War Benedict Crowell led a panel of officers from the armed forces and representatives of the American aircraft industry on a fact-finding tour of Great Britain, France, and Italy. Although Crowell's group had not been charged with making recommendations, it succumbed to the spell of independent air power that was cast on the members in Europe, exceeded its instructions, and overrode the objections of the Navy panelist to call for the creation of a department of aeronautics in the cabinet, thus echoing Mitchell's proposal. Baker chose, however, to ignore the recommendation of what he considered an investigatory rather than advisory mission. Instead of endorsing the view of the future that Crowell had glimpsed in Europe, he accepted the guidance of Pershing and like-minded generals who had proved successful during the recent fighting. The Secretary of War saw no need for institutional change; he concluded that the Army, like the Navy, should continue to control its own aviation, relying on the existing Joint Army and Navy Board for coordination.

Mitchell's drive for independence from the Army was thus frustrated at the outset. In 1917 and 1918, a wartime British government had overcome opposition from the Army and Navy to establish an independent Royal Air Force. Why had Great Britain's leaders accepted an idea now judged too radical on the opposite shore of the Atlantic? The main consideration had been that Germans were bombing London, thus arousing a demand for revenge. If independent, the air arm could unleash bombers of its own against German cities without being diverted by ground commanders to other missions. Once the fighting ended, another factor prompted a cost-conscious government to retain the Royal Air Force as a permanent part of the British military establishment. This consideration was the immense toll of dead and wounded exacted by four years of trench warfare. The Italians listed more than two million casualties, the British some three million, the French six million, and the Germans seven million. Aviation, acting independently of the struggling masses below, held out the promise of carrying the war beyond the battlefield, where bloody stalemate had reigned; by attacking the enemy homeland, a war could be ended at a comparatively small cost in human life, on the part of both the victor and the defeated nation.

The United States suffered 320,000 casualties during the war, a heavy toll considering the brief period of actual combat but slight compared to the losses of the other combatants. Pershing, furthermore, had done precisely what he set out to do, breaking through Germany's outer defenses, although greatly aided by a series of enemy attacks that may have cost Germany 800,000 casualties and assuredly contributed to the exhaustion of an already weary German army. The

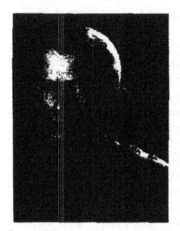

Maj. Gen. William L. Kenly, (left) Chief, Division of Military Aeronautics,
May 1918–December 1918, and Maj. Gen. Charles T. Menoher, (right)
Chief, Army Air Service, December 1918–October 1921.

American Expeditionary Forces had scarcely experienced the frustrations of
trench warfare during some six months of savage fighting, but the armies of
Britain, France, and Germany had fought over much the same terrain for four
painful years. No wonder, therefore, that the British, whose cities had experienced frightening but otherwise ineffectual aerial attack, looked to the airplane
as a means of minimizing bloodshed by avoiding stalemate, whereas Pershing
and many of his American colleagues interpreted the war as a vindication of an
existing doctrine that promised victory on the ground.

The American Army's confidence in its wartime tactics, congressional indifference to aviation as a weapon of the future, and the limitations of the aircraft
then available all combined to defeat Mitchell's first campaign for an independent air force. Instead of creating a department of aeronautics coequal with the
War and Navy Departments, Congress passed and President Wilson signed the
National Defense Act of 1920. Regarded as a crushing blow by Mitchell and his
allies, the new law did change the status of military aviation. Besides recogniz-
ing the Air Service as a combat arm of the Army and authorizing a permanently assigned complement of officers and men, the new legislation bestowed the
rank of major general on the Chief of the Air Service and authorized a brigadier
general to be Assistant Chief. Menoher continued to serve as chief, and
Mitchell, whose wartime promotion to brigadier general had not yet expired,
stayed on as his assistant with that rank. The reorganization act gave the Chief
of the Air Service control over aviation research and development, the procurement of aircraft, and the recruitment and training of personnel, but withheld
from him the command of operational air units. Taking into account the fact that
flying was the hallmark of an air service, and also the attitude of aviators toward

those who were not, the act specified that no more than ten percent of Air Service officers could be nonflyers and specified that aviators would command all flying units. Furthermore, the law attempted to remedy a persistent complaint of the flyers by authorizing flight pay equal to fifty percent of base pay. This last provision was important to the men who daily risked their lives in flimsy aircraft and as a consequence could not buy life insurance at reasonable rates.

Having retained control of the Air Service, the War Department General Staff soon addressed the subject of military aviation as part of its task of helping the Chief of Staff (now General Pershing) establish policy for the Army on professional matters and advise the Secretary of War. The resulting policy lent credence to the view held by most Army aviators, including those who felt that independence was either undesirable or not yet feasible, that only an airman could understand how to use aircraft. As it did with the Regular, reserve, and National Guard divisions, the General Staff parceled out aviation units among nine corps area commanders, all senior ground officers, responsible for the operations and training of all the forces within their assigned geographic regions of the United States. The Chief of the Air Service controlled only the materiel depots and formal schools within a corps area, not the operating squadrons. Consequently, no air officer could practice in peacetime the concentration of aerial forces that had proved so successful over the St. Mihiel salient and in subsequent fighting.

The new blueprint for the postwar organization of the Air Service called for twenty-seven squadrons, including nineteen observation units that had only a limited offensive potential since they normally functioned exclusively as the eyes of the Army. The combat strength of the air arm totaled only four pursuit and four bombardment squadrons, although Menoher, his successor Mason Patrick, and Mitchell persuaded the General Staff to approve the incremental expansion of the pursuit and bombardment squadrons until they totaled twenty in 1923. Observation balloon companies made up the balance of the force. The General Staff originally wanted thirty-two companies of tethered balloons and two of dirigibles, but in 1922 it deactivated the balloon outfits as a economy move, only to resurrect two of them for a brief period. Mitchell enthusiastically supported acquiring dirigibles until the Italian-built *Roma* crashed and burned in 1922, claiming thirty-four lives; following this tragedy the Army airship was little more than a curiosity, although the program lingered until 1937.

While the postwar status of the Air Service was thus taking shape, demobilization proceeded, as throughout the Air Service dozens of officers, including Arnold at Rockwell Field, were expediting discharges and reducing the wartime inventory of aircraft. Before stepping down as Director of Military Aeronautics, Maj. Gen. William L. Kenly had confessed that the return of peace "has created the greatest uncertainty as to the immediate future."[2] This uncertainty persisted beyond Kenly's tenure, as the air arm contracted in size and then tried to subsist on congressional appropriations that, however lavish in comparison to prewar days, barely enabled airmen to keep their planes aloft.

History of the United States Air Force

Immediately after the armistice, the Army began its painful adjustment to peacetime funding, promptly canceling orders for 13,000 planes and 20,000 engines. Aircraft already purchased and excess to the needs of the smaller Air Service were sold if serviceable; if not, they were salvaged for parts or destroyed. The surplus airplanes the Army dumped on the market further depressed an aviation industry whose production was shrinking from a monthly rate in excess of 1,000 planes in November 1918 to less than a third that number in all of 1922. Nor did military orders ease the crisis facing the airplane manufacturers. General Menoher reported in late 1919 that: "Not a dollar is available for the purchase of new aircraft."[3] The flyers would have to make do with what was on hand, even though those machines were rapidly becoming obsolete. Like the rest of the Army, the Air Service had entered a period of austerity that would last until the eve of another world war.

Similarly, the demobilization of wartime officers and enlisted men began almost as soon as the guns fell silent. Since the wartime expansion of the Air Service had been proportionately far greater than that of the rest of the Army—at peak strength the air arm was almost 200 times as large as the prewar organization, but the ground forces were only 20 times prewar size—military aeronautics now had to undergo drastic cuts to achieve balance between the two components. The flyers realized this and worried that they soon would find themselves part of a tiny, ineffective aviation force, for they sensed that the General Staff had little appreciation of the offensive potential of the airplane, a realization that had touched off the abortive attempt to gain independence. The concerns of the airmen seemed justified, as the War Department cut Air Service strength from a wartime high of 20,000 officers, most of them reservists, to a nucleus in 1919 of just 200 Regular officers. At that time, all the Regulars were on detail from other branches of the service, a condition that would prevail until Congress, a year later, acted to establish a permanent complement for the air arm.

The declining state of the Army's aerial auxiliary troubled the General Staff, which appreciated the contributions of aviation on the battlefields of France, but money simply was not available to refurbish the Air Service. In the absence of a clearly defined threat to national security—Germany had been defeated, and only a few naval planners worried about a war with Japan—a gap rapidly opened between the manpower strength that Congress approved in 1920 and the strength it would fund in succeeding years. The National Defense Act of 1920, which established the status of the Air Service as a combat arm, also authorized a strength of 280,000 for the Army, with 1,516 officers and 16,000 enlisted men (including 2,500 air cadets) serving in military aviation. By 1922, economy-minded congressmen had reduced the Army's size to 148,000; by 1926, the authorized total hovered around 135,000. Similarly, the authorized number of Army officers declined from 19,000 in 1920 to 14,000 in 1926. The Air Service, since it was a component of the Army, shared in the reduction, leveling off in

1923 at just 880 officers and 8,229 enlisted men, a strength that would scarcely change for the next three years.

Airmen tended to blame the Army, as an institution, for most of the manpower problems of the Air Service, claiming that the average ground officer had no interest in military aviation. Undoubtedly some officers fit this description, as Ira Eaker discovered when he reported with his aviation squadron for duty in the Philippines. No arrangements had been made to feed his men, and when he broke into a storeroom to obtain canned goods for them, the supply officer reported him to the commanding general. Luckily for Eaker, the general appreciated the display of initiative and decided against a court-martial. Regardless of what the aviators might believe, such incidents represented individual pettiness rather than institutional attitudes.

In shaping policy for the Army and apportioning its resources, the General Staff could do little to increase the size of the Air Service. The War Department had to operate within a precisely defined framework consisting of the overall strength authorized by Congress for the entire Army and the amount of money appropriated each year to maintain that force. Any expansion of the air arm—whether an increase in the number of enlisted men, admission of Regular officers to flight training, or the granting of Regular commissions to reservists—could come about only at the expense of the other arms of the Army which had demonstrated their importance during the recent war. As a consequence, aviation units like the 1st Pursuit Group, whose table of organization called for 101 officers, had but 20. (Of course, demobilization and congressional unwillingness to fund the Army at its authorized strength had a similar impact on the ground forces.)

Pilots had become especially scarce. Deaths in flying accidents and resignations from the Air Service intensified the shortage during the early 1920s. West Point did not produce many volunteers for flight training in those years, but flyers awarded wartime reserve commissions remained in the Air Service after the war, received Regular commissions, and made up for the absence of West Pointers. The wartime reservists who turned Regular included many future leaders of the air arm. George C. Kenney became a Regular officer in 1920; his experience in aviation dated from his student days at the Massachusetts Institute of Technology when he and a fellow student built their own airplane and coaxed it a few feet into the air for a distance of perhaps a hundred yards. Another addition to the permanent Air Service was Muir S. Fairchild, who had learned to fly in Europe and carried out night bombardment missions with the French. Also embarking at this time on a career in military aviation was Barney McK. Giles, who had spent the war at training fields in Texas; his twin brother, Benjamin F., followed his example and in 1924 become a Regular officer in the Air Service. The roster of former reservists obtaining Regular commissions included Ennis C. Whitehead, during the war an instructor at the Issoudun training center, and Kenneth B. Wolfe, who had taught flying in Georgia. Claire L. Chennault entered the Regular service at this time; he became an acknowledged master of pursuit

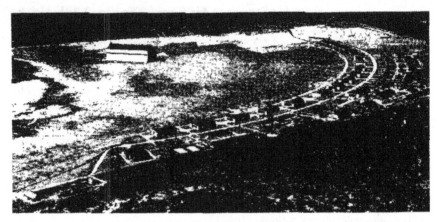

Brooks Field, Texas, 1924.

tactics, retired in 1937 because of physical disability, and returned during World War II, becoming a major general. Yet another addition to the Regular service was James H. Doolittle, who had relieved the boredom of duty on the Mexican border by winning a bet of five dollars that he could sit on the spreader bar between the wheels of a DH–4 while the pilot landed the aircraft. He later gained prominence as a daredevil racing pilot and an aeronautical engineer, left the service, but returned during World War II, rising to the rank of lieutenant general.

In a further attempt to overcome the shortage of pilots, the Air Service continued the aviation cadet program used during the war, though on a reduced scale because of limited funding. Young men who survived an initial screening went directly from civilian life to pilot training and, if they passed the course, were awarded the wings of an Army pilot and commissioned as reserve officers. Some of them were then allowed to serve a few years on active duty with aviation squadrons. Typical classes of the period entered training with 90 to 180 members, a far cry from the 2,500 cadets authorized by the 1920 legislation.

Reserve officers commissioned through the cadet program might serve for a time on active duty and then transfer to the postwar reserve founded in 1919 and confirmed by the National Defense Act of 1920. From some 5,000 pilots in 1920, almost all of them trained for the war, the number enrolled in the reserve increased to almost 7,000 in 1926. (The enlisted reserve proved less attractive, peaking at about 1,000 members in 1926 and declining thereafter.) The growth of reserve pilots was proof of man's fascination with flying in those early days, for the pay was minimal. However, as the pool of pilots trained for World War I grew older and more settled, they lost their enthusiasm for flying; consequently, the number of reserve pilots dwindled to about 1,000 by 1938. Nevertheless, the Air Service and its successor, the Air Corps, continued to provide an appropriate number of Regular officers and enlisted men to help train the organized reserve units.

The Air Service also trained pilots for the National Guard. In 1920, the War Department agreed that each state should establish one observation squadron. One year later, the Air Service began supplying aircraft and instructors, al-

Wright Field, Ohio, 1928.

though the states remained responsible for airfields and hangar space. Unlike the reserve, which initially attracted so many wartime pilots, the National Guard forged slowly ahead in the field of aviation. In 1930, air units could be found in nineteen states, one more than enough to assign one observation squadron to each of the National Guard divisions authorized in the National Defense Act of 1920; but the program did not flourish. In the mid-1930s the National Guard had about 300 pilots and 2,000 enlisted men in the various observation units. Neither the air elements of the National Guard nor those of the reserve would expand appreciably until World War II began in Europe in the summer of 1939.

Despite the scarcity of pilots in the 1920s, training was extremely rigorous. Because the Air Service had far more applicants for flying training than it had funds to accept, it maintained high entrance standards, taking only the best prospects. Even so, only a few survived the ruthless screening during the course of instruction. Charles A. Lindbergh, who made the first nonstop solo flight from New York to Paris, recalled that of the 103 cadets who entered training with him, only 17 graduated from the advanced course. The savage attrition was not limited to cadets, however; Regular officers and reservists also were eliminated during pilot training if their progress was not satisfactory.

After the war, the Air Service streamlined the training programs for pilots and mechanics. By 1922, primary flying training was conducted only at Brooks Field, San Antonio, Texas; after successfully completing that course, student pilots traveled across town to Kelly Field for the advanced course. Scott Field in Illinois was the home of the Balloon and Airship School until 1928, when the school ceased operations. The Technical School at Chanute Field, Illinois, trained aircraft mechanics throughout the interwar years.

Between 1919 and 1922, the Air Service also established professional training programs that were of great benefit to the air arm. In 1919 it created a School of Application at McCook Field in Dayton, Ohio, to provide selected flyers a chance to study the design and maintenance of aircraft and engines. Renamed the Air Corps Engineering School in 1926, it moved to its permanent home at the new Wright Field just outside Dayton soon thereafter. Also in 1919, physicians assigned to the Air Service began receiving training in the medical problems associated with aerial flight; and in 1922, the Army established the School of Aviation Medicine at San Antonio. General Menoher, in 1920, opened the Field Officers School, renamed the Tactical School two years later. This school trained officers for higher command and gave them an opportunity to study tactical employment of aviation.

General Menoher's tenure ended abruptly in 1921, the result of his determination to curb the zeal of his assistant, Billy Mitchell, whose publicity campaigns on behalf of military aviation were by this time overshadowing the Chief of the Air Service and antagonizing senior flag officers of the Army and the Navy. When Menoher presented Secretary of War John W. Weeks a choice between muzzling Mitchell or finding a new officer to head the Air Service, the cabinet officer hesitated, for by courting publicity, Mitchell had become a national celebrity. Menoher promptly accepted a new assignment and was replaced by Maj. Gen. Mason M. Patrick, Pershing's chief of aviation in France, who had testified in 1919 against Mitchell's plan for an air force independent of the Army.

Soon after taking over the Army Air Service, Patrick earned the wings of a junior military aviator at the age of fifty-nine. Although he never flew unless accompanied by a more proficient flyer, his gesture impressed the Army's airmen. Indeed, aviators and ground officers alike respected him, for he knew the problems of both groups and could discuss the issues intelligently. Popular though

Maj. Gen. Mason M. Patrick, Chief, Army Air Service, October 1921–
July 1926, and Chief, Army Air Corps, July 1926–December 1927.

he was, he inherited such chronic problems as the shortage of pilots and the scarcity of modern aircraft in a time of evolving technology, as well as the smoothly functioning system of training that Menoher had established. To provide more officers in the higher grades and ease another problem that hounded him, the General Staff offered to arrange transfers into aviation from other branches of the service, but Patrick refused. He did not want the Air Service to become topheavy with nonflyers. He believed, moreover, that equipment was a greater problem than manpower, declaring that the number of available pilots "was more than ample in view of the materiel available."

As early as 1922, the shortage of airplanes that troubled Patrick was being compounded by the worsening obsolescence of those on hand. The Army, for example, still flew the DH–4, which the Royal Air Force had begun replacing even before World War I. In addition, the fragile construction and hard use combined to limit the span of service for even modern aircraft. Crashes and forced landings were commonplace, and the cautious pilot flying cross-country always watched ahead for a level field suitable for an emergency landing. Engine failure was the cause of many emergencies, although Hap Arnold once had the plywood fuselage of his Le Pere biplane crack lengthwise beneath his feet; luckily the aircraft held together long enough for him to land safely.

Not every pilot was as fortunate as Arnold, for in a given year as many as five percent of the Army's pilots, one in twenty, might die in accidents. Although the number of fatalities per 100,000 flying hours declined from 94 in 1921 to 68 in 1922, the rate rose to 88 per 100,000 during the following year before improving to 35 in 1924 and 27 in both 1925 and 1926. Despite the overall decline, a rate of 27 deaths per 100,000 hours was roughly three times that which would be achieved with the aircraft of the late 1930s.

To the untrained eye, quantity seemed more impressive than quality. In 1921, for instance, a casual observer might well have been impressed by the Army's inventory of almost 3,000 aircraft in storage or assigned to operating squadrons and questioned the need for more. The informed person realized, however, that the overwhelming majority were types designed and built for service during World War I: 1,500 Curtiss Jenny trainers, 1,100 DH–4 observation craft, and 179 SE–5 pursuits. Only 12 of the Army's aircraft were new Martin MB–2 bombers, a type first flown in 1919.

Rapid progress in aeronautical engineering occurred in subsequent years, as the liquid-cooled Curtiss engine permitted a measure of streamlining in fighters and the lighter air-cooled radial engine supplanted the Liberty in bombers; but these advances did not result in the purchase of aircraft in the numbers necessary to offset the effects of accidents and obsolescence. Few airplanes were bought, some 300 accidents of varying severity occurred each year, and obsolete aircraft continued to be discarded. No wonder that the more pessimistic of Army airmen were beginning to believe that normal attrition would soon leave them with nothing to fly.

The Curtiss PW–8.

By mid-1924, the number had dwindled to 1,364 aircraft, with only 754 in commission; the active inventory included 457 observation, 55 bomber, 78 pursuit, and 8 attack planes, the last resembling a cross between the observation craft and the day bomber of World War I. For most of the decade, the total offensive strength of the Air Service based in the United States consisted of the 1st Pursuit Group at Selfridge Field, Michigan; the 2d Bombardment Group at Langley Field, Virginia; and the 3d Attack Group at Kelly Field, Texas. The overseas force consisted of one bombardment and one pursuit squadron in each of the three military departments in Panama, Hawaii, and the Philippines. Until the mid-1920s, the Army air arm got by on equipment left over from the war, for it had no money to do otherwise.

Funding remained a problem for the Air Service throughout the tenures of Menoher and Patrick. For the fiscal year beginning July 1, 1919, Congress, in its rush to demobilize and place the armed forces on a peacetime footing, made available for military aviation only $25 million, a sizable sum by prewar standards but less than six percent of the previous year's funding. Fully aware of the sad state of his inventory, General Patrick made an urgent request for $26.2 million to buy new aircraft in fiscal 1923. The War Department realized that this amount might be a lion's share of the Army budget and asked for only $15 million to avoid favoring aviation at the expense of the other arms that were just as poorly funded, but Congress cut this amount to $12.7 million. Patrick warned that such an inadequate appropriation left the Air Service "entirely incapable of meeting its war requirements," but no conflict seemed likely and his words went unheeded.

For the next fiscal year, 1924, the Air Service received a quarter of a million dollars less and its aircraft continued to deteriorate. Fiscal 1925 brought only slight improvement, an increase to $14,113,000. A discouraged Mason Patrick publicly urged Congress to provide enough money in future appropriations "to supply safe flying equipment for at least existing units and personnel;" but the War Department, the recently established Bureau of the Budget, and Congress each reduced the annual request for funds submitted by the Chief of the Air Service throughout the remainder of the decade.

Of the small number of combat aircraft purchased in the 1920s, pursuit planes received the highest priority. Army flyers shared a belief that air superiority was a necessary prerequisite for all operations, air or ground. Early in the decade, for instance, the Assistant Chief of the Air Service, Billy Mitchell, maintained that control of the air could be won by "the air battles of pursuit aviation."[4] On this issue, but on little else, the General Staff agreed with Mitchell. In 1923 a War Department board recommended that the Air Service, excluding observation craft, consist of sixty percent pursuit, twenty percent bombardment, and twenty percent attack aircraft.

The principal pursuit model of the mid-1920s was the Curtiss PW–8 Hawk single-seat biplane that entered service in 1923. The offspring of a successful racer, it had a top speed of 178 miles per hour, a 335-mile range, and a 22,000-foot ceiling. The Martin MB–2 was the standard bomber, but it was far outclassed in performance by the pursuit planes of the day, a consideration that contributed to the Air Service's emphasis on pursuit. Indeed, the fastest Army bomber of the mid-1920s, the Keystone LB–5, had a top speed slightly in excess of 100 miles per hour, a ceiling of about 13,000 feet, and a combat radius of but 500 miles. Development of the attack aircraft, to be used in low-altitude support

The Martin MB–2.

85

of ground forces, was in its infancy. Through the middle of the decade, the Air Service continued to use modified observation planes for this mission. In fact, the Army's first successful attack plane, the Curtiss A–3 Falcon, was derived from the O–1 observation craft.

Although Menoher and Patrick headed the Air Service during the postwar period of demobilization and cautious spending, it was Mitchell who caught the attention of the public and aroused enthusiasm among the Army's airmen. The ultimate goal of the Assistant Chief of the Army Air Service remained the creation of an independent air force; he considered separation from the Army essential for the effective defense of the nation. He saw his earlier failure to achieve independence as a temporary reverse, a setback that he could overcome by working harder to court public support. Abandoning his earlier concerns about presenting reasoned arguments "on a high plane,"[5] he deliberately sought publicity for himself and the Air Service to enlist the American people, and their political representatives as well, in what he believed was a crusade. Certain of the righteousness of his cause, he cast himself in the role of a knight-errant determined to save the United States from his bureaucratic foes, whose every action he described as ill-informed, evil, or both. Despite his sensationalism and self-dramatization, his intention was to serve his country by teaching it to accept the vision of air power, a term he was in the process of defining. He was more than a propagandist, however, for he remained genuinely interested in the advancement of aeronautical science to improve the aircraft available to the air arm and thus enhance its effectiveness and versatility. Even so, in championing research and development, he never lost sight of the importance of record-breaking flights in generating public and political support for an independent American air force. Mitchell proposed through a bold campaign of publicity and aerial accomplishments to demonstrate that military aviation, in the future if not with the aircraft of the present, could defeat an enemy without the assistance of the Army and Navy, thus refuting the basic and most convincing argument for keeping the Air Service subordinate to the Army.

When Mitchell returned from France, he was thinking of the recent war along with the future independence of military aviation. The earliest project that caught his attention was an armored airplane being developed at McCook Field to support ground forces. Inspired by the wartime armored attack aircraft used by the Germans, the machine was intended to fly at low altitude through a fusillade of small-arms fire, which had proved so deadly to strafing fighters, and attack the enemy in his trenches. Isaac M. Laddon, a civilian engineer, designed two such aircraft, but neither lived up to Mitchell's grandiose expectations, which included the ability to land behind enemy lines and disembark troops. Far from being discouraged because this project failed, Mitchell maintained an active interest in aircraft development while he served as Assistant Chief of the Air Service. He made frequent visits to McCook Field, demanded demonstrations of the new airplanes, and occasionally took the controls himself, although the test pilots there considered him more enthusiastic than skillful in the cockpit.

Besides watching over aircraft development within the Air Service, Mitchell was interested in similar activities overseas. Accompanied by Alfred Verville, an aeronautical engineer, and 1st Lt. Clayton Bissell, a wartime fighter ace, he visited Europe in the winter of 1921–22, conferring with aircraft designers and military airmen. The most important aircraft to result from this tour was the streamlined Verville R–3 racer, which conformed to Mitchell's instructions to build an airplane that did not look like a squirrel cage. Verville fitted the monoplane with a retractable landing gear and proposed using a metal propeller and a radiator that hugged the upper surface of the wing instead of projecting into the airstream and creating drag. Despite Mitchell's interest, the Air Service delayed installing the radiators and never fitted the R–3 with the new propeller; money was saved, but the three aircraft that were built won just one major race in three years of competition.

Although the Air Service failed to capitalize on the Verville R–3, neither wringing the highest speed from it as a racer nor incorporating its best features into a fighter, Army airmen established numerous records for speed, altitude, distance, and endurance, sometimes advancing aeronautical science or the art of flying and always garnering favorable publicity for military aeronautics.

At the same time, Army flight surgeons practicing the new specialty of aviation medicine became concerned about the problems of high-altitude flight. While aeronautical engineers turned to the supercharger and leaded gasoline to enable aircraft engines to operate in thin air at extreme altitudes, the doctors, with help from the same engineers, tried to improve the safety and comfort of pilots. A crude pressurized cabin proved undependable, too heavy, and a dangerous restriction on the pilot's field of vision. Electrically heated flying suits were judged impractical, but heat from the engine could be piped into the cockpit. All in all, however, the test pilots of the 1920s used basically the same equipment as the German bomber crews of World War I—layers of heavy clothing; goggles and masks for protection against the cold; and liquid oxygen, purer than the gas, which vaporized as it warmed and was sucked through a tube. Thus equipped, Maj. Rudolph "Shorty" Schroeder established a series of altitude records; 1st Lt. John Macready, who took over when Schroeder left the Army, reached an altitude of 38,704 feet in January 1926, for a time the world record. The decade had ended before Navy lieutenant Apollo Soucek became the first American aviator to use an oxygen mask while setting an altitude record. Despite the record-setting high-altitude flights, aviation medicine remained in its infancy during the 1920s.

Whatever the scientific value of the various assaults on the altitude record, it was speed that captured the headlines. In 1923, 1st Lt. Russell L. Maughan established a new international speed record of 236.5 miles per hour using an experimental Curtiss racer. During the following year, in a standard Curtiss pursuit, he raced the sun from New York City to San Francisco, taking off at first

Army aviators, from 1919 to 1926, tried to go farther, longer, and higher. **Clockwise from below left:** a Martin MB–1 flew around the rim of the U.S. in 1919; a de Havilland DH–4 refuels another in the 1923 endurance test; a Fokker T–2 flew nonstop across the U.S. in 1923; a Douglas DWC during the 1924 flight around the world; a Curtiss PW–8 flew across the U.S. from dawn to dusk in 1924; a modified Le Pere set an altitude record in 1926.

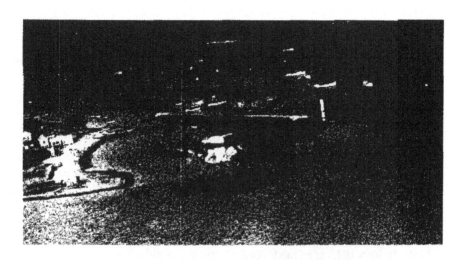

light, landing at dusk, and covering 2,670 miles in 21 hours and 48 minutes, an elapsed time that included five stops for refueling. In 1925, 1st Lt. Cy Bettis, flying the latest Curtiss racer, set a new world speed record in the Pulitzer Cup contest, only to see it broken a few days later in the Schneider Cup event by 1st Lt. Jimmy Doolittle, flying in another Curtiss racer fitted out as a seaplane.

Although an admiring reporter wrote that "General Mitchell . . . talks, thinks, and practices speed," the Air Service of the Mitchell era also tried to exact the utmost range and endurance from its aircraft. In the fall of 1919, for example, two Army pilots and two mechanics flew a Martin bomber 9,823 miles around the rim of the United States, landing frequently for refreshment, repairs, and refueling. In spite of the distance involved, the significance of this feat paled when compared to the accomplishments of First Lieutenants Macready and Oakley G. Kelly. In May 1923, they made the first nonstop flight across the United States, traveling from New York to San Diego in a highly modified Fokker T-2 transport, a 2,500-mile journey that took 26 hours and 50 minutes. In August of that year, emphasis shifted from distance to endurance when, in a flight encouraged by Hap Arnold, First Lieutenants Lowell H. Smith and John P. Richter remained aloft in a DH-4 for 37 hours and 15 minutes, a new world record. They refueled by means of a hose lowered from another DH-4 that served as an aerial tanker.

The greatest of the long-distance projects inspired by Billy Mitchell was the first flight around the world. In April 1924, after the Air Service had established the necessary network of supporting facilities, a flight of four specially built Douglas DWC World Cruisers led by Maj. Frederick L. Martin took off from Seattle, Washington, bound for the Orient and beyond. The bad luck that would recur in Martin's long career—he commanded the Army aviation units in Hawaii when the Japanese attacked in 1941—surfaced for the first time when his World Cruiser crashed in Alaska. He and his mechanic escaped unhurt, but command of the remaining aircraft passed to Lowell Smith. The fact that only two of the original aircraft completed the 175-day, 26,000-mile odyssey did not detract from a brilliant accomplishment for its day. Airmen of five nations had tried to be the first to circle the globe; Mitchell's flyers succeeded.

Distance and endurance flights dramatized the importance of logistics, the responsibility of the Field Service Section. Like the Engineering Division, which dealt with aircraft development and testing, the Field Service Section was located at McCook Field. To support the highly publicized flight around the world, Air Service planners had divided the route into six segments, according to climate. In each segment the section established a temporary depot stocked with spare parts and suitable lubricants. Subsidiary depots, basically refueling points or emergency landing sites, linked the depots. The supplies were shipped in crates made of the same wood as the airframes to facilitate improvised repairs to the aircraft.

Although the flight around the world dramatized their importance, maintenance and supply made possible the day-to-day operation of the Air Service. The Field Service Section operated six depots throughout the United States that were

The six-engine Barling Bomber. The two inside nacelles each have two Liberty engines, one driving a pusher propeller and one driving a tractor propeller; the two outside nacelles contain one Liberty engine each.

responsible for routine distribution of supplies, periodic overhaul of engines and airframes, and the other logistic aspects of military aviation. Besides serving as distribution points for supplies used by operational units, the depots undertook the kind of major repairs that mechanics at the various airfields could not accomplish.

In his heyday as Assistant Chief of the Army Air Service, Mitchell inspired a mixture of pure publicity stunts and actual achievements. He promoted the Transcontinental Reliability Test of 1919 in which competitors worked their way across the country, refueling as many as forty times en route. Like the around the rim flight, it served to publicize aviation rather than promote aircraft development, and Mitchell judged it a success even though seven pilots died in crashes during the competition. Less spectacular but of much greater value was his sponsorship of a model airway linking Washington, D.C., with Dayton, Ohio; the Air Service supervised the placement of beacons, marking of airfields, and preparation of charts.

The combination of pioneer and publicist found in Mitchell was common among Air Service officers. Arnold, as a pioneer, helped establish an aerial patrol to detect fires in the national forests of California and Oregon; as a publicity man, he climbed into a DH–4 to race homing pigeons from Portland, Oregon, to San Francisco, California, and celebrated the Petaluma, California, egg festival by taking a chef aloft in an unsuccessful attempt to cook an egg while in flight. On the one hand, pilots like Doolittle patrolled the Mexican border in search of smugglers or other outlaws; on the other, Spaatz risked his neck at an air show in Montana while trying to sell U.S. Treasury bonds.

The kind of projects that caught Mitchell's fancy revealed a gradual shift in his thinking about air power. Heavy bombers came to absorb the attention he had once lavished on trench strafers and competed for his interest with pursuit

91

planes and racers. His enthusiasm for developing bombardment aircraft culminated in the Barling bomber. Designed by Walter Barling, who had worked as an aeronautical engineer in Great Britain, and fabricated for a cost of $375,000 at the Witteman-Lewis factory in New Jersey, the 21-ton aircraft traveled by rail for assembly and testing at McCook Field. Although it established a short-lived record by carrying a useful load of 8,800 pounds to an altitude of 4,500 feet, the performance of the Barling bomber so deteriorated during two years of testing that it could not struggle across the Appalachian Mountains to reach the Air Service bases on the East Coast. Despite its six Liberty engines, the triplane's weight and aerodynamic drag prevented it from flying faster than 95 miles per hour.

As indicated by his interest in the Barling aircraft, bombers were assuming a more prominent place in Mitchell's thinking. As early as 1915, when only one type of bomber in the world, the Russian *Ilya Mourometz* (designed by Igor Sikorsky), could carry 1,000 pounds of explosives, Mitchell had suggested that military aviation could become America's second line of defense behind the far-ranging ships of the fleet. During his wartime service, he gave scarcely a thought to coastal defense, concentrating instead on massing his forces in France to drive the Germans from the sky and to observe and attack the enemy below. His experience on the Western Front convinced him that combat on land, at sea, and in the air formed three distinct kinds of warfare, that victory in the air was essential to victory on land or at sea, and that only a professional airman could win the war in the air. He therefore argued that the air arm, because of the distinctive nature of aerial warfare, deserved parity with the Army and Navy. The aerial commander, he insisted, should be as free to fight his battle as the commanding general of an expeditionary force or the admiral of a fleet. This reasoning, although logical to Mitchell and his supporters, did not prevail. The air arm remained a part of the Army for reasons of tradition and recent history but also because airmen were claiming parity based on the medium—the skies being as important as the land or seas—rather than on the mission. Military aviation had to have as its purpose something as obvious as the destruction of a hostile army or the sinking of a battle fleet.

One of Mitchell's colleagues at the headquarters of the postwar Air Service, Lt. Col. William C. Sherman, ingeniously addressed the question of mission, suggesting that, just as warships brought victory at sea, morale was the key to success on land, a conclusion that could well have been influenced by the collapse of Germany in 1918. The two-part mission of aviation should therefore be to shatter morale, thus winning the land war, and to sink ships and gain mastery over the oceans. Mitchell seized on the idea of sinking ships and controlling the seas. The seas that concerned him were the coastal waters of the United States; the ships, an invasion armada. In the event of war, American bombers could not cross the ocean, raid the enemy's cities, and destroy the morale of the populace; but aircraft could bomb a naval expedition approaching American shores and attack any hostile troops that actually landed. The airplane, Mitchell reasoned, provided an inexpensive and deadly weapon for coastal defense. Approaching ships presented logical targets for military aviation. Air Service fighters would dispose of any patrols launched from the enemy's aircraft carriers; observation units would locate the enemy; and bombers like the Martin MB–2, which could carry 3,000 pounds of bombs 250 miles or more, would sink even the mightiest battleships. Mitchell claimed that airplanes based on land could intercept and destroy or drive off an invasion flotilla and do so more cheaply than the Navy's battle fleet, an important consideration at a time when wartime spending for national defense was being tailored to fit the needs of peace. If the Air Service could assume the coastal defense mission, traditionally shared by the Army and Navy, aviation would have taken a long step toward becoming an independent service.

Within the U.S. Navy, a group of young airmen and even a few of the older officers of the line realized that warships were vulnerable to aerial attack. They also knew of the struggle in Great Britain between the Royal Navy and the Royal Air Force for control of naval aviation, and, just as Mitchell feared the consequences of entrusting military aeronautics to generals oriented toward land warfare, these naval officers opposed any move to hand the Navy's air arm to a cabinet officer or a chief of air staff who knew nothing about the special needs of the fleet. In short, an air age was dawning in the Navy, but aviators in that service did not want to become part of the federal department of aeronautics and single air force that Mitchell advocated. Rather than seeking an accommodation with the naval aviators, who had deeply felt concerns of their own, Mitchell insisted that air power was indivisible, sovereign over land and sea, and as deadly against the Navy and its ships as against troops on the march. Ruling out the possibility of compromise with the Navy's aviators, he decided to silence the skeptics, humble the Navy, and prove that military aviation could defend the coasts alone by sinking the mightiest of naval vessels, the battleship.

Beginning in 1920 Mitchell concentrated on creating a public climate in which the Navy Department could not refuse to subject an obsolete or captured battleship to aerial attack. A master propagandist, he used every opportunity to argue his case, whether in the hearing rooms of Congress or in the nation's newspapers. However much the Army's leaders may have secretly enjoyed the discomfiture of their naval counterparts, the senior generals did not support Mitchell. As a group, these military officers feared that he was infringing on a mission in which the coast artillery already shared and that he was steering the air arm away from the support of ground troops, important in any future war, to prepare for a seaborne invasion that seemed less probable than another European conflict. Moreover, they resented the way that Mitchell ignored the chain of command and made flamboyant appeals for public support; even General Patrick, who was coming to see the logic of many of his assistant's ideas, had to concede that at times he behaved "like a spoiled brat."

History of the United States Air Force

The Navy was particularly upset because Mitchell challenged the need for increasing the number of large surface ships at the very time naval leaders were struggling to overcome growing public resistance to investing vast sums in a fleet second to none. In 1916, when the realization dawned that Great Britain could conceivably prove as hostile as Germany to the rights of neutral commerce, a massive building program began, only to be suspended when the United States entered the war, so that steel and labor could be used for badly needed destroyers and merchant ships instead of for battleships and battle cruisers. With the return of peace, construction of these capital ships resumed, and the dream of naval expansion intensified the Navy's resentment of Mitchell's activities. Not until February 1922, when the Washington Naval Conference imposed limits on the tonnage of the principal navies of the world, did the vision of a Navy second to none finally dissolve.

Although preoccupied with the expansion of the fleet, the Navy had not ignored the possible effect of aerial bombs on warships. In 1920, ordnance technicians had placed weapons weighing as much as 600 pounds on board the hulk of an old battleship and in the water nearby, exploded them, and photographed the damage. The pictures found their way into the newspapers, stirring up a planes-versus-ships controversy that provided the opportunity for Mitchell's greatest publicity coup, even though aircraft had not dropped the bombs. Taking advantage of the speculation by the press, the congressional curiosity that it aroused, and the Navy's own interest in the subject, Mitchell maneuvered the Navy into allowing the Air Service to attack some obsolete or captured warships, including a battleship. Secretary of the Navy Josephus Daniels expressed the confidence of his service and its contempt for Mitchell when he offered to stand bareheaded on the bridge of any ship the Army attempted to bomb. Fortunately for Daniels, he left office in March 1921 when Warren G. Harding replaced Woodrow Wilson as President and did not have to follow through on his offer. In July 1921, Mitchell's 1st Provisional Air Brigade, based at Langley Field, Virginia, sank each of the targets provided by the Navy, including the *Ostfriesland*, a comparatively modern battleship built by the Germans some ten years before. Mitchell and his fellow Army airmen were overjoyed, even though the tests had been conducted under admittedly artificial conditions.

Before the tests began, the Air Service and the Navy had agreed on a schedule that enabled naval officers to examine the major ships at specified intervals to assess the structural damage from various kinds of bombs. Mitchell, however, was interested only in sinking a battleship with the 2,000-pound bombs fabricated especially for that purpose. Once his Martin MB-2 bombers closed in for the kill, he ignored the agreement, refused to suspend the attack, and sank the *Ostfriesland* by dropping six of the big bombs within twenty-one minutes. The Navy's inspectors had no chance to examine the ship from the time the first bomb fell until the *Ostfriesland* rolled over and plunged to the bottom of the sea.

Mitchell and his allies, the Navy, and the Joint Army and Navy Board all re-

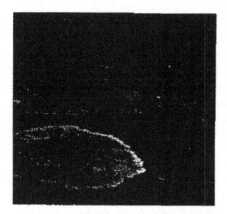

The German battleship *Ostfriesland* suffering a hit and
a miss (left), then turning over (right) before it sinks.

acted differently to the tests. For Mitchell, the sinkings in July 1921, and those
in subsequent tests, proved conclusively that the day of the battleship had ended,
that an independent air force could defend the coasts of the United States and its
possessions more effectively and less expensively than any combination of the
Army's coast artillery and the Navy's warships. He crowed, for example, that
"the future individual equipment of the sailor on a battleship would have to consist of a parachute to come down in after being blown up into the air, a life pre-
server to float on the water when he came down . . . asbestos soled shoes, as the
decks would be all hot, a gas mask to protect him from noxious gases, and a
flash lamp to find his way around the deck and interior of the ship when the
electric lights went out."[6] Meanwhile, spokesmen for the Navy grumbled about
Mitchell's breaking the rules, argued that damage-control parties might well
have stopped the flooding that sank the *Ostfriesland,* and claimed that antiaircraft fire could have eliminated several of the bombers and the projectiles they
carried. The fact remained, however, that bombs had sunk a battleship, and the
realization gradually spread through the Navy that the fleet would need its own
air cover during future wars. Since seaplanes were slow and cumbersome, only
the aircraft carrier could do the job. Like any interservice agency, the Joint
Board tried to compromise. Conceding the obvious, it found that battleships
were in peril when they ventured within range of bombers, but it added that the
dreadnought reigned supreme on the high seas beyond reach of these aircraft.

Emboldened by the success of the bombing tests, Mitchell ground out a succession of speeches and magazine articles that reflected a change in his thinking
concerning the role of an independent air force in wartime. Having shown to his
satisfaction that existing aircraft could sink battleships, he now looked ahead to
the day when an American air force would have vast numbers of bombers with
greater range and carrying capacity than those available. "If we are required to

act against an enemy on land," he predicted, "we may so smash up his means of production, supply, and transportation by bombardment that there is great probability that the armies will never come into contact on the field of battle."[7] Thus he sought to refute the main argument for keeping the Air Service subordinate to the Army, the proposition that aviation did not deserve independence because, unlike the Army and Navy, it could not win a war. Since the end of World War I, Mitchell's views had rapidly evolved. He had returned from France preaching the offensive use of fighters to seize control of the skies. Next, he turned to coastal defense, placing emphasis on the bombers. Finally, he depicted the bomber as an offensive weapon capable by itself of defeating an enemy.

Publicly Mitchell only hinted that the United States might undertake this form of strategic bombardment of an enemy's vital industrial centers and transportation hubs. For his isolationist and somewhat antimilitary American audience, which put greater trust in geography than in the armed forces, he played up the need for air defense to stop such an attack, whether by dirigibles or from aircraft carriers. Whatever his public stance, he believed that air power in the form of the strategic bomber could win a war. In 1923, this belief became the basis of an unofficial manual on bombardment that listed as acceptable military targets the enemy's food and water supplies as well as industry and transportation. The manual stipulated, however, that purely civilian targets would be hit only in reprisal, with the threat of retaliation deterring the enemy from attacking civilian targets in the United States.

While Mitchell campaigned for an independent air force, Patrick was struggling to expand and modernize the Army Air Service. In mid-1922, the chief of the air arm complained to the War Department that his organization had so declined in strength that it was incapable of carrying out even such peacetime duties as training and providing courier service. A formal statement submitted in February 1923 stressed the inadequate size of the Air Service and the flaws in its organization. Patrick criticized the current policy of placing aviation units permanently under the control of the nine corps area commanders and recommended instead that the air arm be divided into two components: observation squadrons serving as integral parts of the ground forces and an enlarged air force of pursuit, bombardment, and attack units that could operate independently of corps area commanders. This latter force was to be directly responsible to the Army's General Headquarters, the body of officers that would help the Chief of Staff function as a military commander in wartime. With a senior airman in charge, the combat elements of the Air Service would thus constitute a General Headquarters air force. Patrick believed that such an arrangement made sense militarily, for it permitted the concentrated employment of Army aviation. He also realized that the establishment of an air force, headed by an airman responsible to the Chief of Staff and his wartime advisers, would be a step toward autonomy, which he consistently defined as the same status for the Air Service within the Army that the Marine Corps enjoyed within the naval establishment.

Whereas Mitchell wanted outright independence, Patrick sought only full responsibility for such matters as administration, the development of weapons and tactics, and promotions.

In response to Patrick's proposal, Secretary of War John W. Weeks convened a board of General Staff officers under Maj. Gen. William Lassiter to consider the suggested changes. Two veteran airmen, Lt. Col. Frank P. Lahm and Maj. Herbert A. Dargue, served on the board, which after two weeks of deliberation endorsed Patrick's views. Specifically, the Lassiter Board called for the creation of a General Headquarters, or GHQ, air force and proposed a ten-year program of recruitment and aircraft procurement to give the Air Service a peacetime strength of 4,000 officers, 25,000 enlisted men, and 2,500 aviation cadets. The War Department adopted the findings of the group as its aviation policy, and Secretary Weeks suggested that Congress consider appropriations for the Air Service and naval aviation as a single package, with the Army air arm receiving the greater share. The Navy, which had just commissioned its first aircraft carrier, a converted collier, rejected an arrangement that subordinated it to the Army in matters of appropriations, and the ten-year plan perished. Since reorganization seemed pointless without the additional men and airplanes, the War Department shelved the part of the plan that called for a General Headquarters air force.

In the meantime, the House of Representatives undertook its own investigation of military aeronautics. On March 4, 1924, the Speaker of the House appointed a nine-man select committee drawn from the Military Affairs and Naval Affairs Committees and chaired by Representative Florian H. Lampert, a Republican from Wisconsin. The Lampert committee began its hearings in October and continued to take testimony until March 1925. Patrick and Mitchell, disgusted by the War Department's failure to negotiate with the Navy in an attempt to resolve the question of funding that blocked the reforms proposed by the Lassiter Board, presented the views of the Air Service, each in a manner that reflected his temperament and goals. An emotional Mitchell, in arguing for a department of aeronautics coequal with the War and Navy Departments, accused some witnesses of lying on orders from their superiors in the Army and Navy, misstated figures supporting his case, and blamed the War Department for the poor condition of the Air Service despite the endorsement of the report of the Lassiter Board. In contrast, Patrick advanced in reasoned terms his proposed "Marine Corps" of the air, an autonomous air arm within the War Department that would assume responsibility for the coastal defense mission to which Mitchell had laid claim. The report of the Lampert committee, not released until December 1925, offered a compromise between the recommendations of the Lassiter Board and Mitchell's views. The committee recommended an immediate expansion of both the Army Air Service and naval aviation and called for the eventual creation of a department of national defense, although it did not specify that such an agency would contain an air arm coequal with the Army and Navy.

Mitchell's headlong attack on the leadership of the Army and Navy during his testimony before the Lampert committee—Sir Hugh Trenchard, Chief of the Royal Air Force Air Staff, observed that Mitchell "tried to convert his enemies by killing them first"—and the speeches he delivered and articles he wrote during 1923 and 1924 cost him his job as Assistant Chief of the Air Service.[8] His four-year tour came to an end in March 1925, and Patrick's request for his retention fell on deaf ears. Indeed, Secretary Weeks had decided that Mitchell's "whole course had been so lawless, so contrary to the building up of an efficient organization, so lacking in teamwork, so indicative of a personal desire for publicity at the expense of everyone with whom he associated that his actions render him unfit for a high administrative post such as he now occupies."[9] Mitchell reverted to his permanent rank of colonel and was sent to Fort Sam Houston at San Antonio, Texas, far from the Washington limelight, as air officer for the VIII Corps Area. Lt. Col. James E. Fechet, commander of the advanced flying school at Kelly Field replaced him as Assistant Chief of the Air Service, assuming the rank of brigadier general.

By the time he departed for Texas, Mitchell had created a devoted following within the Air Service. Arnold, who had recently become the officer in charge of public information for the Air Service, sent encouraging letters to Mitchell at Fort Sam Houston. Spaatz had joined Mitchell in telling the Lampert committee, though less vehemently, that the ills of military aviation could be traced to the War Department. Eaker, an aide to General Patrick, later declared that "except for Mitchell and the little group he inspired we wouldn't have any aviation of consequence." Moreover, Patrick himself absorbed some of Mitchell's theories of air power, if not his insistence on an air arm independent of the Army. In a speech to the students at the Army War College during 1925, Patrick asked his audience how long an enemy could endure with his "industrial establishments, his munitions factories, his means of communication destroyed." This kind of aerial devastation, he declared, "can best be done by an organization that is directed by those who know thoroughly its achievements, its possibilities, and its limitations."[10] Although the organization that Patrick described was to be autonomous within the Army rather than independent, it would wage the kind of strategic bombardment that was occupying an increasingly prominent place in Mitchell's theories.

In spite of being banished to San Antonio, Mitchell did not remain silent. Two accidents provided him the ammunition he needed for a renewed attack on the defense establishment. Sent out on a publicity flight in the late summer of 1925, a time of year when thunderstorms are frequent and severe along the planned route, the Navy dirigible *Shenandoah* encountered violent weather over Ohio and broke up, killing fourteen of the forty-three people on board. Another publicity flight, that of a Navy seaplane from the west coast of the United States to Hawaii, ended when the aircraft vanished. The aircraft and crew were rescued, but not before Mitchell had used the incident in his latest barrage. He

The Navy dirigible *Shenandoah* after its 1925 crash.

charged that accidents like these were "the direct result of incompetency, criminal negligence, and almost treasonable administration of the national defense by the War and Navy Departments."[11]

Calvin Coolidge, who had become President after the death of Warren Harding in 1923, did not share his predecessor's tolerance of public dissent and ordered the airman court-martialed for conduct prejudicial "to good order and military discipline."[12] The trial, held in Washington during November and December 1925, was a national event and promised to become a forum for Mitchell's views on the organization and employment of military aviation. Considering his demonstrated ability to generate and use publicity, Mitchell proved surprisingly inept at advancing his cause during the trial. The narrow issue of his conduct prevented him and his counsel, Representative Frank Reid, an Illinois Republican, from using the

Billy Mitchell during his court-martial in 1925.

proceeding as a forum in which the defendant could expound his views on air power. Found guilty on December 17, 1925, and sentenced to a five-year suspension from duty, Mitchell resigned on February 1, 1926, to continue as a private citizen his fight for an independent air force.

Thus ended the Mitchell era. Between his arrival in France in 1917 and his resignation, he became the dominant figure in the Army air arm, overshadowing his nominal superiors, Menoher and Patrick, and providing a drumfire of publicity, often the result of genuine accomplishments, on behalf of an independent air force. His accomplishments were many, although some, such as his attempt to establish airways for commercial flight, passed almost unnoticed amid the controversy he generated. His interest in aeronautical engineering resulted in aircraft that were advanced for their time. Borrowing from Trenchard, he established the principle that air power should be used for the offense, a doctrine rarely challenged by his successors in the ensuing decades. He declared that airplanes could sink battleships and made good his boast. He inspired the Arnolds, the Eakers, and the Spaatzes, who would command during World War II and whose success in that conflict opened the way to independence.

Mitchell failed to achieve his greatest ambition, the establishment during his lifetime of an independent air force. The reasons for this failure were many: the primitive aircraft of that era were too few and lacked the range and carrying capacity to achieve the decisive results that Mitchell described, the lack of a probable enemy against whom air power could be directed, and especially Mitchell's aggressive tactics. Instead of trying to make common cause with naval aviators, who were largely being ignored by advocates of the battleship when World War I ended, he attacked the Navy as an institution. Similarly, he refused to nourish the War Department's budding interest in aviation, demonstrated by its endorsement of the findings of the Lassiter Board; indeed, his combativeness in the cause of independence thoroughly alienated the Secretary of War.

As a civilian, Mitchell discovered that he no longer captured the kind of bold headlines that he had as a brigadier general. His message, however, remained basically the same. He still envisioned air power as the decisive weapon, with the bomber its cutting edge, and urged that a cabinet officer take charge of all aviation, civil and military, and function as the equal of the Secretary of War and Secretary of the Navy. Although he placed greater emphasis on bombers capable of battering an enemy's "vital centers," he did not overlook other types of aircraft. As a result, even as he encouraged the reading of Douhet, the most extreme advocate of aerial bombardment, he called for a balanced air force and did not endorse the Italian's belief that an all-purpose "battle plane" could fight its way unescorted to the target through swarming fighters, drop its load of explosives, and return to base. Mitchell's ideas still aroused enthusiasm among professional airmen, but the public paid him scant heed. He died in 1936, still hoping to create the public and political pressure that would free the air arm from control by the Army.

Chapter 4

The Coming of the GHQ Air Force, 1925-1935

John F. Shiner

During the decade that began in 1925, the Air Corps looked to a future with better aircraft, the funds to buy them, and greater freedom in using them according to principles devised by airmen. This progress toward independence, identity, and professionalism began in the aftermath of the 1925 court-martial of Billy Mitchell, when President Calvin Coolidge moved to silence an officer with a demonstrated ability to sway the public. Just four years before, when forced to choose between Mitchell, fresh from the sinking of the *Ostfriesland*, and Maj. Gen. Charles T. Menoher, the Chief of the Air Service, the administration of President Warren G. Harding had allowed Menoher to be reassigned, but Coolidge did not shrink from a fight. The new President could not abide insubordination, and his determination—almost an obsession—to hold down spending collided with Mitchell's insistence that the government spend whatever was necessary to establish a modern, independent air force. No wonder that Coolidge decided, little more than two years after succeeding Harding, that Mitchell meant trouble for the administration.

The President's decision to court-martial the outspoken general did not mean, however, that Coolidge was blind to the possibility that the nation's aviation policy needed reform. He was willing to support necessary change provided it was not overly expensive and did not involve a challenge to the administration like Mitchell's accusation that the War and Navy Departments were guilty, in effect, of treason. Even as he moved against Mitchell, Coolidge also confronted the basic issue of aviation policy that Mitchell had raised. By launching a presidentially sponsored investigation of the subject covered by the Lampert committee, Coolidge forestalled the possibility of lavish congressional spending based on that group's findings; by raising the subject of reform, he made it even more difficult for Mitchell to use the court-martial to rally public support for an independent air force. In this fashion, Coolidge proposed to ease a troublesome critic overboard with the least possible splash.

The vehicle for reshaping aviation policy and minimizing the public and political impact of the Mitchell trial was the Morrow Board. Shortly after Secretary of War John W. Weeks had decided to replace Mitchell as the assistant to Maj. Gen. Mason Patrick, the Chief of the Air Service, and some five months before the outburst that resulted in the court-martial, President Coolidge asked Dwight Morrow, a prominent investment banker and close friend, to take charge of an inquiry into the general subject of American aviation. Morrow began familiarizing himself with the topic, so that in September 1925, when Coolidge proceeded against Mitchell, the banker was able to respond immediately to a formal invitation to undertake the study. To serve with him, Morrow chose Arthur C. Denison, a federal judge; William F. Durand, of the National Advisory Committee for Aeronautics; Senator Hiram Bingham, who had organized pilot training during World War I; Representatives James S. Parker, a Republican from New York, and Carl Vinson, a Democrat from Georgia, both members of the Interstate and Foreign Commerce Committee; Maj. Gen. James G. Harbord, who had been on Pershing's wartime staff and was then president of the Radio Corporation of America; Frank F. Fletcher, a retired admiral and an advocate of naval aviation; and Howard E. Coffin, who had been in charge of aircraft production throughout much of the war and also had served on the postwar Crowell Commission. The board's technical advisers included Maj. Leslie MacDill of the Air Service, who had served in France as a staff officer and as the commander of an aerial gunnery school. The group, known officially as the President's Aircraft Board, began holding public hearings on September 21, five weeks before the first session of the Mitchell court-martial. The President directed the committee to produce a report by the end of November, which, he believed, would ensure its appearance before the military court could announce a decision.

The testimony before the Morrow Board contained little that was new. General Patrick again proposed an Air Corps that enjoyed the same autonomy within the Army that the Marine Corps did in the Navy Department. Lt. Col. Benjamin D. Foulois, by this time in command at Mitchel Field, New York, supported Patrick in words almost as strong as those he used in 1919: "I am convinced that aviation will never reach its proper place in the scheme of national defense so long as it remains under the control of the War Department General Staff."[1] The basic theme of the testimony by Air Service officers was the inability or unwillingness of ground officers, and by implication battleship admirals, to use aviation effectively. As Maj. Horace Hickam said: "I am confident that no general thinks he can command the Navy, or no admiral thinks he can operate an army, but some of them think they can operate an air force."[2] Although tame in comparison to Mitchell's accusations, this testimony was motivation enough for an administration disposed to make minor concessions to prevent something it considered worse. Scarcely a week after Patrick repeated his plea, originally made two years earlier, for an Air Corps patterned after the Marine Corps, he was directed to prepare such a plan and circulate it for comment within the War Department.

Meanwhile, the press and the public were looking forward to the fireworks that Billy Mitchell seemed certain to ignite in his testimony before the Morrow Board, but what he said proved disappointing. Mitchell spent much of his time reading aloud from his book, *Winged Defense*, a hastily assembled compilation of the ideas presented in his articles and speeches, instead of confronting his adversaries as he had before the Lampert committee. Possibly he considered the court-martial, which began after the board ended its public hearings, a better platform; if so, he failed to realize how severely the procedural rules governing the trial would inhibit his ability to introduce the issues of air power and an independent air force.

Unless he was patently outrageous, as Mitchell had been before the Lampert committee, an officer normally enjoyed immunity from reprisal when testifying before Congress. He might even depart from the official line in responding to a question, provided he clearly labeled the heretical views as his personal opinion. The War Department refused, however, to tolerate unauthorized leaks to the press, and during 1925 a handful of officers in Patrick's headquarters had more or less openly provided reporters with information favorable to Mitchell and his cause. When the War Department ordered them punished, Maj. Henry H. "Hap" Arnold, recently returned to Washington, became the scapegoat. He was driven off to the wilderness of Fort Riley, where he had barely escaped death fourteen years earlier, to take charge of the small aviation detachment there.

Meanwhile, the Morrow Board completed its work and issued a report that resulted in the illusion, if not the reality, of radical reform. The group's findings appeared before the Mitchell court-martial reached a decision and before the Lampert committee released its findings, which included a more substantial change, albeit at some unspecified time in the future. Whereas Lampert and his colleagues spoke vaguely of an air arm joined with the Army and Navy in a department of defense, the Morrow Board advocated, and Congress approved, in the form of the Air Corps Act of 1926, the establishment of an Air Corps within the Army. The new organization did not, however, have the sort of autonomy Patrick sought. It resembled the Army's Signal Corps or Quartermaster Corps rather than the Navy's Marine Corps. The bureaucratic equal of the Army's technical services and combat arms, the Air Corps was authorized two additional

Maj. Gen. James M. Fechet (left), Chief, Army Air Corps, December
1927–December 1931, and Brig. Gen. Benjamin D. Foulois,
Assistant Chief, Army Air Corps, December 1927–December 1931.

brigadier generals besides the assistant chief (one in charge of materiel and the
other training) and was assured of representation on the War Department General
Staff. The Air Corps Act also included the other major recommendations of the
Morrow Board: a new Assistant Secretary of War responsible for military aviation and a five-year program of expansion that would increase the Air Corps from
its actual strength in mid-1926 of 996 officers, 8,447 enlisted men, 153 aviation
cadets, and 1,451 aircraft (only 1,292 fit for combat) to 1,650 officers, 15,000 enlisted men (including 2,500 air cadets), and 1,800 serviceable airplanes. Thanks
to the Morrow Board and a cooperative Congress, President Coolidge had spread
over five years the costs of an overhaul of military aviation. Yet, the commitment
to modernization and expansion was not all that firm; each year Congress would
have to vote the necessary money, in effect exercising the right of annual review.

The five-year program to improve the Air Corps would go forward under new
military and civilian leadership. General Patrick retired in November 1927 and
was replaced by Maj. Gen. James E. Fechet, who had become the assistant chief
when Mitchell was sent to Texas. Although Fechet had studied mechanical engineering at the University of Nebraska, he cultivated the image of a rough-hewn
ex-cavalryman, which indeed he was, for he had left college after three years,
joined the cavalry, and earned a Regular commission in 1900 during the
Philippine Insurrection. He learned to fly in 1918, when the Air Service was in
the throes of its wartime expansion. Before retiring, Patrick selected an assistant
chief for Fechet, giving the assignment to Foulois, who had obtained the backing
of the governor of his home state, John H. Trumbull of Connecticut. Foulois had
unsuccessfully marshaled similar political support in hope of succeeding
Mitchell as assistant chief, but this sort of lobbying apparently was not unusual

104

F. Trubee Davison ,
Assistant Secretary of War for Air,
July 1926– March 1933.

enough to cause hard feelings between Fechet, who got Mitchell's old assignment, and Foulois, who had tried for it and failed. Not only did the two officers work together harmoniously, but Fechet made a special effort to groom Foulois to succeed him. The third member of the triumvirate that directed the growth of the Air Corps was F. Trubee Davison, the new Assistant Secretary of War for Air, who had been a naval aviator during World War I. Davison had crashed in New York harbor, so severely injuring his legs that afterward he walked with a limp and carried a cane. These three struggled to follow the blueprint for expansion laid out in the Air Corps Act of 1926, sometimes with the assistance of Ira Eaker, now a captain, who functioned as their aide and personal pilot.

As soon as the Morrow Board's recommendations had become law, the Air Corps drew up the necessary plans covering acquisition, construction, and internal reorganization for each successive increment of the five-year plan. Once the expansion was completed, the Air Corps would have one air wing on the East Coast, another on the West Coast, one in the southern United States, and one each in Panama and Hawaii. In addition, one air group would be located in the northern United States and another in the Philippine Islands. The projected wings would each consist of three groups, each with three squadrons. The bombardment wings were to have 150 aircraft and the pursuit or attack wings 280. Fechet's planners also provided for the necessary schools and depots to support this expanded fighting force. The War Department approved the Air Corps plan, which became the official objective of the five-year program. By June 1931, as scheduled, the Air Corps had organized all of the wing and group headquarters, but they and the 67 existing squadrons remained grossly understrength in men and aircraft. Expansion and modernization had not proceeded as planned.

Neither President Coolidge nor Congress was eager to spend the money necessary to carry out the expansion program. The initial funding was delayed until the fiscal year beginning on July 1, 1927; while the administration quibbled over such legalistic points as the definition of a serviceable aircraft. During 1927 and 1928, the executive branch did not ask for, nor did Congress appropriate, funds for the Air Corps to expand to 1,800 airplanes or to build the installations needed to support them, for despite the Air Corps Act, President Coolidge remained a steadfast advocate of economy in government. The man who replaced him in the White House in March 1929, Herbert Hoover, shared Coolidge's dedication to cutting federal expenditures and almost immediately focused on the armed services as the place to begin. The collapse of stock prices during Hoover's first year in office signaled the beginning of a major depression in the United States. As the crisis deepened and spread throughout the world, tax revenues dried up, and Hoover tried in vain to restore prosperity, first through cuts in spending. Military leaders tended to accept Hoover's economic orthodoxy, which emphasized the need for a balanced federal budget, and as a result became increasingly reluctant to oppose cuts in military expenditures as the depression grew worse.

The Army Air Corps thus found itself committed to a program of renovation and expansion mandated in 1926, but it was frustrated during subsequent years by a lack of funds. Less attuned than the more senior generals to economic principles, the Army's airmen expected the War Department to argue their case convincingly and salvage the expansion program regardless of the condition of the economy and the overall size of a shrinking Army. Under different circumstances, the War Department might well have fought to expand the Air Corps if the entire Army could have grown. However, after 1931, military appropriations declined sharply and recovered very slowly; and it seemed folly to feed aviation while starving the rest of the service. Because of the Army's overall condition, the Chief of the Army Air Corps did not receive the money needed to expand to a force of 1,800 aircraft. From July 1927 through June 1932, a period embracing five fiscal years, Patrick and Fechet asked for an aggregate of $183 million for military aviation, but before sending the Army's annual budget requests to Congress, the Secretary of War inflicted a succession of cuts that reduced aviation's share to $126 million. During these years, the amount actually appropriated totaled $167 million, and expenditures were about $157 million, some $26 million less than the Chiefs of the Air Corps had sought. The aviators tended to blame the leadership of the Army for the cuts in funding and considered this yet another example of the General Staff's lack of interest in military aviation, apparently ignoring the fact that by the end of June 1932, the air arm received more than 20 percent of the Army's budget, an increase of more than eight percent since fiscal year 1926.

In mid-1930 President Hoover, facing declining federal revenues, intensified the growing discord between the Air Corps and the General Staff by ordering the Army not to spend $65 million of the $509 million already appropriated by Congress for fiscal year 1931. The Air Corps vigorously protested its share of the reduction. Finally, the General Staff relented and restored $2 million, taking the funds from the other combat arms, but angering those receiving additional cuts, who could see no reason why the aviators should receive special treatment.

Although the Air Corps did not obtain the 1,800 airplanes authorized in 1926, the aircraft inventory did grow from slightly fewer than 1,300 usable aircraft when the law was passed, to approximately 1,475 serviceable aircraft by 1931. This was no small feat considering the struggle for funding and the normal five-year operational life of military aircraft. The accident rate also cut into the inventory: 149 aircraft were wrecked in 1926, 104 in 1927, 86 in 1928, 117 in 1929, and 152 in 1930.

Like aircraft, manpower lagged behind authorizations during the five-year expansion plan. The Air Corps Act of 1926 had authorized substantial increases in the numbers of officers and enlisted men, but the executive and legislative branches both opposed adding to the overall strength of the Army. As was true of funds, increases in Air Corps manpower had to come at the expense of the other components of the Army, which were also understrength. The War Department nevertheless transferred to aviation a sizable number of authorizations for enlisted men, again causing resentment in the combat arms that lost the vacancies. Between July 1927 and July 1931, the enlisted strength of the Air Corps grew from 9,079 to 13,190.

Increasing the commissioned strength of the Air Corps while keeping the total number of Army officers constant at 12,000 presented an even more difficult problem. Spaces for enlisted men could readily be shifted to nonflying specialties in aviation, but 90 percent of the officers had to be qualified aviators. The Army needed only a limited number of new Regular officers each year to fill the few vacancies that occurred. By 1930, West Point graduates filled this need, but comparatively few wanted to learn to fly. During a typical year of the five-year expansion, only about 90 of perhaps 250 new second lieutenants volunteered for pilot training after graduating from the Military Academy—too few to enable the Air Corps to meet the objective of 1,650 officers. Army aviation's other principal source of Regular officers was members of other arms and branches who volunteered for pilot training and transferred into the air arm after earning their wings. From these two sources and the pool of air cadets who had learned to fly and been commissioned in the reserve, the commissioned strength increased from 960 officers on July 1, 1927 to 1,266 on July 1, 1930, but it gained only an additional 100 officers during the next five years. Commissioned strength remained stable at about 1,300 because the number of officers who volunteered and qualified as aviators only offset the attrition caused by resignations and by accidents, which killed 227 pilots and crewmen from 1926 through 1930. The leaders of the Air Corps wanted to cure the officer shortage by awarding Regular commissions to more of the hundreds of cadets who graduated annually from the pilot training program, but this was impossible because of the ceiling of 12,000 officers imposed on the Army and the necessity of commissioning all graduates of the Military Academy who wanted to serve.

Disappointing though it was, the collapse of the five-year program of expansion and modernization had at least one beneficial side effect. On the eve of a

Boeing P–12 pursuit aircraft.

rapid advance in aviation technology, the Air Corps was not saddled with too many aircraft that would soon be obsolete. Just beyond the horizon lay all-metal, multiengine bombers and monoplane fighters, aircraft whose performance would far surpass the performance of the lumbering bombers and biplane pursuits of the late 1920s.

Of those aircraft actually acquired during the five-year program, the most important tactically were the pursuits, which remained the basic type for performing the essential task of driving the enemy from the skies. As the 1930s began, the Air Corps was equipping its fighter units with the highly maneuverable Boeing P–12 biplane, which had a top speed of 194 miles per hour, half again as fast as the best fighters of World War I. Despite all the talk of coast defense operations in which bombers would sink battleships, the development of bombers proceeded slowly during the late 1920s. The top speed of the latest Keystone bomber and of the Curtiss XB–2, which underwent testing in 1928, did not exceed 115 miles per hour, compared to the 99 miles per hour of the Martin bombers that Mitchell had used to dispatch the target ship *Ostfriesland*. The service ceiling of both the Curtiss and Keystone bombers was about 15,000 feet and the radius of action no more than 400 miles.

The Air Corps began an organizational restructuring during the five-year program designed to improve the development, acquisition, and maintenance of equipment; to raise the level of proficiency; and to develop a sense of professionalism among its officers. In 1927, the Air Corps shifted both its aeronautical research center and its logistics agency from McCook Field to the new Wright Field, five miles northeast of the city limits of Dayton, Ohio. McCook

Curtiss B–2 Condor bomber.

Field, only a mile or two from downtown Dayton, was too crowded—"This field is small, use it all" read a sign emblazoned ou one of the buildings there. Shortly before the move, as a result of the Army reorganization of 1926, the new Air Corps created a Materiel Division to exercise control over both logistics and research and development. The new command, headed by a brigadier general, assumed responsibility for aeronautical engineering, supply, industrial planning, the disposal of surplus material, procurement, repair, and maintenance. William E. Gillmore, a specialist in supply and personnel who had learned to fly after the war, became the division's first chief, but in 1929 he exchanged assignments for one year with Foulois, the Assistant Chief of the Air Corps.

Much of the logistic activity took place at four major depots within the United States: Fairfield, Ohio; Middletown, Pennsylvania; San Antonio, Texas; and San Diego, California. At these depots, civilian technicians and cadres of enlisted men and officers performed major repairs on all types of aircraft. Because the flying squadrons had neither trained mechanics nor equipment for much more than routine maintenance and minor repair, more substantial work could be done only at the depot serving the geographic area where the unit was based. At first, the depots repaired airplanes only if an inspection revealed some serious deficiency. In 1930, however, the Materiel Division developed a far more efficient system, routinely bringing aircraft to the depots for inspection and overhaul every twelve to twenty-four months, depending on the type of airplane. The four depots in the continental United States also were responsible for salvaging parts from aircraft that had exceeded their normal useful life of five years. Overseas depots in Hawaii, Panama, and the Philippines performed the same tasks of inspection, repair, and salvage; and Scott Field, Illinois, became the site of a depot exclusively for lighter-than-air craft.

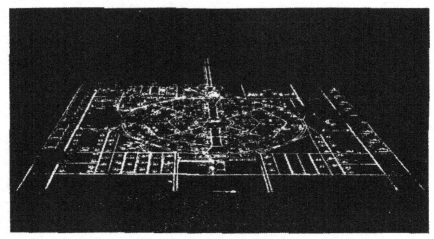

Randolph Field, Texas, in 1931, shortly after it opened.

Until the Materiel Division was created, the Office of Chief of the Air Service supervised all aircraft procurement from Washington. Afterward, the Procurement Section purchased aircraft and all other Air Corps equipment, except for experimental items or those supplied by the Army. The section negotiated contracts; and some of its personnel, working out of four (later three) procurement offices nationwide, attempted to ensure the air arm received what it had bargained for. The Procurement Section was responsible for buying, storing, and distributing supplies and spare parts, but it proved only marginally effective in carrying out these tasks. This lack of success resulted partly from meager funding but also from a policy of assigning flyers temporarily to duty as supply officers without the benefit of formal training. Another handicap was the tremendous volume of items, especially Liberty engines, left over from the war, a glut that still was choking the logistic system when the Air Corps was established in 1926.

Like the rest of the air arm, the new Materiel Division profited from the training system established even before the creation of the Air Corps in 1926. The old School of Application, for example, received the more accurate title of Engineering School in 1926 and the following year moved, along with the Materiel Division, from McCook Field to Wright Field. Meanwhile, the trend toward the centralization of pilot training continued, even though a new school for primary training opened at March Field, California.

In August 1926, the Air Corps established a single organization at San Antonio, the Air Corps Training Center (forerunner of the Air Education and Training Command), to supervise the training of pilots for heavier-than-air craft. Commanded by Brig. Gen. Frank P. Lahm, the center supervised the primary flying training at Brooks Field and the new school at March Field, the advanced flying training program at Kelly Field, and the School of Aviation Medicine at Brooks Field. By the time the decade ended, pilot trainees received instruction for an entire year—eight months in the primary course and four in advanced training. In June 1930, the Air Corps dedicated Randolph Field, Texas, the so-called West Point of the Air, which during the following year became the headquarters for the Air Corps Training Center and the site of all primary flying training, although the advanced school remained at nearby Kelly Field. In one sense this label did not reflect reality, for the training center was not the equivalent of the U.S. Military Academy, nor did it foreshadow the U.S. Air Force Academy, established in 1954. In another sense, however, Randolph Field performed a function similar to that of West Point, for through the Military Academy the Army renewed its officer corps, and through this training center the Air Corps renewed its cadre of pilots, whose particular skill made the air arm unique among the Army's components.

Whereas training at Randolph Field started an officer on a flying career, the Air Corps Tactical School, especially after its move in 1931 from Langley Field, Virginia, to Maxwell Field, Alabama, taught him to think in terms of air power. Each year a class of perhaps fifty officers convened at the school to investigate all aspects of military aviation by means of field problems, formal lectures, and free-for-all debates that often were pursued after hours outside the classroom. Inspired initially by Mitchell and probably at least aware of Douhet, a cadre of

Map problem class at the Air Corps Tactical School, Maxwell Field, Alabama.

students and faculty members developed a theory of aerial warfare that emphasized the long-range bomber almost to the exclusion of other types of aircraft. The Tactical School eventually went beyond Mitchell, who had believed in balanced forces, strong in bombers, but capable also of air defense and the support of land armies. A doctrine emerged from the Tactical School that the bombers of the next war would be able to fight their way to the industrial and administrative centers of the enemy and destroy the very means of making war, avoiding a long and bloody land campaign aimed at defeating the hostile army. In effect, a few airmen were describing a new way to fight a war, a substitute for the traditional strategy of bringing the enemy's army to bay and destroying it, as American generals had done with varying success in the Civil War and World War I.

The typical advocate of the independent use of air power did not resemble Carl von Clausewitz, who in the 1820s had drawn on the experiences of a lifetime of campaigning to search for principles governing the rational use of force in furthering national policy. Instead, this airman tended to be a comparatively junior officer, commissioned during the recent war or immediately afterward and interested in the swift and overwhelming application of force, whatever the political considerations. However, like the veteran Prussian soldier who had composed *On War*, the young American aviator did tend to view warfare as an abstraction or ideal. The concept of war presented by Clausewitz was rooted in his past, mainly in the campaigns fought against Napoleon; in contrast, the vision described at Maxwell Field existed in the future, when military aviation moved beyond the restrictions of existing technology. In a time of fragile biplanes, primitive equipment lent an aura of unreality to the claims made for strategic bombing; but during the decade beginning in 1925, the emerging doctrine of air power coincided with advances in aeronautical engineering that promised to provide the means of carrying out an independent bombing campaign.

In 1926, the year that the five-year plan was announced, the instructional manual in use at the Air Corps Tactical School declared that military aviation could support the Army directly, as it had during World War I, or indirectly by attacking targets far distant from the battlefield to destroy the enemy's will to fight. At the time, Maj. Oscar Westover, the commandant of the school, already had the reputation of avoiding any direct challenge to War Department policy. Indeed, he once declared he would never advance his own ideas if they conflicted with those of his military superiors. Because of this deference to authority, Westover found himself, and not for the last time, caught between War Department doctrine that Army aviation, regardless of its means of employment, always supported the ground forces and his enthusiasm for long-range bombardment, which he shared with many of his fellow airmen. The War Department continued to define victory in terms of the destruction of the hostile army and the occupation of enemy territory, but Westover, along with Fechet, held that air power could demoralize and defeat an enemy whose army was intact and territory inviolate.

112

Given the performance of the few bombers acquired under the five-year plan, to envisage aerial bombardment as the instrument of victory required a large amount of faith, but a succession of officers at the Air Corps Tactical School kept the belief alive. By the time the vision of an orderly five-year expansion had vanished, instructors like Capt. Robert Olds and 1st Lt. Kenneth N. Walker were teaching that bombardment was the "basic arm of the Air Force" and that its logical targets were the enemy's industrial and transportation centers and his lines of supply and communication. Looking far beyond the biplane bombers of the time, the school's bombardment faculty was insisting that "a well organized, well planned, and well flown air force attack . . . cannot be stopped."[3] For the first time, American proponents of strategic bombing quoted the Italian theorist Douhet, although a translation of his basic work, *Command of the Air*, was not published in the United States until 1942.

Despite the increasing fascination with the big bomber, pursuit aviation remained the most exciting branch of military aviation. When he climbed into the open cockpit of a biplane like the Boeing P–12 or Curtiss P–6, the fighter pilot inherited the mantle of Rickenbacker and the other aces of World War I. No wonder that so many of the best pilots gravitated toward pursuit squadrons, including several officers who would become prominent bomber commanders during World War II: Eaker, Haywood S. Hansell, and Curtis E. LeMay. In contrast to the agile pursuit, the bomber was slow and required a crew of three or more; however much this aircraft appealed to the makers of aerial doctrine, it did not afford the kind of flying that would ignite the imagination of the young eagle fresh from pilot training or the youth eager to learn to fly. Even attack aviation, which combined speed, maneuver, and the danger of flying at treetop height, attracted its share of bold young men, among them John R. "Killer" Kane, who would earn the Medal of Honor commanding bombers in World War II.

As the glamour of pursuit aircraft would suggest, most military aviators considered flying an adventure, as did much of the civilian populace, and the Air Corps took advantage of every opportunity to display to the public the equipment that tax money had purchased. The aerial maneuvers held in the spring of 1931 gave the air arm an opportunity to impress the public and also to test its men and aircraft, its senior commanders, and its methods of supply and maintenance. General Fechet, who was grooming Foulois to replace him, temporarily concentrated all available attack, bombardment, and pursuit craft to form a provisional air division of some 600 aircraft under the command of his intended successor. This force accumulated approximately 38,000 hours of flying time in exercises over major cities in the Great Lakes region and along the Atlantic coast. Each exercise, which required the use of several airfields, consisted, weather permitting, of a massed flight over the city and an air show staged at one of the local fields by a demonstration team. At New York City, for instance, the improvised air division used five airports on Long Island to mount a massed aerial flight that followed the Hudson River past the recently built

George Washington Bridge, while the aerial show took place at Floyd Bennett Field, one of the five Long Island airports.

Impressive though it seemed as it droned overhead, the division consisted of a hodgepodge of aircraft, including many trainers and observation craft in addition to the combat types, and therefore was not a very potent force. Yet, the maneuvers demonstrated that massed training was possible, provided excellent experience in logistics and centralized command, gained some needed publicity for the Air Corps, and impressed both President Hoover and Gen. Douglas MacArthur, the Army Chief of Staff. Perhaps more important, the 1931 maneuvers provided the pattern for massed aerial operations in defense of the United States, showing that an Air Corps officer, assisted by his staff, could gather units from all over the country, support them logistically and administratively, and conduct operations that required precise timing and reliable communications.

Besides taking part in maneuvers, the Air Corps retained its interest in long-distance and endurance records and the publicity they generated. Because the

Aircraft gathered for the 1931 maneuvers at Fairfield Air Depot, near Dayton, Ohio.

Refueling of the *Question Mark* over southern California.

air arm was pressed for funds, it could no longer afford to build the racers, as it
had during the Mitchell era, and engage in the systematic quest for speed
records; fortunately, long-distance flying did not require so heavy an investment
in aircraft development. One of the barriers crossed by Army airmen was the
Pacific Ocean between California and the Hawaiian Islands, the area where a
forced landing by a Navy seaplane helped push Mitchell to make the accusations that led to his court-martial. On June 28, 1927, a month after Charles
Lindbergh flew nonstop from New York to Paris, First Lieutenants Lester J.
Maitland and Albert F. Hegenberger flew their Fokker C–2 trimotor, the *Bird of
Paradise*, some 2,400 miles from Oakland to a landfall on the island of Kauai,
then to a safe landing on Oahu. The flight, which lasted just under 26 hours, tested not only the reliability of the machine but the navigational skill and the sta-
mina of the two officers as well, for had they strayed even three and one-half degrees off course, they would have missed Kauai and vanished over the ocean.

Eighteen months later, Air Corps pilots set a new world endurance mark of
almost 151 hours using the aerial refueling technique developed by Army flyers
a few years earlier. Between January 1 and 7, 1929, Maj. Carl "Tooey" Spaatz,
Capt. Eaker, 1st Lt. Harry Halversen, 2d Lt. Elwood R. "Pete" Quesada, and
Sgt. Roy Hooe flew their Fokker C–2 transport, the *Question Mark*, back and
forth between Los Angeles and San Diego. Two Douglas C–1 transports took
turns refueling them with a hose lowered from the tankers through a trap door
in the top of the *Question Mark*. During one hookup Spaatz was showered with
gasoline when the end of the hose pulled away from the special tank inside the
fuselage. While the *Question Mark* sought smoother air, other crew members
pulled off his clothes and rubbed him down with oil-soaked rags to prevent the

high-octane fuel from burning him. Spaatz suffered only minor injury, but he presented a memorable sight, wearing only a coat of oil and a parachute during the remainder of the fuel transfer. The Air Corps had again demonstrated that aircraft could be refueled in midair, but the most important aspect of the flight was that the Wright engines had run smoothly for the equivalent of 11,000 miles. Reliable engines held the key to long-range operations, whether by bombers attacking an approaching fleet or commercial transports carrying passengers.

In terms of future application, perhaps the most important experiments conducted during the early years of the Air Corps dealt with flying in bad weather or darkness. Although a private foundation financed development of radio beacons and receivers, the dangerous job of testing them fell to Army airmen. Chosen to conduct the test was 1st Lt. Jimmy Doolittle, who had flown a DH–4 coast-to-coast, established speed records, attended the Massachusetts Institute of Technology, and received one of the first doctorates in aeronautical engineering granted in the United States. In September 1929, Doolittle made a complete flight from takeoff through landing with a hood over the cockpit, flying only by instruments. He relied on a radio beacon to line up for the final approach and a marker beacon near the field to tell him when to cut power to gradually descend the last 200 feet to the ground. Later, Maj. William C. Ocker and Capt. Carl Crane further advanced the art of instrument flying, writing *The Theory and Practice of Blind Flight*.

Despite massed maneuvers, record flights, and theorizing about strategic bombardment, the bombers of the period were incapable of carrying the war to the enemy. For that matter, no hostile power loomed on the horizon; the United States, regardless of the economic depression, remained dominant in the Western Hemisphere; and the oceans afforded protection from Japan and Italy, which were beginning to exhibit ambitions to become at least regional powers. If the air arm were to emerge from the shadow of the Army, it needed a mission that would take into account the limitations of existing equipment and geopolitical reality. During the final year of Fechet's tenure, just such a mission appeared—aerial coast defense, to which Billy Mitchell had laid claim a decade earlier by sinking battleships in various bombing tests. The assignment did not result from aggressive lobbying on the part of the Air Corps, but from the momentarily congruent interests of the Army and Navy. The high command of the Army wanted to clarify the responsibilities it shared with the Navy in coastal defense, and the leadership of the Navy hoped to free naval aviation from what, at that moment, seemed an onerous task. Consequently, Adm. William V. Pratt, the Chief of Naval Operations, and General MacArthur, the Army Chief of Staff, in January 1931 reached an agreement that, in the admiral's opinion, would enable naval aviation to sever its ties to the coast, allowing naval aviators to accompany the battle fleet anywhere in the world. Pratt believed that mobility, made possible by the aircraft carrier and seaplane tender, was far more important than

116

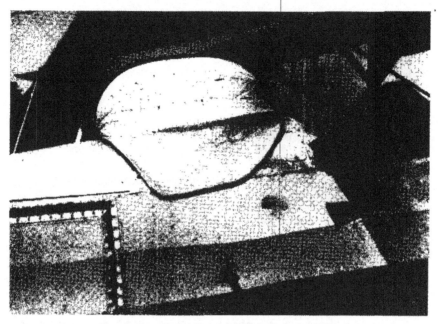

Hooded cockpit used for blind flight in 1929.

coastal patrol from bases ashore. The Navy's General Board, the rough equivalent of a general staff, endorsed the importance of mobility, but feared that Pratt had gone too far and made an agreement that would permit the Air Corps to seize control of all coastal air bases. As a result, the Navy watched closely for signs of "aggression" by the Air Corps.

Army airmen immediately prepared a demonstration of their ability to defend the coast with land-based bombers. In the summer of 1931, plans called for an old freighter, the *Mount Shasta*, to be anchored in shallow water within easy range of Langley Field and serve as a bombing target until blown to pieces. When the Virginia fisheries commission complained about the likely effect of high explosives on fishing in the area, the Air Corps had the hulk towed out to sea where Langley-based aircraft could sink it. Although those involved were reluctant to admit afterward that they had wanted publicity, the attack on the rusting freighter began taking on the importance of Mitchell's bombing of the *Ostfriesland*. Bad weather on August 11 prevented a force of nine bombers led by Maj. Herbert A. Dargue from finding the *Mount Shasta*. Three days later, in clear skies, the airmen located the target and attacked, but the 300-pound bombs that Dargue had selected were inadequate to sink the hulk. A Coast Guard cutter had to send the battered freighter to the bottom to prevent its becoming a hazard to shipping. Although the *New York Times* graciously suggested that 1,000-pound bombs could easily have sunk the ship, partisans of the Navy gleefully

117

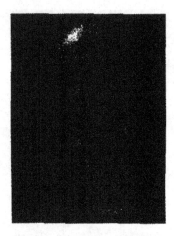

Maj. Gen. Benjamin D. Foulois,
Chief, Army Air Corps,
December 1931–December 1935.

attributed the failure not to light bombs or the bad weather on the first day but to the inability of Army airmen to find a ship at sea, which naval aviators did on a routine basis. "I cannot help but feel," said Hap Arnold, that the *Mount Shasta* fiasco "will have a very detrimental effect on this newly assigned Coast Defense project."[4]

Foulois, who in December 1931 succeeded Fechet as Chief of the Air Corps, also was alert to the possible consequences of the failure to sink the *Mount Shasta* and moved quickly to correct the operational flaws that the test had revealed. He proposed establishing a coast defense school at Bolling Field, Washington, D.C., but the cost of the venture and the jurisdictional prerogatives of other branches, like the coast artillery, aroused opposition within the War Department. General MacArthur intervened, however, and for two years students at Bolling Field conducted theoretical exercises on locating and intercepting hostile ships. On the West Coast, bombers at Rockwell Field tested the tactics developed at Bolling Field.

Although the Air Corps had the mission of aerial coast defense and was acquiring the necessary tactics and navigational techniques, Foulois did not yet have an organization that could rapidly mass men and aircraft against a threat from the sea. Here Fechet's careful preparation of his successor demonstrated its value, for during the 1931 maneuvers Foulois had commanded such a force, and the new Air Corps Chief intended to establish such a centrally controlled strike force on a permanent basis. He proposed to give substance to the theory, advanced by General Patrick, that combat squadrons, excluding observation units, should be removed from the control of the corps area commanders; assigned to a GHQ Air Force that was responsible to the Army's General Headquarters, or GHQ; and commanded by an airman directly responsible to the Army Chief of Staff. Foulois called for the country to be divided into defense zones, each with a permanent patrol force that would search as far seaward as the range of its aircraft would permit. Once Army patrol planes had located the hostile fleet, the strike force would concentrate against the approaching enemy. According to the Foulois plan, the air arm would operate independently of the coast artillery, the mobile ground forces, and, thanks to the Pratt-MacArthur agreement, the Navy as well. Only when the hostile ships became vulnerable to Army coastal batteries would air power revert to a supporting role.

As he had when he proposed establishing a school to train his airmen in coast defense, Foulois again trampled on the toes of the coast artillery and other branches of the service. Moreover, his idea of establishing a centralized strike force and permanent aerial patrols, like the ill-fated five-year plan, enlarged aviation's share of the Army budget and threatened the equitable division of funds among the components. Yet, some senior officers outside the Air Corps accepted the need for a degree of independent aerial operations in time of war, even though they shared the belief that aviation should give priority to assisting the ground forces. The counsel being given the Chief of Staff was clearly divided— military aviation remained under the peacetime control of the corps area commanders to strengthen the bond between air and ground forces, but the War Department nevertheless was encouraging massed aerial maneuvers in preparation for war.

Once again General MacArthur proved amenable to change. In January 1933, he issued a policy letter, "Employment of Army Aviation in Coast Defense," that soothed the sensibilities of the other branches while endorsing the basic theme of the Foulois plan.[5] The Chief of Staff did not mention defensive zones and permanent patrols, but he did sanction long-range aerial reconnaissance far from shore and also acknowledged that a consolidated aerial striking force would be employed against an enemy approaching by sea. In brief, the policy letter endorsed the concept of independent air operations, if the hostile fleet was still far from the coast, but allowed the senior ground commander to take charge of the aerial strike force whenever he deemed necessary.

Foulois and his subordinates were not displeased with the policy letter and the measure of independence it implied. They had come to believe, however, that they formed the nation's first line of defense, and new all-metal bombers on the drawing board lent substance to that belief. Army aviators insisted that, if properly equipped, organized, and employed, air power could repel an invasion force without the help of coast artillery or naval forces. Consequently, the Chief of the Air Corps continued to ask the General Staff for authorization to undertake the detailed planning that would make this kind of coastal defense possible.

MacArthur, who had consistently supported the air arm insofar as funds permitted, went beyond the general subject of coast defense when, in June 1933, he invited Foulois and the Air Corps staff to participate in writing specific air defense plans based on the "color" war plans drafted jointly by the Army and Navy to deal with emergencies involving a variety of nations, each color designating a different enemy. Initially, the Chief of Staff suggested that the Air Corps make recommendations for the employment of a GHQ air force against Red (Great

Britain), Red-Orange (Great Britain allied with Japan), and Green (Mexico), but he settled on Tan (Cuba) because of unrest on that island. The response submitted a month later sent the General Staff into a collective rage, for Foulois and his fellow airmen chose to use the occasion to ignore budgetary constraints and plead for an expansion to 4,500 aircraft. Nor was the planning itself particularly inspired, for the best the Air Corps could do was to argue the general principle that, whoever the foe, the aerial strike force would respond by operating independently of the Army and Navy to launch seaward patrols within permanent defensive zones and attack the enemy ships after the patrols found them.

General MacArthur understandably disapproved of the Air Corps plan, but he did not lose patience with Foulois. Perhaps the Chief of Staff sensed that the Air Corps, by making a reply that did not address the question, was trying to call attention to the overall status of military aviation and the uncertainty that persisted despite MacArthur's recent letter on coast defense. Whatever the reason, on August 11, 1933, MacArthur directed the Deputy Chief of Staff, Maj. Gen. Hugh A. Drum, to head a special committee to review and revise the plan submitted by the Office of Chief of the Air Corps. The Drum Board, which included Foulois and four ground-oriented generals, rejected the Air Corps plan—the expansion because it cost far too much and bore no relationship to any probable threat to the United States and the insistence on independent action because it clashed with the view of the General Staff on the proper role of military aviation. The board's final report, released in October 1933, played down the aerial threat to the United States and emphasized that actions of the Air Corps in coast defense would be part of a broader Army counterinvasion plan. Having bowed to Army doctrine, the board endorsed the importance of long-range reconnaissance and attacks on an invasion fleet "by a properly constituted GHQ Air Force" before the enemy ships could reach their objective. A heritage from World War I, the Army GHQ, to which the GHQ Air Force would report, was to come into existence in time of war to supervise the training of the new American Expeditionary Forces and serve as the staff of its commander, presumably the Army Chief of Staff. Although General Drum and his colleagues rejected out of hand the Air Corps request to expand to 4,500 aircraft, the board did recommend that the air arm consist of 2,320 aircraft (an increase of more than 50 percent), with 980 of them assigned to the GHQ Air Force. This recommendation represented a declaration of principle, however, rather than an expansion plan, for the increase was not to occur at the expense of the rest of the Army—which meant that for the time being it would not happen at all.

Foulois sounded an unusually harmonious tone during the proceedings of the Drum Board, in part because he was outnumbered by ground officers but also in the hope that his cooperative attitude would influence the panel's report. These tactics apparently paid off, for the final report could not have troubled him. The Drum Board supported the Air Corps claim to aerial coast defense, which involved independent operations at least during the initial or long-range phases.

Furthermore, the board accepted in principle the expansion of the air arm and, in approving a GHQ Air Force, recognized the need for a consolidated aerial striking force that would train in peacetime for massed operations in time of war.

To Army airmen, acquiring the coastal defense mission and establishing permanent aerial patrols radiating outward from shore seemed perfectly logical, but to many naval aviators, defending the coast with land-based aircraft was a mission that the Navy should never have surrendered. To complicate matters further, Admiral Pratt, who had yielded the mission to the Air Corps, retired in 1933 and the chief of the Bureau of Aeronautics, Rear Adm. William A. Moffett, died in the crash of the dirigible *Akron* the same year. Their successors, Adm. William H. Standley as Chief of Naval Operations and Rear Adm. Ernest J. King as bureau chief, felt the Navy should control all aircraft operating over the sea, whether flying from mobile aircraft carriers and seaplane tenders or from fixed bases ashore. Since Admiral Standley considered aerial coast defense rightfully a Navy mission, the new Chief of Naval Operations ignored his predecessor's agreement with General MacArthur and treated responsibility for coast defense as an open issue. This turn of events angered the leaders of the Air Corps, who urged the War Department to oppose what they considered a direct encroachment on the acknowledged responsibilities of the air arm. The General Staff wanted to resolve the conflict without alienating the Navy. After lengthy negotiations, the two services in 1935 reached a compromise worded so ambiguously that both the Air Corps and Navy could claim responsibility for aerial operations against an invasion force. The 1935 agreement and the resulting lack of interservice cooperation on aerial coast defense persisted until the Japanese attacked Pearl Harbor six years later.

In one sense, the short-lived coast defense mission served a purpose, for it helped justify the creation of the GHQ Air Force. The Drum Board was the first official agency of the War Department since the Lassiter Board of 1923 to endorse the establishment of such an organization. The conversion of the Army's leadership from indifference to approval resulted from a two-year effort by Foulois and his staff. Throughout the campaign, they advanced three basic arguments. First, a General Headquarters Air Force was an absolute necessity for coastal defense. Second, the air arm should be organized in peacetime for wartime employment, and current war plans called for concentrating its major combat elements. Third, as Foulois himself had shown in the 1931 maneuvers, the Air Corps should train as it would fight, not in nine separate elements, one in each corps area, but as a large, centrally directed strike force responsible through its commander to the Army Chief of Staff. The inescapable conclusion was that a GHQ air force should be formed at once and begin in peacetime to prepare for war.

Military aviation had passed through two stages since World War I. The first, dominated by Billy Mitchell, had been characterized by flamboyance and controversy, which sometimes obscured genuine advances in aeronautical science.

History of the United States Air Force

Although he had a considerable gift for alienating those with whom he disagreed, Mitchell inspired devotion among his followers, engendering a belief in himself and in the future of air power. Such was his magnetism that the Coolidge administration tended to regard him with awe even as it opposed him, overestimating his following with the public and giving military aviation the status of the Air Corps, which the President and his advisers might otherwise have withheld. Under the guidance of Patrick in the final years of his tenure, and under both Fechet and Foulois, the Air Corps fared better than the rest of the Army, despite miserly administrations constrained for much of the period by a depressed economy. Government fiscal policy and the depression frustrated the five-year plan of modernization and expansion, and aircraft technology was only beginning to catch up with the ambitious theories of strategic bombardment being formulated at the Air Corps Tactical School. Nevertheless, regard for the Air Corps and its theory of air power grew within the War Department. Evidence of this changing attitude came on October 12, 1933, when General MacArthur approved the report of the Drum Board. The GHQ Air Force was formally established under the command of Westover, now a brigadier general, in his role as Assistant Chief of the Air Corps, but neither men nor aircraft were actually assigned. Before the new command could evolve from an organizational chart to a genuine organization, a crisis arose that tested the leadership and flying skills of the Air Corps.

In February 1934, President Franklin D. Roosevelt, who had taken office in March of the previous year, abruptly canceled the airmail contracts between the Post Office and the commercial airlines, creating an emergency that delayed the establishment of a fully functioning GHQ Air Force. A special committee of the Senate, which for several months had been investigating the airmail contracts let during the last two years of the Hoover administration, unearthed enough evidence of fraud and collusion to persuade the President that the agreements were invalid and should be abrogated. Before the Chief Executive issued a formal directive to this effect, he had postal officials consult Foulois to determine if the Air Corps could temporarily haul the mail, as the Air Service had done experimentally in 1918. Exhibiting what came to be called a "can do" attitude, the Chief of the Air Corps hesitated not at all before answering yes. Not only did he consider President Roosevelt's request tantamount to an order, he realized that the publicity resulting from a successful operation might help obtain some badly needed appropriations for the Air Corps.

On February 9, Foulois impulsively committed his Air Corps to a task that required flights at night and in bad weather, but the average Army pilot lacked experience in this kind of flying. Since aerial combat was a daytime, fair weather activity in which speed and visibility were most important, Army aviators rarely flew at night or in marginal weather; after all, as one veteran of World War I pointed out, "In war we must see our objective." The Army's open-cockpit airplanes did not normally carry blind flying instruments or even ra-

Thomas-Morse O–19 used for carrying the air mail at Denver, Colorado.

dios. The leaders of the Air Corps realized the seriousness of the problem and directed that artificial horizons, gyro compasses, and radios be installed in the aircraft assigned to carry the mail, but flight instruments were not readily available and mechanics unfamiliar with their operation sometimes installed them incorrectly.

Experience and equipment were just part of the problem, for the Air Corps had become the prisoner of ease and habit. Except during major maneuvers, such as those in 1931, the men of the Air Corps lived a relatively pleasant life, caught up in an easy routine. Although enlisted men formed at 6:30 a.m. each weekday for a roll call before breakfast, officers normally did not arrive for duty until about an hour later. Flying began at about 8:00 a.m. and continued until 11:30 a.m. when the officers went to lunch. The pilots usually relaxed at the officers' club until about 1:30 p.m. and then returned to the office, hangar, or flight line for another two hours. At about 3:30 p.m. the duty day normally ended. Nearly all officers had their weekends free, as well as a half day off on Wednesdays, and almost no one worked at night.

The Air Corps, however, encouraged the use of this leisure time for education. To help flyers take advantage of their spare time, the Air Corps Tactical School operated an extension program, and the *Air Corps Newsletter*, a mimeographed compilation of news, gossip, and professional notes prepared at Air Corps headquarters, suggested publications that an Army aviator might read with profit. Material from either source tended to be narrowly professional, addressing such topics as aerial tactics and strategy (the main concerns of the tactical school), aeronautical engineering, safety, and aerial navigation. Some officers returned part-time to college, among them 2d Lt. Curtis E. LeMay, and the usual field of study was some branch of engineering.

Despite the combination of ease and opportunity, there were disadvantages to life in the Air Corps. Flying was inherently risky, and reductions in flying hours made in the interest of economy slowed the development of skill even as it reduced the exposure to danger. Pay was another source of irritation. In response to the depression, Hoover had required the military to take unpaid leave, and Roosevelt substituted a 15 percent pay cut, which lasted into 1935. Even so, the servicemen lived in quarters supplied by the government, their wives shopped at exchanges or commissaries that charged from 25 to 40 percent less than local stores, and military men had regular pay, albeit less than before the depression, at a time when almost five million families, one in six, were destitute, dependent on charity or government programs of relief.

Foulois faced the challenge of organizing his Air Corps, shifting its units from comfortable military bases to spartan civilian airports, ridding it of the lethargy caused by routine, and sending it to do a twenty-four-hour-a-day job for which it was not even remotely prepared. Further, he had only a short time to do so. On the day that the Chief of the Air Corps agreed to fly the mail, the President revoked the existing contracts. Ten days later, commercial airmail service ended and Army pilots took over the routes. Foulois, his assistant chief, General Westover, and his small staff had to acquire hangar and office space along the various routes, arrange for refueling, assign pilots and maintenance men and arrange living quarters for them, and press into service aircraft with cargo capacity that varied from perhaps twenty-five pounds in the P–12 pursuit to a ton in the new Martin B–10 and Boeing Y1B–9 monoplane bombers, both faster than the biplane pursuit. Westover took charge of the airmail operation, establishing three geographic zones and appointing commanders—Arnold in the western, Hickam in the central, and Maj. Byron Q. Jones in the eastern. The airmen were determined enough, as demonstrated when Jones vowed, "We'll carry the mail, don't worry about that, unless an elephant drops on us. If it does, we'll cut it up and ship it out as mail."[6] Determination was not enough, however, for unexpected problems surfaced—some types of aircraft proved ill-suited to carrying the mail; mechanics arrived at airfields, but their tools did not; and enlisted men had to sleep on boards in drafty hangars because decent quarters were not available and money for subsistence was approved only grudgingly. Nevertheless, the Army Air Corps began flying the mail on February 19 as scheduled.

Unfortunately, the weather did not cooperate, and the United States was hit by some of the worst late winter weather in its history. A blizzard disrupted the first day's operations from the Rocky Mountains to the East Coast; and throughout the rest of the month, snow, rain, dense fog, and icy gales prevailed over much of the nation. Aircraft parked on ramps could not be started when the oil congealed, carburetor icing shut down engines in midflight, and pilots unused to instrument flying became disoriented in fog or clouds. Foulois imposed strict flight safety rules, but these scarcely damped the enthusiasm of his aviators, who were all eager to prove they could carry out the assignment, many unaware of the danger they faced. The odds were against them in their struggle with darkness and the elements, for valor and eagerness could not make up for inexperience and the lack of equipment needed for blind flying. During the first week of the operation, a series of crashes killed six Army flyers, fulfilling predictions that the Air Corps was not up to the task. An embarrassed and angry President took steps late in March to let new contracts with the airlines, which would resume service by June 1.

With better flying weather in mid-March and a quickly instituted course in instrument flying, Army aviators did a much better job during the latter weeks of airmail duty. Yet, the overall record of the Air Corps was not good: 12 deaths, 66 crashes, and a completion rate of only 66 percent of scheduled sorties. During the 12 months of the airmail project, about 15 percent more deaths occurred than the average—54 in fiscal 1934 compared to 46 in fiscal 1933 and 47 in fiscal 1935. The fatalities per 100,000 flying hours rose to 14 in 1934 in contrast to 11 in 1933 and 1935. Moreover, 12 of the deaths during fiscal year 1934 occurred during a highly publicized operation, catching the attention of political leaders and the general public.

Despite the poor record, the airmail episode nevertheless produced some positive results. The Air Corps awakened to the need for an extensive program of instrument training. Captain Crane continued working in the field of blind flying, joined by Maj. George V. Holloman and two civilians, Raymond K. Stout and C. D. Barbulesco. Together they devised an automated landing system that brought a plane onto the runway in response to signals from radio beacons on the ground that moved the controls. This frankly experimental technique was successfully tested during 1937, but was never adopted. Until the advent of approach control radar during World War II, the usual aid for landings in fog or dense clouds was a radio beam that guided the pilot. Whether using such a beam or following instructions from a radar operator, the flyer had to emerge from the overcast and locate the runway lights before landing. From its experience in flying the mail, the Air Corps realized the need for reliable radio communications and in 1938 obtained permission from the War Department to establish the Army Airways Communications System. At its inception a network of control towers, navigation beacons, and radio stations at thirty-three sites in a vast arc stretching from New York state through Florida, Texas, and California to Washington state, the system ultimately evolved into the worldwide Air Force Communications Command.

Another result of the airmail operation was the convening of an investigatory body that endorsed carrying out the mandate of the Drum Board to create the GHQ Air Force. Anxious over the adverse publicity spawned by the poor showing of the Air Corps in carrying the mail, Secretary of War George H. Dern appointed a special committee chaired by Newton D. Baker, himself a former Secretary of War, to examine the condition of military aviation. After completing its deliberations, the Baker Board gave its unqualified blessing to the immediate formation of a centrally controlled aerial strike force.

The board's report, issued in July 1934, reflected the War Department's view of Army aviation, for the General Staff closely controlled the scope of the investigation. Indeed, a major from the General Staff set the agenda, took charge of most of the questioning of witnesses, and did not give the aviators a chance to convert the board to the cause of independent air power. The composition of the Baker Board, which included the five members of the Drum Board (Foulois and four senior Army ground officers), provided added insurance that the group would not reach any unorthodox conclusions. The board's chairman, Newton Baker, had opposed independence for the air arm while serving in the cabinet of President Wilson. In all, just three members of the eleven-man panel could be considered genuine advocates of military aviation—Foulois, Jimmy Doolittle, employed by Shell Oil but still a reserve officer, and Edgar Gorrell, president of the Studebaker automobile corporation and a former Army aviator. A firm believer in strategic bombing, Gorrell, immediately after the armistice that ended World War I, supervised the compilation of a history of the Air Service of the American Expeditionary Forces, a task that produced some 280 volumes of reports, histories, and documents.

The recommendations of the Baker Board established an aviation policy that endured for the remainder of the decade. The report confirmed the principal findings of the Drum Board, acknowledging that military aviation was valuable in both offensive and defensive operations, but insisting that the air arm could not become a third service equal to the Army and Navy. The board based its judgment on what the General Staff had been saying for years: within the limits of existing technology, air power could not independently affect the outcome of a conflict and therefore should remain an integral part of the Army.

Instead of recommending independence, the Baker Board proposed the immediate formation of the GHQ Air Force, consisting of all the Army's combat aviation units within the continental United States. The commander of the new organization—a suitable air officer—was to report directly to the Chief of Staff in peacetime and to the commanding general of the American Expeditionary Forces or a theater commander in wartime. Although granting the commander of the GHQ Air Force control over training and operations, the board suggested that airfields and housekeeping elements remain under the jurisdiction of corps area commanders. The Chief of the Air Corps, Baker and his colleagues believed, should continue to supervise supply, procurement of men and equipment, the training schools, and the development of doctrine. The division of authority among corps area commanders, the Commander of the GHQ Air Force, and the Chief of the Air Corps was to cause problems in the future.

Besides advocating the formation of the GHQ Air Force, the Baker Board echoed the call of the Drum Board to build a force of 2,320 aircraft and to recruit or commission enough men to reach the strength of 16,650 specified in the Air Corps Act of 1926. The air arm, however, was not to expand at the expense of the other combat arms, another instance of the Baker Board endorsing the findings of the earlier panel. Baker and his colleagues advocated a number of actions not mentioned in the report of the Drum Board, including additional instrument and night training and an increase to 300 hours per year in the flying time authorized for each pilot, the latter especially significant since aviators had been flying only about half that much because of funding cuts. The reforms in training and flying hours were designed to correct failings that had surfaced during the airmail operation.

Only one member of the Baker Board suggested that the Air Corps not remain a part of the Army, and he dissented in terms far milder than many an airman on active duty might have used. Doolittle said that an air force independent of the Army would be best for the nation, but he, in effect, conceded that the separation could not take place at that time. He therefore recommended that the Army Air Corps have its own budget, its own promotion list, and a command structure autonomous of the War Department General Staff. This minority report made up but one paragraph in a seventy-five-page document that dealt not only with the Air Corps, but with commercial aviation and the aircraft industry as well.

As Doolittle realized—and also Arnold, whose testimony before the board included similar recommendations—the best the Air Corps could expect was implementation of the Drum Board report, which had called for the establishment of the GHQ Air Force and a modest expansion of the air arm. Like Foulois and his fellow airmen, the ground-oriented War Department General Staff was satisfied with what essentially was a compromise between independence and the status quo. As soon as President Roosevelt gave his approval, the War Department began implementing those reforms that did not require legislation. One reason for haste was a desire by the Army's senior leaders to forestall a possible attempt by the recently formed Federal Aviation Commission to make more changes to the status of the Air Corps.

The Federal Aviation Commission also had its genesis in the airmail operation. As a consequence of that embarrassment, Roosevelt asked Clark Howell, editor of the *Atlanta Constitution*, to chair a five-member committee that investigated all facets of American aviation, much as Dwight Morrow and his colleagues had done almost a decade earlier. Because the Howell Commission seemed immune to influence by the General Staff, the War Department feared that the outsiders might undercut the Baker Board's findings by recommending complete independence for the Air Corps. To prevent this, witnesses from the General Staff argued convincingly that the Baker Board's recommendations should be given a chance before additional changes were introduced. The leaders of the Air Corps tended to support the War Department's position, for they were eager to establish the GHQ Air Force so that military aviation could be organized immediately for effective employment.

A few of the lower ranking officers in the air arm shaped a more controversial course during the new investigation. Maj. Donald Wilson, Capt. Robert Olds, Capt. Harold L. George, Capt. Robert Webster, Capt. Claire Chennault, and 1st Lt. Kenneth Walker, most of whom were instructors at the Air Corps Tactical School, believed they were risking their careers by openly advocating independence during their appearances before the Howell Commission. Taken as a whole, the testimony of these young airmen described strategic bombardment as a new method of warfare that could demoralize an enemy and destroy his ability to resist, even though his armies might remain in the field. They argued that to train for and execute this important offensive mission and to defend the United States against hostile air attack, the Air Corps should be separated from the Army. To their surprise, Maj. Gen. Charles E. Kilbourne, the spokesman for the General Staff, graciously congratulated the junior officers for the clear presentation of their personal views, which, he said, would influence his thinking in the future. Distinguishing between the personal views of comparatively junior airmen and declarations of policy by their leaders, Kilbourne ordered that any references to an independent air force be removed from official statements by Foulois and Westover.

The Howell Commission was impressed with the testimony of Walker and the other young aviators but not with that of Billy Mitchell. The former Assistant Chief of the Air Service denounced the GHQ Air Force as a fraud designed to delay real independence, a charge that the Howell Commission ignored. As far as military aviation was concerned, this latest investigatory body was determined to give the GHQ Air Force a chance and, as the War Department desired, did not recommend any organizational changes. In their final report, issued in January 1935, the commission members affirmed that "aircraft have now passed beyond their former position as useful auxiliaries, and must in the future be considered and utilized as an important means of exerting directly the will of the Commander in Chief."[7] The report went on to say that the recent reforms inspired by the Baker Board recognized the increased importance of military aviation but that a further grant of independence beyond the creation of the GHQ Air Force might someday prove necessary.

While Howell's Federal Aviation Commission conducted its investigation, the War Department drew up plans to bring the GHQ Air Force to life. Since the adoption of the Drum Board's report as official War Department policy in 1933, a GHQ Air Force had existed on paper, but the airmail operation and the subsequent convening of the Baker Board had delayed its actual formation. On December 31, 1934, the General Staff announced that the aerial task force would be established on March 1 of the following year. Col. Frank M. Andrews took command with the temporary rank of brigadier general, established his

Brig. Gen. Frank M. Andrews, front, GHQ Air Force Commander, and staff watch aerial review, Langley Field, Virginia, March 4, 1935.

headquarters at Langley Field, Virginia, and assumed control of all Air Corps bombardment, pursuit, and attack aircraft in the United States. By the end of December 1935, he had received another temporary promotion to major general, the same rank as the Chief of the Air Corps. The flying units under the control of Andrews were divided among three tactical wings, one commanded by temporary Brig. Gen. Hap Arnold at March Field, another by Conger Pratt, also a temporary brigadier general, at Langley Field, and the third by Gerald Brant, a temporary colonel, at Barksdale Field, Louisiana.

"Andy" Andrews seemed a good choice to command the GHQ Air Force during the period when it would be testing its wings not only in the sense of flight operations, but also in terms of its relationship with the rest of the Air Corps and the Army corps areas. He was an unassuming, patient individual with a knack for getting along with others. After graduating from West Point in 1906, he had served for eleven years as a cavalry officer before becoming a pilot during the wartime expansion of Army aviation. While Billy Mitchell was sinking battleships and beginning to arouse wrath among the admirals, generals, and civilian officials, Andrews had been serving in Europe as air officer for his father-in-law, Maj. Gen. Henry Allen, commander of the American occupation forces in Germany. After returning to the United States, Andrews served for a time at Kelly Field, site of the Air Service training center, then attended the Tactical School at Langley Field and the Army Command and General Staff School at Fort Leavenworth, Kansas. Since he had little contact with Mitchell until after the court martial, Andrews was not considered a radical, although he was one member of a revolutionary-sounding trio. These friends and golfing partners were Walter "Trotsky" Weaver, Walter "Kerensky" Frank, and "Lenin" Andrews. Although Weaver and Frank may have detected the fire of a rebel in their close friend, to most observers Andrews remained a gentleman, a gracious host, and an accomplished horseman.

The War Department made Andrews, in his new assignment, directly responsible to the Chief of Staff in peacetime and to the designated theater commander in wartime. Although the commander of the GHQ Air Force was responsible for the effectiveness of his organization, he possessed no authority over airfields or other installations, housekeeping elements, procurement, or supply. Following the recommendations of the Baker Board, corps area commanders retained control over bases and support personnel, and the Chief of the Air Corps continued to be responsible for the other two functions. Nevertheless, all combat units now belonged to a single air commander. This in itself was a vast improvement as far as Air Corps officers were concerned, for it permitted the massed employment of air power.

The GHQ Air Force was a compromise between the advocates of air power, who wanted to free the air arm completely from Army control to strike the distant vital centers, and those conservative ground officers who demanded that military aviation remain a branch of the Army, tied to the advance of the land forces. Because the new organization was capable of independent air missions as well as direct support of ground troops, it offered something to both. The aviators praised it because it permitted the concentrated employment of military aviation, unity of command, and standardized training unhindered by the whims of the various corps area commanders; and the ground commanders were satisfied that they would have supporting aviation when needed.

With the activation in March 1935 of this consolidated strike force, the campaign for an independent (or at least fully autonomous) air arm that had been conducted during the past decade and a half all but ceased, much as Foulois had suggested might happen in earlier discussions with MacArthur. This did not mean that the aviators had abandoned the goal toward which Mitchell had struggled. Rather, it indicated that the airmen considered the GHQ Air Force a step toward independence and were willing to give it a chance before renewing the struggle. Arnold, now commanding a wing of the GHQ Air Force, and other senior officers of the Air Corps had another more practical reason for not making waves at this time. As Arnold acknowledged before a congressional committee in 1936, if the air arm received immediate independence, it would be unable to train its own administrative, technical, and base support specialists and could not promptly take over the functions now routinely performed by Army troops.

In trying to turn his GHQ Air Force into a first-class fighting organization, Andrews encountered jurisdictional problems that involved the corps area commanders and the Chief of the Air Corps. He tried first to clarify the relationship of his air force to the corps area commanders. Consequently, in August 1935 he wrote the Deputy Chief of Staff urging that airfields and the support personnel operating them be reassigned from the corps areas to the GHQ Air Force. He pressured the General Staff on the issue in succeeding months, pointing out that it would be all but impossible for him to develop an effective combat force unless he and his commanders controlled the flying facilities and the assigned manpower. The General Staff finally relented, ordering him to assume command of all GHQ Air Force stations and assigned personnel effective July 1, 1936.

This, however, cured just one of the jurisdictional ills. The Chief of the Air Corps continued to control supply, aircraft procurement, Air Corps schools, and the development of doctrine, all matters that directly affected Andrews and his command. Such an arrangement was not troublesome as long as Foulois remained Chief of the Air Corps, for Andrews could work with him even though the two men were not especially close. Foulois had championed the establishment of the GHQ Air Force and believed that its commander should enjoy the kind of authority that Fechet had granted him during the 1931 maneuvers. In short, both Foulois and Andrews believed in shifting control away from Air Corps headquarters, which they envisioned as a purely administrative agency. Since the two officers agreed, their staffs at Washington and at Langley Field worked harmoniously together. The situation changed dramatically when Westover succeeded Foulois in December 1935.

Like Foulois, Westover had begun his career as an enlisted man, but there the similarity ended. Unlike his predecessor, the new Chief of the Air Corps had gone on to graduate from the Military Academy. He was a latecomer to military aviation, compared to Foulois, qualifying as a balloonist in 1921 and two years afterward as an airplane pilot. Walter Frank, Kerensky to Andrews' Lenin, once said that Westover was the only officer in Foulois' headquarters who opposed an autonomous air force. This was unfair, however, for the issue was not autonomy or independence but respect for War Department policy. A rather humorless, austere person, Westover believed in complete loyalty to superior authority, whether to the Chief of the Air Corps or to the General Staff; to denounce Army policy, as Mitchell had done, was unthinkable. Initially the friction between

131

Maj. Gen. Oscar Westover,
Chief, Army Air Corps,
December 1935–September 1938.

Westover and Andrews had nothing to do with either independence from the Army or War Department policy. It arose from a difference in the organizational philosophies of the two men. Whereas Andrews continued to advocate decentralization and the transfer of operational responsibility away from Air Corps headquarters, Westover believed in centralization, insisting that he and his staff keep a tight rein on the GHQ Air Force and every other element of the air arm. Westover's assistant, Brig. Gen. Hap Arnold, differed markedly from the new Chief of the Air Corps in background and personality, but he, too, supported control from headquarters, not merely because he was Westover's deputy but because he believed that centralization was more efficient.

Oriented toward air operations rather than toward the functioning of the Air Corps as a whole, Andrews believed that as the individual responsible for the combat effectiveness of the GHQ Air Force he should direct all the various functions that contributed to its success, whether the procurement of aircraft or the assignment of pilots and crews. In his opinion, the GHQ Air Force should function all but autonomously of Westover's headquarters, leaving its commander free to deal directly with the Army Chief of Staff. In contrast, Westover believed that as Chief of the Air Corps he should control Army aviation in its entirety, and to the dismay of Andrews, he did just that, transferring officers into or out of the GHQ Air Force without consulting its commander and generally ignoring the advice emanating from Langley Field. Both Andrews and Westover tried repeatedly to convince the War Department that each should exercise the authority that he considered necessary, but the General Staff for the time being was unwilling to approve a further reorganization of the air arm.

The conflict between Andrews and Westover evolved from a difference in organizational philosophy into an often bitter clash on the future of air power. Soon after taking over the GHQ Air Force, Andrews became a strong proponent of strategic bombing. By 1937, moreover, he had become disenchanted with the General Staff's dominion over Army aviation and concluded that the air arm had to become a separate service if it was ever to realize its potential to win wars. This view was anathema to Westover, not because he no longer believed in strategic bombardment or the impact of air power but because supporting Andrews meant defying legally constituted authority, which had placed the Air Corps within the Army.

Westover had served thirty-three months as Chief of the Air Corps when an accident ended his life. On September 21, 1938, during an inspection tour of the aviation industry on the West Coast, he was killed when the airplane he was piloting crashed while landing. His death ended the controversy with Andrews but did not resolve the basic issue of who should exercise the ultimate authority over the GHQ Air Force. Arnold, like Fechet, Foulois, and Westover before him, moved from Assistant Chief to Chief of the Air Corps and worked amicably with Andrews, until Andrews was reassigned on March 1, 1939, after four years as Commanding General, GHQ Air Force. Although just as convinced as Westover had been that Air Corps headquarters should exercise unity of command over every aspect of military aviation, Arnold could be tactful, even charming in advancing his beliefs. Compared to Westover, who had been a wrestler in his youth and tended to stalk grimly after his opponent, always seeking the advantage, Arnold was more flexible, willing to accept delay to preserve harmony and avoiding any confrontation he might lose. As a result, the new Chief of the Air Corps waited for the change of command at the GHQ Air Force before taking the issue to the General Staff, where he won the support of the new Deputy Chief of Staff, Brig. Gen. George C. Marshall. On the day that Andrews relinquished command, the Chief of the Air Corps assumed responsibility for the GHQ Air Force, and the new commander, Brig. Gen. Delos C. Emmons, began reporting to Arnold. Marshall had come to believe that the Air Corps did not receive adequate recognition within the Army hierarchy, and he may have seen the concentration of authority in the hands of the Chief of the Air Corps as a means of increasing the prestige of aviation. Whatever the reason, Marshall sided with Arnold, a hunting companion in the Philippines before World War I, against Andrews, whose ability he had come to respect and who was the son-in-law of a general under whom the recently appointed Deputy Chief of Staff had once served.

Between 1925 and 1935, the Air Corps did more than merely survive years of economizing. It obtained a mission, aerial coast defense, that justified the creation of a centrally controlled strike force, the GHQ Air Force, and was seeking another mission, strategic bombardment, that seemed likely to free it from the Army. Although the agreement with Admiral Pratt that gave the Air Corps sole responsibility for coast defense sank in a sea of ambiguity, the GHQ Air Force survived. The relationship of its commander to the Chief of the Air Corps and to the ground officers commanding the corps areas was a subject of debate into the 1940s, but it was certain that the combat elements of the Air Corps would be commanded by a professional airman, whether he reported directly to the Army Chief of Staff, a designated theater commander, or the Chief of the Air Corps. Moreover, professionalism was being encouraged by the Air Corps Tactical School, although the ideas radiating from the faculty and students tended to emphasize strategic bombardment. Indeed, it was becoming increasingly clear that the GHQ Air Force would be built around the bomber. New types of these aircraft were beginning to appear, and the emerging leaders of the Air Corps were believers in strategic bombardment. Some, like Westover, were not especially assertive, but others, like Andrews, argued loudly for the acquisition of huge multiengine bombers. During the remainder of the 1930s, a consensus would arise among the Army's senior airmen that the next war would be fought in Europe, that air power would provide the key to victory, and that the bomber would provide the means of obtaining independence from the Army.

Chapter 5

The Heyday of the GHQ Air Force, 1935-1939

John F. Shiner

B y the mid-1930s, the Army's air arm had become firmly established. Although the GHQ Air Force proved to be a relatively short-lived organizational entity (1935–1939), its brief existence marked another step forward in the growth of the Army air arm. During the late 1930s, the Army Air Corps modernized its aircraft inventory, increased its numbers and striking power, solidified its doctrine, and, in response to growing international tensions, began preparing for the increasingly likely eventuality of hostilities. When open warfare finally erupted in Europe in September 1939, the Army Air Corps stood poised, along with the rest of the U.S. military establishment, to develop into an impressive instrument of modern warfare.

Money remained tight throughout most of the 1930s, as the country struggled with the depression and the War Department struggled to equip an Army that needed everything from semiautomatic rifles for its infantrymen to B–17s for its bomber crews. To acquire the aircraft it wanted, the Air Corps needed a financial windfall, which it surprisingly got in fiscal year 1934. In the budget for 1934, Congress included a direct cash appropriation of $30 million, an increase of $6 million over the preceding year, but President Franklin D. Roosevelt, in an effort to fight the depression by cutting government expenses, imposed a ceiling of $11.5 million on what the Air Corps could spend. In an effort to create jobs, however, the Roosevelt administration, with the other hand, made $7.5 million available to the Air Corps from the Public Works Administration expressly to buy airplanes and inject life into a dying aircraft industry. With this infusion of funds, the air arm was able to purchase 92 badly needed aircraft at a time when an order for even a dozen airplanes might enable a manufacturer to stave off bankruptcy. In the mid-1930s, the General Staff also became concerned over the declining number of aircraft in the Air Corps and made a concerted effort to obtain larger appropriations for the Army air arm. This attitude brought some improvement, for Congress approved almost $30 million again in fiscal 1935 and appropriated more than $45 million for military aviation in fiscal 1936.

Despite the increased appropriations, the lack of funding in previous years continued to take its toll, and the overall strength grew only slowly. While many new aircraft were acquired, even larger numbers of aging airplanes had to be scrapped. The inventory of aircraft in the Air Corps fell to a mere 855 in 1936, more than 100 fewer than the Drum Board had wanted for the GHQ Air Force alone. At the urging of the War Department, Congress in June 1936 authorized the Air Corps to increase its strength to the 2,320 aircraft recommended by the Drum Board in 1933 and the Baker Board in 1934, but the administration refused to request enough money in fiscal 1937 to begin the buildup. Although Air Corps appropriations continued to climb annually from 1936 onward, not until fiscal 1939 did the government provide sufficient money to enable the Air Corps to reach the total number of aircraft that the Baker Board had approved five years earlier.

A new emphasis on competitive bidding also slowed the buying process. Shortly after the Public Works Administration released money for the Air Corps, the executive branch and Congress became intensely interested in military aircraft procurement. The Air Corps Act of 1926 contained clauses requiring competitive bidding in all major purchases of aircraft, but three consecutive Chiefs of the Air Corps—Maj. Gens. Mason M. Patrick, James M. Fechet, and Benjamin D. Foulois—had used loopholes in the law to continue negotiating production contracts. As Foulois explained, negotiation enabled the Air Corps to avoid unreliable firms and ensured that the air arm would receive the best possible airplanes at a reasonable price, since inspectors from the Materiel Division could ferret out instances of excess profits and penalize the offending companies on subsequent orders. In support of Foulois, Reuben H. Fleet, the president of Consolidated Aircraft, told congressional investigators that Air Corps officers had pressured his firm into selling fifty $6,000 airplanes for one dollar each to make up for huge profits on earlier contracting. Indeed, Fleet claimed that the Air Corps had bargained so sharply that the company had lost money in future dealings. On the other hand, William Boeing, founder of Boeing Aircraft, acknowledged during hearings on the airmail contracts that manufacturers made huge profits selling engines and aircraft to the Army and Navy.

As the cancellation of the airmail contracts had shown, powerful sentiment existed on Capitol Hill for economic competition. Conger Pratt, then a brigadier general in charge of the Materiel Division, submitted figures showing that no firm's profits exceeded sixteen percent, but Congress nevertheless forbade the Air Corps to negotiate with individual aircraft suppliers. The recent investigation of the airmail contracts had uncovered rigged bidding; and the fear of similar collusion contributed to the ban on negotiated contracts. At this same time, a Senate committee was investigating the armaments industry and the so-called Merchants of Death, who were charged with subordinating patriotism to profits. In these circumstances, Congress insisted on open bidding, ignoring previous successes in negotiating airplane contracts. The authority to purchase airplanes through negotiated agreements was not restored until after the United States had entered World War II, when aircraft of every type had to be obtained quickly and in vast numbers.

As was true of aircraft, the number of officers also grew slowly, even though the Air Corps by 1933 had almost attained the enlisted strength of 15,000 called for by the 1926 law. Commissioned strength, which had grown only slightly during the first half of the decade, hovered around 1,500 Regulars in mid-1936. Congress finally acted in 1935 to ease the shortage of officers by giving the Secretary of War the authority to grant Regular commissions to some reserve officers and to retain others on extended active duty. Each year for 10 years, 50 reservists would receive Regular commissions after completing flight training, and as many as 1,000 reserve officers would be retained on active duty. The lawmakers, however, delayed voting funds for the program, which did not get under way until 1936. Handicapped by a chronic shortage of money, the Air Corps could not make full use of this authority until 1939, shortly before the outbreak of war in Europe.

In the late 1930s, the bomber enthusiasts in the Army Air Corps held the upper hand in influencing aircraft development and procurement, but they were at a disadvantage in forging an aerial weapon capable of accomplishing offensive purposes. Since the Army Air Corps was part of the Army, the overall needs of the service affected the funds available for aviation, and airmen, despite the glamour of flying, faced an obstacle if they tried to bypass the War Department and appeal directly to the American people. Strategic bombers would prove deadliest if the circumstances of World War I should recur and the Army bombers operate from airfields in the British Isles or France against Germany, the enemy of that war. Obvious though it was, Army airmen could not openly acknowledge the fact, since an influential segment of public opinion in the United States was determined to keep the nation from becoming involved in another European war. Indeed, this very attitude produced neutrality legislation designed to prevent history from repeating itself, and it would have been folly

Boeing B-9, the Army's first monoplane bomber.

for advocates of air power to discuss publicly the bombing of European cities. Consequently, coast defense, hemispheric defense, and the defense of outlying American possessions became the most frequently cited justifications for the development and acquisition of a force of long-range bombers. Yet, the nation's fascination with flying and the hope that aviation might somehow win any unavoidable war cheaply and quickly offset isolationism to some degree and helped the Army Air Corps purchase a series of revolutionary bombers during the 1930s.

The first of the new bombers, the Boeing Y1B–9, proved a disappointment but, despite its failings, signaled an abrupt departure from the kind of wire-braced, fabric-covered biplanes that had been bought during the late 1920s from Keystone and Curtiss. Purchased in limited numbers for evaluation by operational units, this streamlined twin-engine, low-wing monoplane had a top speed of 186 miles per hour, some 50 miles per hour faster than the fastest of its predecessors. Unfortunately, the Boeing firm retained the uncomfortable open cockpit and also demonstrated that it had not fully mastered the art of all-metal construction. The elongated fuselage lacked longitudinal strength, and the metal skin wrinkled so noticeably under aerodynamic forces that the plane earned the nickname "tissue-paper bomber."

Although capable of speeds in excess of 200 miles per hour, the Martin B–10, a second new bomber, revealed failings similar to those of the Boeing when it arrived at Wright Field, Ohio, in 1932 for an evaluation. The Army test pilots detected severe wing flutter in the prototype; but at the engineering center, Maj. Carl F. Greene had studied that very phenomenon and was able to de-

The prototype Martin B–10 (above) evaluated by the Army in 1932 had open crew positions. Production B–10s (right) had closed crew positions and gun turrets in the nose. These B–10s are at Bolling Field in July 1934, before the flight to Alaska.

sign a modified wing of unusual strength. Because of Greene and other Wright Field engineers, who redesigned the aileron cables and insisted on enclosed cockpits and other refinements, the B–10 became the standard Air Corps bomber of the mid-1930s. In 1934 Lt. Col. Hap Arnold led a squadron of these planes on a successful massed flight to Alaska and back, giving heart to those who viewed the B–10 as a weapon for coastal defense, if not as a true strategic bomber.

Carl Greene also contributed to the development of the pressurized cabin, although it was not adopted for bombers until the next decade. He collaborated with John E. Younger, a civilian consultant, and other members of the engineering staff at Wright Field in designing such a cabin for the Lockheed XC–35, tested in 1937. When parked on the apron and pressurized for the first time, the air whistled through hundreds of tiny holes in the cabin, all of which had to be painstakingly sealed. When a final coat of soapy water revealed no bubbles from escaping air, the tests began. At altitudes above 30,000 feet, fluid might congeal

Formation of Boeing P–26 aircraft.

in the hydraulic system, windows frost over, and instruments fail due to the cold, but the pressurization functioned perfectly.

As the Y1B–9, and especially the B–10, would indicate, bombers tended to dominate American aircraft development during the 1930s. In fact, the B–10 outperformed the best Army pursuit plane of its time, the Boeing P–26, an all-metal monoplane that represented a transition in fighter design. Its externally braced wing and a fixed landing gear were inherited from the era of the biplane, but wing flaps had been added to reduce the landing speed. At full throttle the P–26 could attain 234 miles per hour, only marginally faster than the new bomber, and the difference in speed was too little to permit intercepting fighters to locate and catch approaching B–10s.

The superiority of bombers over pursuit aircraft emerged dramatically during Air Corps maneuvers on the West Coast in 1933; when pitted against the new bombers, standard pursuits failed miserably in attempts to intercept the B–10s short of the target. Brig. Gen. Oscar Westover, who commanded the 1933 maneuvers while serving as Assistant Chief of the Air Corps, recommended eliminating pursuits from the inventory because they did not have enough of an advantage in speed over bombers to make consistent interceptions. Westover concluded that "high speed and otherwise high performing bombardment aircraft, together with observation aircraft of superior speed and range and communications characteristics, will suffice for the adequate air defense of this country."[1] Nor did he feel that the pursuit, or fighter, was needed to support offensive operations. Westover firmly believed that "the ability of bombardment aviation to fly in close formation and thus to insure greater defense against air attack . . . warrants the belief that no known agency can frustrate the accomplishment of the bombardment mission."[2]

Local exercises held during 1934 at March Field, California, seemed to vindicate Westover's judgment. Once again, P–26s were unable to scramble and climb fast enough to intercept even one of the attacking bombers. The B–12, basically a B–10 with larger engines, was just too fast for the best Air Corps fighter. This prompted Hap Arnold, who had arranged the test, to report that he doubted that pursuit aircraft could "prevent a formation of modern Bombardment planes from reaching their objective." During the Baker Board hearings, the future chief of Army aviation stated that the future of pursuit aviation "is one of the mysteries nobody can answer right now."[3]

One man was more than willing to provide an answer—Capt. Claire L. Chennault, at the time head of the Pursuit Branch of the Air Corps Tactical School. Quick to take offense and impugn the motives of those who opposed him, he could alienate people as readily as convert them, and his lack of polish as a speaker and leathery features tended to conceal his tactical genius. Having flown pursuit planes since 1921 and thought deeply about the part they could play in a future war, he was infuriated by the attitude that prevailed in the Air Corps as a result of the exercises conducted in 1933 and 1934. In an eight-page critique of Arnold's report, Chennault pointed out that the P–26 was inferior to the more recent foreign pursuit aircraft, while the B–12 was the world's newest and finest bomber. He argued that the maneuvers, instead of proving the invulnerability of the bomber, demonstrated the need for improved interceptors, suitable tactics, and an effective ground control system—the combination that prevailed a few years later in the Battle of Britain. Chennault adamantly maintained that gaining air superiority remained the first function of an air force and that pursuits were crucial to this mission. This held true, he believed, whether the ultimate objective was to protect the United States from invasion or to carry out a strategic air campaign against the heart of a hostile nation. Not content with theoretical argument, Chennault developed and tested an experimental air defense system that included ground observers, a communications network linked to a control center, and interceptors standing alert on the ground. His ideas influenced a handful of young fighter pilots, but senior officers tended to consider him more a nuisance than a prophet. By the time he retired in 1937 because of physical disability, the leadership of the Air Corps—typified by Arnold, Frank

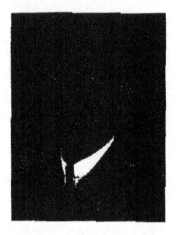

Capt. Claire L. Chennault,
Instructor, Air Corps Tactical School,
July 1931–July 1936

Andrews, and Kenneth Walker—shared the conviction that the long-range bomber solved virtually all problems of aerial warfare.

Between 1936 and 1939, new fighters did appear, of course, including the supercharged but unwieldy Consolidated P–30, a two-place aircraft that served mainly to demonstrate the superiority of the single-seat pursuit. The Air Corps also added 77 Seversky P–35s and 210 Curtiss P–36s to its inventory beginning in 1937. Vast improvements over the P–26, each had an enclosed cockpit, a retractable landing gear, and a top speed in excess of 300 miles per hour. Yet both were lightly armed, poorly armored, and hardly a match for the new bomber designs that culminated in the Boeing B–17 Flying Fortress, for almost a decade the premier American bomber.

Until his retirement late in 1935, Maj. Gen. Benjamin D. Foulois worked to convince the General Staff of the need for long-range bombers, the kind of aircraft that he believed could destroy an enemy's potential for war and gain victory with minimal help from the Army or Navy, producing independence for the air arm. In mid-1933, he had asked the War Department to approve research funds for an experimental bomber able to carry a ton of bombs 5,000 miles at a speed of 200 miles per hour. He soft-pedaled strategic bombing—despite his personal belief in this form of aerial warfare, he realized it was not yet an acceptable justification in the opinion of the General Staff—and emphasized the defensive value of such an airplane, which could deploy rapidly to protect either coast, Panama, Hawaii, or Alaska.

Foulois was somewhat surprised when the War Department early in 1934 approved the experimental bomber, called Project A. The decision may have been an effort to undercut one of the recurring attempts by Representative John J. McSwain, a Democrat from South Carolina, to legislate independence for the air arm. In any event, Boeing won the design competition that followed and began work the following year on the XB–15, but the bomber did not take to the air until 1937, and test flights revealed that it was stable but slow, really too heavy for the four 880-horsepower engines available at the time. Nevertheless, Project A contributed to other Boeing designs, including a seaplane for transoceanic passenger service, and afforded the company valuable experience in the fabrication and assembly of large aircraft.

Boeing was not, however, the only American manufacturer pioneering in construction of huge aircraft. Project A, kept secret until the XB–15 rolled from the factory, was not yet finished when the War Department in October 1935 authorized Project D—the development of an even larger bomber that could carry 2,400 pounds of explosives 8,000 miles. The Douglas Aircraft Company won the contract, but the resulting aircraft, the XB–19, did not fly until 1941. With a 212-foot wingspan and a gross weight of 80 tons, it lacked adequate power, the same basic shortcoming as the XB–15, although, like the Boeing product, the XB–19 provided engineering knowledge that would benefit future aircraft designs.

During June 1934, as Project A was taking shape, but before the award of the contract for Project D, the Air Corps informed aircraft manufacturers that it was not looking for another experimental type, but for a new, standard multiengine bomber. The Office of the Chief of the Air Corps specified that the aircraft carry a ton of bombs, have a minimum combat radius of 1,020 miles, and attain a top speed of 250 miles per hour. The competitors had until August 1935 to deliver a prototype to Wright Field to compete for an order that could be for as many as 220 airplanes, depending on the unit price. The Glenn L. Martin Company entered a more powerful version of the B–12, and Douglas submitted a newly designed aircraft, the XB–18, powered by two engines like the Martin entry. Only Boeing departed from this conventional approach by building a large, four-engine bomber inspired in part by design studies for a four-engine transport and in part by the initial work on the XB–15. Bristling with machinegun positions enclosed in metal-ribbed plastic, the new bomber was nicknamed the Flying Fortress.

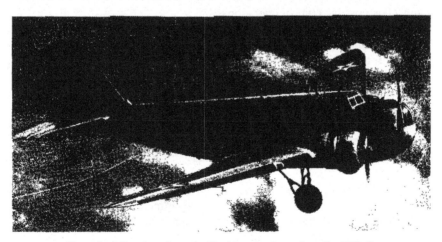

Douglas' first bomber, the B–18, was based on the DC–2.

History of the United States Air Force

The Boeing 299 (eventually designated the B–17) made an impressive debut. In August 1935, the prototype flew the 2,100 miles from the Boeing plant near Seattle, Washington, to Wright Field at an average cruising speed of 232 miles per hour, completely outclassing its competition. Foulois, the Chief of the Air Corps; Westover, his deputy; and Andrews, who commanded the GHQ Air Force, rejoiced at the prospect of purchasing a bomber that could carry out truly strategic operations as well as serve as an effective instrument of coast defense. Unfortunately, the prototype of the B–17 was destroyed in a crash on October 30 during the competition. An investigation revealed that the pilot had attempted to take off without disengaging the gust locks that protected the elevators and rudder from damage by strong winds. Even though structural failure had not contributed to the accident, the Air Corps was forced to exclude the plane from the competition because the crash occurred before the completion of the formal evaluation. To the disappointment of the believers in strategic bombing, the Douglas B–18 was declared the eventual winner, and the Army ordered 90 of them.

General Andrews, as commander of the GHQ Air Force, took the lead in an attempt to obtain a few B–17s immediately. He wanted at least thirteen of the advanced bombers for an operating squadron. The Office of the Chief of the Air Corps gave its full support to a proposal by Andrews to earmark the B–17s for operational testing, designating them Y1B–17s, so that a small quantity could be purchased without violating the requirements for competitive contracting. With the approval of the War Department, the Air Corps signed a contract with Boeing in January 1936 for thirteen B–17s fitted with superchargers for high-altitude flight. The first of the bombers was delivered one year later; the last of the initial group entered service in August 1937. The Army Air Corps had gained its first truly long-range bomber, but in numbers too few to have much impact on possible combat operations.

Between 1936 and 1938 the question of buying additional B–17s became a burning issue between the Army and its Air Corps. General Andrews was the driving force behind an effort to designate the four-engine, long-range Boeing as the air arm's standard bomber. Even before the delivery of the first of the original thirteen B–17s, Andrews, the GHQ Air Force Commander joined Westover, the Chief of the Air Corps, and Arnold, the Assistant Chief, in urging the War Department to purchase immediately enough of the planes to equip two bombardment groups. Secretary of War Harry H. Woodring, reflecting the thinking of the General Staff, refused because the B–17 was both unproven and costly.

Despite the Army's unwillingness to invest in so many of the big bombers, Andrews, in June 1937, presented the War Department with a study arguing that all future bombers should be four-engine models because of safety, a ferrying range sufficient enough to reinforce the Hawaiian Islands and other American outposts, and a longer radius of action for reconnaissance and heavy bombing

144

Wreckage of the Boeing 299 (B–17 prototype) at Wright Field, Ohio.

in support of coastal defense operations. A year later, he was describing long-range bombers as "the principal striking force in air operations." For the time being, he cautiously continued to avoid arguing the case for the heavy bomber in terms of its value as a strategic weapon, for he realized that neither the public nor Congress was ready to think in terms of offensive rather than purely defensive forces. Instead, he insisted that planes like the B–17 provided the nation with the best possible defense, for they enabled his GHQ Air Force to destroy a hostile invasion force far from shore.

The ground-oriented leaders within the Army saw things differently. Gen. Malin Craig, who succeeded MacArthur as Chief of Staff in 1935, was reluctant to spend large sums for expensive four-engine bombers, although he agreed to the purchase of twenty-six improved B–17Bs with funds carried over from fiscal 1938 and to include another thirteen of the B models in the budget for fiscal 1939. He would do no more, since the amount spent on one B–17 roughly equaled the cost of two B–18s, and this twin-engine aircraft could perform the two missions approved for the Air Corps—coast defense and the support of ground operations. From Craig's point of view, allowing the Air Corps to acquire large numbers of four-engine bombers would merely encourage its fascination with strategic bombing, which remained untested and of dubious value. Nor did the General Staff want an air arm committed to buying expensive and glamorous four-engine aircraft and competing for scarce funds with the ground forces, which desperately needed such unexciting articles as rifles and mortars. In short, three considerations moved Craig and the War Department to oppose a heavy investment in B–17s: first, the purchase of B–17s would reduce the number of aircraft that could be bought, when numbers were important to reassure Congress and the public; second, the long-range B–17 might divert the Air Corps from the support of ground forces; and third, the measured growth and balanced rearmament of the entire Army might be jeopardized by too great an investment in B–17s for the air arm.

A lack of unity within the Air Corps was partially to blame for its problems in obtaining groups, rather than squadrons, of B–17s. Westover and Arnold believed the air arm needed more of these bombers, but they also acknowledged the importance of acquiring fighters or attack aircraft and did not support Andrews in his campaign to invest in B–17s to the exclusion of twin-engine types. To those who sided with Andrews, Westover seemed overly willing to compromise to preserve harmony with the General Staff. In 1937, these critics complained, Westover counseled the War Department to delay buying more four-engine bombers until it had time to study the issue closely, even though Arnold, his Assistant Chief, lent vocal support to the need for more B–17s. The year before, in 1936, Arnold had talked personally with the Chief of Staff, General Craig, unsuccessfully urging him to include 20 B–17s in the initial draft of the fiscal 1938 budget. Although more outspoken than Westover, Arnold was no more willing than the Chief of the Air Corps to wage a fight to the finish, for he, too, failed to share Andrews' vision of an Air Corps with a bombardment force composed almost exclusively of airplanes like the B–17. Besides overestimating the impact of a force of B–17s on the course of a ground campaign, Andrews may have overlooked two other points: the shortages of modern equipment that handicapped branches of the Army other than the Air Corps and the possibility that neither congressional appropriations committees nor the electorate, in their fascination with numbers, might be able to understand the advantage of buying a few truly excellent aircraft instead of many that were merely adequate.

Despite conflicts between money and numbers, between strategic air warfare and support for ground operations, and between modernizing the Air Corps and rearming the rest of the Army, the War Department produced a five-year program of aircraft procurement that would begin in fiscal 1940. Secretary of War Woodring intended to provide a systematic means of at last expanding the Air Corps beyond 2,320 airplanes, the number established by the Baker Board in 1934. When it was presented in March 1938, the Woodring program called for the purchase of 144 four-engine bombers, 266 twin-engine bombers, 259 attack aircraft, and 425 pursuits. The Secretary of War authorized the Air Corps to buy 67 of the four-engine aircraft in fiscal 1940, 48 more in the following fiscal year, and the remaining 29 later.

The future of the B–17 was far from assured, however; by July 1938 the decision to purchase some five squadrons of the aircraft in 1940 had been reversed. The change resulted in part from an unrelated proposal by Westover to begin developing a new long-range bomber that would ultimately replace the B–17. This move called attention to two subjects that the General Staff still

General Andrews, behind microphone, welcoming the crew
of the first B–17 to arrive at Langley Field (March 1937).

questioned: the B–17 and research and development for the Air Corps. Given a
chance to reconsider, the War Department decided that the funds earmarked in
the Woodring program for the purchase of the first 67 B–17s could buy as many
as 300 attack aircraft, which Craig and the General Staff considered more valuable than the big bombers to an Army that was being rebuilt literally from the
ground up. Consequently the purchase of B–17Cs, improved models of the
B–17Bs already on order, was postponed beyond June 1940. The War
Department similarly delayed the start of research and development on a new
four-engine bomber, decreeing that such spending in fiscal 1939 and 1940 be
"restricted to that class of aviation designed for the close support of ground
troops and the protection of that type of aircraft"—in effect attack aircraft, fighters, and twin-engine bombers.[4] One of the previously authorized experimental
bombers, the XB–15, had been flying since January 1938, and Westover won an
exception for the other, the XB–19, which looked to a reluctant General Staff
like a strategic bomber, pure and simple, and not a weapon of hemisphere defense; but work on a possible replacement for the B–17 would have to wait until
fiscal 1941.

As they had so often in the past, Army airmen tried to enlist public support
for a particular project, in this instance the B–17. On May 12, 1938, in what he
described as a routine coast defense exercise, Andrews sent three B–17s to in-

B–17s from Mitchel Field, Long Island, New York, intercept
the ocean liner *Rex* at sea, 725 miles east of New York City.

tercept the Italian ocean liner *Rex*. The commander of the GHQ Air Force
sought to demonstrate that his B–17s could locate and attack a hostile fleet far
from American shores. After securing the cooperation of the steamship line and
arranging extensive press and radio coverage, the general launched his small
force from Mitchel Field, New York. The navigator of the lead B–17, 1st Lt.
Curtis E. LeMay, directed the interception of the *Rex*, ably calculating the ship's
course and speed from its last reported position earlier in the day and making visual contact 725 miles east of New York City. The National Broadcasting
Company provided an announcer who described the event from one of the aircraft, while reporters looked on and Maj. George W. Goddard took photographs.

The GHQ Air Force had provided dramatic evidence that the B–17 could be
a valuable weapon for coastal defense, but the lesson was lost on the Army's
leadership, which interpreted the flight as an attempt to create public pressure
to divert money from other branches of the service for the purchase of Flying
Fortresses. Similarly, the Navy tended to be less concerned about what an aircraft like the B–17 could do than about the challenge it posed to the Navy's mission of aerial coast defense. After the interception of the *Rex*, the Army Chief
of Staff gave oral orders restricting future Air Corps flights to within 100 miles
of shore. Army airmen believed General Craig's order resulted from a Navy
protest; but whatever the motivation, the Chief of Staff did not put the 100-mile
limit in writing and proved amenable when Arnold and Andrews tried to get the
restriction lifted. Craig readily agreed that the General Staff would consider requests from the Air Corps to exceed the limit for specific exercises, and approval was all but automatic. In June 1938, for instance, only a month after the

rule went into effect, the General Staff allowed three B–17s from Langley Field, Virginia, to intercept a ship 300 miles out to sea. Later in the year, Craig authorized the commander of the GHQ Air Force to approve exceptions to the 100-mile limit, in effect rescinding it.

Even though the War Department was understandably reluctant to invest in large numbers of the expensive heavy bombers that the aviation industry had succeeded in developing during the 1930s, the theory of strategic bombardment became an article of faith within the Air Corps and was receiving grudging recognition from the General Staff. Members of the bombardment faculty at the Air Corps Tactical School had preached for years that air power could annihilate an enemy's defending fighters by attacking his aircraft factories and airfields and by shooting down his interceptors. Having thus gained control of the skies, an armada of strategic bombers could destroy both the enemy's warmaking capacity and his will to resist, forcing him to sue for peace. This theory was now embodied in the new B–17.

However, in 1935, while serving as Chief of Staff, General MacArthur voiced the opinion of the General Staff in his annual report: "So far as tactical and strategic doctrine is concerned, there exist two great fields of Air Force employment; one fully demonstrated and proved, the other conjectural."[5] He considered as proven those tasks involving direct cooperation with ground forces: air superiority, close air support, interdiction, observation, reconnaissance, and air transport. MacArthur felt, as did most of his contemporaries in the ground forces, that "the more conjectural use of the Air Force involves its employment against unarmed centers of population and industry."[6] Although he insisted that "the sentiment of this country will always repudiate and forbid the unprovoked initiation of this kind of war by our own forces," he acknowledged that the new GHQ Air Force should be able to conduct such an air campaign in defense of the nation.[7] He made it clear, however, that he wanted the Air Corps to concentrate on its responsibilities for supporting ground troops, however much officers like Arnold or Andrews may have believed in the heavy bomber as a kind of ultimate weapon. MacArthur's description of strategic bombardment as conjecture resulted from study, reflection, and experience. Strategic bombing had never proved itself in wartime. World War 1, however, had demonstrated the importance of military aviation to ground armies, and it would be a fatal blunder to divert men and aircraft needed for tasks of proven value to fly missions that at best were important only theoretically. Moreover, the Chief of Staff, as shown by the careful phrasing in his annual report, had to be wary of arousing opposition in the press or in Congress by speaking too directly about a bombing offensive, especially one directed at an enemy's industrial cities.

Cautious though MacArthur was, the General Staff of the mid-1930s did not have a closed mind on the topic of strategic air warfare, a fact demonstrated in 1935 by the Chief of the War Plans Division, Brig. Gen. Charles E. Kilbourne. Over the years, Kilbourne had frequently clashed with Foulois and his subordinates in the Office of the Chief of the Air Corps, but this did not blind him to the need for an aerial doctrine that would satisfy the airmen and the rest of the Army. He sponsored a draft statement, prepared by his staff section, that tried to reconcile the traditional ground officer's view of aviation as an auxiliary with the claims of the advocates of air power that bombing could defeat an enemy. Kilbourne's draft conceded that military aviation, acting alone, could control a "weak and disorganized people" but added that the ability of air power to break the will of a well-organized nation "has never been demonstrated and is not accepted by members of the armed services."[8] To win a war against a modern state, the statement declared, the U.S. Army would have to occupy the enemy's territory. Although this task could be "greatly assisted" by military aviation, air power alone could not win such a conflict.

Kilbourne's draft, however, did not rule out strategic bombing. Instead, it spelled out four types of operations where an air force could assist the ground forces: those beyond the sphere of influence of ground forces, those in immediate support of ground forces in a campaign, those in defense of the coast or land frontiers, and those in defense of rear areas. Although the draft called for the destruction of enemy aviation as the primary objective in operations beyond the reach of ground troops, it listed such other strategic targets as lines of communication, factories, refineries, and powerplants or other public utilities. By referring to targets whose destruction would affect the enemy's overall ability to wage war, General Kilbourne was endorsing strategic bombardment should circumstances prove appropriate.

The Air Corps responded favorably to Kilbourne's proposed aerial doctrine. Despite some opposition from bombardment enthusiasts at the Air Corps Tactical School, who did not believe the paper placed enough emphasis on strategic bombing, Foulois and his staff offered only minor changes that slightly accented the importance of air power. The Chief of the Air Corps returned the revised draft to the General Staff in February 1935 and suggested it be used as the basis for a revision of training regulation TR–440–15, *Employment of Air Forces in the Army*. The General Staff took his advice and in October of that year published a new version containing doctrine for aviation that, for the first time, was basically acceptable to ground officers like MacArthur and Kilbourne and to airmen like Foulois and Andrews.

The Air Corps continued to focus on strategic bombing for the remainder of the decade. New equipment permitted the refinement of bombing doctrine, for both the Sperry Company and an inventor named Carl Norden produced optical bombsights that, when coupled to an automatic pilot, could produce unprecedented accuracy. Gone were the days of improvisation when Maj. Hugh J. Knerr tried to improve accuracy by sighting with cord tied crosswise in the bomb bay and pulling on other strings tied to the pilot's arms to guide him left or right. The new sights enabled the Air Corps to think in terms of daylight precision bombing by comparatively few aircraft in tight formation instead of massive raids, either by day or in concealing darkness, in which many bombers saturated a wide area. As the decade ended, stories circulated that, with the Norden sight, a bombardier could hit a pickle barrel from 10,000 feet, but as Arnold discovered during tests in the California desert, the barrel had to be half the size of the San Joaquin Valley.

By the late 1930s, the Air Corps had forged the strategic bombing doctrine with which it would enter World War II. Because good visibility was necessary for precision attacks, the bombers were to operate during daylight, flying at high altitude to neutralize antiaircraft fire and maintaining a compact formation to mass their mutually reinforcing defensive fire against enemy interceptors. Long-range fighter escort seemed unnecessary because of the firepower built into the bombers; moreover, it seemed technologically impossible to build a fighter able to carry enough gasoline to have the range necessary to escort the bombers and still be nimble enough to fight off interceptors. A consensus was emerging at the Air Corps Tactical School that the destruction of interceptors by gunners on board the bombers and the leveling of the factories building engines and airframes would produce air superiority in short order. Once the bombers dominated the skies, they could destroy with pinpoint accuracy the industries vital to the enemy's war effort, winning a victory quickly and cheaply. However, the theory had not yet been tested against the best of the modern pursuits and new ideas about air defense systems.

American Army airmen were not alone during the 1930s in their preoccupation with strategic bombing. In Great Britain, J. F. C. Fuller, a pioneer of armored warfare who retired from the army to become a respected commentator on military matters, contemplated aerial attacks on London that collapsed the foundations of society, causing riot, insurrection, and *"complete industrial paralyzation."* A disaster such as Fuller described seemed progressively more likely after January 1, 1933, when Adolf Hitler, the leader of the National Socialist (or Nazi) Party, became chancellor of Germany. In 1934, Hitler established a dictatorship, during the following year repudiated the essence of the Treaty of Versailles that had restored order to western Europe after World War I, and in 1936 sent troops into the Rhineland, demilitarized by the Versailles agreement. With each passing year, therefore, the danger of war increased.

Even as the shadow of German bombers fell across the British Isles, the independent Royal Air Force remained confident that its own bombers, Britain's principal weapon of aerial warfare, would always get through to inflict unbearable damage on the nation's enemies. Range was not considered a problem, for a future conflict was expected to follow the pattern of World War I, enabling British bombers to operate from French soil. Lumbering biplane night bombers were giving way to fast monoplanes, some fitted with power-operated gun turrets, that were believed able to fight their way by daylight through swarming interceptors to destroy an enemy's centers of transportation, production, and communication. Moreover, the British aircraft industry was at work on the next generation of bombers, four-engine types that could carry tons of high explosives from the United Kingdom directly to targets on the continent. New methods of detecting aircraft and destroying the bombers did little to shake the confidence of those who flew them—not even radar, which emerged from the laboratories in the mid-1930s, nor fast, heavily armed defensive interceptors like the Hawker Hurricane and Supermarine Spitfire. The belief of Lord Trenchard in the offensive use of military aviation persisted long after his retirement, and the bomber seemed the best means of carrying the war to the enemy.

The attitude of German airmen toward strategic bombing reflected geography, Hitler's leadership, and the nation's industrial resources. Germany's *Luftwaffe*, kept secret until March 1935, remained independent of the army and navy, but tied to land operations. Although aware of the strategic potential of the bomber, Hitler's airmen did not prepare for this kind of warfare as enthusiastically as the Americans and British. A number of considerations prevented Germany from creating an air force modeled to any great extent on the strategic air warfare teachings of Giulio Douhet, but a principal factor was hesitancy on the part of German professional airmen and soldiers to accept Douhet's assurance that strategic bombardment could win a war quickly. This skepticism stemmed from their awareness of Germany's vulnerability to invasion; while strategic bombers were destroying the industrial and governmental centers of London, Paris, or even Moscow, hostile troops might seize portions of Germany, consolidating their grip before German bombing took effect. Since German territory had to be defended, the *Luftwaffe* could not embrace strategic bombardment and ignore the needs of the ground forces. Furthermore, Hitler saw no pressing need for a long-range, multiengine bomber, even though he repeatedly threatened to level the cities of those in western Europe who dared oppose him. He believed that fast light bombers and dive bombers, perhaps operating from forward airfields overrun by the armored forces, could make good the promise of destruction. Finally, the German aircraft industry was better adapted to the production of smaller aircraft, as demonstrated after 1937 when the Heinkel firm began its struggle to build a long-range bomber, the unsuccessful He 177, an ingenious attempt to overcome the lack of sufficiently powerful engines. To minimize drag while developing the horsepower needed for an airplane with a loaded weight in excess of thirty tons, the builder used two nacelles, each containing two engines geared to turn a single propeller; the problem of cooling remained unsolved, however, and engine fires were common.

Douhet, whose theories had spread even to the United States, was honored as a prophet in his native Italy by a government that lacked the resources to follow his doctrine. The pageantry and bombast of Benito Mussolini, the Fascist dictator who had ruled since 1922 and fancied himself a skilled airman, could not conceal the fact that Italy had neither the oil nor the other raw materials necessary to develop a major air force. The nation's *Regia Aeronautica* was an independent air arm; but its comparatively few modern aircraft, although adequate for colonial wars or a possible conflict with some smaller west European state like Austria or Yugoslavia, lacked the performance to wage aerial warfare against a major European nation.

"Douhet has no partisans in France," said Gen. Maxime Weygand on the very eve of a new European war. "There is something in these bombardments of defenseless people behind the front that smacks of cowardice which is repugnant to the soldier."[9] All questions of gallantry aside, the French realized their cities were vulnerable to bombing and hoped to avoid initiating a form of warfare with potentially disastrous consequences. Nor was France's *Arméee de l'Air* in fighting trim. An independent force, although in wartime its commander would report to a supreme commander drawn from the army, it was in the throes of rebuilding after years of spartan budgets and not all its new aircraft were working out as expected. One bomber, for example, was so overweight that it could not remain aloft if one of its two engines quit.

For a time, the Soviet Union displayed an interest in long-range bombers, even experimenting with giants that could carry one or more fighters to the vicinity of the target, but military aviation remained an integral part of the Red Army. Before the 1930s ended, the senior officers who had directed the bomber program aroused the suspicions of Joseph Stalin, the Soviet dictator, who had them executed in a purge of the armed forces. The theory of strategic aerial warfare apparently died with them, for support of ground troops gained the highest priority.

In Japan, as in the United States, both the army and navy had air arms. During the 1930s, the Japanese concentrated primarily on exploiting China as a market for goods and a source of raw materials, using whatever military force was necessary when the nation resisted. Since the Chinese were just beginning to industrialize, attacking airmen found few truly strategic targets. Separated by vast distances from targets of potential enemies suitable for strategic bombardment, for example, the United States, the Japanese showed little interest in long-range bombers, although they developed large seaplanes for maritime reconnaissance. As events proved, Japan learned to make limited strategic use of carrier-based aircraft instead of producing the long-range landplanes the United States had developed.

Such in general were the obvious characteristics of the major air forces of Europe and Asia in the late 1930s. Of them all, Great Britain's Royal Air Force had the strongest interest in strategic air warfare. Independent of the Army and Navy and able to compete with them as an equal in the struggle for funds, the Royal Air Force, in Trenchard's words, had as its aim to crush the enemy's means of resistance by attacking divergent targets. These objectives, he elaborated, included means of communication and transportation and factories producing everything from "boots to battleships." As demonstrated by the policy, from 1936 to 1939, of buying three bombers for every fighter, the Royal Air Force was an offensive weapon and the Bomber Command its cutting edge.

History of the United States Air Force

In the end, the steadily deteriorating international climate provided the most compelling reason for the growth and modernization of the Army Air Corps during the late 1930s. After consolidating his grip on Germany, defying the Treaty of Versailles, and rearming, Hitler intervened in the Spanish Civil War, which erupted in 1936. Mussolini, whose troops had just overrun Abyssinia and made it an Italian colony, joined Hitler in supporting a revolution against the legally constituted government of the Spanish republic, a recently formed coalition in which the communists formed the dominant element. Republican Spain received aid from sympathizers in the United States, Great Britain, and France—although those three governments remained neutral in the conflict—and from the Soviet Union. This assistance proved insufficient, for the republic was overthrown and replaced by a military dictatorship headed by Francisco Franco. The triumph of Franco enhanced the stature of Fascist Italy and Nazi Germany; indeed, late in 1936, after Franco had launched his revolution, Mussolini coined the term "Axis powers," boasting that all Europe would henceforth revolve on a Rome-Berlin axis. During that same year, Japan showed its affinity for the European dictatorships by signing the Anti-Comintern Pact, an ill-defined pledge to cooperate with Germany in opposing the Communist Third International, which was dedicated to spreading the Soviet ideology throughout the world.

Emboldened by the inaction of France and Great Britain against German rearmament, the Italian conquest of Abyssinia, and the intervention in Spain, Hitler in 1938 took control of Austria and bullied the western powers into allowing Germany to absorb a part of Czechoslovakia, a prelude to the occupation of the rest of that unfortunate country in spring 1939. Hitler made his moves in the shadow of his air arm, the *Luftwaffe*, which inspired a morbid fear of aerial bombardment among the European democracies. Italian attacks on defenseless Abyssinian villages, Japanese air raids on crowded Chinese cities, and German attacks on Spanish towns fed concerns for national survival that were rooted in the bombings of World War I. The government of Great Britain, for example, anticipated 200,000 civilian casualties in London alone during the first two weeks of a sustained aerial bombardment.

President Roosevelt realized the importance of military aviation as a weapon of war and a symbol of power. In dismembering Czechoslovakia, Hitler had pointed to the *Luftwaffe* as the instrument of destruction to be loosed upon those who opposed him; the President now turned to the airplane as the visible sign of American resolve. According to Hap Arnold, appointed Chief of the Air Corps in September 1938, Roosevelt firmly believed that "airplanes were the war implements that would have an influence on Hitler's activities."[10] Vastly increased production would serve as a warning to the German dictator, possibly deterring further aggression, and provide a source of aircraft not only for the American armed forces but also for the French and British who, at the time of the Czech crisis, had not been prepared to defy the *Luftwaffe*.

The Heyday of the GHQ Air Force, 1935–1939

Maj. Gen. Henry H. Arnold,
Chief, Army Air Corps,
September 1938–June 1941

At a secret meeting in the White House on November 14, 1938, Roosevelt outlined his program for aerial expansion to Arnold; Craig; Brig. Gen. George C. Marshall, the new Deputy Chief of Staff; and a few other officials. The President surprised those present by talking in terms of an Air Corps of 20,000 planes and an aircraft industry capable of producing 24,000 planes per year. Conceding that Congress probably would not approve an Air Corps of more than 10,000 planes, Roosevelt established as his immediate goal 7,500 combat aircraft and 2,500 trainers that, he believed, would serve notice to Hitler. Arnold later described the President's call for expansion of the air arm as the most important event in the history of the Air Corps, a "Magna Carta" for air power, which liberated military aviation from the arbitrary ceilings on manpower and aircraft recommended by investigative agencies like the Baker Board and imposed by legislation. Congress seemed sufficiently alarmed by events in Europe to vote the money for some degree of expansion beyond the Baker Board's 1934 figure of 2,320 planes. Consequently, Roosevelt's expansion program, though by no means a blank check, promised rapid growth based on military realities, with the Air Corps assuming a prominent position within the American defense establishment.

As he worked on a formal proposal for congressional funding of the plan, Arnold was both pleased and troubled by the President's enthusiasm. The Air Corps had long sought expansion so that it could become an effective force, but 10,000 airplanes (actually some 8,000 plus the 2,000-odd already authorized) would mean little unless they were accompanied by more pilots, support personnel, and airfields. The President, however, seemed concerned only with numbers of aircraft, assuming that once aircraft production increased, the Air Corps would somehow absorb the new equipment. Arnold realized that so abrupt an increase would be self-defeating; the new airplanes had to be part of an orderly, across-the-board buildup that included facilities and trained men.

Actually, in proposing an Air Corps of 10,000 planes, the President was merely testing the waters, which proved uncomfortably warm. He ultimately adjusted his proposal, heeding the advice of senior officers of the General Staff, who shared Arnold's misgivings about absorbing the aircraft and warned against upsetting the balance of rearmament, and the intuition of his own political supporters in Congress, where isolationist tendencies survived and opposition was forming. Draft legislation prepared by Arnold and the War Department that would have expanded the Air Corps to 10,000 aircraft yielded to a new plan that reduced the amount of money earmarked for aircraft so that other elements of the Army could modernize. As a result, when the President presented the new program in a special message to Congress on January 12, 1939, he declared that the worsening international conditions made the Baker Board's goal inadequate and asked for 6,000 airplanes, 4,000 fewer than he had proposed in the secret meeting eight weeks earlier.

In practice, the target for the revised expansion program fell short even of 6,000 aircraft, leaving considerable cushion for a more orderly development of an institutional structure for Army aviation. The current inventory (less those aircraft declared obsolete) and aircraft already authorized for purchase but not yet delivered totaled about 2,500 airplanes. New orders would total only some 3,000 units and thus enlarge the Air Corps to 5,500 aircraft. By thus trimming his request, Roosevelt avoided the heated public debate over rearmament and possible involvement in a European war that a more ambitious program might have caused. Following the advice of Arnold and the senior members of the General Staff, the President agreed that slightly more than half of the $300 million that Congress made available for the Air Corps be used to purchase aircraft. The total actually spent for this purpose, $186 million, bought 3,251 airplanes, increasing the Air Corps inventory to 5,500, as the President had intended. The balance of the appropriation was devoted to overcoming the most serious obstacles to expansion: a lack of men to operate and maintain the new equipment, a shortage of training facilities, and a need for more operating bases. The addition of these airplanes was just a start, however; Roosevelt had not abandoned his goal of 20,000 aircraft revealed during the November 14 meeting, although he would approach it in a series of comparatively small increments, if necessary.

In the spring of 1939, nine of ten Americans surveyed in a Gallup poll favored an immediate increase in American aerial strength. Those who supported the President agreed that the time had come to shore up the nation's defenses, and they believed that he was behaving cautiously and responsibly, as demonstrated by his willingness to purchase 3,251 new aircraft instead of the 10,000 once mentioned in newspaper speculation. This sampling of public opinion did not, however, deal with questions of war or peace and involvement or isolation, so that some of those who responded in the affirmative might well have believed that the President's actions would help America remain aloof from Europe's troubles.

Air Corps planners worked feverishly in the winter of 1938–39 to devise a plan for orderly expansion. Arnold's first step was to transfer to his headquarters several experienced officers to pool their abilities in determining how the Air Corps should proceed. This group included Lt. Cols. Carl Spaatz, Joseph McNarney, and Ira Eaker; Maj. Muir Fairchild; and Capt. Laurence S. Kuter, individuals who would play leading roles in the aerial campaigns of World War II. Since manpower had to parallel the expansion to 5,500 airplanes, the planners decided that the enlarged Air Corps should consist by June 1941 of 48,000 officers and men, with an appropriate number of airfields, maintenance depots, and training centers. Arnold promptly initiated an intensive recruiting program and began offering tours of extended active duty to reserve pilots. Halfway to its goal by September 1939, the Air Corps then consisted of 2,058 Regular officers, 669 reserve officers, and 23,779 enlisted men.

The rapid increase in personnel necessitated a radical overhaul of the training process. Between 1919 and 1939 the largest number of pilot training graduates during one year had been 246; because of expansion, the Air Corps would need 1,200 new pilots annually. Arnold realized existing facilities would be inadequate for such large numbers, and he arranged contracts with nine of the best civilian flying schools to provide primary flight training beginning in mid-1939. The Air Corps supplied the aircraft and a cadre of supervisors, but all the instructors were civilians. Trainees who successfully completed the 12-week primary program went on to Randolph Field, Texas, for basic flight training and then to Kelly Field, Texas, for advanced training, both conducted by members of the Air Corps. Despite the specialized skills required for long-range bombers like the B–17, the air arm made no move until 1941 to establish schools to train navigators or bombardiers; in 1939, these skills were learned through on-the-job training in GHQ Air Force units.

To handle the large influx of new enlisted men, the Air Corps changed its technical training program considerably. All such training had formerly taken place at Chanute Field, Illinois; beginning in late 1939, new recruits first completed a basic course at Scott Field, Illinois, before going on to specialized instruction at either Chanute or the recently completed Lowry Field in Colorado. Supplementing the work of these three installations, the Air Corps arranged in 1939 for some enlisted men to be trained as mechanics at civilian technical schools and aircraft factories. As it had during World War I, this approach helped ease the training burden at a time when the Army air arm was woefully short of facilities. Even though the Air Corps was building new training bases as quickly as possible, it not only retained the civilian-operated training programs, it expanded them.

Any expansion of the Air Corps had to be shaped by prevailing ideas about how to employ the new air force, and in the late 1930s, those ideas also took much firmer shape. The doctrine of daylight strategic bombing had fired the imagination of airmen like Andrews and Arnold, but it did not yet seem wise to talk publicly of an air offensive against a European enemy, even though President Roosevelt was deeply troubled by Adolf Hitler's conquests of Austria and

Czechoslovakia. In deference to a lingering desire for isolation from Europe and its recurring wars, American defense policy at first had to emphasize protecting the United States, its outlying possessions, and the Western Hemisphere. Moreover, a genuine threat had appeared in South America, where German-operated firms raised the possibility of economic penetration followed by political subversion and the establishment of bases for operations against the United States. In 1938, Arnold, while Assistant Chief of the Air Corps, perceived this danger and gained Westover's approval for the Air Corps Board, a study group located at Maxwell Field, Alabama, to determine how military aviation could best enforce the Monroe Doctrine. A month after Arnold became Chief of the Air Corps, the hurriedly prepared study reached him, and he immediately approved its call for a force of long-range heavy bombers as the Air Corps contribution to the defense of the hemisphere.

With Congress in 1939 approving the expansion of the air arm, Secretary of War Woodring appointed a War Department board, with Arnold in charge, to investigate the issue of using aircraft for hemispheric defense. Arnold's group elaborated on the work of the Air Corps Board, which called for the use of air power to deter the Germans from setting up bases in Latin America or to destroy the Axis bridgehead if deterrence failed. Like the Air Corps Board, the War Department panel concluded that long-range heavy bombers were essential to defend the hemisphere effectively, adding that the Air Corps needed outlying bases to extend its radius of action. The new Army Chief of Staff, General Marshall, reviewed these recommendations on September 1, 1939, the day Hitler's forces invaded Poland and started World War II. In one of his first actions after transitioning from deputy to Acting Chief of Staff to Chief of Staff, Marshall approved the study, noting that it established "for the first time" a specific mission for the Air Corps that was wholly consistent with American defense policy. Hemisphere defense, viewed as an extension of national defense, became an official policy of the United States. President Roosevelt's new faith in military aviation as a symbol of American determination and a weapon of war, along with Marshall's recognition of the importance of air power in hemisphere defense, undermined the position of those on the General Staff who had opposed the purchase of additional long-range bombers. With General Marshall's full endorsement, the Air Corps now had a mission requiring the purchase of large numbers of B–17s and a greater investment in the development of improved bombers for the future.

Letting contracts for new airplanes proved to be easier than having them actually roll from the factory, for the aircraft manufacturers needed time to prepare for sustained production. In September 1939, the Air Corps had only 23 B–17s, with about 100 more on order. To avoid the mistake made during World War I of fixing too soon on a few designs, the War Department early in 1939 authorized Arnold to find a second source of long-range bombers, and he asked the Consolidated Aircraft Company to begin work on the XB–24, prototype of the wartime Liberator bomber. Air Corps doctrine, which held that long-range bombers could fight their way to their assigned targets and by destroying them cripple an enemy state, and the perceived needs of hemisphere defense coalesced in the purchase of the Flying Fortress and the Liberator.

The primacy of the strategic bomber in Air Corps thinking affected the design of the pursuit planes acquired as a result of the 1939 expansion program. By 1939, the 300-mile-per-hour P–36 had become the mainstay of the Army's pursuit aviation, but it lacked a supercharger for high-altitude fighting, was lightly armed and poorly armored, and tottered at the edge of obsolescence. The Air Corps, however, had already let contracts for the Bell P–39, of which only the prototype was supercharged; the Curtiss P–40, basically a P–36 with a liquid-cooled engine; and the Lockheed P–38, intended as a high-altitude interceptor. As money for expansion became available, the Air Corps quickly ordered 524 P–40s (in addition to 200 already being purchased out of regular appropriations for fiscal 1939), along with 13 YP–38s and 12 YP–39s—the Y prefix indicating that these aircraft, like the Y1B–9 and Y1B–17 before them, were for operational testing. Only the P–38, with its two supercharged engines, came close to matching the performance of the latest German and Japanese fighters, although the P–39 and P–40 performed useful service at low and medium altitudes. Since it had become an article of faith that formations of bombers could protect themselves against interceptors, none of the three fighters had the range necessary to escort the new B–17s and B–24s, although the addition of external fuel tanks soon enabled the P–38 to fly escort missions. Basically, the American pursuits of this era were designed to gain air superiority in combat at low or medium altitude and to support ground troops.

Attack aviation also experienced growth as a result of Roosevelt's expansion program, but a consensus within the Air Corps held that attack aircraft—those whose primary job was the support of ground forces—were less important than either long-range bombers or pursuit aircraft. In 1936 the single-engine Northrop A–17 became the standard attack model, but within three years the Air Corps took steps to acquire a larger, faster replacement. The Air Corps eventually selected the twin-engine Douglas A–20 and ordered 186 as part of the 1939 rearmament effort. Meanwhile, the Air Corps contracted for test models of the North American B–25 and Martin B–26, creating a class of aircraft designed to fill the void between the high-altitude, long-range strategic bombers and the low-altitude attack types. The Air Corps signed production contracts for 183 B–25s and 201 B–26s in fiscal year 1940, before either plane was flying.

As the decade ended, the Air Corps was rapidly expanding, laying the foundation for its growth into the world's most powerful air force by the end of World War II. The most dominant characteristic of this foundation was the Air Corps' commitment to the long-range bomber as a truly decisive weapon, able to win victory with a minimum of help from the Army, Navy, or other forms of military aviation, and its tendency to consider air power and strategic bombing

Attack and pursuit aircraft of the late 1930s: A–20 (top), P–36 (middle), P–38 (right above), P–39 (left above), and P–40 (left).

Bombers of the late 1930s: (opposite page, top to bottom): B–17, B–24, B–25, and B–26.

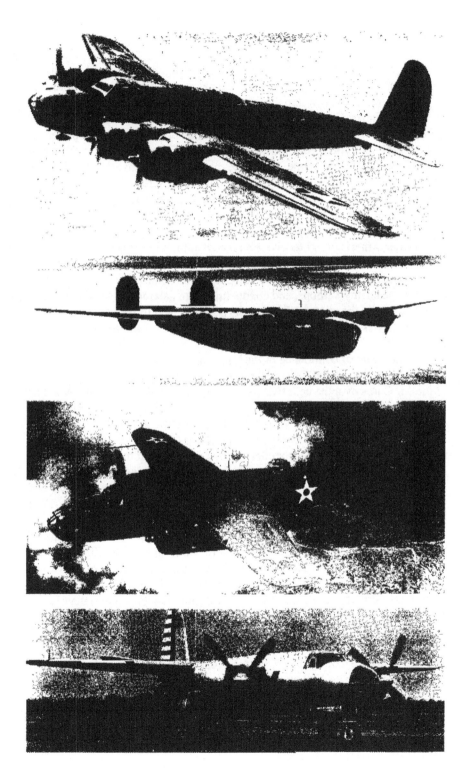

161

as synonymous. Although a few dissenters challenged the vaunted invulnerability of the new four-engine bombers, the skeptics did not prevail. Moreover, airplanes like the B–17 fit into the existing strategy of national and hemispheric defense. Unlike Great Britain, bombed during World War I and within easy striking distance of continental Europe, the United States had never experienced aerial attack and could rely on the protection of two vast oceans. Whereas Britain's vulnerability compelled the Royal Air Force to invest in air defense, developing new interceptors and establishing a radar screen, the U.S. Army Air Corps looked to the big bombers to intercept an approaching invasion force, flying aircraft, if necessary, to bases in the Panama Canal Zone, in Hawaii, Latin America, or even the Philippines. While aircraft like the B–17 carried the war to the attacker, American fighters were expected to function generally as they had in the previous war—gaining control of the skies over the battlefield (perhaps a hostile beachhead in the Western Hemisphere or in some overseas possession), harrying the enemy's troops, and conducting reconnaissance. Given the degree of confidence in the strategic bomber, its accuracy, and its capacity for self-defense, there was no reason to believe that pursuit aviation would have to do otherwise.

A further vote of confidence in the long-range bomber came in the summer of 1939 from a board that General Arnold had convened to determine the needs of the Air Corps over the next five years. Brig. Gen. Walter G. Kilner, who had served with Foulois during the Mexican expedition and who had been in charge of training in France during World War I, chaired the group, which included Spaatz, an advocate of bombardment, and Charles A. Lindbergh, who had just returned from an informal inspection of the *Luftwaffe* and the German aircraft industry. The Kilner Board recommended, among other things, that by 1944 the Air Corps acquire two new heavy bombers—ultimately the Boeing B–29 and Consolidated B–32—bigger, deadlier, and with greater range than the B–17 or the B–24.

Although in the midst of expansion, the Army Air Corps was small compared to the major European air forces that went to war in September 1939. General Arnold commanded some 26,000 officers and enlisted men equipped with about 800 first-line combat aircraft. In contrast, Germany's *Luftwaffe* had about 3,600 comparable aircraft, the British almost 2,000, and the French more than 1,700. Despite the recent advances in American aviation technology that had produced airplanes like the B–17, despite centralization of the aerial striking force in the GHQ Air Force, and despite the President's obvious interest in military aviation, the U.S. Army Air Corps was not yet the equal of the air forces of Europe. It remained for the war itself to push the Air Corps to the forefront.

Part II

World War II, 1939-1945

Chapter 6

Reaction to the War in Europe

Bernard C. Nalty

W hile the Air Corps expansion of 1939 was beginning, Europe went to war. The United States reacted to the outbreak of war in Europe initially with cautious neutrality. As the expansionist campaigns of both Germany and Japan widened, however, the United States exhibited greater and greater opposition to those campaigns and greater and greater support for those fighting against the Germans and Japanese. The United States accompanied this shift from neutrality to outright opposition with a dramatic buildup of its military forces. For the Army Air Corps, this meant an even greater expansion, further reorganization, development of plans for the defense of U.S. interests and possibly even offensive operations against Germany or Japan (or both), deployment of forces, and shouldering new missions. How well the Air Corps carried all this out would determine how ready it would be should the United States find itself actually drawn into the war.

The war broke out when, after annexing the remainder of Czechoslovakia in the spring of 1939, Hitler turned covetous eyes toward Poland, an ally of France and Great Britain. Persuaded by their past inaction that the European democracies would not come to the aid of Poland, Hitler negotiated a nonaggression pact with Joseph Stalin in August that gave Germany a free hand there. With diplomacy removing the danger of Soviet intervention on behalf of his intended victim, Hitler attacked on September 1. From the beginning, air power played a crucial role in shaping the nature and course of the conflict.

Although Hitler, like Stalin, had expected Poland's allies to back down, both France and Great Britain honored their commitments and declared war against Germany. The entry of Britain and France into the war did not, however, lead to bombs falling mercilessly on London, Paris, or Berlin, as the military commentators had so confidently predicted. A form of mutual deterrence gripped western Europe, rooted in both the technological limitations of the bomber and the real, if exaggerated, fear of its effectiveness. As events soon proved, most of the bombers of 1939 lacked the range, durability, firepower, and navigational equipment to reach distant and defended targets. For example, fear of Hitler's *Luftwaffe* might discourage intervention on behalf of Czechoslovakia; but when war came, his bombers did not mount a sustained offensive against London or even Paris. Moreover, fear of air attack had inspired prudent defensive measures, as well as temporary appeasement, on the part of the European democracies. During the time of mounting tension after the Czechoslovakian crisis of 1938, all the future belligerents set up civil defense organizations of varying effectiveness, designated bomb shelters, emplaced antiaircraft guns, and deployed fighters. The British, who experienced the heaviest bombing of the World War I combatants, issued gas masks to civilians, allocated hospital space for thousands of casualties from aerial attack, and prepared to evacuate children from the cities; and only Britain had a functioning radar network when the war began. The fear that motivated such preparations proved groundless, for the anticipated waves of bombers did not appear over the capitals of western Europe, at least not during the early months of the conflict. The governments of France and Great Britain shared a dread of the effect of aerial bombing on their own urban populations that caused them, at least temporarily, to abstain from initiating air attacks on German cities. Hitler, in the meantime, proved reluctant to embark on an air war; not until the British had made ineffectual strikes against German warships did the *Luftwaffe* retaliate, attacking the same kind of targets with equally dismal results.

While Poland alone felt the lash of unrestrained air power, Hitler's *Luftwaffe* used its aircraft as planned, mainly in support of advancing armored and infantry forces. German bombers gutted Warsaw, the Polish capital, primarily to extinguish the last spark of resistance to German ground forces and only secondarily to demoralize the French and British. During the fighting in Poland, the *Luftwaffe* followed a doctrine, based partly on experience in the Spanish Civil War, that called for aviation to cooperate closely with rapidly moving ground forces. A key element in these tactics was the Messerschmitt Bf 109 fighter, with its top speed of 350 miles per hour and armament consisting of one or two 20–mm cannon and a pair of machineguns. This nimble airplane had the assignment of gaining aerial superiority so that bombers could destroy not only defen-

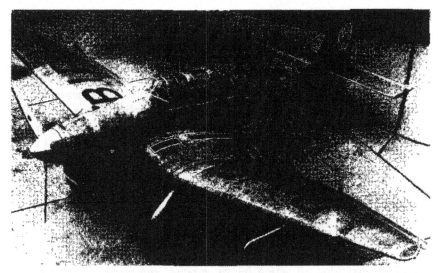

German Junkers Ju 87 Stuka.

sive positions on the battlefield but also the airfields, supply depots, transportation hubs, and factories capable of sustaining resistance to the German advance. The fighters operated in pairs, the two aircraft so spaced that they could maneuver either in unison to mass their fire or separately to protect each other. Two such teams worked together, flying close enough for mutual support but far enough apart for independent action. Although scarcely revolutionary—a decade earlier Claire Chennault, then a captain in the Army Air Corps, had experimented briefly with a formation of six fighters in three mutually supporting pairs—the four-plane German formation became the model for air forces throughout the world.

Hitler's airmen destroyed more than three-fourths of the combat aircraft of the ill-equipped Polish air force. Once the German fighters had gained mastery of the skies, aircraft like the Junkers Ju 87B dive bomber attacked the centers of resistance. The air battles proved costly to the aggressors, however, with the *Luftwaffe* losing only some fifty fewer aircraft to fighters, antiaircraft fire, and accidents than the number of Polish aircraft it claimed to have destroyed. Nonetheless, the Polish campaign served as grist for a Nazi propaganda mill that presented the invasion as a model of cooperation between military aviation and ground forces, a flawless example of *blitzkrieg*, or lightning war, as Germany in five weeks overwhelmed its much weaker eastern neighbor. While the Germans surged forward, the Soviet Union attacked from the east, seizing the share of Polish territory allotted it in a secret protocol to the Soviet-German Nonaggression Pact.

The boasts of Hitler's propagandists concealed serious weaknesses that soon would emerge to trouble the *Luftwaffe*. Production planning, for instance, remained geared to a short war, fought with the basic kinds of fighters and bombers already rolling from the assembly line. In such a conflict, neither numbers nor obsolescence would pose a problem, and there seemed no need to expand the manufacture of aircraft or radically improve the existing models. Although Germany turned out some 8,000 planes during 1939, compared to 7,000 in the United Kingdom, the monthly rate of British production by year's end exceeded German. Nor did the *Luftwaffe* have a long-range heavy bomber in production. None had seemed necessary when Hitler first began thinking seriously of a war in Europe, and even now the ability of mechanized forces to advance rapidly seemed likely to place medium bombers like the Heinkel He 111 or the Dornier Do 17 within striking distance of most worthwhile targets, whether tactical or strategic.

The *Luftwaffe* found new targets during 1940. In April German forces shattered the calm that had settled on Europe following the conquest of Poland, attacking Denmark and Norway, both neutral nations. The attack against Denmark scarcely tested German aviation, for the small nation was overrun in a matter of hours. The conquest of Norway, however, proved hard-fought, requiring closely coordinated action by air, ground, and naval forces. First the Germans destroyed the Norwegian air force, catching its few aircraft on the ground. Then, in conjunction with amphibious landings, parachute troops seized key airfields so that trimotor Junkers Ju 52 transports could land men to capture nearby objectives. The Allies responded by landing British, French, and Polish troops at various places on the Norwegian coast, but only at Narvik in the far North did they establish a strong beachhead.

Although limited in range and carrying capacity, Hitler's bombers had battered and demoralized the defenders, first of Poland and then of Norway. In conjunction with the ground forces, the *Luftwaffe* struck again during the spring of 1940. On May 10, as Allied forces were trying to maintain a bridgehead in Norway, German troops invaded Holland and Belgium, both neutrals, and knifed through the defenses of France. Against the French, the *Luftwaffe* gained control of the air and then served mainly as aerial artillery as it had in Poland. French aviation tended to live up to the prewar estimates of its commander, Gen. Joseph Vuillemin, who expected to lose two-thirds of his force in the first sixty days of sustained fighting. So complete was German mastery of the air that antiaircraft fire and fighters shot down at least forty of the seventy-one obsolescent light bombers that tried to attack the pontoon bridges carrying German armor across the Meuse River. Elsewhere the Germans combined ingenuity with boldness. In Belgium they used gliders to place assault troops atop Fort Eben Emael, capturing that underground redoubt; in Holland, as in Norway, they employed parachute troops and airborne infantry to seize airfields. Elements of the Dutch air force challenged the troop-carrying Ju 52s, shooting down several before Bf 109s could intervene, but the stubborn gallantry of the Dutch resistance collapsed after German bombers destroyed the central part of Rotterdam, duplicating the earlier devastation of Warsaw.

The deadly cooperation of German air, infantry, and armor overwhelmed the opposition on the continent of Europe. On June 4, 1940, the last British troops sent to reinforce France withdrew, escaping by sea from Dunkirk under cover of Royal Air Force fighters; and within the week, the Allied expedition to Norway had reembarked at Narvik. France accepted surrender terms on June 22, and the resulting armistice left Hitler the master of western Europe.

Before the Battle of France had ended, Italy, since May 1939 bound to Germany in the so-called Pact of Steel, at last entered the war, as, in the words of President Roosevelt, "the hand that held the dagger . . . struck it into the back of its neighbor."[1] In the Far East, moreover, the Anti-Comintern Pact gave way in September 1940 to stronger diplomatic bonds when Japan joined its anti-Comintern partners, Germany and Italy, in the Tripartite Pact, becoming the third of the Axis powers. The new agreement bound all three to join forces against any current nonbelligerent, obviously the United States, which might intervene in either the European war or the Sino-Japanese conflict. Great Britain now stood alone against the combined might of Germany and Italy, while in the Orient, the danger increased of Japanese aggression against British, French, and Dutch colonies.

The immediate threat to Britain's survival came from the German divisions that had thrust across France and now stood poised at the English Channel, awaiting orders to invade the British Isles. Before Hitler could launch an invasion, however, the *Luftwaffe* had to seize control of the skies. The Germans. who had greatly underestimated the capacity of the British aircraft industry to replace losses, attempted an aerial war of attrition by trying to lure the Spitfires and Hurricanes of the Royal Air Force Fighter Command into battle against numerically superior forces and wear down British resistance. In such a struggle, however, the *Luftwaffe*'s principal fighters had severe limitations: the Bf 109 lacked the endurance to protect bombers over the United Kingdom or engage in sustained aerial combat, while the twin-engine Messerschmitt Bf 110, which had the necessary range, lacked maneuverability.

At the outset, Air Marshal Sir Hugh Dowding had only some 650 fighters with which to defend the British Isles, but technology provided him with the information he needed to employ his force to deadly effect. Intent to exploit fully the capabilities of the primitive radar systems of the day, the British had established a chain of radar stations along the Channel coast that helped provide information on incoming German attacks that enabled control centers to mass fighters to meet a threat. Dowding received further critical information from Ultra, a source of intelligence that intercepted, decoded, and translated radio messages encrypted on the standard German Enigma enciphering machine. In the critical sector that embraced London, Dowding relied on radar and Ultra to intercept the German raids with adequate strength, but no more, so that he could maintain a reserve of fighters. When the battle began, he instructed his pilots to avoid massive dogfights with the escorting Messerschmitts and break through

British ground control radar that directed interceptors toward attacking aircraft.

to destroy the bombers before they reached their targets. In one of the most decisive actions of the Battle of Britain, Eagle Day, August 15, 1940, the *Luftwaffe* dispatched almost 1,500 bomber and fighter sorties to lure the Hurricanes and Spitfires aloft and destroy them, but ended up losing more than three times as many aircraft as the defenders.

Although attrition failed on Eagle Day and in similar air actions, the Germans twice stumbled on tactics that were far more dangerous to Fighter Command than the campaign of attrition, but each time reverted to their original plan. Despite successful attacks on coastal radar installations in preparation for Eagle Day, the *Luftwaffe* failed to mount a continuing effort to blind the British defenders, even though the 350-foot high antennas made conspicuous and vulnerable targets. Then, beginning on August 30, the enemy feinted toward the cities and concentrated on Fighter Command's airfields, inflicting heavy losses in aircraft. Again, however, the Germans did not follow through with a continuing effort against the fighter airfields. After September 3, since German intelligence concluded that the *Luftwaffe* had all but destroyed Dowding's force, the attacks shifted to London and attrition resumed.

By the end of September, Fighter Command had prevailed, though by the narrowest of margins. Because of radar, Ultra, modern fighters, and aggressive pilots, the British shot down twice as many airplanes as they lost. Moreover, while the Germans maintained their leisurely pace of aircraft production throughout the Battle of Britain, aircraft production in the British Isles accelerated, so that Fighter Command had more serviceable aircraft on hand when the battle ended than when it began. The British also won the battle of attrition of highly trained pilots. Since the fiercest action took place over the United Kingdom, most of the Fighter Command pilots who parachuted or made crash landings returned to duty; many of the Germans who took to their parachutes came down in British territory and became prisoners of war. So important were trained pilots that both air forces set up rescue services to retrieve men from the waters of the channel; indeed, with the approval of Prime Minister Winston Churchill, the British ignored the red cross insignia to fire on the white-painted German seaplanes engaged in rescue work. Determined to recover as many as possible of its highly trained airmen, the *Luftwaffe* camouflaged its rescue aircraft and provided fighter escort.

On September 17, Ultra revealed that Hitler had postponed the invasion of the British Isles. The *Luftwaffe*, which had failed to gain the necessary control of the air, shifted its strategy from attrition by day to bombing cities by night. Since the weakened German fighter force could no longer protect the lightly armed bombers in daylight, the enemy had no choice but to resort to unescorted nighttime raids, but the bombers were too few and carried loads too small to force Britain out of the war. Although causing heavy damage and spectacular fires in London, Coventry, and elsewhere, the night attacks failed to destroy either British industry or morale. The intensity of the attacks peaked by the end of 1940; and during the following year' Hitler turned his attention elsewhere, overrunning Yugoslavia in March, defeating a British expeditionary force in Greece, advancing into Egypt in April, and on June 22, 1941, invading the Soviet Union.

As the threat posed by Nazi Germany grew, the United States increasingly sided with Hitler's enemies and favored increases in military strength and readiness. As early as the Czechoslovakian crisis of 1938, the President had anticipated the outbreak of war in Europe and taken certain basic precautions, such as

Firemen standing amid rubble caused by German bombing.

asking Congress for funds to expand the Air Corps. He reacted to the initial on-slaught against Poland by proclaiming neutrality, declaring a limited national emergency, and issuing an executive order calling for modest increases in the strength of the Army and Navy. Then, on May 16, 1940, before the Battle of Britain had begun, while German armies still were surging through France, President Roosevelt called for a force of 50,000 planes divided among the Army, Navy, and Marine Corps. In choosing this figure, he looked beyond the needs of the American armed forces and estimated the effect of requests for air-craft from the British, who had failed to provide an aerial umbrella for Allied operations in Norway, and from the French, whose air force was being over-whelmed by the *Luftwaffe*. The number, however, represented a dramatic ges-ture rather than a concrete goal, a rallying cry rather than a definite program. Aware of the true state of the nation's aircraft industry, which had barely begun to expand, Roosevelt called attention in his announcement to the need for greater manufacturing capacity to create and sustain so large an armada. The President's call to action resulted in immediate orders for 11,000 Army aircraft and the drafting of plans for an air arm of 54 groups, totaling more than 200,000 officers, air cadets, and enlisted men.

The orders prompted by President Roosevelt's stirring call—enough, Arnold said, "to stagger any mere officer"—at first went unfilled. As late as November 1940, six months after the Chief Executive established a general objective of 50,000 aircraft, an entire week's production of the American aviation industry amounted to fewer than 50 military aircraft, two combat types and the rest train-ers. Obviously, the United States could not rearm and simultaneously supply the air forces battling the Axis powers without increasing production.

Fortunately, a banker thoroughly familiar with airplane manufacturing would soon take the oath of office as special assistant for aviation matters to Secretary of War Henry L. Stimson. Robert A. Lovett joined the War Department in 1940 and in March of the following year became Assistant Secretary of War for Air, a position Roosevelt had left vacant since 1933. In one of his first actions as as-sistant secretary, Lovett surveyed the American aircraft industry, comparing its techniques with those he had observed during recent visits to Europe, for pro-duction would be his main concern.

As the fighting raged in Europe, President Roosevelt realized that the exist-ing Army-Navy Munitions Board, even with the creation of a panel dealing with aircraft production, had such strong ties to the American military services that it could not deprive them of warplanes to assist the Allies, a policy that he be-lieved absolutely necessary. He solved the impasse by invoking a law passed during World War I and created the National Defense Advisory Commission, with himself as nominal chairman. Actually dominated by three men—William S. Knudsen, the president of General Motors, Sidney Hillman, an official of a major labor union, the Congress of Industrial Organizations, and Edward Stettinius, Jr., the chairman of the board of U.S. Steel—the commission became

Robert A. Lovett,
Assistant Secretary of War for Air,
April 10, 1941–December 8, 1945

an industrial planning agency, through trial and error easing the impact of increased defense spending on the economy, especially the aircraft industry. Although far from infallible (it once questioned the feasibility of trying to mass-produce the B–17), the commission established workable priorities, arranged for distribution of critically needed raw materials, and successfully mobilized the resources of the automobile industry for aircraft production. Early in 1941, the commission was replaced by the Office of Production Management under Knudsen and by the War Production Board after the attack on Pearl Harbor. General Arnold, who would appoint Knudsen a wartime lieutenant general in charge of materiel services for the Army Air Forces, later declared: "With his arrival in Washington, the Air Force production problems decreased as each day passed, and many of my headaches gradually disappeared."[2]

Chaos within the aircraft industry had barely begun to yield to order when new demands arose. Comparing the transfer of military equipment to the loan of a garden hose to help a neighbor put out a fire, President Roosevelt in March 1941 persuaded Congress to pass the Lend-Lease Act. This legislation enabled the Chief Executive to make weapons available to Great Britain, requiring only that any surviving items be returned after the war, an example of financial legerdemain that made it possible for the recipient to acquire weapons without using already depleted credit for outright purchases. China promptly became eligible to borrow war materials in this fashion, as did the Soviet Union after Hitler attacked in June 1941. By the time the war ended, Great Britain and its commonwealth had received some 26,000 airplanes through lend-lease, the Soviet Union 11,450, and China almost 1,400. An additional 4,000 went to other nations fighting the Axis powers. As the volume of production increased, General Arnold would have fewer worries about competition for the military aircraft leaving the assembly line. Until that happened, however, lend-lease complicated production planning, for to Arnold's dismay, executive arrangements with Great Britain, China, and the Soviet Union siphoned off equipment needed by the Army air arm.

Gradually the aircraft industry enlarged plant capacity and amassed the work force that would enable it to exceed the President's goal of 50,000 airplanes. Production gathered momentum, especially in 1941, so that between the outbreak of war in Europe and America's entry into the conflict, the number of aircraft available to the Army Air Forces increased from 2,500 to 12,000. Perhaps the most important contribution of the manufacturers during this period was a tenfold increase in training craft from 700 to almost 7,000. In 1939, the Army accepted a monthly average of fewer than 100 aircraft; during 1940, monthly acceptances rose from 250 in January to more than 800 in December; and in 1941, the number accepted soared from slightly more than 1,000 in January to 2,500 at year's end. The Army's inventory of combat aircraft, held in check by the need for trainers and the demands of lend-lease, nonetheless reflected the increasing tempo of production, for example, the number of B–17s rose from 22 in September 1939 to almost 200 when Japan attacked in December 1941. Fighter strength also increased during this period from not quite 500 to more than 1,600; of these first-line pursuits, fewer than 100 were P–38s, at least 300 were P–39s, and the rest were P–40s. From 1939 through 1941, the number of military airplanes annually emerging from American factories increased from 2,141 to more than 19,000; but the most spectacular growth, to a peak annual volume almost 45 times the 1939 rate, was yet to come.

At the same time that the United States was dramatically increasing the size of its air forces, it also took the first halting steps toward harnessing technological development for increasing the capability of those forces. As early as October 1939, Leo Szilard, a Hungarian-born physicist who had fled Germany when the Nazis came to power, sought to prod President Roosevelt into action on a project with overtones of science fiction—the development of an atomic

Lockheed P–38 assembly line.

bomb. Because Roosevelt had no science adviser to direct an inquiry into the feasibility of making an atomic bomb, the topic of nuclear fission languished for seven months, while an ad hoc uranium committee reviewed the possibilities raised by Szilard's letter. The difficulty in harnessing the talents of busy civilian scientists to work on a military project of uncertain value helped persuade the President to establish an organization to manage scientific projects of this sort. At the urging of Vannevar Bush, a mathematician and engineer, Roosevelt invoked another World War I law and, in the spring of 1940, created the National Defense Research Committee. Under the direction of Bush, the committee, absorbed during the following year into the Office of Scientific Research and Development, served to marshal the resources of American science, first for national defense and later for victory. The Office of Scientific Research and Development would participate in a number of projects, especially in electronics and armaments, that proved of great importance to the Army Air Forces.

Such breakthroughs lay in the future, however. In September 1939, the American government thought in terms of defense, whether national or hemispheric, and relied on geography rather than technology for protection from aerial attack. No radar scanned the skies and no control centers directed interceptors against hostile bombers. Although the U.S. Navy had pioneered the development of radar, the United States lagged behind Britain in tactical applications. As late as 1941, Maj. Gen. Henry H. Arnold, chief of the air arm, denounced the American product as "no good" and recommended trying to purchase radar from Great Britain. Granted that the American sets had definite weaknesses—a susceptibility to jamming, for instance—the greatest advantage of foreign radar may have been the skilled operators rather than the sets themselves. In any event, production continued in the United States, and by the end of November 1941 the Army was sufficiently confident of the equipment to begin installing it on both coasts and in Panama, Hawaii, and the Philippines.

In the autumn of 1939, the aircraft of the U.S. Army Air Corps compared unfavorably with those of the air forces of Europe, except for the B–17, unequalled as a high-altitude daylight bomber. The Army had, for example, no fighter that could match the British Spitfire or the German Bf 109 in high-altitude performance. The P–38 Lightning with its supercharged engines could climb as high as the European types, but lacked their maneuverability; and the lack of a supercharger restricted the ceiling of both the P–39 and P–40. Neither the Air Corps nor the American aviation industry had made progress toward the development of a turbine, or jet, engine for aircraft. Engineers at Wright Field, Ohio, the center of prewar research and development, had tried gearing a supercharger to the drive shaft of a piston engine, using the exhaust to help turn the propeller blades and increase power, but nothing came of this experiment until the appearance of the so-called compound engine after World War II. In the absence of any challenge from the United States, Germany and the United Kingdom took the lead in developing jet aircraft.

History of the United States Air Force

The failure of the Air Corps to become involved in the prewar development of radar or jet engines cannot be attributed to General Arnold, who had an abiding interest in technology and often solicited the help of prominent scientists. In 1939, for instance, he became aware of rocket experiments in the United States and recruited Theodore von Kármán, a Hungarian-born specialist in aerodynamics at the California Institute of Technology, to head a project designed to develop rockets capable of helping heavily laden bombers take off from short runways. The team headed by von Kármán produced solid-propellant rockets that could be attached to an airplane and ignited by the pilot to help hurl the craft into the sky. This technique of jet-assisted takeoff underwent a successful test in the summer of 1941. Some three years later, Arnold selected von Kármán to survey the status of German aviation and determine the development projects needed to make the United States dominant in the skies after the war had ended.

The air arm turned to von Kármán but ignored Robert Goddard, who in this national emergency proposed to develop an explosives-laden, long-range missile for attacking distant targets. Brig. Gen. George H. Brett, in charge of the Materiel Division at Wright Field, turned down the idea. Such a one-shot weapon, Brett argued, would prove less accurate and efficient than a bomber, which could fly a number of missions. The decision reflected the priorities of the time. Ignoring questions of accuracy and economy of use, the Air Corps remained so short of aircraft that any diversion of resources into missile development might well have proved a mistake.

The growing force of aircraft had to be manned and maintained. General Arnold and his advisers faced the task of overseeing the frenzied expansion of a prewar air arm that numbered about 25,000, including reserve officers who participated to varying degrees in annual training exercises. The Air Corps of 1939 had operated 76 installations (including 21 major bases or depots), produced fewer than 1,000 graduates from flight training courses, and graduated about 1,500 enlisted men from technical schools. These figures represented a vast increase from the mid-1930s, but Army aviation had to expand still further in terms of both manpower and facilities to absorb its share of the increased American aircraft production.

The air arm needed equipment of every sort—bases, ranges, and men—and it needed them simultaneously. Civilian flight and technical training schools participated in the buildup. For example, the number of primary flight training schools under contract to the Army increased from nine in 1939 to twenty in 1940, to forty-one the following year, and to a maximum of fifty-six in 1943. Also, eight civilian institutions joined the technical training centers at Lowry Field, Colorado, and Chanute Field, Illinois, in producing technicians. Pan American Airways took part in the training effort, providing instruction in meteorology and navigation until the Air Corps could set up schools of its own.

The number of installations increased to a peak of over two thousand in 1943—what had been a cornfield or cotton patch in 1939 became a paved run-

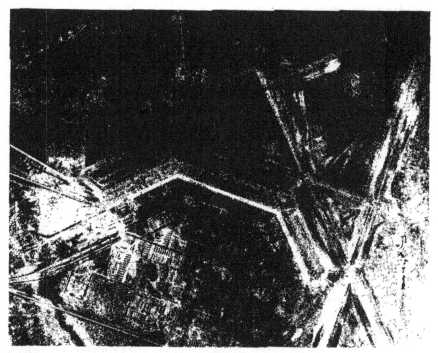

Douglas Army Air Field, Douglas, Arizona, was one of hundreds of training
fields that were created from empty land, completed their missions during
the war, then closed immediately after the war. Douglas, active for just
over three years, opened in July 1942 and closed in October 1945.

way, while tracts of wilderness served as gunnery or bombing ranges. Included
in this growth were the Army's flight training centers, which came to incorporate both new military airfields and existing civilian fields taken over during the
national emergency. The expanded training facilities began offering courses of
instruction for sorely needed bombardiers and aerial gunners. The network of
air installations within the United States, valued at $100 million in 1940, grew
in five years to a complex worth 30 times that amount and covered land equal
in area to the states of New Hampshire, Vermont, Massachusetts, and
Connecticut combined. The expansion, moreover, absorbed almost 30 percent
of the amount spent by the War Department during the period for domestic military construction.

Typical of the new training bases was Thunderbird Field near Phoenix,
Arizona, an installation operated under contract to the Army by a firm headed
by Leland Heyward, a theatrical producer, actor's agent, and private pilot, and
John H. Connelly, who had served in the Air Service during World War I and
taught flying for the Civil Aeronautics Administration. Flight operations began

in March 1941, three months after ground was broken for the project. The most substantial of the field's hurriedly built structures were the hangars, where mechanics—some of the less experienced earning only 75 cents an hour—worked by night to prepare the aircraft for the next day's flying. The first class at Thunderbird Field numbered 59 cadets; by the fall of 1945, when the last class graduated, some 20,000 pilots from 30 nations had trained at Thunderbird Field and two nearby airfields operated by the same firm.

Despite the excellent weather in Arizona, learning to fly was dangerous. One student, for example, overshot the runway on a solo flight, landing smoothly but somersaulting into a dry irrigation ditch. As the pilot hung head-down in his safety harness, a would-be rescuer asked if he was all right. The embarassed student answered that he was unhurt, but wouldn't recommend the maneuver to any one else. Although this trainee survived uninjured and graduated, others were less fortunate, including one cadet who died because he set his altimeter incorrectly and plowed into the desert on a moonless night, the instrument showing that his airplane was at 1,000 feet.

Airfields and training courses meant nothing without technicians, students, instructors, and men to perform administrative and housekeeping chores—all grouped in the general category of manpower. The personnel strength of the air arm kept pace with construction projects and aircraft purchases, reaching 43,000 at the end of 1939 and approaching 100,000 in 1940. By December 1941, almost 300,000 men wore the insignia of the Army Air Forces. The number of graduates from flight training increased by about 800 percent in 1940, reaching 8,000 during that year and 27,000 in 1941. The various technical training courses produced ten times as many specialists in 1940 as in 1939, almost 15,000, and about 42,000 the following year. Not only did greater training opportunities become available for enlisted men, in 1940 nonflying officers began to graduate from courses in engineering, administration, weather, photography, communications, and armaments. The vast majority of the new technicians enlisted for a specific term, which the government might extend, or received reserve commissions to serve during the emergency.

The reserve provided a means for rapidly enlarging an officer corps that, by the end of 1940, had an active duty strength of approximately 6,000. Of this total, roughly 40 percent were Regulars, 40 percent were reservists, and the balance were officers on detail from other elements of the Army, such as the Quartermaster Corps. By July 1941, the Army Air Corps had mobilized all the reservists willing to volunteer for extended tours of duty and was beginning to call up the others. As the prewar pool of reservists shrank, civilians with needed skills, successful air cadets, and graduates of other Air Forces schools received commissions in the reserve, with orders to report immediately for active duty.

The 19 observation squadrons that formed a part of the National Guard made a lesser contribution to national defense than did the reserve. In 1939, the Air

Corps successfully resisted a congressional proposal to expand the aviation component of the National Guard, persuading legislators that it would be a mistake to divert resources from the expansion of the Regular air arm. Consequently, in September 1940, when President Roosevelt mobilized the National Guard, only 468 pilots responded to the call.

Despite its rapid expansion, the Air Corps tried to avoid increasing the number of noncommissioned pilots. During 1940, it retained about two dozen graduates of pilot training courses who had served on active duty as reserve officers and then agreed to stay on as enlisted men, primarily to fly transports. However, congressional pressure intensified for more enlisted pilots, largely to save money, and the War Department was urging a lowering of educational standards for flight school. By the summer of 1941, the Air Corps had decided to combine acceptance of additional enlisted pilots with a change in educational requirements. Abandoning the policy that candidates for flight training either present proof that they had completed two years of college or pass an equivalent examination, the Army began accepting high school graduates, who trained as enlisted men and graduated as sergeant pilots. The program for noncommissioned pilots satisfied Congress and expanded the pool of potential flyers by lowering the required level of education.

The training of pilots, whether officers or sergeants, and of air crewmen, along with the need for specialists in totally new fields, overwhelmed the experienced cadre that had kept the Air Corps functioning during the 1930s. A shortage of instructors and the shift from professional education to training for service in a national emergency forced the Air Corps in 1940 to shut down its Tactical School at Maxwell Field, Alabama. Two years would pass before the Army Air Forces established a School of Applied Tactics at Orlando, Florida, to familiarize officers with staff duties and the managerial, as well as operational, aspects of air warfare.

Acquisition of large numbers of aircraft and trained men to fly and maintain them did not necessarily produce true air power. The critical issue was whether the role of military aviation would ultimately be defined by ground officers or airmen. Fortunately, on the eve of war a ground officer became Chief of Staff who accepted the airplane as a strategic as well as tactical weapon and had confidence in the leadership of the air arm. The Army Air Forces might not have become a truly effective instrument of warfare except for the cooperation and mutual respect between Arnold and Gen. George C. Marshall, the new Army Chief of Staff. The two officers struck an informal bargain: Arnold would not use American rearmament as a vehicle for obtaining independence from the Army and Marshall would see to it that aviation received the degree of autonomy within the Army that Arnold believed necessary for strategic as well as tactical operations against the enemy. Although a powerful advocate of the air arm, Marshall did not endorse the establishment of a separate air force in the midst of a national emergency, for he hoped to avoid any disruptive organizational changes. Military aviation was to remain a part of the Army, at least for the duration of the war, but the Chief of Staff intended that airmen enjoy sufficient freedom to function efficiently and imaginatively. Arnold, who respected the Chief of Staff and felt assured of Marshall's continuing cooperation, declined to take advantage of the interest in air power inspired by the success of the *Luftwaffe* and made no attempt to rally congressional support for independence. "Right at this minute," the Air Corps chief conceded to a fellow officer in 1940, "it looks to me as if it might be a serious mistake to change the existing setup when we are using every facility available to take care of the present expansion of the Air Corps."[3]

Even as he advised against seeking immediate independence, Arnold urged the Chief of Staff to grant aviation greater autonomy within the War Department. In brief, Arnold sought appointment as Deputy Chief of Staff for Air, one of three deputies responsible for ground forces, aviation, and services for the expanding Army. In this position, Arnold would continue to serve as Air Corps chief and have a deputy of his own to direct the GHQ Air Force. Although concerned that the plan might lead to the separation of the Air Corps from the rest of the Army, the General Staff did not reject it out of hand, for the appointment of Arnold as deputy for air, even though his authority would remain largely unchanged, should satisfy civilian critics, who complained that air power was not getting its due.

General Marshall tried to please both the General Staff, who tended to look on air power as another weapon for the commander on the ground, and the airmen, who argued that aviation was decisive in its own right. In November 1940, the Chief of Staff installed Arnold, who remained Chief of the Air Corps, as his acting deputy for aviation, but reversed the policy adopted the previous year and removed the GHQ Air Force from Arnold's control. Instead of reporting to the Chief of the Army Air Corps, as it had for eighteen months, this aerial striking force now came under the authority of the Army's General Headquarters, reverting to the original chain of command. When the GHQ Air Force began functioning in 1935, its basic mission had been to train in peacetime to fight during a future war as the air arm of the commanding general of the Army. The future, it was assumed at that time, would repeat the recent past, with a commanding general modeled after Pershing taking charge of the American Expeditionary Forces. To prevent the kind of friction that had arisen between Pershing in France and Peyton C. March, the Chief of Staff at Washington, the Army Chief of Staff was expected to assume command overseas, assisted by a wartime General Headquarters or GHQ. In 1940, an Army GHQ was organized, but neither an armed enemy nor an expeditionary force overseas existed. Consequently, what was envisioned as an operational headquarters became immersed in training and deployments, duplicating the work of the War Department General Staff and inserting itself between the GHQ Air Force and the Air Corps chief. Awkward though the arrangement was, the Army GHQ exercised control over the GHQ Air Force for more than a year. That such an organizational structure survived as long as it did reflected both Arnold's willingness that "the present organization be given a chance to prove itself before any adjustments are made" and his harmonious relationship with Marshall.[4]

Although they might be postponed for a time, changes to the cumbersome system were inevitable. By the end of December 1940, Brett, now a major general and Acting Chief of the Air Corps, had revived Arnold's earlier proposal to reorganize the Army along functional lines, with deputy chiefs of staff for the air, ground, and service components. In March 1941, Marshall accepted the proposal, but only for aviation. He wanted one officer, General Arnold, to have complete responsibility for Army aviation, ending the informal arrangement whereby Arnold dealt with Marshall and the General Staff concerning plans, policy, and operations and Brett, as acting Chief of the Air Corps, assumed responsibility for research and development, manpower and administration, acquisition, and maintenance. In June 1941, the War Department adopted a regulation that reshaped military aviation as the Chief of Staff desired. Arnold became the Chief of the U.S. Army Air Forces, which consisted of two elements, the Air Corps and the Combat Command. The former continued to perform administrative and other support duties; the latter replaced the GHQ Air Force, which vanished into history. Both reported to Arnold, who made any interpretation of the boundary between support and operations. The new Chief of the U.S. Army Air Forces resembled a chief of staff for Army aviation, ultimately responsible for the functioning of the entire organization, including its contribution to the war plans and intelligence estimates adopted by the War Department.

In spite of this surface similarity between his role as Chief of the Army Air Forces and Marshall's as Army Chief of Staff, Arnold's authority was closely circumscribed; his writ did not extend beyond the Air Forces, and even here it was not absolute. For example, the Army GHQ remained athwart the lines of authority extending from Arnold's office to the Combat Command and to the Air Forces units overseas, which were controlled by the Army commander in the particular theater. Arnold, however, remained Marshall's deputy, the principal spokesman for air power in the highest councils of the Army and, as yet largely by invitation, the adviser to the President on military aviation.

In carrying out his duties, Arnold benefited from the assistance of a newly created Air Staff, formally organized to deal with the usual military specialties like operations, intelligence, and logistics. The Air Staff, a title borrowed from the British, in June 1941 replaced the varying number of advisers who, over the decades, had helped the Chief of the Air Service and the Chief of the Air Corps. As soon as the new agency began functioning, Lt. Col. Harold L. George of the Air War Plans Division spearheaded an effort to enhance the status of the Air Staff, particularly the status of his office. He proposed that his division formulate all plans dealing with military aviation, to make it, in effect, an aviation di-

Mitchel Field, Long Island, New York.

vision of the War Department General Staff. The War Plans Division of the General Staff reacted by denying that the new Air Staff had any role whatsoever in War Department planning, but that interpretation did not prevail. A compromise was reached that defined the Air Staff as the staff of a commander, in this case Arnold, who was subordinate to the War Department, and guaranteed the right of the Air War Plans Division to submit its views to the War Plans Division of the General Staff. Once the United States had entered the conflict, the War Department encouraged the assignment of Air Forces officers to joint and Anglo-American planning groups, as well as to the Operations Division, as the General Staff's planning body came to be called.

While the Air Staff was finding a niche in the planning process, the two principal components of the Army Air Forces, the Combat Command and the Air Corps, undertook their assigned duties. As successor to the GHQ Air Force, the new Combat Command consisted of four regional air forces: the First at Mitchel Field, Long Island, New York; the Second at McChord Field, Washington; the Third at MacDill Field, Florida; and the Fourth at March Field, California. The First and Fourth Air Forces were to provide the nucleus for air defense in the event of war, and the other two would become combat training commands.

Meanwhile, the Office of Chief of the Air Corps became responsible for the Materiel Division and the Maintenance Command. The latter had been created in the spring of 1941 to take over the supply and maintenance activity formerly performed by components of the Materiel Division. In October, the Maintenance Command became the Air Service Command, but continued to concentrate on maintenance and supply and remained subject to the Office of Chief of the Air Corps until that office disbanded in 1942. By the time the war ended, the Materiel Command (formerly Division) had consolidated with the Air Service

182

Command to form the Air Technical Service Command, testimony to the difficulty in separating responsibility for such closely related matters as procurement, supply, and maintenance.

Another concern of the Office of Chief of the Air Corps was the training of aviators, crew members, and technicians. The inability of Randolph Field, Texas, to accommodate flight training for an expanding air arm led in 1940 to the establishment of three training centers, each serving a specific part of the nation, that produced navigators and bombardiers, as well as pilots. Supervision of the three regional centers shifted, following a 1942 reorganization, from the Office of Chief of the Air Corps to the new Flying Training Command. The Technical Training Command, set up in 1941, addressed the task of instructing technicians. Two years later it incorporated with the Flying Training Command to form the Army Air Forces Training Command.

Unfortunately, flaws soon appeared in the arrangement that produced the Army Air Forces. The relationship between Arnold's Air Staff and the War Department General Staff was still being defined; and within the air arm, the distinction between combat and service components tended to blur. However, although not fully satisfactory from the standpoint of either ground or air forces, the 1941 reforms did ensure that the Chief of the Army Air Forces had continued access to General Marshall and, in advising the Chief of Staff, benefited from information gathered and processed by a staff of his own.

A further reform, effected in March 1942, eliminated the Air Forces Combat Command and the Office of Chief of the Air Corps. It also made Arnold the Commanding General of the U.S. Army Air Forces, with full responsibility over aircraft development, procurement of men and machines, training, administration, and all forms of support not provided by the Army's technical services. The functional reorganization that Arnold had been advocating since 1940 also went into effect at that time, after a committee on reorganization headed by Maj. Gen. Joseph T. McNarney of the Army Air Forces formally endorsed the changes. Acting on the recommendations of McNarney and his colleagues, the Army Chief of Staff established the Army Ground Forces and the Services of Supply (in 1943 redesignated the Army Services Forces), which took their places alongside the Army Air Forces. This overhaul eliminated the Army GHQ, an administrative obstacle that had stood between Arnold's headquarters and the commands responsible to him.

The Air Staff continued to function after the 1942 reorganization as it had since its creation the year before. As a matter of policy, General Arnold tried to bring to military specialties such as planning or intelligence the administrative techniques that he had come to admire in his dealings with the aircraft industry. The marriage of business efficiency and military staff work began in 1941 when Arnold sought to resolve contradictory statistics generated by various staff sections and speed the flow of accurate information throughout the headquarters. These early efforts led to the establishment of the wartime offices of organizational planning and statistical control, which cut across the functional boundaries of the Air Staff (personnel, logistics, and the like), gathered data from a variety of sources, resolved contradictions, and solved problems involving various staff agencies. In designing and manning these and other offices, Arnold called upon qualified civilians, visiting management consultants who evaluated his staff procedures and businessmen, lawyers, and public relations specialists commissioned in the reserve and assigned to jobs requiring their skills.

Before the emergence of the Army Air Forces and the Air Staff, military aviation played a minor role in American strategic planning. The Air Corps did not have suitable planning agencies, and its interests tended toward doctrine and equipment rather than war plans. For instance, in 1933, when Gen. Douglas MacArthur, the Army Chief of Staff, asked Maj. Gen. Benjamin D. Foulois, the Chief of the Air Corps, to participate in war planning, Foulois used the occasion to plead for the modernization and expansion of military aviation, which he considered more important than drawing up plans to defeat a hypothetical enemy. As the war drew the United States closer, however, the Army Air Forces began playing an increasingly larger role in both strategic planning and in developing the necessary arrangements with the British and others for supporting and, if need be, joining in the war against the Axis.

Before the outbreak of war in Europe, the Joint Army and Navy Board, the predecessor of the Joint Chiefs of Staff, examined the existing national strategy in the light of Germany's growing military might and reports of increased German economic and diplomatic activity in Latin America, Italy's ambitions, and Japan's aggression in China. Shortly after the invasion of Poland, Army and Navy planners sought to revise the joint war plans to meet a changing threat. Each of the old plans had been directed at fighting a war against a single enemy and were designated by a color—orange for Japan, red for Great Britain, or black for Germany—although a single document might deal with two enemies, as in the short-lived Red-Orange Plan. The replacements for the color series were called rainbow plans because they addressed a combination of enemies, the Axis powers of Germany, Italy, and Japan. The new plans varied in scope from Rainbow 1, the defense by the United States, acting alone, of the Western Hemisphere and the outlying American possessions, to Rainbow 5, which called for the United States and its Allies to defend the hemisphere, retain control of the Pacific in the face of aggression by Japan, and defeat Germany and Italy before launching a final offensive against the Japanese. By the summer of 1941, Rainbow 5 emerged as the basic statement of American strategy because it reflected the state of the world. Germany, with Italy as a junior partner, dominated Europe, and Japan was testing the declining strength of the colonial powers—Great Britain, the Netherlands, and France—that Germany was fighting or had defeated.

As the strategic consensus was taking shape, War Department planners gave increasing thought to one aspect of Rainbow 5, a coalition war in Europe, the kind of conflict that had been studied in Army schools since World War I. In planning for war in Europe, military aviation played an important role, for fighting there afforded opportunities not only to support the Army's ground forces but also to test the theory that an industrial nation like Germany could be bombed into submission. In contrast, the Army Air Forces figured scarcely at all in the kind of warfare that most interested the Navy, which had prepared for a battle to control the Atlantic, over which the Army would sail to fight in Europe, and for the final offensive against Japan. Conditioned by the history of World War I, naval planners anticipated a renewed threat from German submarines, but two decades of drawing up Orange Plans for a war against Japan fought by battle fleets, aircraft carriers, and amphibious troops also conditioned their thinking.

The creation of the Air Staff gave Army aviation its first full-time planning agencies, but Air Forces planners made only a limited contribution to the initial work on the Rainbow series. When it became apparent that Great Britain would be an ally if the United States became involved in the war, Anglo-American planners met at Washington from late January until early March 1941 to discuss a mutual strategy. Army airmen played a more important part in these talks with the British than they had in shaping a purely American strategy because Great Britain's Royal Air Force was a separate service, the equal of the Royal Army and Navy, and after the defeat of France air power became the sole means of carrying the war to Germany. Since aviation provided the only club for battering Hitler, discussions with the British required the participation of a high-ranking American airman who could deal directly with the representatives of the Royal Air Force. As a result, McNarney, then a colonel assigned to the War Plans Division of the War Department General Staff, served in the American delegation during the conversations at Washington with the British planning group. A self-styled "fire eater," McNarney believed that in the event of war, the Anglo-American alliance should immediately undertake operations aimed at "reducing the war-making capability of the Germans" to prevent a British collapse.[5] The staff discussions, however, were not an appropriate forum to undertake a commitment for action, not even the loose collaboration—essentially basing Army bombers in the United Kingdom but under American control—that McNarney advocated. Lacking the authority to endorse a binding course of joint military action, the officers from the two nations could talk only in general terms, mainly about global strategy, and the conversations produced agreements in principle rather than specific results. The two nations promised to exchange military missions and agreed that the British would have a priority claim on the aircraft produced at American factories, unless the United States entered the war. They also endorsed McNarney's proposal that, in the event the United States went to war against Germany, American bombers would operate from British bases under American command but in collaboration with the Royal Air Force Bomber Command. The conferees further recommended that Anglo-

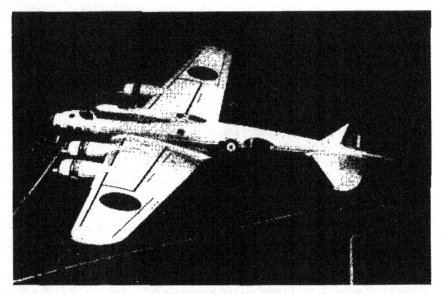

British Boeing B–17C.

American strategy in any coalition war should be to concentrate on the defeat of Germany first and, only after Hitler's downfall, the defeat of his Allies, the premise of Rainbow 5, the basic American war plan.

The confidence of airmen like McNarney in daylight strategic bombing, which helped prompt the agreement concerning the employment of American bombers based in the British Isles, remained unshaken despite an evaluation by the Royal Air Force of the Fortress I, a B–17C mounting seven hand-operated machineguns and carrying the Sperry bombsight instead of the more accurate Norden. After twenty-two missions that began in May 1941—including strikes against Brest in France and Narvik in Norway—only twelve of the original twenty Fortresses survived, and these were transferred to Coastal Command for antisubmarine patrol. For the British, the results of this test confirmed a lesson they had learned earlier in the war: unescorted bombers could not survive by day against enemy fighters. Without a long-range escort, the Royal Air Force shifted to night operations, sacrificing bombing accuracy for survival. The fate of the Fortress I, however, did not discourage Army Air Forces planners, who believed that the planes had gone into combat too few at a time to mass defensive fire or obtain a destructive bombing pattern.

The Army Air Forces, secure in its belief that the strategic bomber could carry the war to the enemy, began arranging to dispatch a military mission to the United Kingdom, as decided during the Anglo-American conversations at Washington. The War Department selected a veteran airman, Maj. Gen. James E. Chaney, to represent the Army in Britain. General Chaney, who arrived in

186

London in May 1941, seemed a logical choice because the first Army contingents likely to arrive in the British Isles would be aviation squadrons and because of the contacts he had made among the leaders of the Royal Air Force during his recent service in Britain. While an air observer in 1940, he had correctly interpreted the Battle of Britain as a triumph for the Royal Air Force and the key to British survival. In connection with his study of that struggle, he examined the air defenses of the United Kingdom, searching for techniques that Army airmen could use in protecting the United States and its overseas outposts or, if the United States became Britain's ally, in helping defend the United Kingdom.

Aided by a small staff, Chaney devoted his second tour of duty in Britain to making tentative arrangements for bases that Army airmen could use, should the United States and the United Kingdom become allied in the fight against the Axis. In preparing a possible wartime command structure for American air forces, General Chaney unsuccessfully opposed Arnold's concept of a theater air force that combined fighter, bomber, and service elements under the centralized control of a single air officer responsible to the overall theater commander. More sensitive to advice from the British than to the views of his superiors, Chaney favored local autonomy and proposed organizing the air components geographically as well as functionally—an interceptor command in Northern Ireland, for example, and a bomber command in England—with the principal combat forces largely responsible for their own maintenance and other services.

Army Air Forces planners began giving more definition to their plans when President Roosevelt, on July 9, 1941, not quite three weeks after Germany had invaded the Soviet Union, asked the Army and Navy for estimates of the "overall production requirements needed to defeat our potential enemies." The War Plans Division of the General Staff received the task of framing the Army's response; and Clayton Bissell, a former aide to Mitchell and now a lieutenant colonel assigned to the War Plans Division, asked for help in preparing an Air Forces annex to the estimate. The Air War Plans Division requested, however, that it be allowed to prepare an Air Forces plan on its own. Arnold endorsed the proposal, and the War Plans Division, already working at capacity, agreed to delegate the task. Beginning on August 4, Lieutenant Colonel George, the chief of the Air War Plans Division, and three of his fellow officers—Lt. Col. Kenneth N. Walker, Maj. Haywood S. Hansell, Jr., and Maj. Laurence S. Kuter—drew up the division's first major plan, AWPD/1, or Air War Plans Division plan number one. Drafted by advocates of strategic bombing, the document went far beyond estimating production requirements, offering nothing less than a plan for defeating Germany by means of aerial bombardment.

The Army Air Forces planners accepted the basic strategy of defeating Germany first in the event of a two-front war, a concept incorporated in Rainbow 5 and recommended by the Anglo-American staff planners during their recent discussions in Washington. The basic American strategy called for American air forces to contain the Japanese in the Pacific, the defense of the Western Hemisphere, and the defeat of Germany; but not until Germany had been beaten would decisive operations begin against Japan. This basic strategy of defeating Germany first required an Army air arm of slightly more than two million men, about 135,000 pilots or members of air crews and the rest performing technical or administrative duties. The total number of aircraft envisioned in AWPD/1 exceeded 63,000, with almost 7,500 heavy bombers, including the B–17 and B–24, the even larger Boeing B–29 and Consolidated B–32 (neither of which had yet flown), or a truly intercontinental type, still in the planning stage, that emerged after the war as the Consolidated B–36.

George and his colleagues declared that 6,800 medium, heavy, and very heavy bombers based in Europe and North Africa could knock Germany out of the war by destroying 154 key industrial targets. Moreover, long-range bombers could strike at the heartland of Germany even though German forces dominated Europe and the Mediterranean and were knifing deep into the Soviet Union. The ability of the bomber to defy distance persuaded the Air Forces planners that Great Britain, instead of serving as the base for an invasion of the continent, might function more effectively as the site of the airfields from which bombers could destroy the industries on which the German war effort depended. Although firm believers in victory through strategic bombardment, the authors of AWPD/1 did not rule out an invasion of Europe from the British Isles for two reasons. First, to do so would trigger a clash over doctrine that might prove fatal to the plan, since the War Department General Staff, which normally reviewed any document like AWPD/1, remained committed to the principle that victory resulted from destroying an enemy's army and seizing his territory and not from leveling his industries. Second, the officers who prepared AWPD/1, however confident they were that air power could prevent the bloodshed of a land campaign, had to concede that bombing would not bring the war to a swift conclusion because of the time needed to mass 6,800 bombers, especially since the largest were not yet in production. Consequently, the framers of the plan proposed that an interim force, consisting of 3,800 bombers, would carry the war to Germany while the striking force grew to its maximum size.

The Air Plans Division realized that building even the interim force, let alone the full armada of 6,800 bombers, would require a mighty effort by the American aircraft industry, for in the summer of 1941 the Air Forces had on hand fewer than 700 bombers of all types—light, medium, and heavy. Assuming that the problems of production would be solved, as indeed they were, the planners felt that a growing force of American bombers could neutralize the German fighter force by destroying engine and airframe plants and shooting down interceptors in aerial combat. Having won air superiority, the American air forces could then attack the nation's electrical power grid, considered a vital target because its generators served the entire economy, cripple the transportation network, and destroy the oil industry. Only when these war industries had been battered and Germany stood at the abyss of defeat, would the Americans engage in attacks to shatter civilian morale. AWPD\1 abandoned the principle rooted in Douhet's writing that civilian morale would collapse under heavy bombing, perhaps because of the continued resistance shown by the British populace despite the German bombardment. The plan proposed instead that attacks directed at morale serve as a coup de grace for an enemy mortally wounded by the destruction of his industries.

Of all the systems of targets proposed in 1941, only the oil industry proved both vital and vulnerable to high-altitude strategic bombing. Given the belief in the pinpoint accuracy of daylight bombardment that prevailed among bombing enthusiasts when AWPD/1 was written, the power grid seemed a logical target, but events defied logic: the generating plants proved hard to locate and hit, transmission lines were among the first things repaired after an urban attack, and the large hydroelectric dams required special bombs that had to be dropped from a height of about fifty feet, bombs too bulky for B–17s or B–24s. Consequently, the power grid did not come under sustained attack. The offensive against German transportation proposed in AWPD/1 did not begin until late in the war when the advancing ground troops brought such targets within range of tactical aircraft and Allied dominance in the skies permitted heavy bombers to attack with greater accuracy from comparatively low altitude. As for German morale, which became a collateral target of the transportation campaign, the planners in 1941 were correct in emphasizing timing, for the civilian populace held up surprisingly well under aerial attack, at least as long as suffering and sacrifice seemed likely to bring victory or at least avoid a worse disaster than bombing. Not until hope had vanished did morale collapse.

In determining the force to be employed and the targets to be destroyed, the Air Forces planners reviewed the experience of the Royal Air Force in its brief attempt to bomb Germany by daylight and concluded that accuracy would prevail despite bad weather. Although acknowledging that only an average of five days per month would provide the cloudless skies needed for precision attacks, George and his fellow officers believed that German industry could nevertheless be leveled because 90 percent of the bombs directed at a particular factory on those clear days would explode within 1,250 feet of the aiming point, an unattainable degree of accuracy. The planners did not foresee the use of the radar bombsight—far less precise than the optical kind, but necessary when weather obscured the target—that increased the number of days when bombing was possible, but reduced accuracy. During the bomber offensive, crews undertook five or fewer missions from the United Kingdom against Germany during just six months out of 32, a result of the increased use of radar, but even using the Norden sight under the best conditions of visibility, bomber formations could get 90 percent of the bombs directed at a target no closer than a mile from the aiming point, four times the anticipated dispersion. A number of factors contributed to the lack of pinpoint accuracy—antiaircraft fire, winds, fighter opposition, and the practice of having a formation release its bombs simultaneously.

The framers of AWPD/1 also erred in their assumption that German industry in the weeks following the invasion of the Soviet Union was already producing at full capacity; Hansell later described the German economy of that period as "presumably drawn taut" by the demands of a two-front war. Such was not the case. Despite his failure to subdue Britain, Hitler clung to the notion that his war against Stalin would be short and victorious. To avoid risking discontent among the populace by demanding sacrifices he believed unnecessary, the German dictator permitted production of civilian goods at the expense of weapons for his armed forces. The fatal weakness of the wartime German economy was not that it was overextended in 1941, but that it mobilized far too late in what proved to be a war for national survival.

Confident of the vulnerability of German industry and the accuracy of American bombing, the planners nevertheless feared—correctly as events would prove—that strategic bombers might be diverted from powerplants, oil refineries, and rail centers to attack less important targets. Because of unavoidable delays in marshaling a decisive force of bombers and the preferred strategy of the ground-oriented Army, they reasoned that an invasion of Europe might be undertaken, and such a campaign would inevitably require air support. To meet this need without shifting the B–17s and other bombers from their most rewarding targets, the Air War Plans Division proposed creating a force of light bombers, attack aircraft, and dive bombers to support the ground forces.

Although some General Staff officers considered strategic bombing, as set forth in AWPD/1, to be an unproven theory and possibly dangerous because it might interfere with the modernization and expansion of the ground forces, General Marshall decided the plan had merit. He therefore sent it out of channels to Secretary of War Stimson, a recent convert to air power, who endorsed its views. Circumstances, however, prevented the plan from reaching the President's desk. Shortly before the Chief Executive was to have an explanation of AWPD/1 and the aerial strategy behind it, the United States entered the war. By the end of December 1941, an Anglo-American conference at Washington had accepted the spirit of the plan, even though it lacked President Roosevelt's formal endorsement, largely because aerial bombardment was the only means of carrying the war to Germany.

With the increasing importance of air power in a war against Hitler's Germany, General Arnold, as head of the Army Air Forces, rapidly became the voice of American air power in dealings with the British, functioning as the American counterpart of the Chief of the Air Staff, Royal Air Force, even though the American air arm was not yet independent and its chief was a subordinate of the Army Chief of Staff. Arnold's unique status enabled him to become a member of the wartime Combined Chiefs of Staff, the Anglo-American agency that provided strategic advice to President Roosevelt and Prime Minister

President Roosevelt and Prime Minister Churchill on the deck of the HMS *Prince of Wales* at Argentia, Newfoundland, in August 1941. General Arnold is at the far left, and General Marshall is at the right behind Churchill.

Churchill. Arnold's place among the Combined Chiefs resulted from Marshall's belief in him and in the effectiveness of military aviation, as well as from the presence of a representative of the independent Royal Air Force. Because of Arnold's work with the Allied war council, when President Roosevelt in 1942 organized the Joint Chiefs of Staff to replace the Joint Army and Navy Board, the Commanding General of the Army Air Forces became a member, even though he was not, in the strict sense of the term, a chief of staff. His colleagues on the Joint Chiefs were Marshall, the Army Chief of Staff and Arnold's nominal superior; Adm. Ernest J. King, Commander in Chief, U.S. Fleet (and later Chief of Naval Operations as well); and Adm. William D. Leahy, Chief of Staff to the President.

Arnold's transformation from Chief of the Army Air Forces to a peer of the Army Chief of Staff and Commander in Chief of the U.S. Fleet essentially began at a meeting of the Anglo-American political and military leadership at Argentia, Newfoundland, in August 1941. There, President Roosevelt and Prime Minister Churchill conferred with their principal military advisers, covering the concepts discussed earlier in the year at Washington by the group of Anglo-American planners that had included Colonel McNarney. The British outlined possible actions, such as driving the Germans and Italians from North Africa, in the event America became their ally; but the Americans carefully avoided making any clear-cut military commitment. Given the armament and state of training of the U.S. Army and the Army Air Forces, Roosevelt's planners concluded that the United States could best help the British at this time by remaining a nonbelligerent and providing aircraft and other war materials. During the conference, Churchill referred to the new hard-hitting armored formations he hoped to employ in defeating the Germans. The British armed forces were attempting to apply lessons learned from Germany's earlier conquests. So, too, was the United States Army, which tried to imitate the *blitzkrieg* tactics foreshadowed in Poland and France, but not really perfected until the invasion of the Soviet Union.

The effort to keep pace with German tactical development included the issuance on April 15, 1940, of a new War Department field manual, FM 1–5, *Employment of Aviation of the Army*. The work of a board of air and ground officers headed by General Arnold, the publication covered a broad spectrum of air operations, declaring that strategic bombing could "deprive the enemy of essential war materiel" but also setting forth principles for tactical operations. When supporting ground forces, for example, aviation was most effective against the enemy's "rear areas"; troops on the battlefield presented a less profitable target, especially if dispersed or entrenched. The manual stated that, in general, control of aircraft supporting ground operations was to be centralized in the headquarters of the theater commander under an airman who advised the commander on the use of air power. If he believed it necessary, the theater commander could dedicate or attach aviation units to subordinate ground commanders, who would assign them missions. In brief, the manual endorsed strategic bombing, acknowledged that centralized control under an airman would increase efficiency, but left ground-oriented commanders ultimately responsible for employing Army aviation.

In an attempt to learn from recent German experience, the Army experimented, especially in the Louisiana and North Carolina maneuvers of 1941, with the use of aviation in cooperation with artillery, infantry, and armor. The maneuvers might conceivably have clarified the relationship of airmen to ground commanders, whether subordinates taking orders or equals collaborating on an agreed course of action, but the lack of aircraft and suitable radios prevented a real test of the precepts in FM 1–5. The greatest benefit of the maneuvers proved to be the opportunity for a number of relatively junior officers to gain the experience with large units that paid off when they became wartime commanders or senior staff officers.

German success also inspired a series of precautionary moves by air units to safeguard the Western Hemisphere and the supply lines to Great Britain and the

Bell P–39 Kingcobras, marked with the Soviet red star,
wait at Nome Air Base, Alaska, for ferrying to Europe.

Soviet Union. The units assigned to protect the Panama Canal and its approaches formed the Caribbean Air Force (later the Sixth Air Force), which, following an exchange of base rights for old American destroyers, began establishing airfields on the British possessions of Jamaica, Antigua, St. Lucia,
Guiana, and the Bahamas. In Alaska, preparations were less extensive, partly a
result of the inhospitable climate. The recently established Air Field Forces,
Alaska Defense Command (precursor of the Eleventh Air Force) possessed a
handful of fighters and twin-engine bombers, most based near Anchorage. Work
had begun on several new airfields, including those which would prove useful
to deliver lend-lease aircraft for the Soviet Union to use against Hitler's forces.

To help protect the Atlantic sealanes that were necessary for Great Britain's
survival, the Army sent a squadron of P–40s to Iceland, which had agreed in
July 1941 to allow American marines to relieve the British occupation force.
The fighters arrived on board the aircraft carrier USS *Wasp* in August. In addition, a few bombers flew maritime reconnaissance missions from Gander Lake,
Newfoundland, searching the North Atlantic for German U–boats prowling restricted waters and for survivors from torpedoed ships. The principal activity in
this region dealt, however, with the development of the air bases, weather stations, and communications facilities that would enable American-built bombers
to reach the United Kingdom.

Although construction of the Greenland air bases had not yet begun in the
summer of 1941, bombers manufactured in the United States began flying the
Atlantic from Gander to Prestwick, Scotland, in 1940. However, until the pas-

193

sage of the Lend-Lease Act, a "cash-and-carry" policy governed military sales, and British crews had to pick up aircraft at the factories. Late in May 1941, President Roosevelt directed Secretary of War Stimson to "take full responsibility for delivering other than PBYs [naval patrol planes] to the point of ultimate takeoff."[6] As a result, Army Air Forces crews began flying the planes from the place of manufacture to terminals where British airmen or American civilians took over for the transatlantic flight.

This change in policy served as the charter for the Army Air Forces Ferrying Command, which specialized in the delivery of aircraft. The new organization, forerunner of the wartime Air Transport Command, soon broadened its activity to include an airline that carried diplomatic mail and official passengers between the United States and Great Britain. Before 1941 ended, two Ferrying Command B–24s, their bomb bays converted into passenger compartments, flew an American mission headed by W. Averell Harriman, financier and diplomat, to Moscow via Newfoundland and Scotland. One of the aircraft returned by crossing Africa and the South Atlantic; the other, piloted by Maj. Alva L. Harvey, continued around the world, arriving in the United States by way of Australia.

The ferry route across the North Atlantic could not have functioned without accurate weather forecasting and reliable communications. Beginning with a station at Gander Lake in March 1941, elements of the Army's Airways Communications System soon bounded across the ocean, establishing control centers and navigational aids in Labrador, Greenland, Iceland, and finally the United Kingdom. The Army Air Forces also called on its weather service, which employed some fifty persons along the route, to gather and interpret data and sometimes to fly long-range weather observation missions. British and Canadian meteorologists, along with Danish meteorologists serving in Greenland and Iceland, gave the North Atlantic operation an international character.

Besides using the northerly route across the Atlantic, which the British nicknamed the Arnold Line in honor of the Chief of the Army Air Forces, passengers and lend-lease aircraft or other war materiel might travel from the United States to Natal, Brazil, span the Atlantic to the west coast of Africa, and cross that continent to the Sudan. The South Atlantic route, pioneered by Pan American Airways, had barely commenced operation when the United States entered the war. In November 1941, following a variant of the South Atlantic line, the Ferrying Command initiated service to Cairo and surveyed a further extension to Basra on the Persian Gulf.

Europe was not the only area of conflict in the late 1930s and early 1940s. In the Far East, Japan was engaged in its own campaign of expansion in China and Southeast Asia. American planners were well aware of the danger in the Far East, but they remained committed to the view that Germany was the more immediate and dangerous threat and that sustaining the resistance of Great Britain was key to victory over Germany and, in the long run, Japan as well. This view was aptly summarized in Adm. Harold R. Stark's aphorism that "if Britain wins decisively against Germany we could win everywhere; but that if she loses . . . while we may not lose everywhere, we might, possibly, not *win* anywhere." American eyes were fixed on Hitler in 1940 and 1941, and justifiably so, but the threat from Japan was not ignored.[7]

The Japanese were trapped in circumstances that made war with the United States an increasingly attractive gamble. Japan was committed to the subjugation of China, not necessarily occupying that vast country but eliminating effective resistance and exerting economic domination. The continuing war in China, even as it promised economic rewards, consumed scarce resources and forced Japan to look elsewhere for replenishment. The fall of France enabled Japan to employ political pressure on the French colony of Indochina, obtaining rice, coal, and rubber to sustain the fighting in China and acquiring access to ports and airfields. Whereas Hitler scored victories of sobering magnitude, the Japanese nibbled away at China and Indochina, occasionally killing Americans, as in the sinking of the gunboat *Panay* in 1937. Even though Japan always offered suitable apologies and expressed a desire for peace, the gradual southward expansion of the Japanese empire continued until, during July 1941, the economic exploitation of Indochina gave way to armed occupation. The Roosevelt administration reacted by imposing a freeze on Japanese assets in the United States, a course of action that Great Britain and the Dutch government-in-exile adopted. The impounding of funds prevented Japan from purchasing oil from the United States or from the Dutch colonies, and only such distant sources as Latin America and the Middle East seemed likely vendors of fuel for the war in China. In contrast, the oil of the poorly defended Netherlands East Indies lay near at hand, although any move in that direction would require the neutralization or conquest of the Philippines. That, in turn, could be assured only by the defeat of the American Pacific Fleet, which Roosevelt had shifted during 1940 from San Pedro, California, to Pearl Harbor, Hawaii, to deter Japanese aggression in the western Pacific. Instead of

Pearl Harbor, Hawaii, before the war. The white bouys
at right center mark the battleship anchorage.

195

discouraging Japanese ambitions, the freeze of funds and resulting embargo on the sale of oil convinced the more militant of Japanese leaders that war with the United States was all but inevitable.

Located on the flank of a Japanese line of advance that seemed directed toward Malaya and the oil fields of the Netherlands East Indies, the Philippine Islands were in mortal peril. Since the initiative lay with Japan, the United States tried to make the best possible use of whatever time remained. "Due to the situation in the Far East," Secretary of War Stimson recommended, "all practical steps should be taken to increase the defensive strength of the Philippines."[8] In carrying out Stimson's proposal, the Army Air Forces now reinforced the Philippines, while at the same time contributing to the defense of the Western Hemisphere and helping the British. "Early in 1941," General Arnold recalled, "the over-all policy on war defenses in the Pacific was fundamentally changed." Under the previous policy, "troops in the Philippines would hold out as long as they could on their own," but it seemed possible in mid-1941 that the islands "would not only be defended but reinforced."[9] Transfers of men and equipment to the islands had to be weighed, however, against needs elsewhere, for the new policy sought to discourage Japanese aggression without causing serious disruption of American actions directed toward Europe.

Contributing to the decision to reinforce the islands was the apparent progress made by General MacArthur, the retired Army Chief of Staff, in creating a Philippine military establishment. The general believed that by 1946, when the commonwealth was scheduled to become independent of the United States, it would be strong enough to oppose successfully "any conceivable expeditionary force."[10] A key element in this future array would be 100 fast bombers, able to cooperate with a flotilla of torpedo boats in opposing any invasion armada. MacArthur had 100 trained pilots but only some 40 obsolete aircraft for them to fly. In July 1941, the War Department sought to build on the foundation MacArthur had prepared by recalling him to active duty and placing him in command of the newly created U.S. Army Forces in the Far East, mobilizing the Philippine Army, and strengthening the American contingent in the islands. MacArthur's air element—initially called Air Forces, U.S. Army Forces in the Far East, and commanded by Brig. Gen. Henry B. Clagett—underwent a change of name and commander, in November 1941 becoming the Far East Air Forces under Maj. Gen. Lewis H. Brereton.

Critical to the defense of the Philippines, and the British and Dutch possessions as well, was the B–17. Indeed, the confidence shown by American airmen in the Flying Fortress, which the Royal Air Force had found so disappointing in Europe, helped persuade the War Department that the islands could be defended. Secretary Stimson maintained that a force of these bombers could form a cheap and effective deterrent to Japanese aggression in the region, a means by which the Philippines might become a "self-sustaining fortress capable of blockading the China Sea by air power."[11] The hope also existed that, if the United States

Clark Field, Philippines, in 1939.

should go to war with Japan, the Soviet Union would permit American bombers to shuttle between Luzon and Vladivostok, attacking the Japanese home islands en route. No such agreement was forthcoming, however, from a nation reeling from the German onslaught and unwilling to risk a two-front war by antagonizing Japan.

With a ferry range in excess of 2,000 miles, the B–17 could fly to the Philippines and avoid the risk of travel by freighter through the Japanese Bonin group or the Carolines, Palaus, Marshalls, and Marianas—the former German colonies entrusted to Japan after World War I. On September 5, 1941, nine B–17Ds of the 14th Bombardment Squadron, led by Maj. Emmett O'Donnell, Jr., took off from Hickam Field, Hawaii, bound for Clark Field, near Manila. En route the planes landed at Midway Island, Wake Island, Port Moresby in New Guinea, and Darwin, Australia. The Wake Island-Port Moresby leg crossed the Japanese-controlled Caroline Islands, so the crews maintained radio silence, flying by night at 26,000 feet, an altitude believed beyond reach of Japan's fighters. During the final segment, Darwin to Clark Field, the weather turned bad, but the squadron reached its destination on September 12, Philippine time, landing safely in a driving rain. Another 26 B–17s, led by Lt. Col. Eugene Eubank, arrived in November to add to the striking power of Far East Air Forces. Meanwhile, to avoid flights over the Japanese-ruled islands, construction began on a South Pacific route from Hawaii to Christmas Island, Canton Island, Nandi in the Fiji group, Noumea on New Caledonia, and Townsville, Australia.

To protect the deterrent force of B–17s gathering in the Philippines, the War Department built up the defensive elements of the Far East Air Forces. By December 1, General Brereton had about 100 P–40s, plus 68 obsolete Seversky P–35As and Boeing P–26As. A radar site at Iba Field and a web of ground observers fed information by telephone and telegraph to an interceptor command at nearby Nielson Field, which could launch fighters from any of the six airfields in the vicinity of Manila. The B–17s might derive further protection by operating from airstrips beyond the range of Japanese bombers based on Formosa (now Taiwan). Taking off from grass runways at Del Monte on the island of Mindanao, the Flying Fortresses could stage through Clark Field to attack an invasion fleet.

Late in 1940, the War Department also began dispatching modern fighters to Pearl Harbor, where the Pacific Fleet stood by to discourage Japan's southward expansion. The principal mission of the Hawaiian Air Forces, commanded since November 1940 by Maj. Gen. Frederick L. Martin, was to protect the Pearl Harbor naval base, and shortly after General Martin's arrival, Navy aircraft carriers began delivering P–36s and P–40s, so that by December 1941 the Hawaiian Air Forces had ninety-nine P–40s, along with thirty-nine of the older P–36s and fourteen of the obsolete P–26s. In addition, a small contingent of bombers operated from the island of Oahu—thirty-three obsolete B–18s, twelve modern Douglas A–20A attack aircraft, but only twelve B–17D heavy bombers. Unfortunately, reinforcement of the Philippines absorbed B–17s that might otherwise have strengthened the defenses of Pearl Harbor.

Despite the arrival of the new fighters, General Martin had two concerns, dispersal and reconnaissance, that defied solution. The shortage of available land frustrated his plan to disperse the aircraft on small airstrips throughout the

Hickam Field, Hawaii, 1940.

Hawaiian chain. A lack of long-range bombers or patrol craft prevented the execution of a joint search plan drawn up in collaboration with the naval air command. Based on the assumption that the "most likely and dangerous form of attack on Oahu would be an air attack," the plan called for "daily patrols as far seaward as possible through 360 degrees," a task that could not be carried out, except briefly during an emergency, with the aircraft available.[12] Thus far Hawaii's defenders perceived no immediate danger, save possibly from sabotage. Ironically, an alert against sabotage caused the Army to concentrate its aircraft at the main bases and park them together to ease the task of guarding them, instead of dispersing them and building revetments to reduce the danger from air attack. In focusing on thwarting saboteurs, however, the garrison became preoccupied with an insignificant threat. The real danger would come from the skies, for Japan had already decided to launch a carrier attack against Pearl Harbor if the Americans made no concessions by the deadline that Japan had set.

The Japanese carrier task force approaching Hawaii hoped to deliver a strategic blow that would destroy the ability of the United States to wage war in the Pacific until Japan had carved out an empire rich in the natural resources needed for modern warfare and created an impenetrable defensive perimeter to protect it. Without the Pacific Fleet, the American armed forces could neither reinforce the distant outposts of Guam, Wake, or the Philippines nor frustrate Japanese plans to seize the oil and other raw materials of the Netherlands East Indies (now Indonesia) and Malaya (now a part of Malaysia). Because of the vast distances of the Pacific, Japan used aircraft carriers to bring short-range bombers, fighters, and torpedo planes within striking distance of the target. For the Japanese, such an operation represented a desperate gamble: the carriers might be detected before launching their aircraft, damage to the American fleet might prove superficial, and the United States had the resources and manpower to recover from even a successful strike. Already gathering momentum to supply the needs of Great Britain, the Soviet Union, and China, the American industrial juggernaut had the potential strength to overwhelm Japan before the riches of the conquered territory could be exploited. But the Japanese succumbed to arguments of necessity—with oil imports restricted, Japan would never be stronger, only weaker—or to beliefs in racial or national superiority, which held that the Americans as a people lacked the courage to accept the loss of life necessary to break through Japan's outer defenses.

During this period of heightening tension, American cryptanalysts were decoding Japanese diplomatic messages and charting the breakdown of peaceful relations between the two countries; and this intelligence, called Magic, provided evidence of the increased likelihood of war. Because the Japanese might attack the Philippines, Malaya, the Netherlands East Indies, or possibly the Soviet Union, already at war with Germany, the fighting could erupt almost anywhere in the Pacific. The distribution of Magic information was poorly coordinated—messages that might have sounded alarms in Hawaii failed to reach commanders there and warnings that did arrive were not shared between the Army and Navy. One of the best informed of American officials, Secretary of War Stimson, later acknowledged that, although not completely surprised by the attack, he had been worried that Japanese aggression would most likely take place in the Southwest Pacific but was astonished "at the Japanese choice of the greatest American base as a point of attack."[13] The strike force destined for Hawaii steamed undetected toward its objective.

Despite its advantage in industrial potential, the United States in December 1941 remained unprepared to fight an air war against the Axis powers. Of some 12,000 aircraft of all types, the Army Air Forces had sent just 913 combat models overseas—636 pursuits, 61 B–17s and B–24s, 157 medium bombers, and 59 light bombers. This total included some 300 warplanes based in the Philippines or en route there, another 200 in Hawaii, fewer than 40 in Alaska, and almost 250 in the vicinity of the Panama Canal, with the rest divided among Iceland, Greenland, and Newfoundland. Although American planners accepted the premise that Germany would be the main enemy if the United States went to war, not one Army bomber was based within range of any German city. The Japanese homeland lay beyond the range of American bombers based in the Philippines, neither suitable aircraft nor airfields existed in China for attacking Japan, and the Soviet Union remained deaf to requests for the use of bases near Vladivostok. The American forces already mobilized, trained, and deployed overseas merely foreshadowed the nation's vast resources in manpower, industrial capacity, and raw materials. It would take many months of herculean effort and bitter experience before the United States could organize, equip, train, and employ an air force that could carry out its myriad missions and meet the Axis air forces on equal terms.

Chapter 7

The Army Air Forces in Desperate Battle, 1941-1942

Bernard C. Nalty

War came suddenly to the Pacific. At 7:55 on Sunday morning, December 7, 1941, the first wave of carrier-based Japanese aircraft attacked the Pearl Harbor Naval Base and other military installations on the island of Oahu, including Wheeler and Hickam Fields. Three of the six mobile radars on the island had been operating that morning, but two shut down as scheduled fifty-five minutes before the attack. At the remaining site, two Army operators, practicing after the normal surveillance period, detected a large formation of aircraft approaching Oahu. However, the only officer still on duty at the information center that interpreted radar sightings concluded that they were either Navy aircraft returning from American carriers at sea or the B–17s that Maj. Gen. Henry H. Arnold, Chief of the Army Air Forces, had seen off from California the previous night.

At Wheeler Field the commanding officer, Col. William J. Flood, had completed a hundred earthen revetments for his fighters, but because of an alert against possible sabotage by Japanese living in Hawaii, the airplanes were lined up in the open, wingtip-to-wingtip, when the enemy struck. The strafing fighters roared past so low that Flood claimed he could see the pilots smiling as they destroyed the American aircraft. Officers and enlisted men tried to push the least damaged of the P–36s and P–40s into the revetments before exploding gasoline tanks turned the entire apron into a sea of flame. Few of the fighters could be saved; Wheeler Field, Flood said later, was "a pitiful, unholy mess."[1]

The second wave of attackers, which arrived not quite an hour after the first, encountered aerial opposition from a few Army fighter pilots. These included 2d. Lt. George S. Welch, who, with five other pilots of the 47th Pursuit Squadron, drove to the auxiliary airstrip where their fighters were parked, took off, and climbed into a melee in which friendly antiaircraft fire proved almost as dangerous as Japanese aircraft. Welch, flying a P–40, shot down four of the enemy, 2d. Lt. Kenneth A. Taylor got two more, and P–36 pilots from Wheeler Field reported two other victims.

The B–17s en route from Hamilton Field to the Philippines flew into the midst of the air battle. The twelve aircraft—two of the original fourteen had turned back early in the flight—carried no ammunition; the weight saved had been invested in extra gasoline. To compensate for the additional fuel stored aft of the center or gravity, the armor had been removed from the crew positions and placed, along with the guns, forward in the fuselage, leaving the planes utterly defenseless. Despite enemy fighters, friendly antiaircraft fire, and fatigue caused by the long flight, all the Flying Fortresses landed, one on a golf course, and only one was damaged beyond repair.

Within three hours after the first bombs fell on Pearl Harbor, the Japanese had sunk or badly damaged eight battleships of the Pacific Fleet and ten lesser ships. Intended as a deterrent to war, the naval concentration instead attracted the Japanese, who killed 2,335 American servicemen and wounded 1,143 at the cost of 29 aircraft and their crews. The Hawaiian Air Force had more than a third of its aircraft destroyed and others sustained damage in varying degrees, leaving about 80 airplanes in flyable condition. The death toll among General Martin's airmen exceeded 200 with more than 300 wounded. Although surprised and battered, the Americans had fought back. Sailors and soldiers fired at the Japanese with everything from .45 caliber pistols to 5-inch guns. Pilots like Welch and Taylor had knifed into the milling enemy aircraft; and amid the destruction at Hickam Field, General Martin, bleeding internally from an ulcer, was planning how his surviving airplanes might locate and attack the Japanese.

Word of the raid on Pearl Harbor had already reached Washington when Japanese emissaries delivered a note severing diplomatic relations. On December 8, the United States declared war on Japan; three days later, both Germany and Italy entered the conflict as allies of the Japanese. The United States would fight the kind of war envisioned in Rainbow 5, as a partner in a coalition arrayed against the three Axis powers—Germany, Japan, and Italy—with the defeat of Germany taking precedence. For the present, however, victory remained a distant goal. The American losses at Pearl Harbor cleared the way

Wheeler Field, Hawaii, after the Japanese attack.

for the limited expansion that Japan desired, and the dramatic suddenness of the attack made even the West Coast of the United States seem vulnerable. At the same time, German submarines preyed on shipping along the East Coast and revived concern for the security of the Panama Canal.

Instead of launching the kind of offensive operations described in AWPD/1, the Army Air Forces found itself fighting a series of desperate defensive actions. It had no usable airfields within striking distance of Japan and did not yet have the crews and aircraft to take advantage of the British bases within range of Germany and Italy. The authors of AWPD/1 had concluded that an interim force of 3,800 bombers—859 B–26s or B–25s, 1,600 B–29s or B–32s, and the rest B–17s or B–24s—would be needed to carry the war into Germany, while the Army Air Forces obtained and deployed the 6,800 bombers believed necessary to defeat Hitler. To wage a worldwide war against the Axis, the air arm had just 332 B–25s and B–26s on hand at the end of December 1941 and added only another 1,500 in all of 1942. The total number of B–17s and B–24s available on December 31, 1941 amounted to a mere 287, although an additional 1,900 were on hand a year later. Moreover, the prototypes of the B–29 and the B–32 did not fly until the summer of 1942. Aircraft production was increasing, but to assemble in Europe and North Africa a force of 6,800 or even 3,800 bombers for the defeat of Germany remained beyond the capacity of the air arm when the first year of fighting ended. The need for bombers to harry the advancing Japanese, patrol the sealanes, and complete the crew training necessary for sustained and effective aerial warfare further complicated the systematic concentration of air power against Germany.

The War Department moved swiftly to reinforce the Hawaiian Islands, the Air Forces sending 46 B–17s in the weeks following the Japanese attack. Although Gen. George C. Marshall, the Army Chief of Staff, and Adm. Harold R. Stark, the Chief of Naval Operations, agreed that the Navy should assume command over long-range reconnaissance from the islands, the Hawaiian Air Force (redesignated the Seventh Air Force in March 1942) retained 18 of the bombers as a strike force to attack any Japanese task force that the reconnaissance craft might locate. The danger of a Japanese invasion of the islands seemed to have passed by the end of December, however, making men and materiel earmarked for the defense of Hawaii available to protect the supply line to Australia; and the urgency that had characterized the earlier reinforcement of the islands abated. Supposedly committed to maintaining a force of 96 heavy bombers in Hawaii, the War Department dragged its feet, apparently out of concern that the aircraft would be used exclusively for long-range reconnaissance. Not until the spring of 1942, when American intelligence detected a threat to Midway Island, some 1,100 nautical miles northwest of Hawaii, did any appreciable number of heavy bombers arrive in the region.

During the early months of 1942, the West Coast of the United States seemed even more vulnerable than Hawaii to a sudden Japanese raid. Erroneous reports of warships off California and recurring false radar sightings contributed to the uneasiness. Then, on the night of February 23, 1942, a Japanese submarine shelled an oil refinery near Santa Barbara, California. Concerned that the shelling was intended to divert attention from some more dangerous attack, the local commander held most of his aircraft in reserve and dispatched only three Army bombers, which conducted a search but failed to locate the submarine. Early on the morning of February 25, when radar indicated aircraft approaching Los Angeles, a blackout went into effect and, although no interceptors took off, searchlights and bursting shells illuminated the skies over the city, as antiaircraft batteries fired some 1,400 rounds. Rumors of flaming Japanese bombers crashing into the city proved groundless; the only damage was self-inflicted: shell fragments punctured roofs, traffic accidents occurred in the blacked-out streets, and the excitement contributed to at least one fatal heart attack. A subsequent investigation indicated that weather balloons released in the city and picked up by radar had caused the panic.

Despite the fierce barrage thrown up to meet the phantom raiders during this so-called Battle of Los Angeles, the defenses of the West Coast were extremely porous. When Arnold left March Field, California, for Washington, D.C., on the afternoon of December 7, he made sure that the squadrons based in the area were on wartime alert; indeed, he could do little else until he returned to his desk and began shifting reinforcements westward. In the days immediately after the attack on Pearl Harbor, the bases defending California, Oregon, and Washington had only 14 B–17s (intended for the Philippines), some 75 medium bombers, and 45 pursuits. Arnold concluded that the greatest immediate need was for fighters, and within three weeks, he sent an entire group of P–38s from Selfridge Field, Michigan. The buildup continued, and by the spring of 1942, more than 400 fighters and almost 300 bombers operated from airfields on the Pacific Coast.

Not only were aircraft scarce on the Pacific seaboard during the early months of the war, radar coverage of the region was inadequate, as demonstrated by the false alarm that triggered the barrage over Los Angeles. At the time of the Pearl Harbor attack, the radar network functioning on the West Coast consisted of just ten sites. Robert Watson-Watt, a British expert on radar, arrived in the United States to study the nation's air defenses and found grave flaws in the coverage of the Pacific approaches. Some senior commanders, he reported, did not understand the value or the limitations of radar, either rejecting it as a gimmick or embracing it as the universal solution to all problems of defense. Furthermore, the coastline was long and difficult to cover, especially since no aircraft as yet carried radar capable of detecting ships on the surface of the sea. The equipment seemed crude by British standards and the operators inexperienced. The radar network on the East Coast shared these basic shortcomings, but both would improve.

The threat of aerial attack rapidly abated on both coasts; although in the fall of 1942, the Japanese submarine *I–25* twice launched a small float plane to drop incendiary bombs in the forests of Oregon, but setting just one insignificant fire. The occasional attack by Japanese submarines on coastal shipping, scarcely comparable to the far deadlier German U–boat campaign, required only a few medium bombers. Ironically, in view of the hurried defensive measures following the attack on Pearl Harbor, the only Japanese aerial threat to the continental United States came in the last year of the war, well after training had replaced air defense as the principal concern at the Army airfields in the western United States. Between November of 1944 and May 1945, more than 9,000 hydrogen-filled paper balloons soared aloft from Honshu in Japan's home islands. The prevailing winds carried the balloons eastward to release high explosive or incendiary devices over American territory, but the offensive accomplished little. Of 285 balloons known to have reached the United States, most deposited their bombs in remote areas along the West Coast, though a few penetrated as far east as Nebraska, Iowa, and even Michigan. The only known casualties were six picnickers killed when they accidentally detonated a bomb that had landed near Bly, Oregon.

Germany's declaration of war brought the same sort of confusion and hectic reinforcement to the East Coast that the attack on Pearl Harbor caused on the West Coast. Arnold reinforced the air defenses on the Atlantic seaboard, although not to the extent that he did along the shores of the Pacific. Germany had no carrier task forces, but the danger existed, though laughably remote in retrospect, that German bombers might fly suicide missions across the ocean, light planes mount raids from submarines, or the pro-Nazi French colonial officials send the aircraft carrier *Bearn*, anchored at Martinique, to launch its complement of American-built dive bombers against the cities of the eastern United States. Since the spring of 1941, the armed forces tried, with increasing urgency, to create an air defense system along the Atlantic. By the time the nation went to war, the plotting rooms were ready, a few fighters stood by at airfields in the coastal states, and the first of several thousand spotters, mostly civilians, had received training and taken their places at observation posts. Although the entire system had undergone a few not very realistic exercises, it lacked two key elements: a radar warning net and a mechanism for coordinating antiaircraft batteries with intercepting fighters. Fortunately, thirteen radar sites stood took ready for occupancy when the war began, and within a month twenty-seven sets swept the skies along the coast.

As it began to take shape, the warning network produced an occasional false alarm. On December 9, for instance, P–40s took off from Mitchel Field to intercept raiders reportedly headed for New York City, and the schools there sent children home to find shelter from nonexistent bombs. Because air raid sirens had not yet been installed, most New Yorkers remained unaware of the supposed danger and no panic ensued. Over the months, the threat of aerial attack failed to materialize, and the emphasis had shifted by 1943 from defense to training for combat overseas.

After learning of the Japanese attack on Pearl Harbor, Lt. Gen. Frank M. Andrews, the former chief of the GHQ Air Force and now the commanding general of the Caribbean Defense Command in Panama, alerted his forces and dispatched reconnaissance aircraft, then demonstrated both confidence in his troops and calmness in the midst of crisis by making sure that he was seen attending a motion picture on the first night of the war. On December 10, Andrews shifted twenty-five P–40s from Puerto Rico to Panama, and another eighty fighters arrived in the Canal Zone by the end of the month. The activation of additional radar sites contributed to the effectiveness of the planes, which were dispersed and camouflaged at the airfields on the isthmus. Mistaken reports of approaching Japanese ships caused momentary alarm, but no attack took place. Indeed, the only major action in the Caribbean area not involving submarines occurred in Puerto Rico, when a merchant ship unaware of the outbreak of war approached the island. The vessel's unannounced appearance—its radio was dead—and the accidental discharge of a rifle ashore convinced local authorities that the enemy was invading. Army planes took off from Borinquen Field and strafed what they thought were landing craft in the adjacent bay, and shore gunners also engaged the nonexistent assault force.

Unity of command had been a problem in Panama, where the same division of authority that contributed to the Pearl Harbor disaster prevailed on the eve of war. In the autumn of 1941, General Marshall had resolved to establish a command responsible for the overall defense of the Panama Canal and its ap-

206

proaches. Because aviation figured so prominently in plans to locate and destroy an attacker, the Army Chief of Staff wanted General Andrews, in whom he had special confidence, to take charge. The Navy did not agree, however, and the local naval district remained independent of the Army's Panama Department, with the commanders of the two organizations coordinating their defensive activity.

After the attack on Pearl Harbor revealed the inadequacy of such an arrangement, Secretary of War Stimson raised the issue at a cabinet meeting, and President Roosevelt promptly agreed that greater unity of command was necessary for the security of the canal. Taking a map of the existing Caribbean Com-mand, the Chief Executive wrote "Army" over the Panama sector and "Navy" over the outer perimeter that stretched from Cuba through the West Indies.[2] As a result of the President's decision, General Andrews, as commander of the Caribbean Command, exercised unified command over the Canal Zone, its western approaches, and the waters immediately to the east, while the Navy provided a commander for all forces in Jamaica and beyond.

Whether in the Caribbean, on the Gulf Coast, or along the Atlantic seaboard, German submarines posed a deadly threat, at times sinking tankers or merchantmen within sight of shore. Essential though it was, the campaign against the U–boat bore no resemblance to the prewar interception of the *Rex*, a passenger liner that followed a prescribed course and schedule, or the attacks on surface warships that proponents of the GHQ Air Force had envisioned when they spoke in the mid-1930s of aerial coast defense. Rarely surfacing during daylight except to increase speed or recharge their batteries in an emergency, the submarines were essentially invisible given the technology of early 1942. All that the airmen knew for sure was that the raiders would try to attack individual ships or convoys in the shipping lanes used by merchant vessels. Until depth charges and radar became available, aircrews had to search the seas with binoculars while flying B–17s, B–18s, and even A–20s that carried general purpose bombs.

Initially the Army aircraft flew routine patrols in areas of U–boat activity, sometimes passing over a sector and then doubling back in the hope of catch-

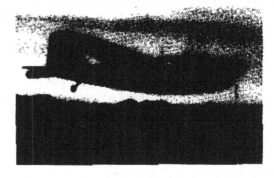

Douglas B–18 equipped with magnetic anomaly detection equipment in the tail for locating submarines.

ing any unwary captain who might have surfaced after the bomber passed. Beginning in May 1942, aircraft joined antisubmarine vessels in escorting coastal convoys. The Navy's long-range patrol bombers proved better suited than Army bombers for this role because of their lower cruising speed and greater endurance. Antisubmarine missions, whether escort or patrol, sank few U–boats, but the aircraft harassed the enemy, forcing the boats to remain underwater during the day and, after the introduction and widespread use of airborne radar, to dive frequently at night also. When submerged, submarines traveled on battery power, which reduced speed, range, and the probability of finding and attacking Allied ships. Running beneath the sea added to the discomfort of the crews, whose members by the end of a cruise were scraping a layer of mold from their bread and even the canned goods seemed to smell and taste of diesel oil. Although actual sinkings were rare, the unceasing threat of aerial attack reduced the effectiveness of the submarines.

During the critical spring of 1942, Army airmen fighting the war against German submarines operated under Navy control, receiving their assignments from the commanders of the Gulf, Eastern, or Caribbean Sea Frontiers. The arrangement proved awkward, however, for the naval staffs often were uncertain about the availability of Army Air Forces units, the training of the crews, or the condition of the aircraft. At last, in the spring of 1943, Adm. Ernest J. King, reorganized the war against German submarines. King, who had become Commander in Chief, U.S. Fleet, in December 1941 and succeeded Stark as Chief of Naval Operations in March 1942, persuaded the Joint Chiefs of Staff to establish the Tenth Fleet, a command post located in the Navy Department that exercised centralized authority over the antisubmarine campaign. Naval officers retained control over Air Forces bombers, and the Air Forces assumed clearly defined responsibility not only for providing trained squadrons but for aircraft maintenance as well. This revised arrangement lasted but a few months, for it satisfied neither Arnold, who wanted to use Air Forces bombers to attack shipyards instead of individual submarines, nor King, who not only was seeking bombers of his own but disliked dealing on equal terms with the Commanding General of the Army Air Forces, whom he regarded as at best a satellite member of the Joint Chiefs of Staff. In mid-1943, Arnold and Maj. Gen. Joseph T. McNarney fashioned an agreement with Vice Adm. John S. McCain to remove Army heavy bombers from naval control. In effect, the Air Forces diverted new, radar-equipped B–24s to the Navy in return for the squadrons flying antisubmarine missions.

Improvisation characterized the Battle of the Atlantic, especially in its early months. Civilian pilots in privately owned light planes searched the coastal waters of the United States for submarines. In the hands of the Navy, strategic bombers designed for the Army Air Forces became successful long-range patrol craft, helping drive the enemy from American shores, from the waters off Iceland and Greenland, and from the Bay of Biscay. The greatest piece of im-

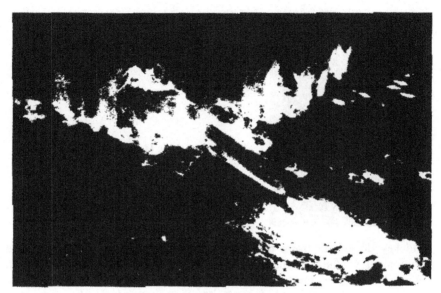

Caught on the surface, and straddled by bullets,
a German submarine dives for cover.

provisation, however, was the escort carrier, a converted merchantman that, beginning in 1943, accompanied the transatlantic convoys into the most dangerous midocean areas, providing continuous air cover throughout the passage. Antisubmarine warfare profited, moreover, from the work of cryptography analysts who helped locate the German wolf packs and discover their plan of attack.

Securing the East Coast of the United States and protecting the Atlantic sealanes were tasks included in Rainbow 5, the basic American war plan, which also called for essentially defensive operations in the Pacific, operations designed to contain Japan until the defeat of Germany. Even had the American planners decided otherwise, the disaster that befell the Pacific Fleet at Pearl Harbor would have forced the United States onto the defensive against Japan. American forces in the Pacific tried to relieve the garrison at Wake Island but turned back short of the objective; as the planners of the attack on Pearl Harbor had intended, the crippling of the Pacific Fleet cleared the way for a series of Japanese victories.

The Japanese blow to the Philippines proved as devastating to Army aviation as the attack on Pearl Harbor had been to the Navy's battleships, even though Gen. Douglas MacArthur's headquarters at Manila knew of the raid on Oahu within an hour after the bombs started falling there. Precisely what happened on the morning of December 8 on the island of Luzon, across the international date line from Hawaii, remains concealed in the fog of war: the principals have died

Maj. Gen. Lewis H. Brereton,
Commander, Far East Air Force,
November 1941–February 1942.

and key documents were destroyed during the Japanese conquest of the Philippines. On the one hand, Maj. Gen. Lewis H. Brereton, the air commander, insisted that he recommended an immediate strike against the airfields on Formosa (now Taiwan) with the 18 B–17s at Clark Field, warning at the time that the bombers could be destroyed unless they went into action promptly. On the other, General MacArthur and his chief of staff, Maj. Gen. Richard K. Sutherland, denied that Brereton made any such request. In fact, both went further: MacArthur, five years after the fact, argued that an attack on Formosa would have been suicidal and Sutherland claimed that the bombers should not have been at Clark Field but at Del Monte on the island of Mindanao, beyond the reach of the enemy. What emerges is that an attack was proposed by someone, that Brereton supported the idea even if he did not originate it, and that the operation was postponed to permit a last-minute reconnaissance to obtain aerial photographs that would supplement the inadequate charts of Formosa available to the American flyers. Also, if the attack had been delayed until the following day, some of the B–17s would have been shifted for the night to a nearby auxiliary airfield and brought back to Clark Field before dawn. Such a delay seemed likely at the time, for the bomber commander, Lt. Col. Eugene Eubank, did not receive orders for a photographic mission over Formosa until mid-morning of December 8, and by then the enemy was stirring.

Early morning fog paralyzed most of the Japanese squadrons based on Formosa, so that only a small formation of army aircraft could take off and bomb targets in the vicinity of Lingayen Gulf, some seventy-five miles north of Clark Field. The hundred-odd Japanese navy bombers scheduled to leave the ground at seven in the morning remained fog-bound until ten; and by then radio monitors on Formosa were picking up indications that Brereton was launching his bombers. The Flying Fortresses had indeed taken off, but only to avoid being caught on the ground during an attack on Clark Field. General Arnold recalled that before leaving the West Coast for Washington he had obtained access to the transpacific telephone and cautioned Brereton against allowing the enemy to catch the American aircraft parked on the tarmac and destroy them, as had happened in Hawaii. At about eight, probably in reaction to the Japanese army bombers approaching the Lingayen Gulf rather than as a consequence of a call from Arnold, the two squadrons of B–17s roared aloft to remain out of harm's way for more than two hours. While the bombers were in the air, orders reached Clark Field for an attack on Formosa, photo reconnaissance or none, and the first of the B–17s began landing at about eleven o'clock to refuel and load bombs. Unfortunately, the Clark-based fighters that had taken off earlier when the Japanese formation passed Lingayen Gulf had also landed and were refueling.

By that time, the sun had burned away the fog over Formosa, enabling the main force of enemy aircraft to take off for an attack on Clark Field. Once the formation made its landfall, observers began reporting its progress toward the Manila area. The information center at Nielson Field realized that Clark Field was among the targets and issued a warning that arrived too late to save either the fighters or the bombers. When the raiders appeared, the P–40s were preparing to take off, while the B–17s remained parked on the apron. Two waves of Japanese bombers and one of strafing fighters wiped out the Flying Fortresses on the ground at Clark Field (the sole survivor was airborne on reconnaissance), and only three of the P–40s managed to do battle, downing three or four hostile fighters. Iba Field also came under attack at this time, and there, too, the destruction was all but complete. During the first morning of the war, General Brereton's command lost roughly half its aircraft, including seventeen of thirty-five B–17s, at a cost to the Japanese of only seven fighters.

Had the prewar dispersal plan been carried out, all of the B–17s would have been based at Del Monte on Mindanao, safely out of range of the enemy on Formosa, until conditions permitted them to stage through Clark Field and take the offensive, but General Brereton had not taken this precaution. He later explained that, in anticipation of the arrival of the Flying Fortresses that had just set out from California (and encountered the Japanese over Pearl Harbor), he chose to base about half of his existing B–17s at Clark Field, which was better equipped than Del Monte and located near MacArthur's headquarters at Manila. The latest reinforcements would land at Del Monte and bring that primitive airfield to full operating capacity, accommodating two-thirds of his expanded force of B–17s. General Sutherland remembered things differently, however; he blamed Brereton for disobeying an order to concentrate the bombers on Mindanao, but no copy of such an order has survived and no disciplinary action was taken against the Air Forces officer, who later had important assignments in North Africa and Europe. In his memoir, *Global Mission*, written almost a decade after the attack on Clark Field, Arnold confessed that he had "never been able to get the real story of what happened in the Philippines."

The surviving bombers at Del Monte and elsewhere continued to fight, manned by crews and serviced by mechanics who subsisted on canned corned beef from quartermaster stores and pineapple grown on Mindanao. Until Clark Field became untenable, the B–17s staged through it, as three bombers did on December 10 to attack the Japanese invading northern Luzon. The pilot of one, Capt. Colin Kelly, became one of the first heroes of the air war against Japan. He remained at the controls of his B–17C while swarming enemy fighters shot it to pieces, sacrificing his life so that the surviving crew members could parachute from the doomed bomber. Kelly's crew erroneously received credit for sinking a battleship, but at best his bombardier, Cpl. Meyer Levin, may have scored near misses on a cruiser. A lack of training in ship identification, the combined fear and excitement of aerial combat, and utter confidence that the bomber could sink a battleship helped cause the error. Although the target probably escaped with little or no damage, Kelly's action saved the lives of six crew members; he was a hero at a time when the nation desperately needed heroes.

Abandoned as a permanent base for B–17s by the end of December, Del Monte served in January as the staging area for B–17s operating out of the Netherlands East Indies against targets in the Philippines. In April, within a month of the surrender of the American forces in the Philippines, a force of ten B–25s and three B–17s arrived at Del Monte from Port Darwin, Australia. One of the Flying Fortresses attacked Japanese-occupied Manila by night, but its bombs exploded harmlessly in the bay. The B–25s, however, were more successful in harassing Japanese coastal shipping off Mindanao; at best, this gallant mission did little more than annoy the enemy.

Although the defenders of the Philippines had adequate warning, Japanese air power had again destroyed a deterrent force, wiping out the B–17s at Clark Field as efficiently as it had crippled the battle fleet at Pearl Harbor. Before the war, one of the American fighter pilots at Clark Field had written his sister that they were doomed from the start, expecting the small air force to which he was assigned to be overwhelmed by the Japanese. He believed the islands could hold out for an indefinite period, but the defense of the Philippines lasted only six months and ended with an American surrender.

Despite the succession of victories—Pearl Harbor, Wake Island, Hong Kong, Singapore, the Philippines, and Burma—Japan was fighting a limited war in terms of resources and strategic aims, making devastating use of its available manpower and material. Critically short of oil, steel, rubber, and aluminum, Japan invested what it had in a series of bold operations designed to capture what it needed so badly. For example, by using the 48 million barrels of oil husbanded as a reserve, Japan hoped to acquire a virtually limitless supply in the Netherlands East Indies.

Japan had no aircraft capable of strategic bombing from bases on land. Even if these bombers had been available, the vastness of the Pacific would have protected the continental United States from aerial bombardment just as that same ocean now protected Japan from U.S. wrath. Unable to achieve decisive results against the American heartland, the Japanese had used the aircraft carrier to ex-

An aircraft of the Pearl Harbor attack force launches from a carrier.

tend the range of their bombers and neutralize the Pacific Fleet at a single stroke. With the American fleet out of the war, at least temporarily, carrier forces and short-range army aircraft supported the succession of operations designed to gain for Japan the foodstuffs of the Philippines, the rubber and ore of Malaya, and the oil of the Nether-lands East Indies and Burma. Having conquered all this, Japan intended to establish a defensive perimeter so strong that the United States would hammer away unsuccessfully until the American people lost heart and accepted the existence of this newly fashioned Japanese empire.

Such was the scenario of the Japanese militarists who dominated the government of Japan, breaking any political combination arrayed against them. To the most belligerent of these leaders, war with the United States entailed few risks, for they believed that the Japanese warrior spirit would prevail. This confidence reflected the combination of racism and nationalism that for a generation or more had disturbed relations between the United States and Japan. Whereas racists in the United States had considered the Japanese unfit to immigrate and incapable of being absorbed into American society, Japanese militarists staked the country's survival on a vaunted racial and national superiority. The Japanese fantasy failed to take into account American industrial capacity, which in 1941 dwarfed that of Japan; the leaders of the island nation had reduced war to a test of wills. Adm. Isoroku Yamamoto, who inspired the attack on Pearl Harbor, respected the industrial power of the United States, but he could not overcome the optimism of those who believed that Japan could defend its line of outposts until a disheartened America negotiated a peace giving the Japanese control of the oil and other essential resources they had conquered.

Just as most Japanese leaders tended to be contemptuous of the United States, many in the West were supremely confident of their own abilities and

213

armaments, certain that Japan could neither produce first-rate weapons nor use them effectively. Yet, to the surprise of the Allies, the Japanese had developed modern aircraft to carry out the strategy of limited war. British naval officers on board the *Repulse* and *Prince of Wales* in December 1941 did not realize that the enemy possessed a land-based torpedo bomber until twin-engine Mitsubishi G3M2s skimmed the surface of the South China Sea to release the deadly missiles that helped sink these warships. Nor did American airmen heed Claire Chennault's warning of a deadly new Japanese naval fighter, the Mitsubishi A6M, also called the Zero fighter because of its designation of Zero-Sen or type 0. While flying for the Chinese government, Chennault's American Volunteer Group, the Flying Tigers, encountered the fast, nimble, long-range airplane and discovered that designer Jiro Horikoshi had given it the ability to turn more tightly than any Allied aircraft. As the Flying Tigers discovered, and others soon learned, American pilots had to avoid dogfights and use their greater diving speed and overwhelming firepower to pounce on the Zero, which obtained its range and quickness by sacrificing armor, structural strength, and self-sealing fuel tanks.

When the battleship *Arizona* exploded and sank to the bottom of Pearl Harbor, Japanese flying schools produced about 2,000 pilots in a year, a total divided almost equally between the army and navy. In contrast, the U.S. Army Air Forces alone graduated some 11,000 pilots in 1941. At this time, Japan had about 2,700 modern aircraft, half with the army and half with the navy. This force was overwhelmingly superior to the few hundred planes, many obsolete, that the Allies in 1941 and 1942 could muster in the far Pacific; moreover, many Japanese pilots had honed their skills against the Chinese. As a result, Japan had a clear advantage in men and equipment at the outset. Japanese leaders, however, failed to anticipate the attrition in men and machines that war with the United States would bring and maintained production schedules and training programs geared to the desultory fighting in China, where the Japanese held the initiative, rather than to a defensive war across the breadth of the Pacific.

Japanese Mitsubishi Zero.

The Army Air Forces in Desperate Battle, 1941-1942

As Admiral Yamamoto realized, Japanese productive might did not approach that of the United States. During the last three years of peace in the Pacific, American aircraft production had increased more than quadrupled, from 6,000 units per year to more than 26,000, while Japan's annual output rose by a mere 600 aircraft to not quite 6,000. By 1944, the year of peak production for both countries, the United States turned out 96,000 airplanes, more than three times the Japanese total. The army and the Imperial Japanese Navy further hampered production by refusing to standardize aircraft components. The army, for instance, used a 24-volt electrical system throughout the war, but the navy did not follow suit until 1945. Both services developed a .50 caliber machinegun, but the two weapons used a different cartridge. The army and navy steadfastly refused to enter into joint development or production ventures, even though these would have conserved manpower, plant capacity, and scarce materials.

Ignoring the limited capacity for building aircraft and training pilots, Japan had risked its very existence in an attempt to wrest from Great Britain and the Netherlands those natural resources essential for modern warfare and then fight the United States to a standstill. For a time the gamble seemed to pay off, as the Japanese carved out an empire that embraced Malaya, the Netherlands East Indies, the Philippines, and the islands of the central Pacific. Allied propaganda in that dismal period frequently depicted Japan as an octopus, its head at the home islands and its tentacles stretching toward Alaska, Hawaii, Australia, and India. The Allies could find few sources of consolation: the gallant but unsuccessful fight for Wake Island; the tenacious defense of Luzon, where a few American and Filipino airmen—men like Boyd D. Wagner, Russell Church, and Jesus Villamor—against overwhelming odds, attacked shipping and airfields as long as their aircraft survived and then fought as infantrymen; and Burma, where Chennault's American Volunteer Group and their P–40Bs won heartening victories in the air, even though the Japanese triumphed on the ground. Wake Island surrendered in December 1941, and by mid-May the enemy had overrun

A group of P–40s flown by American volunteers under Chennault in China.

Bataan peninsula and the island fortress of Corregidor, the last two outposts on Luzon, and had driven the Allies out of Burma.

From the doomed Philippines, Brereton and Brig. Gen. Henry B. Clagett flew to Australia, where until February 1942 they were the senior airmen trying to re-organize the remnants of the Far East Air Force. Maj. Gen. George H. Brett, in China on a tour of inspection, received orders to assume command of the American forces in Australia and almost immediately was promoted to Lieutenant General. He had scarcely taken charge when he was appointed Deputy Supreme Commander of a new American-British-Dutch-Australian Command headed by a British general, Sir Archibald P. Wavell. In his capacity as Wavell's deputy, General Brett had no direct control over the employment of American troops. As a result, General Brereton, the senior American officer after Brett, temporarily became the U.S. Army commander in Australia, although he also acted as Deputy Chief of Air Staff for Wavell's command. In April 1942, after General MacArthur arrived in Australia from the Philippines and assumed command of the new Southwest Pacific Area, Brett became his air officer.

Airmen like Brett and Brereton had little to work with in trying to stop the Japanese advance. Typical of the problems they faced was the fate of the men and aircraft carried in a convoy originally bound for the Philippines but diverted to Brisbane, Australia, immediately after the attack on Pearl Harbor. The ships carried 18 P-40s; 52 crated Douglas A-24s, the Army version of the Navy's SBD dive bomber; and the 8th Materiel Squadron, which formed the ground echelon of a B-17 group under orders to proceed to the Philippines. Although trained to maintain the new B-17Es of the 7th Bombardment Group, which the outbreak of war had stranded en route to the Philippines, the materiel squadron helped assemble the fighters and dive bombers delivered by the convoy. Since the combat elements of the B-17 group were scattered from Hawaii to Java as reinforcements, the materiel squadron never rejoined its parent organization. The A-24s, moreover, were slow in getting into the fight for Java because the firing switches for the two forward-firing machineguns were missing, possibly discarded with the crates in which the aircraft had arrived. In keeping with his style of management, General Arnold personally directed the shipment of replacements for the missing solenoids, which were available only in the United States. To make assurance triply sure, he shipped 312 of the switches, three times the number needed: 104 by air across the Pacific, another 104 by transpacific sea convoy, and the final 104 by air across the south Atlantic and Africa.

Although Java-based B-17s did damage Japanese shipping anchored at Davao on the island of Mindanao, those bombers, the recently arrived A-24 dive bombers, and the fighters sent to the Netherlands East Indies were all unable to check the Japanese onslaught. In a daring, perhaps foolhardy, attempt to strengthen the Allied forces in the embattled Dutch colony, 32 precious P-40s were loaded as deck cargo onto the USS *Langley*, the former coal carrier that had been converted into the Navy's first aircraft carrier, but Japanese air-

216

craft sank the ship as it tried to steam in daylight from Australia to Java. By the end of February 1942, defeat was certain. On March 2 the American air units withdrew from the Netherlands East Indies, and a week later the Dutch surrendered. The combined American-British-Dutch-Australian Command, responsible for the defense of the approaches to Australia, lacked the resources for its task.

When the Netherlands East Indies passed from Dutch to Japanese control, planning had already begun to avenge, at least symbolically, the defeat at Pearl Harbor. Two naval officers, Captains Francis S. Low and Donald B. Duncan, suggested attacking Tokyo with Army medium bombers launched from an aircraft carrier some 500 miles from the target, a proposal that General Arnold enthusiastically endorsed. Such a mission, however, presented grave danger not only for the bomber crews but also for the officers and men of the ships involved—the carrier *Hornet*, which would launch the strike; the *Enterprise*, whose air group would defend the task force; and the escorting warships. Coaxing a heavily loaded bomber from a rolling deck posed a challenge to the best of pilots, even though the aircraft carrier would be steaming into the wind, reducing the required takeoff speed. Once airborne, the bombers would require precise navigation to locate the assigned targets and continue to designated airfields in China, where they would reinforce the American warplanes already operating in that country. Before the airmen faced these perils, the small naval task force would have to penetrate undetected through hostile seas, sailing where no American surface ship had dared to go since the outbreak of war and in the process risking two of the seven first-line aircraft carriers then in service. To lead the mission, General Arnold selected Lt. Col. James H. Doolittle, who gathered a force of 16 B–25Bs and trained their crews.

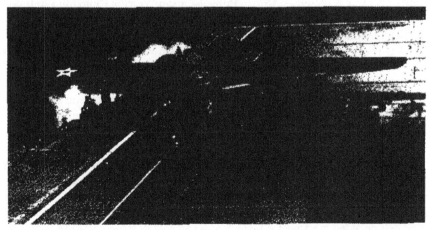

When they took off, the left wings of Doolittle's B–25s had to extend beyond the left side of the carrier for the right wings to clear the island.

En route to the launching point off Japan, the task force encountered Japanese patrol craft. The task force commander, Vice Adm. William F. Halsey, Jr., proposed to dispatch the bombers at once, and Doolittle agreed, even though the *Hornet* was more than 100 miles farther from shore than planned. At an air base in Florida, Doolittle's pilots had practiced taking off from a runway marked to represent a carrier's flight deck; now they faced the real thing. On the morning of April 18, 1942, Doolittle released the brakes and sent the first B-25 thundering down the flight deck into a 40-mile-per-hour gale. His bomber clawed its way upward and led the force to Japan, where 13 of the raiders bombed Tokyo, while the other three attacked Kobe and Nagoya. After bombing Japan, the B-25s headed for China, but bad weather and the additional fuel consumed because of the early launch forced the crews to abandon or crashland all the planes but one, which touched down safely not in China as planned but at Vladivostok in the Soviet Union. Three of Doolittle's 79 airmen died in crash landings or parachute jumps, and Japanese patrols took eight prisoner. Of those captured, three were executed by firing squad and another died in confinement, but the other four survived a brutal imprisonment.

Intended to satisfy President Roosevelt's desire to strike directly at Japan, thus boosting American morale and possibly shaking Japanese confidence, the raid inflicted trifling damage. It did demonstrate that the United States could deliver an occasional jab against the Japanese—as the Navy already had in raiding recently captured Wake Island, enemy bases in the Marshall group, and the enemy's beachhead in northeastern New Guinea—while gathering strength for a knockout blow against the Germans in Europe. Doolittle's attack had no effect on Anglo-American strategy, except to enable President Roosevelt to suggest that the bombing of Japan might have diverted Japanese naval forces from the Indian Ocean, where a foray had aroused British Prime Minister Winston Churchill's unfounded concern about possible cooperation with Germany in the vicinity of Suez.

The boldness of the Doolittle raid stung the Japanese, who reacted in three ways. The army promptly organized air groups for the defense of Japan against future air attacks, and some 250 aircraft were dedicated to this role when the bombing of the home islands resumed in June 1944. The April 1942 attack also ensured the army's enthusiastic participation in an attempt to extend the far-flung defensive perimeter by seizing Midway Island as the naval leadership had been demanding. Finally, Japanese troops in China mounted an offensive that soon overran the airfields where the B-25 crews had intended to land. The Chinese government at Chungking (now romanized as Chongqing), headed by Generalissimo Chiang Kai-shek (Jiang Jieshi), may have foreseen such a reaction, for it had agreed only reluctantly to the Doolittle raid.

Shortly after Doolittle's flyers bombed Japan, Navy signal intelligence specialists decoded message traffic indicating an enemy move early in May against Port Moresby in southeastern New Guinea. As the time approached, the defenders shifted their aircraft carriers to meet the threat and sent Army bombers to search seaward. Some of these B–17s did detect a Japanese screening force and dropped a few bombs without effect, but land-based bombers took no part in the main action. The Battle of the Coral Sea, fought on May 7 and 8, 1942, was a struggle between American and Japanese carrier aircraft. Although the U.S. Navy lost a large carrier, more than 60 planes, a destroyer, and a tanker, American naval aviators sank a light carrier and damaged a bigger one, depriving the enemy of the air cover necessary for the assault on Port Moresby, which the Japanese canceled.

The Battle of the Coral Sea had scarcely ended before decoded Japanese radio traffic revealed an impending attack on Midway Island, an operation designed to draw out and destroy what remained of the U.S. Pacific Fleet, while at the same time extending the defensive belt protecting Japan and ensuring against repetition of the Doolittle raid. A carrier task force, trailed by a formation of battleships and an invasion group, approached Midway, while other Japanese naval units prepared to attack the Aleutian Islands, thus diverting attention from the main objective. Alerted by the decoded messages, Adm. Chester W. Nimitz, the Commander in Chief, Pacific, marshaled three carriers against the four that spearheaded the assault.

Since he was responsible for repelling the enemy thrust, the admiral exercised operational control over Maj. Gen. Clarence L. Tinker's Seventh Air Force, which had risen from the ashes of General Martin's Hawaiian Air Force. Tinker wanted to attack Wake Island, a likely staging area for the enemy, but his B–17Es lacked the range. Instead, Admiral Nimitz sent seventeen of the Flying Fortresses and four B–26 medium bombers, hurriedly fitted out to drop torpedoes, to Midway, where they came under the operational control of a Navy air officer.

The B–17s, led by Maj. Walter C. Sweeney, opened the battle on June 3, following a sighting by a Navy patrol aircraft. The bombers attacked the troop transports bound for Midway, but caused no damage. The next morning, after Navy flyers had located the enemy's carriers, the four B–26s attacked with torpedoes, losing two of their number to antiaircraft fire but inflicting no damage on the warships. A formation of B–17s en route to attack the transports received orders to hit the carriers instead, but once again the bombs fell harmlessly into the sea. By the time the Battle of Midway ended on June 6, the B–17s had dropped some 300 bombs during 55 sorties, but failed to score a single hit, demonstrating that the strategic bomber, using conventional high-altitude tactics, posed little danger to warships under way.

A struggle between carrier task forces like the recent engagement in the Coral Sea, the Battle of Midway was a victory for the dive bomber. Navy aircraft of this type fatally damaged three Japanese aircraft carriers in a span of just three minutes on the morning of June 4. That afternoon they crippled the fourth carrier, which its crew had to scuttle on the following day; and on June 6, they sank a cruiser already damaged in a collision. The enemy, moreover, used dive bombers in conjunction with torpedo bombers to damage an American aircraft carrier, USS *Yorktown*, which finally succumbed to submarine attack. The American ship-building industry had the capability to replace the *Yorktown*, but Japanese shipyards lacked the capacity and the steel to restore to full strength the mobile striking force that had triumphed during the early months of the war. Besides the ships, the battle of Midway cost the Japanese navy its cadre of veteran pilots who had won victories from Pearl Harbor to the Indian Ocean; because of Japan's limited training establishment, this was a staggering loss.

Despite the success of the dive bomber at Midway (not to mention Germany's earlier use of the Ju 87 Stuka), this type of craft proved incompatible with General Arnold's vision of air power, even though he had reluctantly equipped one bombardment group with the very type used so successfully by the Navy in this battle. A misplaced confidence in the ability of the heavy bomber to sink warships from high altitude affected the general's judgment, but he had other and sounder reasons for preferring other types of aircraft. For short-range missions, the fighter could double as bomber; besides being faster than a light bomber or dive bomber, the fighter-bomber could deal on equal terms with enemy fighters once it had dropped its bombs. For any sort of interdiction, range was a dominant consideration, since Army aircraft, unlike those of the Navy, operated from immobile bases, and the larger Army aircraft could fly farther. Twin-engine types like the B–25 or A–20 had greater range, carried heavier loads of explosives, and possessed more formidable armament than the Navy's SBD dive bomber or its Army equivalent, the A–24; moreover, the second engine provided a margin of safety.

The American dive bombers had claimed the last of their victims in the seas beyond Midway, when four B–24s arrived at the island. These bombers, which had greater range than the B–17, enabled General Tinker to attempt an attack on Wake Island. Aside from the real possibility of interception by the Japanese, the flight itself was dangerous, requiring precise navigation, flawlessly operating engines, and careful husbanding of fuel. Fitted with extra gasoline tanks, the bombers took off on the night of June 6 for a dawn strike, flying westward beneath an overcast that prevented the navigators from using the stars to maintain course. The aircraft could not find the tiny atoll, and only three had enough fuel to return to Midway; the B–24 that disappeared into the Pacific carried General Tinker.

To divert attention from Midway and also to extend their defensive perimeter, the Japanese attacked the Aleutian Islands with an invasion force that included two aircraft carriers. Faced with this secondary threat, Admiral Nimitz placed Brig. Gen. William O. Butler's Eleventh Air Force under the control of Rear Adm. Robert A. Theobald, who incorporated the Army airmen into the task force charged with defending Alaska. On June 3 and 4, Japanese aircraft took off from the fog-enshrouded light carriers, but on both days found clear skies over the target, the American base at Dutch Harbor. A break in the weather enabled General Butler's aircraft to attack the carriers, but neither B–17s nor torpedo-carrying B–26s inflicted any damage. Besides bombing the American base at Dutch Harbor, the Japanese occupied two undefended islands, Kiska and Attu, but the hostile presence in the Aleutians proved short-lived. United States forces recaptured Attu in May 1943, and the enemy abandoned Kiska in July of that year.

Although described by the more imaginative military analysts as a spear aimed at the vitals of the Japanese octopus, the Aleutians remained a secondary theater of operations throughout the war, and with good reason. The weather proved sullen and given to unexpected rage, and the island chain afforded few good sites for airfields. At Adak Island, Army engineers overcame problems typical of base construction in the Aleutians when they drained a bog, scraped down to the subsurface gravel, and managed to build a mile-long runway surfaced with pierced-steel planking. Drainage there remained a problem, however; a foot of water might collect on the metal surface so that aircraft often took off and landed in clouds of spray. At all the Aleutian airstrips the steel planking was vulnerable to fierce gales that could dislodge the interconnected strips and peel them back like the skin of a banana. In these circumstances, the air offensive from Alaska, far from being decisive, consisted mainly of harassing raids against Paramushiro, the Japanese naval base in the Kurile Islands.

Despite the American victories in the Coral Sea and at Midway, the Japanese octopus seemed alive and menacing, with tentacles that might yet choke off the supply line to Australia and possibly enfold the continent in deadly embrace. The defense of Australia under General MacArthur therefore took on a critical importance. As MacArthur's air officer, General Brett attempted to create a supply and maintenance service to absorb the new squadrons being rushed into the Southwest Pacific Area while he simultaneously harried the Japanese advance across the Owen Stanley Mountains of New Guinea toward Port Moresby. The theater commander grew impatient with these efforts, however, and requested a replacement to take over the Allied Air Forces and also its American component. As Brett's replacement, Arnold chose Maj. Gen. George C. Kenney, who arrived in August 1942. Unlike the hard-pressed Brett, Kenney was an innovator with an "earthy sense of humor, a mastery of colorful though not always quotable language, and a fine sense of the dramatic."[3] Apparently those were the

Gen. Kenney (left) and Gen. MacArthur in early 1944. Kenney served as MacArthur's air officer from August 1942 until the end of the war.

Brig. Gen. Kenneth N. Walker, who
helped develop bombing doctrine
before the war, was awarded the
Medal of Honor posthumously.

qualities needed to get along with MacArthur. "Sometimes," wrote General
Arnold, "we had to guard against the wrong mixture of human 'chemical,'" and
the Brett-MacArthur compound obviously failed. In contrast, General Kenney
gained the confidence of the theater commander, insisted on direct access to
him, and remained MacArthur's air officer for the rest of the war.

The war in the Southwest Pacific proved frustrating for advocates of strategic bombardment like Brig. Gen. Kenneth N. Walker, who had helped shape prewar bombing doctrine at the Air Corps Tactical School and now headed Kenney's
bomber command. Bombers were few, and thousands of miles of ocean separated their bases from the Japanese heartland. Instead of delivering massive blows
against vital industrial targets to defeat Japan, the handful of B–17s available in
the Southwest Pacific bombed heavily defended advance bases like Rabaul on
the island of New Britain in the hope of disrupting shipping, destroying supplies,
and downing fighters, all in an effort to check the Japanese advance. Determined
to lead by example in these trying times, Walker insisted on flying on missions
against Rabaul and was killed during one of the attacks. His sacrifice earned him
the Medal of Honor.

Although long-range bombing could contribute little during the early months
of the war against Japan, aerial reconnaissance proved especially important to
the defense of Australia and its vulnerable supply line. Capt. Karl Polifka led a
flight of F–4s (P–38Es stripped of armament and fitted with cameras and additional fuel tanks) that commenced operating from Australia in April 1942. At
times the distances that had to be flown were too much even for the long-range
F–4s; furthermore, an unarmed aircraft might not survive if intercepted by
Japanese fighters over one of the more distant targets. As a result, fully armed
B–17s and B–25s exchanged bombs for cameras on long-range flights that were
likely to encounter enemy aircraft. For example, Flying Fortresses of the 40th
Reconnaissance Squadron, later rechristened the 435th Bombardment Squadron,

flew missions over Rabaul; and when the United States launched a counterthrust into the Solomon Islands, the unit's B–17s not only photographed the initial objective but also carried two officers of the assault force, the 1st Marine Division, on a personal reconnaissance flight.

In the Pacific, the United States checked the Japanese advance in the battles of the Coral Sea and Midway and gathered strength for limited offensive operations on the periphery of Japan's conquests. In the war against Germany, American forces adhered to a defensive strategy, fighting the U–boat, a weapon that had threatened to isolate the British Isles in 1917 and presented that threat again in 1942. At the same time, the United States shipped men and weapons to the United Kingdom in preparation for assaulting continental of Europe. Since building an invasion force took time, air power, which could be mustered more quickly, would strike the first American blows against Germany. This aerial striking force, however, would inevitably have fewer bombers that the final objective of 6,800 or the interim goal of 3,800 set forth in AWPD/1, the blueprint for bombing Hitler into submission drafted in the summer of 1941.

The new Eighth Air Force drew the assignment of carrying the war to the enemy. In the hectic weeks after Pearl Harbor, Prime Minister Churchill, in casting about for a quick way of exerting pressure on Germany and Italy, had proposed occupying French northwest Africa, and General Arnold created the Eighth Air Force to take part in the operation. A British defeat in the Libyan desert and a shortage of shipping doomed Churchill's plan to open up the western Mediterranean, making the new air force available for operations elsewhere. Meanwhile, Arnold rejected Chaney's proposal to organize the Britain-based American air forces by functional commands, separated geographically, and obtained Marshall's approval for centralized control under an air officer for the theater. Maj. Gen. Carl Spaatz, the officer whom Arnold had chosen to command the Army Air Forces in Great Britain, asked for the Eighth Air Force, and Arnold agreed.

Selected to lead Spaatz's bomber command in the British Isles, Brig. Gen. Ira C. Eaker established a headquarters at High Wycombe, a girls' school that had once been a manor house, completed the network of bomber bases General Chaney had begun, and set up a training program. Eaker tried insofar as possible to pattern his organization after the Royal Air Force Bomber Command, led by Air Marshal Sir Arthur Harris. Chaney argued, however, that Eaker should report to him, as the senior Army (and Army Air Forces) officer in the British Isles and in effect the acting theater commander. Chaney did not realize that the issues of organization and command were settled; his was a temporary assignment. Marshall had decided on Maj. Gen. Dwight D. Eisenhower to head the European theater, and the Chief of Staff had also approved Arnold's choice of Spaatz to command the theater air force.

With the fight against Germany initially an air war fought almost exclusively with bombers, Spaatz had the authority to deal directly with the leaders of the

Maj. Gen. Carl A. Spaatz (left) and Brig. Gen. Ira C. Eaker.

Royal Air Force. In this sense, the Eighth Air Force, although a component of the U.S. Army Air Forces, enjoyed a status comparable to Great Britain's independent air service, while Eaker's VIII Bomber Command resembled the Royal Air Force Bomber Command under Harris. As agreed a year earlier at the Argentia conference of August 1941, the two allies would cooperate in an aerial campaign designed to wear down Germany in preparation for the kind of cross-channel invasion that Marshall and Eisenhower believed necessary for victory. The American airmen proposed to bomb Germany by day in carrying out an overall aerial strategy decided by the Combined Chiefs of Staff and transmitted to Eighth Air Force headquarters by the Joint Chiefs of Staff. When Spaatz arrived, the VIII Bomber Command had not yet proved itself; the men, equipment, and tactics remained untested. Moreover, British airmen, because of their own lack of success in daylight bombing, tended to doubt that the American could bomb Germany by day without incurring disastrous losses.

Daylight bombing was an integral part of Air Forces doctrine and training, but Sir Charles Portal, Chief of Air Staff for the Royal Air Force, was eager to add the weight of American bombs to the deadly tonnage already raining down by night on Germany. When German defenses first compelled the Bomber Command to abandon daylight raids and seek the concealment of darkness, British airmen had tried to destroy oil refineries and other fairly compact targets, only to discover that the raiders seldom found their objectives. An examination of 600 photographs taken from individual bombers at the time they released their bombs revealed that only 10 percent dropped their loads within five

224

Sir Charles Portal,
Chief of Staff,
Royal Air Force.

miles of the assigned target. Since air crews could not find and attack a particular structure by night, Bomber Command had to find a different target for the
heavy bombers. Navigators could find German cities and bombardiers aim precisely enough to damage an urban area; consequently, industrial cities, rather
than specific factories, became the target of British night attacks. In addition,
Air Marshal Harris believed that "city-busting," or area bombing, could destroy
the urban infrastructure of houses, shops, and utilities that supported the
German war effort, satisfying Churchill's demand for results and possibly making an invasion unnecessary. Indeed, nighttime area bombing yielded impressive results, as Harris tried to "de-house" German workers by incinerating the
industrial cities where they lived. Guided by new navigational beacons, his
crews burned the north German towns of Lubeck and Rostock, and on May 30,
1942, he dispatched a thousand bombers to devastate Cologne. Both Harris and
Portal believed that American crews could readily adopt British tactics of flying
through the darkness in loose bomber streams, aiming at either flares or fires set
by incendiary bombs instead of at features on the ground.

Neither the failure of British daylight raids nor the desolation being wrought
by night shook the resolve of Arnold, Spaatz, and Eaker to bomb during the day.
For them daylight precision bombing was an article of faith, and the same deep-
seated belief influenced Chaney's analysis of the German nighttime bombing of
Britain. His study concluded that from the fall of 1940 through the spring of
1941 the *Luftwaffe* had relied on small formations to make night attacks on
sprawling urban targets, instead of massing its bombers by day against truly essential industries. The Americans, Chaney declared, could avoid Germany's
mistakes by dispatching a succession of large formations that could fight their
way through the fighter screen to destroy vital factories, bombing them accurately by day instead of merely dumping munitions at night. Losses would be
greater in daylight than in darkness, but the improvement in accuracy would
more than compensate for the increased casualties. Rather than offering new in-

225

sights, Chaney's report served as a summary of Army Air Forces doctrine on strategic bombardment.

Although persuaded by their own bitter experience that daylight precision bombing could not succeed, the leaders of the Royal Air Force agreed that Spaatz should have the chance to prove them wrong. Sir Archibald Sinclair, Secretary of State for Air, summarized this view when he declared that, inasmuch as the Americans were determined to attack Germany, "It would be a tragedy if we were to frustrate them on the eve of this great experiment." Should daylight bombing somehow succeed, Sinclair envisioned an air war in which the British would "send a thousand bombers over Hamburg one night" and the Americans "follow with five or six hundred bombers the following day, and, if the weather is kind, for us to follow up with a large force of heavy bombers the next night—and then go on bombing one city after another in Germany on that scale."[4] Even Sinclair had his doubts that the Eighth Air Force would prove successful, but Generals Spaatz and Eaker could be sure of an opportunity to demonstrate the soundness of prewar bombardment doctrine once the necessary men and planes were available.

Ships carrying ground elements of the Eighth Air Force began arriving in the United Kingdom in May 1942, and the first airplane, a B–17, landed in Scotland on July 1. The buildup encountered unavoidable delays, however. Ships for the ground elements proved scarce, the transoceanic communications network had the teething problems of any new and complex technology, and bomber pilots needed extra training before they learned to watch fuel consumption and trust their navigators during an Atlantic crossing that used the new airfields in Greenland. A bomber shepherded each fighter formation, and when none of the big airplanes was available to navigate for a P–39 group, the pilots and ground crews sailed in one convoy, while the fighters waited for space in another.

Further delays occurred after the men and machines—accompanied by the first items in a mountain of spare parts and maintenance equipment—reached their destination. Rushed across the Atlantic though not yet ready for combat, bomber crews had to undergo additional training in such basic skills as gunnery, radio communication, and aerial navigation. Next they flew practice missions that taught them to fight at 25,000 feet, breathing oxygen and enduring biting cold while maintaining a tight defensive formation. As the bomber men sharpened their techniques under the leadership of Col. Frank A. Armstrong, Jr., fighter groups underwent indoctrination by the Royal Air Force. The P–39 unit whose planes were waiting for shipment from the United States acquired British Spitfires and underwent a period of familiarization that delayed their entry into combat. Meanwhile, the Eagle Squadrons, three Royal Air Force squadrons made up of American volunteers, transferred to the U.S. Army Air Forces, temporarily retaining their Spitfires and becoming the 4th Fighter Group.

Among the first American aviation units to reach the British Isles was the 15th Bombardment Squadron (Light). Although trained as an attack unit for

Martin Baltimore medium bomber, produced primarily for the RAF.

supporting ground forces, the squadron received orders to retrain, under the British, as a night-fighter outfit flying a version of the A–20 light bomber fitted with high-intensity searchlights. Technology improved, however, and radar replaced the searchlight, depriving the squadron of a mission. The Americans therefore resumed bombardment training in Douglas Boston III attack bombers, the equivalent of the American A–20A, borrowed from the British. On July 4, 1942, to commemorate the national holiday, six crews from this squadron took part with British airmen in an attack against German airfields in Holland. The first American raid mounted from the United Kingdom was scarcely a success, for only two of the Eighth Air Force Bostons managed to locate, bomb, and strafe the assigned target. The Americans, moreover, lost two planes to antiaircraft fire and the British lost one, downed by the combined efforts of flak and German fighters.

More than a month passed before the VIII Bomber Command's B–17s were ready to deliver their first strike against Nazi-occupied Europe. On August 17, General Eaker flew one of the 12 Flying Fortresses that bombed the Sotteville marshaling yard at Rouen, France. Colonel Armstrong led the raid; his copilot that day was Maj. Paul W. Tibbets, an officer destined for a mission of far greater significance before the war ended, for he would drop the atomic bomb on Hiroshima, Japan. Although at most a small-scale demonstration of the destruction to come, the flawlessly executed attack produced heartening results. Only one German fighter slipped through the four squadrons of escorting Spitfires, and this lone aircraft caused no damage. The bombing proved accurate, and all twelve B–17s returned with, at worst, a few holes from shell fragments.

Admittedly a mere pinprick to the enemy, the Rouen attack symbolized American determination to join in the bombing offensive. As the advocates of daylight precision attack conceded, many more aircraft would be needed before

Consolidated B–24 Liberator bombers at a desert strip in North Africa.

formations large enough to defend themselves and inflict serious damage could penetrate far into Germany on a regular basis. As B–24s and additional B–17s arrived in England, they went into action against rail centers and aircraft factories in France, Dutch shipyards, or the heavily defended submarine pens along the French coast.

Despite the important role assigned it in the air war, the Eighth Air Force did not drop the first American bombs on a target in Europe. That honor went to a detachment of B–24s led by Col. Harry A. Halversen, a veteran of the endurance flight of *The Question Mark* in January 1929. Halversen's group originally had the mission of bombing Japan; but the enemy, as a consequence of the Doolittle raid, overran the bases in China projected for the B–24s. The Halversen force therefore received orders to terminate its journey in Egypt and strike a blow to aid the Soviet Red Army, hard pressed by Hitler's invaders. The target of this ambitious raid was Ploesti, Rumania, where huge refineries supplied fuel for the German war machine. The attack, delivered by a dozen aircraft bombing through an overcast at dawn of June 10, 1942, proved ineffectual. The unsuccessful raid on Ploesti led, however, to one of the more ingenious escapes of World War II. A B–24 piloted by 1st Lt. Eugene L. Ziesel ran low on gasoline and landed at Ankara in neutral Turkey where authorities interned the crew. Ziesel convinced his captors that the bomber's engines had to be run up every few days to keep them from deteriorating. Each time he used less fuel than the amount the Turkish mechanics had put in the tanks, and when a large enough surplus had accumulated he took off and flew to an Allied air base. A week after returning to combat, Ziesel and his crew were killed during an attack on Naples, Italy.

Even as Halversen's bombers were attacking Ploesti, German forces led by Field Marshal Erwin Rommel advanced on the Suez Canal. To help meet this emergency, these B–24s began bombing the Libyan ports of Tobruk and Benghazi in an effort to disrupt enemy supply lines. Aircraft bound for the China-Burma-India Theater by way of the Sudan joined the colonel's bombers to form the nucleus of a new command. Late in June 1942, General Brereton, who had been ordered to leave the Southwest Pacific and organize a bomber command in India, exchanged that assignment for command of a hurriedly assembled U.S. Army Middle East Air Force.

Except for the B–17s and B–24s, Brereton's squadrons were attached to the Western Desert Air Force, commanded by Air Vice Marshal Sir Arthur Coningham. Coningham's force helped to check Rommel at El Alamein, Egypt, in July and hurled him back in October and November; but the American aircraft, not even 10 percent of the total, played only a minor role in the action. During the victory at El Alamein and the westward advance that followed, Coningham and the ground commander, Gen. Bernard Law Montgomery, maintained a joint headquarters in which aviation and ground elements had equal voices. The status of British tactical air power in North Africa as an equal of the ground force reflected the independence of the Royal Air Force but did not provide a satisfactory precedent for an independent American air force. Granted that the fighter-bomber was essential to victory on the battlefield, it could not win a war by itself, whereas American leadership expected the strategic bomber to do just that and provide an irrefutable argument for a postwar air arm coequal with the Army and Navy. Although Coningham's success could not justify an independent American air force, his accomplishments did demonstrate that an independent air arm, the Royal Air Force, could cooperate effectively with ground forces.

In the western desert, cooperation was the watchword between Coningham and Montgomery, although the two strong personalities eventually clashed in France. At El Alamein, the air officer massed his Allied aircraft to the deadliest effect, hitting supply lines and airfields—indeed, for a time maintaining almost a constant patrol over the bases used by an exhausted *Luftwaffe*—instead of tying his airplanes to the battlefield. Exposure to the cooperation between Coningham and Montgomery influenced General Brereton, whose command became the Ninth Air Force in November 1942. Within months, in fact, Coningham's methods would serve as a model for air-ground cooperation in the United States Army.

Three great battles marked, as events would prove, the limits of Axis success: Midway in June 1942, Stalingrad from August 1942 to February 1943, and the breakthrough at El Alamein in late October and early November 1942. Decisive though they appear in retrospect, at the time they served at most as portents of eventual victory. Winston Churchill in November 1942 thought that perhaps marked the beginning of a change of fortune for the Allies, saying that, "Before Alamein we never had victory; after Alamein we never had a defeat." The defensive phase of the war had ended for the Allies. Although America's ability to produce vast quantities of weapons and recruit and train the men to use them had only begun to make itself felt on the battle fronts in 1942, the United States soon began to perform the function that President Roosevelt had proposed in

1940, becoming the "vast arsenal of democracy," turning out endless tons of arms and equipment for its expanded armed forces and those of its allies. Nowhere was the nation's genius for production and management more evident than in the wartime growth of the Army Air Forces in terms of both modern aircraft and trained manpower.

Chapter 8

Building Air Power

George M. Watson, Jr.

The building of American air power, foreshadowed by President Franklin D. Roosevelt's response to the Munich crisis of 1938, involved several kinds of vigorous and sustained efforts. Aircraft had to be manufactured in massive numbers, designs improved, and new models developed as necessary. The Army Air Forces had to set up a worldwide logistics network to supply, maintain, and repair the vast aerial armada thus created. The service had to recruit and train manpower—a term that by the end of the war included women—and then had to take care of those who had been recruited, sustaining their morale and providing for their health and welfare.

The manufacture of airplanes, rather than the training of men and women, set the pace for the creation of American air power to fight World War II. Simply put, the air arm could neither train, nor deploy, nor fight without aircraft, and the inventory seemed unlikely to grow rapidly because of the sluggish rate of the nation's aircraft production. In 1939, when fighting broke out in Europe, firms in the United States produced just 2,141 military airplanes, about half of Japan's output, one-fourth of Germany's, two-thirds of France's, and one-third of Great Britain's. An obviously feeble American industry faced the challenge of providing not only the clouds of aircraft that President Roosevelt believed would warn Adolf Hitler not to arouse the wrath of the United States but also those needed by the nations arrayed against the German dictator. Following the adoption and expansion of the lend-lease program, aircraft production became even more important when the United States, as the President vowed in December 1940, became the great arsenal of democracy, sustaining the war against the Axis powers while at the same time rearming.

Of all the combatants in World War II, only the United States succeeded in building the numbers and kinds of aircraft necessary to wage every form of aerial warfare—whether strategic, tactical, land-based, or carrier-based—and to supply the air services of its allies as well as those of its own armed forces. The Soviet Union, for example, had a labor force, raw materials, and plant capacity rivaling the United States; but the German invasion forced the displacement of factories out of the war zone, and Soviet authorities chose to concentrate on tactical aviation for support of the Red Army. America's other major ally, the United Kingdom, lacked the resources in workers, materials, and machines to produce an adequate number of aircraft for every purpose. Once the Battle of Britain had been won, the British increased the emphasis on bombers, enlisting science to help them find and destroy German cities. The Axis powers, most of all Italy, were handicapped by shortages of raw materials for the construction and operation of aircraft. Although not fully mobilized until midway through the war, German industry demonstrated great ingenuity, despite mounting Allied pressure, but could not overtake the United States except in such narrow specialties as jet and rocket propulsion and synthetic fuel. After overrunning western Europe and large tracts of the Soviet Union, Germany failed to integrate the resources of these regions, except for labor drafts either forced or voluntary, into the production effort. Similarly, Japan failed to reap the benefits of its early conquests, due in part to submarine warfare and an unexpectedly rapid Allied counteroffensive. Nor could the Japanese fully mobilize their aircraft industry.

Whereas Hitler believed his people could have both guns and butter and was reluctant to make demands on Germany's aviation industry (he refused, for instance, to insist on multiple shifts or to encourage German women to work in the factories), President Roosevelt forced the American firms to extend themselves, in part by establishing production goals that seemed unattainable even to him. In 1939 he had spoken boldly of turning out 10,000 aircraft per year, although he had to settle at the time for a third that amount in new construction; and in May of 1940 he announced a goal of 50,000 planes. In response to the Japanese attack on Pearl Harbor and the declarations of war by Germany and Italy, he demanded that the American aircraft industry build 60,000 airplanes in 1942 and 125,000 during 1943. The new Assistant Secretary of War for Air, Robert M. Lovett, could not believe that turning out 125,000 aircraft in a single year was a realistic objective. He compared this goal to "asking a hen to lay an ostrich egg," suggesting that it was "unlikely you will get the egg, and the hen

Lt. Gen. Henry H. Arnold,
Chief, Army Air Forces,
June 1941–March 1942.

will never look the same." Lt. Gen. Henry H. Arnold, Chief of the Army Air Forces, insisted, however, that the effort was worthwhile: "If we can induce her to lay it, I for one feel that we must accept the wear and tear on the hen."[1] Arnold reflected the belief of the Chief Executive that with enough effort what was impossible today might well become feasible tomorrow. The President acknowledged that his objective of 50,000 aircraft, announced in 1940, had come "out of the air," but he was less interested in near-term results than in expanding future production as much as humanly and technologically possible, in creating enthusiasm, and in raising morale. True, Roosevelt often settled for less than he demanded, but industry eventually came within 30,000 aircraft of meeting his most ambitious goal, attaining a peak output of 96,000 aircraft in 1944.

Although he dealt with possibilities rather than realities in announcing his production goals, the President kept in close touch with the views of the military concerning their actual aircraft requirements. In the summer of 1941, this contact had resulted in AWPD/1—Air War Plans Division plan number one—which proposed that the Army Air Forces expand in the event of war to 60,000 planes and 2,100,000 men. In August 1942, Roosevelt asked for a new estimate that reflected more accurately the needs of a coalition war against Germany, Japan, and Italy. Specifically, he wanted an estimate of "the number of combat aircraft by types that should be produced for the Army and our Allies . . . in 1943 in order to have complete air ascendancy over the enemy."[2] As in the case of the previous year's presidential request for production requirements, the Air War Plans Division of the Air Staff undertook a response. Although wartime reassignments had broken up the team that had turned out AWPD/1, Arnold summoned one of its members, Haywood Hansell, now a brigadier general, from England to take charge of the new study, called AWPD/42. In answering the President's question, General Hansell's group called for the production of some 75,000 airplanes and 8,000 gliders, intended for an Army Air Forces numbering 2,700,000 men, along with 8,000 aircraft for America's allies. Omitted from the

233

list of aircraft was the intercontinental bomber proposed in AWPD/1; instead of investing in the B–36, the Army Air Forces would use the B–17 and B–24 to carry the war to Hitler's Germany, with the B–29 or B–32 appearing in time to batter Japan from bases in China or on the islands of the far Pacific.

Besides answering the basic question, Arnold's Air Staff planners, as with AWPD/1, used a presidential request for projections of aircraft production as the occasion for a statement of aerial strategy. For the most part, AWPD/42 reaffirmed the earlier views on bombing Germany into submission. The list of critical targets increased by 23 to 177, an expansion that reflected the addition of three war industries—submarine construction, aluminum production, and the manufacture of synthetic rubber—to the "target systems" contained in AWPD/1: electric power; transportation; oil; and the *Luftwaffe*, including fighters, bases, and aircraft factories. With the Battle of the Atlantic far from won, submarine construction ranked second in importance only to the neutralization of the *Luftwaffe*. If American airmen destroyed all 177 targets, Hansell's group insisted, "the effect would be decisive and Germany would be unable to continue her war effort."[3] Enemy morale received scant mention, possibly because Air Marshal Sir Arthur Harris of the Royal Air Force's Bomber Command had laid claim to city busting, which combined the physical destruction of cities with the demoralization of their inhabitants.

In drafting AWPD/42, General Arnold's planners included an estimate of 33,000 aircraft manufactured for the Navy, a figure based on official projections rather than specific interservice coordination. Even more rashly, the Army airmen proposed a coastal command of their own, numbering 640 heavy and medium bombers, that would patrol the waters off North and South America, Iceland, and the Azores in search of submarines. Adm. Ernest J. King, the Chief of Naval Operations, found the idea of an Army Air Forces hemispheric patrol especially annoying, for he had just wrested from a reluctant Arnold a share of bomber production so that Navy airmen could fly long-range antisubmarine missions. Always sensitive to the fact that Arnold was not a true service chief like Gen. George C. Marshall, Army Chief of Staff, and himself, King raised strong objections to the Air Forces' meddling in Navy matters and prevented the Joint Chiefs from formally adopting the plan, which nevertheless served as a statement to what the Army Air Forces saw as its needs and its strategy against Germany.

President Roosevelt's pressure to increase aircraft production would have proved fruitless had American industry as a whole not been ideally suited to mass production, whether of refrigerators and automobiles or tanks and aircraft. In contrast, the Axis powers were ill-prepared for the battle of the assembly line. Poor in natural resources, Italy had never been capable of large-scale production, and tension between nonpolitical managers and doctrinaire Fascists frustrated attempts at innovation. In Germany, conservative industrialists resented the intrusion of Nazi ideologues, and efficiency also suffered because veteran craftsmen tended to resist change. Only a first-class organizer (and Nazi stalwart) like Albert Speer could realize the potential of Germany's factories. In Japan, the army and navy set production policies for much of the war; when the nation at last turned to its industrialists, it was too late. Unaffected by ideology like the German and Italian firms or militarism like the Japanese, American aircraft and engine manufacturers provided in astonishing numbers the equipment necessary for victory in the air, turning out in 1944, the last full year of the fighting, some 96,000 airframes and 256,000 aircraft engines, almost half again the number of airframes produced by the Axis nations and two and one-half times as many engines. The Army Air Forces accepted about half of the 320,000 aircraft built in the United States between July 1940 and August 1945 and three-fourths of the 800,000 engines; but a part of this mountain of equipment, like some of the B–24s used for antisubmarine patrol, was turned over to the Navy or made available to America's allies.

As befit an industrial giant whose strength lay in the mass production of durable goods, the United States was blessed with managers who could apply assembly-line techniques to huge bombers (though with mixed results) and even to ships. The automobile industry had its Henry Ford, his son Edsel, and William S. Knudsen, the General Motors executive who helped advise the President on issues of production and later became a lieutenant general in charge of materiel for the Air Forces. Men like J. H. "Dutch" Kindleberger of North American Aviation and Henry J. Kaiser in shipbuilding knew how to bring workers, raw materials, and finished components together in the proper place and sequence.

The civilian within the War Department who bore the greatest responsibility for aircraft purchases and production, Assistant Secretary Lovett, was a lawyer, however, rather than a manager. His legal work for the aviation industry gave him a familiarity with production methods, costs, and profits. His experience enabled him to judge the feasibility of production goals and harmonize the plans of the air arm with those being shaped for the entire Army by General Marshall and Under Secretary of War Robert P. Patterson, who did for the Army Ground Forces and Service Forces what Lovett did for the Air Forces.

The impressive production effort began chaotically. Scarcely had the fighting broken out in Europe when the Army air arm found itself competing with the British and French for new aircraft. The collapse of France in 1940 did not ease the situation, for Roosevelt subsequently agreed to assist China and the Soviet Union. General Arnold objected from the outset to sharing America's slender aerial resources, voicing his complaint so strenuously that President Roosevelt, according to Arnold's recollection, reminded the airman that "there were places to which officers who did not play ball could be sent, such as Guam."[4] In a sense, the Air Corps profited from agreeing, however reluctantly, to the release of aircraft, for Britain and France provided data on combat performance that led to such improvements as increased firepower and armor. Nor did the diversion

Curtiss P–40 aircraft with British markings.

weaken the American air forces as much as Arnold had feared, for the best air-craft of 1940 or even 1941 were not necessarily the best in 1943 or 1944.

The President's desire to aid foreign nations had the greatest impact on the availability of fighters. The United States transferred more than 17,000 of these aircraft during the course of the war. The types diverted in the greatest numbers to the various Allies were P–39s and P–40s, adequate fighters when designed be-fore the war but soon outperformed by more modern types. Similarly, General Arnold sacrificed some 7,000 light bombers or attack aircraft, half either A–20s intended for the Air Forces or versions of that successful airplane designated specifically for export. Included in the shipments to America's allies, however, were almost 3,000 aircraft for which the Army Air Forces had no plans: Lockheed's A–29 Hudson, Martin's A–30 Baltimore, and Vultee's A–31 Ven-geance dive bomber (manufactured as the A–35). Thanks to mass production, these transfers, along with the shipment of some 2,000 B–24s and 3,000 C–47s, had little long-term effect, although in the early months of the war, before huge numbers of aircraft began emerging from the assembly lines, the absence of the A–20s, P–39s, and P–40s may well have hampered the Air Forces. On balance, however, American manufacturers met the needs of both lend-lease and the armed forces of the United States.

Although Roosevelt announced unrealistic goals for aircraft production, he took concrete action to increase productive capacity so that they might ulti-mately be reached. Beginning in 1940, his administration provided incentives for aircraft builders, minimizing the financial risk to the manufacturer. Since American firms had struggled for survival during the depression of the previous decade, they proved reluctant to invest in additional plant capacity that might not be needed if Great Britain collapsed or the United States avoided involve-ment in the conflict. Roosevelt's answer was to build the factories at govern-ment expense and allow private corporations to operate them; by the end of the

236

war, the Air Forces had used War Department funds appropriated for the purpose to contract for 34 major plants. Although nine contracts were either canceled or amended to incorporate other financing, the total investment by the government approached $1.5 billion, some 20 times the amount spent on the entire Air Corps in 1939. Additional money, perhaps another $1 billion, was spent on lesser facilities, tools and other equipment, and the expansion of existing plants. Thanks in large measure to federal expenditures, the amount of floor space devoted to the manufacture of airframes, engines, and propellers increased more than 13-fold from some 13 million square feet in 1940 to a maximum of about 175 million square feet in December 1943.

Besides building factories and leasing them to aircraft manufacturers, the Roosevelt administration persuaded Congress to ease restrictions on excess profits, to grant tax advantages to airplane builders, and to lift the ban on negotiated contracts that had caused Maj. Gen. Benjamin D. Foulois such embarrassment when he was Chief of the Air Corps in the 1930s. Congress enacted the reforms piecemeal during the wartime years. The substitution of negotiation for time-consuming competition and the awarding of tax breaks were obvious measures for meeting the demand for increased production. The subject of excess profits proved far more complex. Although profit was perhaps the strongest of incentives, some restrictions had to prevail, for war profiteering posed a real threat to the nation's sense of purpose and to its economy. A congressional investigation revealed, for example, that one company, which owed its very existence to government loans and its success to military contracts, charged the Army and Navy more than twice the usual amount for its product, a starter for aircraft engines. The excess profits in this case found their way into bonuses for executives and welfare or morale programs for the workers. Abuses like this caused the government to insist on renegotiating contracts if profits seemed outrageous, but establishing a margin of profit applicable throughout the aircraft industry proved impossible. Such factors as the volume of manufacture, the availability of labor and material, the urgency with which a product was needed, and the extent of the government's investment in tools and buildings had to be considered before making accusations of profiteering. Thus it happened that Douglas Aircraft, when it first began operating plants owned by the government, could legally realize a profit in excess of fifty percent on its corporate investment, seven times the average of firms using company-owned plants and machinery.

As it had in 1917, the American automobile industry shared in the expansion of aircraft production, acquiring the use of new factories built by the government for the manufacture of aircraft or converting existing ones to that purpose. Once again the government sought to take advantage of the techniques of mass production perfected by the auto builders. In contrast to World War I, these practices proved more adaptable to the making of all-metal airplanes than they had to the handcrafting of the wood-and-linen products of an earlier generation. As an airplane manufacturer, the automobile industry concentrated on fabricating wings or other structural components for aircraft assembled by others. Only Ford and the Eastern Aircraft Division of General Motors participated on any large scale in the final assembly of airplanes, Ford building Consolidated B–24s for the Army Air Forces and General Motors making Grumman aircraft for the Navy.

Ford's government-built plant at Willow Run, Michigan, applied the methods of mass production to building the entire airframe of the B–24 and installing the bomber's four engines. In their desire to apply the techniques with which they were most familiar, Ford production engineers planned to use dies to form bomber parts from aluminum, just as automobile components were shaped from steel. Unfortunately, aluminum lacked the rigidity necessary for the efficient use of this process, especially when being formed into large parts. Unlike steel, the more flexible aluminum required repeated stampings and an increased investment of time before the desired shape was attained. Also, components of the B–24, including such major items as the vertical stabilizer, changed to reflect experience in combat, and radical changes required new dies. In contrast, a successful type of automobile might require only cosmetic adjustments during a production run of two or more years. Although the plant at Willow Run became highly efficient in terms of weight produced per worker, the number of finished aircraft remained disappointingly few. Indeed, by March 1944, monthly production barely exceeded 400 bombers, roughly two-thirds capacity, but given the success at other factories and the progress on the battlefield, the projected manufacture of 600 bombers per month at Willow Run proved unnecessary.

What did not change from one war to the next was the success of the nation's auto builders in converting to the production of aircraft engines. Packard, which built Liberty engines in World War I, now manufactured under license the British Rolls Royce Merlin that powered the P–51 escort fighter. General Motors, Ford, and Nash built Pratt and Whitney products, while Dodge and Studebaker were licensed by Wright Aeronautical. Automobile firms turned out more than 40 percent of the engines built for American aircraft between July 1940 and August 1945.

The old aircraft factories, the new ones built by the government, and those converted to the manufacture of airplanes would have been useless had the industry been unable to recruit and retain an adequate work force. As the aircraft industry grew larger, the nature of its work force changed. From 200,000 in 1940, most skilled craftsmen, the number of workers soared beyond 2,000,000 in 1944, declining the following year below 1,500,000 as a result of cutbacks in production that began even before the war ended. Most of the new workers were unskilled, though thoroughly trained in the repetitive work that contributed to the fabrication of an airplane, and many were women. The preponderance of unskilled (or at most semiskilled) labor reflected the triumph of the assembly line, on which much of the construction of the airplanes became a suc-

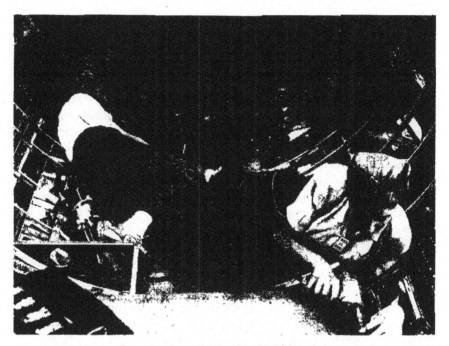

Construction of a Boeing B–17 bomber.

cession of simple procedures that required attention to detail rather than competence at metal working or some other craft. Although most of the workers had limited skills, workers with industrial experience were necessary to keep the production line moving. Officials of the Selective Service System acted to prevent individuals with these abilities from leaving the factory to join the armed services, as many craftsmen had done during the early months of World War I. Persons holding essential jobs remained exempt from military service, and federal authorities urged workers about to enter the armed forces to remain at the plant for as long as possible. Since the work force had to be kept intact, the Army Air Forces saw to it that a new project was waiting when an existing contract ended. Industrial planners tried to avoid periods of idleness, even when a factory retooled for a different product. This policy sustained morale in the work force by providing continuity and reduced the tendency of employees to move from one firm to another and force the old employer to hire and train new workers before resuming production. The measures taken to preserve the numerical strength, skills, and morale of the work force demonstrated the importance attached to aircraft production, the recognition that providing the weapons of aerial warfare was as important as using them.

In an aircraft industry whose greatest strength (aside, perhaps, from its very size) was a unique capacity for mass production, the issue of quantity versus quality arose early in the war. Should the Army Air Forces settle for good or insist on the best? Was it better to turn out large numbers of adequate aircraft immediately or to accept the unavoidable delay in attaining the maximum volume of production in order to obtain a superior airplane? The Director of Requirements on the Air Staff, Maj. Gen. Davenport "Johnny" Johnson, commander of a pursuit group during World War I, endorsed quality: "Fifty 100 percent aircraft are of more value than a hundred 50 percent aircraft in actual combat."[5] His words went unheeded, for in 1943 the Air Forces delayed the appearance of the Douglas A–26 light bomber to continue volume production of three similar, adequate, but less effective aircraft—the North American B–25, Martin B–26, and Douglas A–20. Similarly, Vultee's A–35 Vengeance dive bomber remained in production even through neither the Army Air Forces nor the Navy had any plans for them; however, America's allies received the Vengeance through Lend-Lease, and it saw action with the British in Burma.

With a few admittedly important exceptions, the Air Forces relied throughout the war on variations of the types of aircraft on hand in December 1941 when the Japanese attacked Pearl Harbor. Some of the newer aircraft, moreover, evolved directly from earlier ones; for instance, the A–26 descended from the A–20, and Bell Aircraft's P–63 was a supercharged and more powerful variant of the P–39. Not so the B–29, for this four-engine giant was a daring departure, a truly revolutionary aircraft rushed into service with a minimum of testing. In retrospect, General Arnold termed the B–29 a $3 billion gamble, but a gamble that paid off.

In the spring of 1940, after a design competition, Boeing and Lockheed received contracts for preliminary work on a very long-range bomber. Lockheed soon abandoned the project, but Boeing, the manufacturer of the XB–15 and B–17, produced an aircraft that, despite recurring overheating problems with its 2,200-horsepower radial engines, emerged as the most formidable bomber of World War II. Collaboration between Wright Aeronautical, the engine manufacturer, and Army Air Forces technicians at Wright Field resulted in modifications that increased the volume of air passing around the cylinders and solved the overheating problem, which occurred in the second bank of cylinders in the twin-row radial engine. Nicknamed the Superfortress, the B–29 boasted a number of novel features. A pressurized cabin, identical in principle to that devised by Col. Carl Greene and his colleagues at Wright Field in the mid-1930s, enhanced crew efficiency in bombing from high altitude; and remotely controlled turrets blended smoothly with the cylindrical fuselage to create a minimum of aerodynamic drag. Twice as heavy as the B–17, the Superfortress carried a crew of 10 and up to 10 tons of bombs, about two tons more than the maximum bombload of the latest model of B–17. A fuel capacity of some 9,500 gallons, compared to 3,600 gallons in a B–17 fitted with tanks in the bomb bay, gave the new bomber a ferry range in excess of 5,000 miles. Although B–29s based in India, heavily laden with fuel, once flew 4,000 miles to bomb a refinery on Sumatra and return, a typical combat mission required a round-trip flight of no more than 3,200 miles.

Comparable in size and performance to the Boeing B–29, the
Consolidated B–32 Dominator had little impact during the war.

When Lockheed canceled work on its long-range bomber to concentrate on
production of the P–38, the Air Forces turned to Consolidated Aircraft, builder
of the B–24 Liberator, for an alternative in the event the B–29 should fail. The
substitute that emerged was the B–32 Dominator, which started out as an enlarged Liberator with a pressurized cabin. Stability problems forced the manufacturer to replace the twin stabilizers originally chosen with a large, single vertical stabilizer, thus delaying development. With the Superfortress already entering service, the expense of pressurizing a second bomber no longer seemed
justified, and this feature was abandoned. When the war ended, the Army Air
Forces had taken delivery of some 3,700 B–29s but only 118 B–32s.

Two new fighters, the Republic P–47 and the North American P–51, entered
service after Pearl Harbor and performed with deadly effect against the Germans
and Japanese. The P–47 Thunderbolt made its debut in 1942, more than a year
after the prototype had flown, a delay that stemmed from difficulties in linking a
turbosupercharger to the 2,000-horsepower Pratt and Whitney radial engine.
Until jettisonable auxiliary fuel tanks became available, the P–47D suffered the
handicap of short range. Few pilots complained, however, about its durability or
firepower, for the six-ton Thunderbolt stood up well in combat and carried eight
.50 caliber guns. The ability of the heavy airframe to withstand punishment and
the augmentation of the machineguns with rocket launchers and bomb pylons
converted later models into deadly weapons for ground attack. American factories turned out more than 15,500 of these aircraft for the Army Air Forces.

The North American P–51 Mustang filled a need that most of the prewar Air
Corps planners had not anticipated, becoming the premier long-range escort
fighter of the war. With a normal loaded weight of about five tons, the Mustang
weighed less than the P–47. The greatest asset of the P–51 was its ability to fly

as far as Stettin or Munich in Germany or Prague in Czechoslovakia, engage in aerial combat with enemy interceptors, and return to England. The addition of a large permanent fuel tank in the fuselage and jettisonable tanks under the wings gave the fighter its spectacular range. Originally designed for the British who wanted an improvement over the P–40, the airplane went into production in the spring of 1941 and at first attracted little attention, largely because of an Allison engine that lacked a supercharger for high altitude performance. Allied airmen became enthusiastic, however, after an American air attaché in London called attention to the fighter's true potential. Maj. Thomas Hitchcock, a pilot in the Lafayette Escadrille during World War I and a horseman in civilian life, suggested "cross breeding" the P–51 with the Merlin engine that powered the Spitfire.[6] When Rolls Royce engineers substituted their supercharged Merlin for the original Allison, they doubled the altitude at which the airplane could fight and increased its speed beyond 400 miles per hour. Armed with six .50 caliber guns, the Mustang could now do battle at high altitude over targets deep in Germany. Although production eventually exceeded 14,500 aircraft, the P–51 was not ready in time for the critical air battles over Germany during the summer and fall of 1943, a failure that General Arnold conceded was "the Air Force's own fault" for ignoring the possibilities inherent in this design.[7]

Other new aircraft that appeared during war included the P–61 night fighter and C–46; C–54, and C–69 transports. Northrup built about 700 P–61 Black Widows—twin-engine, twin-boom aircraft—which replaced the P–70, a nightfighter version of the A–20. The radar-equipped Black Widow, comparable in size to a medium bomber, had the speed, endurance, and firepower—as many as eight 20–mm cannon and .50 caliber machineguns—needed in a night fighter. Curtiss-Wright manufactured some 3,000 C–46 Commandos, the heaviest and

Northrop P–61 Black Widow night fighter.

largest of the twin-engine transports, but the C–46 saw only limited action before 1944 because of the tendency of its 2,000-horsepower Pratt and Whitney radial engines to overheat. Once that problem was solved, another surfaced: the hydraulic system was vulnerable to fire from the ground. More successful were the thousand-odd Douglas C–54 Skymasters that the Air Transport Command used on transoceanic flights. The Lockheed C–69 Constellation, a four-engine aircraft like the Skymaster, showed great promise, but only 14 were built during the war.

Despite the late emergence of these successful aircraft, many of the types that helped contain the advancing Axis forces fought on until victory. The B–17 and B–24 served throughout the conflict, with the Air Forces accepting some 12,600 Flying Fortresses and more than 18,000 Liberators. The Douglas A–20 remained in production into 1944; the government purchased more than 7,000 before Douglas began producing the improved A–26. North American B–25 and Martin B–26 medium bombers entered the inventory as late as 1945; the Air Forces accepting almost 10,000 B–25s and slightly more than 5,000 B–26s. The Army bought the last of almost 10,000 Bell P–39s in 1944, turning then to the greatly improved P–63, also built by Bell, of which some 3,000 were accepted. A large proportion of the P–39s and P–63s were included in lend-lease deliveries. The final P–40 of more than 13,000 rolled from the Curtiss factory in 1944; and Lockheed ended P–38 production in 1945, with total acceptances approaching 10,000.

Emphasis on production diverted resources from research and development. Although useful concepts were tested—flying wings, wooden construction, and tail-first canard designs—the Air Forces, the National Advisory Committee for Aeronautics, and the aircraft industry concentrated on wringing the best performance from existing engines and airframes. As a result, the aerial gunner of 1945 might sit inside a power-operated plexiglass turret instead of battling the slipstream to manipulate his weapon as gunners did four years earlier, but he would still be a member of a B–17 crew. Similarly, the metal bead and ring gunsight fixed to the cowling of a P–40B gave way in later models to a device that reflected the sight picture onto the windscreen. Typical of the subordination of research and development to production was the saga of the jet fighter. The Army Air Forces and the aircraft manufacturers ignored the possibilities of the jet engine and set about perfecting the piston types, while others, primarily the British and Germans, examined this new means of propulsion. Once the British handed over the fruits of their research, however, Bell turned out a test aircraft, the XP–59, in just 13 months from the signing of the contract until first flight; and Lockheed designed and built the prototype for an operational jet fighter, the P–80, in an incredible 143 days.

The miracles of mass production would have been meaningless if the aircraft turned out in such an impressive volume had not met the current needs of combat: victorious fighters or effective bombers could, in one short year, become vic-

The Bell XP–59 Airacomet, the United States' first jet-powered aircraft.

tims with disheartening frequency. Changes had to made to aircraft like the P–38 or the B–17 to incorporate the lessons learned in battle. Typical of this process was the Flying Fortress. The B–17D of 1941 had a range of 2,500 miles and relied on seven hand-operated machineguns for its protection, whereas the most modern, the G model, could fly a maximum of 3,700 miles—the result of additional fuel tanks in the wings—and had eight of its 13 machineguns in power-driven turrets. Similarly, the last of the P–40s, due mainly to improvements in the Allison engine, surpassed the 1941 version by a factor of 10 percent in range (for a maximum 1,050 miles with a jettisonable tank), speed (increased to 343 miles per hour), and service ceiling (raised to 31,000 feet) and could carry more than twice the original bombload (now 1,500 pounds). The long service rendered by many of the types of aircraft on hand when Japan plunged the United States into war resulted from significant modifications to the basic design. Some models required changes to improve stability, to aid maneuverability, or to compensate for greater weight. Fighters in particular had to have increasingly more powerful engines, some fitted with water injection to improve combustion and thus provide a brief but dramatic surge of power in emergencies.

Modifications were absolutely essential; the question was where should the airplanes be modified. In terms of the efficient use of manpower, the assembly line was the best place, but frequent changes disrupted production and choked off the supply of aircraft at the source. Another possibility was modification centers, but these, too, had their drawbacks, for airplanes were taken out of service and worked on in comparatively small numbers by a large force of workers. Consequently, the Air Forces tried to employ the best features of both. Modification centers, most operated by the aircraft industry, prepared airplanes for service in a particular theater or climate and made changes that were either minor or so important they could not be postponed. Changes requiring retool-

244

ing were made at the factory and might take the form of a fairly complete re-design—such as the B–17D with a small vertical stabilizer and no power-operated gun turrets that emerged as the B–17E with a new tail and two power-operated turrets—or the simultaneous incorporation of several minor changes that might already be underway, one or two per aircraft, at the modification centers. To take advantage of the efficiency of the assembly line, the Air Forces grouped a number of minor refinements and designated them with a block number, so that the basic P–38G became a P–38G–1, or perhaps a P–38G–10, depending on the changes that had been made during manufacture.

Of all the post-production modification projects, the most ambitious involved the B–29 with its trouble-plagued 18-cylinder Wright engines. The first 150 of these planes, destined for India and China, could not leave the training site at Salina, Kansas, because late delivery or misrouting of parts had prevented needed modifications. General Arnold and a trusted specialist in maintenance and logistics, Maj. Gen. Bennett E. Meyers, arrived at the Kansas airfield, and Meyers promptly located the missing items, borrowed a work force from the Boeing plant at nearby Wichita, and set up an improvised modification center that enabled the Superfortresses to enter combat. Whatever his flaws of character—he eventually went to prison for diverting Air Forces funds to his own use—Meyers proved a masterful organizer. The first of the bombers was fully modified in about two weeks, and after six weeks, the last of the group had departed for the Far East.

Whether buying aircraft or modifying them, the agency of the Air Forces that dealt directly with the aviation industry was the Materiel Command, which

The B–29's powerful, complex, twin-row Wright R–3350 air-cooled engine was susceptible to fires caused by inadequate cooling.

evolved from the prewar Materiel Division. When Hitler invaded Poland in 1939, the Materiel Division exercised responsibility over most aspects of logistics— buying airplanes, overhauling aircraft in need of extensive repair, purchasing items of supply unique to the air arm, and distributing everything from motor oil to canned meat. The division's experimental engineering section, working close- ly with airplane manufacturers, handled research, development, testing, and eval- uation. The Air Corps obtained from the Army's technical services supplies used in common with other branches. The Quartermaster Corps, for instance, provid- ed food and uniforms, the Signal Corps radios, and the Ordnance and Chemical Corps furnished the various kinds of munitions used in aerial warfare. The dis- tribution of supplies, regardless of source, was the task of the Materiel Division's Field Service Section, which operated four major supply and storage depots throughout the United States. Combat elements of the GHQ Air Force drew their supplies from these depots, which also had maintenance facilities to undertake any aircraft repairs that the operating unit could not perform. During the rapid buildup of the air service that preceded America's involvement in the war, General Arnold decided that the combined tasks of maintenance, procurement, and supply would overwhelm the Materiel Division. In April 1941, therefore, he created the Maintenance Command to handle the routine purchase, storage, and distribution of supplies and to perform maintenance at all air bases, thus freeing the Materiel Division to concentrate on developing and acquiring airplanes and the equipment installed in them. Unfortunately, the change preceded by a few months a reorganization of Army aviation that entrusted support functions to the Air Corps and operations to the Combat Command. Supply and maintenance soon became a source of friction between the two.

Lt. Gen. Delos C. Emmons, chief of the new (and short-lived) Combat Command, resented having elements of the Air Corps operating supporting units on bases otherwise controlled by his organization. General Arnold in Oct- ober 1941 sought to resolve the issue by converting the Maintenance Command into the Air Service Command, with the authority to establish service units at all installations, although those located on Combat Command bases would be sub- ject to the administrative control of the base commander. Administrative control was not enough, however, for base commanders continued to resent serving as hosts to elements of another command; from the point of view of the local com- mander, he was supporting the very unit that was supposed to be supporting him. In January 1944, some twenty-one months after both the Air Corps and the Combat Command had disappeared as organizations, the commanding officers of bases obtained full control over the maintenance and supply units located on their airfields; but the Air Service Command continued to set the standards for the work of the units (called subdepots), largely through periodic inspections and the issuance and enforcement of technical orders establishing procedures.

The March 1942 reorganization of the War Department that abolished the Air Force Combat Command and the Office of Chief of the Air Corps also confirmed the status of the Air Service Command and elevated the Materiel Division to the organizational level and title of a full-fledged command. The basic distinction between the two remained the same—the relationship of their activity to the airplane. The Materiel Command developed and bought aircraft and engines and, in doing so, maintained cadres of engineers, inspectors, and auditors at the various factories throughout the country. The Air Service Command dealt directly with aircraft only in repairing them and processing the spare parts ordered by the Materiel Command; otherwise, it developed and purchased equipment unique to the air arm but not installed in aircraft—items like auxiliary power units for starting aircraft engines—and dealt with the process of supply by ordering, accepting, sorting, forwarding, and salvaging almost everything used by the Air Forces. In accomplishing its duties, the command established a network of depots and subdepots that handled both maintenance and supply. Even before the transfer of the subdepots to local control in January 1944, units overseas were subject to the technical supervision of the Air Service Command but were otherwise under the direct control of the numbered air force operating in the region, like the Eighth Air Force in the United Kingdom or the Fifth in the Southwest Pacific.

At its peak strength in late 1943, the Air Service Command operated 11 major depots and 238 subdepots in the United States. These were supplemented as necessary by special depots that functioned as central supply warehouses for critically needed items. The most serious problem facing the service command in carrying out the tasks of maintenance and supply was inventory control, a chore done manually with only the aid of the primitive punched-card business machines of that era. Duplicate serial numbers, lost documentation, and crates of supplies that were simply stacked and forgotten plagued the system throughout the war.

At the outset, the Air Service Command and the Materiel Command seemed to have a clear-cut difference in responsibilities, but the distinction tended to blur as the war progressed, especially in dealing with spare parts for aircraft and engines. The Materiel Command determined the quantity of parts, but the Air Service Command placed the actual order, arranged the production schedule, stored the parts, and distributed them. As a consequence, spare parts were sometimes unavailable when needed, for the service command had to take into account the availability of warehouse space and shipping, along with the needs of the users as established by the materiel specialists. Because of this administrative tangle and because an ideally suited officer was available to sort it out, the headquarters of the Army Air Forces decided to reintegrate the activities of both commands. General Knudsen, chief of the Materiel Command, had been an executive of General Motors, a member of the original National Defense Advisory Committee, and head of the prewar Office of Production Management. On the basis of this experience, Arnold selected him to command the new agency, the Air Technical Service Command, which combined the Air Service Command

and the Air Materiel Command. The official merger of the two organizations took place on September 1, 1944, some three years after the materiel and service functions were separated, but the actual consolidation moved slowly to avoid disrupting wartime projects.

The Air Service Command, and later Knudsen's Air Technical Service Command, undertook the daunting task of shipping war materiel overseas for temporary storage and distribution to the combat forces. During 1942, as the United States built up the overseas stocks that would enable the Allies to contain the enemy and take the offensive, the shipment of cargo remained comparatively simple, for speed was the main consideration. The basic strategy was to defeat Germany first, so the United Kingdom was the likely destination and New York City the most heavily used port of embarkation. Rommel's advance into Egypt in the spring of 1942 and the invasion of Northwest Africa later in the year caused a temporary diversion of men and cargo from Great Britain, but New York remained the principal port. As the war expanded and the volume of deliveries increased, special organizations had to be created to ensure the orderly dispatch of cargo. Beginning in 1943, supplies destined for Air Forces units outside the United States passed through the Atlantic or Pacific Overseas Air Service Commands. When the materiel arrived in the intended theater of operations, it moved through a network of depots and subdepots modeled after the network in the United States but operated by the numbered air force in each theater.

Until early 1943, during the period the overseas buildup was beginning and the great danger was too little of everything rather than too much of anything, the Army Air Forces relied upon automatic resupply to maintain stocks in the various theaters. Unfortunately, the tables governing shipments could not keep pace with changing circumstances, so that a supply officer might find himself inundated with items he did not need. As a result, once the initial frenzy to build and sustain adequate stockpiles had passed, the Air Forces reduced the use of automatic shipments, introducing a requisition system based on locally determined requirements.

After the supplies and spare parts reached their destination, the depot or subdepot that stored and issued them had a section that conducted aircraft maintenance. A large, centralized maintenance operation in the United States performed the extensive and time-consuming jobs that could not be done within the flying unit or at the local subdepot, completely rehabilitating an unserviceable aircraft if necessary. A major center required a large number of workers, but since each operation was divided into a series of comparatively simple tasks, like production work on an assembly line, the average individual level of skill did not have to be great. Rather than tie up thousands of trained Air Forces mechanics to man the domestic depots, General Arnold found it easier to hire civilians, many of them women, who possessed or could learn the skills necessary for airframe or engine repair. Uniformed technicians instead operated the centers in the combat zones and more remote centers unattractive to civilian em-

Members of the 834th Aviation Engineer Battalion prepare a new strip.

ployees. The civilian work force engaged in logistics activity, including aircraft
maintenance and repair, increased from 5,500 in 1939 to a peak slightly in excess of 300,000 by the spring of 1943; and the Army Air Forces obtained the services of still other civilians by letting contracts to airlines and other elements
of the aviation industry.

Every depot and subdepot had its share of soldiers, members of the Army's
technical services assigned to a variety of jobs from driving trucks to operating
the laundry. Realizing that an independent postwar air force would be responsible for all technical and housekeeping duties, Arnold's air arm tried gradually to absorb many of these tasks. Besides acquiring the base laundries from the
Quartermaster Corps and sharing in the administrative functions of the Adjutant
General, the Air Forces obtained authority over the development, procurement,
and maintenance of all electronic equipment, thus taking over functions exercised by the Signal Corps throughout much of the war. The service provided by
another component of the Army, the Corps of Engineers, required skills in earth
moving and heavy construction and could not be absorbed in similar fashion by
the Air Forces. Before the United States entered the war, General Arnold had
proposed that the engineers train and equip units to perform lighter construction
in building, repairing, and camouflaging airfields in the combat theaters.
Experience during the Army maneuvers in 1941 demonstrated the value of these
aviation engineers, and a battalion was serving at Hickam Field, Hawaii, when
the Japanese attacked in December. Units of this sort attained a peak wartime
strength of almost 118,000 in February 1945; they served in every theater of
war, although sometimes under the direction of the theater engineer officer
rather than the senior airman. When commanded by the theater engineer, the

aviation engineers tended to function like other elements of the Corps of Engineers and lost their distinctive character.

The output of the American aircraft industry, aided by the vast yet efficient logistics complex that evolved during the war, enabled the Army Air Forces to get replacements for operational losses, accidents, and obsolescence. The number of aircraft on hand increased by more than sixfold, from some 12,000 aircraft at the end of December 1941 to more than 25,000 at the farthest extent of the Axis advance in 1942 to a peak of more than 79,000 in the summer of 1944. Just as aircraft factories were useless without workers, the huge aircraft inventory of the Army Air Forces could accomplish nothing without the hundreds of thousands of men and the comparatively small number of women with such diverse jobs as pilots, members of aircrews, weather observers, engine mechanics, or as teletype operators. To fly, support, and maintain its aircraft, the Air Forces in June 1945 had 2,282,259 persons in uniform, almost one-fourth the aggregate strength of the Army, 15 times the number of airmen and officers on duty six months before the Japanese attacked Pearl Harbor, and three times the number serving in the air arm six months after the fighting began.

This growth doomed for the duration of the conflict, if not forever, the principle that pilots should dominate the air arm in numbers, as well as in authority. The Air Corps Act of 1926 had decreed that 90 percent of the Regular officers should be pilots—aeronautical engineers and even navigators were pilots first and specialists second—but no such policy could apply to a large and semiautonomous branch of service in which temporary officers by far outnumbered the Regulars. For example, wartime growth multiplied paperwork, and administration soon became a major problem for the Army Air Forces, as it absorbed many of the tasks formerly done by the Army's Office of the Adjutant General. Further complicating both administration and the training of administrators was the transfer of qualified officers experienced in both paperwork and flying, who with the outbreak of war were eager to trade their desks for the cockpit. As early as 1942, therefore, General Arnold felt compelled to authorize the creation of an Officer Candidate School, largely to produce specialists in administration. Established at Miami Beach, Florida, though eventually moving to Maxwell Field, Alabama, the course graduated some 30,000 lieutenants during the war. In addition, the Army Air Forces commissioned individuals directly from civil life, usually because they possessed some needed skill or profession. Direct commissions went to lawyers, businessmen, public relations executives, doctors, and others. The commissioning of nonflying administrators for wartime service was but one element in the shift from what had been a small corps of career officers composed almost totally of pilots to a large officer corps with numerical preponderance of nonpilots or part-time pilots commissioned for the duration of the war because they had special skills related directly or indirectly to aerial flight.

Two examples of the need for these specialists were the Army Air Forces Weather Service and the Army Airways Communications Service, both of which expanded from small peacetime organizations located mainly in the United States and its overseas possessions to worldwide operations essential to an effective air arm. The creation and early expansion of the Army Air Forces Ferrying Command triggered a demand for up-to-date weather information and reliable communications in areas like South America, Central Africa, and Greenland. From some 60 specialists in 1940, the weather service expanded within four years to about 4,000 meteorologists and weather observers serving in such diverse locations as China, the islands of the Pacific, and the airfields of Sicily and Italy. Communications teams accompanied Air Forces units into every theater, providing radio links and navigation aids vital to the air war. Radio operators endured tropical disease, air raids, and fatigue as they not only manned their equipment but also sometimes doubled as infantry, defending against infiltrators or stragglers. By the end of the war, the 49,000 specialists of the communications service operated a network of some 800 radio stations, 570 control towers, 200 message centers, and 1,300 navigation aids.

As the prewar Air Corps became the wartime Air Forces, pilots and support specialists were assigned to noncombat flying that nonetheless helped carry the air war to the enemy. Originally intended to ferry aircraft from factories in the United States to transfer points where British crews took over for the Atlantic crossing, the Ferrying Command evolved during the war into a global organization with 80 percent of its air routes outside the continental United States. Redesignated the Air Transport Command, it ultimately operated about 3,000 aircraft, flying passengers and cargo some 935 million miles. Besides carrying men and cargo, the Air Transport Command continued to deliver aircraft to combat theaters ranging from England to India. Indeed, ferrying crews delivered more than 250,000 airplanes (although those shuttling among several commands were counted each time they changed hands), in the process flying more than 600 million miles but losing just 1,000 aircraft to accidents or hostile action.

In recruiting and maintaining an organization that had a peak wartime strength of 2,400,000 and embraced hundreds of military specialties other than piloting an aircraft, the leadership of the Army Air Forces employed categories of persons normally excluded in peacetime. For example, pressure from Congress forced a reluctant General Arnold to agree in 1940 to accept blacks and admit them to flight training, although on a racially segregated basis in keeping with War Department policy. Concerned that accepting blacks, at a time when most aspects of American society remained racially segregated, would result in turmoil within the air arm and thus reduce its efficiency, he tried to minimize contacts between the races by establishing a flight training center at the Tuskegee Institute, a relatively isolated college for blacks in rural Alabama that already trained civilian pilots. The black pilots and crews trained at this one location, where black mechanics serviced their aircraft, and black administrative clerks typed and filed their reports and requisitions. As a result, every black flying unit trained from scratch, without the benefit of a veteran cadre to whom the

251

Tuskegee aviation cadets and their instructor.

younger officers and men could look for advice. Despite the handicaps imposed by racial segregation, the Army Air Forces organized four fighter squadrons, which formed the 332d Fighter Group, and four medium bombardment squadrons, incorporated into the 477th Bombardment Wing (Medium). The bomber crews saw no combat, but the fighter pilots destroyed or shared in the destruction of 108.5 German aircraft.

Roughly six percent of those serving in the Army Air Forces were black Americans, with the vast majority draftees who did not fly aircraft or maintain them but instead manned labor or housekeeping units that patched roads, mended roofs, and cut grass at air bases or manhandled supplies at logistics depots. Their duties were boring, their leadership indifferent, and their morale poor. Restricted to a small range of activity, they had little opportunity for promotion or hope of transfer to fields more clearly related to winning the war. The dissatisfaction bred by this treatment needed only a shove or racial slur to result in violence. At Bamber Bridge in the United Kingdom, for instance, an armed clash erupted after white military police forcibly arrested a black airman for being out of uniform at a village pub. Clearly the Air Forces, reflecting the policy of the Army and the attitudes of a racially segregated nation, did not make full use of the abilities of those the blacks serving in its wartime ranks.

Women, too, had an opportunity to contribute to the success of the wartime Army Air Forces. On May 15, 1942, President Roosevelt signed a bill creating a Women's Army Auxiliary Corps, later redesignated the Women's Army Corps.

Eighth Air Force map table showing positions of long-range fighters.

Since the air arm was part of the Army, the women volunteers were eligible to serve there, and in January 1945 the number doing so reached 29,323, the maximum wartime strength, of whom about 20 percent served outside the continental United States. Blacks, although eligible to enlist, accounted for less than three percent of the women in the Army Air Forces.

The so-called Air WACs received various assignments during the war. Initially, most joined the aircraft warning service where they replaced some 6,000 unpaid women volunteers at air defense centers on both coasts. Once the threat of aerial attack on the United States had abated, the women soldiers received different assignments. By January 1945, enlisted women served the Air Forces in more than 200 categories of jobs, while female officers carried out more than 60 kinds of duties. As impressive as the number of jobs might seem, roughly half the women in the Army Air Forces performed administrative or clerical tasks. As file clerks, typists, or stenographers, they did basically what they had done as civilians, though they now were subject to military discipline and had to know procedures, organizations, and terminology unique to the Army. Women kept flight records, for example, helped process men and equipment for transfer overseas, and served as dispatchers or operated information desks at air terminals. In the entire Women's Army Corps, no more than 20 individuals were qualified as aircrew members for noncombat flights, though others sometimes went along as radio operators. At least one woman earned the title of crew chief, responsible for the maintenance of a specific airplane, and one flight line was staffed with women mechanics as an experiment. Eventually the number of women mechanics surpassed 1,200.

Two WASPs at the controls of a Boeing B–17 at Buckingham Field, Florida.

Another wartime program assigned women pilots to ferry aircraft and perform other flying duty, usually in the United States. Two such groups of civilian volunteers merged into the WASP—Women Airforce Service Pilots. The members were subject to military discipline during training but held no rank and did not, as their director, Jacqueline Cochran, complained, have even "the right to a military funeral."[8] The Army Air Forces accepted fewer than 1,900 of the 25,000 who applied to become WASPs, but of those who entered, 1,074 completed their indoctrination and began flying. A total of 37 died in accidents and 36 sustained injuries of varying severity. Although ferrying planes was their first and principal duty, they also towed targets at gunnery school and served as instructors at flight schools. By the time the Air Forces, facing a surplus of male aviators, disbanded the WASP in December 1944, the women had flown about 60 million miles on operational duty.

Women also played an important, if more traditional, role as nurses. By 1944, some 6,500 Army nurses served in the Air Forces, most assigned to military hospitals. About 500 flight nurses cared for critically wounded soldiers during air evacuation missions, helping to reduce the mortality rate and thus contributing to higher morale among combat troops. Nurses accepted for flight duty had to undergo an eight-week training course so strenuous as to persuade one observer that each graduate should have received a medal. The curriculum, for instance, required the nurses to crawl the length of an infiltration course while machinegun fire cracked overhead.

The demand for manpower, which resulted in a lowering of the barriers that had excluded entire groups from the Air Forces, also led to an easing of standards, whether for draftees or aviation cadets. The Selective Service System tried to assign each of the services a share of the draftees who had scored poorly on the general classification test, but the Air Forces, because of the need for so many enlisted technicians, accepted a smaller proportion than the Army Ground Forces. Besides accepting a number of draftees with lower scores that it would have preferred, the air arm had to adjust downward the standards for admission to pilot training. For example, the minimum age for pilot training was reduced from twenty to eighteen years, and the required two years of college could be waived for applicants who passed a general educational test. Moreover, high school graduates who had never attended college could become cadets with the understanding that they would serve as sergeant pilots rather than as commissioned officers after completing the required training. Instead of sergeants, some became flight officers, as the Air Forces called its flying warrant officers, and a few were commissioned. One of this talented few was Charles E. "Chuck" Yeager, first pilot to fly faster than the speed of sound, who became a fighter ace, set aviation records, and eventually retired as a general officer.[9]

So overwhelming was the response to the call for air cadets that the Army Air Forces began using an enlisted reserve as a manpower reservoir to hold qualified volunteers, subject to the draft, who could not immediately be accommodated at cadet training facilities. The enlisted reserve also served as a means to retain the civilian instructors at primary flying schools like the Thunderbird Field complex in Arizona. Since these instructors performed just the one task, normally at a single base, and were not available for combat, Secretary of War Henry L. Stimson declined to offer them commissions, leaving them subject to the draft. If they wished to continue with the essential job of teaching others to fly, they had to choose between enrolling in the reserve or accepting direct commissions as flight instructors in the Navy. The latter course, which removed them from the Air Forces program, often proved more attractive.

As in the Air Corps of the interwar years, the pilot remained the most important (although no longer the most numerous) of officers in a vastly expanded and greatly diversified wartime air arm. Pilot training began with preflight instruction; and early in the war, all cadets received this indoctrination at a replacement center, with about 175 hours devoted to physical training, drill, organized athletics, and classroom instruction that included an introduction to meteorology, mathematics, photography, wireless telegraphy, map reading, and the recognition of Allied and enemy ships and aircraft. Because the existing Army preflight schools could not absorb all the men seeking to enter the aviation cadet program, General Arnold made arrangements with colleges and universities, largely devoid of male students because of the war, to teach portions of the curriculum. Faculty members taught the academic aspects of preflight training like mathematics and meteorology, and officers assigned to each detachment handled the purely military instruction, including map reading and radio commu-

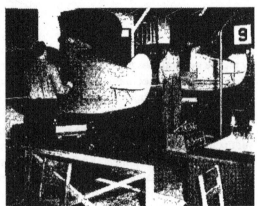

Pilot training: new trainees arrive at Replacement Center (top left), trainees learn instrument flying in Link trainers (top right), trainees and instructors discuss flights (left above), a solo in a North American AT–6 (left below), and prospective bomber pilots trained in Curtiss AT–9s (bottom).

Training: navigator (top left), turret gunner (top right), bombadier (right), and aviation engineers (bottom), who are diving for cover as a P–40 from another base practices a low-level run.

nication. During 1944, when the backlog of cadets diminished to manageable size, the Air Forces ended the college program.

From preflight training, future pilots entered primary training, where they learned to fly a docile, but rugged, airplane like the Boeing PT–17, usually under the tutelage of a civilian instructor. To complete this phase of instruction, which required from 60 to 65 hours in the cockpit, the student had to solo and perform certain elementary maneuvers like inside loops and rolls. For a time, the Flying Training Command tried to introduce fledgling pilots to night flying during primary training, but few cadets could meet the challenge, and the subject was postponed until basic training, the next phase of instruction.

During basic training, almost always administered by uniformed instructors, trainees mastered the military applications of the fundamental techniques learned in the earlier phase. Flying an aircraft like the Vultee BT–13, students spent 70 to 75 hours at the controls, practicing aerobatics, formation flying, and daylight navigation. During basic training, future pilots first encountered the sensations of blind flying in the Link trainer, a simple flight simulator named for its inventor, Edwin A. Link. Seated beneath a hood, which prevented him from looking outside, an individual student followed the instructions received over earphones; manipulated the controls, which caused the machine to rotate on a pivot; and learned to trust aircraft instruments rather than his own senses. Because trainees had to absorb so much so quickly, the curriculum for basic training changed several times, with less emphasis sometimes placed on formation and instrument flying to permit greater attention to aerobatics and with aerobatics sometimes yielding time to instruction in blind flying.

Basic training marked a watershed, for successful graduates afterward began to specialize in single-engine or multiengine aircraft. Those selected to fly fighters received advanced training in the single-engine North American AT–6, whereas future bomber or transport pilots faced the challenge of a twin-engine type like the Curtiss AT–9 or Beech AT–10. During advanced training, all cadets returned to the Link trainer, since instrument flying formed an important part of the curriculum, and received further instruction in aerial navigation. The potential fighter pilots (some of whom, depending on the needs of the moment, would become copilots in bombers or transports) devoted much of their seventy hours in the air to practicing aerobatics and gunnery. The cadets received their wings after advanced training and, with the exception of those few that already held commissions or became sergeant pilots or flight officers, received the wartime rank of second lieutenant in the Army Air Forces.

Graduate pilots then entered transition training, an extension of the advanced course emphasizing combat skills. Subjects included more gunnery and aerobatics for fighter pilots, who devoted about 10 of their 30 hours in the cockpit flying obsolete aircraft like the P–40. Bomber and transport pilots spent 100 hours at the controls, did further work on instrument flying, and received an introduction to the aircraft they would be assigned to fly, perhaps the B–17 or the

C–47. Next in the normal course of events came assignment to an operational unit in the United States for combat training, followed by duty overseas. Chuck Yeager called combat training a "gruesome weeding out process" from which only the best survived.[10] Thirteen pilots who entered combat training with him died in crashes caused by stalling when making too tight a turn at low speed and low altitude, by cutting it too close while buzzing the Nevada wasteland and hitting the crest of a ridge, or by failing to recover from a high-speed dive. Including transition and combat training, the average American pilot spent about a year preparing for combat, logging about 400 hours in the air before going into battle. In contrast, by mid-1944 German aviators received perhaps 150 hours of training and Japanese fewer than 100.

The number of weeks devoted to pilot training for Army aviators changed during the war. The preflight course, originally a four-week indoctrination, finally stabilized at ten weeks, largely because of the importance of subjects like meteorology and aircraft identification and the need of many cadets for additional instruction in mathematics. While the program lasted, cadets assigned to training detachments at colleges could remain on campus for as long as five months before reporting for the next phase of training. Otherwise, acceleration was the watchword until victory drew near. In the summer of 1939, the Air Corps reduced the cycle of primary, basic, and advanced training from twelve months to nine; it declined during the following year to seven months, with thirty weeks of actual instruction, and to twenty-seven weeks after the United States entered the war. Not until March 1944, did the trend reverse and the time allotted for training return to thirty weeks. As a general rule, the less the demand, the longer and presumably more thorough the course of instruction, regardless of the specialty being taught.

During World War II, 193,000 men emerged from advanced training to receive the silver wings of a pilot in the Army Air Forces. Another 124,000, almost 40 percent of the total, began primary training but failed at some stage of the process or became victims of accidents. The number undergoing flight training at any given time reflected the anticipated needs of the service. In December 1943, the total peaked at 74,000, which resulted in too many pilots and caused the air arm to begin reducing the number of cadets accepted until only 5,000 were in training when the hostilities ended.

Some who did not complete the course received the opportunity to train for other positions within aircrews. Most bombardiers, in fact, acquired their specialty after elimination from pilot training. Until 1940, no formal school for bombardiers existed; enlisted men and the few nonpilot officers learned this skill while serving in bombardment squadrons. During 1940, however, the Air Corps opened a school for instructors at Lowry Field, Colorado; and in 1941, graduates began teaching the subject, following a curriculum that at first lasted twelve weeks but was extended to eighteen and finally to twenty-four weeks as the demand for bombardiers decreased. Once again, the less the need for a particular specialist, the greater was the time invested in training.

Although the almost 45,000 graduates of bombardier training learned the rudiments of navigation, success depended on demonstrating the ability to put bombs on a target. The cadets trained with the Norden sight, for a time the Sperry as well, or with a different type intended for lower medium-altitude attack. Perched on the A–2 simulator—a wheeled, self-propelled, steel scaffold—students scored their first hits on paper targets placed on the floor of a hangar. After this introduction, they dropped dummy and practice bombs from a Beech AT–11 fitted with a bombsight and an automatic pilot. During subsequent training, bombardiers learned the characteristics of the planes in which they entered combat and became qualified aircrew members.

The Air Corps had provided some instruction in aerial navigation since the early 1930s, but the courses that were functioning when the war began could not produce the necessary number of graduates. Until the expanded Army schools could begin operating, Pan American Airways taught students at its facility in Florida. Mastering a curriculum that lasted 18 weeks (20 weeks after December 1944), more than 50,000 students learned four basic methods of aerial navigation. The first method, dead reckoning, involved the computation of the speed and heading necessary, allowing for the effect of wind, to follow a charted course. A second technique, pilotage, required the use of general compass headings in conjunction with checkpoints visible from the air. The other two methods, celestial navigation and radio navigation, relied on the use of the stars and the sun or on radio signals from known locations on the ground to keep the aircraft on course. Emphasis throughout the period of instruction rested on practical solutions rather than theory, with each trainee flying about 20 missions totaling 100 hours.

Both navigators and bombardiers received some training in flexible gunnery, since in most bombers they had this additional duty. All enlisted men in a bomber crew served as aerial gunners, whether this was their primary function or a collateral task, as with radio operators and some armorers or mechanics. The 297,000 graduates of gunnery courses usually received six weeks of training. First, they fired at fixed or moving targets at ranges on the ground; they then went aloft in trainers like the Lockheed AT–18 to engage towed targets or use gun cameras against maneuvering fighters. An attempt to fire frangible bullets at heavily armored P–63 fighters proved unsuccessful; the reduced charge in the cartridge fouled the machineguns, and the flying targets proved susceptible to damage from hits in unarmored spots or the ingestion of bullet fragments into the cooling system.

Gunners manning the remote-control turrets of the B–29 required additional specialized instruction, for in that airplane only the tail gunner actually aimed and fired his guns from inside a turret. The other gunners aimed through plexiglass bubbles on the fuselage and fired the weapons electrically. An officer with the rating of bombardier manned a scanning station atop the fuselage and served as "gun captain," coordinating the defensive fire.[11] The two waist gunners in B–29s received additional training, one as an electrician, the other as an armorer, and between them they made emergency repairs to the firing circuits or the guns.

The B–29, besides requiring specially trained gunners, had a flight engineer who inspected, monitored, and adjusted the four temperamental engines and the oxygen and hydraulic systems. Instructors trained by Lockheed Aircraft conducted basic and advanced courses for flight engineers that lasted a total of 29 weeks. About 7,800 airmen completed the training, which like the bombardier and navigator courses resulted in a commission for those who graduated.

The emergence of airborne radar in bombers and night fighters created a need for other new courses of instruction. Since B–17s, B–24s, and B–29s used radar to attack targets obscured by cloud or darkness, some 7,600 graduate bombardiers or navigators received the additional 10 weeks or more of instruction that qualified them in the techniques of radar bombardment. Another 500 officers, graduates of a course in communications, became radar countermeasures specialists and learned to frustrate enemy efforts to track bomber formations. Similarly, 1,000 men trained to become radar operators in night fighters; most were aviation cadets dropped from pilot training but were commissioned or appointed warrant officers after the nine-week radar course.

Aircrew survival and mission success depended in large measure on the mechanics who kept the airplanes flying, individuals with skills that included engine overhaul, sheet metal work, and radio repair. Between the attack on Pearl Harbor and the cessation of hostilities, almost 1,400,000 persons had some kind of technical training, an indication of the importance of these specialists. Before the war a single technical school at Chanute Field, Illinois, had produced all the mechanics the Air Corps needed, no more than 900 graduates per year; but the wartime Army Air Forces relied heavily on contractors to train the vast number of technicians it needed. The prewar graduates, moreover, worked on airframes,

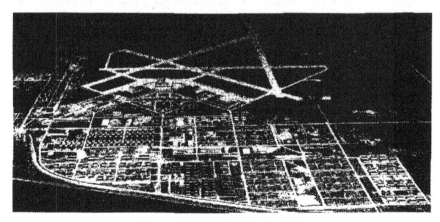

Chanute Field, Illinois, in 1943.

engines, and comparatively few aircraft accessories like radios, hydraulics, or electrical systems. In the 1930s, one mechanic could perform almost every job on any aircraft, but this was not so during World War II. New warplanes were not only more numerous but far more complex, with accessories that included power-driven gun turrets (sometimes operated by remote control), radar, a pressurized cabin in the B–29, engine superchargers, and components made of magnesium, a more difficult material to work with than aluminum. In recognition of the growing complexity of the modern airplane, students concentrated not only on a single skill, like sheet metal work or engine repair, but also on a specific category of aircraft. The advent of radically different aircraft like the B–29, the helicopter, and the jet-propelled P–80 required the preparation of new courses designed exclusively for each type and its components.

Throughout the war, service schools, including the one at Chanute Field, usually taught fundamentals to the mechanics, who then received further training from contractors, either in private institutions or at aircraft factories. During the first six months of 1942, the number of private institutions under contract increased from nine to 16, among them the Curtiss-Wright Technical Institute, the Boeing School of Aeronautics, Parks Air College, and the Embry-Riddle School of Aviation. The number of mechanics in training approached 8,000 at midyear, and the courses dealt with such specialties as engines, sheet metal work, instruments, hydraulics, and propellers.

Specialists in electronic fields also received training at service schools and from contractors. Enlisted radio operators and repairmen trained at Chanute Field; but officers specializing in radio communication received their initial instruction at Chanute Field until 1943, then at Yale University, and at Scott Field, Illinois, beginning in 1944. Radar training began at the Massachusetts Institute of Technology, where a few officers attended classes in 1941. As the use of radar became more common, schools opened at Scott Field; Truax Field, Wisconsin; and Boca Raton Army Airfield, Florida. A basic course in electronics, eventually required before radar training, was offered at Chanute Field, Harvard University, and the Massachusetts Institute of Technology.

The Army Service Forces, which provided technical services to the Ground Forces and the Air Forces, also provided instruction in certain specialties needed throughout the Army. Cooks, bakers, and supply clerks graduated from schools operated by the Quartermaster Corps. Pay clerks received training from the Finance Corps, and Air Forces chaplains trained at Harvard University under the auspices of the Army Chaplain Corps. The Ordnance Corps taught men to fuze and handle high-explosive bombs, and the Chemical Warfare Service trained airmen to work with fire bombs, although the Air Forces taught the repair and maintenance of aerial machineguns and cannon. Weather was of vital interest to the entire Army, but the air arm needed unique kinds of data and therefore trained its own weathermen. During the war, the Air Forces began exerting greater control over courses in chemical munitions, finance, and military police procedures in preparation for the day when the service became independent and no longer relied on the Army Service Forces.

Like the elements of the Army Service Forces that trained cooks, clerks, and munitions handlers, the Army Medical Service helped provide specialists for the Air Forces. As before the war, the Army Medical Service shared in the training of doctors and nurses, offering general instruction in medical subjects likely to be encountered throughout the Army. The Air Forces then took over the training program, sending newly assigned doctors to its School of Aviation Medicine, where they became flight surgeons, and training officers of the Army Nurse Corps in subjects related to military aviation. The Air Forces also operated schools where enlisted medical technicians and hospital stewards received instruction in health, hygiene, and first aid.

Important wartime advances in aviation medicine included the use of transports fitted with litters to fly the wounded to well-equipped hospitals away from the combat zone, the development of effective and reasonably comfortable oxygen masks, and the improvement of electrically heated flying suits. Less successful were attempts to develop an ejection seat for fighter pilots and an inflatable corset or "G-suit" that maintained an adequate supply of blood to the brain by not allowing blood to collect below the heart, thus preventing blackouts in violent aerial maneuvers.[12] A few of the G-suits, so called because they compensated for the effect of forces several times the pull of gravity, appeared before the fighting ended, but not the ejection device. To compensate in part for the lack of an ejection seat, the Air Forces substituted the bailout bottle, a portable metal container for oxygen fastened to the parachute harness that enabled a pilot to breathe at high altitude while escaping from a damaged airplane and parachuting to safety. Flight surgeon William R. Lovelace II tested the bottle by making a parachute jump, his first, from an altitude of 40,000 feet. The experiment confirmed that the principle was correct but also revealed that parachute harnesses would have to be strengthened and the oxygen container attached more securely.

Assisted by nurses, medical technicians, psychologists, and psychiatrists, the flight surgeon held the key to medical care within the Air Forces, examining those seeking to enter and caring for those accepted. Because the requirement for academic training had been relaxed to obtain more cadets, the medical service developed a battery of psychological and medical tests designed to eliminate at the outset those unlikely to complete pilot training. After interviewing instructors, graduates, and nongraduates, psychologists prepared a multiple-choice test believed capable of measuring a cadet's aptitude for flight training or other instruction. Scores helped determine whether a cadet might train to be a pilot, begin immediately to master the duties of a bombardier or navigator, or be rejected for instruction as an aircrew member. General Arnold insisted that the tests were well worth the cost of less than five dollars per candidate, and the failure rate in pilot training of roughly 40 percent did represent an improvement over the 50-percent attrition during World War I, when psychological testing was not attempted. Moreover, many of those barred from entering pilot training, along with a good many of those who were eliminated during the course, succeeded in becoming navigators or bombardiers, contributing to the efficient use of manpower.

The basic function of the flight surgeon in the bombardment or fighter group was to determine not only if a man was physically able to fly but whether he could still function as part of a fighting team. Besides caring for the flyer's immediate medical needs, flight surgeons had to diagnose and treat the stress encountered in aerial combat, whether affecting the mind, body, or both. The sudden transition from an airfield in rural England to an air battle five miles above Germany intensified the stress of waging a fight for life that lasted from a few minutes to several hours, a fight in which cold or a lack of oxygen could prove as deadly as fire from antiaircraft guns or fighters. Indeed, as Air Forces physicians soon discovered, stress, though difficult to diagnose, could disable a man just as surely as wounds from bullets or shell fragments. The average doctor serving as a wartime flight surgeon had little previous experience with psychosomatic reactions, since the tensions of peacetime were far different from those of war. Yet, the surgeons, aided by psychiatrists and psychologists, discovered how to help the airmen through the worst times, and commanders came to treat the effects of stress as a medical rather than a disciplinary problem. Cooperation between medical specialists and flying commanders contributed to a remarkable stability among bomber crews—only 1.5 percent of the crew members were grounded permanently either for reaction to stress or for other causes that did not involve physical injury. Another small group, fewer than three percent, were removed temporarily from flying status but returned to the air war over Germany.

For some members of bomber crews, personal armor proved a simple, but effective, means of reducing anxiety and stress by providing the wearer some degree of protection against death or disability. If possible, a crewman donned both an infantryman's steel helmet and a newly developed vest or apron that could stop shell fragments or ricocheting bullets. Col. Malcolm C. Grow, the Eighth Air Force Flight Surgeon, launched the study that analyzed the kinds of wounds suffered by bomber crewmen and resulted in the development of body armor.

In their early efforts to deal with victims of stress, Eighth Air Force flight surgeons found that the absence of a fixed combat tour contributed to anxiety or emotional breakdown. Crew members facing disheartening rates of attrition needed a goal, a sense of making progress toward relief from the demands of aerial combat. As a result, in March 1943, General Eaker, then in command of the Eighth Air Force, announced a tour of duty of 25 missions for bomber crews and 150 to 200 operational flying hours for fighter pilots. Even so, bomber crewmen in particular remained haunted by the thought that the odds were heavily against them. Curtis E. LeMay, while a brigadier general in the Eighth Air

Force, used rough calculations and determined leadership to inspire resignation, if not confidence, among the bomber forces he commanded in Europe during 1943. Col. Charles B. Thornton of General Arnold's statistical control unit adopted a different approach in 1944, when he tried to demonstrate mathematically that a crew member flying from the United Kingdom had about a 60 percent chance of completing his tour and a 50 percent chance of surviving if shot down, a combination that resulted in an 80 percent prospect of survival. Thornton's numbers, however, may have been reflected an overly optimistic view of the collapse of German resistance. A postwar analysis of six bombardment groups flying missions against targets in Europe examined the fate of 2,051 crewmen who began a cycle of 25 missions and discovered that by the time of the last mission 1,295 had been killed or reported missing and another 197 were ill or recovering from wounds. Clearly, other commanders had good reason to follow Eaker's example and establish a standard combat tour for each theater. Because circumstances varied, policies differed from one theater to another and within a given theater according to the particular time. In the Mediterranean Theater of Operations, typical bomber crews had to fly between 50 and 60 missions and fighter pilots 300 hours or more, but in the Pacific 500 to 600 hours constituted a tour in either bombers of fighters. The China-Burma-India Theater had no announced policy at all.

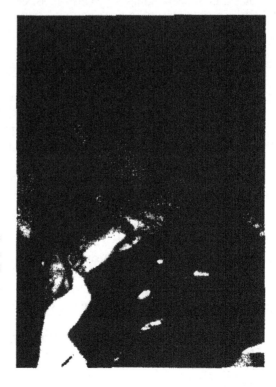

Crewman struck in the back by a 20-mm explosive projectile with the armored vest that saved his life .

Rest and recreation supplemented the effect of the fixed tour. Throughout the world, the Army Air Forces medical service established rest centers where airmen could escape the stress of war. The prospect of visiting such a center depended on the theater of operations and the tempo of the war; in the Pacific, the Fifth and Thirteenth Air Forces tried to schedule leave every three months, whereas in Eighth Air Force in Europe the interval varied from two to five months. According to one official and somewhat breathless account, individuals sent to these facilities might spend "idle pleasant days while the mysterious 'healing force of nature' accomplished what no scheduled rehabilitation could ever do."

Another means of easing anxiety, raising morale, and saving the lives of trained airmen was the Air-Sea Rescue Service operated jointly by the Army Air Forces and the Navy. Lacking a rescue organization early in the war, the Air Forces assembled and trained one in a remarkably short time. In England, Army airmen supplemented the work of the Royal Air Force, and during 1943 rescue units of the two nations saved about 28 percent of the Eighth Air Force crews that went down off the coast of Britain. The proportion saved increased as the war continued, reaching as high as 90 percent in a single month as the fighting neared an end. By March 1945, 1,972 American flyers had been saved by British and American rescue units in the North Sea, the English Channel, and other waters surrounding the British Isles. On the opposite side of the world, ships or rescue aircraft picked up half the B–29 crewmen reported to have crash landed between the Mariana Islands and Japan. Indeed, the rescue effort in support of the bombing of Japan became so immense that on the final B–29 mission of the war, some 2,400 men, about one fourth of those taking part in the operation, manned rescue aircraft.

Unlike the tightly structured military society of the 1920s or 1930s, the wartime air arm was diverse in background and outlook, composed overwhelmingly of wartime airmen whose service in uniform represented a temporary aberration rather than a career. As a result, the armed forces had to ease the transition of the citizen soldier from civil society to life in uniform by making a special effort to preserve some of the amenities he was used to. Chaplains and agencies such as the Red Cross and Army Emergency Relief helped in time of personal crisis or family emergency by offering counsel, or even small amounts of cash. Morale also benefited from recreational activities sponsored by Army Air Forces Special Services. This organization presented movies, supplied athletic gear, ran hobby shops, distributed scarce radios and phonographs, and in conjunction with the United Service Organization arranged for professional entertainers to perform at air bases. Special Services sponsored athletic competition at bases everywhere, with the Eighth Air Force alone having over 500 basketball teams.

Nor was education ignored. Commanders encouraged enrollment in the United States Armed Forces Institute or other correspondence courses. Sym-

Downed airmen are helped aboard a Consolidated
OA–10 Catalina rescue seaplane.

phony concerts and operatic performances were available for men stationed
near Naples, and airmen in Britain could learn to appreciate the art in the gal-
leries there. Indeed, almost everywhere base education sections arranged off-
duty sightseeing tours; supplied and ran libraries; published newspapers; and
distributed news maps, copies of officially sponsored publications like *Stars
and Stripes* and *Yank*, and commercial newspapers and magazines.

Because of its sudden growth, which involved the acquisition of vast tracts
of land and extensive construction, and the heavy investment in advanced technology as well as in manpower, land-based American air power, when un-
leashed in World War II, could not provide an inexpensive means of victory, as
Douhet, Mitchell, and other visionaries had predicted. In part the high cost resulted from a lavish use of materials, an expansible work force, increased plant
capacity, and a program of subsidies that encouraged a greater volume of production than was absolutely necessary. At no time did the aircraft industry have
to slight the Army to favor the Navy or slight the bomber to favor the fighter.
Few hard choices proved necessary once production took priority over long-
range development. Indeed, production took on a life of its own, sometimes
churning out aircraft far in excess of American needs, although useful to the nation's allies, and providing alternatives to unproven weapons like the B–29.
Prodigal as well as prodigious, aircraft production typified a war effort that
mass-produced everything from rifles to merchant ships.

To build and sustain air power and employ it in a worldwide conflict required
vast expenditures. Between July 1940 and the cessation of hostilities in August

History of the United States Air Force

1945, the Army Air Forces accepted equipment worth $43.5 billion, roughly 37 percent of the amount spent by the War Department for military procurement. Actually the air arm's share of the cost was even larger, for elements of the Army Service Forces (which embraced the technical commands) purchased a variety of items for use by the Air Forces. The Army Ordnance Corps, for example, provided high-explosive bombs and rockets, the Chemical Warfare Service supplied fire bombs, and the Signal Corps furnished a great deal of radio and radar equipment. Because of this assistance from the Army Service Forces, the Air Forces could devote almost 83 percent of its procurement funds to the purchase of aircraft, some of them transferred to the U.S. Navy or to the armed forces of Allied governments.

The U.S. Treasury reported that from September 1939 until the fighting ended in 1945 it released $160 billion to the War Department. Spending patterns suggest that the Army Air Forces used roughly $50 billion or about 30 percent of the total, a sum that does not take into account either War Department expenditures on industrial facilities for aircraft manufacture or items the technical services supplied for to the air arm. The War Department invested a comparable proportion of its uniformed manpower in military aviation. The strength of the Air Forces fluctuated between 23 and 31 percent of the total serving in the wartime Army, reaching a peak in excess of 2,300,000 men and women in 1944. The Air Forces suffered 52,173 killed in action and 63,209 wounded, approximately 12 percent of the Army's 936,259 battle casualties, which vindicated the belief that it would cost fewer lives to wage aerial warfare than to fight a land campaign. Casualties per hundred men in uniform stood at five and one-tenth for the Air Forces but ten for the rest of the Army. In addition to battle deaths, however, the Air Forces lost 13,093 officers, enlisted men, or cadets in fatal aircraft accidents, a total almost 30 percent of the number killed in combat.

The actual deployment and use of this large and costly air force changed as the war progressed. Until late 1942 Army aviation gathered strength while helping check the Axis advance, a sharp contrast to the decisive role envisioned in earlier decades by enthusiasts for air power. Once the Allies stopped the enemy and the necessary programs of production, logistics, and recruitment, and training reached peak efficiency, the Army Air Forces assumed the status of an offensive weapon in the execution of a war plan calling for the defeat of Germany and Italy as the necessary prelude to victory over Japan. Beginning in 1943, land-based air power struck its first blows, blows that increased in destructive power throughout 1944 as the war entered its final decisive phases.

Chapter 9

The Defeat
of Italy and Germany

Bernard C. Nalty

Part of what British Prime Minister Winston Churchill called the end of the beginning—the end of the defensive war for the Allies and the beginning of the offensive—was the invasion of French Northwest Africa. In this operation, called Torch, the Anglo-American allies, using the ships, men, and aircraft immediately available to them, sought to gain control of the Mediterranean Sea and divert the German forces plunging deep into the Soviet Union. As early as the Argentia conference in August 1941, the prime minister had raised the possibility of such an operation if the United States should go to war. Again, during a visit to Washington shortly after the Japanese attack on Pearl Harbor, Churchill and his military advisers proposed an African landing, preferably at the invitation of French colonial authorities, in conjunction with a British advance across the Libyan desert. This plan never came to fruition, however, because a German counterattack hurled the British back into Egypt.

After relegating the North African invasion to an academic exercise, the Combined Chiefs of Staff, at the urging of Gen. George C. Marshall, Army Chief of Staff, and the American Joint Chiefs of Staff, addressed the possibility of storming ashore in France and establishing a permanent lodgment there, either to relieve German pressure on the Red Army and provide a secure base for future operations in Europe or to take advantage of a sudden collapse of the Hitler regime. The British, although willing to plan for an invasion with these limited purposes, were wary of actually attempting it, and rightly so. An estimate of the men and machines available in the near future revealed that the Anglo-American forces could not overcome determined opposition and seize a beachhead in France, and a vicious fight seemed certain, since the Nazis gave every indication of having firm control of Germany and seemed likely to remain in control for the near future. Because some sort of offensive seemed necessary in 1942, at least to distract the Germans who had driven deep into the Soviet Union, the Combined Chiefs of Staff endorsed an invasion of French Northwest Africa. The planners expected light resistance to landings there, since the colonial government seemed likely to side with the Americans and British. An advance eastward from the invasion beaches could not only force Hitler to shift men and materiel from the Soviet Union to Africa but also cut off the German and Italian divisions in Egypt, which in the autumn of 1942 still posed a threat to the Suez Canal.

Planned in part to compel the Germans to reapportion resources, the assault on French Northwest Africa forced the British and the Americans to realign some aviation units. The earlier invasion proposal had resulted in the creation of the Eighth Air Force, which deployed to the United Kingdom when the operation was cancelled. With the decision to actually launch the attack, some Eighth Air Force units already in the United Kingdom, along with fighter and bomber groups that otherwise would have joined the Eighth Air Force there, moved to Africa. The Rouen strike of August 17, 1942, had not yet taken place when Lt. Gen. Henry H. Arnold, the Commanding General of the Army Air Forces, notified his commanders in England that the very group chosen to make the attack would soon be en route to North Africa, along with another B–17 group, a minimum of three Eighth Air Force fighter groups, and much of its medium and light bomber strength. These units, with other units from the United States, formed the Twelfth Air Force, commanded by Brig. Gen. James H. Doolittle, recently returned from leading the April 1942 strike against Japan.

Operation Torch began on November 8, 1942, when American troops landed at Casablanca, Morocco, and Oran in western Algeria, while British forces seized the city of Algiers, to the east. Reflecting the initial geographic separation, each national contingent had a different air organization—Doolittle's Twelfth Air Force supported the Americans and Air Marshal Sir William Welsh's smaller Eastern Air Command the British—an arrangement that continued during the advance eastward into Tunisia. The division of the air component according to nationality violated the spirit of War Department doctrine which endorsed the principle that an airman should exercise centralized control of military aviation within a theater of operations. The arrangement for Northwest Africa had originated with Maj. Gen. Carl Spaatz, ironically the air

Lt. Gen. Dwight D. Eisenhower (left), Commanding General,
European Theater of Operations, and Maj. Gen. Carl A.
Spaatz, Commander, Eighth Air Force, summer 1942.

officer of the European Theater of Operations as well as the commander of the
Eighth Air Force, who expressed concern that the more experienced British airmen would dominate their American counterparts in an Anglo-American command structure. Consequently, unity of command over air power during the expedition existed only insofar as Welsh and Doolittle took their orders from Lt.
Gen. Dwight D. Eisenhower, the Allied commander for Operation Torch.

Besides linking the efficient use of air power to centralized control within the
theater, War Department doctrine also recognized the importance of collaboration at the operational level between the senior ground commander and the senior airman. The appropriate manual, FM 31–35, *Aviation in Support of Ground
Forces*, adopted in April 1942, specified that an air support command, part of a
theater air force, would specialize in flying missions for the principal combat
force within that theater, such as a field army. The air support commander, who
operated from the army headquarters, advised the ground commander on the
employment of tactical aviation. Ideally, the airman and the army commander
formed a team, the ground officer identifying critical targets and the aviator explaining how air power might be used and then issuing orders for whatever
strikes the two decided were necessary. The ground commander, however, made
the final decision whether to attack a particular target. To ensure a rapid response by the supporting aircraft, the airman might assign an element of the air

support command to assist a specific corps or other ground formation; and whenever circumstances required him to make such an assignment, the air support commander also established control elements at the corps command post. The manual specified that, even though certain aircraft supported a particular ground unit, the corps commander or other ground officer did not assume command of the squadrons, which remained under the control of the airman in charge of the air support command. If communications should fail, for instance, and the air support commander became unable to employ his aircraft effectively, he might attach some of his squadrons to a ground unit, and the commander of that organization would assign them missions. The manual advised, however, that instances of actually attaching aviation units to ground forces would be comparatively rare.

On the day after the landings in Morocco and Algeria, German troops began arriving in Tunisia, disembarking from trimotor Junkers Ju 52 transports, as many as fifty of which landed at Tunis in a single day. Meanwhile, Field Marshal Erwin Rommel retreated westward from El Alamein in Egypt toward Tunisia where he intended to join forces with the units arriving by sea as well as by air. To frustrate the German plan, the Allies attempted a rapid advance from the Torch beachheads, but poor roads, a shortage of trucks, rain, unreliable communications, and stiffening resistance impeded the ground forces. Allied airmen fared little better, for the combination of rain and unpaved airfields often immobilized their airplanes in the mud, while German fighters, the Bf 109 and the newer Focke-Wulf Fw 190, operated from all-weather surfaces that shed the rain and enabled the *Luftwaffe* to gain mastery of the Tunisian skies.

As early as the end of November 1942, Eisenhower became concerned that the Twelfth Air Force, elements of which had to deploy all the way from the Atlantic coast of Morocco to the eastern reaches of Algeria, moved too slowly in occupying its designated forward bases. Moreover, the Eastern Air Command had failed to provide the kind of air support that the senior British ground commander, Lt. Gen. Kenneth A. N. Anderson, demanded. Since he had no senior airman at hand in Northwest Africa, Eisenhower conferred with Spaatz at Gibraltar, then summoned him to Northwest Africa, and on December 3 appointed him Acting Deputy Commander in Chief for Air of the Allied forces in the region. Brig. Gen. Ira C. Eaker assumed command of the Eighth Air Force, and Spaatz functioned as an adviser and trouble shooter for Eisenhower. In his new assignment, Spaatz sped the deployment of aviation engineers to eastern Algeria, where they set to work on new airfields, and arranged for Doolittle to attach some light bombers to Welsh's Eastern Air Command.

In December 1942, while Spaatz was trying, as Eisenhower's acting deputy for air, to bring a degree of unity to the employment of aviation, Air Chief Marshal Sir Arthur Tedder, the Air Officer Commanding, Middle East, showed a representative of the Army Air Forces how the Royal Air Force supported ground operations. Personal observation of the command structure in

272

Air Chief Marshal Sir Arthur Tedder (left), Air Officer
Commanding, Middle East, and Air Vice Marshal
Sir Arthur Coningham, Air Officer Commanding,
Western Desert Air Force

Northwest Africa had convinced Tedder that the existing air organization was
almost crazy, with Doolittle and Welsh maintaining separate headquarters, both
some distance from Eisenhower's command post. To demonstrate the importance of collaboration between ground and air, Tedder took Brig. Gen. Howard
A. Craig, who headed the Air Support Command of Doolittle's Twelfth Air
Force, to see how the air and ground staffs interacted at Cairo. When Craig's airplane developed engine trouble, Tedder found time to give the American a tour
of the headquarters of the Western Desert Air Force, which supported the advance of the British Eighth Army, under Gen. Bernard Law Montgomery, from
El Alamein toward Tunisia. The commander of the Western Desert Air Force,
Air Vice Marshal Sir Arthur Coningham, made use of a system of air support
that had been evolving since the battle for France in 1940. British soldiers and
airmen cooperated at every level of command, beginning at the top where
Montgomery and Coningham maintained their headquarters at the same location, their planners working in tents a few yards apart. Elsewhere in the command structure, army officers trained as air liaison specialists served at the various air and ground headquarters, trying to create an understanding of what air
power could do and what the troops needed. A joint control center, staffed by
soldiers and airmen, maintained direct communication between the ground unit
needing support and the aviators providing it. This center served as a clearing-
house for requests from army units, culling out those that could not be fulfilled
for lack of resources or other reasons and sending the rest to Coningham's headquarters. Every level of command within the Eighth Army had a communication
center capable of contacting the joint control center.

Besides introducing Craig, and through him Spaatz, to a mechanism for air support that became a model for the Americans, Tedder and Coningham helped influence Eisenhower to choose an air officer for the Northwest African theater. As Spaatz had feared when he argued against such an appointment, Eisenhower gave serious consideration to a British officer, Tedder, before deciding on Spaatz, who was more familiar with the existing command arrangements and the problems they had caused. On January 5, 1943, Spaatz took command of the Allied Air Forces in North Africa.

The appointment of Spaatz did not ensure cooperation and efficiency in providing air support for the ground forces. Aircraft remained in short supply as the new year began, a result in part of a shortage of spare parts and a lack of adequate maintenance facilities. The Twelfth Air Force at mid-January could muster only about half its authorized number of aircraft, and not all of these could support the war on the ground. Despite a near obsession with air cover, the senior American ground commander, Lt. Gen. Lloyd R. Fredendall of II Corps, got along well with General Craig, whose XII Air Support Command flew missions for the unit. German air attacks had impressed Fredendall with the need for an aerial umbrella overhead, and on one occasion he insisted that British night fighters patrol the daytime skies above his sector in an obvious misuse of the aircraft.

The shortage of suitable airplanes and the American general's well-known insistence on air cover may have caused him to be blamed for the rejection of a request from the 242 Group of the Royal Air Force to take over support missions for which the Northeast Air Command did not have the necessary aircraft. According to the British, General Craig had turned down the request because the only available fighters, P–39s, did not have sufficient range for the mission. Doolittle, however, believed that Fredendall had made the decision, complained that Craig was not standing firm against the ground officer, and requested that Spaatz look into the matter. Although Spaatz was content merely to remind Fredendall that the air support commander served at corps headquarters to prevent the ground commander from making "damn fool decisions," Craig's days were numbered, for Doolittle had decided that he was a better staff officer than air support commander. When Craig fell suddenly ill, Doolittle replaced him with Col. Paul Williams, who got along as well with Fredendall as Craig had. "General Fredendall and General Patton," the colonel reported, "both stated in substance 'Don't wait for us to order air missions, you know what the situation is, just keep pounding them.'"[1]

Like the XII Air Support Command under Craig and Williams, the Eastern Air Command also suffered from a shortage of aircraft. Its resources stretched to the breaking point, Welsh's organization could not take advantage of the network of air liaison officers and control specialists—which the British termed the "tentacles" of the control system—and duplicate the air-ground team that, under Montgomery and Coningham, had driven the Germans and Italians back from El Alamein. Moreover, Air Marshal Welsh and the senior British ground commander, General Anderson, disliked each other, rarely exchanged views, and

274

maintained separate headquarters. Had the two officers been more willing to co-operate, they might have made better use of the available aircraft; however, collaboration, no matter how enthusiastic, could not have compensated for the scarcity of aircraft that persisted into 1943.

At the beginning of the year, the Anglo-American allies in Northwest Africa did not have enough first-line aircraft to defend the ports and bases in Algeria, seize control of the skies over Tunisia, attack German lines of communication and supply, and support the advance on the ground. Existing American doctrine acknowledged the need to establish air superiority, but the German superiority in numbers and bases proved difficult to overcome. Consequently, the drive into Tunisia bogged down, for the Allies could not advance on the ground while the enemy still controlled the air.

While the American and British forces, and the French troops now fighting alongside them, gathered strength to renew the attack and the Germans lashed out with limited counterattacks, the Anglo-American military and political leadership met at Casablanca, between January 18 and 24, to shape the immediate course of the war against Hitler. The Combined Chiefs of Staff agreed during the sessions to a reorganization of the Allied command structure for operations throughout the Mediterranean region. Eisenhower became the overall commander in chief, with British officers assuming command of the major components for land, sea, and air. Tedder took over the Mediterranean Air Command, which had three principal elements: the Northwest African Allied Air Forces, under Spaatz; The Malta Air Command; and the Middle East Command. Organized according to function, the Northwest African Air Forces consisted of strategic, service, training, aerial reconnaissance, coastal patrol, and air support of tactical elements. Doolittle assumed command of the strategic arm, built around the bomber command of his Twelfth Air Force. Eisenhower chose Coningham to head the air support element, designated the Northwest African Tactical Air Force and made up of the XII Air Support Command and the Northeast Air Command, in the expectation that the British airman could ensure the same cooperation between air and ground in Tunisia that had characterized the fighting in Egypt and Libya. Coningham denied, however, that the term "cooperation" described the relationship between the British Eighth Army and the Western Desert Air Force. "I submit," he told Eisenhower and other senior commanders, "that we in the Eighth Army are beyond the cooperation stage, and that work is so close that we are, in effect, one unit."[2]

On January 26, two days after the Casablanca Conference ended, while Coningham prepared to change assignments, Eisenhower appointed an airman to take over Allied air support operations until the British officer arrived. Brig. Gen. Laurence S. Kuter, who had helped write AWPD/1 in 1941 and served most recently as Eisenhower's air officer, took charge of the Allied Air Support Command, the title used during the period of transition. Kuter still directed tactical aviation when the Germans launched a series of counterattacks, including a thrust by Rommel that on February 19 overwhelmed Fredendall's troops dug in at Kasserine Pass. By the time Coningham assumed command of the Northwest African Tactical Air Force on February 23, the bad weather that had hampered Allied airmen ended, and Rommel was retreating through the pass.

Armed with Eisenhower's endorsement of his plan to centralize control over tactical aviation and strike a balance between efficiency and effectiveness acceptable to airmen and ground commanders, Coningham immediately set about making the system work. A survey of the situation in Tunisia convinced the British officer that the Allies had been trying to do too much with too little. He did not, as late as the end of February, have enough aircraft to defend the rear areas, maintain over the battlefield the kind of aerial umbrella that Fredendall had wanted, and at the same time to attack the enemy from his front lines all the way to his distant ports and depots. Instead of massing for a decisive effect, tactical aviation had struck scattered and ineffectual blows that cost the Allies vitally needed men and aircraft without doing serious harm to the enemy. The air marshal's experience in the desert fighting convinced him that tactical air power could make its greatest contribution to the destruction of an Axis army by sending its limited number of aircraft beyond the front lines, attacking airfields, gaining control of the air, and then disrupting supply lines and battering the enemy's frontline positions. After he took charge of all Allied tactical aviation in North Africa, he demonstrated once again the belief in the offensive, a hallmark of the Royal Air Force, which had characterized the operations of Maj. Gen. Sir Hugh Trenchard over the western front during World War I. Coningham's dedication to offensive operations, along with his insistence on collaboration between airmen and ground commanders, provided an example for American leaders like Brig. Gen. John K. Cannon and Brig. Gen. Elwood R. Quesada and greatly influenced American tactical doctrine.

Air Marshal Coningham's reforms signaled the triumph of the principle of centralized control of tactical aviation. Experience in the Northwest African Tactical Air Force validated the principles tested in Egypt and Libya. In Tunisia, an air officer in continuous consultation with the senior ground commander controlled all the tactical aircraft available to support the operation, and this number increased as spring approached and brought better flying weather. Coningham's first responsibility was to seize control of the skies, using his squadrons offensively to forestall enemy air attacks; afterwards, he could employ his forces to isolate the battlefield and batter enemy strongpoints. Centralization, the basic concept underlying Coningham's success, also formed a part of existing American aerial doctrine, although an exception permitted aircraft to be attached to a particular ground unit and take orders from its commander.

Even though able thus far to work amiably with as prickly an individual as Montgomery, Coningham within six weeks ran afoul of Lt. Gen. George S. Patton, Jr., who had replaced Fredendall after the defeat at the Kasserine Pass. The new commander of II Corps soon became convinced that his American troops did not receive enough air support under Coningham's centralized arrangement. When Patton complained in his daily situation report of April 1, 1943, that "Total lack of air cover for our units has allowed the German air force to operate at will," Coningham replied in kind, angrily charging that Patton's troops were not "battleworthy." Since a quarrel between the two might jeopardize the harmony between air and ground that Coningham's appointment was supposed to promote, Tedder, the senior Allied airman in the theater, ordered his subordinate to apologize, and Coningham did so. The last word, however, belonged to Patton, who was meeting with Tedder and Spaatz when four strafing German fighters, apparently flown by pilots who did not realize that Coningham ruled the skies, interrupted the discussions. Asked how he had got the *Luftwaffe* to cooperate in demonstrating his point, Patton answered, "I'll be damned if I know, but if I could find the sons of bitches who flew those planes, I'd mail each one of them a medal."[3]

Although Patton continued to grumble about the tactical air support his soldiers received, air power was helping turn the enemy's North African bridgehead into a trap for more than a quarter million soldiers and their commander, Col. Gen. Jurgen von Arnim, who had assumed overall command when Rommel departed for Germany. Ultra intelligence, which decoded messages sent using the standard German enciphering machine, often revealed not only departure times but also the cargo carried, enabling Allied aircraft to prey on the supply ships that threaded their way through narrow channels in the Axis minefields planted between Sicily and Tunisia. Ultra also helped Allied airmen intercept the Junkers trimotors and the six-engine Messerschmitt Me 323s carrying men and cargo across the Mediterranean. Indeed, communications inter-

North American B–25 Mitchell medium bombers intercept a
flight of Junker Ju 52 transports over the Mediterranean.

277

cepts set the stage for the so-called Palm Sunday massacre, April 18, 1943, when the North African Air Forces claimed the destruction of fifty to seventy transports and sixteen escorting fighters.

Lessons learned from the Tunisian fighting, which ended with the Axis surrender on May 12, 1943, inspired a new War Department field manual, FM 100–20, *Command and Employment of Air Power*. Influenced by the command structure used so successfully by Air Marshal Coningham, the publication declared that "land power and air power" were "co-equal and interdependent," that neither was "an auxiliary of the other." After issuing this declaration of equality and interdependence, the document rejected the practice of attaching air units to ground commands and stated more clearly and forcefully than its predecessors that "control of available air power must be centralized and command must be exercised through the air force commander" to realize the flexibility and effectiveness of the aerial weapon. By listing air superiority as the "first requirement for the success of any major land operation," the new manual called attention to earlier doctrine, which had been ignored in the headlong advance into Tunisia after the invasion of Northwest Africa.

Some Air Forces officers found fault with the new statement of doctrine. For example, Brig. Gen. Orvil A. Anderson, a high-altitude balloonist and also an advocate of strategic bombing, complained that it should have treated air power as an indivisible whole instead of discussing the strategic, tactical, air defense, and service functions within the theater air force. Regardless of objections like his, the publication had implications for every aspect of air power and did more than merely establish the relationship of air and ground commanders in a campaign like the recent fighting in North Africa or the forthcoming invasion of France. Since air and ground were coequal, the senior Air Forces officer in the United Kingdom had the same status as the commanding general of the ground forces, with equal access to the theater commander. The airman could present the case for every application of air power just as the army commander might argue the merits of any operation on the ground. Arnold and the other leaders of the Air Forces believed that strategic bombardment, if given the chance, could utterly cripple the enemy; recognition of air as the equal of ground seemed an important step toward making sure that the bomber would have the opportunity to attack German industry. Once the bombing of German factories had produced the anticipated result, this success would justify the postwar emergence of Army aviation as an independent service.

The Army Air Forces considered strategic bombardment the most effective manifestation of air power; indeed, the commanders and crews of the B–17s and B–24s served as Arnold's shock troops in both the war against Hitler and the drive for postwar independence. During 1942, however, the few bombers available to the Eighth Air Force could inflict very little damage on Hitler's Fortress Europe. For example, the attacks on the submarine bases along the Atlantic coast of France, which began in October 1942, proved fruitless, for not even the

2,000-pound general purpose bomb, the largest that American aircraft carried, could penetrate the concrete-roofed structures that sheltered the U-boats. At year's end, British leaders were again questioning the value of daylight bombing. Would the Americans, they wondered, not make a greater contribution to victory if they abandoned daylight precision attack and joined the Royal Air Force Bomber Command in raids on German cities by night? In January 1943, when Roosevelt and Churchill met with the Combined Chiefs of Staff at Casablanca, this question surfaced once again. The British prime minister demanded an explanation why not one American bomb had yet fallen on Germany. Eaker stepped forward to save the day for the Air Forces and its doctrine of daylight bombing. Summoned from England to defend his Eighth Air Force and its tactics, he ignored the disappointing past, described a future when Americans by day and British by night would "soften the hun for land invasion and the kill," and persuaded Churchill to allow the daylight attacks to continue. The prime minister, with his gift for the dramatic, recast Eaker's arguments into a slogan, a ringing pledge to "bomb the devils 'round the clock."[4] Persuasive though Eaker had been, Churchill proved a willing listener. The British leader did not consider daylight bombing a critical issue at this time; the Americans, he believed, should have an opportunity to try such tactics, provided they did not close their minds to night bombing in the event daylight attacks failed.

In sharing his vision of day and night attacks, Eaker did not foresee a centrally directed Anglo-American air campaign, but rather a coordinated offensive, with his Eighth Air Force operating on its own, although receiving guidance and advice from the British. Had he proposed a truly unified campaign, the logical choice as commander would have been Air Marshal Harris of the Royal Air Force Bomber Command. Eaker worried that the veteran British airman, if placed in charge, would take advantage of his access to Churchill and try to arrange the diversion of the Eighth Air Force from the daylight precision bombardment of industries to area attacks on cities by night. At Casablanca, General Marshall, the Army Chief of Staff, sided with Eaker and the other American airmen. Marshall viewed the bombing of Germany as an indispensable means of preparing for an invasion of Europe, and he also realized that the Allies could not mount so ambitious an amphibious assault in the immediate future, which left the bomber the only weapon capable of carrying the war to the enemy. More important, Marshall had confidence enough in Arnold and the Army Air Forces to insist that the Americans control their own bombing tactics, subject only to operational guidance from the British and overall direction from the Combined Chiefs of Staff. The British agreed, thus ensuring that the Eighth Air Force would be able to begin daylight precision attacks.

The Anglo-American Combined Chiefs of Staff promptly established a purpose and priorities for a Combined Bomber Offensive. The directive approved at Casablanca called for the "progressive destruction and dislocation of the German military, industrial, and economic system, and the undermining of the

Maj. Gen. Ira C. Eaker (left), Commander, Eighth
Air Force, December 1942–January 1944, and
Air Chief Marshal Arthur T. Harris,
Air Officer Commanding, Bomber Command.

morale of the German people to a point where their capacity for armed resistance is fatally weakened."[5] Broad enough in purpose to embrace both daylight
precision attacks on factories and night raids designed to burn out cities, the
Casablanca Directive gave first priority to disrupting submarine construction.
The directive also called for campaigns against aircraft manufacture, the transportation net, oil production, and other elements of German industry. Ironically
in view of the inclusion of enemy morale as a target, the Allied leaders at
Casablanca adopted unconditional surrender as their ultimate aim. While military officers drew up a bombing campaign intended at least in part to undermine
German morale, Churchill and Roosevelt slammed the door on a negotiated
peace and endorsed a policy that might deny Germany an alternative to fighting on despite the aerial bombardment that lay ahead.

General Eaker and his staff immediately set to work on a more detailed plan
for carrying out the bomber offensive approved at Casablanca. The resultant
Pointblank Directive, ratified in principle by the Combined Chiefs of Staff during a May 1943 conference at Washington, D.C., adjusted priorities by acknowledging the importance of gaining air supremacy. The document, however, designated the bomber itself as the means for attaining this end through attacks on airplane plants and the destruction of German fighters in aerial combat.
This concept, in addition to reflecting prewar American doctrine on bombardment, recognized existing reality—at this time the Allies had no fighter capable of escorting missions deep into Germany.

The principle underlying the Anglo-American effort remained coordination
rather than centralized control. The Pointblank Directive assumed, rather than

280

insisted, that Air Marshal Harris would make selective nighttime strikes on cities housing the same industries that General Eaker proposed to hit by day. The British airman remained a free agent who persisted in his distrust of what he called panacea attacks on supposedly vital elements of the enemy war machine. The air marshal preferred to wage a nighttime offensive against the towns where German workers lived, disrupting their rest and destroying their homes, although in the process he might set fires that consumed the factories that employed them. The Combined Bomber Offensive thus came to consist of two efforts based on similar intelligence and economic data, but only loosely coordinated, one designed to destroy industrial plants by day and the other to raze whole towns by night. Together they choked off German production almost completely. According to estimates made after the war by the Federal Republic of Germany, the around-the-clock bombing destroyed more than three million dwellings and killed more than a half million civilians.

An Anglo-American planning committee, taking into account the agreed strategy of the Combined Chiefs of Staff, produced a list of daylight and nighttime targets. In making specific recommendations, the American members of the planning committee reviewed the general military situation and the findings of the Committee of Operations Analysts. Established by Arnold, this latter committee tried to determine, often using the American economy as a model, what industries were truly critical to the German war effort. The British Air Ministry and the Ministry of Economic Warfare also provided data on the German industrial base. Other sources of information included aerial photography, which helped assess bombing results as well as identify targets; reports from recently arrived refugees; and even prewar analysis by attaches at Allied embassies.

At most, however, the Anglo-American planners created an illusion of collaboration in the Combined Bomber Offensive. Harris did not consider himself bound by the agency's work and retained final responsibility for choosing the cities to be bombed. On a particular night, he might or might not attack a city containing an industry like ball bearing production or aircraft manufacture that the Eight Air Force was trying to destroy by day. At times, Harris chose to cooperate, especially in the latter part of the war, but the choice remained his.

Once a mission ended, analysts reviewed the results, again using aerial photographs, though a particularly successful strike might inspire radio traffic vulnerable to Ultra code breaking. In the case of bombing results, the British tried in general to relate urban destruction to German morale and industrial manpower, whereas American researchers sought a connection between gutted factories and overall military effectiveness. Whatever the perspective, an accurate assessment of the impact of the bombing proved difficult.

Throughout the war, American airmen continued to insist that their heavy bombers were destroying German war industries rather than urban areas surrounding the factories. Since the writing of AWPD/1 in the summer of 1941,

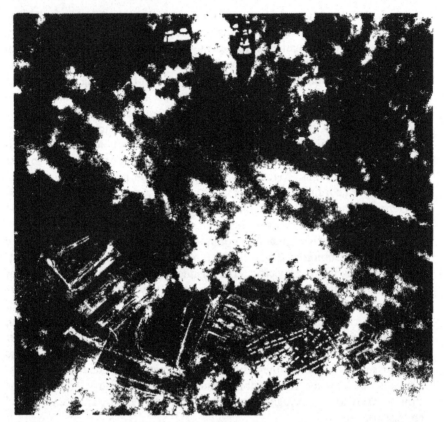

U.S. bombs fall toward harbor at Wilhelmshaven, Germany, January 1943.

Army Air Forces planners had tended to regard attacks on civilian morale as a coup de grace for an enemy already in his death throes. They remained wary of striking such a blow as late as the spring of 1945, when General Eaker wrote, "we should never allow the history of this war to convict us of throwing the strategic bomber at the man in the street." His main concern, however, may have been the postwar reputation of an independent air force rather than the fate of the German populace. Years later, he would concede that there was "no strong moral sentiment among the leaders of the Army Air Forces" concerning the bombing of Germany; the objective of these senior officers was to defeat Hitler and the Third Reich.[6] As Spaatz later declared, objections to area bombing or other forms of aerial attack aimed directly or indirectly at civilian morale arose strictly from considerations of effectiveness: the extent it would hasten the destruction of the German war machine, thus saving the lives of Allied soldiers, sailors, and airmen. An ethical debate did occur at lower levels among the officers who recommended targets, with officers like Brig. Gen. Charles P. Cabell and Col. Richard D'O. Hughes arguing that, insofar as equipment and tactics permitted, only military targets should be bombed.

In actual practice, however, daylight bombing proved too inaccurate to destroy with surgical precision a military installation or armaments plant in an urban setting. With clear skies, a formation using the Norden sight could place almost ninety percent of its explosives within a one-mile radius of the aiming point, which meant that the bombs landed inside a circle with an area of slightly more than three square miles. This was not the legendary kind of accuracy that placed the bomb in the pickle barrel, but it was not all that bad considering that a whole formation dropped its bombs when the lead bombardier released his. Radar, used to bomb through cloud cover, proved less than half as accurate as the Norden sight. The dispersal of production among hard-to-pinpoint urban sites and the destruction of structures that served as visual reference points in many cities also reduced accuracy against industrial targets, so that Eaker's man in the street, living near his place of work, may not have realized he was being spared, if indeed that was the general's main concern.

In the weeks following the Casablanca Conference, the American dropped too few bombs to give rise to questions of ethics—the Eighth Air Force had barely begun to carry the war to Germany. On January 27, 1943, a force of B–17s, prevented by thick cloud from bombing Vegesack, attacked Wilhelmshaven, conducting the first raid by American heavy bombers on a target in Germany. Other attacks followed, directed at shipyards building submarines and, as time passed, against aircraft plants and other factories farther inland.

Because the P–38s had gone from the United Kingdom to North Africa, the escort mission devolved on the Republic P–47 Thunderbolt, a new fighter flown for the first time some six months before the United States went to war. Although durable and heavily armed, these Thunderbolts had only early versions of the new jettisonable fuel tanks and could not operate beyond Aachen, at the German border. On long flights, whether deep into Germany or to distant targets in France, the bombers had to rely for escort on YB–40s, B–17s carrying extra machineguns, ammunition, and armor instead of bombs. Unfortunately, these aerial dreadnoughts failed because they could not keep pace with formation, especially during the return flight when the weight of bombs no longer slowed the other aircraft.

During the summer of 1943, bomber commanders decided that the best defense was a disciplined formation that permitted the massing of .50 caliber fire from many Flying Fortresses or Liberators. The basic formation of that period, the awe-inspiring but cumbersome combat wing, consisted of three 18-plane groups, each with three squadrons, arranged to present a frontage of 7,000 feet, a height of about 1,000 feet, and a depth in excess of 1,800 feet. Maneuvering so large a formation proved awkward, with planes farthest from the pivot point of a turn roaring along at full throttle in a desperate effort to maintain station and those near the pivot wallowing at near stalling speed. As a result, when fighter protection improved, the combat wing disappeared, replaced by a 36-plane group, which remained the standard alignment until supplanted by an even more flexible 27-plane formation in 1945.

Escorting P–47s still had to turn back near Germany's western border when General Eaker, on August 17, 1943, launched strikes against the ball bearing plants at Schweinfurt and a Messerschmitt aircraft factory at Regensburg. Plans had called for the Regensburg force to take off first, attack its target, and turn southward to land in North Africa. Then, before the *Luftwaffe* interceptors that had opposed the first mission could land for fuel and ammunition, the Schweinfurt force would thunder across Germany, returning to England after dropping its bombs. Unfortunately, fog disrupted the timing of the two raids.

The force bound for Schweinfurt could do nothing until the mists cleared. While the crewmen waited at their planes for word to take off, their thoughts focused on the day's mission, an ordeal that would last some seven hours, unless cut short by mechanical failure or enemy action. Since they would fly at altitudes where the air temperature might drop to fifty degrees below freezing on the Fahrenheit scale, the men wore either bulky, heavily lined clothing or the new and unreliable electrically heated flight suits. Neither the E or F model of the B–17 could generate enough surplus electrical current for more than a few of the heated suits, and the wiring in those actually used proved dangerously fragile. A break anywhere cut off heat throughout the entire garment, so that a failure in the boot could result in frostbitten fingers. Similarly, a gunner who, in trying to clear a jammed weapon, removed one of the heavy gloves worn with the old suit also ran the risk of frozen fingers and possible amputation. The extreme cold, moreover, could freeze oxygen lines, causing loss of consciousness and, ultimately, death.

Bomber crews faced dangers other than cold, as they roared along at a ground speed that could exceed 200 miles per hour. German fighter pilots and antiaircraft gunners used all their skills to destroy the plane and kill the men inside. A B–17 might vanish in a streak of flame; a pilot might turn his head and find the copilot mangled by bullets or shell fragments; a direct hit could tear away the tail gunner's compartment and send it, along with the man inside, tumbling earthward.

Even as the men of the Schweinfurt force waited and thought of the battle to come, the 146 B–17s of the Regensburg force began taking off despite the fog. German radar detected the formation as it assembled over England, and Fw 190s intercepted the flight as the P–47 escort neared the limit of its endurance. Other German fighters joined in, attacking from various directions or remaining beyond range of defensive machineguns and launching 210–mm rockets to scatter the bombers. Lt. Col. Beirne Lay, Jr., a staff officer who had volunteered as copilot on one of the Flying Fortresses, welcomed a chance to take over the controls, after watching helplessly as fighters tore into the massed B–17s; the mechanics of flying diverted his attention from the swarming interceptors.

A B–17 flies over smoke from earlier bombing runs on the
aircraft plant at Regensburg, Germany, August 1943.

Fourteen bombers went down before the formations reached Regensburg and
encountered the radar-controlled antiaircraft defenses. Despite the attacking
fighters and the German barrage over the target, bombing accuracy proved excellent.

German fighter controllers expected to direct further attacks as the Regensburg force returned to England, but to their surprise, the B–17s headed instead
for North Africa, where they landed at primitive airfields in Tunisia. A suitable
target soon appeared on the early warning radars, however, for at midmorning,
the 230 B–17s assigned to bomb Schweinfurt began assembling over the British
Isles. Having replenished fuel and ammunition, the German fighters now attacked the formation bound for the important ball bearing factories. The number of haystacks burning on farms below puzzled one of the navigators, until he
realized he was seeing the funeral pyres of B–17s shot down by the enemy.
Antiaircraft batteries put up a barrage over the target itself, and fighters resumed
the attack during the return flight.

During the day's two raids, the defenders shot down 60 of General Eaker's
bombers, almost one-sixth of the B–17s assigned to the day's mission or about
one-fifth of the 306 B–17s that actually bombed Regensburg and Schweinfurt,
while another 27 B–17s sustained serious damage. A total of 601 officers and
men were killed, captured, or interned in a neutral country. These losses raised

Two B–17 bombers with radar antennas replacing the ball turrets.

the possibility that the Flying Fortresses and Liberators would prove incapable of penetrating Germany's defenses without fighter escort. Faced with similar evidence, the Royal Air Force Bomber Command had halted daylight operations and concentrated on night attack. Not so the Americans. Eaker and his colleagues gave no serious thought to abandoning daylight precision bombing, not only because of the formidable task of retraining crews and modifying aircraft but also because of an abiding belief that doctrine would prevail.

Despite this confidence, the Eighth Air Force did investigate British methods. Brig. Gen. Fred L. Anderson, who led Eaker's bomber command, had already flown as an observer on a few night missions. Then, after the loss of forty-five B–17s on a raid against Stuttgart in September, one squadron of Flying Fortresses participated with the Royal Air Force Bomber Command in seven night attacks, with an average of five aircraft flying on each and a total of two lost. During the first week of October, this familiarization project ended; although the squadron continued to fly at night, it dropped propaganda leaflets rather than bombs. The night bombing experiment ended in part because of the difficulties the crews encountered in adapting to a radically different kind of operation, but the principal reason was Eaker's conviction that, given enough airplanes and crews, the Eighth Air Force could fight its way in daylight to any target within bomber range and return without suffering crippling losses.

What effect did the strikes against Regensburg and Schweinfurt have on the enemy? The Eighth Air Force had hurt the German war machine at Schweinfurt, if not at Regensburg. The accurate attack on the Messerschmitt plant damaged most of the main buildings but, according to Albert Speer, Hitler's minister of armaments and war production, had "only minor consequences."[7] Much of the machinery escaped serious damage, and the aircraft firm went ahead with plans to disperse among nearby villages and towns hard-to-locate shops that would man-

Radar-led bombers release their bombs at a completely cloud-covered target .

ufacture aircraft components for assembly at Regensburg. In contrast, the less precise bombing at Schweinfurt temporarily reduced German ball bearing output by some thirty-eight percent, complicating an existing shortage and forcing Speer to increase production elsewhere and draw on reserve stocks. By October, however, manufacturers in Germany produced more ball bearings than before the August bombing.

After a brief period of recuperation, the Eighth Air Force returned to Germany. The tempo of operations rapidly increased until the bombers flew three missions deep into Germany in a single week, culminating on October 14 in a second raid on Schweinfurt. Escorted a short distance by P–47s, a formation of 291 B–17s started eastward against increasingly savage opposition. Defying fighters and antiaircraft fire, 228 Flying Fortresses succeeded in bombing the target, causing damage that reduced ball bearing production an estimated 67 percent.

For a second time within 60 days, daylight bombing had disrupted the critical ball bearing industry, but to Speer's amazement the Allies did not follow up the attack. Two factors brought about this unexpected reprieve: first, no central authority existed to overcome Air Marshal Harris' scorn for panacea targets and compel him to unleash Royal Air Force Bomber Command against Schweinfurt and other centers of ball bearing production; and second, the *Luftwaffe* controlled the skies over Germany. The Eighth Air Force suffered dismaying losses on the second mission against Schweinfurt—60 out of 291 B–17s, more than one in five, failed to return. The day's toll brought the number of bombers shot down in a single week to 148, each carrying a ten-man crew. Eaker could, with justification, announce: "Now we have got Schweinfurt," but his command had paid a staggering price.[8]

History of the United States Air Force

The losses among B–17 crewmen proved crippling, at least for the immediate future. General Eaker had entered October with some 700 B–17 crews on hand. Even though the mid-October losses cut deeply into this force, new arrivals increased the total assigned to more than 800 crews by the end of the month. These strength figures were misleading, however, for the inexperienced men had to be integrated into squadrons and acquire the skills of the veterans they replaced, a process that took time. Compared to the problems of absorbing reinforcements, aircraft repair moved swiftly, an important consideration since less than a third of the planes that took off in the second Schweinfurt mission returned without serious damage. Earlier experience had prompted the Eighth Air Force to transfer responsibility for the repair of major battle damage from the operating groups to central depots, and combat units performed only those jobs they could finish within 36 hours, so that the workload would not overwhelm the available mechanics.

Eaker remained confident that, given the investment of several weeks for training, the Eighth Air Force would again launch hundreds of bombers against distant targets as it had before the second raid on Schweinfurt. Against Emden on November 2, his bombers used radar for the first time to attack through cloud cover, and this innovation promised to increase the number of days that the reconstituted bomber force could attack Germany.

Unaffected by Eaker's optimism, Arnold believed the Eighth Air Force was recovering too slowly from the October battles. To provide fighter additional escort, Arnold sent P–38s, replacing those diverted to the Mediterranean, and sent the first of the new P–51Bs, which had even greater range. Modifications to shackles and pylons enabled the P–47 to carry two underwing jettisonable tanks, plus a larger one beneath the fuselage, thus increasing fuel capacity some fifty percent. Even as he tried to improve the quality of the fighters available to the Eighth Air Force, Arnold became convinced that the root of the problem was less a lack of fighter cover than a failure of leadership. From the vantage of Air Forces headquarters, Eaker's bomber crews seemed to be spending too much time training in the United Kingdom or flying what amounted to practice missions, and airworthy bombers remained on the ground because the men who flew them were on leave, recovering from the ordeal of combat. Arnold wanted new and firmer hands in control of the daylight bombing offensive, so in January 1944 he sent Eaker to the Mediterranean, appointed General Doolittle to command the Eighth Air Force, and entrusted the American role in the Combined Bomber Offensive to Spaatz, as Commander of the newly created U.S. Strategic Air Forces in Europe.

Eaker's arrival and the departure of Spaatz and Doolittle were the latest in a series of changes in the Mediterranean area during 1943. Operations in that theater diminished in importance as the time approached for an assault across the English Channel against the heavily defended coast of France. Brereton's Ninth Air Force, which had conducted some strategic operations, became exclusively

The Defeat of Italy and Germany

a tactical air force. After handing over most of its combat elements to the Twelfth Air Force in September, the Ninth established itself in the United Kingdom, received new fighters and other aircraft, and began preparing to support the assault across the Normandy beaches. To replace Brereton's command, the Twelfth Air Force, at that time under Spaatz (prior to his leaving for the United Kingdom), reconstituted itself as a tactical force, while the XII Bomber Command formed the nucleus of the new Fifteenth Air Force, a strategic command headed by Doolittle until his departure for Great Britain.

By the end of the year, a major shift of senior commanders between the United Kingdom and the Mediterranean had taken place. Not only had Spaatz gone to Great Britain to direct the entire American strategic bombing offensive and Doolittle accompanied him to take over the Eighth Air Force, but Eisenhower, with Tedder as his deputy, had also gone to London to assume command of the planned Allied invasion of Europe. Tedder's departure from the Mediterranean opened a vacancy for Eaker, whose administrative skill and ability to work with the British Arnold continued to value, however disappointed he was with the recent efforts of the Eighth Air Force. On January 15, 1944, Eaker replaced Tedder in command of the Mediterranean Allied Air Forces. General Cannon took over the Twelfth Air Force and Maj. Gen. Nathan F. Twining the Fifteenth, which was a part of the U.S. Strategic Air Forces that Spaatz now commanded from the United Kingdom. Spaatz arranged, however, to route his orders to Twining by way of Eaker, who might modify them if circumstances required.

Eaker's new headquarters occupied a palace at Caserta in Italy, where Allied troops were advancing doggedly northward. The Casablanca Conference, which in January 1943 had approved the Combined Bomber Offensive, also set in motion a series of events that within the year carried Allied forces across the Mediterranean and about three-fourths of the way from the toe of the boot-shaped Italian peninsula to Rome, the capital city. At Casablanca, the Anglo-American leadership had looked beyond victory in Tunisia, which at the time was far from won, and decided to take advantage of the momentum gained in North Africa by seizing the island of Sicily and opening the Mediterranean to Allied convoys. Sicily, however, proved a stepping stone to further conquests, for the Allies invaded Italy and forced that nation to turn against the Axis. What began in 1943 as a means of maintaining pressure on Germany, using troops that might otherwise have been idle during the immediate future, became a full-scale land campaign, weakening the Axis but also tying down Allied divisions and aircraft that could have been preparing for an invasion of France followed by a thrust into the heart of Germany.

Although Sicily was the first objective decided on at Casablanca, an obstacle lay in the path of the North African forces, which Eisenhower commanded until he left for the United Kingdom in January 1944. Astride the sea route between Tunisia and Sicily loomed the island of Pantelleria, its volcanic features stud-

289

The Pantelleria harbor after the attacks in June 1943.

ded with a hundred gun emplacements, an outpost too dangerous to ignore. After a series of harassing attacks, a massive aerial bombardment began on June 1, 1943, lasting 10 days and totaling more than 4,800 tons of bombs, with naval gunfire adding to the deluge of explosives. A preinvasion hammering by warships and aircraft followed, and when landing craft carrying the assault force started shoreward on June 11, the Italian defenders raised the white flag of surrender.

During the battle of Pantelleria, the Tuskegee-trained black airmen of the 99th Fighter Squadron, the first blacks ever to fly for the Army, made their debut in aerial combat. Initially, the pilots seemed unsure of themselves, a result of racial segregation, for the black squadrons had no cadre of veteran flyers to serve as a steadying influence for the younger men. All the Tuskegee pilots had about the same number of flying hours, and only one, Lt. Col. Benjamin O. Davis, Jr., a 1936 graduate of West Point, had any appreciable experience as an officer or familiarity with Army procedures. As a result, black units entered combat at a distinct disadvantage and at the outset performed poorly compared to squadrons that had veteran leaders with many hours in the air. As time passed, however, efficiency improved, and by war's end black fighter pilots successfully and routinely escorted bombers from Italy deep into Germany. In *Those Who Fall*, his memoir of wartime service as a bomber pilot, John Muirhead paid tribute to the Tuskegee airmen, describing how they suddenly appeared, exactly on schedule, and stayed with the bombers all the way to the target, during the final minutes ig-

Lt. Col. Benjamin O. Davis, Jr.,
Commander,
99th Fighter Squadron.

noring the concentrated antiaircraft fire that usually discouraged both American escorts and German interceptors. They were, wrote Muirhead, "the best of shepherds."

Operations from Italy lay some months in the future, however. After Pantelleria came Sicily, invaded by air and sea following systematic aerial attacks that tried to isolate the island from Italy and prevent intervention by the *Luftwaffe*. On the night of July 9, 1943, hours before the next morning's amphibious landings, British troops in gliders and American parachute infantry approached the beachhead their countrymen planned to seize. High winds and inexperience on the part of the crews of the C–47s towing the gliders contributed to errors in navigation that caused 121 of the 133 gliders to miss the designated landing zone, with 65 of them coming down at sea. Despite this tragedy, the glider-borne troops seized and held an important bridge leading inland from the invasion beaches. At Gela, almost 65 miles to the west, wind and navigational error also scattered the almost 3,500 American paratroops, but did not prevent them from making contact with the force landing by sea.

The Troop Carrier Command of the Northwest African Tactical Air Force staged two other major airborne operations during the Sicilian fighting. On the night of July 11, another mission near Gela ended in failure because Allied ships, unaware of the approaching formation, opened fire on the C–47s, twenty-three of which failed to return to their North African bases. The airborne troops landed over a wide area and suffered casualties that General Eisenhower considered "in excess of any damage inflicted on the enemy." Nor were friendly antiaircraft gunners advised of the final drop, on July 13, when a combination of Allied and German fire shot down fourteen transports carrying British parachutists and drove off almost twice that number before the troops could jump. The airborne force succeeded, however, in recapturing a bridge over the Simeto River, some twenty miles northwest of Syracuse. No wonder that an analysis of airborne operations in Sicily emphasized the need for planning by a single head-quarters, further training in aerial navigation, and the proper use of identification signals within clearly defined flight corridors.

Despite the confusion that hampered airborne activity, Allied air power rapidly gained control of the skies over Sicily and southern Italy. This aerial superiority could not, however, prevent the Germans from conducting a carefully planned withdrawal across the narrow Strait of Messina to the Italian mainland. Antiaircraft fire from the beaches and from the evacuation craft prevented fighters and medium bombers from pressing their daylight strikes. The Germans feared high-altitude bombardment from beyond the reach of the defending batteries, for a night strike by British Wellington medium bombers had temporarily disrupted operations on the Sicilian beaches, but the Wellingtons and the American heavy bombers concentrated on ports along the Italian coast where intelligence incorrectly reported the evacuees were landing. By holding out until mid-August, the Germans gained time to send additional forces into Italy and prepare, if necessary, to take over the defenses manned by increasingly dispirited Italian troops.

During the battle for Sicily, American strategic bombers returned to Ploesti, attacking from rooftop height the refineries in and around town. For the August 1 raid, General Brereton assumed control of five B–24 groups—two from his own Ninth Air Force, two on loan from the Eighth Air Force, and one that had been scheduled to join General Eaker's command. After training against a mock-up of the target constructed in the Libyan desert, Brig. Gen. Uzal G. Ent led 177 bombers on the long flight from North Africa. Near the coast of Greece, fate intervened; the B–24 carrying the lead navigator for the expedition plunged suddenly into the sea and exploded. Another aircraft dived low to look for survivors, could not catch up with the formation, and returned to Africa, carrying with it the alternate for the navigator killed in the crash.

Shortly after the bomber went down, the surviving aircraft crossed the coast of Europe and came under surveillance by German radar. The early warning network had gone on alert when the enemy intercepted and decoded a radio message advising Allied forces that a large formation was flying northward from Libya, a warning designed to prevent antiaircraft gunners from firing on the friendly bombers. German control centers tracked the Americans until the approaching aircraft descended too low for radar coverage. As the bombers drew near, antiaircraft crews around Ploesti manned their weapons, and fifty-two interceptors, flown by Germans or Rumanians, took off to do battle.

As the bombers neared the target, they had to turn at a particular village and head directly for the refineries. To pick out the proper landmark required precise navigation, and here the death of the lead navigator and the absence of his alternate proved decisive. Two of the attacking groups turned at the wrong village and followed a course toward Bucharest, Rumania's capital, rather than Ploesti. The crews soon realized the mistake and changed headings, their B–24s

However dramatic the Consolidated B-24 raids were at Ploesti, as these two photos demonstrate, they were costly in men and materiel. Because of their courage under fire, five of the raiders received the Medal of Honor.

flying in ragged clusters instead of the prescribed formations. In doing so, they approached the refineries from the wrong direction and bombed targets assigned to other groups. The navigational error brought the two groups over the deadliest of the area's antiaircraft defenses, forcing the gunners on board the aircraft to open fire, not at interceptors, but against batteries on the ground. Maj. Norman Appold, a pilot, credited George Barwell with silencing three of six 88–mm antiaircraft guns firing directly at one of the groups. Barwell, a British officer and instructor in aerial gunnery who had volunteered for the mission, knocked out the antiaircraft guns from the top turret of Appold's B–24. The defenses that challenged the bombers were ingenious and deadly. For example, two parallel formations of B–24s that had made the proper turn to Ploesti were skimming the farmland on either side of a rail line when the sides of several boxcars dropped to reveal antiaircraft guns that opened fire in both directions. Beyond this antiaircraft train, some of the crews found their assigned targets already in flames, bombed by aircraft in the groups that had got lost, and had to brave dense smoke and exploding delayed-action bombs to deliver attacks of their own. Second Lieutenant Lloyd D. Hughes flew his B–24 through a wall of flame that ignited gasoline streaming from punctured fuel tanks; the crew managed to drop the bombs, but only two gunners survived when the aircraft cartwheeled and exploded during an attempted crash landing.

The turn toward Bucharest had temporarily confused the enemy fighters, but they arrived in time to attack the last American groups approaching Ploesti. Other German fighters intercepted the B–24s over the Ionian Sea on the flight back to Benghazi and shot down four bombers that had survived the earlier battles. In all, 54 of the B–24s either failed to return or crashed while trying to land, for a loss rate in excess of 30 percent, and the roster of killed or missing listed more than 500 names. More than 100 of the missing, however, actually were prisoners of war, captured after parachuting safely or surviving crash landings or ditchings at sea. The cost in lives and machines proved out of proportion to the results achieved, for the enemy compensated for the damage by using idle refining capacity. Moreover, no follow-up attack discouraged repair crews or added to the destruction. Whatever its results, the mission demanded the ultimate in skill and courage. Five officers received the Medal of Honor. Colonels Leon Johnson and John R. "Killer" Kane survived to receive theirs for leading their groups through savage antiaircraft fire, flame, and smoke to drop their bombs on the refineries. Posthumous awards commemorated three others—Lieutenant Hughes, Maj. John L. Jerstad, and Lt. Col. Addison L. Baker—who sacrificed their lives to guide burning aircraft to the assigned targets.

Despite the losses, the bombardment groups that had hit the refineries were back in action within two weeks. On August 13, they sent sixty-five B–24s to bomb an aircraft factory at Wiener Neustadt in what had been Austria, the first raid on Hitler's Reich from bases in Libya. After flying through dense clouds, the bombers encountered light opposition at the target, losing two of their number but damaging hangars and other buildings.

Meanwhile, the battle for Sicily was coming to a successful end. An advance into Italy seemed the next logical step, since it would enable the Allies to maintain pressure on Germany and take advantage of an obvious Italian willingness to abandon the Axis and even take up arms against Germany. Mussolini was overthrown on July 25, 1943, and even as the new government announced that the war would continue, its representatives began negotiating with the Allies. By the time British forces landed on September 2 at the heel and toe of the Italian boot, King Victor Emmanuel had secretly agreed to surrender. Increasing German strength around Rome forced the last-minute cancellation of a planned American airborne descent on the capital to protect the King and his fellow conspirators, who nevertheless went ahead with their plan. On September 8, a spokesman for the group announced that Italy had capitulated. The king and the others managed to escape from Rome, found a haven with the Allies, and formed a government that, on October 13, declared war against Germany. Meanwhile, the Allies landed at Salerno on September 9 in an attempt to capitalize on Italy's surrender by quickly seizing nearby Naples, a task that took three hard-fought weeks.

In General Eisenhower's phrase, air power "went flat out" in support of the Salerno landings.[9] An American airman, Maj. Gen. Edwin J. House, served as fighter director during the amphibious assault, controlling all such aircraft, whether land-based or flown from British carriers. Unfortunately, Allied fighters based on Sicily operated at the end of their tether over Salerno, so that after the first few days their lack of time on station and the need for unremitting attacks on German ground forces caused rents in the aerial umbrella. Through these gaps the *Luftwaffe* mounted raids, harassing the hard-pressed Allied troops and scoring hits with radio-guided bombs on three warships; but the enemy airmen did not prevail. Transport aircraft parachuted reinforcements onto the beachhead, while Allied fighters and bombers helped break the German grip on the heights dominating the beaches. Allied air power then spearheaded the advance inland.

Falling back from Salerno, the enemy exploited winding, rain-swollen streams and mountainous terrain to slow the advance toward Rome. The fighting in the Mediterranean region underwent yet another change, from an, at times, fumbling land campaign in North Africa, to the swift conquest of Sicily, to what promised to be a long and difficult land campaign in Italy. Although the capture of airfields near Foggia in the southern part of the Italian peninsula brought strategic bombers closer to targets in Germany, Austria, and Rumania than they had been when flying from Libya, Italy remained in the shadow of the United Kingdom, as far as Allied strategy was concerned. From Great Britain would come the invasion of the European continent and the air offensive that contributed to its success. Nevertheless, a bitterly contested advance up penin-

A Lockheed F–5 reconnaissance plane flying past enemy installations before the Allied landing at Anzio casts its shadow on the beach.

sular Italy continued simultaneously with the bombing raids launched from England and the other preparations for invading France.

One week after Eaker began his new assignment in the Mediterranean Theater, the Allies attempted an end run around the main line of resistance to capture Rome. The landing at Anzio on January 22, 1944, caught the Germans off guard but failed to break through to the Italian capital. Allied aircraft had cratered nearby airfields and attempted to isolate the battlefield by attacking overland lines of communication, but the air strikes did not prevent men and machines from reaching the hills overlooking the beachhead. Hitler succeeded in massing troops from as far away as Yugoslavia and bottling up the invasion force.

An attempt to advance from the south to join forces with the Anzio beachhead encountered determined German resistance, especially in the vicinity of Monte Cassino, site of an abbey that traced its history to the sixth century. Convinced that the Germans had posted observers at the monastery to direct artillery fire, the Allied commanders trying to break through the defenses asked that the structure be destroyed. During a final aerial reconnaissance, Eaker and another American general thought they saw a radio antenna and several German soldiers on the monastery grounds. In fact, the enemy soldiers had not entered the gates, although they had established positions some fifty yards from the abbey's walls.

During the bombing of the abbey at Monte Cassino, exploding
ammunition threw up a cloud of smoke 1,500 feet high.

After dropping warning leaflets, one of which found its way into the hands
of the abbot, American airmen attacked the mountaintop on the morning of
February 15, 1944. Some 250 bombers dropped about 600 tons of high explosive, with Allied artillery adding to the destruction. The bombardment began before the monks or the civilians who had taken refuge with them could react to
the warning and flee, and the bombs and artillery shells took an unknown toll
among the noncombatants. Afterward, German troops dug in among the ruins
of the monastery, converting Monte Cassino into a redoubt. Despite the failure
of the first bombardment, General Arnold urged Eaker to return with all the
bombers at his disposal, breaking up "every stone . . . behind which a German
soldier might be hiding."

The commanding general of the Army Air Forces was determined that air
power shatter the stalemate in Italy to prevent ground commanders from gaining control of tactical aviation and attempt to divert strategic bombers from the
offensive against German industry. Eaker, however, favored a different use of air
power to achieve Arnold's goals. Pointing out that Spaatz endorsed his idea, he
proposed the "cutting of communications, road and rail, and the destruction of
enemy coastal shipping to a point where he cannot possibly supply his . . . divisions." The Allies called this aerial campaign Operation Strangle.[10]

Intended to "reduce the enemy's flow of supplies to a level which will make
it impractical to maintain and operate his forces in Central Italy," Strangle reflected the theories of Solly Zuckerman, professor of anatomy in peacetime
Great Britain who had become a pioneer in the field of operations analysis, but
American airmen and intelligence specialists also made a contribution. Zuckerman argued that marshaling yards formed the Achilles' heel of railroad trans-

A bridge, and a train on it, brought down during Operation Strangle.

portation, whereas the Americans proposed concentrating on chokepoints, especially bridges. Operation Strangle tried to do both, for it sought to disrupt rail transportation by attacking railyards, rolling stock, and railroad bridges throughout an interdiction zone that extended from Rome to Florence and irregularly across the breadth of the peninsula. Disruption of rail service would force the enemy to rely on trucks, which were judged to be in short supply and vulnerable, at least during daylight, to air attack.

Strangle began as scheduled in March 1944 and soon produced important results. Tactical aircraft, assisted at times by heavy bombers, battered the marshaling yards, but the Germans easily repaired the damage. In addition, most freight traffic originated north of the Alps so that raids on railroad yards in Italy had no impact on the organization of trains and dispatching of cargo. In contrast, attacks on railroad bridges proved crippling, for to repair the twisted ruins of such structures required engineering skill, heavy equipment, and the use of scarce steel. Until work crews could repair a viaduct, the enemy had to shift cargo from freight cars to trucks. During the day, fighter-bombers attacked the roads and highway bridges that the motor convoys used and strafed the trucks. Only during darkness could trucks safely travel the highways of Italy, for the Allies had no aircraft capable of night interdiction, but doing so meant that a comparatively short journey might have to be broken into several nighttime segments. The resulting delay, along with the limited cargo capacity of trucks compared to railroad cars, prevented the Germans from adequately replenishing stocks of ammunition depleted in the steady fighting. Strangle did not force the Germans to withdraw, but during Operation Diadem, when the Allied troops before Cassino successfully attacked to link up with those at the Anzio beachhead,

298

the ammunition shortage, which could not be made good because of continued interdiction of roads and rail lines, reduced the Germans powers of resistance. Monte Cassino fell to the Allies in mid-May and Rome on June 4.

During the six months that saw the cracking of the German defenses south of Rome and the occupation of that city, the air campaign from the United Kingdom had rapidly intensified. Doolittle assumed command of the Eighth Air Force at a time when its fortunes were on the rise. Because of increased production and accelerated training programs in the United States, at the end of January 1944 he had twice the number of B–17s and B–24s and bomber crews that Eaker had commanded at the end of October of the previous year. Far more important, however, was the growing number of P–51 Mustangs. Even though the Ninth Air Force, a tactical organization, received the first group of P–51s to reach the United Kingdom, these aircraft escorted strategic bombers of the Eighth Air Force on missions deep into Germany. The new fighter gave Doolittle what Eaker had lacked—a fast, maneuverable fighter that, thanks to jettisonable fuel tanks and a new permanent tank behind the cockpit, could protect bombers to Berlin and beyond.

The appointment of General Spaatz to direct the American strategic air forces in Europe demonstrated that daylight precision bombing would continue despite the reverses suffered in October 1943. Although Eaker's British associates regretted the departure of a personable and undoubtedly competent commander, Spaatz soon came to exert greater influence in Anglo-American councils than his American predecessor or such British airmen as Harris or Air Chief Marshal Sir Trafford Leigh-Mallory, the Commander in Chief, Allied Expeditionary Air Forces. The influence wielded by Spaatz resulted from his harmonious and militarily successful relationship with Eisenhower, who, as the war in Europe neared an end, ranked Spaatz as one of his two best generals, and also from the fact that Arnold selected him and held him in high regard.

The P–51 contributed immensely to the revival under Spaatz of daylight bombing offensive, as demonstrated in January 1944 by Maj. James H. Howard, a Ninth Air Force Mustang pilot. On a single escort mission, Howard downed three enemy fighters and damaged three others, singlehandedly breaking up an attack on a formation of bombers and earning the Medal of Honor. The escort fighters had their shortcomings, however. The P–51 had poor cockpit ventilation and an uncomfortable seat that could combine to cause fatigue on a long flight; and the oil for the superchargers in the P–38 could congeal in the extreme cold, leaving the Allison engines gasping for air at a time when the pilot needed maximum power. Even when their aircraft functioned perfectly, tired or overly aggressive pilots could push their fighters beyond performance limits. Capt. John T. Godfrey, credited with destroying sixteen and one-third German aircraft, attempted too violent a maneuver in the thin air at high altitude and, according to an eyewitness, tumbled end over end before regaining control of his P–47. Whether the fighter was a P–51 Mustang, P–38 Lightning, or P–47

North American P–51 long-range escorts in the sky over Europe.

Thunderbolt, aerial combat six miles above the soil of Germany demanded a finely tuned machine and the full attention of an alert and well trained pilot.

As the American fighters increased in number and improved in performance, Spaatz attacked Germany with aircraft from the Fifteenth Air Force based in Italy and from Doolittle's Eighth Air Force, now stronger and better equipped than it had been under Eaker. The renewed offensive was governed by a February 1944 modification of the Pointblank Directive, which gave overriding priority to the destruction of the German fighter force. To accomplish this end, the American strategic bombers launched Operation Argument, a coordinated attack on the German aviation industry. Between February 20 and 25, 1944, the Eighth Air Force dispatched some 3,300 bomber sorties and the Fifteenth Air Force about 500 against targets from Regensburg and Steyr in southern Germany, to Tutow near the Baltic coast, and to Posen in Poland. During this so-called Big Week, the B–17s and B–24s dropped 10,000 tons of bombs on factories manufacturing airplanes or aircraft components and also on the ball bearing plants at Schweinfurt. Air Marshal Harris' night bombers, though engaged in a sustained attack on Berlin, mounted five raids on cities connected with the aircraft industry, following up the American daylight strikes on Steyr, which produced both aircraft components and ball bearings, and on Schweinfurt. American bomber losses averaged six percent during Big Week, roughly one-third the loss rate suffered in the October 1943 missions against similarly distant targets. The improvement resulted in large measure from the 3,500 or more long-range fighter sorties flown to protect the B–17s and B–24s.

Speer and his associates feared one aspect of the Big Week attacks more than any other, for they believed that the destruction of the ball bearing industry, which had belatedly begun to disperse its manufacturing facilities, could cripple the German war machine. Once again production plummeted as a result of the bombing, but Allied airmen again failed to pursue a potentially decisive campaign. "As it was," the German armaments minister later wrote, "not a tank, plane, or other piece of weaponry failed to be produced because of lack of ball bearings."[11]

The German aircraft industry responded quickly to Big Week and the threat of systematic air attack. The various firms dispersed their factories and plants and agreed to devote efforts to turning out a few critically needed types. As their American counterparts already had done, German manufacturers now sought to avoid making minor design changes on the assembly line, shifting this work to modification centers. After an abrupt decline early in 1944, Speer and his colleagues marshaled a labor force, set up small and widely separated factories, and succeeded in increasing fighter production from 1,300 planes in January to 1,600 in April and to 3,000 in September of that year. In achieving these impressive totals, Germany built single-engine fighters almost exclusively, since this type was desperately needed to defend the Reich. The United States, however, produced more than twice as many aircraft, in categories ranging from light observation craft to the heavy bombers battering Germany, and five times the number of aircraft engines. Moreover, the United States had the fuel and the time to train replacements for the pilots and crews lost in combat. At most, Speer managed to reduce to some extent the numerical odds against the *Luftwaffe*.

Attrition among German pilots, who could not be replaced because a shortage of fuel hampered training, helped neutralize the effect of Speer's efforts. Even before Operation Argument and the Big Week signaled a systematic attack on the aircraft industry, the combination of aerial combat against American daylight raids; sustained operations against British night attacks; action in North Africa, Sicily, and Italy; and the continued heavy fighting in the Soviet Union resulted in severe losses among fighter pilots. Indeed, during 1943 the monthly attrition rate in the fighter squadrons peaked in July at 16 percent, before declining as winter approached and the air war diminished in intensity. In that single year, the *Luftwaffe* lost some 35,000 of the 49,000 pilots and other aircrew members killed or missing since the war began. The year's heavy toll testified to the increasing impact of the Combined Bomber Offensive. Since the conquests of 1940 and the unsuccessful air campaign against the British Isles, Hitler had ignored western Europe, using the *Luftwaffe* to further his conquests in the Balkans, Greece, Crete, North Africa, and the Soviet Union, but in 1943 the Third Reich began to experience the fury of aerial warfare. The Royal Air

Force Bomber Command destroyed Hamburg in a terrible fire storm, and not even the losses inflicted on the Eighth Air Force at Schweinfurt in August and October could offset the gathering strength of its bomber command.

In 1944 the effect of attrition on the *Luftwaffe* worsened as the hundreds of attacking Allied bombers became thousands, and the long-range P–51 appeared in ever increasing numbers. Losses among German fighter pilots continued, with some 2,200 dead or missing between January 1 and the end of May, when the rate of attrition reached 25 percent. During all of 1944, almost 21,000 pilots and crewmen were lost out of a pool of aviators that had shrunk in size and skill from the force that had been available a year earlier. Increased fighter production thus proved a hollow triumph, for in a statistical sense, *Luftwaffe* fighter units underwent a complete numerical turnover of single-engine pilots during the first five months of 1944. Only the ablest (or luckiest) survived to fly the aircraft that German industry produced, as new pilots joined fighter squadrons in rapid succession, their brief careers averaging 30 days or less.

When German fighter production began its increase under Speer's prodding, Allied heavy bombers that might otherwise have attacked this industry had to deal with radical new weapons that the enemy developed and deployed. Photographic confirmation of these so-called vengeance weapons came during the summer of 1943, when a British reconnaissance pilot brought back film that revealed two large rockets lying on trailers at a research center in the Baltic hamlet of Peenemünde. On the night of August 17, within hours of the first American raid on Schweinfurt, Bomber Command attacked the site, causing damage that delayed the appearance of the V–2 long-range rocket. Later that same month, the Eighth Air Force joined in the campaign against the vengeance weapons, an undertaking eventually called Operation Crossbow, sending B–17s to bomb a massive concrete structure at Watten, France, that intelligence had linked to the rocket program.

As the threat grew more ominous, the diversion of bombers became more frequent. Aerial reconnaissance soon discovered that at various places in western Europe the Germans were building flat-roofed hangars, inclined ramps, and sheds with a gently curved shape that resembled a ski placed on edge. These "ski sites" stored, serviced, and launched another vengeance weapon, the V–1, a pilotless, jet-propelled flying bomb. As the number of launch facilities for the two new weapons proliferated, Crossbow intensified, so that from December 1943 to June 1944 American and British aircraft had dropped some 36,000 tons of bombs on V–1 and V–2 installations. This bombardment did not prevent the enemy from launching the first V–1 on the morning of June 13, 1944, and the first V–2 on September 8. Attacks by these two vengeance weapons lasted until March 1945, despite air raids on launch sites, propellant factories, and plants manufacturing V–1 and V–2 components. General Spaatz even experimented with missiles of his own, war-weary bombers loaded with explosives and directed by radio signals against V-weapons sites. The *Luftwaffe*, in turn modified

The V–1 flying bomb (top), launch of a V–2 (middle), and a V–1 just before it impacts in London.

some of its bombers to launch the V–1, and the less mobile V–2 continued to menace British towns and the Belgian port of Antwerp, a supply conduit for the advancing Allied armies. The last vengeance weapon exploded in Antwerp on March 28, 1945, and in London a day later.

Although reluctant to do so, both Doolittle and Harris diverted some of their heavy bombers in an attempt to neutralize Hitler's V-weapons. Harris was especially concerned about shifting targets, since Bomber Command late in 1943 had launched the Battle of Berlin, a series of 16 night raids that ended on March 24, 1944. "We can wreck Berlin from end to end," he had declared, "provided the USAAF [United States Army Air Forces] will come in on it."[12] The Eighth Air Force, however, continued to hit the German aircraft industry, while at the same time taking part in Crossbow, and had to delay its first Berlin strike until March 4. As it turned out, raiding Berlin by daylight actually reinforced the campaign against the aircraft industry, for the *Luftwaffe* felt compelled to fight in defense of the capital, giving the pilots of the long-range Mustang an opportunity to accelerate the attrition of the German fighter force. Unfortunately, the first American attack on Berlin fell victim to bad weather, for out of 300 bombers just 29 succeeded in finding the cloud-covered city and bombing one of its suburbs, and then only because they failed to hear the recall order. Indeed, weather had become such a hindrance to planned operations that the Eighth Air Force began sending P–51 fighters on last-minute reconnaissance missions to check on conditions over primary and alternate targets. Despite this practice, clouds impeded bombing accuracy on three additional missions flown between March 6 and March 22 against industrial targets in Berlin and its suburbs. Aircraft losses suffered in these strikes varied from ten percent to two percent per mission; the raid of March 6 proved the deadliest, with 69 bombers shot down out of 672 that reached the target.

During the Anglo-American raids, which inflicted serious damage on Berlin, the night fighters protecting the city proved deadlier than the daytime defenses. Royal Air Force bomber losses, some five percent on the earliest missions, had nearly doubled by the time the aerial battle of Berlin ended. Moreover, a long-range mission to Nuremberg, flown in bright moonlight on the night of March 30, inflicted moderate damage at a prohibitive cost. Bomber Command lost 95 of 782 aircraft, 743 crewmen killed or wounded, and 159 taken prisoner. Even more disheartening than the losses was the fact that a strenuous and costly night campaign, which included the attacks on Berlin, had failed to produce decisive results; Germany fought on, and Hitler continued to rule in spite of the destruction within the capital and in other cities throughout the nation. By early April 1944, the defenders controlled the night skies over Germany, although only briefly, as events would prove. The British bomber crews needed time to rest and regroup, as General Eaker's had after the second Schweinfurt attack.

Although Germany had proved resilient under air attack, Spaatz continued to believe that bombing could defeat the enemy without the need of an invasion, provided that the bombers crippled an industry vital to the German war machine. As Speer later acknowledged, ball bearing plants formed such a target, but the Allies failed to press the advantage gained at Schweinfurt during August and October 1943 and again in February 1944, giving the enemy time to move machinery to small, widely separated factories less vulnerable to aerial bombing. Early in March 1944, General Spaatz revived a target that the British had tried unsuccessfully to attack four years earlier, one that American planners had included in AWPD/1. He proposed the destruction of the German oil industry, believed to consist of fifty-four refineries and synthetic fuel plants. The approach of D-Day for the invasion of France interfered with his plans, however. Eisenhower, Tedder, and Leigh-Mallory believed that an attack on the oil industry, decisive though it might be in the long run, would take effect too slowly to undermine German resistance to the invasion. They favored employing both strategic and tactical aviation on targets other than oil production that were more directly related to the German defense of the Normandy beaches. What Eisenhower and his staff had in mind was an attack on the transportation system that would isolate the defenders of the coastline from their inland sources of supply and reinforcement.

To demonstrate the importance of destroying the oil refineries, Spaatz, at Arnold's suggestion, resorted to subterfuge. At a time when Tedder and Leigh-Mallory were determined to use the American strategic air force against transportation, Spaatz directed the Fifteenth Air Force in Italy to attack the marshaling yard at Ploesti, knowing full well that the pattern of the bombing would include some of the oil refineries. On April 5, 1944, the bombers attacked Ploesti for the first time since August of the previous year, and the results were so encouraging that Spaatz had the target hit again on the 15th and 24th. Invoking the autonomy that Spaatz allowed him as commander of the Mediterranean Allied Air Forces, Eaker gave the Fifteenth Air Force permission to continue attacking the oil industry. Meanwhile, Spaatz tried to persuade Eisenhower to approve sending the Eighth Air Force after synthetic fuel plants deep inside Germany. The airman argued that attacks on oil production would make an immediate contribution to the success of the invasion by destroying enemy aircraft, since the *Luftwaffe* had no choice but to defend its source of fuel. In addition, the destruction of the oil industry would ultimately hobble the German armed forces, depriving them of mobility as well as air cover. Eisenhower surely realized that Spaatz wanted nothing less than an offensive against the oil industry, but he was confident that the airman would also support the invasion when directed. As a result, the supreme commander raised no objection to attacking oil production even though D-Day for the Normandy invasion was fast approaching. After a three-week delay because of bad weather, 800 bombers struck eight oil manufacturing plants on May 12, at a cost to the Eighth Air Force of 46 bombers and 10 escorting fighters.

Ultra intercepts revealed that these first systematic attacks on the petroleum industry produced immediate results. Decoded radio traffic disclosed that the Germans were shifting antiaircraft units from centers of aircraft manufacture to protect oil refining and synthetic fuel production. In addition, messages began referring to an incipient shortage of aviation gasoline that might soon require cutbacks in training flights. Speer later acknowledged that the May 12 attacks had signaled "a new era in air warfare," the beginning of a campaign that ultimately "meant the end of German armaments production."[13] Although the raids on the oil industry may have sounded a death knell for Hitler's Reich, actual burial lay months in the future. Conservation measures helped keep the machines of war moving, and as many as 350,000 workers struggled to repair production facilities so that the output of fuel could continue.

A diplomatic success now promised to benefit the oil campaign and the entire bombing offensive. Since entering the war, the United States had tried to persuade a wary Soviet Union to provide bomber bases for raids on Germany and Japan. Although not yet willing to provoke the Japanese, with whom Stalin had entered a nonaggression pact in 1941, the Soviet government at last allowed American strategic bombers to use its airfields for attacks against German territory. Fifteenth Air Force bombers flew the first such mission on June 4, 1944, returning to Italy a week later, but bad weather persisted during the stay in the Soviet Union, and the group, led by General Eaker himself, struck just three targets. On June 21, the Eighth Air Force joined in, attacking a synthetic fuel plant near Berlin en route to Soviet air bases in the Ukraine. A German high-altitude reconnaissance aircraft followed the formation bound for the airfield at Poltava, and a raid that night destroyed forty-three of a hundred-odd B–17s and fifteen of seventy P–51s. In spite of this disaster, shuttle bombing continued throughout the summer, but Soviet bases became less important as Allied troops advanced from the invasion beaches toward Germany's western border. When Soviet officials refused to cooperate in efforts to drop supplies to noncommunist Polish resistance forces in Warsaw—the Eighth Air Force received permission for just one such mission using the Ukrainian airfields—the shuttle campaign came to an end.

Despite the encouraging results of the early attacks on refineries and synthetic oil plants, which successful shuttle bombing might have magnified, the Eighth Air Force was unable to throw its full weight into the oil campaign. Until the Allies gained a lodgment on the continent, General Eisenhower had the authority to use strategic bombers for missions that would contribute to victory on the battlefield. To assure the success of the Normandy invasion, air power based in Great Britain had to maintain control of the skies, won in a six-month battle of attrition against German interceptors, and keep the enemy from bringing reinforcements to the beachhead. The transportation plan advocated by Tedder and Leigh-Mallory aimed at isolating the Normandy battlefield. The critical element in this undertaking consisted of cutting the rail lines that could carry German forces, especially the armored divisions, to reinforce Hitler's coastal defenses, the so-called Atlantic Wall. As he had in Italy, Zuckerman advanced his theory of attacking railyards and destroying repair facilities and rolling stock. Leigh-

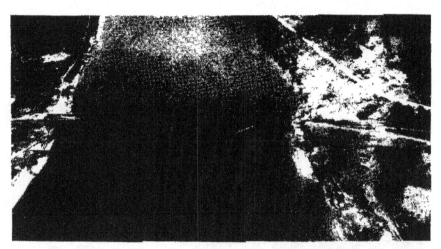

The destroyed Pont du Graviere railroad bridge on the Seine River.

Mallory endorsed this action and urged that American strategic bombers concentrate on the rail hubs in France. Spaatz, although he liked and respected Zuckerman, believed that the analyst was wrong; what had happened during Operation Strangle in Italy convinced the American officer that the proper targets should he bridges and viaducts, which Ninth Air Force medium bombers and fighter-bombers could destroy without the help of B–17s and B–24s diverted from strategic targets or Crossbow operations. The argument dragged on until a trial raid demonstrated the vulnerability of the bridges. Brereton's Ninth Air Force, using a plan devised by Brig. Gen. Frederic H. Smith, Jr., sent out a force of B–26s and P–47s that damaged three of the bridges that crossed the River Seine and destroyed a fourth, a 650-foot steel railroad span at Vernon. As a result, Leigh-Mallory became belatedly enthusiastic about attacking this kind of target, and by D-Day the Allies had cut every bridge across the Seine, immobilizing the German troops and supplies still northeast of the river.

The invasion required special efforts from aerial reconnaissance as well as fighter and bomber squadrons. Just before D-Day, Capt. Charles R. Batson skimmed the Normandy beaches in an F–5, a photographic version of the P–38, returning with 130 bullet and shrapnel holes in the aircraft and only one engine still functioning. A strip camera that exposed film continuously, the brainchild of Col. George C. Goddard (who had photographed the interception of the liner *Rex* in 1938), enabled the intelligence specialists who examined Batson's handiwork to locate obstacles and other beach defenses. Besides covering the invasion beaches, American reconnaissance pilots, flying F–5s or faster, stripped-down variants of the British Spitfire or twin-engine de Havilland Mosquito, carried out high-altitude missions over Germany, bringing back pictures that helped locate such targets as synthetic fuel plants or provided evidence of bomb damage.

307

Invasion beach at Normandy with Allied aircraft overhead.

On June 6, 1944, D-Day for the invasion of France, the *Luftwaffe* managed to fly perhaps 100 sorties to oppose the 8,000 Allied fighters, bombers, and troop transports taking part in the operation. The forward airfields that the Germans intended to use had been put out of action by bombing, and the *Luftwaffe* squadrons based in the area had suffered crippling attrition, in May losing 712 aircraft in combat and 656 in accidents attributable mainly to inexperienced pilots. Within 36 hours of the Allied landings, the enemy rushed some 200 fighters to France, increasing the total strength in that category by about one-third, but the airfields being built to replace the ones bombed into uselessness were not yet ready. Although German fighter strength increased to 800, even this number was too few; the *Luftwaffe* did succeed in launching as many as 500 sorties in a single day, but within two weeks of the invasion, Allied airmen had destroyed almost 600 German aircraft, the bulk sorely needed fighters.

The *Luftwaffe* failed to impede the amphibious assault, the predawn airborne operation that preceded it, or the consolidation of the landing sites. Once the invasion force had carved out a beachhead, Allied tactical aircraft eclipsed the heavy bombers in contributing to battlefield success, but the Eighth Air Force bombers occasionally had to come to the aid of the man with the rifle. At St. Lô, France, for instance, some 1,500 B–17s and B–24s helped sever local enemy communications and kill, wound, or stun the German frontline soldiers. Unfortunately, errant bombs caused 102 American casualties, including Lt. Gen.

Lesley J. McNair. The tragic accident contributed to a delay between the bombing and the infantry attack that enabled the defenders to recover from the initial shock and resist bitterly, if unsuccessfully.

Following the breakout at St. Lo, the enemy counterattacked before dawn on August 7 at Mortain, overran the town, and cut off an American infantry battalion. Thanks to a warning from Ultra and some determined American opposition, the Germans failed to reverse the tide of battle. Fighter-bombers intervened after daylight, alerted by Ultra to the routes assigned the enemy units, and took a heavy toll in armor moving toward Mortain. Although the Germans persisted for almost a week, they never generated the striking power to punch through the American lines, a failure that resulted mainly from the attacks by P–47s on enemy tanks during the first day of the counterattack.

During the thrust across France, the Ninth Air Force supported the operations of Lt. Gen. Omar N. Bradley's 12th Army Group, made up of the First Army, under Lt. Gen. Courtney H. Hodges, and the Third Army, commanded by General Patton. The IX Fighter Command, with some 1,500 P–47s, P–38s, and P–51s divided among 18 groups, had organized into two tactical air commands specializing in fighter-bomber operations. General Brereton, who commanded the Ninth Air Force until Maj. Gen. Hoyt S. Vandenberg succeeded him during the course of the campaign, assigned one such command to each American army. The IX Tactical Air Command, under General Quesada, a veteran of the flight of *The Question Mark* in 1929 and the North African fighting of 1943, supported Hodges' forces, and Brig. Gen. Otto P. Weyland's XIX Tactical Air Command worked with General Patton's army. Each tactical air command established its headquarters at the army command post, following the practice adopted in North Africa. The IX Bomber Command, with 11 groups of medium bombers and attack aircraft, remained under Ninth Air Force control, available to assist any element of the army group. Fighters from the Eighth Air Force at times lent a hand, but their pilots lacked experience hitting targets in close proximity to friendly troops and therefore usually flew interdiction missions.

In supporting the two armies, the tactical air commands followed the principle of cooperation between air and ground forces, with neither subordinate to the other. Coordination between air and ground took place at every level from the army and tactical air command headquarters downward through corps, division, and regiment or combat command, to battalion. At each headquarters, an appropriate number of airmen were available to advise the commander and plan the support he required. Requests for air support were usually consolidated at a division headquarters, then were submitted to corps headquarters, and ultimately to the tactical air command. The commander of a battalion or larger unit sometimes called for strikes in conjunction with a planned attack or merely asked that fighter-bombers, when available, attack a specific target. He might, however, face a threat requiring an immediate strike, in which case the fighter control center at the tactical air command could divert aircraft from less important missions.

Maj. Gen. Elwood R. Quesada (left), Commander,
IX Tactical Air Command, and Brig. Gen. Otto P. Weyland,
Commander, XIX Tactical Air Command.

Whether dispatched according to plan or diverted from another strike, the aircraft came under the control of an airman in a control party, who cooperated with the unit commander in directing the attack without unnecessarily endangering friendly troops. As had been the practice in Italy, these parties normally used jeeps, equipped with radios capable of communicating with the pilots overhead. General Quesada, however, modified the practice, placing an airman and his radio inside a tank within an advancing armored column and assigning a specific number of fighter-bombers to escort the unit. Whenever the tanks encountered opposition, the controller identified the source of the resistance, pointed it out to the pilots, and the fighter-bombers pounced on it.

Generals Quesada and Weyland frequently assigned entire groups of fighters—forty-eight aircraft or more—to provide support for a specific division on a given day. Dedicating fighter-bombers to cooperate with a particular ground unit reflected the Allied preponderance in the sky, a degree of dominance undreamed of at the time of Kasserine Pass. The practice did not conflict with the doctrine that had evolved from the experience in North Africa, for the fighter-bombers remained under the control of an airman, not the division commander. The fighter control center might divert any or all of the aircraft to meet some emergency, and a tactical control party provided by the Army Air Forces directed the actual strikes. Instances of friction between airmen and ground commanders proved rare, partly because the overwhelming aerial resources at the disposal of the Americans ensured that help would come, weather permitting, but also because the aviators at every operational level, from Quesada or Weyland to the officer with a radio in a jeep or tank, cooperated fully with their counterparts in the ground forces.

By the time the battlefront stabilized along the eastern border of France, the Ninth Air Force had brought over from England its combat squadrons, command structure, and logistic base. Aviation engineer units landed in Normandy at midmorning of D-Day to begin work on the first in a network of 241 airfields—some rebuilt, others carved out of farmland—that ultimately extended from the invasion beaches into Holland, Luxembourg, and Germany. The IX Service Command also moved to the continent, but it could not simultaneously provide maintenance for combat units, distribute supplies, and operate a supply line extending from the French seaports. As a result, early in 1945, Maj. Gen. Hugh J. Knerr, deputy for logistics to General Spaatz, took charge of a newly designated Air Technical Service Command in Europe, which delivered supplies, weapons, and munitions. General Knerr also consolidated under his direction the repair, modification, and maintenance of all Eighth Air Force and Ninth Air Force airplanes. Logistic problems arose—the supply system, for instance, could hardly stay abreast of consumption when transporting fuel by air, road, or pipeline across the French countryside. Nonetheless, the Ninth Air Force managed to keep a greater percentage of its planes in action from airfields on the continent than it had from bases in England. Contributing to this increase was the decline of Germany's fighter force and a consequent reduction in battle damage.

Meanwhile, the Fifteenth Air Force, after launching the oil offensive, concentrated on support for the invasion of southern France. In preparation for this operation, which began on August 15, 1944, heavy bombers attacked military installations in a region stretching from Genoa, Italy, to Marseilles, France, isolating the assault beaches and inland drop zones located midway between the two ports. As in Normandy, paratroops led the way, followed by amphibious forces. The principal source of air support for the advance northward from the beachhead was Brig. Gen. Gordon P. Saville's XII Air Support Command, operating initially from airfields in Corsica taken from the Germans shortly after Italy's surrender. Early in September, troops that had landed in southern France joined with the armies advancing from Normandy, forming a single front from the English Channel to the Swiss border.

Following the breakout from Normandy in late July, Marshall and Arnold advised Eisenhower to use his airborne divisions, which formed a theater reserve, in conjunction with the advancing ground armies. Brereton became a key figure in any such action, for after leaving the Ninth Air Force, he assumed command on August 8 of the First Allied Airborne Army. His new headquarters drafted plans for 18 operations of varied complexity, all canceled as unnecessary when the Allies surged forward on the ground. When the Allied offensive lost momentum, General Montgomery obtained control of Brereton's force on September 10 and began drawing up plans for the airborne troops to vault the Rhine at Arnhem in the Netherlands and outflank the main defenses of Germany's industrial heartland, the Ruhr Valley. On September 17, 1,500 transports and 500 gliders, protected by more than 1,300 fighters, crossed the North Sea to land some 20,000 troops by parachute and glider. Recovering from their initial surprise, the Germans encircled the British force at Arnhem, rushing antiaircraft batteries into place to cut the air route that provided supplies and reinforcements. At the same time, the enemy stopped an armored column trying to advance along the highway leading to Arnhem and the Rhine. During the fighting, some 250 Eighth Air Force B–24s parachuted cargo to American airborne troops holding the critical bridges over which the British tanks had to pass, delivering the supplies accurately despite heavy antiaircraft fire and ill-defined drop zones. In spite of the persistence in delivering supplies by air, the daring operation, called Market Garden, ended in failure, as the British abandoned the isolated bridgehead at Arnhem.

While Allied forces liberated France, but suffered a setback in Holland, Anglo-American bombers hammered away at German petroleum production. Although still skeptical of the value of industrial targets recommended by specialists in economic warfare, Harris eventually enlisted Bomber Command in the oil offensive. Taking advantage of radar and radio beams as aids to accurate bombing, his men dropped roughly forty percent of the total bomb tonnage directed at oil production between April 1944 and the end of the war. The British, however, did almost all their bombing of this industry after November 1944, for Harris often derided the notion of panacea targets and only reluctantly attacked something that might fall in that category. "I still do not think it was reasonable at the time to expect that the campaign would succeed," Harris wrote; "what the Allied strategists did was bet on an outsider, and it happened to win."[14] The long-shot victory that he spoke of came in a race that pitted German engineers dedicated to maintaining oil production against Allied airmen determined to choke it off as completely as possible. Synthetic fuel plants proved hard to destroy and difficult to locate on radar. Frequent layers of cloud kept the Allies from hitting them often enough to stop production entirely; indeed, the British sometimes had clearer skies at night than the Americans encountered in daylight. Air power did succeed, however, in reducing production to a mere trickle. Soviet ground forces also contributed to the victory, overrunning the battered refineries at Ploesti in August 1944 and thus freeing the Fifteenth Air Force to bomb synthetic oil plants in southern Germany, Poland, and Czechoslovakia. German efforts to conserve fuel for essential operations became so desperate that in the autumn of the year Speer discovered fighters grounded in good flying weather, student pilots logging only one hour a week in the air, and horses pulling trucks over the roads of northern Italy.

As the German war effort began to feel the impact of the oil offensive, the *Luftwaffe* introduced a pair of revolutionary fighters, one of which, had it appeared sooner, might have prolonged the war, though it could not have changed the eventual outcome. The more formidable of the two was the world's first operational turbojet interceptor, the Messerschmitt Me 262. Heavily armed and

312

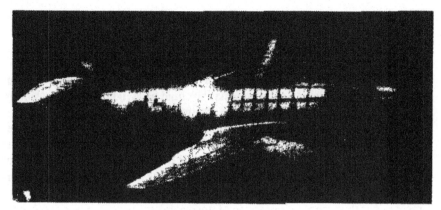

Messerschmitt Me 262.

faster than conventional aircraft, this fighter flew its first sorties in April 1944 and saw increasing service during the summer and early autumn. At the time, the Royal Air Force had only a mere handful of its new Gloster Meteor jets, and an American jet fighter suitable for combat did not appear until 1945. The German aircraft industry succeeded in producing some 1,500 Me 262s and might have turned out even more of them sooner, had the program not encountered a series of delays resulting from indecision about the role of the airplane—whether fighter or fast bomber—and difficulty in developing reliable engines. Continuing engine problems and a lack of trained pilots—the latter a result of attrition over the years and a shortage of fuel to train replacements—reduced the effectiveness of the few hundred Me 262s that did enter combat.

The other fighter was the rocket-powered Messerschmitt Me 163, an interceptor capable of speeds approaching 600 miles per hour. After streaking to an altitude of 30,000 feet, the Me 163 quickly exhausted its chemical fuel in a few high-speed passes at a bomber formation, then glided to earth, landing on a metal skid beneath the fuselage. In an overly hard landing, the plane tended to flip over, detonating any of the highly volatile fuel that remained in the tanks. The rocket-powered fighter made its combat debut late in July 1944, but slow production, with fewer than 300 actually accepted for service, and the need for exceptionally skilled pilots imposed an impossible demand on a *Luftwaffe* that was desperate for time and had few such veterans after five years of war.

Although Germany's ground forces had suffered the same kind of attrition as the *Luftwaffe*, the Third Reich fought stubbornly on two fronts as the Allies advanced from east and west. The only hope, Hitler believed, lay in prolonging resistance until differences between the Soviet Union and the western democracies sundered their alliance. To gain time he proposed a counteroffensive launched from the concealment of the Ardennes, a region of woods and river gorges that extended from the German border into Belgium and Luxembourg,

313

in the hope of recapturing the port of Antwerp. On December 16, 1944, the enemy lunged forward, carving out an extensive salient and triggering what came to be called the Battle of the Bulge.

German reliance on telephone and telegraph reduced the volume of radio traffic, but Ultra nevertheless acquired a number of intercepts, which unfortunately proved ambiguous. The information could have indicated the possibility of a major counterattack or merely the creation of a strategic reserve to meet future American thrusts. Given the Allied optimism of the moment, the latter seemed far more probable. Bad weather hampered aerial reconnaissance in the weeks preceding the attack, but photographic evidence and visual sightings of enemy movement by road and rail multiplied. This intelligence, open to interpretation as was that obtained through Ultra, could have indicated reinforcement rather than preparations for an offensive. In any event, the wooded Ardennes seemed an unlikely springboard for a winter counterattack by an army believed to be approaching exhaustion.

As the enemy counterattacked, his pilots displayed unexpected aggressiveness, at times forcing American fighter-bombers to jettison their explosives and engage in aerial combat, but the greatest problem for Allied airmen was not so much the *Luftwaffe* as the winter weather. Even so, neither surprise nor the persisting cloud cover enabled the German thrust to gain its initial objective, the Meuse River, for American troops clung to key positions, including the Belgian village of Bastogne. On December 23, the skies cleared and the full weight of Allied air power, including Eighth Air Force fighter and bomber units temporarily under the operational control of General Vandenberg's Ninth Air Force, pounded the German salient and the supply lines sustaining it. Allied aircraft attacked the roads and rail lines carrying German troops and supplies, bombed German fighter airfields, and parachuted supplies into Bastogne. For five days, the Allies took advantage of good weather to dominate the skies over the battlefield, but wind and blowing snow limited air activity during the last three days of December. By the end of the year, however, air power had disrupted the flow of men and materiel to the German forces, although a month of fighting remained before the Americans and British could restore the front lines of mid-December.

Once the bad weather that ended the year had abated, the *Luftwaffe* took a last desperate gamble to seize the aerial initiative in western Europe. On January 1, 1945, a force of almost 900 German planes attacked 11 Allied airfields in Belgium, Holland, and northern France. The enemy avoided the use of radio in planning and coordinating the operation, a measure designed to prevent a surge in the volume of message traffic that might alert the Allies to the likelihood of imminent attack, and the absence of radio transmissions unintentionally neutralized Ultra. Having thus frustrated Allied intelligence and achieved tactical surprise, the Germans destroyed about 150 Allied aircraft, though at an excessive cost to themselves. Perhaps a third of the attacking planes failed to return,

314

some shot down by German antiaircraft gunners, who, kept ignorant of the operation for security reasons, assumed that any large formation had to be American or British. The Allied losses had little effect on the course of the war, for seemingly endless streams of replacements were leaving American aircraft factories; but Germany, despite its miracles of airplane production, could not replace the fuel burned or, given the lack of gasoline for training, the pilots shot down.

The Ardennes counteroffensive and the aerial attacks of January 1, 1945, gained Germany a little time, but the hoped-for split among the Allies failed to develop. Hitler's armed forces had wasted their carefully husbanded stores of petroleum and were now burning fuel almost as fast as the battered oil industry could produce it. The flurry of action in December and January did, however, create an illusion that Germany remained capable of savage counterthrusts, and this belief affected Allied planning. British and American bombers therefore pursued the oil campaign, preventing a resurgence of that industry, and resumed an attack on railroad transportation throughout a rapidly shrinking Reich.

The final transportation campaign, begun in the fall of 1944, represented an attempt to duplicate within Germany the success that air power had enjoyed against French railroads during the preparations for the Normandy landings. Although the systematic bombing of the bridges across the Seine had played a dominant part in disrupting rail transportation in France, marshaling yards and rail centers in Germany at first received the greatest attention, largely at the insistence of Zuckerman and Tedder. The bridges across the Rhine escaped attack because of their sturdy construction, their powerful antiaircraft defenses, and, most of all, because the Allies hoped to use them for the assault on Germany. The Battle of the Bulge intervened, but the transportation campaign resumed early in 1945. By that time, however, the Allies had aircraft enough of every type to attack almost any target within Germany, whether a synthetic oil plant, a railyard, a bridge, or even a string of boxcars at a siding. Zuckerman, still advocating bombing rail centers, hoped to continue the kind of attacks on transportation begun before the Ardennes fighting and expected a clash with Spaatz, the champion of the oil offensive. No confrontation occurred, however, for Spaatz now had so many men and aircraft that he could do whatever was asked of him without worrying about priorities. Actually, the transportation campaign gave his bombers a target to attack by radar when bad weather concealed the synthetic oil plants. The sprawling railyards tended to be located in areas identifiable on radar, whereas the compact oil facilities all too often disappeared amid the radar return from urban areas. The oil offensive depended on decent weather and visual aiming with the Norden sight, but Spaatz's strategic forces could bomb the switching yards through an overcast. Moreover, the broad expanse of rails presented a suitable target for formation bombing, and any bombs that missed the mark had some effect, since they landed among warehouses, factories, and homes. The campaign against German transportation, far from in-

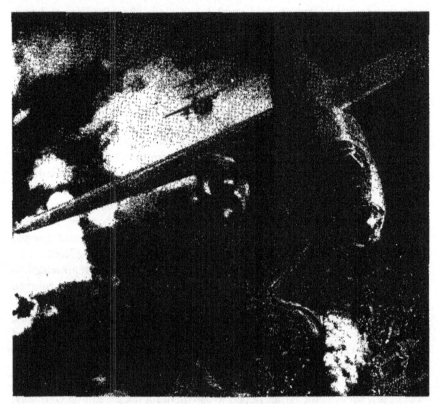

Martin B–26 Marauders hit the railyards at Haslach, Germany.

terfering with the oil offensive, increased the number of days when the B–17s and B–24s could attack worthwhile targets. As the spring of 1945 approached, airmen like Spaatz and Tedder no longer faced hard choices; they had the aerial resources to carry out a transportation campaign without easing pressure on the oil industry.

The attacks on transportation facilities rapidly intensified. While Harris employed Bomber Command, by day as well as night, to cut the canals and railroads that linked the coal mines and factories of the Ruhr to the rest of Germany, American strategic and tactical aircraft hit railroad centers throughout the nation. As more and more transportation targets collapsed in rubble and twisted steel, the number of genuine rail hubs not yet attacked rapidly declined. Minor railroad junctions became targets, and civilian morale at last came under attack, especially by the Allied fighter-bombers, which demonstrated to many Germans who had thus far escaped the worst consequences of Hitler's madness that the *Luftwaffe* could no longer protect them. On February 22 and 23, American airmen conducted two operations, grouped under the code name

316

Clarion, that in effect extended the war to the undamaged towns along Germany's rail system by attacking hundreds of viaducts, marshaling yards, repair shops, railroad stations, and roundhouses. The transportation campaign, including the two Clarion operations, delivered new destruction almost daily and fatally disrupted the German rail system, forcing the trains to move cargo circuitously and slowly, bypassing damaged switching yards and trackage until repairs were made.

During the final phase of the war, the German air force was so crippled by lack of fuel and the death or capture of trained pilots that American and British airmen rarely encountered formidable resistance except in the vicinity of Berlin. Elsewhere the Anglo-American allies could apply crushing force against whatever targets they chose. Several factors influenced the use of air power during the early months of 1945, including the overwhelming might of the Allied strategic air forces; a new assessment of German strength caused by the Ardennes attack, the appearance of the jet fighter, and the persistent threat from the vengeance weapons; and the destruction of major industrial centers, which catapulted lesser targets into prominence. The considerations helped seal the fate of Dresden, set ablaze by a British night attack on February 13, then pounded by American bombers in daylight on the 14th and 15th and again on March 2.

"Dresden," a Royal Air Force briefing officer intoned before the February 13 mission, is "the seventh largest city in Germany" and also "by far the largest unbombed area the enemy has got." Although famed for its china, the city had developed into what the briefer described as "an industrial city of first-class importance." Dresden, he continued, also had a special strategic value, for "like any large city with its multiplicity of telephone and rail facilities," it would prove "of major value for controlling the defence of that part of the front now threatened by Marshal Konev's breakthrough."[15] The advance of Soviet forces under Marshal Ivan S. Konev focused special attention on Dresden, an industrial city containing several factories that produced armaments or military equipment and a large railroad marshaling yard through which men and supplies must pass to oppose the Red Army. Dresden had for some time occupied a place on Bomber Command's list of possible targets, but other industrial cities, many now in ashes, lay nearer at hand. Harris had not loosed his bombers against the city because the long flight might well have resulted in severe losses when the German night defenses were at their deadliest. Now those defenses had crumbled, except around Berlin. The bombing of Dresden had become feasible and militarily useful.

Dresden could be bombed and seemed worth bombing, but for the attack to actually take place depended on the interaction of other circumstances, principally Anglo-American hopes of striking a final aerial blow to knock Germany out of the war and a meeting of the Allied leaders—Roosevelt, Churchill, and Stalin—scheduled for Yalta in the Crimea during February. To end the war, American and British planners suggested a massive attack on Berlin, Operation

Thunderclap, but Harris broadened the proposal to include Chemnitz, Leipzig, and Dresden, three rail centers largely untouched by bombing. Spaatz agreed but with reservations. The American officer persuaded the Royal Air Force Chief of Air Staff, Sir Charles Portal, who represented the Combined Chiefs of Staff in directing the bomber offensive, that attacks on the cities added by Harris to Operation Thunderclap should wait until the Red Army had advanced far enough to benefit from the resulting disruption of German lines communication and supply.

Looking to the impending conference at Yalta, Churchill would tolerate no delay. When he prodded his advisers about plans for "blasting the Germans in their retreat from Breslau [now Wroclaw, Poland]," roughly 140 miles east of Dresden, Portal mentioned the bombing, as weather permitted, of Berlin, Dresden, Chemnitz, Leipzig, and possibly other cities.[16] The purpose of the attacks had changed, however, from driving the last nails into the coffin of the Reich, the purpose of Thunderclap, to disrupting German transportation in support of the Soviet advance.

Pressured by Churchill somehow to impede the German retreat, the British military delegation arrived at Yalta ready to bomb Berlin and the various rail hubs of eastern Germany. During the meetings, Col. Gen. Alexsey Antonov, the acting Soviet armed forces chief of staff, suggested that it would be of great help if the American and British bombers could "paralyze the junctions of Berlin and Leipzig."[17] Since Dresden also lay on a rail line over which German reinforcements traveled eastward, it, too, became a target, even though it was not specifically nominated by Soviet authorities.

A decade later, when the communist press of East Germany denounced the attack on Dresden as an Anglo-American atrocity, Antonov's remarks formed the basis for a response. Ignoring the earlier Allied interest in Dresden—Harris considered it a worthwhile target, and the Americans had bombed it twice, once as a target of opportunity and again to damage the railroad yards—U.S. officials tried to turn the tables declaring flatly that the attack, about which a Soviet satellite complained so bitterly, had resulted from a Soviet request. Antonov's statement at Yalta, and the fact that no objection was forthcoming when an American liaison officer told his Red Army counterpart of the planned raid on Dresden, served as evidence that Soviet authorities had asked for the bombing. Antonov, however, had not singled out Dresden, and the Soviet liaison officer, who worried mainly about the accidental bombing of Konev's troops, would not have been troubled by a strike on a city that lay some seventy miles from the nearest Red Army column.

The unfortunate city, with its factories and railroad complex, became the target of a typical Royal Air Force nighttime urban area raid on February 13, followed on successive days by two American daylight attacks on the rail stations and the marshaling yard. A fuel-starved *Luftwaffe* proved incapable of defending Dresden, the Allied advance on the ground had overrun the early warning radar sites, and the heavy antiaircraft batteries had been moved to guard more important industries elsewhere. Testimony to the weakness of the defenses was the fact that the 1,200 British and American bombers that attacked during the three days lost less than one percent of their number. Dresden's fire service proved as feeble as the fighter and antiaircraft defenses and could not deal with the fire storm generated by the nighttime bombing, which consumed the heart of the city and killed most of the estimated 35,000 persons who perished during the three raids. Cloud cover hampered daylight bombing accuracy by forcing the Eighth Air Force crews to rely on radar or fleeting glimpses of reference points on the ground and thus contributed to the loss of life. A vital railway bridge escaped destruction, however; and since the bridge remained intact, and rails and roadbed were easily repaired, train traffic resumed three days after the third raid. Dresden's war industry, never a specific objective of the attacks, recovered, according to Speer, "with comparative rapidity."

Speer's attitude toward city busting changed during the war. He feared in 1943 that a half dozen attacks on the scale of the raid that set Hamburg ablaze would cause Germany to collapse, but he soon realized that he had underestimated the resilience of the populace. He acknowledged, however, that a series of attacks, like the three successive bombings in February that consumed so much of Dresden, caused "a considerable shock effect," although by this time a mood of fatalism deadened the impact on the German people. Looking back on the war, Speer advised the victorious Allies that bombing is more effective on "economic targets" than population centers.

Dresden, Germany, following the Allied attacks in February 1945.

Berlin, Germany, in August 1945.

As Dresden lay in ruins, Allied armies moved into position to crush Hitler's Reich. One final airborne assault, Operation Varsity, took place on March 24, 1945, as Anglo-American parachutists and glider troops landed near Wesel, Germany, in conjunction with an amphibious crossing of the Rhine. The smoke that screened the landing craft from German gunners also blanketed some landmarks that defined the airborne landing zones, but poor visibility did not disrupt the operation. German antiaircraft crews inflicted casualties, however, and the Curtiss-Wright C–46 transport proved likely to burn if fuel or hydraulic lines were punctured. Except for the antiaircraft fire, the transports and gliders encountered little opposition; Allied heavy bombers had battered all nearby airfields before the attack, and *Luftwaffe* fighters could offer no more than token resistance. As in the previous year's airborne landings in Holland, Eighth Air Force bombers dropped supplies to the Varsity assault force.

The Allied forces that had landed in Normandy and southern France now launched their final drive, which carried them to Lubeck on the Baltic, the Elbe River, Pilsen in Czechoslovakia, Linz in Austria, and the Brenner Pass leading into Italy, where the German defenders surrendered on May 2. As Allied armies crushed the Third Reich, the *Luftwaffe* could do little more than harry the waves of aircraft that ranged ahead of the relentless advance, cratering roads and rail lines, shattering bridges, and destroying trucks and horse-drawn wagons. When German resistance stiffened, P–47 fighter-bombers and fast bombers like the B–26 helped pound the enemy into submission. At last, after Hitler's suicide as Russian troops overran Berlin, Germany accepted defeat. On the morning of May 7, 1945, at Reims, France, *Generaloberst* Albert Jodl, a member of the

320

German high command, signed a surrender agreement, ratified on the following day in a ceremony amid the ruins of Berlin.

Before Allied troops had landed in Normandy, Spaatz and Arnold looked ahead to an analysis of the role that strategic bombing would play in the eventual defeat of Germany. The desire to concentrate on strategic air warfare reflected the relationship between the bomber and the future independence of the air arm. Should an unbiased panel conclude that aerial bombardment had proved decisive against the Third Reich, the Army's historic strategy of defeating hostile armies on the battlefield would have to yield to a policy of destroying, through air power, an enemy's capacity to make war. Since the inquiry that Arnold sought would affect future relationships among the armed services, it could not remain solely an Army Air Forces project, but he wanted the Air Forces in control. He therefore proposed that the Joint Chiefs of Staff assign to the Army Air Forces overall responsibility for conducting the investigation, with the Navy, Army Ground Forces, and Army Service Forces "represented in such proportion as deemed advisable for their immediate needs and in order that impartiality be assured."[18] The key to Arnold's plan was the proposal of proportionate representation; as far as the Combined Bomber Offensive was concerned, the Navy had not participated, and its main interest could only be the relationship of aerial bombardment to German submarine warfare. Since the future of his service would not be jeopardized by an investigation of the air war against Germany, Adm. Ernest J. King, Chief of Naval Operations, readily agreed to Arnold's call for the study.

Under the supervision of Franklin D'Olier, an insurance company executive, the U.S. Strategic Bombing Survey set to work in the spring of 1945, examining evidence mainly from American and German sources, sometimes at great risk to the investigators. For instance, on May 4, just three days before the German surrender at Reims, fire from an enemy roadblock killed one Army enlisted man and one civilian and wounded two other civilians. A German mine that had gone undetected exploded on May 20, killing a civilian and a soldier, and wounding two civilians. Despite the occasional danger, more than a thousand persons gathered, winnowed, and analyzed information for a study that had two purposes. Its Air Forces sponsors believed it would provide documentation to demonstrate the decisiveness of strategic bombing and thus justify an independent air force within the postwar armed forces, while at the same time yielding data helpful in planning the air war against Japan.

The survey of the bomber offensive in Europe produced detailed reports on the impact of the bombing on various aspects of German industry, but the findings were narrow in scope. Arnold kept the British from participating, possibly because he wanted to avoid debate about day versus night or industries versus cities that might have detracted from the overall analysis, and the Soviet Union routinely denied access to industrial sites occupied by its troops. Despite the limitations, the investigation revealed a number of errors in judgment on the part of planners. In retrospect, too many tons of bombs were wasted against the all-but-indestructible submarine pens, and too few devoted to crippling the ball bearing industry. Mistaken, too, was the judgment that airframes rather than engines formed the Achilles' heel of the aircraft industry. The survey, however, confirmed the importance of the oil offensive, although conceding that the constricting effect on German operations appeared more slowly than anticipated. The investigation pointed out, moreover, that the attacks on the transportation net within Germany had taxed the enemy's ingenuity to the utmost and offset the advantage obtained by dispersing factories.

The question that remained unanswered was whether the Allies could have avoided these mistakes or corrected them at the time they were made. Given the importance of the antisubmarine campaign in the early months of the war and the inability of bombers and escorting fighters to hit shipyards in Germany, the submarine bases in France could not have been ignored. Similarly, when the ball bearing industry was most vulnerable, the Eighth Air Force lacked the strength to sustain a destructive series of attacks, and Harris refused to participate. The defeat of the *Luftwaffe*, more a result of attrition among its fighter pilots than the "dehousing" of aircraft workers or the leveling of the factories that employed them, facilitated both the oil and transportation offensives. Had the oil offensive begun in the fall of 1943, when bombers were fewer and long-range fighters nonexistent, the results would have been insignificant and the losses among airmen severe. Similarly, an effective transportation campaign had to await Allied domination of the sky and the advance by the ground forces that brought swarms of fighter-bombers within range of Germany's railroads and canals. Victory might have come earlier, however, if Harris had joined wholeheartedly in a coordinated Anglo-American bomber offensive, attacking the centers of ball bearing production in 1943, for example, or joining the oil offensive in the spring of 1944 instead of later in the year. Yet, a bigger role by Harris in 1943 might conceivably have resulted in his dominating the Combined Bomber Offensive, and this the Americans did not want.

Out of the mountain of evidence came a cautious conclusion, hedged with qualifications and disappointing to those who had hoped for a flat declaration that strategic bombing had won the war. Despite its focus on strategic bombardment, the survey concluded that "Allied air power"—the combined efforts of Allied tactical and strategic forces—"was decisive in western Europe." The report did credit the strategic bomber with bringing "to virtual collapse" the industrial underpinning of the German armed forces, but it added that the breakdown of war production occurred after the Normandy invasion so that the "full effect . . . had not reached the enemy's front lines when they were overrun by Allied forces."[19] In short, the analysts tried to evaluate the contributions of air power within the context of a combined air, ground, and naval campaign, concluding that the Army Air Forces had made an essential contribution to victory, even though it had not won the war by itself.

By incorporating both tactical and strategic aviation under the overall heading of air power, the survey acknowledged the impact of the fighter-bombers, medium bombers, and attack aircraft that supported the Allied advance into Germany. For example, as Patton's troops advanced through the Lorraine region of France they rarely saw, according to the Army's official history of that campaign, "more than a single German plane at a time, although they may have been subjected to a short night bombing or heard a few enemy reconnaissance planes chugging overhead in the darkness."[20] In contrast, German troops had to endure even worse aerial pressure than the *Luftwaffe* had once imposed on the armies of Poland or France. Air power immobilized and demoralized Germany's soldiers, whether massing for the counterthrust or on the defensive. During the American advance through Lorraine, fighter-bombers routinely hit the stone houses that the defenders had turned into pillboxes, breaking open the structures, then following up with fragmentation bombs and napalm; when German antiaircraft batteries massed against this threat, Army field artillery destroyed them. The mutual relationship between air and ground extended beyond the battlefield itself. For instance, the *Luftwaffe* fighter shot down over Berlin could not strafe troops in France, nor could tanks affect the land battle if they sat immobilized on flatcars stopped by a bombed railroad bridge or starved for fuel never produced because bombs had reduced a refinery to rubble. Events thus supported the soundness of the survey's judgment in treating air power as the sum total of its components.

Although fully aware, as their overall conclusion indicated, of the relationship between tactical and strategic aviation, the analysts who prepared the survey tended to ignore some of the more unconventional uses of long-range bombers. During attempts to seize a bridgehead across the Rhine in Holland in 1944 and in Germany in 1945, heavy bombers dropped supplies to the airborne forces. In the summer of 1944, General Doolittle diverted bombers from the offensive against German industry to deliver arms and equipment to French partisans, with as many as 180 B–17s taking part in a single drop. Aircraft based in the Mediterranean performed similar work, though on a lesser scale, infiltrating agents and delivering supplies to resistance forces in Italy, Yugoslavia, and Greece.

Air power, the Strategic Bombing Survey revealed, had not lived up to the expectations of prophets like Douhet or Mitchell, who expected a bolt from the blue that destroyed some vital industry and rendered the enemy powerless to resist, even though his army and navy remained intact. Air power turned out to be a savage and all-consuming hurricane rather than a lightning strike, a bludgeon rather than a rapier. In Europe, the air war became a long and bloody struggle for control of the skies so that bombers could burn cities and level industries by night and day. Until the summer of 1943, the *Luftwaffe* enjoyed air superiority by night over Germany, but Bomber Command put an end to this mastery when it destroyed Hamburg, using a variety of navigation and bombing aids, new aim-

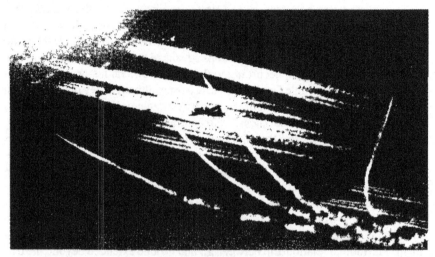

Sky-writing over Germany: bombers left the straight lines; the curved contrails came from fighter escorts sweeping up above the bombers.

ing techniques, and metallic strips that frustrated radar. The enemy fought back, however, improving fighter tactics and regaining air superiority over the Reich in the spring of 1944. German dominance did not last; losses of crews and aircraft, a dwindling supply of fuel, and the Allied capture of radar sites along the channel coast shifted the nighttime balance permanently in favor Bomber Command. The struggle to control the skies also took place in daylight. The Americans gained air superiority over Germany early in 1944, benefitting from the P–51 long-range fighter, from a highly efficient aircraft industry untouched by war, and from a training establishment that at peak capacity could turn out more graduates than the Air Forces could absorb. Against this formidable combination, the *Luftwaffe* never regained the mastery of the skies it had exercised in 1943; not even a marvelous jet fighter, the Me 262, could redress the balance of aerial power.

Germany, moreover, began too late to create the production base necessary to wage war on several fronts simultaneously. The nation's industries performed capably enough when the war was a series of rapid conquests from the channel coast to the gates of Moscow but failed, under the pressure of sustained bombing, to meet the demands of a defensive war in which Germany had to disperse its air power to meet danger from many quarters instead of concentrating it for a single campaign. When leaders of the *Luftwaffe* warned of the swelling volume of American aircraft production, Hitler dismissed the figures as mere fantasy, joking that if the numbers were correct he would have to go on the defense in the East and concentrate all of Germany's resources on air defense. His answer to the threat of bombing was not defense but revenge in the form of rockets and flying bombs, projects that absorbed labor and scarce materials needed for less spectacular weapons. The projections of American production proved real, however; Hitler's reaction was fantasy.

In short, the survey recognized that, throughout the fighting in Europe, the Army Air Forces, despite the autonomy that Marshall had given its leaders, had indeed remained a part of the larger Army, American, and Allied war machines. Operationally, Army airmen diverted strategic bombers to support the invasion, the breakout from the beaches, and the Battle of the Bulge. Administratively, too, the Air Forces remained a part of the Army. Allowed for much of the war to receive a disproportionately large share of the draftees who had scored highest on the general classification test, the air arm had to adjust its manpower policy once the War Department realized that it had underestimated the size of the ground forces needed to win the war. Even before the Ardennes counteroffensive resulted in unexpectedly heavy casualties and made the shortage even worse, the Air Forces helped make up the deficit. During 1944, the War Department transferred some 24,000 air cadets, already surplus to the projected needs of the Air Forces, to the Army Ground Forces for retraining as infantrymen and also sent another 6,000 potential pilots or air crewmen to the Service Forces. The 65th Infantry Division, which reached Europe in January 1945, included 1,100 former aviation cadets, described as "bright, brawny youngsters," most of whom became "excellent soldiers." The Air Forces also exchanged men with the Ground and Service Forces, trading those fit to serve overseas for men qualified for duty only in the United States. The transfers and exchanges accompanied a sharp reduction in the acceptance of air cadets, which made additional men available through the Selective Service System for assignment to the combat arms of the Army Ground Forces.

Although the Air Forces eventually had an excess of manpower and could help the hard-pressed Ground Forces, the growth that created this surplus nevertheless represented a valuable investment. Until the cross-channel invasion, the airplane was the only weapon with which the Americans could carry the war to Germany. During these months, air power provided an immediate return in terms of damaging the Germany war machine, forcing the *Luftwaffe* onto the defensive, and tying down or destroying fighters that otherwise might have strafed Soviet troops, British soldiers in North Africa, or the invading armies that eventually stormed ashore in Normandy. A decision to limit the size of the Army Air Forces earlier in the war might have made additional ground forces available in the United Kingdom, but without the mastery of the skies that overwhelming numbers of aircraft and airmen provided, the troops might have remained in the British Isles long after June 6, 1944. The idle armies would have served mainly as a source of irritation to the Soviet Union, by far the principal ground combatant in the war against Hitler, for the troops in Britain could have influenced only indirectly the great battles that would have been fought on Germany's Eastern Front. As it turned out, by the time the Anglo-American divisions were powerful enough to shatter the Atlantic Wall, Allied air power had crushed the *Luftwaffe*, giving the invasion flotilla and the forces that fought their way through France and into Germany a freedom from aerial interference undreamed of as late as 1943. The compilers of the Strategic Bombing Survey correctly interpreted the American war against Germany as essentially an indivisible effort; a combination of weapons, techniques for their manufacture and employment, and manpower that ultimately overwhelmed the enemy. In the final days of the war against Japan, however, a new aerial weapon would appear, the atomic bomb, a device so dreadful that it again raised the possibility that air power could not merely defeat an enemy in conjunction with ground and naval forces but could by itself utterly destroy the foundations of a hostile society.

Chapter 10

Victory over Japan

Bernard C. Nalty

The basic Anglo-American strategy against the Axis called for remaining generally on the defensive in the Pacific, defeating Italy and Germany first, and then bringing overwhelming might to bear against Japan, whose surprise attack had plunged the United States into the war. Once the purely defensive phase of the war against the Japanese ended, the Allies launched a series of limited offensives designed at first to improve the security of Australia and later to prevent the enemy from consolidating his defensive perimeter. Although limited in scope and commitment, these operations at the time seemed daring indeed. In January 1943, Admiral of the Fleet Sir Dudley Pound, First Sea Lord and a member of the British delegation at the Casablanca Conference, suggested allowing Japan to disperse its forces throughout the vast Pacific, since, in his opinion, no major objective like the Philippines could be retaken until the defeat of Germany permitted the transfer of Allied troops from Europe. Yet, even as the admiral proposed giving up the initiative in the Pacific, limited attacks in New Guinea and the Solomon Islands had already begun to reverse the course of the Pacific war. Under the cover of air power, operating from aircraft carriers or captured islands, the Allies would advance on Japan at a pace which pessimists could only have found amazing. In August 1942, the American 1st Marine Division took a tentative step on what became the road to Tokyo by invading Guadalcanal and a few neighboring islands in the southern Solomons, an operation intended mainly to protect the sea and air routes between Hawaii and Australia. Except for the diversion to the Pacific of some B–17s, the Solomons venture at its outset imposed no great strain on the buildup in Europe and did not challenge the strategy of defeating Germany first.

The location of the Solomons did, however, cause controversy over command arrangements in the far Pacific. Since the ultimate objective of the campaign begun at Guadalcanal was Rabaul, on the island of New Britain and west of the boundary between the South Pacific and Southwest Pacific Areas, Gen. Douglas MacArthur, in command of the Southwest Pacific, sought to direct the entire operation. Regardless of the relationship of Rabaul to the existing boundary, Adm. Ernest J. King, the Chief of Naval Operations, refused to entrust precious aircraft carriers to an Army officer, especially to one who intended to use them within range of Japanese land-based air power. Consequently, the Solomons became a Navy sector under Vice Adm. Robert L. Ghormley, the South Pacific commander. Ghormley, in turn, remained a subordinate of Adm. Chester W. Nimitz, the Commander in Chief, Pacific Fleet, with headquarters in Hawaii. Like Nimitz, Ghormley placed naval officers in key positions throughout his headquarters. For example, Rear Adm. John S. McCain exercised operational control over all aviation units, Army as well as Navy or Marine Corps, and prescribed their training and doctrine. Army airmen objected to placing their squadrons under this all-embracing authority, fearing in particular that naval officers would assign the B–17s missions incompatible with Army Air Forces doctrine and retrain the crews accordingly. To safeguard the status of Army aviation in an essentially naval headquarters, War Department planners agreed to appoint an airman, Maj. Gen. Millard F. Harmon, as commander of Army forces assigned to the South Pacific.

Although he exercised administrative rather than tactical control, General Harmon, backed by his superiors at Washington, guided training and doctrine along paths acceptable to Army airmen. He also exerted influence over the employment of B–17s, resisting insofar as the military situation permitted attempts by Admiral McCain and his successor, Rear Adm. Aubrey W. Fitch, to use the Flying Fortresses on search missions at the expense of attacks on bases like Rabaul. Ultimately, General Harmon succeeded in obtaining for the South Pacific a full-fledged air force, which assumed tactical control of Army aviation in the theater. Activated in January 1943 and entrusted to Maj. Gen. Nathan F. Twining, who had been Harmon's chief of staff, the new Thirteenth Air Force remained under the operational control of a naval officer throughout the campaign in the southern Solomons. In July of that year, when the war moved into the central Solomons with the invasion of New Georgia, Twining became the Commander, Air, Solomons, replacing a naval officer. At year's end, when he departed for the Mediterranean theater, Twining handed over the organization to Maj. Gen. Ralph J. Mitchell of the Marine Corps.

The fighting for the Solomons began at Guadalcanal in the summer of 1942 and ended in the spring of 1944 with the repulse of the last Japanese counterattacks on Bougainville, almost 400 miles to the northwest. Launched by Admiral Ghormley, the campaign proceeded after October 1942 under the direction of Adm. William F. Halsey, Jr., whose task force had launched Jimmy Doolittle's B–25s against Japan in April 1942. A few Army B–17s had bombed the beaches in preparation for the landing at Guadalcanal, and aircraft like these contributed in varying degrees to the victory there and to subsequent successes, usually by bombing distant airfields or anchorages. Although high-altitude attacks on warships rarely proved effective, the Japanese credited a flight of B–17s with surprising the destroyer *Mutsuki* and sending it to the bottom when it stopped to take off troops from a sinking transport. More successful in the waters around the Solomons was a squadron of SB–24s, Liberator bombers fitted with radar for nighttime bombing from low altitude. The unit, commanded by Col. Stuart P. Wright, arrived at Guadalcanal in August 1943 and quickly demonstrated its effectiveness against surface ships that presented a sharp radar image against the background of the open sea.

During the early fighting ashore at Guadalcanal, the Army airmen based there operated on a shoestring, hard-pressed for maintenance and relying on the Bell P–400, an export model of the P–39, which excelled at strafing but climbed sluggishly and lacked the oxygen equipment necessary to do battle with the Japanese Zero. At the outset, Japanese bombers made daily raids, with warships at times adding to the weight of the bombardment, in an attempt to knock out Henderson Field, the airstrip on Guadalcanal taken over from the enemy and named in honor of Maj. Lofton Henderson, a Marine Corps aviator killed in the Battle of Midway. Although these blows occasionally staggered the Americans, Army airmen joined Marine and Navy flyers in seizing control of the skies over the Solomons and slaughtering the reinforcements the Japanese were ferrying by sea to Guadalcanal. The aircraft of the Army Air Forces flying from the island came to include P–39s and P–38s, and these, along with all the other fighters based there, came under the operational control of a Marine Corps airman.

In April 1943, with Guadalcanal secured and preparations under way for attacking New Georgia, Japanese message traffic yielded another important secret to American cryptanalysts: Adm. Isoroku Yamamoto, the commander in chief of the Japanese Combined Fleet and the architect of both the raid on Pearl Harbor and the expedition against Midway, planned to visit the island of Bougainville. Although no other source of information, such as routine aerial reconnaissance, could readily conceal the breaking of the Japanese naval code, American planners decided that the admiral's real and symbolic value to the enemy outweighed the possibility of compromising an important source of intelligence. On April 18, 1943, the anniversary of Doolittle's raid on Tokyo, Maj.

Henderson Field, Guadalcanal, Solomon Islands, 1944.

John W. Mitchell led sixteen P–38s (one other blew a tire trying to take off and still another turned back after experiencing engine trouble) to the farthest extent of their combat radius and succeeded in intercepting the two bombers carrying Yamamoto and his inspection party and the six Zero fighters escorting them. In a wild aerial battle that began low over the jungle and continued offshore, both bombers were shot down and Yamamoto killed.

The tangle of conflicting reports by the pilots involved has taken years to sort out and remains the object of debate despite the reports of various panels that have tried to re-create the day's events. When the P–38s returned from the mission, Capt. Thomas G. Lanphier claimed one bomber, as did 1st Lt. Besby F. Holmes, and 1st Lt. Rex Barber claimed two. Until Japanese testimony became available, the Americans assumed that a third bomber had been present, so Barber, Lanphier, and Holmes each received credit for destroying one. When Japanese sources revealed after the war that only two bombers carried the admiral and his staff, an attempt was made to correct the record by crediting Barber with sharing in the destruction of both, collaborating with Lanphier in downing the bomber that carried Yamamoto and with Holmes in shooting down the other aircraft. This decision has not gone unchallenged, even though it reflected statements by both Japanese and American eyewitnesses and took into account the performance characteristics of the P–38.

The failure in March 1944 of a Japanese counterattack in the jungles of Bougainville, the island where Yamamoto died, ensured the security of the Allied lodgment there and decided the Solomons campaign. Meanwhile, General MacArthur's forces in the Southwest Pacific had approached Rabaul from its opposite flank, a drive during which air power protected a series of amphibious landings, helped disrupt Japanese traffic on the sea lanes, and contributed to the neutralization of the bastion on New Britain. The American aer-

330

ial organization assigned to MacArthur's theater was the Fifth Air Force, organized in September 1942 under the command of General Kenney, who also headed the Allied Air Forces, Southwest Pacific Area. Kenney established a close relationship with MacArthur, who sent the airman as a representative to various strategic planning sessions and also used him as an emissary to the leaders of the Republican party in an unsuccessful attempt to obtain the Presidential nomination in 1944. In gaining MacArthur's trust, Kenney sold the theater commander on a basic concept of aerial attrition, which began with operations "to

Rabaul Harbor, New Britain, following a raid by B-25 bombers.

take out the Jap air strength until we own the air over New Guinea," and then made the plan work. Once Kenney's flyers had destroyed enough enemy aircraft in aerial combat or by bombing airfields, MacArthur's land and amphibious forces could advance, always moving in the shadow of Allied fighters and bombers.[1]

Despite the vast distances over which men and aircraft had to travel to reach the Fifth Air Force, the productive capacity of the United States and the increasing security of the sea route to Australia enabled Kenney to seize and maintain air superiority over the Japanese. American air forces in the Southwest and South Pacific surpassed 1,000 aircraft of all types by January 1943, more than 2,000 by December of that year, and reached 5,500 by the time the war ended. By then, the Far East Air Forces, consisting of the Fifth Air Force and the Thirteenth, had advanced into the Philippines and was preparing for the invasion of Japan. As early as the end of 1944, the inventory of aircraft flown by Kenney's Far East Air Forces outnumbered the total available to the Japanese throughout the entire Pacific; and once opened, the gap widened.

During the battle for New Guinea, Kenney's varied responsibilities and the tenuous communications between Australia and New Guinea persuaded him to entrust combat operations to a Fifth Air Force advance echelon located at Port Moresby and commanded by his deputy, Brig. Gen. Ennis C. Whitehead. The relationship between the Allied Air Forces, Southwest Pacific Area, and the Fifth Air Force remained informal, since Kenney and some of his staff officers held the same assignment in both. The willingness to delegate authority and the interchangeability of assignments between the senior officers at Allied and American air force headquarters persisted after June 1944, when Kenney assumed command of the Far East Air Forces.

In keeping with Kenney's views on the use of air power to seize control of the skies before advancing on the ground or by sea, General MacArthur's drive toward Rabaul began with a concentration of forces under an aerial shield that extended only as far as eastern New Guinea. The struggle for that island had barely begun in 1942 when the C–47 emerged as the only form of transportation able to defy the mountains and jungle that hampered movement there. With the passing of time, these aircraft flew in reinforcements from Australia, evacuated the wounded, and carried men and supplies across the Owen Stanley Mountains as the war moved farther away from Port Moresby. In September 1943, Army Air Forces C–47s dropped Australian and American parachute troops at Nadzab during an Allied drive toward the island's northeast coast. Nine months later, as the New Guinea campaign drew to a successful close, transport aircraft dropped some 1,500 paratroops at Noemfoor Island off the northwest coast.

The effective use of unarmed C–47s depended, however, on control of the air, which Kenney's flyers extended over all of New Guinea by early 1943 and ultimately pushed all the way to the Philippines. The fighter was essential to this success. Starting with a few P–400s, P–39s, and P–40s, General Kenney's fight-

Allied soldiers board a C–47 at a field near Port Moresby, New Guinea.

er command soon acquired P–38s, P–47s, and in 1944 a few P–61s. The last of these types, the Northrop Black Widow, was the most effective night fighter to reach the Air Forces squadrons in the Pacific for use against aerial harassment after dark. With the arrival of the newer day fighters, which eventually included the P–51, American pilots no longer complained that they always seemed to be attacking from below because their aircraft lacked the power to climb above Japanese formations.

Interception formed only a part of the fighter pilot's duties, though always a dangerous one. Indeed, these operations might prove fatal even when what looked like enemy bombers on the radar actually proved to be a fast moving, late afternoon thunderstorm. The flyers, after returning from the false alarm, would have to land on rain-slickened metal planking, made all the more dangerous by gusty wind and gathering darkness. Many sorties, however, consisted of attacks on Japanese infantry strongpoints, invisible from the cockpit of a P–39 and marked only by a burst of tracers fired into the jungle by an Australian spotter

333

plane. Days sometimes passed before the Americans learned the results of such a strafing attack. A note of congratulations might arrive from an Australian unit fighting its way along a ridge in New Guinea or, better yet, a messenger bringing with him a present from the ground commander—whiskey to help relieve the boredom and discomfort of a forward airfield or to overcome the fear caused by a close call over Rabaul or a surprise bombing attack on the base.

Important though it was, the fighter or fighter-bomber provided just one of the weapons that enabled General Kenney to defeat Japanese air power. Low-flying A–20s destroyed parked enemy aircraft by dropping 23-pound fragmentation bombs fitted at the general's suggestion with small parachutes that slowed descent and enabled the attackers to escape the hail of metal when the devices detonated. Delayed-action high-explosive bombs from B–25s and Kenney's few B–26s cratered runways, and low-altitude strafing by bombers and fighters added to the toll among Japanese aircraft. Maj. Paul I. Gunn, a former naval aviator commissioned from civilian life during the recent fighting in the Philippines, and Jack Fox, a technical representative of North American Aviation modified several B–25s, creating especially deadly strafers. Instead of the usual glassed-in bombardier's compartment, their attack version had a solid nose and eight forward-firing machineguns capable of unleashing a torrent of fire against parked airplanes, barges, or small ships. Gunn again applied his ingenuity in July 1943, when a new model of the B–25 fitted with a 75–mm gun arrived in the Southwest Pacific. He strengthened the air frame and the metal skin to withstand the recoil of this weapon and increased firepower by adding four forward-firing machineguns.

Besides attacking enemy air power, General Kenney directed an interdiction campaign designed to neutralize Rabaul and disrupt the passage of supply convoys bound for New Guinea. In 1942, while en route to Australia, Kenney had become interested in skipbombing, the dropping from masthead height of a de-

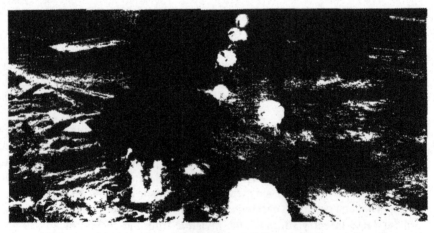

Fragmentation bombs with parachutes fall onto Japanese aircraft.

layed-action bomb that would carom off the surface of the sea, penetrate the thin hull of a merchantman, and explode inside, fatally rupturing plates or igniting the cargo. The strafing model of the B–25 proved well suited to skipbombing, an aptitude demonstrated during tests in which even B–17s participated. The experiments revealed, however, that when dropped from a few hundred feet, a delayed-action bomb proved more accurate and did as much damage to a freighter as the same kind of bomb skipped from the surface of the sea. In January 1943, after the B–17s and B–24s that routinely attacked Rabaul reported that enemy shipping was gathering there, an entire squadron of B–25s, fitted out for strafing, began practicing low-altitude bombing.

As the Japanese transport and escort vessels were dropping anchor in Rabaul harbor, the men who had broken Japan's naval code again helped to shape the course of the Pacific war, for they pieced together the orders for an infantry division to embark at the beginning of March on a convoy bound for New Guinea. Intensified aerial patrols sighted the ships, and Allied planes—American B–17s, A–20s, and B–25s and Australian Bristol Beauforts and Beaufighters—made coordinated attacks under fighter cover provided by P–38s. Descending below 10,000 feet, Flying Fortresses set fire to one transport, which its crew had to abandon; but the B–25s proved even deadlier, attacking with delayed action bombs from the height of a victim's mast and claiming hits with 17 of 27 bombs dropped. In this action, the Battle of the Bismarck Sea, Allied air power sank 12 of the 16 ships in the convoy, killing approximately half the 6,000 troops on board. In all, fewer than 1,000 soldiers reached New Guinea, the other survivors returning to Rabaul, which remained in Japanese hands for the rest of the war. Although the U.S. Marines established themselves on the island of New Britain, the Allies bypassed Rabaul. Even without the conquest of this stronghold, American and Australian forces had broken Japan's outermost shield; ahead lay the Philippines and perhaps Formosa.

Although the Allies surged forward in the Southwest Pacific, they experienced only modest success in the China-Burma-India Theater. In Burma, especially, the war began badly. By mid-1942 the Japanese had overrun the British colony, inflicting on its defenders what the American commander there, Lt. Gen. Joseph W. Stilwell, described as "a hell of a beating." While the ground forces tried to regroup in China and India, Chennault's Flying Tigers, some of whom followed their commander into the Army Air Forces, and elements of the Tenth Air Force, operating from India, persisted in harassing the Japanese. The war on the Asian mainland now divided into two related campaigns: one to reconquer Burma and the other to defeat the enemy in China and carry the war to his home islands. The common link was the need to open a highway through Burma to carry supplies from India to sustain the land and air operations in China.

The reconquest of Burma would take time, for the operation had a low priority in the worldwide allocation of resources. For example, the buildup of the

335

Tenth Air Force had been delayed to provide the aircraft needed to deal with Rommel's threat to the Suez Canal, and its recently appointed commander, General Brereton, went to North Africa in June 1943 to take charge of American air units there. In August, Brig. Gen. Clayton L. Bissell took over the Tenth Air Force, which at this time exercised control over Chennault's China Air Task Force, succeeding Brig. Gen. Earl L. Naiden, the interim replacement for Brereton. Because Japan had closed the Burma Road, over which military cargo reached China, the fighting there, whether on the ground or in the skies, depended on airlift. Bissell reorganized the command to include a ferrying group, which became the India-China Wing of the Air Transport Command, responsible for the airlift to China.

Because of differing national priorities and competition for scarce supplies, two tangled lines of responsibility emerged within China, Burma, and India. Vice Adm. Lord Louis Mountbatten functioned as supreme Allied commander for Southeast Asia, including Burma, while Generalissimo Chiang Kai-shek (now romanized as Jiang Jieshi), the leader of Nationalist China, exercised similar authority in China. General Stilwell served as U.S. Army commander within the China-Burma-India Theater, a largely administrative assignment, as deputy to Lord Mountbatten, and as chief of staff to the Generalissimo. Although sent to the China-Burma-India Theater to command the Army Air Forces component, Maj. Gen. George E. Stratemeyer served initially as deputy to Lord Mountbatten's air commander. The American airman coordinated the efforts of the Tenth Air Force, the Fourteenth Air Force (commanded from its inception by Chennault as a major general), and the air transport wing flying cargo across the Himalayas. Late in 1943, General Stratemeyer at last assumed command of an operational organization when Lord Mountbatten selected him to direct the Western Air Command, made up of the Tenth Air Force and the Royal Air Force's Bengal Command.

A unique set of circumstances thrust Stratemeyer into this ramshackle command structure. Stilwell wanted a theater air officer but he did not want Chennault, who disagreed with him on matters of strategy and supply and had appealed over his head in an attempt to influence the President. Both Marshall and Arnold were wary of Chennault, who did not seem to understand the logistic difficulty of fighting an intensified war on the Asian mainland. Stratemeyer, senior to Chennault, served as Arnold's Chief of the Air Staff and in that capacity had visited China on an inspection tour that dealt specifically with problems of supply. The difficult and ill-defined assignment went to Stratemeyer because he was experienced in staff work, familiar with logistics in the theater, and satisfactory to Stilwell, Arnold, and Marshall.

As the confusing organizational pattern took shape, American airmen based in India, sometimes aided by bombers and crews borrowed from Chennault, protected the air route across the Himalayas and attacked ports and railroads in Burma. When neutralizing airfields that threatened the airlift or destroying railway bridges, the older P–40s, no longer suitable for dogfights, delivered 1,000-pound bombs with such accuracy that pilots nicknamed them "B–40s." Newer models of the P–40, better adapted to dealing with enemy fighters, helped defend the aerial supply line over the Hump, as the spine of the Himalayas was called, but Japanese fighters for a time remained so dangerous that Brig. Gen. William B. Old, in charge of the airlift in the latter months of 1943, had to route the transports northward to avoid interception.

The Allies, however, soon gained control of the skies over Burma as the Japanese struggled unsuccessfully against the rapidly expanding American and British air forces. By the end of 1943, General Stratemeyer possessed both the authority to employ air power as circumstances might dictate and the means to hurt the enemy. In contrast, the Japanese were making many of the same errors in Burma that the Americans had made in North Africa, trying to do too much with too little and thus forfeiting the initiative. A need to divert aerial strength, at the time that the Americans and British were increasing theirs, compounded the woes of the Japanese. Bombers, for example, that had launched a promising series of raids on Calcutta, India, suddenly departed so they could oppose General MacArthur's advance.

Control of the air enabled the Allies to move at last against the enemy in Burma. Although a lack of resources ruled out a proposed amphibious assault to recapture the port of Rangoon, Lord Mountbatten set in motion a less ambitious offensive provisioned by air and designed principally to safeguard the aerial supply line and secure the right-of-way for a new road into China. This scaled-down Burma operation began early in 1944 with two Allied thrusts. On March 5, a mixed force of Burmese, British, and Indian troops under British Brigadier Orde Wingate raided behind Japanese lines in northwestern Burma; and a month later, General Stilwell attacked in the northeast with a predominately Chinese force that included 3,000 American infantrymen commanded by Brig. Gen. Frank D. Merrill.

From the standpoint of air power, Brigadier Wingate's effort was the more spectacular, for an air task force led by Col. Philip G. Cochran landed some 10,000 men and pack animals in jungle clearings beyond enemy lines. After the initial assault, American and British aircraft dropped perhaps three million pounds of cargo to sustain the attack. Even as they were supplying these soldiers, commanded by Maj. Gen. Walter D. Lentaigne after Wingate's death in a B–25 crash, the transports had to fly the first of more than 12,500 reinforcements and 20,000 tons of supplies to outposts successfully resisting a Japanese offensive west of the area where Lentaigne's troops operated.

Although Stilwell did not rely so heavily on aircraft for mobility and supply, air power did some of the same things for him—flying supply, strike, and reconnaissance missions—that it was doing for Wingate and Lentaigne. Inside stable and reliable C–47s, quartermaster soldiers, who a few days earlier had driven trucks or operated laundries, pushed bundles of food, fuel, medicine, and

Gurkha paratroopers wait beside the C–47 transport that
will carry them to the jump zone near Rangoon, Burma.

ammunition out of the cargo doors onto parachute drop zones established
below. Aerial photographs helped pinpoint battlefield targets and the trails the
enemy used for supply and reinforcement. Because the jungle restricted fields
of fire and hampered the registration of artillery, fighter-bombers did the work
of howitzers. When the strike controller assigned to each of Stilwell's major
units could not pinpoint a Japanese position, he made radio contact with a low-
flying observation plane that then guided the attacking aircraft to the target.
Stilwell's men captured Myitkyina airfield and, weeks later, the village itself.
Unfortunately, by the time Stilwell's troops seized the latter objective on August
3, 1944, Burma had reverted to a minor battlefield compared to the islands of
the Pacific and advance through the jungles seemed scarcely worth the effort.

Like Burma, which became a backwater area of the war, China did not prove
to be the springboard for decisive operations against Japan. The enemy offensive following the Doolittle raid had deprived American airmen of bases within bombing distance of Japan, and supply proved a critical problem. Until northern Burma could be reconquered and a new highway built to China, cargo that
had already traveled halfway around the world faced an dangerous flight across
the Himalayas. Overworked C–47s, supplemented by their commercial counterparts, Douglas DC–3s (obtained from the Chinese national airline), replaced
truck convoys in supplying both the American aerial effort and the armies of
Chiang Kai-shek. To guide the heavily laden transports over the Himalaya
Mountains, Air Forces communications specialists set up the first elements in a
network of nine radio stations extending from the Indian province of Assam to
Kunming in China. Understandably, this primitive aerial route did not approach

A Curtiss C–46 Commando flying the Hump route through the Himalayas.

the volume of cargo that might have arrived by highway had the Japanese not intervened.

During January 1943, the airline over the Hump had delivered less than 1,500 tons of freight, but a move to double the size of the transport fleet with new and larger aircraft inspired estimates that the monthly volume would reach 4,000 tons by November. The new aircraft, after all, included the C–87, a cargo version of the B–24, and the C–46, both of which had greater capacity than the C–47. Chiang Kai-shek, however, demanded an apparently unrealistic 10,000 tons each month, and President Franklin D. Roosevelt insisted that this goal be met by September 1943. Testimony to the danger facing the airmen who tried to meet this objective took the form of several "huge black blotches" that Brig. Gen. William H. Tunner saw at the end of the runway at Chabua in Assam when he took command of the airlift in the summer of 1944. "Each was a lasting memorial," Tunner later wrote, "to a group of American airmen, the crew of a plane that had crashed and burned on the spot."[2] Despite serious handicaps—frequent mechanical failures in the unproven C–46, crew fatigue caused by overwork and primitive living accommodations, and a feeling that a hard and dangerous job was going unrewarded—the aerial supply line met the President's goal by November 1943, just two months beyond his deadline. Moreover, in the last six months of 1944, the fleet of transports and the number of flights per month into China available to Tunner more than doubled, pushing the volume of cargo delivered in December beyond 30,000 tons.

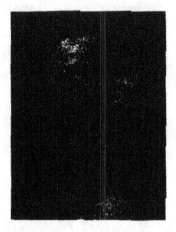

Maj. Gen. Claire L. Chennault,
Commander, Fourteenth Air Force.

Before this period of rapid growth—indeed, when the route over the Hump had barely begun to function—Chennault began campaigning to expand the air war in China. Ignoring his dependence on aerial supply and airfields defended by ground forces, he insisted that air power could do more to defend China and defeat Japan than the Chinese infantry divisions that Stilwell proposed to equip and train. Bypassing his theater commander, the airman in October 1942 assured President Roosevelt that, if given command of an American air force in China with as few as 147 operational fighters and bombers, he could take the offensive, destroy enemy air power over China, and carry the war to Japan. Since Chennault proposed to break the Japanese hold on the mainland without jeopardizing Chiang's postwar plans for using the American-equipped divisions against the Chinese communists, the Nationalist leader endorsed the Chennault plan, which would divert supplies from the ground forces to the air war. Unlike Chennault and Chiang, Stilwell emphasized the importance of employing China's vast manpower against the Japanese, regardless of the effect on the postwar balance of power between the Nationalists and communists. Although willing to concede the importance of military aviation to operations on the ground, Stilwell doubted that the volume of supplies arriving over the Himalayas could sustain the ambitious air offensive and at the same time permit the development of airfields, the organization and training of ground forces, and the reopening of an overland supply route through northern Burma.

General Marshall and Secretary of War Stimson, two persons whose judgment the President greatly respected, shared Stilwell's misgivings and supported a strategy of building a Chinese army and reopening the Burma road. Furthermore, Arnold, the Commanding General of the Army Air Forces, returned in February 1943 from a visit to China convinced that neither Chennault nor Chiang Kai-shek understood the complexity of mounting a sustained aerial campaign in that region. The Chinese leader, however, remained unwavering in his support of Chennault, and Roosevelt yielded to both Chiang's insistence and his own abiding impulse to support the person who promised immediate results, in this case Chennault, instead of backing Stilwell, who always seemed to be preparing for a decisive action, but sometime in the future. In March 1943, Chennault's China Air Task Force became the Fourteenth Air Force, and the commander of the new organization confessed to a friend, "I feel just like the fellow who said he wanted an elephant and then got one. I suppose I can figure out how to handle it as time goes on."[3]

Handling the elephant proved more difficult than Chennault anticipated. By the summer of 1943, his aerial offensive had begun, but the increased activity—including attacks on coastal shipping, ports, and troop concentrations—prompted a savage reaction. Far from collapsing as expected, the enemy threatened for a time to seize control of the skies over China and neutralize the airfields from which the Fourteenth Air Force mounted its attacks. The timely arrival of fresh pilots and improved fighters enabled Chennault to retain air superiority, but the Chinese ground forces soon faced disaster of a magnitude that jeopardized not only Chennault's air offensive but also another undertaking that the Allied military leadership considered more likely to produce truly decisive results.

The air war that Chennault waged in China paled in comparison to the campaign planned for a force of B–29s based in that country. At the Quebec Conference of Allied leaders in August 1943, American planners first proposed using airfields in China to launch the new bombers against Japan in an aerial offensive designed to help win a victory over Japan just one year after the defeat of Germany. Despite the logistic problems involved, Allied planners had selected China because Chiang's armies already controlled the territory where air bases could be built within B–29 range of the home islands. In the summer of 1943, amphibious forces probing Japan's outer defensive perimeter were an estimated year or more away from objectives within striking distance of the enemy homeland. At the time of the Quebec Conference, therefore, China seemed the best choice for launching the bombing campaign, although attacks might follow from the Mariana Islands in the central Pacific, perhaps as early as December 1944. The B–29 offensive from China, the so-called Matterhorn project, seemed so important that in November 1943 Arnold vetoed a plan to stage B–24s through bases in eastern China and hit targets in the Sasebo-Nagasaki region of Japan because he did not want to dramatize the vulnerability of the Japanese home islands to air attack.

In the latter part of 1943, with B–29 attacks from China a part of the Allied agenda, the monthly volume of cargo airlifted over the Himalayas approached 10,000 tons, a foreshadowing of the vast increase that occurred in 1944. Encouraging as this progress was, the flight over the Himalayas remained but one piece in a complicated logistic mosaic. Materiel destined for Allied units in India and Burma, as well as China, choked Calcutta, the major port in the region. Chennault, moreover, planned to launch his Fourteenth Air Force on an expanded air campaign in 1944, increasing its consumption of fuel and munitions. At the same time, Stilwell sought to arm and train additional Chinese divisions, warning that these troops might well be needed to stop a Japanese offensive in eastern China triggered by the intensified air war. In brief, no one guarantee that even the rapidly expanding volume of cargo crossing the mountains could satisfy a competition for supplies made all the keener by the coming of the B–29s.

In earmarking the B–29 for the war against Japan, General Arnold faced the unpleasant prospect of entrusting to theater commanders inexperienced in strategic air warfare a weapon so deadly that it might well force Japan to surrender. Because of distances, aircraft available, and kinds of targets, not MacArthur in the Southwest Pacific, nor Stilwell in China and Burma, nor Nimitz in the Central Pacific had employed the land-based bomber in quite the way that the advocates of air power had championed. Consequently, Arnold proposed that he retain control of the new bombers and direct their activity from Washington. After all, the air arm could ensure its future independence by bombing Japan into submission, and the B–29 fleet seemed capable of doing just that, provided an experienced airman employed it properly. At Arnold's urging, the Joint Chiefs of Staff assumed operational control of the B–29 offensive, appointing the Commanding General of the Army Air Forces to exercise "executive direction" in their name. The Twentieth Air Force, the designation of the striking force of B–29s, consisted of two bomber commands. The XX Bomber Command would attack from China, under the command of Brig. Gen. Kenneth B. Wolfe, who had helped bring the new aircraft through a series of development crises, the most difficult caused by overheating and fires in the huge engines. After the conquest of the Mariana Islands, the XXI Bomber Command, led by Brig. Gen. Haywood S. Hansell, would operate from airfields in that island chain.

Learning the intricacies of a complicated and largely unproven airplane caused frustrating delays for the men of the XX Bomber Command, organized in November 1943, some five months before the Twentieth Air Force, the headquarters to which it would report. By the spring of 1944, however, a modification center in Kansas was correcting defects in 150 of the bombers and turning them over to their crews for the flight across Africa to India. From India, the B–29s staged through the Chengtu (Chengdu) region of China, where some 75,000 laborers used picks and shovels to turn valuable agricultural land into airfields. Meanwhile, the cargo reaching China by air increased in volume because of the more efficient use of the additional transports flying out of India. Following schedules devised by Lt. Col. Robert S. McNamara, later to become Secretary of Defense, B–29s doubling as transports aided in delivering fuel and other cargo from India to bases in China. McNamara operated a statistical section, patterned after the statistical control unit at Air Forces headquarters, that kept track of all the variables affecting the supply effort—gross and net loads, aircraft available, and the time required to load and unload—and adjusted schedules accordingly.

While the stockpiles grew larger at Chengtu, the bombers conducted badly needed training flights and carried out an ineffectual practice mission from India against Bangkok, Thailand. Training soon became a luxury, however, for Japanese forces were advancing in eastern China, trying to overrun the airfields from which Chennault's Fourteenth Air Force launched its attacks, especially the strikes against coastal shipping. When the enemy surged forward on the ground, threatening to overwhelm the Chinese defenders, Chennault had to intervene, and the air war intensified further, rapidly using up the stocks of fuel and munitions he had accumulated for his operations. General Stilwell promptly arranged to give the Fourteenth Air Force a larger share of the tonnage arriving from India, but weeks would pass before the cargo, in effect diverted from General Wolfe's B–29s, reached General Chennault's squadrons. Although the possibility of a Chinese collapse seemed far from remote, the Joint Chiefs of Staff denied Chiang Kai-shek's request that the Fourteenth Air Force immediately begin drawing on the supplies already flown into China for use by the XX Bomber Command, an indication of their reluctance to delay the bombing of Japan, a project in which the United States had already invested so much effort.

With Allied prospects on the ground in eastern China growing progressively bleaker, General Wolfe's bombers made their first attack on Japan, doing minor damage to the steel mills at Yawata on the night of June 15, 1944. The effort, however, cut deeply into fuel stocks and, because of the long full-power climb to bombing altitude, resulted in engine wear that required extensive overhaul. Repairs to the engines took excessive time, since little depot assistance was available and enlisted crew members had to do much of the work. When he could not deliver powerful blows in rapid succession, as General Arnold demanded, General Wolfe returned to the Materiel Command, replaced by a veteran of the strategic air war in Europe, Maj. Gen. Curtis E. LeMay.

Whereas his predecessor had at times used darkness rather than self-defending formations to frustrate enemy fighters and radar to compensate for poor accuracy in visual bombing, General LeMay at the outset insisted on developing skill in formation flying and daylight bombing techniques so that his new command could use the precision tactics which his B–17s had employed over Europe. In stepping up the tempo of flight operations, the new commander profited from improvements in the functioning of the aerial supply line. General Tunner made good a promise to deliver more cargo, especially gasoline. The arrival in the theater of thirty-three C–109s, a tanker version of the B–24, increased the amount of fuel flown into China, even though the aircraft had a dangerous tendency to leak gasoline vapor, which collected in the fuselage, needing only a spark to turn the tanker into a flying torch.

General LeMay's efforts to improve bombing effectiveness sometimes paid off in heavy destruction, as at the Anshan steel mills in Manchuria, but he could not conduct continuous attacks. Supply proved an insurmountable obstacle, and emergencies required the diversion of effort from industrial targets. Indeed, an

A Boeing B–29 at a base in India and the bombs it will
carry to a Japanese target on the Malay Peninsula.

incendiary raid on the docks at Hangkow (Hangzhou), China, delivered to slow
the enemy's advance on the Fourteenth Air Force bases, proved to the one of the
most devastating B–29 attacks thus far. Thanks partly to the strike on Hangkow,
the Japanese drive outran its supply lines early in 1945. Matterhorn bombing
missions from the airfields at Chengtu ended in January, although the B–29s
continued to fly from India under the operational control of Lord Mountbatten.
Twice afterward the bombers staged through Chengtu to sow mines in the waters off Shanghai, China, but otherwise bombers from Chengtu attacked targets
in Southeast Asia inside a triangle formed by Rangoon, Burma; Cam Rahn Bay,
Indochina; and Palembang on Sumatra.

The results achieved by the XX Bomber Command did not live up to expectation. In all, the organization flew forty-nine missions, fifteen against Japanese
industries in the home islands, Manchuria, or Formosa. Fortunately for the
Allied cause, the pace of the war in the Pacific had so accelerated that, by the
time XX Bomber Command flew its first mission against Yawata, amphibious
forces were in the process of seizing airfield sites in the Mariana Islands that
could sustain a massive bomber offensive against Japan from another direction.

The B–29 campaign from China formed part of a general increase in the
tempo of the fighting in the Pacific that had been decided on at the Quebec
Conference of August 1943. The conferees agreed that, while preparations went
ahead to mount a B–29 offensive from China, Admiral Nimitz should attack
westward through the Central Pacific toward the Marianas and General
MacArthur bypass Rabaul and fulfill his promise to return to the Philippines.
The Combined Chiefs of Staff expected the strategic air campaign from China

Maj. Gen. Willis H. Hale,
Commander,
Seventh Air Force.

to be entering its second year before completion of airfields for additional B–29 raids from the Marianas or possibly Luzon.

During the advance toward the Marianas, the Army Air Forces, rather than shift B–17s and B–24s from the South or Southwest Pacific to support an offensive in the Central Pacific, sent squadrons directly from the United States, an acknowledgment by General Arnold that the offensives northward from New Guinea and westward from Hawaii, for the time being, enjoyed equal importance. The new bombers, which began arriving in the fall of 1943 after the Quebec Conference, reversed a decline in Seventh Air Force strength, for beginning shortly after the Battle of Midway it had been releasing B–24 units for service elsewhere in the Pacific. In December 1942, during the period of eclipse, Maj. Gen. Willis H. Hale, the Seventh Air Force commander, bombed Wake Island, accomplishing the goal that had cost General Tinker's life. By the following summer, General Hale's bombers ranged as far as the Gilbert Islands, staging through the Ellice group. The Central Pacific drive began in the Gilberts in November 1943, with an amphibious assault on Tarawa, the occupation of Abemama, and the conquest of Makin Atoll. For the campaign in the Gilberts, General Hale's airmen flew bombing and photo reconnaissance missions (and fighter patrols after the objectives were seized) under the operational control of a Navy task force commander, Vice Adm. John H. Hoover.

Early in 1944, following the hard-fought victory in the Gilberts, American amphibious forces advanced into the Marshall Islands. General Hale's fighters and bombers, some based at recently captured Tarawa, attacked several targets in the Marshalls, including Kwajalein Atoll. After seizing Kwajalein and nearby Majuro Atoll early an February, American forces captured Eniwetok Atoll at the western end of the Marshall chain and hit the Truk Islands of the Caroline group with a carrier strike that forced units of the Japanese Combined Fleet to seek a safer anchorage. The conquest of Eniwetok, declared secure on February 20, 1944, completed an unexpectedly swift advance that avoided a long, bloody struggle for the Marshalls and accelerated the war by some six months. As the fighting moved closer to Japan, General Hale's command joined the Thirteenth Air Force in neutralizing Wotje and Maloelap in the Marshalls and Truk in the Carolines, where the enemy struggled eeaselessly to repair cratered runways and keep those once-formidable bases in the war.

Although harassing Truk and other bypassed Japanese bases became a principal mission of the Seventh Air Force, Hale's airmen also participated in the invasion of the Marianas. Prior to the attack, Seventh Air Force bombers escorted photographic missions, flown by the Navy's reconnaissance version of the Liberator, over Guam and Saipan, two of the objectives. On June 22, 1944, one week after the landings at Saipan, a squadron of P–47s took off from two escort carriers, landed ashore, and began operating from a captured airfield. The Thunderbolts used rockets, machinegun fire, and 500- or 1,000-pound bombs to attack Japanese redoubts impeding the advance of marines or soldiers on Saipan, Guam, and Tinian. The P–47s also served as daytime interceptors, with P–61s patrolling at night. The attack on the Marianas paid important strategic benefits; it not only obtained B–29 base sites sooner than originally planned but also lured the surviving Japanese carriers into a major action, the Battle of the Philippine Sea. During one aspect of this engagement—an air battle called the Marianas Turkey Shoot—American naval aviators downed some 243 aircraft from enemy carriers, in effect destroying the corps of naval aviators that the enemy had reconstituted after the Midway disaster of June 1942.

While the Central Pacific forces in just eight months advanced some 2,000 miles from the Gilberts to the Marianas, General MacArthur consolidated his grip on New Guinea and obtained the bases needed for a return to the Philippines. His troops occupied Morotai Island, a stepping-stone to the south-

A reconnaissance photograph of Saipan before the Allied landings.

ern Philippines, and units from the Central Pacific seized two islands in the Palau chain, securing airfields from which to fend off aerial incursions from the enemy-held Carolines. Resistance at Peleliu in the Palaus smoldered until late November, after B–24s had begun using the runway there to attack targets in the Philippines.

Morotai, along with Sansapor and Owi off the north coast of New Guinea, provided runways from which B–24s of the Fifth and Thirteenth Air Forces raided the oil refineries at Balikpapan, Borneo. General Kenney failed, however, to obtain B–29s for these attacks, even though he had arranged for the construction at Port Darwin, Australia, of an airfield to accommodate them. Arnold and the other members of the Joint Chiefs of Staff remained determined to use the new bombers exclusively against Japan's home islands. Even the smaller Liberators, however, caused serious damage in their five raids against Balikpapan. To deal with the fighter opposition there, General Kenney sent P–38s and P–47s on sweeps over the refineries and used them as bomber escorts. As became standard for long, overwater missions in the Pacific, American submarines served as lifeguards along the route, picking up airmen who ditched at sea.

Even as General MacArthur's offensive gathered momentum, questions arose within the Joint Chiefs of Staff of the wisdom of becoming entangled in the Philippines, where the fast carrier task forces would sacrifice much of the

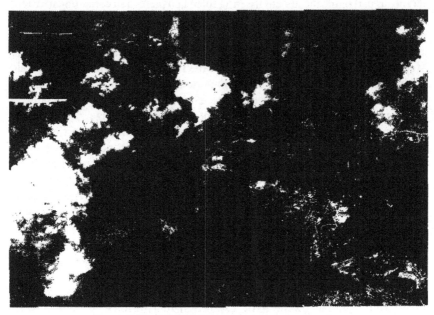

Consolidated B–24 Liberators over the burning
oil refineries at Balikpapan, Borneo.

mobility they had demonstrated in the Central Pacific. Some felt that Allied forces should ignore the entire island chain, or at least avoid Luzon, and strike directly at Formosa. MacArthur insisted on seizing Mindanao in the Southern Philippines and later reconquering the principal island of Luzon; he argued that the United States owed a "great national obligation" to the Filipinos, who had remained "overwhelmingly loyal to the American cause." Ignoring this debt of honor, he warned, would "admit the truth of Japanese propaganda to the effect that we had abandoned the Filipinos and would not shed American blood to redeem them." The general's view prevailed. During a conference held in July 1944 at Pearl Harbor and attended by General MacArthur, Admiral Nimitz, and President Roosevelt, the Chief Executive is supposed to have referred to the invasion of Mindanao and then asked: "Douglas, where do we go from here?" According to this story, the answer was: "Leyte, Mr. President, and then Luzon." Actually, during September carrier strikes in the southern Philippines revealed that Japanese air power in the region was weaker than assumed, enabling the general to accelerate his plans. He bypassed Mindanao and attacked Leyte, immediately to the north, on October 20, 1944, rather than in December as originally planned.[4]

Leyte promised airfield sites that General MacArthur needed to continue executing his amphibious operations under the cover of land-based aircraft, but the promise almost went unfulfilled. Except at Tacloban, where aviation engineers serving as part of the theater engineering force laid pierced steel matting to extend runways built by the Japanese, construction bogged down in a sea of mud as the seasonal rains began. Hard work at last triumphed over weather, but completion lagged far behind schedule. Years later, General MacArthur's Chief of Engineers, Maj. Gen. Hugh J. Casey, commented on the flooding of Leyte's roads and airfields, declaring, "One thing that was important and I had to personally impress on all our Engineer officers was drainage. Somehow or other . . . they'd build an airdrome or what-not but not give sufficient attention to drainage."[5]

As in the Marianas, the Japanese employed their remaining carriers in defense of the Philippines, but these ships, short of aircraft and all but devoid of trained pilots, served merely as bait to draw their American counterparts away from Leyte. The Japanese aircraft carriers fulfilled this suicidal mission, sacrificing four of their number but attracting the full attention of the American fast carriers. While the carriers courted destruction, two other Japanese forces converged on Leyte. American battleships intercepted one and defeated it, but the other force attacked the escort carriers supporting the Leyte beachhead and their destroyer screen. Navy aircraft, launched to attack the rapidly approaching task force, could not return to the damaged or violently maneuvering carriers and had to land at Tacloban, where Army aviation ordnancemen hung bombs on them so they could renew the battle. Overestimating the force opposing him, the enemy commander retired after sinking one escort carrier, two destroyers, and a destroyer escort. Army B–24s helped speed the Japanese on their way, drop-

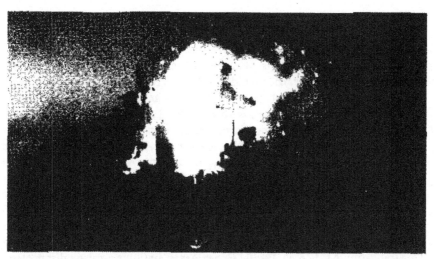

The battleship *New Mexico* takes a direct hit from a Japanese kamikaze.

ping bombs close to the flagship and delivering the coup de grace to a cruiser already badly damaged in a related action.

Besides risking his navy off Leyte, the enemy unveiled a new weapon, the kamikaze or divine wind, named for the storm that had scattered a Mongol invasion fleet bound for Japan in 1281. The originators of this modern kamikaze hoped to defeat another invasion force by crashing planes or boats into American warships, exchanging a few lives for the lives of hundreds. Kamikaze tactics, and the subsequent development of special suicide weapons like a rocket bomb containing more than a ton of explosives, indicated desperation as well as resolve. At the time of the attack on Pearl Harbor, a Japanese pilot logged roughly 300 hours during training. Now, as the war drew ominously nearer Japan, pilots who had flown as many as 100 hours became increasingly rare. Since 100 hours could not prepare a man for aerial combat with the Americans, the Japanese decided to capitalize on their average airman's willingness to die for his emperor and country. Members of this special corps would receive just enough flight training, as little as 15 hours, to enable each to fly a single suicide mission.

The Japanese army and navy had, of course, launched ambitious programs to replace flyers killed in action or stranded on bypassed Pacific islands, but the efforts failed. Dwindling stocks of gasoline hampered flight training; because of American submarines, the flow of petroleum from the East Indies declined so sharply that during 1944 the enemy began experimenting with alcohol as a fuel extender. As the war approached a climax, Japan had on hand about 1.5 million barrels of aviation fuel—refined gasoline, some of it spiked with alcohol, and synthetic fuel, none of it rated higher than 87 octane. This reserve compared poorly to the 4.2 million barrels of gasoline, mostly smoother firing 92 octane, on hand when the fighting began in 1941. Japanese authorities decided to invest much of their diminished supply in suicide attacks by a group of ill-trained pilots flying, in many cases, obsolete airplanes.

Before the kamikaze corps went into action off Leyte on October 25, sinking an American escort carrier, bulldozers had carved out the first of the airfields in the Marianas for the strategic bombing of Japan. On Saipan, aviation engineers, although short of equipment, had enlarged a former Japanese airfield in time for the first B–29 Superfortress to land there on October 12. At the controls was General Hansell, who, during his tours in the Air War Plans Division, had helped prepare the basic plans of the wartime Army Air Forces, AWPD/1 and AWPD/42. Work at Guam proceeded more slowly, impeded by Japanese resistance, by competing demands such as the building of a naval base, and by the selection of one airfield site so remote that engineers had to built a road to reach it. The Navy construction battalions on Tinian made more efficient use of their men and equipment after General Harmon—who served as the Commanding General, Army Air Forces, Pacific Ocean Areas, until his airplane disappeared over the Pacific early in 1945—persuaded Admiral Nimitz to concentrate on one field at a time, rather than divide the effort between two air bases. By the end of November 1944, facilities in the Marianas could support the hundred-odd B–29s available to Hansell's XXI Bomber Command.

After a half dozen disappointing practice missions against the fortified islands of Truk and Iwo Jima, General Hansell received a directive to attack an aircraft factory just ten miles from the emperor's palace at Tokyo. An unarmed B–29, fitted with cameras and redesignated an F–13A, conducted a last-minute reconnaissance, and on November 24, after a week's delay caused by rain and adverse winds, Brig. Gen. Emmett O'Donnell, a veteran of the fighting in the Philippines, led 111 bombers aloft from Saipan's runways. As the bombardiers aimed visually through broken cloud or with radar, jet-stream tail winds propelled the B–29s over the target at almost 450 miles per hour and blew the bombs from their intended trajectories. For the first time, American airmen had encountered the winds of the high-altitude jet stream. Of the 88 aircraft that released their bombs, only 24 succeeded in aiming at the plant itself rather than at an alternate target, and just 45 bombs exploded on the factory grounds. The enemy brought down one of O'Donnell's Superfortresses, the victim of an apparent ramming by a damaged fighter.

For almost three months, from the training mission against Truk in late October 1944 until his last attack on Japan in January 1945, Hansell drove his men—perhaps too hard, he later suggested—to improve accuracy and increase the tonnage of bombs on the target in a high-altitude precision campaign directed mainly at the Japanese aircraft industry. Unfortunately, the jet stream caused insolvable problems, affecting not only the speed of the aircraft over the target but also the dispersal of bombs, which might pass from a swiftly moving current of air to a slower layer moving in a different direction. Also, mechani-

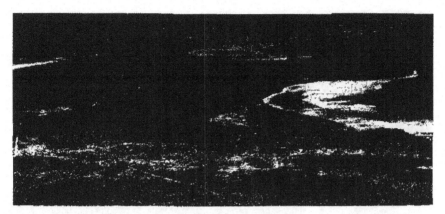

In August 1944, this part of Guam was wilderness, except for a small
Japanese fighter strip (above); one year later, it was Harmon Field.

cal problems, usually with the engines, caused as many as one aircraft in five to
turn back short of the target. At last, aided by calm weather, Hansell's B–29s on
January 19, 1945, delivered a devastating attack that cut production at a
Kawasaki airplane plant near Kobe by an estimated ninety percent, the final raid
before Arnold removed him as commander of the XXI Bomber Command.

In Washington, Arnold decided well before this last attack that the B–29 of-
fensive against Japan had reached a dead end. As he had removed an old friend,
Ira Eaker, in the aftermath of the second raid on Schweinfurt, he now summoned
LeMay from China to replace Hansell at the head of the XXI Bomber Command.
In early December, Arnold dismissed the notion that he was "putting the heat on
Possum," using Hansell's nickname, but by the end of the month he had decided
that Hansell had lost too many B–29s and inflicted too little damage upon Japan.[6]

The declining confidence on Arnold's part occurred as the target planners at
Washington were losing their enthusiasm for the kind of high-altitude precision

351

Maj. Gen. Curtis E. LeMay (left), new commander of the XXI Bomber Command, and Brig. Gen. Haywood S. Hansell, Jr., departing commander.

bombardment that Hansell was determined to conduct. The emphasis now shifted from leveling manufacturing plants to igniting flimsy houses, which would fuel raging fires in the congested Japanese cities; whole towns rather than individual factories became targets. As early as December 18, 1944, immediately after LeMay's B–29s had burned out the waterfront at Hangkow, China, Brig. Gen. Lauris Norstad, the Twentieth Air Force Chief of Staff, called for an experimental incendiary raid upon Nagoya, Japan. Although reluctant to divert bombers from precision attacks on airframe and aircraft engine plants that produced airplanes for the kamikazes, Hansell sent his B–29s against Nagoya on December 22. The squadrons relied on radar to bomb through dense cloud and obtained no better results with incendiaries than they usually achieved with high explosives. A second incendiary attack on the city, carried out on January 3, ignited fires that sent smoke billowing to 20,000 feet but scattered blazes failed to converge and therefore did not create the kind of firestorm that might have incinerated Nagoya and many of its inhabitants.

However disappointed Arnold may have been with the results of the high-altitude bombing, whether high explosives or incendiaries, Hansell had succeeded in improving both the bombing accuracy of his crews and the mechanical reliability of the aircraft they flew, although the winds at high altitudes over Japan still scattered carefully aimed bombs and the B–29s continued to require careful maintenance, especially if the complex engines were subjected to hard use.

Not the least of Hansell's accomplishments while leading the XXI Bomber Command was his creation, in collaboration with the Navy, of a rescue network for the crews of B–29s that went into the ocean between the Marianas and Japan. The odds for survival rose dramatically, despite an occasional setback such as occurred in January 1945, when rescuers saved just 13 of 135 airmen. Over the entire bombing campaign, however, rescue aircraft and submarines retrieved half of the 1,300 crew members who crash landed at sea during the command's missions against Japan.

More important for the survival of B–29 crews than the rescue organization was Iwo Jima. The Japanese used the volcanic island for an early warning radar site and a staging base for a succession of air strikes against the Marianas, including a night attack on December 7, 1944, that destroyed three Superfortresses and damaged twenty-three. Both B–29s and Marianas-based Liberators bombed Iwo Jima, but eventually marines had to storm its beaches. In American hands the island became a radar outpost for the Marianas, a fighter base for the defense of those islands and for escort missions over Japan, and an emergency airfield for disabled Superfortresses.

Neither the aerial bombing of Iwo Jima, conducted with varying intensity over two months, nor a three-day preparatory bombardment by carrier aircraft and warships could destroy the underground defenses that honeycombed the island. The marines landed on February 19, 1945, and, though a captured airfield began functioning on March 6, fighting continued until April 4, with more than 25,000 Americans killed or wounded. The cost in lives and suffering nevertheless seemed justified, especially in view of the number of airmen making emer-

North American P–51 Mustangs lined up on the number 2 strip on Iwo Jima.

gency landings at Iwo Jima. By the time the war ended, more than 2,000 B–29s, each with 11 men on board, had made emergency landings on the island. Although many of these aircraft might have limped to the Marianas or ditched successfully, Admiral King, the Chief of Naval Operations, estimated that the number of lives saved equaled or exceeded the 6,000 lost in capturing Iwo Jima.

During the fight for Iwo Jima, B–24s from the Marianas hit suspected enemy strongholds, and P–51s took off from the recently captured airfield on the island to bomb and strafe as the marines inched forward. Despite these Army Air Forces contributions, Navy and Marine Corps airmen flew most of the close air support missions at Iwo Jima. Army pilots carried more of the burden in the Philippines, where the Far East Air Forces, along with some Marine Corps units, helped General MacArthur bypass other objectives nearer at hand to attack Mindoro, invade Luzon, and finally mop up the enemy on the southern islands like Panay, Cebu, Negros, and Mindanao.

Landings on the island of Mindoro, an intermediate objective between Leyte and Luzon, took place on December 15, 1944. Aircraft moved onto an airfield site in time to launch fighters and medium bombers against a Japanese task force of two cruisers and six destroyers approaching from Cape St. Jacques, Indochina, to contest MacArthur's latest operation. Harassment by aircraft from Mindoro apparently forced the enemy to be content with an ineffectual hit-and-run shelling of the beachhead. After parrying this Japanese thrust, Fifth Air Force fighters and bombers from airfields on Mindoro and Leyte followed up carrier raids against Luzon by attacking bridges, road traffic, and rail lines. In the wake of these preparations, American forces landed on January 9, 1945, coming ashore at Lingayen Gulf and advancing toward Manila. Army fighter-bombers, reinforced by Marine Corps dive bombers under Fifth Air Force operational control, responded to instructions radioed by mobile control parties with the advancing troops. Army C–47s dropped parachuting reinforcements and landed drums of gasoline for the columns moving on Manila and dropped paratroops in the assault upon Corregidor, a small island in Manila Bay. Once MacArthur gained control of Luzon, he turned his attention to mopping up the bypassed Japanese in the southern Philippines, where Army and Marine Corps airmen supported American infantrymen and Filipino guerrillas.

The American lodgment on Luzon, besides freeing troops for action in the southern islands, further constricted the supply artery carrying oil from the Netherlands East Indies to Japan. Tankers and other ships now ran a gauntlet of air power as they plied the China Sea, coming under attack whether under way or in port. Despite the increasing effectiveness of aircraft, submarines remained the deadliest weapon against enemy shipping, especially oil tankers. When American intelligence learned that the Japanese used alcohol processed from sugarcane on Formosa to blend with a diminished supply of gasoline, bombers—including for a time the new Consolidated B–32—attacked the distilleries there.

Paratroopers of the 503rd Regiment jumping onto Corregidor Island, Philippines.

Instead of Formosa, Okinawa in the Ryukyu Islands became the next objective, for Okinawa was small enough that a lengthy land campaign would not be necessary yet was large enough to accommodate the bases needed for an assault upon Japan's home islands. From airfields on Okinawa and nearby Ie Shima, bombardment groups that had finished off a battered Germany could join the Marianas-based B–29s in devastating Japan. During the battle for Okinawa, which lasted from April 1 to June 21, 1945, fighter squadrons of the Army Air Forces served under the operational control of a Marine Corps officer, Brig. Gen. William J. Wallace. The Army airmen tried to prevent kamikazes based on Formosa or the Japanese island of Kyushu from attacking American ships off Okinawa. Although LeMay had already begun the systematic fire-bombing of Japanese cities and was reluctant to interrupt the campaign, the kamikazes posed so great a threat that the Joint Chiefs of Staff, for a period of five critical weeks,

A North American B–25 attacks a Japanese destroyer in the China Sea.

355

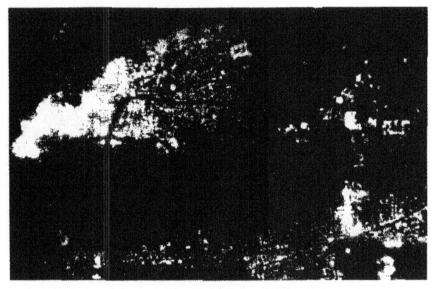

Flames engulf a Japanese city following an incendiary attack.

empowered Admiral Nimitz to use the B–29s for bombing the airfields on Kyushu the suicide pilots used and the factories that produced aircraft for them.

The incendiary raids promised to be the kind of decisive aerial bombardment that would vindicate the advocates of strategic bombardment by consuming Japan's cities and with them the nation's capacity to resist. In Europe, where the Strategic Bombing Survey tried to evaluate the effect of American strategic bombing even as the air war there drew to a close, the bomber offensive had neither taken the place of an invasion nor prevented the Germans from fighting tenaciously as Allied ground forces tightened the noose about the Third Reich. Against Japan, already short of food and oil, Arnold believed that bombardment could force a surrender, thus avoiding an invasion and a long and bitter ground campaign. To win the victory before the impending assault upon Japan, LeMay, who shared his commanding general's vision, abandoned the daylight precision bombing that he had conducted in Europe and embraced the British theory of nighttime area bombing.

The change in tactics evolved gradually as various officers, including General LeMay, reviewed the indecisive results of the earlier attacks and studied the reports of tests conducted in the United States demonstrating the vulnerability of Japanese houses to incendiary attack. LeMay became convinced that area bombing with incendiaries would prove far more effective than precision attacks. Not only were the houses built of inflammable materials, the tinder-like residential areas encroached on vital factories, and the industries themselves tended to be concentrated in comparatively few cities. LeMay believed,

Daytime shows the complete devastation from an incendiary attack.

moreover, that a system of cottage industry existed in the towns, with households working at home on components of various weapons. Since the fire departments in those cities did not meet European standards, they could not deal with the kind of conflagrations that had overpowered better equipped fire fighters at Hamburg and would soon do so at Dresden. Fire raids would kill or injure Japanese workers, destroy their homes and the factories where they worked, and convert the labor force into a demoralized mob of refugees.

American planners showed little concern for the average Japanese citizen, whose German counterpart Eaker had expressed a reluctance to bomb. This difference in attitude resulted at least in part from a desire to avenge Pearl Harbor and retaliate for Japanese wartime atrocities, among them the execution of airmen captured after the Doolittle raid of 1942 and the brutal treatment of American prisoners of war in the Philippines. The wanton murder of American and Filipino captives during the death march from the Bataan peninsula on Luzon to prison camps elsewhere on the island came to light after an Air Forces pilot, Capt. William E. Dyess, Jr., and a few fellow prisoners escaped and, with the aid of Filipino guerrillas, eventually returned to the United States. Other factors influencing the air war against Japan undoubtedly included the lack of widely shared ethnic, cultural, or religious ties with the populace. Perhaps the most powerful argument for unrestrained attack was the refusal of the Japanese to surrender, even when facing overwhelming odds and certain death—an attitude the Americans considered fanatical. In the Marianas, for instance, civilians, including women and children, had chosen suicide rather than internment, and enemy sailors and airmen had become kamikazes, willing to ram B–29s, dive aircraft into warships, or ride explosives-laden boats or manned torpedoes to certain death. By the spring of 1945, American planners looked forward with dread to an assault upon the home islands in which the entire populace would rise up and fight to the death. Estimates of Americans killed and wounded in this kind of fight to the death varied from 31,000 in the first 30 days of an invasion of Kyushu to as many as 268,000 in overrunning the entire island town by town.

Having selected the incendiary bomb as the decisive weapon that would prevent such carnage, the question arose how best to deliver it. Hansell's high-altitude attacks had proved disappointing because the incendiaries produced widely scattered fires, a consequence of the ballistic characteristics of the bombs, the comparatively long time they took to fall to earth, and the variable winds that influenced their trajectory. LeMay solved the problem of isolated blazes by attacking at low altitudes, where the winds of the jet stream did not blow. Because Japanese radar was easily jammed and incapable of precise control over either interceptors or antiaircraft guns, the B–29s could attack at low level by night with near impunity. The lack of effective aerial opposition would, moreover, enable the Superfortresses to substitute bombs for the weight of defensive weapons and ammunition. Finally, low-altitude attacks meant that more B–29s would be available for combat, since the new tactics eliminated a long climb at nearly maximum power, easing the strain on the engines and reducing the frequency of time-consuming maintenance.

General LeMay began burning out Japanese cities on the night of March 9–10, 1945, sending more than 300 bombers against Tokyo at altitudes between 4,900 and 9,200 feet. Some 2,000 tons of incendiaries, which achieved a density of 25 tons per square mile, destroyed more than 250,000 buildings, left a million persons homeless, killed more than 83,000, and injured almost 41,000. The attacking force lost 14 bombers to antiaircraft fire but none to fighters, and five crews were rescued at sea.

Despite some setbacks—due to shortages of incendiaries, failure at times to concentrate a sufficient weight of bombs in the designated areas, and diversions because of the Okinawa campaign—the XXI Bomber Command persisted in its urban bombardment. By mid-June the attacks had reduced to ashes an area of more than 250 square miles divided among six cities, with some 40 percent of the destruction in Tokyo. LeMay's airmen paid a price to achieve this widespread devastation. On the night of May 25, for instance, during a raid on the capital city, a combination of mechanical failure and enemy action downed 26 B–29s, and another 100 of the 502 Superfortresses that bombed the target sustained battle damage. LeMay reacted to the losses by resuming daylight raids, using an escort of P–51s from Iwo Jima to neutralize Japanese fighters and flying the incendiary-laden B–29s at an altitude beyond the reach of antiaircraft guns. He thus reverted to the bombing tactics that Hansell had tested in January, but with a larger force than Hansell had been able to muster. LeMay could

A Boeing B–29 Superfortress drops mines into the waters near Japan.

launch 500 or more B–29s, escorted by about 100 fighters, on daylight fire raids that achieved a degree of saturation about as destructive as the low-altitude night strikes. Besides setting ahlaze the major cities hy day or by night, the bombers flew precision strikes against industrial targets, sometimes using radar by night or in cloudy weather, and continued the mine laying begun early in 1945.

As the bombing increased in fury, Nimitz called on the B–29s to step up this campaign of aerial mine laying and help isolate Japan from the resources of its shrunken empire. Arnold and his advisers agreed, though reluctantly, for to them Japanese industry and industrial cities seemed more important targets than shipping. The admiral, however, viewed the mining of coastal waters as a means of sealing the chinks in a blockade that, he believed, could force Japan to surrender without the need of an invasion. Arnold, who hoped to achieve the same end through aerial bombardment, decided to divert B–29s to mine laying to prevent the Navy from absorbing by default a mission requiring long-range, land-based bombers needed by the Air Forces. The same code-breaking organization, now operating from Guam, that had obtained the intelligence essential for the victories at the Coral Sea and Midway, intercepted and decoded Japanese radio messages dealing with shipping and thus obtained information for sowing the minefields.

A major factor in the success of the B–29, whether in laying mines or leveling cities, was the rapidly improving logistic support received by the Marianas-based units. A planned maintenance facility took shape on Guam by mid-February 1945, after American soldiers and airmen had brought order to a mile-long agglomeration of shipping crates that had accumulated over the months. Following the establishment of the Guam Air Depot, the monthly total of aircraft unable to complete sorties because of mechanical failure declined from twenty-two percent in December 1944 to an average of some seven percent in July and August 1945. Similarly, the tally of bombers grounded for lack of spare parts dropped from almost thirteen percent in December to two-tenths of one percent when the fighting stopped.

In July 1945, Gen. Carl Spaatz assumed responsibility for directing the day-to-day air war waged against Japan by the strategic bombers of the Twentieth Air Force and, once it arrived from the United Kingdom, the Eighth Air Force as well. The attempt to persuade the Joint Chiefs of Staff to appoint an overall commander for air operations had been frustrated until early in 1945, when the Army and Navy agreed to apportion the final effort against Japan according to service. Once the Joint Chiefs of Staff assigned General MacArthur responsibility for land operations against the home islands and Admiral Nimitz command of the war at sea, they decided that Spaatz should take charge of land-based strategic aviation. The Chiefs, with Arnold as their executive agent, coordinated the strategic campaign under Spaatz with the aerial operations conducted by Kenney for MacArthur's invasion forces and those carried out by Nimitz's carrier aircraft. On July 25, Arnold relinquished command of the Twentieth Air Force to LeMay, who served as commander until Twining replaced him on August 2.

Before the first B–29s had attacked Japan from China in the summer of 1944, Arnold looked ahead to a new weapon, the atomic bomb, which was taking shape in the minds of some of the nation's leading scientists. About all that Arnold knew for certain about the revolutionary bomb was that it would be heavy and bulky, requiring a B–29 to drop it. In the summer of 1944, the

Commanding General of the Army Air Forces launched a program to produce the skilled B–29 crews—backed by maintenance, ordnance, and security specialists—that would drop the weapon when it became available. Col. Paul W. Tibbets, a veteran of the first B–17 mission against Nazi-occupied Europe, assumed command of the 509th Composite Group, built around the 393d Bombardment Squadron, commanded by Maj. Charles W. Sweeney. Tibbets stripped the unit's B–29s of all defensive armament except the tail guns to save weight, thus increasing speed and carrying capacity. Little could be done, however, to modify the planes to accommodate the atomic bomb; instead the scientists, working under the guidance of J. Robert Oppenheimer, a physicist who taught at the University of California and the California Institute of Technology, had to tailor their product to fit the bomb bay of the B–29.

Crew training took place at Wendover Field in western Utah, with the group's bombardiers dropping inert test models of variously shaped atomic weapons. Later, crews flew the bombers to Batista Field, Cuba, where they practiced overwater navigation and radar bombing. In June 1945, after the ground echelon had boarded a ship bound for the western Pacific, the aircrews began the long flight to Tinian. Among the aircraft was a B–29 fresh from the Glenn L. Martin factory at Omaha, Nebraska, a bomber that Colonel Tibbets would name *Enola Gay* after his mother.

Meanwhile, the laboratories at Los Alamos, New Mexico, had produced two kinds of atomic weapons. One was a gun or uranium type, detonated by firing one mass of uranium through a gun barrel into another to create a self-sustaining chain reaction. The other, an implosion or plutonium bomb, released its energy when an explosive outer shell drove a layer of plutonium inward to form a critical mass. The various components of the gun-type weapon left Los Alamos for the Marianas beginning on July 14. Two days later, on the morning of the 16th, the fireball from a test version of the implosion device lit the predawn New Mexico sky to midday brightness, demonstrating that the power of the atom dwarfed the destructiveness of chemical explosives.

Even before this successful test, a debate as to the wisdom and morality of using the bomb had begun among the scientists working on the weapon. For example, Leo Szilard, who had been instrumental in starting the development program, now feared that use of the bomb would introduce a new and more horrible form of warfare, thus encouraging future Hitlers to arm themselves with these weapons before attacking their neighbors. The issue soon narrowed, however, to a choice between demonstration and destruction, whether to demonstrate the fury of the bomb and overawe Japan's leaders, perhaps by obliterating an island in Tokyo Bay, or to accomplish the same result by leveling an actual city. A panel of scientists, on which Oppenheimer served, concluded that the saving of American lives outweighed the possible danger of future aggression and that no effective demonstration was feasible. If an announced detonation ended in a misfire, Japanese resistance would be strengthened rather than undermined. The surest way of saving American lives, the panel members believed, was to drop the bomb on a Japanese city, and they recommended this to the Interim Committee on the Atomic Bomb, headed by ex-Senator James F. Byrnes, the personal representative of Harry S. Truman, who had become President on the death of Franklin Roosevelt in April 1945.

Preparations for an atomic attack went forward as the debate among the scientists came to an end. From Tinian the 509th Composite Group flew a series of missions dropping practice bombs on Japan. Filled with high explosives, the orange-painted, five-ton "pumpkins," as they were called, had ballistic characteristics like the atomic weapons. These missions enabled the bombardiers to sharpen their skills, while at the same time conditioning the enemy to accept as routine the appearance of one or two B–29s over a major city. Aiming visually and occasionally using radar, the group dropped thirty-seven of the practice bombs.

As preparations for dropping the atomic bomb reached this advanced stage, Arnold became convinced that it would not be needed. Influenced by a visit to LeMay and also by the preliminary findings of the Strategic Bombing Survey of Germany, the Commanding General of the U.S. Army Air Forces concluded that incendiary and high-explosive weapons could force Japan to submit, so that neither an invasion nor an atomic bomb would prove necessary. He tried to arrange for LeMay to describe for the Joint Chiefs of Staff the rapidly accumulating devastation resulting from the current bombing campaign, but a planned meeting of Allied leaders at Potsdam, near Berlin, was approaching, and the agenda of the Joint Chiefs proved too crowded to permit such a briefing. During the seventeen-day conference at Potsdam—in the presence of the other Joint Chiefs, Secretary of War Stimson, and President Truman—Arnold raised the possibility of defeating Japan without using the atomic bomb. General Marshall declined, however, to gamble that continued conventional bombing could defeat so determined an enemy and insisted that the atomic bomb afforded the only possible alternative to invasion. Arnold thus found himself out of harmony with Marshall, whom he admired and respected. Rather than make an issue of his confidence in the cumulative effect of high-explosive bombs and incendiaries, Arnold deferred to the Army Chief of Staff. Marshall's advice reinforced Stimson's views, the recommendations of the Interim Committee, and Truman's own belief: the atomic bomb should be dropped on a Japanese city in the hope of shocking the enemy into surrender before the invasion, now scheduled for November 1945.

Over Hiroshima on August 6, 1945, the gun-type device, nicknamed Little Boy, fell clear of the bomb bay on the *Enola Gay* at 8:15 a.m. local time and detonated seconds later, after Colonel Tibbets had whipped the B–29 through a diving turn. A ball of fire appeared in the sky, and a mushroom cloud of smoke and debris came writhing upward. At the base of the cloud, a combination of blast, fire, and lethal radiation killed at least 70,000 persons, leveling the heart of the city.

A B–29 of the 509th Composite Group prepares for a night mission from Tinnian (above), the mushroom cloud from the atomic bomb dropped on Nagasaki (right), and the Enola Gay (below), the B–29 that carried the atomic bomb dropped on Hiroshima.

History of the United States Air Force

The destruction of Hiroshima did not compel Japan to sue immediately for peace. Describing the nature of the weapon dropped on Hiroshima as unleashing the "force from which the sun draws its power," President Truman warned that Japan faced a "rain of death from the air, the like of which has never been seen on earth."[7] Nevertheless, despite the annihilation of one city and the possible destruction of others, the badly divided Japanese government proved incapable of action. Some of the nation's leaders saw no choice but surrender. Others, although realizing the futility of further resistance, feared that surrender would result in the execution of the emperor, an unacceptable consequence. A small faction advocated fighting to the death as a matter of national honor. Hopes, however faint, that the Soviet Union might mediate on Japan's behalf continued to delude a segment of the leadership until August 8, when Stalin declared war. The very paralysis that afflicted the Japanese government at this critical time created an illusion of suicidal determination, which concealed the nation's desperate condition and persuaded the United States to drop its only remaining atomic bomb.

The primary target for the implosion weapon, called Fat Man, was Kokura, a steel manufacturing center, which Major Sweeney found obscured by cloud. He therefore turned his borrowed B-29, *Bock's Car*, normally flown by Capt. Frederick C. Bock, toward Nagasaki, the alternate target. At 10:58 a.m. local time on August 9, the bomb exploded at the proper altitude but almost two miles wide of the mark, an error that stemmed from Sweeney's bombardier relying on radar until the clouds suddenly parted, then hurriedly switching to visual aiming. Once again a mushroom cloud marked the devastation of a large city. The nature of the terrain—Nagasaki lay among hills and ridges, whereas Hiroshima occupied a saucer-like plain—gave some shelter from the blast and helped reduce the number of deaths, though as many as 35,000 perished that morning.

Atomic bombs had destroyed two cities, killing more than a hundred thousand persons, and Russian forces were overwhelming the defenses of Manchuria. Emperor Hirohito realized that Japan's situation was hopeless. Although uncertain of the treatment he would receive at the hands of the victorious Allies, he chose to intervene in the deliberations of government, invoking the moral authority of his office and defying the tradition that made him a spokesman for his ministers rather than a ruler in his own right. "I have given serious thought to the situation prevailing at home and abroad," he told the cabinet, "and have concluded that continuing the war can only mean destruction for the nation and a prolongation of bloodshed and cruelty in the world."[8] Not even the emperor could at a single stroke overcome those officials who, obsessed with notions of honor, tried to foment a mutiny in their determination to avoid the humiliation of surrender. He did prevail, but the maneuvering took time, and, to American eyes, progress toward a cease-fire seemed to stall. As a result, after suspending the air war on August 11, President Truman approved its resumption three days later. Beginning at daylight on August 14, and on into the evening, more than

1,000 Army Air Forces bombers attacked targets in Japan, the last returning to base as President Truman was announcing that hostilities had ended.

After the atomic bomb had been tested in New Mexico, but before the devastation of Hiroshima, General Arnold proposed that the United States Strategic Bombing Survey, which was then completing its assessment of the air war against Germany, address the topic of the impending defeat of Japan. The existence of the new bomb may have helped prod the general into action, for some investigation of its effect on the course of the war seemed inevitable, and the Strategic Bombing

After the surrender, B–29s from the Marianas parachuted food and supplies to Allied prisoners still held in Japanese camps. B–29s on Saipan, (above) take on food and clothing, while a POW camp near Nagasaki, plainly marked to assist the pilots, (below) shows the shadow of a B–29 passing over it.

Survey seemed ideally suited for the task. Since the group would examine the atomic bomb in the context of strategic bombardment, looking on it as an aerial weapon capable of inflicting severe damage rather than as a scientific phenomenon, Arnold believed that the survey's investigation would produce the raw material for additional arguments to gain independence for the air arm.

Late in August, President Truman signed the formal authorization for Franklin D'Olier, survey chairman, and his colleagues to study the defeat of Japan. The investigation, however, soon devolved into a struggle between the survey's Military Analysis Division, under Maj. Gen Orvil A. Anderson, and the Naval Analysis Division, headed by Rear Adm. Ralph A. Oftsie, a veteran naval aviator. Unlike the Combined Bomber Offensive in Europe, the aerial campaigns of the Pacific war involved carrier-based naval aviation along with Army strategic bombers and tactical aircraft, the Army squadrons usually operating from islands captured by amphibious assault. Because of the interrelationships among air, sea, and ground, a finding that strategic bombing had defeated Japan would greatly strengthen the case for an independent air force. Conversely, an affirmation of the importance of carrier operations might weaken the argument for independence and ensure the future of naval aviation. In his desire to strengthen the case for an independent air force, Anderson lumped all forms of aviation, whether land-based or carrier-based, Army or Navy, into the general category of air power, which, he insisted, had dominated operations on land and at sea. Oftsie, determined to prevent an independent air force from absorbing naval and Marine Corps aviation, stressed the role of the aircraft carrier in both the great naval battles like Midway and the amphibious assaults that brought land-based American bombers within range of Japan. After months of recrimination between the two divisions, the survey published first a revised version of the report by Oftsie's group, which had been approved by a representative of General Anderson, and eight months later, in July 1947, Anderson's version of the war against Japan, which still lacked the concurrence of Admiral Oftsie's division. The survey labeled both documents, albeit in comparatively small print, as products of the respective divisions and described them as supporting documents rather than formal reports.

For their part, D'Olier and the senior directors tried to avoid taking sides in the quarrel between the Army Air Forces and the Navy with its portents for the future of the defense establishment. As it had in dealing with the conflict in Europe, the survey treated the war against Japan as a unified effort involving the mobilization and application of force in a variety of forms. In the case of the Japanese homeland, however, the investigators concluded that the most violent kind of force, the atomic bomb, had merely propelled the enemy toward an inevitable end, unconditional surrender. According to the survey, the United States "underestimated the ability of our air attack, coupled as it was with blockade and previous military defeats, to achieve unconditional surrender. . . . Having entered the war inadequately prepared, we continued all-out mobiliza-

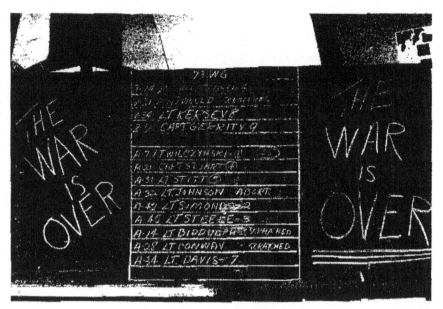

Mission board of the 73d Bombardment Wing on Saipan, August 16, 1945.

tion of all resources to bring ever increasing pressure on Japan beyond the time when this was reasonably required."[9]

The Japanese had relied on distance, as well as fierce resistance along the outer perimeter of their newly conquered empire, to wear down the United States, hoping to force the acceptance of an empire that embraced the natural resources necessary for Japan's survival as a great military and naval power. American air and amphibious forces breached that perimeter, bypassing important strongholds and advancing to within striking distance of the home islands. The heavy bombers then devastated a homeland ill-prepared for such an aerial onslaught. The B–29s burned whole cities, in the process razing irreplaceable factories, while attacks on shipping by submarines and aircraft deprived Japan of the raw materials essential for modern war, especially the oil vital to training and combat. Whether based on land or shipboard, whether applied by the Army Air Forces, the Navy, or the Marine Corps, air power had reduced the enemy's aerial and naval strength, diminished his overall resources, and helped bring him to the brink of surrender.

Such in brief was the nature of the war against Japan. The caution displayed by the Strategic Bombing Survey in assessing the role of aviation reflected the complex nature of the interrelated air, land, and sea operations in the Pacific theaters. For General Arnold, however, the survey's conclusions merely reinforced his belief that the Army Air Forces should be and would be an independent service. Uncertainty might shroud the overall effect of the atomic bomb on the future of warfare, but the land-based B–29, the only available aircraft that could carry the atomic bomb, had dropped two of these weapons with devastating results, and this fact could not be changed by the Navy's arguments on behalf of the aircraft carrier, or so Arnold and his followers believed in the hour of victory. The next task, now that the war had been won, was to convert this vision of independence into reality.

Part III

Building the
Air Force,
1945-1950

Chapter 11

The Quest for Independence

Herman S. Wolk

In February 1946, an era ended with the retirement of Henry H. Arnold, whose career extended from the fragile Wright biplanes to the B–29 and the atomic bomb. He had served in military aviation from the days when it was part of the Signal Corps through its emergence as the Air Service, the Air Corps, and finally the Army Air Forces. He had directed the Army Air Forces throughout World War II, helped shape American and Allied strategy as a member of the Joint Chiefs of Staff and the Anglo-American Combined Chiefs of Staff, and late in 1944 received the five-star rank of General of the Army. During his almost thirty-nine years of commissioned service, he had been a manager, administrator, and commander in peacetime and time of war, though he never led men in actual combat. Whatever his assignment, he had consistently thought in terms of applying to aerial warfare the latest advances in technology and aeronautical science.

Although scarcely a technician—he had once designed and built a donkey cart for his children but neglected to install brakes with near-disastrous results—he appreciated the impact of science and technology on military aviation and sought the advice of scientists and engineers. For example, he recruited

Theodore von Kármán, one of the great talents in the field of aerodynamics, who helped design a huge wind tunnel for the Army air arm and worked on solid-propellant rockets to help heavily laden aircraft take off. During the war, Arnold made use of von Kármán's abilities and those of other scientists and engineers like radar specialists Edward Bowles, Lee DuBridge, and David Griggs. After having lunch with Arnold and several scientists, General of the Army George C. Marshall, the Army Chief of Staff, asked what the airman was doing in their company. Arnold replied that he was using the scientists to help develop advanced aircraft that Air Corps engineers could not develop by themselves. Although he cultivated his contacts among the scientists because he needed their talents, Arnold nevertheless inspired genuine admiration among them. Years after their collaboration, von Kármán described Arnold as "the greatest example of the U.S. military man—a combination of complete logic, mingled with farsightedness and superb dedication."[1] This remains a striking tribute, even though von Kármán's judgment may have been influenced to some extent by the sense of importance, even camaraderie, that a scientist could be expected to feel when singled out by a military leader in time of crisis.

In making use of von Kármán and other scientists and engineers, Arnold was looking far beyond victory in World War II. At times, his vision may have jolted his fellow generals in the Army Air Forces, who were concentrating on winning the air war with weapons that were already in hand or soon would be. Even before the Allies had recovered from the German counteroffensive of December 1944, Arnold called together his principal staff officers, all veteran pilots, and urged them to look twenty years into a future shaped by aeronautical science and technology. "For the last twenty years," he told them, "we have built and run the air force on pilots. But we can't do that any more."[2] In the future, Arnold believed, the scientist and engineer who designed the radical new weapons would become increasingly important, perhaps dominating the air arm as the pilot now did.

Such was Arnold at his boldest; over the months, however, he devised a program for the future that posed less of a challenge to the existing order than he had in his informal remarks of December 1944. His staff almost certainly contributed to the new plan, and his vision may have been dimmed by the caution of his advisers, even as his vigor diminished as a result of the cumulative effect of a series of heart attacks suffered over the years. In November 1945, the last of Arnold's three reports on the conduct of the air war against the Axis afforded an insight into "air power and the future." The general looked ahead to the existence of "three autonomous services, each of which has an equal and direct share of the total responsibility." The independent air force, with the Army and Navy, would form a single "balanced United States military organization" that, according to Arnold, ensured economy and efficiency by eliminating the duplication of effort by the different armed forces.[3] The Joint Chiefs of Staff were to retain their wartime form, which included the uniformed heads of the land, sea,

372

General of the Army Henry H. Arnold,
Commanding General, Army Air Forces,
March 1942–February 1946.

and air forces and a chief of staff to the President, the job filled by Fleet Adm. William D. Leahy during the conflict and immediately afterward.

The new air force, like the existing Army Air Forces, would emphasize strategic bombardment, including long-range fighter escort, for, as Arnold pointed out, "It is conceivable that there will always be one industry, such as the oil industry in Germany, so necessary to all phases of the national war-making ability that its destruction would be fatal to the nation."[4] He did not, however, deny the need for balance since as his air force of the future would also be capable of defending against enemy bombers and attacking hostile ground forces, carrying out these missions by night and day, regardless of the weather. Reconnaissance would be essential, as would air transport, including the dropping and supplying of airborne troops, weather forecasting, and communications.

The near future, Arnold predicted, would see the introduction of new weapons and techniques. These would take their place alongside the atomic bomb, which had already demonstrated at Hiroshima and Nagasaki its ability to level structures and kill people throughout many square miles. "Aircraft, piloted or pilotless," he said, "will move at speeds far beyond the velocity of sound." Guided missiles would travel thousands of miles to destroy their intended targets, but "until such time as guided missiles are so developed that there is no further need for manned aircraft, research in the field of 'conventional' aircraft of improved design must continue."[5] He also foretold the appearance of target-seeking antiaircraft missiles, completely reliable communications, equipment for truly all-weather operations, and the aircraft and delivery techniques to supply airborne forces with whatever supplies or equipment they might need.

Because of the potential importance of these and related developments, Arnold proposed a continuation of the strong federal programs of research and development begun during the war. His air force of the future would require a permanent advisory panel of prominent scientists who would do for it what von

373

Kármán and others had done for the Army Air Forces. Arnold further believed that the independent air force should "have the means for recruiting personnel who have full understanding of the scientific facts necessary to procure and use the most advanced equipment," so that it could benefit from the guidance of its science advisers and "accomplish applied research" on its own or in collaboration with civilian scientists and private firms.[6] He suggested, moreover, that the independent air arm should sponsor basic or theoretical research that had no direct or immediate benefit to military aviation, but he opposed the building of laboratories or the training of officers to conduct this kind of experimentation.

Concerning the training and assignment of personnel, Arnold's vision of the future saw no radical departures from policies in effect during the recent conflict. His appreciation of the comprehensive nature of modern war did, however, prompt him to suggest the slaughter of at least one sacred cow, the belief that headquarters should be run by veteran pilots. He predicted that the Air Staff of the future would not be composed exclusively of command pilots, the staff of tomorrow would have to include officers skilled in production, in business methods, in economics, and in technology. Yet, even as he alluded to the need for peacetime staff officers with these skills, he was expressing general satisfaction with the technical and flying training administered during World War II and with the method of assigning officers and men. Despite his endorsement of wartime training methods, he did not believe the armed forces would ever again have the time that had been available in 1940 and 1941 to mobilize and train the reserve components. Consequently, the air arm would have to make certain during peacetime that reservists and members of the Air National Guard were ready for immediate service in an emergency.

As Arnold prepared to step aside, work began on the organizational structure of the postwar Army Air Forces, which was entering a period of transition that should, if all went well, result in independence, if not necessarily in the exact air arm that Arnold had described. The new Army Chief of Staff, General of the Army Dwight D. Eisenhower, decided that the Air Forces should include three separate commands, each charged with one of the major functions of air power, which he enumerated as strategic bombardment, air defense, and support of the ground forces. He was especially interested in the tactical support of the Army, as a result of his experience as wartime supreme commander in Europe. Although Maj. Gen. Elwood R. Quesada, who had commanded tactical aviation forces in North Africa and Europe and now served on the Air Staff, thought he detected a conspiracy by the Army Ground Forces to gain control of the tactical air forces, Eisenhower's philosophy of air support was rooted in the concept of mutual dependence between air and ground. He believed that air support was absolutely essential to the success of operations on land and that control of the air, which permitted effective support of ground forces, was best gained by aviation units operating under an air commander who knew how to employ military aircraft to the greatest advantage. Far from endorsing the capture of avia-

Gen. Carl A. Spaatz,
Commanding General, Army Air Forces,
March 1946–September 1947.

tion by the ground forces, as Quesada feared, Eisenhower declared, "the Army does not belong in the air—it belongs on the ground."[7]

In mid-January 1946, based on his discussions with Eisenhower, Gen. Carl Spaatz, who formally became commanding general early in February, decided to reorganize the Army Air Forces but only by creating components that could be absorbed by an independent air force. In this fashion he hoped to avoid a postwar reorganization as part of the Army followed by a second restructuring once independence had been gained. He set up three major operating commands—the Strategic Air Command, the Tactical Air Command, and the Air Defense Command—reflecting not only the three basic combat missions that had evolved during World War II but also the basic organization that Eisenhower favored. Spaatz subsequently denied that he had yielded to pressure from the Army high command in taking this functional approach. "Eisenhower and I thought along the same lines about this thing," he recalled. "I certainly would not call it pressure." Concerning the creation of a tactical command dedicated to the support of ground armies, Quesada, who took over the new Tactical Air Command in March 1946, declared that Eisenhower and his successor as Chief of Staff, Gen. Omar N. Bradley, "were assured by Spaatz that the Air Force would always honor and always meet its commitments to the Army to provide strong tactical air forces. Spaatz made that commitment to Eisenhower and it was a very strong commitment."[8]

The peacetime reorganization took effect on March 21, 1946, and the major commands thus established reported directly to General Spaatz, as the Commanding General, Army Air Forces. The headquarters of the Continental Air Command, originally a planning group for demobilization but later a catchall for combat units not deployed overseas, became the headquarters of the Strategic Air Command, under Gen. George C. Kenney. Initially located at Bolling Field, Washington, D.C., Kenney's headquarters moved to Andrews Field, Maryland, in October 1946. Its mission was to conduct long-range glob-

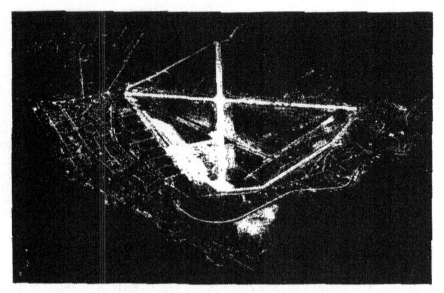

Langley Field, Virginia, 1945.

al air operations and to be responsible for "maximum range" reconnaissance.
The Air Defense Command, activated at Mitchel Field, New York, was headed
by Lt. Gen. George E. Stratemeyer. Its missions, besides the obvious one of defending the United States against air attack, included protecting coastal shipping, training the Air National Guard, and administering and training the Air
Reserve and the Reserve Officer Training Corps. The Tactical Air Command
was activated at Tampa, Florida, under General Quesada, who subsequently
moved his headquarters to Langley Field, just outside Hampton, Virginia, to be
near the headquarters of the Army Ground Forces at Fortress Monroe in
Hampton and of the Navy's Atlantic Fleet at nearby Norfolk, Virginia. The mission of Quesada's command was to support ground or naval forces and, if necessary, assist the Air Defense Command. Quesada was determined that his organization would become so proficient that after the air arm gained its independence "the Army would be the first to admit that the tactical air forces
[being] under the jurisdiction of the United States Air Force was to their benefit."[9] Besides the three combat commands, the Army Air Forces (and later the
independent air force, as well) consisted of the Air Materiel Command (formerly the Air Technical Services Command), the Air Training Command, the
Air University (formerly the Army Air Forces School), the Proving Ground
Command, the Air Transport Command, and the overseas theater commands.

In this postwar structure, the intermediate headquarters between a combat
command and its operating wings or groups was a numbered air force. Of the
sixteen wartime air forces, eleven were retained in the three new combat com-

mands; the other five were disbanded. The Strategic Air Command assumed direction of the Eighth and Fifteenth Air Forces; the Tactical Air Command, the Third, Ninth, and Twelfth; and the Air Defense Command, the First, Second, Fourth, Tenth, Eleventh, and Fourteenth. Although Spaatz hoped to retain all sixteen air forces, he simply did not have the resources to man and operate them.

Early in 1946, Spaatz created the Air Board. He intended that the group consider and recommend policy at the highest levels of the Army Air Forces and report directly to the Commanding General. The members were not to involve themselves in day-to-day operations or activities so that they would have the time and objectivity for impartial deliberations. Unfortunately, the Air Board, in its actual operations, did not achieve this goal. As established in February of that year, the Air Board consisted of the entire uppermost echelon of the headquarters of the Army Air Forces, the heads of major commands, and prominent retired general officers, most former commanders. Because of its composition, some members of the board were forced to comment on matters in which they were deeply involved and about which they consequently found it difficult to offer impartial observations. Nevertheless, the board played a major role in shaping policy for many of the key postwar issues.

Spaatz also directed that plans be drawn up for reorganizing the reserve components of the Army Air Forces. The War Department's basic plan for the postwar military establishment reflected the belief of General Marshall, the wartime Chief of Staff, that it was unrealistic to expect the nation to maintain a large peacetime force. The postwar military establishment would therefore include the National Guard and the Organized Reserve Corps, both ready in case of emergency to reinforce the ranks of a small Regular Army. As part of the Army, the Air Forces adopted a congruent arrangement, consisting of a small active duty force backed by National Guardsmen and reservists. The Air National Guard, established in April 1946 as an important part of the air arm's postwar organization, performed for military aviation the same function that the National Guard did for the ground forces and service forces. In keeping with Marshall's conviction that the postwar Army should depend on the citizen-soldier, the Air National Guard would provide a source of organized combat units capable of mobilizing rapidly and quickly attaining wartime readiness. By the end of June 1947, the assigned strength of the Air National Guard totaled 10,000 officers and men, and 257 squadrons had received federal recognition. Meanwhile, the Air Defense Command was administering a reserve program composed largely of inactive reservists, not affiliated with any unit, who were available in an emergency, though not necessarily well trained. Of more than 500,000 reservists carried on the rolls in the summer of 1947, 80 percent were inactive.

Such was the structure Spaatz imposed on the military organization that Arnold had entrusted to him. The Army Air Forces, however, looked more impressive than it actually was, for the substance of its wartime air power was vanishing. Indeed, in the same report in which he had described the powerful independent air force of the future, Arnold took note of the rapid progress of demobilization, for disbanding the forces that had defeated the Axis was the immediate task facing all the armed services. Millions of men and women, willing enough to serve in wartime, were eager to return home. Nor had there appeared by the end of 1945 any threat to American security that might give pause to the political leaders, indeed, to the populace as a whole, in the call for rapid demobilization. While Arnold pondered the future, the Army Air Forces that had fought the war disappeared in the nation's eagerness to resume the ways of peace. "We did not demobilize," complained Brig. Gen. Leon Johnson, who had earned the Medal of Honor at Ploesti, Rumania, in 1943 and in late 1945 was serving as a personnel specialist on the Air Staff, "we merely fell apart . . . it was not an orderly demobilization at all. It was just a riot, really."[10]

In terms of numbers, the rapid mustering out tore the Air Forces apart. Between V-J Day in August 1945 and April 1946, its strength fell from 2,253,000 to just 485,000 and declined by May 1947 to a postwar low of about 304,000. Among the enlisted men, the most skilled tended to be the first to leave, thus depriving the air arm of highly trained maintenance technicians, who could take advantage of a favorable civilian job market. Between January 1945 and October 1946, the number of experienced mechanics dropped from 350,000 to 30,000. No wonder that General Spaatz, who had gradually assumed Arnold's duties between the end of hostilities and Arnold's retirement, complained of "almost hysterical demobilization" and cited a "rising curve of flying accidents due to loss of experienced ground crews."[11] Although desperately short of aircraft mechanics, other enlisted technicians, and even gunners, the Army Air Forces soon found itself with more pilots, bombardiers, and navigators than it could use. Consequently, many officers in these categories, although willing to remain on duty, were forced to leave as the air arm began reducing its strength from a wartime maximum in excess of 2,000,000 to a peacetime authorization of just 400,000.

Like manpower, the armada of aircraft that American industry had produced during the war began vanishing once the fighting ended. After all, airplanes had little military value without crews to man them and technicians to keep them in the air. At the height of the conflict, in June 1944, the Army Air Forces had about 79,000 aircraft of all types. After the defeat of Japan, the air arm flew thousands back to the continental United States from overseas and placed some in storage. The service turned another 35,000 over to the Reconstruction Finance Corporation, the federal agency disposing of surplus property, and halted production lines, even scrapping airplanes that were in the process of being assembled. As a result, by December 1946 the inventory of aircraft dwindled to approximately 30,000, less than half the number on hand in mid-1944, and during 1947 the total dropped to about 24,000, only 18 percent ready for action. The operational aircraft flew from 177 airfields, just 21 more than were in service in 1940 and a dizzying drop from the wartime maximum of 783 in late 1943.

Hundreds of bombers—B–17s, B–24s, B–25s, and B–26s—lined up at
Walnut Ridge AAB, Arkansas, wait for salvage and destruction crews.

Military leaders complained about the possibly disastrous effects of the pell
mell rush to demobilize. Looking back from the vantage of 1948, Spaatz preferred "not to speculate on what might have happened only one year after V–J
day, when the combat readiness of AAF first-line planes dropped very low, if
our Air Force had been called on to resist or to suppress a recurrence of combat
activity from an uncontrolled element in one of the occupied countries."[12] As
the stampede to civilian life was in progress, the Joint Chiefs of Staff were fully
aware of the steep decline in the overall military strength of the United States.
Indeed, they thought it would take well over a year to reconstitute American
military might to even a fraction of its recent power. General Marshall, the
Army Chief of Staff while the armed forces were in headlong decline, recalled
that the demobilization was injurious. Yet, even Marshall, who considered it a
serious error not to have planned a more gradual and systematic reduction, had
to concede that it would not have been possible, in the flush of victory and with
no clearly perceived danger at hand, to have maintained a large military force.

A threat soon materialized, however, in the form of the Soviet Union. By the
end of 1945, it had become clear that once Hitler's Germany had been defeated, the sense of common purpose that had held together the alliance between the
capitalist West and the communist East could not be maintained. Relations de-
teriorated so thoroughly and so quickly that on March 5, 1946, in an address at
Westminster College in Missouri, Winston Churchill, a year earlier voted out of
office as Prime Minister, could declare, "From Stettin in the Baltic to Trieste in
the Adriatic an iron curtain has descended." East of that line, the Soviet Union
exerted an influence that varied from guidance and direction to outright domination. One Soviet satellite, Yugoslavia, and a potential satellite, Austria, would
escape the Moscow orbit, but that lay months in the future. For the present,

Churchill seemed ominously correct when he warned of continued Soviet expansionism; his response to the danger consisted of a call for military and diplomatic cooperation between the two English-speaking democracies to disabuse Joseph Stalin, the Soviet dictator, of any "temptation to ambition or adventure" and to provide "an overwhelming assurance of safety" for the western democracies.[13]

In Iran, Stalin did back away from one adventure, suppressing his nation's ambitions in the face of diplomatic pressure from the Iranian, British, and American governments and the recently established United Nations. A border dispute between communist Yugoslavia and Italy was settled to the satisfaction of the western powers, but the Soviet Union persisted in demanding concessions from Turkey, and a powerful communist faction was waging a civil war in Greece. President Truman and his advisers were concerned about a Soviet irruption into the eastern Mediterranean. Consequently, when the British advised Washington that they could no longer afford to support the Greek government, Truman offered a program of American aid to both Turkey and Greece. On March 12, 1947, he called on Congress to provide $400 million in assistance to the two nations during fiscal 1948. In doing so, he enunciated the so-called Truman Doctrine, declaring that "it must be the policy of the United States to support free peoples who are resisting attempted subjugation by armed minorities or by outside pressure," indeed, to "assist free peoples to work out their own destinies in their own way."[14] The assistance and support, he assured a cooperative Congress, would be rendered through economic and financial aid, and within six weeks the funds had been voted.

Even as Greece and Turkey were being subjected to a military threat, the nations of western Europe, their economies ruined by the war, faced hunger, unemployment, currency inflation, and possible collapse. In both France and Italy tightly disciplined communist parties seemed ready to take charge. To help Europe regain its economic strength, Secretary of State Marshall, the Army's wartime Chief of Staff, in June 1947 called for a program of assistance, the so-called Marshall Plan. As in the case of aid to Greece and Turkey, Congress voted the funds requested by the administration to promote European recovery.

American demobilization and the division of Europe into rival political camps took place in the shadow of the atomic bomb. In the United States, social scientists like Bernard Brodie and Arnold Wolfers declared that the atomic bomb had revolutionized political relationships and military affairs. Nor did they consider it possible that the weapon could remain an American monopoly; indeed, Brodie expected that within five to ten years other nations would develop the bomb, which in his opinion had altered the very nature of war. In future conflicts, the crucial difference made by the atomic bomb would be the tremendous destruction that could be inflicted in a short time. "A world accustomed to thinking it horrible that wars should last four or five years," Brodie observed, "is now appalled at the prospect that future wars may last only a few days."[15]

Victory might no longer be worth the price. Assuming the use of atomic weapons, Brodie predicted that the United States would never again be able to fight a major war without suffering enormous destruction. National survival thus rested on the ability to discourage potential aggressors by the threat of nuclear devastation, by what Wolfers termed "a policy of determent," or deterrence, as it came to be called.

With the Army Air Forces evaporating in the warm sun of demobilization and the nuclear arsenal increasing slowly, the atomic bomb had little immediate effect as either a deterrent or an actual weapon of war. Nevertheless, the air arm had to organize, plan, and train to use it. In late 1945, therefore, Army Air Forces headquarters, influenced by the findings of a board formed by Arnold and headed by Spaatz, decided to designate all heavy bombardment units as elements of the atomic strike force, thus heeding the advice of Lt. Gen. Ira Eaker, the Deputy Commanding General of the Army Air Forces, who warned that if one wing were singled out as a special atomic unit, money for the rest of the heavy bomber force would be drastically reduced by an economy-minded Congress. Eaker conceded, however, that the resources were not available for all groups to train simultaneously; initially a single unit—a wing headquarters and three groups of four B–29 squadrons each—should prepare for atomic operations and maintain readiness for war. On January 2, 1946, Lt. Gen. Hoyt S. Vandenberg, now a member of the Air Staff, recommended to Eaker that the first atomic unit be built around the 58th Bomb Wing. The wing's first combat element would be the 509th Bomb Group, which had leveled Hiroshima and Nagasaki, although other groups would subsequently join. This force, which formed the key element of the new Strategic Air Command, was to have the most proficient crews and mechanics, receive the latest aircraft and equipment, maintain constant readiness, and be able to deploy in short notice to begin wartime operations in a matter of days. Because "the atomic bomb is a major weapon to be employed," Vandenberg believed that the group would have to be located "relatively near" the Manhattan District Project's assembly and storage facilities. To ensure security in the handling of the bombs and coordination between the strike force and the fabrication center, the 509th was stationed at Roswell, New Mexico, reasonably close to the Los Alamos complex, but far enough away that an attack on just one base could not destroy both bombs and bombers.[16]

Vandenberg also suggested that, in an emergency, atomic strike units be moved to "suitable operating bases" overseas where everything would be ready for them except the bombs. The atomic weapons, he believed, should not be sent with the units but should "remain in the United States until such time as they are to be actually used against the enemy." This reflected a continuation of the policy that had governed the dropping of the atomic bombs on Hiroshima and Nagasaki. The decision—including, Vandenberg believed, "the times of attack and targets"—would be made by the Commander in Chief. Once the President

Roswell Army Air Field, New Mexico, 1944.

decided to use the weapons, a transportation squadron under control of the wing headquarters would deliver the bombs and a fully equipped assembly team to the theater of operations.[17] General Spaatz approved this concept on January 7, 1946, and the 58th Bomb Wing was designated the first atomic strike force in the Army Air Forces.

In planning for a possible atomic war, the Joint Chiefs of Staff faced demobilization and a lack of atomic weapons, the same problems that hampered preparations by the Army Air Forces. Other considerations arose quickly, such as the probable duration of the American monopoly on atomic bombs, which the Joint Strategic Survey Committee in October 1945 predicted would last at least five years. Once the Soviet Union had developed a bomb, according to the American planners, the United States would be especially vulnerable since so many of its industrial cities were clustered along the coasts. In contrast, the Soviet Union, because of the distance an attacker would have to fly over its territory before reaching the truly vital inland targets, seemed less vulnerable to fear from an atomic attack. Successfully waging war against the Soviet Union, the Joint Chiefs of Staff concluded in 1946, would require sound intelligence, especially on the factories built east of the Ural Mountains during the German invasion, and the development of forward bases to place the B–29 within range of these distant targets. Because of the limited number of bombs and the difficulty of delivering them, land and sea forces would have to seize, develop, supply, and protect the advance bases for the bombers. This interdependence served as an argument for a balanced array of air, ground, and sea forces with which to fight the Soviet Union.

Although calling for balance among the armed forces, the Joint Chiefs of Staff realized that the United States could not hope to match the Soviet Union in conventionally armed ground forces and would have to resort to atomic weapons early in any conflict. In June 1946 this reasoning produced an interim plan, called Pincher, which recommended an atomic air offensive at the onset of war with the Soviet Union, even though there were no more than nine atomic bombs available at this time and roughly twenty B–29s to carry them, the aircraft of the 509th Bomb Group modified for the purpose. Obviously such an uncertain strategic concept looked to the future. More securely rooted in the present was Makefast, an Army Air Forces plan completed in September 1946 and based on the ideas contained in the Pincher concept. Makefast did not have an atomic weapons annex, an acknowledgement of the fact that the firm intelligence necessary for detailed target lists was lacking and that the Atomic Energy Commission, the civilian agency which manufactured and had custody over the weapons, had not amassed a large enough stockpile for the kind of atomic offensive envisaged in Pincher.

Along with these first attempts to plan for atomic warfare, the Army Air Forces addressed the problem of advance bases for the B–29s by experimenting with polar operations. In November 1945, four B–29s flew the 6,553-mile flight from Hokkaido, Japan, to Washington, D.C., demonstrating, in theory at least, that the arctic wastes of the polar region were no barrier to air power. Flying over the area proved simple, however, compared to living, conducting operations, and maintaining aircraft in the snow and cold. During tests begun late in 1946, B–29s of the Strategic Air Command, equipped for conventional bombardment, tried unsuccessfully to operate from Alaskan airfields in winter when

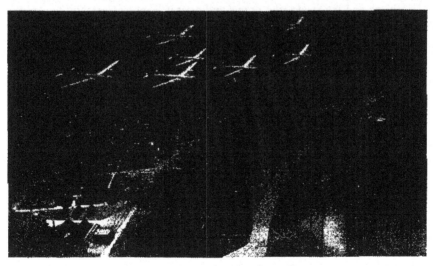

A flight of B–29s over RAF Scampton.

temperatures plunged to lower than 40 degrees below zero Fahrenheit, temperatures that congealed engine oil and froze the rubber in tires.

Besides launching the unsuccessful experiment in the frozen North, Spaatz in 1946 arranged with Air Marshal Sir Arthur Tedder of the Royal Air Force to prepare five bases in East Anglia for B–29s in the event of a crisis with the Soviet Union. Tedder also agreed to have two of these bases, Sculthorpe and Lakenheath, equipped to handle atomic weapons. However, neither bombers nor personnel—skilled mechanics and trained crews alike—were available at this time to occupy the British airfields, and the atomic stockpile remained in New Mexico in the custody of the Atomic Energy Commission. Late in 1946, after two American transports had at separate times strayed across the Yugoslav border and been shot down, W. Stuart Symington, the Assistant Secretary of War for Air, wanted an entire group of B–29s available in Europe to discourage incidents like these. He had to settle for six of the aircraft, which arrived in November, toured western Europe briefly to show the flag, and returned to the United States. Even this gesture would have been impossible without spare parts cannibalized from bombers that did not participate in the flight, demonstrating again the inability of the Strategic Air Command to deploy bombers across the Atlantic.

Not until the summer of 1947 could the Strategic Air Command begin deploying bombers to Europe on a regular basis for short tours of duty at airfields in Germany. Later that year planning began for a so-called balanced occupational force that included three fighter, one reconnaissance, and four troop carrier squadrons, as well as sufficient air base units to meet the needs of the B–29s rotating from the United States for temporary duty in Germany. Although the public associated the B–29 with atomic weapons as a result of the attacks on Hiroshima and Nagasaki, the crews and aircraft sent to Germany lacked the training and equipment to drop these weapons. The actual atomic strike force continued to train in the southwestern United States.

The first B–29s deployed to the Pacific on a rotational basis in the summer of 1947. Late in the following year a shortage of fuel forced a reduction in flying hours and threatened to disrupt the practice of rotating the bombers overseas. As though acknowledging the comparative importance of the two regions in the minds of American planners, the Strategic Air Command continued sending bombers to Europe even as it suspended the rotation of bombers to the Pacific. The westward deployments resumed in January 1949 after a two-month pause, as the B–29s regularly reinforced the fighters, light bombers, and reconnaissance aircraft scattered from Hawaii to the Philippines, Okinawa, and Japan.

Four major events absorbed the energies of the postwar air arm. Simultaneously with the rush to demobilize, the restructuring of the Army Air Forces, the collapse of the wartime alliance (which increased the possibility of war), and the first efforts to create an atomic strike force, Spaatz and his fellow airmen took up Arnold's quest for an air force independent of the Army. The dominant

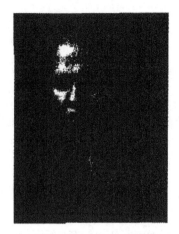

General of the Army George C. Marshall,
Army Chief of Staff,
September 1939–November 1945.

questions relating to independence dealt, of course, with the relationship of the air arm to the Army and Navy, but other related matters were also being resolved. One basic question was the probable nature of any future war, whether it would be fought by citizens recruited and trained for the purpose or by the force under arms when the conflict began. Another was the size of the air arm—whether a part of the Army or an independent department—and a third was the relationship of an air force to the Army and Navy.

The need to choose between a comparatively large force in readiness and a small cadre capable of expansion in time of emergency was dramatized by the debate over a program of peacetime Universal Military Training, in which young American males would serve for perhaps two years on active duty and then spend several years in a reserve. Marshall, while Army Chief of Staff, was enthusiastic about the idea, for he believed that the citizenry would refuse to shoulder the cost of a large standing army but would accept the inconvenience of maintaining the less costly pool of reservists. The past two wars had been won by millions of soldiers, sailors, marines, and airmen inducted from civilian life. Augmented to some degree by mobilized reservists and National Guardsmen, this nation in arms had been trained and then led by a cadre of experienced officers and noncommissioned officers. What Marshall proposed to do was to substitute reservists with some degree of peacetime training for the raw recruits of World War I and World War II, thus bringing the armed forces to wartime strength and proficiency with a minimum of delay. President Truman also favored the plan, at least in part because he felt that young Americans would benefit from the discipline, education, and health care they would receive while undergoing the mandatory instruction.

The leadership of the Army Air Forces was less enthusiastic. Some support existed for the program; in fact, Arnold had endorsed the concept during a speech at an American Legion convention in 1944, but he soon found compelling reasons for opposing the plan. First, a large pool of men with only rudimentary training, however useful to the Army, would be of little value to an air force that relied on skilled pilots and highly trained technicians employing the latest products of aviation science. Second, the development of the atomic bomb indicated that the next war might well begin with a sudden onslaught, a nuclear Pearl Harbor so extensive and so violent that the kind of mobilization that occurred during the two world wars would be impossible; such a war would have to be fought by the forces under arms when the bombs began falling. In the end, the specter of atomic war destroyed Universal Military Training, for even if the program were adopted, the United States would face the additional expense of maintaining the active duty armed forces, including a retaliatory arm equipped with aircraft and atomic weapons, in a state of constant readiness so that aggression could be deterred or punished. As the months passed, the public and Congress accepted the idea that an air force, instantly ready for combat, was a convenient and effective substitute for the reservoir of military manpower that Marshall and Truman tried unsuccessfully to create.

Debate over the size of the postwar Army Air Forces began while the proposal for Universal Military Training still flourished; and during the final months of his tenure as commanding general, Arnold had to argue against including the trainees, at various times expected to number anywhere from 70,000 to 200,000, in the total strength of the air arm. Even discounting the effects of Universal Military Training, plans for the postwar Army Air Forces varied greatly in manpower and total number of flying groups. Those clearly tentative documents considered by the War Department in 1943 reflected an uncertain view of the future in which the peacetime Army might number between 1,500,000 and 1,700,000. Using these figures, Air Forces planners submitted for departmental approval a proposal calling for 530,000 men and 105 groups of combat aircraft—21 groups in the Atlantic, 58 in the Pacific, and 26 in the United States, the Caribbean, and Alaska. By the summer of 1944, however, a new consideration had surfaced—the premise that an effective international security organization would take shape after the war. Consequently, the Air Forces obtained approval from the War Department to plan for a postwar force of 75 combat groups and 635,000 men. The increase in manpower, even though the number of flying groups declined, stemmed from a belief on the part of Air Staff planners that an independent air force would assume many functions from the Army, including antiaircraft artillery. In the spring of 1945, the future of the air arm seemed less settled when General Marshall established for planning purposes, not as an absolute ceiling, a postwar Army Air Forces of just 120,000 men and 16 groups. This figure may well have been a trial balloon, inflated by the general's own enthusiasm for Universal Military Training and the interest shown in the plan before the advent of the atomic bomb. If so, it rapidly went flat, punctured by Arnold's argument that such a plan represented "disarmament in air strength" and by the changing public and congressional attitudes toward the proposed training program.[18]

When Universal Military Training collapsed, the Army Air Forces settled on a postwar goal of 574,000 men and 70 combat groups, with the largest concentration of manpower located in the United States—in training, acting as potential replacements, or serving as administrators—but most of the groups, 59 of the 70, based in Europe and the Pacific. The War Department approved this latest plan in August 1945 but, as demobilization gathered momentum, had to recant and impose a ceiling of 400,000 officers and men, a figure that General Eisenhower, who had just replaced Marshall as Chief of Staff, approved in December. The total of 400,000 remained valid as long as the aggregate strength of the Army was not reduced below 1,000,000. The Air Forces might organize 70 groups within that authorization, but a sizeable proportion would have to be skeletal organizations. A strength of 70 groups, fully manned and equipped, became both an objective and a battle cry for the air arm when it did become independent.

Within the War Department General Staff, tentative planning for an independent air force began as early as 1943, when General Marshall called for a study of the subject and referred the resulting document to the Joint Chiefs of Staff for their consideration. In effect, the War Department sought to transpose wartime experience in the major theaters to the national level, establishing a single defense department with coequal elements controlling air, sea, and ground forces. The idea of a postwar reorganization took hold, exciting interest in Congress as well as in the Army and Navy, and causing Robert Lovett, at that point still Assistant Secretary of War for Air, to predict "a bitter struggle with the High Command and particularly the Navy in getting the postwar set-up properly made so that airpower is recognized as a coequal arm."[19] A report of the Committee for Reorganization of the National Defense, set up by the Joint Chiefs of Staff, dramatized for the leaders of the Army Air Forces their differences with the Navy. Although four of the five officers on the committee, including one naval officer, recommended the formation of three coequal armed forces in a single department headed by a civilian cabinet officer, the committee's chairman and senior naval member, Adm. James O. Richardson, dissented and defended the status quo. The admiral expressed fear that the Navy might lose naval aviation to the new air force and possibly lose the Marine Corps to the Army. Other senior admirals—among them the wartime naval triumvirate of Admirals of the Fleet Ernest J. King, the Chief of Naval Operations; Leahy, the Chief of Staff to the President; and Chester W. Nimitz, the Commander in Chief, Pacific Ocean Areas—feared that the kind of centralization foreshadowed by the report would undermine the effectiveness and status of their service, subjecting its programs to review by officials who either misunderstood or opposed them. Obviously defense reorganization was too complex and far-reaching an issue to achieve an easy consensus among the Joint Chiefs of Staff. As a result, both the Navy Department and War Department produced plans of their own.

In the summer of 1945, Secretary of the Navy James V. Forrestal commissioned a special report on reorganization to be prepared under the supervision of his friend Ferdinand Eberstadt, an investment banker who had served on the War Production Board and as chairman of the Army and Navy Munitions Board. The Eberstadt Report, submitted in September of that year, proposed the formation of an independent air force but opposed a single department of national defense, instead recommending coordination among the services by means of joint committees formed within the organization of the Joint Chiefs of Staff. Although Forrestal had requested the report, he nonetheless had serious reservations about its contents. The Secretary of the Navy opposed an independent air force, suggesting the Army might give its air arm even greater autonomy within the War Department rather than have it reconstituted as a third component of the armed forces. In effect, Forrestal would have continued to divide appropriations between the Army and Navy, as had been done during the war, with the Army drawing on its share of the overall defense appropriations to fund an autonomous air force. Like the Eberstadt panel, Secretary Forrestal disliked the idea of a single secretary of defense on the grounds that the appointee would wield excessive power, but he did not believe that the system of coordination through committees, proposed by Eberstadt, would actually work. As a substitute for these committees, he suggested a security council that included the President and representatives of the War, State, and Navy departments; a resources board to coordinate mobilization; a central intelligence agency; and a munitions board to handle procurement and logistical planning. Forrestal, moreover, was not convinced that the unification of the armed forces in a single department would save money compared to the system of Army-Navy cooperation that he favored.

For Arnold in particular, the idea of leaving the air arm's budget within that of the Army was entirely unacceptable. During the years of economizing prior to World War II, he had participated in struggles over money that had pitted the Air Corps against the other components of the Army. Since austerity seemed likely to recur, he considered it essential that military aviation be able to present its own request for funding to the Bureau of the Budget and Congress without an internal review within the War Department. The kind of strong secretary of defense favored by Arnold and the other leaders of the Air Forces would have the power to resolve the inevitable disputes over funding for the individual services in a manner that would reflect the emergence of land-based air power as the one genuinely decisive weapon of modern war. This the Joint Chiefs of Staff or their committees could not do because the ground, sea, and air forces, at least in theory, had equal influence. Reliance on the Joint Chiefs of Staff or their committees, the airmen feared, would result in endless debate instead of decisions acknowledging the importance of land-based air power.

Perhaps, thought Arnold, the naval opposition could be reassured, if not converted to the point of view of the Army's airmen. Aware of loose talk by his colleagues—statements such as "Who needs a Navy?" that were intensifying the fears of naval officers for the future of their service—he offered assurances con-

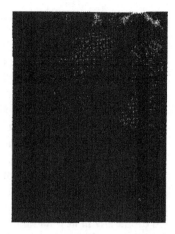

General of the Army Dwight D. Eisenhower,
Army Chief of Staff,
November 1945–February 1948.

cerning naval aviation. He was, he declared, opposed to bringing aircraft carriers under air force control, although areas of overlapping responsibility would exist where the division of responsibility between the established department and the new one would blur. In instances like these—land-based maritime patrols and possibly flight training—the strong secretary of defense, which the Army Air Forces hoped to establish atop the defense pyramid, would award the function to one of the disputants.

In the quest for independence, the Air Forces had strong support from General Marshall who, throughout his tenure as Chief of Staff of the Army, shared Arnold's belief that a powerful civilian authority would be needed to head a new defense department. Although coordination by committee had worked reasonably well during the war, Marshall believed that peacetime, with the certainty of fiscal restraints and the resulting competition for funds, would require a vigorously led defense establishment, whose civilian secretary could fashion a single budget and defend it before the Bureau of the Budget and Congress. Marshall was concerned about the duplication of effort and cost in the present system, arising from what he perceived as the Navy's penchant for self-sufficiency—the combination of land-based and carrier-based aviation, amphibious ground forces, and the fleet itself—during what he was certain would be a period of financial austerity. For the military establishment to conduct itself in what Marshall considered a sound, efficient manner, the civilian secretary of defense would have to redirect naval thinking from self-sufficiency to collaboration with the land and air forces. Under the centralized kind of management that Marshall favored, the Joint Chiefs of Staff would become a planning agency, formulating strategy and policy for consideration by the secretary of defense, Congress, and the President.

To write the War Department's plan for organizing a single department of national defense, Marshall formed a committee headed by Lt. Gen. J. Lawton Collins, a veteran of the fighting in the Pacific and Europe, who had the dual as-

389

signment of Deputy Commanding General and Chief of Staff in the headquarters of the Army Ground Forces. Collins forwarded the group's report to the Army Chief of Staff in October 1945. The so-called Collins plan—based on the Report of the Committee of the Joint Chiefs of Staff on the Reorganization of National Defense, with which Admiral Richardson had disagreed—recommended the creation of a single department of national defense headed by a civilian secretary, the appointment of a civilian under secretary and a uniformed chief of staff for the armed forces, and the statutory ratification of the Joint Chiefs of Staff, which President Roosevelt had organized in 1942 in an exercise of his wartime powers. Under this plan, the Joint Chiefs of Staff would formulate a budget proposal to be sent through the secretary of defense to the President. The report of the Collins committee codified the views of the Army and the Army Air Forces and established a structural framework, if not the exact working relationships, incorporated eventually in new national security legislation.

After succeeding Marshall as Army Chief of Staff, Eisenhower threw the weight of his great prestige behind the unification of the armed forces into a single defense department. Like his predecessor, Eisenhower advocated the creation of an independent air force as part of the new defense structure, an idea he considered so logical that he said, referring to the Army, "No sane officer of any arm would contest that thinking." Elaborating on this point, he told the general staff in December 1945 that, although "there can be other individual opinions" concerning the status of military aviation, it "seems to me to be so logical from all our experience in this war—such an inescapable conclusion—that I for one can't even entertain any longer any doubt as to its wisdom."[20]

While the drive toward independence gathered momentum, the War Department, including the Army Air Forces, underwent a postwar reorganization of its own. As part of the transition from Air Forces to air force, General Arnold wanted the Air Staff to be made coequal with the War Department General Staff, thus placing the air arm on an organizational plateau above the ground forces and service forces, the other functional components of the Army. Arnold also wanted the Army to have two chiefs of staff, one for ground and service forces and the other for the Air Forces. Although the reorganization did not include these major points—the Commanding General, Army Air Forces did not become the peer of Eisenhower nor did the Air Staff become the equal of the War Department General Staff—the structure that was established in June 1946 and remained in effect until the creation of an independent air force in 1947 did provide somewhat greater autonomy for the Army Air Forces. The commanding general of the air arm received the authority to nominate fifty percent of the members of War Department's general and special staffs. Furthermore, Spaatz, as Arnold's successor, assumed responsibility for preparing budget estimates and justifying them before the Budget Advisory Committee of the War Department, the first step in the appropriations process that involved the Bureau of the Budget and Congress. Since this arrangement was clearly temporary and

President Truman, with Gen. Spaatz (center) and Lt. Gen. Eaker looking on, signs proclamation designating August 1, 1946, as Air Force Day.

Eisenhower was irrevocably on record in favor of an independent air force, Spaatz saw no need to quarrel with the reorganization plan.

Beset by the crumbling of the wartime alliance between communism and democracy, threatened during the transition from war to peace by the danger of inflation in the United States and economic collapse abroad, President Truman faced problems more intricate and potentially more dangerous than defense reorganization, but he could not ignore this issue in the unsettled postwar world. As he said in retrospect, "One of the strongest convictions which I brought to the Presidency was that the antiquated defense setup . . . had to be reorganized quickly as a step toward insuring our future safety and preserving world peace." Like most military and political leaders of the time, he attributed the disaster at Pearl Harbor in large measure to the absence of a unified command. Not only did he move swiftly to rectify this lack of unity, he intended that the new defense establishment should reflect his belief that "Air power has been developed to a point where its responsibilities are equal to those of land and sea power." He therefore recommended in December 1945 that Congress approve legislation to create an independent air force, an equal of the Army and Navy in a new department of defense. Truman's reorganization plan resembled the Collins report inasmuch as it urged the appointment of a civilian cabinet officer, aided by a uniformed chief of staff, to head the defense establishment instead of relying on the Joint Chiefs of Staff or some similar agency to coordinate the nation's defenses, as a number of prominent admirals were advocating. The President realized that true unification would depend on more than mere legislation. "It will require," he said, "new viewpoints, new doctrine, and new habits of thinking throughout the departmental structure."[21]

The new thinking that the President hoped for evolved all too slowly. His presentation of his own reorganization plan failed to break the deadlock between the Navy's official position favoring coordination and the view shared by the Army and the Army Air Forces that a cabinet officer would have to exert control over national defense. Forrestal responded to the Truman plan by taking a firm stand against it. "As the President knows," said the Secretary of the Navy, "I am so opposed to the fundamental concept that I do not believe there is any very helpful observation that I could make on the draft you referred to me."[22] The controversy, by again showing the inability of the Army and Navy to unite behind the President, may have strengthened Truman's belief that coordination would not work.

In January 1946, the Senate Military Affairs Committee responded to the President's call for defense reorganization by creating a subcommittee to write the necessary legislation. Appointed as advisers to the subcommittee were Maj. Gen. Lauris Norstad, Assistant Chief of Air Staff, Plans, and Vice Adm. Arthur W. Radford, Deputy Chief of Naval Operations (Air). The choice of an Army airman and a naval aviator probably reflected the fact that much of the Navy's resistance to the reorganization of the defense structure focused on the possible encroachment by an independent air force on naval aviation. After rejecting the first eight bills drafted by the subcommittee, the parent committee in April accepted one that included features of both the Eberstadt report and the Collins plan, though it hewed in general to President Truman's ideas. In May the committee recommended this bill to the Senate.

The Navy, however, continued to oppose the legislation, and the Chief Executive became increasingly perturbed. In mid-May 1946 he told his Secretaries of War and the Navy, Robert P. Patterson and Forrestal, to have a unification proposal on his desk by the end of the month. Aided by Symington and Eberstadt, the two cabinet officers forwarded to the President eight points on which they agreed: no military chief of staff, which Truman had proposed to assist the secretary of defense called for in his plan; statutory confirmation of the Joint Chiefs of Staff; formation of a national security resources board, a council of common defense (like the subsequent National Security Council), and a central intelligence agency; and the establishment of centralized agencies for supply and procurement, research and development, and military education and training. Despite the broad agreement, three major issues as yet defied compromise: the power of the secretary in the single department of defense; whether the Army Air Forces should become a separate department and, if independent of the Army, its relationship to the Navy's air arm; and finally the future of the Marine Corps. Aside from the question of an independent air force, the issues boiled down to a choice between coordination and centralized control within the proposed defense establishment. Basically, the Navy advocated a system of coordination between the naval establishment as it currently existed, which included naval aviation and the Marine Corps, and the other armed forces; decisions would be reached by consensus through the Joint Chiefs of Staff and joint committees. In contrast, the War Department recommended a civilian secretary of defense with the authority to make decisions of policy and administration, decisions that, the Navy believed, could conceivably jeopardize its air and amphibious components.

Hovering in the background was the question of roles and missions—how, for example, the Navy and an independent air force should divide responsibility for various aspects of aviation. Although the leadership of the Army Air Forces had foresworn any designs on carrier aviation or routine administrative flights by Navy airmen, both Arnold and Spaatz wanted control of land-based maritime patrols, even though during World War II responsibility for antisubmarine patrols had been surrendered to the Navy, along with the necessary number of long-range bombers. This controversy continued into the spring of 1946 with no hope of resolution by the Joint Chiefs of Staff. General Eisenhower, the Army Chief of Staff, and Fleet Admiral Nimitz, King's successor as Chief of Naval Operations, agreed in May to cease considering this issue, which had thus far stymied negotiations. The general had become convinced that issues like this, dealing with service roles and missions, would have to be decided by the President once the basic question of reorganization had been settled.

Despite the failure to resolve the matter of land-based maritime air patrols, once Patterson and Forrestal had accepted the eight points, Truman prodded the Army and Navy into agreeing on the framework of a defense department headed by a civilian, essentially the structure described in the Senate bill. Establishing the mechanism for bringing three separate departments, each responsible for its own administration, under the overall control of a secretary of defense took precedence over sorting out roles and missions. Although the Navy continued to oppose the Truman plan, in July 1946 the Joint Chiefs of Staff told Norstad, now the Director of Plans and Operations on the War Department General Staff, and Vice Adm. Forrest P. Sherman, Deputy for Operations on Nimitz's staff, to draft a unification plan.

For much of his career, Norstad had been a staff officer rather than a commander, serving as a wartime adviser to General Arnold, as an operations planner in the headquarters of the Northwest African Air Forces and later the Mediterranean Allied Air Forces, as Chief of Staff, Twentieth Air Force, and then as a planner on the postwar Air Staff before moving to the War Department General Staff. Sherman, in contrast, had commanded the aircraft carrier *Wasp*

Maj. Gen. Lauris Norstad, Director of Plans and Operations, co-author of a plan for the unification of the armed services.

when it was sunk by a Japanese submarine and later in the war led a division of fast carriers before receiving an assignment to the Navy Department. Whatever their differences in experience, both were advocates of air power, Sherman of its carrier-based applications, and Norstad of land-based aviation. The two officers first tackled the issue of the organization of unified theater commands, an issue brought sharply into focus during the war in the Pacific where General MacArthur and Admiral Nimitz had controlled separate theaters, one dominated by the Army and the other by the Navy. Norstad and Sherman drew up a plan that the Joint Chiefs of Staff and then President Truman approved during December 1946. It established seven unified commands, each under a single commander but consisting of components of more than one service: the Atlantic Fleet and the Far East, Pacific, Caribbean, European, Alaskan, and Northeast Commands. Even as they approved the unified theater commands proposed by Norstad and Sherman, the Joint Chiefs noted that the Strategic Air Command, created in March 1946, had been designated a specified command, reporting to the Joint Chiefs of Staff and presumably to a secretary of defense when that office became a reality.

Having disposed of the topic of theater commands, Norstad and Sherman, with the help of Assistant Secretary of War for Air Symington, turned in January 1947 to the thornier subjects of functions and organization. The resulting draft provided the basis for an agreement between Secretary of War Patterson and Secretary of the Navy Forrestal on the status of the civilian secretary in the defense establishment, but not on the assignment of missions, which came to be handled separately from the subject of organization. The two cabinet officers agreed to support legislation that formed a comprehensive national security establishment consisting of an office of the secretary of national defense and offices of the secretary of the Army; the secretary of the Navy, whose domain would continue to include naval aviation and the Marine Corps; and the secretary of the air force, with each of the three departments having a uniformed chief as well as a civilian head. Although incorporated into the department of national defense, all three of the departments would be administered as individual entities by the appropriate service secretaries.

In spite of the progress toward an organizational framework, the issue of coordination versus direction still lingered. Forrestal continued to urge that the secretary of defense be a coordinator, with limited authority, who would work through the civilian secretaries at the head of each service. In contrast, Eisenhower and Spaatz wanted a secretary of defense with substantial authority to make decisions. At last a compromise was reached, and after extended hearings, the Senate and House passed a unification bill. On July 26, 1947, President Truman approved the National Security Act of 1947, which created the National Military Establishment, including the Office of Secretary of Defense and the Departments of the Army, Navy, and Air Force.

The new law tried to accommodate the views of Forrestal on the one hand and of Spaatz and Eisenhower on the other. Although the Secretary of Defense received the authority to exercise general direction and control over the three military departments, as Spaatz and Eisenhower had recommended, his writ was far from absolute. Not only did the law contain a clause reserving to the service secretaries all the power not granted to the Secretary of Defense, it gave the civilian heads of the services the right to appeal decisions of the Secretary of Defense, taking their complaints directly to the Director of the Budget or the President, provided only that they notified the Secretary of Defense of their dissent. In this instance, Forrestal had clearly prevailed, for thanks to the right of appeal, the Secretary of Defense on most key issues would coordinate policy instead of establishing it.

The act also authorized a number of other agencies dealing with national defense. As they had during the war against the Axis, the Joint Chiefs of Staff would provide strategic planning and direction for the armed forces. A National Security Council was established to advise the President on a broad range of issues; in time of crisis it could be supplemented by a War Council made up of the Secretary of Defense, the service secretaries, and the uniformed chiefs of the Army, Navy, and Air Force. To prevent a repetition of the lapses in disseminating information that had helped the Japanese achieve surprise at Pearl Harbor, a Central Intelligence Agency would channel intelligence evaluations to the National Security Council. A Munitions Board, with all three services represented, was to coordinate the production, procurement, and distribution of armaments, much as its predecessor had done during the war. A Research and Development Board, with members from the three services, would chart the requirements for research and development. Finally, a National Security Resources Board would advise the President on questions of industrial, civilian, and military mobilization. These various components of the National Military Establishment, taken together, formed the framework for an integrated approach to national security. If every element functioned as planned, this orga-

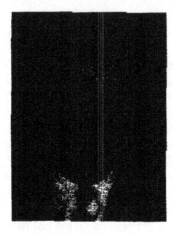

James V. Forrestal,
first Secretary of Defense,
September 1947–March 1949.

nization would be able to determine long-range plans and policies and be able to react to sudden crises.

In agreeing to the formation of the National Military Establishment, Secretaries Forrestal and Patterson had forwarded to President Truman a draft of an executive order setting forth the responsibilities of the three armed forces. If Forrestal had won the debate on coordination versus direction, he made a minor concession in that roles and missions were not included in the basic law, as he had recommended, but were made the subject of Presidential directives. On the same day that Mr. Truman signed the new National Security Act, he issued Executive Order 9877, "Functions of the Armed Forces," which delineated the duties of the Army, Navy, and Air Force exactly as Patterson and Forrestal had defined them. In general, each was responsible for the medium—air, ground, or sea—in which it operated, although the naval establishment retained an air arm and the Marine Corps.

President Truman wanted Patterson to head the reorganized defense establishment, but the Secretary of War declined, explaining that he had some time earlier resolved to leave government service. The Chief Executive thereupon turned to Forrestal, choosing as the first Secretary of Defense a man who, while Secretary of the Navy, had acceded only reluctantly to the establishment of an independent Air Force and its incorporation in the department he would head. Precisely because of this reputation for wariness, Forrestal, as Secretary of Defense, might be able to persuade reluctant naval officers to support the National Security Act. After naming Forrestal, Truman chose as his service secretaries three veterans of the War and Navy Departments. John L. Sullivan, Under Secretary of the Navy, became Secretary, replacing Forrestal; Kenneth C. Royall, an Under Secretary of War, became the first Secretary of the Army; and the President selected Symington, the former Assistant Secretary of War for Air, to take office as the first Secretary of the Air Force.

As the fitting climax to a career that began at the U.S. Military Academy and extended from the aerial battles over the Western Front in one world war to the

General Carl A. Spaatz, first
Chief of Staff of the Air
Force, and General Hoyt S.
Vandenberg, who succeeded
Spaatz on April 30, 1948.

bombing of Germany and Japan in another, General Spaatz became the first
Chief of Staff of the United States Air Force. General Vandenberg, who had
served as Deputy Commanding General, Army Air Forces, took over as Vice
Chief of Staff, U.S. Air Force. Whereas Spaatz was linked to strategic bombardment, Vandenberg, the nephew of Republican Senator Arthur H.
Vandenberg of Michigan, had earned a brilliant wartime reputation for his handling of tactical aviation. Brig. Gen. William F. McKee, named Assistant Vice
Chief of Staff, was truly an anomaly in an Air Force that prized flying skill, for
he was an administrator rather than an aviator. He had transferred from the coast
artillery into the Army Air Forces and had made his reputation as a trou-
bleshooter for General Arnold.

The Air Force at last had won its independence, becoming the equal of the
Army and Navy in the National Military Establishment (soon to be redesignated the Department of Defense). The leaders of the new Air Force had wanted a

strong Secretary of Defense to whom they could make the case for air power, using arguments based on strategic bombardment during World War II and the growing belief in atomic deterrence to obtain a suitably large share of the available appropriations. What they got was not a unified and strongly led defense establishment but what was, in effect, a confederation of the three armed forces in which each might appeal an unfavorable decision to the President or his principal budget officer. Nor was the naval leadership pleased with a system that promised a three-way division of resources instead of the old division between Army and Navy. The postwar Navy, in spite of the resulting fiscal constraints, might to some degree continue to exercise the kind of mobility and striking power it had demonstrated during World War II; to do so, however, would require not merely the retention of air and amphibious forces as provided for in the basic legislation but also a share in the atomic mission, thus far a monopoly of the Air Force and its predecessor, the Army Air Forces. Even the Army had cause for concern; it had supported independence for military aviation, giving up its own tactical air support in return for a promise of responsiveness that could be affected by future appropriations and the internal priorities of the Air Force. The misgivings of the Army, Navy, and Air Force, the appeals mechanism incorporated in the new law, and a growing realization of the ambiguities in the Presidential directive assigning functions among the armed forces combined to ensure a tempestuous start for the reorganized defense establishment.

Chapter 12

Framing Air Force Missions

Warren A. Trest
George M. Watson, Jr.

The new National Military Establishment came into being on September 17, 1947, when James V. Forrestal took the oath as Secretary of Defense. On the following day, as Forrestal watched, W. Stuart Symington was sworn in as Secretary of the Air Force, along with the other newly designated service secretaries; all the principal civilian authorities were now formally installed. On September 26, Gen. Carl Spaatz, previously the Commanding General, Army Air Forces, became the first Chief of Staff of the Air Force. Symington and Spaatz were the leaders, civilian and military, who charted a course for the new service. During their tenure, the Air Force adopted the basic organization that has persisted over the years: a headquarters, with a staff consisting of deputies who both advised and carried out policy and special assistants; a network of major commands and lesser agencies, both operating and supporting; and the operational commands overseas. A struggle with the Navy over the atomic mission subsided, so that by mid-1950, the Air Force, by now under different leadership, assumed certain responsibilities, among them the deterrence of nuclear war, that it has carried out ever since, albeit with changes in equipment, emphasis, and funding. Deterrence, however, was but a single aspect of an evolving national policy, and the Air Force had to devote its resources to the others: the containment of communism, for example by going to the aid of West Berlin; and regional collective security, best exemplified by the North Atlantic Treaty Organization.

A small group of civilians and military men formed the Office of the Secretary of the Air Force, which advised Symington. The Secretary of the Air Force might also consult the Air Staff, if the need arose, although this predominantly military agency existed primarily to advise the Chief of Staff and help execute his policy. As the civilian chief of the Air Force, Secretary Symington maintained the division of labor between operations and administrative support that had emerged after Robert A. Lovett became Assistant Secretary of War for Air in 1940. Lovett, whose law practice familiarized him with the inner workings of the aircraft industry, had focused his talents on the critical subject of airplane manufacture, helping provide the Army Air Forces with the equipment it needed during a period of hectic expansion. Similarly, Symington believed that his main job was not operational but supportive—not deciding what kinds of weapons the Air Force needed or how they should be used, but obtaining the appropriations needed to acquire them. As he described it, his task was "to get as much of the pie as I could for the Air Force."[1] Both men concentrated on supporting the air arm: Lovett at a time when money was plentiful, but production only beginning to increase, and Symington at a time when the challenge lay in obtaining the necessary funds.

Because of changed circumstances since Lovett's day, the first Secretary of the Air Force represented the service in a series of bitter battles over the distribution of appropriations and the assignment of roles and missions among the three departments of the reorganized defense establishment. Instead of worrying about profits, delivery deadlines, stockholders, and labor, as he had when president of Emerson Electric, a Missouri firm that during World War II had built gun turrets for bombers, he found that he had to satisfy Congress while at the same time meeting the needs of the Air Force. In the new role he developed shrewd political instincts, which eventually would make him a senator and a Presidential hopeful.

The civilians most directly involved in the day-to-day management of the Air Force were Symington's principal assistants, all of whom had either practical or theoretical knowledge of business techniques. Arthur S. Barrows, the Under Secretary of the Air Force, had helped direct Sears, Roebuck and Company, perhaps the most successful of American merchandisers. One of the assistant secretaries, Cornelius Vanderbilt Whitney, had served as an officer or director of various enterprises and as a member of General of the Army Dwight D. Eisenhower's wartime staff. The other assistant secretary, Eugene M. Zuckert, for a time an instructor at the Harvard Graduate School of Business Administration, had worked for Symington at both the Surplus Property Administration, which the Missouri businessman once headed, and the office of Assistant Secretary of War for Air.

W. Stuart Symington, first Secretary of the Air Force and
General Carl A. Spaatz, first Chief of Staff of the Air Force.

While still the Commanding General, Army Air Forces, Spaatz had thought
about reorganizing the Air Staff to assign the heads of the various sections responsibility for broad functional areas. Besides having the Air Staff gather information and channel it upward for a decision, he wanted the organization to
help carry out the policy that he adopted, dealing directly with the commands.
A study by civilian specialists in business management confirmed the wisdom
of reducing the number of staff officers to a comparative few and making them
deputies who could act in the name of the Air Force Chief of Staff. Initially, the
new Air Staff consisted of Deputy Chiefs of Staff for Materiel, for Operations,
and for Personnel and Administration, along with the Air Comptroller. The
comptroller's functional areas embraced cost control, statistical control, the
budget, and program analysis. The title of personnel and administration defined
that deputy's areas of responsibility; but operations included such diverse subjects as communications, guided missiles, intelligence, training, and requirements, as well as the obvious ones of plans and operations. Besides supply, procurement, and research and development, materiel dealt with atomic weapons,
installations, and industrial planning. The new Air Force made a conscious effort to limit the size of the special staff, which handled technical matters or
problems of acute but probably temporary importance, although retaining the
Air Board and the office of Air Inspector. Proponents of the new system insisted it reflected the principle that "the organization shall be fitted to the job, rather
than the job to the organization," a slogan that concealed the arbitrary, almost
capricious, assignment of responsibilities to the various staff sections, espe-

401

cially the office of Deputy Chief of Staff for Operations.[2] Consequently, the organization of the Air Staff began to change almost from its inception, a process that has continued over the decades.

A major scandal, especially shocking because it involved a valued associate of General of the Army Henry H. Arnold, helped determine the composition of the office of the Inspector General, as the Air Inspector came to be called. Incorporated in that section of the special staff was an Office of Special Investigations to keep watch over the loyalty and conduct of servicemen and civilian employees. A postwar investigation of wartime contracting revealed that Lt. Gen. Bennett E. Meyers, the officer responsible for speeding the B–29 into combat, had created a bogus company, granted it wartime contracts for work that was never done, and pocketed the money. For his breach of trust, Meyers was dismissed from the service, and for persuading a witness to commit perjury during a Senate investigation, he received a sentence of three to five years in a federal prison. This incident, which became national news in the fall of 1947, persuaded Symington to establish an agency to prevent similar instances of fraud or impropriety within the Air Force and its civilian work force. For a chief of the investigative agency, he turned to J. Edgar Hoover, Director of the Federal Bureau of Investigation, obtaining the services of Joseph F. Carroll, one of Hoover's assistants, who had been assigned as an investigator for Symington's surplus property office. Carroll assumed the rank of colonel and became the first director of the new Office of Special Investigations.

The three major combat commands inherited from the Army Air Forces—the Strategic Air Command, Tactical Air Command, and Air Defense Command—changed once the Air Force gained its independence from the Army. The Strategic Air Command emerged as the most important of the three since it was responsible for deterrence and, should deterrence fail, for waging atomic warfare. Indeed, its emergence began during the debate on President Harry S. Truman's plan for defense reorganization, before there was an Air Force, when the overseas deployment of B–29s, even though the aircraft were incapable of dropping nuclear bombs, seemed important to Army airmen, not only for training but also to dramatize the validity of their claim to independence. The Pincher plan, the earliest concept for an atomic war issued by the Joint Chiefs of Staff, acknowledged the importance of the Strategic Air Command; but the Army Air Forces, in its Makefast war plan, admitted that it lacked the bombs and targeting data to fight the kind of war outlined in the Pincher document. By late 1947, after the Air Force had become independent of the Army, the Strategic Plans Committee of the Joint Chiefs of Staff was working on Broiler, a concept that called for using atomic bombs to destroy industrial and governmental centers in the event of war with the Soviet Union. In May of the following year, the Joint Chiefs approved, as a guide for planning by the individual services, an emergency war plan called Halfmoon that was based on the belief that atomic attacks on cities could compensate for the Soviet Union's advantage in man-

Gen. George C. Kenney (left), Commanding General of Strategic Air
Command, and Maj. Gen. Clements McMullen, Deputy Commander.

power. Adhering to this concept, the Air Force produced Harrow, a plan that tar-
geted atomic weapons against specific cities in the Soviet Union. The plan was
unrealistic, however, since it failed to reflect either the small size of the atomic
stockpile or the operational status of the Strategic Air Command, which could
not have delivered the weapons called for in the plan.

Even if the war plans of 1947 had been less ambitious or had an adequate
number of atomic bombs been available to conduct extensive attacks, the
Strategic Air Command was poorly prepared for combat. The bombardment
squadrons suffered the consequences of an ill-conceived plan inaugurated by
Maj. Gen. Clements McMullen, the organization's deputy commander, and approved by Gen. George C. Kenney, the commander, that was intended to produce a strategic striking force in the image of the Air Corps of the 1930s.
According to their theory, the Strategic Air Command would be a small outfit
operated almost exclusively by pilots who had "cross-trained" for other flying
duties, like navigation, and also doubled as staff officers. Unfortunately, the
cycle of training and retraining produced versatile individuals rather than efficient crews, and the burden of carrying out, seemingly at random, any assignment in any airplane while also struggling with logistics, engineering, or administration sorely tested the morale of the officers serving in the command.

Despite the turmoil caused by cross-training and the treatment of group or
wing staff assignments as additional duties, the Strategic Air Command enjoyed
a clear primacy within the Air Force. As its prestige rose, that of tactical aviation declined. Evidence of the change in relative status came on December 1,
1948, when the Air Force established the Continental Air Command, under Lt.
Gen. George E. Stratemeyer, to serve as a coordinating agency for tactical aviation, air defense, and the training of the Air National Guard and Air Force

Reserve. During World War II, Stratemeyer had been assigned to the China-Burma-India Theater, where at one time he reported simultaneously to a half-dozen officers of three different nationalities, a haphazard arrangement that foreshadowed the arbitrary grouping of missions that characterized the Continental Air Command. The principal attraction of the new command was its promise of economy in a time of tight budgets. As Stratemeyer acknowledged after assuming command, the Air Force could not afford separate organizations, fully manned and equipped, to fly tactical support missions for the Army, provide air defense, and train the reserve components. Since the Air Force was responsible for the three missions, the only way to carry them out within the budget approved by Congress was to use, insofar as possible, the same men and aircraft for all three.

As head of the Continental Air Command, Stratemeyer controlled the resources of the Tactical Air Command and the Air Defense Command, thus creating a reservoir of men and aircraft that he could employ as circumstances dictated. He formed six air forces, one in each army area (as the old corps areas were now known), and made the commanders responsible for the proficiency of the assigned Air Force, Air National Guard, and Air Force Reserve units. He retained authority over all the active duty squadrons assigned to the Continental Air Command and, in theory at least, could shift them as required to either the Air Defense Command or the Tactical Air Command, which existed as headquarters. In actual practice, the threat of a Soviet air attack meant that a certain number of fighter squadrons had to stand by to defend the nation and therefore were not available for tactical missions. Otherwise, the fighter, light bombers, and tactical airlift units remained in the United States, ready for deployment overseas or participation in exercises with the Army. For a joint exercise, the Continental Air Command pulled together an appropriate number of squadrons, returning them to normal duties when the exercise ended, but the same units rarely worked together in successive maneuvers. The rotation of Air Force units from the United States to overseas and from routine assignments training the reserve to exercises with the Army disrupted continuity, so that air and ground units could not develop the kind of teamwork characteristic of World War II. The badly flawed arrangement lasted until November 1950 when the Truman administration, fighting a war in Korea, began spending more for defense and separate organizations for air defense and tactical aviation again became feasible. The Tactical Air Command and Air Defense Command regained their old status independent of the Continental Air Command, which continued to administer the reserve components until it was disbanded in 1968.

The other major commands with roots in the Army Air Forces emerged from the transition to independence more or less intact. The Air Materiel Command, Air Training Command, and Air Proving Ground Command continued to operate as they had under the postwar Army Air Forces. Located at Eglin Air Force Base, Florida, the Air Proving Ground Command tested armaments, aircraft, and

Maxwell Field, Alabama, 1944.

tactics under conditions of simulated combat. The Air Training Command did exactly what the name implied, focusing as it had since its inception during World War II on teaching individual skills ranging from flying and navigation to engine maintenance and equipment repair. Established in 1946, the Air University absorbed and expanded the work of the postwar Army Air Forces School. This major command, a descendant of the Air Corps Tactical School, developed doctrine, concepts, and long-range objectives, besides providing professional education for officers, who might progress through a succession of schools as they advanced in rank and responsibilities. The mission of the Air University embraced the coordination of the courses taught in all Air Force schools, including those operated by the Air Training Command. Under the general guidance of the Air University (and after April 1950 under its direct control), the Air Force Institute of Technology concentrated on various aspects of engineering. The Air University retained responsibility for the Air War College, Air Command and Staff School, and Special Staff School and took over the supervision of the School of Aviation Medicine at Randolph Air Force Base, Texas.

While thus adopting an organizational structure suited to the needs of independence, the Air Force continued to absorb the support and housekeeping functions provided by the Army Service Forces, a transition begun during World War II. Adhering to a deadline set by Secretary of Defense Forrestal, the Air Force completed the process within two years of separating from the Army. At the end of that time, airmen had replaced soldiers in maintaining records; were operating every aspect of the bases taken over from the Army Air Forces, including the base exchanges; and were serving on promotion and decoration boards.

The support and housekeeping units transferred from the Army included large numbers of blacks, who, with little prospect of more interesting or useful duty, had provided a source of uniformed labor for the racially segregated service. Also incorporated in the new Air Force was the 332d Fighter Group, commanded by Col. Benjamin O. Davis, Jr., a graduate of West Point, who learned to fly at Tuskegee Army Airfield and fought in World War II. This group was composed exclusively of blacks, as had been required by War Department directives, and no one—pilot, mechanic, or clerk—had any real chance for transfer or advancement. The policy of racial segregation thus demonstrated that it was inefficient as well as unjust, for it required the duplication of facilities and units, curtailed assignments, and not only reduced opportunities for blacks but also undermined their morale.

A faction within the Air Force therefore urged that race no longer be a consideration in training, assignment, or promotion. The principal advocate of change was Col. Noel F. Parrish, a white officer who had commanded the training detachment for blacks at the Tuskegee Army Airfield during the war. Some senior officers dismissed Parrish as a kind of fanatic, but a number of others were recommending the same policy, among them Lt. Gen. Idwal H. Edwards, the Deputy Chief of Staff for Personnel, and two of his fellow members of the Air Board, Lt. Gen. Jimmy Doolittle and Maj. Gen. Follett Bradley, both recently retired. Confident that racial segregation could not survive, Edwards quietly began laying plans for the racial integration of the Air Force, convincing those leaders who had formerly supported segregation, as reflecting a national consensus, that public opinion and national policy were about to change. As a result, when President Truman in July 1948 issued an executive order that in effect integrated the races throughout the armed forces, the Air Force was already moving toward that goal. Secretary of the Air Force Symington, a long-time proponent of racial integration, placed Assistant Secretary Zuckert in charge of compliance with the Presidential directive. The "unbunching" of members of exclusively black units and their reassignment throughout the Air Force proceeded smoothly, largely because of the preparations made by General Edwards and the close supervision exercised by Col. Jack Marr, his deputy for the project.

To symbolize its separation from the Army, the Air Force adopted for its officers and enlisted men a blue uniform inspired by that of the Royal Air Force. Unfortunately, too few were on hand to outfit everyone simultaneously, and as a result Army khaki or olive drab and even the officer's "pinks and greens" continued to be worn as late as 1950. During this time of transition, an enlisted clerk, who transferred from an Army finance office to the Air Force counterpart, might work at the same desk and continue to wear the same uniform, merely putting on different insignia.

Part of the legacy of the Army Air Forces was an interest in science and its application to aerial warfare. In 1944 General Arnold asked his old acquaintance Theodore von Kármán to follow the advancing Allied armies and direct a survey of Germany's wartime accomplishments in aeronautical science. The result, entitled *Where We Stand*, compared German and American progress and

Theodore von Kármán, Chairman, Scientific Advisory Group, November 1944–March 1946, and Chairman, Scientific Advisory Board, March 1946–December 1954.

inspired Arnold, who at the time was recovering from a heart attack, to telephone from his sickbed and ask for a more detailed forecast of the future of aerial warfare. Von Kármán and his colleagues set to work in the fall of 1945 and produced thirty-three monographs, bearing the collective title *Toward New Horizons*, which became available in a preliminary form by the end of the year. The introductory volume, *Science, The Key to Air Supremacy*, addressed the increasing importance of science and technology as an era of rockets and jet aircraft dawned; the other thirty-two dealt with specific areas of research and development. According to von Kármán's own appraisal, the thirty-three volumes formed "the first exhaustive report of its kind in the history of the American military" and "definitely made the point that the Air Force was the major defense arm of the nation and that defense was clearly dependent on a continuous input of technological and scientific progress."[3] Among other recommendations, he and his team called for the development of supersonic aircraft and guided missiles and for close cooperation between the air arm and the nation's scientists.

During his study of wartime aviation development in Germany, resulting in *Where We Stand*, von Kármán not only headed the investigative group but served as the chief of the Scientific Advisory Group, which reported directly to General Arnold. When von Kármán went to Europe, a cadre of scientists remained behind, available to Arnold for consultation. After his return, the entire group set to work on *Toward New Horizons*. When this project was finished, the Scientific Advisory Group joined in the general demobilization, meeting for the last time in February 1946.

The organization was soon revived, however, as the Scientific Advisory Board, again under von Kármán's leadership. One of the recommendations set forth in *Toward New Horizons* called for the establishment of a panel of distinguished scientists, assisted by a full-time clerical and administrative staff, that could provide the air arm with "a cross section of the nation's scientific thought." Maj. Gen. Curtis E. LeMay, at the time the Deputy Chief of Air Staff,

Research and Development, in the headquarters of the Army Air Forces, strongly supported this proposal, and the new Scientific Advisory Board convened for the first time in June 1946. Instead of reporting directly to General Spaatz, the new commanding general, as the Scientific Advisory Group had to his predecessor, the board advised LeMay, the Air Staff officer responsible for research and development. After the Air Force was established, the reorganization of the Air Staff eliminated the office of Deputy Chief of Air Staff, Research and Development, and entrusted the function to the head of a directorate under the Deputy Chief of Staff, Materiel. Rather than see the Scientific Advisory Board buried at this lower level of the staff hierarchy, General Spaatz accepted the recommendations of von Kármán and Maj. Gen. Laurence C. Craigie, the new Director of Research and Development, and had the board report directly to the Chief of Staff.

In another attempt to gain access to the nation's leading scientists, General Arnold, before his retirement, proposed investing some $10 million from the Air Forces procurement budget in a civilian organization where engineers and scientists could study the role of air forces in modern war. In March 1946, the Air Materiel Command let the first contract to the new agency, Project Rand (its title a contraction of research and development), which was a part of Douglas Aircraft. According to General LeMay, the Deputy Chief of Staff, Research and Development, Rand provided "a continuing program of scientific study and research on the subject of air warfare with the purpose of recommending to the Air Force preferred methods, techniques, and instrumentalities for this purpose."[4] Because its ties to a particular aircraft manufacturer, Douglas, represented a potential source of embarrassment, Rand reconstituted itself as an independent, nonprofit corporation, with the Air Force as its principal customer.

The creation of the Scientific Advisory Board and the launching of Project Rand were attempts to go outside the air arm and draw on the skills and wisdom of the nation's most prominent engineers and scientists. To take full advantage of this talent, the new Air Force required a sound internal organization for research and development. One of the first questions to arise after separation from the Army and reorganization of the Air Staff was whether a full-fledged deputy chief of staff or a less prestigious director should deal with research and development. This was part of a larger issue affecting the composition and autonomy of the Air Materiel Command, which was responsible for supply, maintenance, and procurement and for research and development as well. The debate was between those who believed that Air Force headquarters should exercise closer supervision over the command and those who believed it should not and between those who believed that logistics and research and development were incompatible in the same agency and those who believed those functions belonged together.

Lt. Gen. Benjamin W. Chidlaw, who headed the Air Materiel Command, saw no need for change. He advocated a strong program of research and develop-

General Hoyt S. Vandenberg,
Air Force Chief of Staff,
April 1948–June 1953.

ment and cooperated closely with the Scientific Advisory Board, which provided all the guidance he thought he needed in this field. His own experience led him to join other officers with a similar background in opposing both closer supervision from Air Force headquarters and the loss of control over research and development, which he viewed as the beginning of a unified process that included procurement, maintenance, and supply. Even though territorial imperative may have played a large part in shaping their attitudes, Chidlaw and his like-minded fellow officers remained convinced that the Air Materiel Command in its present form was logically organized and efficient.

At Air Force headquarters, however, the leadership had become convinced that the command was slighting research and development in carrying out its several duties. From the perspective of the Pentagon, the machinery for research and development seemed in need of a complete overhaul. In the spring of 1949, Gen. Hoyt S. Vandenberg, who had succeeded General Spaatz as Chief of Staff on April 30, 1948, asked the Scientific Advisory Board to propose an "ultimate plan" for organizing Air Force research and development. A committee headed by Louis N. Ridenour, a physicist and the dean of the graduate school of the University of Illinois, accepted the assignment and recommended "the establishment of a Research and Development Command separate from the Materiel Command" and a reorganization of the Air Staff to include a deputy chief of staff to represent research and development.[5] Although Vandenberg acknowledged that the panel of engineers and scientists had offered a sound solution, he did not believe that Ridenour's group, of which retired General Jimmy Doolittle was the only truly military member, had the prestige or authority necessary to put the recommendation into effect. For this sensitive task, Maj. Gen. Muir S. Fairchild, the Vice Chief of Staff, turned to the Air University and a board of officers headed by Maj. Gen. Orvil A. Anderson. From the deliberations of the Anderson committee emerged the Air Research and Development Command, which would conduct the never-ending quest for new and improved weapons and equipment, leaving the work of procurement, maintenance, and supply in the hands of the Air Materiel Command. Although not an ideal solution—a further realignment of research and development and logistics activities would prove necessary in a dozen years—the reform adopted in January 1950 represented an improvement over the structure inherited from the Army Air Forces.

Even as it adjusted its organization for research and development, the Air Force acquired several new jet aircraft, the fruits of development projects already completed. The jet turbine had several advantages over piston engines. It was able to burn a fuel similar to kerosene, which was cheaper than the highly refined and leaded 100-octane gasoline required by the latest piston engines; it was simpler to maintain than the complicated twin-row radial engine, which was the most powerful piston engine ever built; and it avoided the inevitable loss of efficiency experienced by the propellers of that era when aircraft speed exceeded 450 miles per hour. Some of the newer jets incorporated the results of wartime German research that von Kármán and his colleagues had made available to American engineers. Perhaps the most important of these innovations from the standpoint of aerodynamics was the sweptwing, which delayed the buildup of drag as aircraft approached the speed of sound. Two new aircraft incorporated this feature, the Boeing B–47 bomber and the North American F–86 fighter. (Since June 1948, the designation of "F" for fighter had replaced "P" for pursuit.) The six-engine B–47 also contained some uniquely American ideas; the jet engines were slung in pods from the German-developed sweptwing to minimize the danger of structural damage in the event of fire and to serve as a mass balance to prevent the thin wing from twisting as it flexed during high-speed flight. Another new jet, the Republic F–84 Thunderjet, entered service as a straight-wing fighter-bomber but was redesigned into a radically different sweptwing aircraft, the F–84F Thunderstreak.

Along with the Boeing B–52, an eight-engine, sweptwing bomber that was still on the drawing board, the F–86 Sabrejet, the B–47 Stratojet, and the F–84F were the aircraft of the future, the result of merging the aerodynamic developments of Hitler's Germany with improved, American-built jet engines. Although more powerful and reliable than the engines that had powered the first generation of jets like the American Lockheed P–80 (now the F–80), the latest turbines had a high rate of fuel consumption compared to piston types, accelerated less swiftly than the combination of piston engine and constant-speed, variable-pitch propeller, and developed thrust enough for large aircraft only if several were used—six, for example, in the B–47 with a weight comparable to the four-engine B–29, or eight in the projected B–52, which would be a much heavier bomber.

The older aircraft serving alongside the new jets included the F–80, the first operational American jet fighter; the B–29, designed for World War II; the B–50, an improved version of B–29; and the B–36, an intercontinental bomber that had begun taking shape on the drawing board in 1940, when the German conquest

Boeing B–47 Stratojet, here shown in a reconnaissance version.

of the British Isles seemed possible. Since the United Kingdom survived to provide airfields for B–17s and B–24s, the propeller-driven B–36 was not needed during the war, and the first of the huge bombers, which had six 3,500-horsepower pusher engines and when empty weighed twice as much as a B–29, did not take to the air until 1946. Three years passed before the B–36, with the addition of four jet engines mounted in pods beneath the wings, two engines per pod, could attain the speed demanded of a first-line bomber. The Air Force's first jet light bomber, which doubled as a reconnaissance craft, the North American B–45 Tornado, was designed before engineers fully appreciated the importance of the sweptwing. At that time, there were no jet transports, for the thirst of the jet engines of the late 1940s made it impossible to strike a satisfactory balance between the weight of fuel and cargo capacity.

North American
B–45 Tornado.

A KB–29 fuels an F–84 using the probe-and-drogue method (above); a KB–29 pumps fuel to another B–29 using the flying boom (below).

To compensate for the ravenous fuel consumption of the early jets, the Air Force began using a British-developed system of aerial refueling, an admittedly crude method that required the crew of the bomber taking on fuel to use a grapnel to capture a hose trailing from the tanker and insert the nozzle in a filler pipe. This technique evolved into the so-called probe-and-drogue method, used mainly for fighters, in which a tanker trailed one or more hoses, each terminating in a basket-like receptacle. When taking on fuel, the pilot maneuvered to insert a pipe fixed to the aircraft into the center of the basket. Once contact had been made, the fuel began flowing from the tanker, usually a modified B–29, into the tanks of the fighter. Although a number of its aircraft used the probe-and-drogue method, the Air Force preferred the American-devised flying boom, a telescoping tube fitted with two small vanes for stability that is steered from a tail compartment in the tanker into a receiver in the other aircraft.

Although acquiring newly developed aircraft and devising techniques for their use, the Air Force could not buy them in the numbers its leaders considered necessary. Even before the passage of the National Security Act of 1947, Spaatz and Symington had called for expansion to 70 groups, a goal first established by the Army Air Forces in the summer of 1945, but an objective that collided with President Truman's economic policy. The fear of a postwar depression had given way by 1948 to concern over inflation, which the Chief Executive proposed to control by cutting federal spending, without reducing overall tax revenue, and applying the surplus thus generated to the federal debt, which as a result of the war had increased more than fourfold from $56 billion at the time of Pearl Harbor to $252 billion by December 1945. Two factors jeopardized Truman's plan—the intent of congressional Republicans to make high taxes an issue in the approaching Presidential election and the spiraling cost of modern weapons. For example, the workhorse bomber of World War II, the mass-produced B–17, cost an average of $218,000; whereas the few B–36s that had entered service carried a price tag of $3.6 million each. Although the iron curtain had already descended across eastern Europe and communist forces were overrunning China, the President continued to insist on holding new defense expenditures to about $10 billion during fiscal year 1949. He was concerned that the economic consequences of a sudden expansion of the armed forces, especially the purchase of massive quantities of expensive new equipment, would undermine his plan for controlling inflation.

Whatever his concern about high cost of aircraft, Truman could not ignore air power. The wartime glamour of aerial warfare still lingered in the public consciousness, as did an appreciation of the powerful contribution that military aviation had made to victory over the Axis, and congressional support for the new Air Force was strong. The attitude on Capitol Hill resulted, to a great extent, from Secretary Symington's remarkable skill at pleading the case for air power before the various senators and representatives and the voters who elected them. Under conflicting pressures to spend on aircraft and to economize, Truman in September 1947 convened the Air Policy Commission under Thomas K. Finletter, an attorney and wartime special assistant to the Secretary of State, to investigate the question of investing in air power. Three of the panel's other members—Palmer Hoyt, a newspaper publisher; John McCone, an engineer and businessman; and Arthur D. Whiteside, a specialist in investments—shared Finletter's lack of practical experience in aviation. Only George P. Baker, an economist who had served for two years on the Civil Aeronautics Board, had any acquaintance with the subject, and his dealt with its commercial aspects.

The Finletter commission heard more than 150 witnesses in some 200 sessions. Symington, Spaatz, and other representatives of the Air Force testified to the decisiveness of land-based bombers against Japan and Germany and maintained that the turbulent postwar world required that the Air Force be composed of 70 combat groups. Navy witnesses disputed the Air Force version of World War II, citing the role of the fast carrier task forces in the war against Japan and emphasizing the importance of retaining control of the seas, and argued that it was folly to rely in the future on a single weapon, the strategic bomber. Forrestal,

413

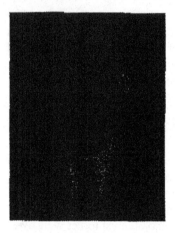

Thomas K. Finletter, head of the Air Policy Commission and Secretary of the Air Force, April 1950–January 1953.

who hoped to achieve a balance among the services and avoid an expansion of the Air Force at the expense of the others, testified accordingly, warning that the nature of the next war defied prediction and might turn out to be a conflict in which land-based air power would prove far less effective than it had in World War II. In addition, he echoed President Truman's warning of the possibly dangerous economic consequences of intemperate investment in armaments. The commission sided with the Air Force instead of with Forrestal, recommending an expansion to 70 groups. Finletter and his colleagues also favored a modernization of naval aviation, although they were more assertive in endorsing the 70-group Air Force. While the President's panel was arriving at these conclusions, a Congressional Aviation Policy Board, headed by Senator Owen Brewster, a Republican from Maine, was going over the same subject as the Finletter commission, and hearing many of the same witnesses; it also recommended expansion of the Air Force to 70 groups. President Truman, however, remained unconvinced of the need for 70 groups. He did not release the Finletter report until after he submitted his fiscal 1949 budget in January 1948 and was content to point out that more than $5 billion, about half of the money he was seeking for national defense during the coming fiscal year, would be spent on the various aspects of aviation in the armed forces, including training, manpower, and facilities, as well as aircraft procurement.

There the subject rested until February 1948, when the communist faction seized power in Czechoslovakia, excluding from the government those democratic elements that had thus far survived. On March 5, Gen. Lucius D. Clay, U.S. Military Governor in Germany, sent a message to Washington in which he revised his earlier estimate that war between the United States and the Soviet Union was "unlikely for at least ten years" and warned of "a subtle change in Soviet attitudes which I cannot define but which now gives me the feeling that it may come with dramatic suddenness."[6] This warning did not, it was later revealed, reflect Clay's estimate of the situation in Europe; instead, the general was trying to help the armed forces, especially the Army, rally political support for additional appropriations.

The message from Clay, along with the communist coup in Czechoslovakia and the first signs of interference with Western access to Berlin, which was divided into American, British, French, and Soviet sectors even though it lay inside the Soviet occupation zone of Germany, prompted the administration to ask Congress for a supplemental appropriations bill that would divide slightly more than $3 billion among the armed forces. The additional money would strengthen the Army and Navy while at the same time increasing the Air Force from 48 to 55 groups. Congress was thus being asked to consider two separate bills to fund the nation's defense during fiscal 1949, the supplemental appropriations legislation introduced in March and the regular request received in January. In the hope of simplifying the deliberations, Forrestal persuaded Congress to combine all the funds for aircraft procurement contained in the two requests (a total of about $1.5 billion, $725 million in the March submission and the rest in the January proposal) and consider this amount separately as an aircraft procurement bill supplemental to the legislation submitted in January.

During the hearings on the supplemental appropriations bill introduced in March, Symington made a determined effort to get the money for an Air Force of 70 combat groups. After Forrestal had warned that American weakness might encourage the ambitions of Joseph Stalin, the Soviet dictator, just as French and British indecision in the late 1930s had whetted Hitler's appetite for conquest, Secretary of the Army Kenneth C. Royall asked, in effect, for a balanced strengthening of all the armed forces, and spokesmen for the Navy requested an infusion of manpower. Symington then made his appeal, citing the reports of the Finletter and Brewster panels, as he called for funding the full 70 groups. Not even the entire $3 billion, he declared, could give the nation the kind of Air Force that it needed, but for the present he would accept $850 million from the supplemental request as an initial investment in American air power. He warned the Secretary of Defense, "The press, Congress, and the people are sold on this Air Force program."[7] Any rearmament effort that did not begin with a 70-group Air Force could not be adopted, Symington said, and to ignore this was to invite Congress to defy the administration and enact a plan of its own.

Secretary of Defense Forrestal, impressed by Symington's warning, went to the White House and obtained what he interpreted as Presidential approval to add $500 million to the $3 billion supplemental request (from which $725 million had been shifted to the aircraft procurement bill). The additional $500 million would, among other things, enable the Air Force to expand to 66 groups, if not to the full 70, largely by retrieving aircraft from storage and refurbishing them. The prospect of $3.5 billion added to the defense appropriation for fiscal 1949 sharpened the administration's fears of deficit financing and rampant inflation, causing Truman to substitute only about $159 million for the extra $500 million that Forrestal thought he had been promised.

415

Symington was mistaken if he truly expected Congress to seize the initiative, make the Air Force the foundation for rearmament, and compel President Truman to expand the service to 70 groups. The legislative branch proved as cautious as the executive in its approach to economics. The total supplemental appropriations for the Department of Defense finally equaled the $3 billion Truman initially requested in March plus the $159 million additional he agreed to (less the $725 million being considered separately as aircraft procurement), and Congress approved only that amount. In passing the basic defense appropriations bill submitted by the administration in January 1948, the legislators reached a compromise with Forrestal and the President that involved trimming some nonoperational programs. Only in dealing with aircraft procurement did Congress show signs of behaving as Symington had predicted, voting $822 million more than the President had sought. This additional money, which Representative Carl Vinson, a Democrat from Georgia, described as a down payment on a 70-group Air Force, represented a gesture of support rather than a genuine investment, for the aircraft procurement bill specified that the President would have the final word on spending the extra funds. When he signed the bill into law, Truman declared that he would not spend any money that he had not requested, thus holding expenditures for aircraft for all the services to about $1.5 billion.

In spite of the increasing tension as the Soviet Union and its satellites began waging a cold war against the Western democracies, President Truman hoped to avoid the kind of panicky spending on rearmament that might disrupt the American economy. He persuaded Congress to revive the Selective Service System, an expensive program although less so than a large standing army, and obtained supplemental appropriations for fiscal 1949, but it was his withholding of the additional funds for new aircraft that demonstrated the real priorities of the Truman administration. The soundness of the economy took precedence over rearmament whenever a choice had to be made. After the November 1948 election returned Truman to office in apparent vindication of his policies, he continued to concentrate on preventing inflation, in part by trying to keep defense expenditures below $15 billion annually. In theory, the Air Force share of such an amount, which Forrestal intended to divide as equally as possible among the services, would maintain 55 groups; in reality, further cuts in the appropriations enacted for fiscal 1950 and proposed for fiscal 1951 held the total strength to 48 groups.

During the struggle over money, Secretary Forrestal had to insert himself into the budget process, beginning with the supplemental appropriations bill for fiscal year 1949. However, the National Security Act, and his own inclination, restricted him to the role of a negotiator, trying to persuade the Army, Navy, and Air Force to accept what he considered a balanced division of funds within the total that the President was willing to request from Congress. In this process his chief adversary was Secretary of the Air Force Symington, who maintained that any nearly equal distribution worked to the disadvantage of his department, which, because of the decisive effect of air power, deserved the lion's share.

A Miltary Air Transport Service C–74 at Kelly AFB, Texas, receiving
cargo for Alaska (above); passengers from three services wait
at the Wright-Patterson AFB, Ohio, terminal (below).

Despite the divisive nature of the battle for funds, Forrestal claimed one victory for the principle of unification within a single department of defense—the
consolidation of the Air Force Air Transport Command with the Naval Air
Transport Service. He assigned a high priority to the project, which came to
fruition on June 1, 1948, when 40 transports from the Navy joined 600 from the
Air Force to form the Military Air Transport Service, which also included the
weather and rescue components of the Air Force. The new command was responsible to the Secretary of Defense, who made the Air Force his executive

agent. The first commander of the Military Air Transport Service was Air Force Maj. Gen. Laurence S. Kuter, whose vice commander was a naval officer, Rear Adm. John P. Whitney. Although Forrestal intended that naval officers be eligible to command the transport service, none ever did.

Except for the creation of the Military Air Transport Service, and even there the Navy retained a few transports for its own use, Forrestal had little success in getting the services to apportion missions among themselves, let alone agree to merge similar functions. In the tense climate following the communist overthrow of the Czech government and Clay's war warning, even as President Truman was seeking supplemental appropriations for national defense, Forrestal in March 1948 convened the Joint Chiefs of Staff—General Spaatz, Adm. Louis E. Denfeld, and Gen. Omar N. Bradley—at Key West, Florida, to define more clearly the functions of the armed forces. The agreements reached at Key West and in a subsequent meeting at Washington specified that the Army was responsible for land warfare; the Navy for operations at sea; the Marine Corps for amphibious operations; and the Air Force for air operations, including strategic air warfare. Each service, moreover, had collateral responsibilities to provide the maximum assistance to the others in accomplishing overall military objectives. The functions of naval aviation in support of sea warfare were easily defined, but the Joint Chiefs could not reach a consensus on the Navy's responsibility for assisting the Air Force in strategic air operations. In the absence of such an agreement, the Navy pursued its plans to create a carrier-based atomic strike force. For the naval leadership this seemed a logical evolution from the conventionally armed carrier task forces of World War II, but the leaders of the Air Force saw it as a wasteful attempt to duplicate the mission of the Strategic Air Command. The Key West agreements replaced Executive Order 9877, which had initially delineated responsibilities after the creation of the Air Force. President Truman approved the agreements on April 21, 1948, with the title "Functions of the Armed Forces and the Joint Chiefs of Staff." Since the issue of what the Air Force perceived as the Navy's encroachment on its atomic monopoly had not been resolved, bickering over the strategic air mission would continue.

In August 1948, just four months after the meeting at Key West, Forrestal again conferred with the Joint Chiefs of Staff, including General Vandenberg, who had replaced Spaatz as Air Force Chief of Staff at the end of April. The site of the meeting was the Naval War College at Newport, Rhode Island, and the main topic was the atomic mission. At the time, only the Strategic Air Command of the Air Force, a specified command responsible to the Joint Chiefs, had access to the atomic bomb and flew the kind of aircraft that could drop it. The Navy, however, planned to build a huge aircraft carrier and already was strengthening the decks of the two largest carriers already in service and acquiring or modifying twin-engine bombers to carry atomic weapons. The immediate issue was whether the Air Force should act as executive agent of the Joint Chiefs in the operation of the Armed Forces Special Weapons Project, an

Attendees at the Newport, Rhode Island, conference, August 20–22, 1948
(left to right): Lt. Gen. Lauris Norstad, USAF, Gen. Hoyt Vandenberg,
USAF, Lt. Gen. Albert Wedemeyer, USA, Gen. Omar Bradley, USA,
Defense Secretary James Forrestal, Adm. Louis Denfeld, USN, Vice
Adm. Arthur Radford, USN, and Maj. Gen. Alfred Gruenther, USA.

interservice organization that handled and assembled nuclear bombs released to
it by the Atomic Energy Commission. Since the meeting at Key West, Air Force
leaders had been campaigning to have their service appointed executive agent
because its war plan depended on nuclear bombs. The Navy opposed this idea,
fearing that the Air Force, as executive agent, would deprive the Navy of nuclear
weapons after naval aviation had developed the means of delivering them. At
Newport, Forrestal tried to effect a compromise: in return for assurance that it
would share in the nuclear mission, the Navy agreed that the Air Force, at least
temporarily, would serve as executive agent for the special weapons project.
The upshot of the meeting was that the Air Force, although it continued to bear
primary responsibility for strategic aerial warfare, had to give the Navy access
to nuclear bombs and allow it to participate in the strategic air operations contained in the joint war plans.

Another result of the Newport conference was the establishment of the
Weapons Systems Evaluation Group to provide the Joint Chiefs of Staff with
factual data on the performance and usefulness of various weapons. At the time
the evaluation group began functioning, Secretary Forrestal had strong doubts
that the Strategic Air Command could actually cripple the Soviet Union, con-

sidering the available bombs, bases, and aircraft. Indeed, he predicted that, in any such conflict, naval forces would have to control the seas so that ground forces could seize and defend advance airfields close enough to the Soviet heartland to permit air power to attack "in a decisive, and I repeat decisive, manner."[8] Little wonder that the first assignment handed the Weapons Systems Evaluation Group was a technical analysis of a strategic bombing campaign against the Soviet Union.

By the time the group's report appeared in the spring of 1949, Forrestal was dead. He left office at the end of March of that year, in ill health and discouraged by his inability to deal any longer with the often conflicting military and political demands on the Secretary of Defense. After suffering a nervous breakdown, he was undergoing psychiatric treatment at the Bethesda Naval Hospital in Maryland when he jumped to his death from a window.

The findings of the Weapons Systems Evaluation Group provided the data for a briefing on the effectiveness of nuclear weapons given in January 1950 to President Truman and Secretary of Defense Louis A. Johnson, Forrestal's successor. The briefing officer and director of the evaluation group, Army Lt. Gen. John E. Hull, began by conceding that "logistical deficiencies and expected bomber attrition" would "preclude an offensive on the scale currently contemplated" in the basic war plan.[9] The logistical problems referred to were a lack of overseas bases, the current status of aerial refueling technique, inadequate stockpiles of fuel overseas, and a shortage of airlift to supply the strike forces. The anticipated losses among the bombers, which could vary from thirty to fifty percent, would result, the group concluded, from a lack of recent intelligence on Soviet defenses and insufficient training in taking evasive action over heavily defended targets. Because of the probable attrition, the evaluation group recommended the exclusive use of atomic bombs, enabling the aircraft that did get through to inflict the greatest possible damage. The predicted attrition rate among bombers did not vary according to type, but the long range of the B-36 gave it a distinct advantage over the B-29 and B-50, which required either midair refueling or advance bases. When the session ended, according to an eyewitness, Secretary Johnson smiled and declared that the B-36 had been vindicated, but the President scowled, insisting that the briefing had proved just the opposite.

That the two men, rather than focusing on the generally pessimistic message of the briefing, concentrated on the B-36 bomber, a peripheral issue, reflected the position the B-36 had come to occupy during the previous year as a symbol not only of strategic aerial warfare but of the rivalry between the Air Force and Navy over that mission. The controversy erupted following the cancellation of the contract for the aircraft carrier *United States*, which the Navy's leaders envisaged as the key to their future atomic strike force. The decision to cancel, endorsed by President Truman, traced its origins to a review of the defense budget for fiscal 1950 conducted by Secretary Johnson shortly after taking office.

420

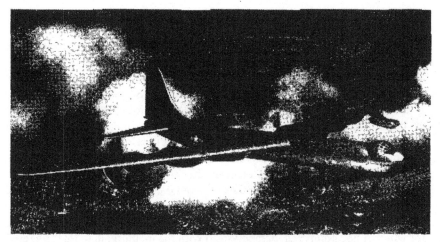

Consolidated B–36 Peacemaker over Ft. Worth,
Texas, with Carswell AFB in the background.

The cost of the carrier—$188 million, of which $43 million appeared in the
budget that was undergoing review—caught Johnson's attention, prompting
him to ask the Joint Chiefs of Staff for their views on the need for the costly
ship. Reflecting the competition for funds in a time of tight budgets, the Joint
Chiefs could not agree, with a sharp division emerging between the Navy and
Air Force. Of the three service chiefs, only the Chief of Naval Operations,
Admiral Denfeld, defended the warship and recommended that work continue.
The Air Force Chief of Staff, General Vandenberg, attacked the project, arguing that the carrier and its aircraft would duplicate the mission of land-based
bombers and prove more vulnerable to attack, since the aircraft carrier, unlike
bases ashore, could be shelled by surface ships, torpedoed by submarines, and
bombed by airplanes. When the cancellation was announced, Secretary of the
Navy John L. Sullivan resigned in protest, and a number of naval officers
mounted a counterattack designed to persuade the American public that the
United States had to be built.

The counterattack was directed against the B–36, for the administration by
canceling the carrier had in effect designated this land-based bomber as the
principal agent of strategic warfare, excluding the Navy from partnership in the
atomic mission. Moreover, the huge bomber seemed vulnerable on several
counts: the pace of development had been so sluggish that General Kenney of
the Strategic Air Command had once counseled scrapping the project and investing in the money in a jet-powered, long-range bomber; the aircraft was slow
and engineers had failed in their attempt to harness exhaust gases to drive a turbine and increase the engine power; Secretary of Defense Johnson, the cabinet
officer who had chosen the bomber over the aircraft carrier, had formerly been

an official of Consolidated Aircraft, the builder of the B–36; and Secretary of the Air Force Symington was a friend of the firm's president. Cedric Worth, a civilian employed in the office of the Under Secretary of the Navy, outlined the Navy's case against the B–36 in an anonymous memorandum that reached the desk of James Van Zandt, a Republican from Pennsylvania and a Navy veteran of both world wars who served on the House Armed Services Committee.

On May 25, 1949, Van Zandt introduced a resolution that a special committee be formed to investigate the allegations of wrongdoing in the procurement of the B–36. This resolution was not adopted, but the House of Representatives did authorize the Armed Services Committee to examine the comparative merits of the bomber and the aircraft carrier after considering the allegations of irregularities in the procurement of the controversial aircraft. Charges of possible political influence in the selection of the B–36 arose because representatives of the Glenn L. Martin Company, loser of the last two Air Force bomber contracts for which it had competed, helped Worth with the memorandum that triggered the investigation. The Armed Services Committee presented a report in January 1950 that absolved the administration and the Air Force of any wrongdoing in awarding the contract to Consolidated Aircraft. Rather, the investigators concluded that the Air Force had bought the bomber because it was the best aircraft available at the time, and the committee's main recommendation was the firing of Cedric Worth, whose memorandum had set the investigation in motion.

In early October, the House Armed Services Committee reconvened the hearings to compare the B–36 with the aircraft carrier that Secretary Johnson had scuttled. This second round of hearings afforded an opportunity to examine the evolving strategy of deterrence, which depended so heavily on the B–36, and had a special timeliness because of the recent defeat of the Chinese Nationalists by the communists and President Truman's announcement in late September that the Soviet Union had detonated an atomic bomb. Unlike the new Secretary of the Navy, Francis P. Matthews, who tried to explain away the controversy as a mere difference of opinion, Vice Adm. Arthur W. Radford, the Commander in Chief, Pacific Fleet, led an array of admirals, Marine Corps generals, and technical experts in unleashing a barrage of criticism against the administration for trying to economize by placing excessive reliance on strategic air power, as embodied in the B–36. The Navy's uniformed witnesses warned that their service was being starved of funds because of a misplaced faith in strategic bombardment. The naval testimony also criticized the Air Force for what was seen as its obsession with strategic air warfare and consequent neglect of tactical aviation and air defense, as shown by the emphasis on the Strategic Air Command and the consolidation of tactical aviation and air defense in the Continental Air Command.

Symington and Vandenberg testified for the Air Force in defense of strategic bombing and the B–36, stressing the role of the long-range bomber in World War II and denying that the aircraft carrier had any place in a strategy of deter-

House Armed Services Committee Chairman Carl Vinson (D-Georgia),
shakes hands with Air Force Secretary W. Stuart Symington (right) after the
committee absolved the Air Force in the B–36 procurement controversy.

rence. The recently appointed Chairman of the Joint Chiefs of Staff, General
Bradley, also testified, questioning whether the Navy had any justifiable
grounds for its bitter protest at the loss of the planned aircraft carrier. The naval
service was not unique in having projects canceled to keep the defense budget
within limits set by the administration, Bradley pointed out, arguing that the Air
Force or Army could "make the same complaint with equal or greater validity."[10] Bradley's strongest censure, however, was directed at those, obviously
within the Navy, who refused to work as a team within the Joint Chiefs of Staff
and publicly rebelled against him as chairman and against the Secretary of
Defense. Indeed, he considered this unwillingness to cooperate with the
Secretary of Defense an assault on the time-honored precept of civilian control
over the military.

In contrast to Symington, Vandenberg, and Bradley, the testimony of
Secretary Johnson was conciliatory and dealt mainly with his responsibilities for
reducing defense expenditures to meet congressionally imposed budget ceilings.
He defended, largely in terms of the potentially adverse economic impact of excessive spending, his decision to cancel the carrier and to cut the budgets of all
the services. Although he endorsed the high priority given to the procurement of

long-range bombers as being required by the President's strategy of deterrence, he suggested that judgment on the usefulness of the B–36 and other weapons be left to the newly formed Weapons Systems Evaluation Group. Finally, the Secretary of Defense echoed Bradley's call for interservice cooperation.

The second series of hearings confirmed the basic finding of the first that the B–36 was the best available bomber, but the opportunity to examine deterrence or compare land-based and carrier-based aircraft slipped away. By emphasizing the issues of teamwork and civilian control, Bradley, and to a lesser degree Johnson, had shifted the focus of the investigation from deterrence and the means of providing it to disobedience, even petulance, on the part of the dissenters. Rightly or wrongly, the committee tended to interpret the concerns expressed by the Navy's witnesses about the nation's basic strategy as the result of anger over the loss of the carrier rather than the product of a different philosophy of warfare.

Although the Air Force successfully defended its procurement of the B–36, there was no winner in the acrimonious debates of August and October 1949. The hearings, like the Key West and Newport conferences of 1948, provided a forum for arguing interservice issues but did little to resolve them. The opportunity for the admirals to present their views in public may have helped ease the Navy's grievances; otherwise, the debate over the B–36 advanced the cause of unification only because it brought a change in naval leadership. Although Secretary Johnson issued an order that no action be taken against officers who testified before the committee, the Chief of Naval Operations, Admiral Denfeld, had made administration policy an issue in his testimony, thus hurling a challenge that Secretary of the Navy Matthews could not ignore. With the approval of President Truman, Matthews removed Denfeld, replacing him with Adm. Forrest P. Sherman, a naval aviator not involved in the B–36 controversy. Earlier Sherman had teamed with Maj. Gen. Lauris Norstad of the Air Force to draft a unification bill, a sign, however faint, that a new era of cooperation might be dawning. Besides removing Denfeld, the administration reprimanded two Navy captains, John G. Crommelin and Arleigh A. Burke, who had been involved in public attacks against Secretary Johnson. Crommelin retired in 1950, but Burke remained on active duty, becoming Chief of Naval Operations, 1955–1961.

The machinery for unifying the nation's defenses, severely tested during the B–36 hearings, had undergone modification earlier in 1949. Recommendations for change had come from a variety of sources: Sen. Millard E. Tydings, a Democrat from Maryland, and the Senate Armed Services Committee that he headed; a committee to promote efficiency in government, chaired by former President Herbert Hoover; and a task force that included Ferdinand Eberstadt, who had played a part in the creation of the National Military Establishment, and Wilfred J. McNeil, Secretary of Defense Forrestal's special assistant for the budget. The thrust of the reform was to enhance the authority of the Secretary of Defense, a change that the Army and Air Force tended to favor and the Navy and Marine Corps to oppose. Although the House Armed Services Committee suspended its hearings on the subject to conduct the first phase of the inquiry into the B–36 program, a reorganization bill emerged from Congress and the President signed in August 1949. The new law confirmed the office of Chairman of the Joint Chiefs of Staff, filled since January by General Eisenhower pending the passage of authorizing legislation, and redesignated the National Military Establishment as the Department of Defense, increasing the powers of the Secretary. The Secretary of Defense had formerly been the first among equals with the Secretaries of the Army, Navy, and Air Force; but he now emerged as the principal adviser to the President on all matters relating to his department with "direction, authority, and control" over the service secretaries, who were by the same law removed from the National Security Council and deprived of their right of appeal to the President or the director of the Bureau of the Budget.[11] When Secretary of Defense Johnson canceled the aircraft carrier *United States*, he had sought in advance the approval of the Chief Executive, thus frustrating an appeal by the Navy; because of the changes enacted in 1949 to the basic national security act, an appeal of this sort was no longer possible.

As was confirmed, or rather left unchallenged, during the Congressional debate concerning the B–36, the United States had embraced a strategy of deterring war by means of the threat of nuclear bombardment. The Finletter report acknowledged as much, declaring in January 1948 that the security of the nation depended on confronting any potential aggressor with "the prospect of a counterattack of utmost violence" using atomic bombs.[12] In November of that year, the National Security Council formally adopted deterrence as official American policy in NSC–20/4, which restated the Finletter commission's finding in slightly different words. The security of the nation, said NSC–20/4, required that the United States maintain, for as long as necessary, sufficient military strength "to act as a deterrent to Soviet aggression." American strategy looked to the atomic bomb to guarantee the peace, but these weapons and the means of delivering them were scarce as the decade of the 1940s drew to an end.

The United States held a monopoly on atomic weapons until September 1949, when the Soviet Union detonated a nuclear device of its own. During this period of atomic ascendancy, according to the writings of David Alan Rosenberg in the journal *International Security*, the number of available bombs varied from nine in the summer of 1946 to 13 a year later and to 50 in mid-1948. Not until the years 1949 and 1950 did a vast increase occur, with the total number of weapons finally approaching 300. As the stockpile grew, the Strategic Air Command modified aircraft to carry the five-ton bombs of that era and trained crews to fly these bombers. Between December 1946 and January 1949, the number of bombers grew from 23 to 121 (8 B–29s, 96 B–50s, and 17 B–36s) and the crews increased from 10 to 150, although the larger total may have included some that were not fully trained. The critically important bomb assembly teams, composed of men from the various services, totaled just seven in

January 1949, a definite improvement since not one had been available three years earlier; nonetheless, just a beginning. Until the striking force and the stockpile of weapons expanded rapidly beginning in 1949, the Strategic Air Command could not have conducted a campaign of atomic bombing that, to be decisive, would have required several times the number of bombers, aircrews, bombs, and bomb assembly teams actually available.

The Navy would not have been much help in a nuclear war; besides being handicapped by the same scarcity of bombs, it was still in the process of preparing to share in the nuclear mission. Even though the *United States* had been canceled, twin-engine Navy aircraft capable of carrying atomic weapons began entering service in 1949. The modified Lockheed P2V–3C, a converted patrol bomber, was ill-suited to carrier operations, but the new North American AJ–1 Savage operated routinely from the largest of the Navy's aircraft carriers. Given the size of the nuclear stockpile and the readiness of the Air Force and Navy, it was no wonder that the atomic bomb played only a peripheral role when a crisis erupted in Europe.

In the spring of 1948, within weeks of the communist seizure of power in Czechoslovakia, the Soviets challenged western access to Berlin. The available nuclear retaliatory force consisted only of some three dozen B–29s with crews in varying stages of training, fewer than fifty atomic bombs, and three weapons assembly teams that were still in training. The attempt to absorb Berlin, however, did not invite overwhelming military retaliation. Instead of sending tanks thundering across a border or even staging the kind of coup that had toppled the Czech government, the Soviet Union merely reinterpreted the understanding, in force since 1945, that allowed the three western allies to travel from the American and British occupation zones in western Germany through the Soviet Zone to the American, French, and British sectors of the city. No written agreement covered road, rail, or barge traffic, leaving these forms of transportation vulnerable to the whim of Soviet officials. The four powers had, however, formally established a network of corridors for aircraft to fly in and out of Berlin. As long as the Soviet Union persisted in a subtle form of aggression, shutting down surface travel but respecting the agreement on air travel, aviation would provide Berlin's only reliable link with the outside. At the time, there was no assurance that airlift could sustain the portion of Berlin occupied by the western powers; no such thing had ever been done. Consequently the Soviet leadership may have assumed that the western sectors would quickly become untenable, presenting France, Britain, and the United States with a choice of abandoning Berlin or remaining there on terms dictated by the Soviet Union.

Soviet pressure on the western sectors of Berlin began in April 1948 with a series of arbitrary restrictions on surface transportation that temporarily halted all cargo intended for the western troops stationed in the city. Meeting this challenge devolved on Curtis LeMay, now a lieutenant general, whose U.S. Air Forces in Europe provided the C–47 transports that, for ten, days kept the garrisons sup-

A line of Douglas C–47s at Tempelhof Airport during the Berlin Airlift.

plied. Based on this experience, LeMay's headquarters at Wiesbaden, Germany, drew up a contingency plan for resuming the airlift if the Soviet Union revived the short-lived blockade. On June 18, Soviet authorities announced new restrictions designed not merely to prevent the delivery of military supplies, but to isolate those parts of the divided city administered by the United States, the United Kingdom, and France. The expanded blockade was described as retaliation for the introduction of new currency in the German territory occupied by the western allies; currency reform, which would destroy the value of the existing occupation scrip, was perceived by the Soviet government as the initial step toward merging the British, French, and American zones into a west German state.

President Truman decided that the United States should meet this latest challenge by mounting an airlift, as it had done during the earlier partial blockade, although air transport would now supply not merely the western occupation forces but every civilian in the American, British, and French sectors of Berlin. At the request of General Clay, who headed the American military government in Germany, LeMay launched an expanded airlift on June 26, 1948, sending his command's C–47s on thirty-two flights from Wiesbaden and Rhein-Main Air Bases through the air corridors with eighty tons of food for the residents of West Berlin. Thus began an operation, in which British and U.S. Navy transports also participated, that frustrated the Soviet blockade, supplying some two million inhabitants of Berlin with food and fuel for almost a year, when other forms of transportation could not be used, and continuing for three months after the surface routes were reopened.

The airlift began with Air Force C–47s flown by troop carrier groups assigned to General LeMay's command. These workhorse transports of World War II were at first reinforced and then replaced by four-engine Douglas C–54s, which had three times the cargo capacity of the older aircraft. The Air Force marshaled the resources of the Tactical Air Command and the Military Air Transport Service, shifting C–54s from as far away as Alaska and the Caribbean to reinforce the units in Europe. Included among the troop transports provided by the Tactical Air Command were a few of the new Fairchild C–82s, twin-boom, twin-engine aircraft that loaded through large doors in the rear of the fuselage and accommodated bulky cargo more easily than either the C–47 or C–54.

Transports were not the only aircraft rushed to Europe as the United States responded to the blockade of Berlin. When Soviet authorities closed the surface routes, the Air Force had only one group of piston-engine fighters in Germany, along with a single squadron of B–29s on a rotational deployment from a bombardment group based at Smoky Hill Air Force Base, Kansas. General Clay urged that the rest of the B–29 group and a group of F–80 jet fighters that were scheduled for deployment to Germany be sent immediately. President Truman approved Clay's request; in July the bombardment group's other two B–29 squadrons joined the squadron at Fuerstenfeldbruck, and the F–80s arrived at Neubiberg in August.

The question of sending B–29s to bases in the United Kingdom arose once again. Initially, the British government was eager to accept the bombers at the bases that Spaatz and Air Marshal Arthur W. Tedder, Chief of the Air Staff, Royal Air Force, had selected in 1946. When the Soviet Union seemed willing to negotiate a settlement of the crisis it had generated, the British hesitated, but the Soviet attitude then hardened and the request for permission to send the bombers was renewed. The British agreed to this request, and President Truman approved the deployment of two groups, but the aircraft were not equipped to carry atomic bombs. Throughout the crisis, the nuclear strike force remained based in the southwestern United States where it continued to train. Presumably Stalin and his advisers realized this and could discount an atomic threat from the B–29s based in England; in any event, the blockade remained in place for ten months after the arrival of the bombers in late July.

Airlift rather than strategic bombardment formed the critical element in the American response to the Berlin crisis. President Truman intended to supply the city until the Soviet Union realized the western powers would not pull out and agreed to negotiations over the question of access. Because the airlift was so important, General Vandenberg directed the Military Air Transport Service to form a task force headquarters to conduct the operation under the overall direction of LeMay's U.S. Air Forces in Europe. Chosen to head the new organization was Maj. Gen. William H. Tunner, a staff officer of the Military Air Transport Service, who had maintained the flow of supplies from India across the Himalayas to China in 1944 and 1945. Late in July 1948, Tunner took over from

Brig. Gen. Joseph Smith, whom LeMay had placed in charge when the airlift began a month earlier.

The complexity of the airlift argued powerfully for the selection of a single headquarters to manage the endless succession of transports that roared along the three narrow corridors to land and unload at Gatow airfield in the British sector; Templehof in the American; or after its completion, at the new Tegel airfield. Although located in the French sector, Tegel was built by the Americans for use by their aircraft during the emergency. Some of the American transports, which were far more numerous than those of the Royal Air Force, began operating from air bases in the British zone of Germany, thus reducing flying time and spreading the volume of traffic more evenly over the western corridors. Regardless of the point of origin or the assigned airport, all aircraft bound for Berlin were handled by flight controllers at the Berlin traffic center. Citing these factors, Tunner easily persuaded LeMay that unified management was necessary, but the British held out for closer coordination of the two national efforts, preferring that solution to surrendering control to the Americans. Not until mid-October 1948, when the approach of winter threatened to complicate the airlift still further, did Tedder and LeMay agree on a combined task force commanded by Tunner with a British officer, Air Commodore J. W. F. Merer, as his deputy. Such was the arrangement inherited by Lt. Gen. John K. Cannon, one of the most prominent tactical air commanders of World War II and a postwar commanding general of the Air Training Command, when he succeeded LeMay as the head of the U.S. Air Forces in Europe.

The coming of winter not only brought bad flying weather but also forced Tunner to devote a disproportionate amount of space to coal, bulky and difficult to handle, though essential to the survival of the city. The change of seasons may have persuaded the Soviet leadership that Berlin was doomed, that transports could not fly through storms and darkness to supply the necessary volume of food and fuel. Whatever the reason, Soviet aircraft harassed the transports but did not attempt to shoot them down. The winter weather proved as bad as expected, but the American and British airmen overcame clouds, fog, and darkness by relying on ground controlled approach radar that enabled a controller at the airfield to guide an incoming aircraft onto a glide path and to within sight of the runway lights. Radar thus made it possible for the task force to synchronize its operations and maintain a steady flow of arriving aircraft, day and night, good weather and bad. Throughout the winter, the controllers brought a stream of transports into Berlin's airfields at three-minute intervals. Each pilot had one opportunity to land; if he could not, he had to return to the point of origin and reenter the cycle.

For the Soviet Union, the blockade of Berlin proved counterproductive. Far from discouraging a union of the western zones of occupation, it was forcing the western democracies toward closer cooperation. Consequently, in the spring of 1949, the Soviet Union entered into negotiations to resolve the question of ac-

429

The Berlin Airlift continued, even though the heaviest snowfall of the year occurred during the operation. These transports are at Wiesbaden Air Base.

cess. The two chief negotiators were Dr. Phillip C. Jessup, U.S. Ambassador to the United Nations, and Jacob Malik, the Soviet representative on the United Nations Security Council. The talks culminated in an agreement, signed on May 5, 1949, that resulted in the lifting of the blockade just one week later, but did not settle the basic issue of freedom of access. Despite the resumption of surface traffic into the city, the airlift continued until September 30 to build up a reserve of food, fuel, and other supplies in the event the Soviet Union reimposed the blockade.

By the time the Berlin airlift ended, the Anglo-American supply effort had resulted in the successful delivery of 2.3 million tons. American aircraft carried roughly 1.7 million tons, of which 1.4 million tons was coal and the rest was food. A monumental achievement, the 15-month airlift was not accomplished without casualties. The sustained operations were surprisingly safe despite crowded airways and bad winter weather, with the accident rate of the airlift forces averaging less than half that of the entire Air Force. Nevertheless, breaking the blockade cost the lives of 30 American servicemen and one civilian in 12 crashes.

The airlift represented a technological triumph in the delivery of cargo by air, but its success ultimately depended on individual courage and dedication and on teamwork from members of the military services of the nations involved. Within the Air Force, nearly every command participated to some degree. Airmen assigned to U.S. Air Forces in Europe supported the operation while, at the same time, they performed routine occupation duties and prepared for possible combat. Although the Tactical Air Command, the Navy, and the Royal Air Force provided transports and crews, the Military Air Transport Service did most of the flying into Berlin, trained replacements to sustain the operation, and flew spare parts and other vital cargo across the Atlantic. The Air Materiel Command provided maintenance and logistic support in the United States, while the Air Weather Service produced timely forecasts throughout the 15-month period. The Army Transportation Corps operated a highly efficient system of ground transportation, with drivers braving Germany's icy winter roads to haul cargo from the port of Bremerhaven to the airfields from which the transports took off. The Army Corps of Engineers built and maintained runways and constructed the new airfield at Tegel. In addition to the direct participation of its transports, Navy tankers carried fuel and oil across the Atlantic. To keep the airlift going, military and civilian mechanics worked around the clock at maintenance depots in Germany and England, and technicians in the United States conducted a complete overhaul of every transport after it completed 1,000 hours flying time in the Berlin corridors. Hundreds of French and British military personnel and civilians joined refugees displaced by World War II in loading and unloading the aircraft.

On one level, the Berlin crisis demonstrated the importance of radar control of transport operations in bad weather and at night and the need for large aircraft capable of delivering bulky cargo, but it had other consequences, both military and diplomatic. The confrontation over Berlin, and the heightening tensions that had preceded it, raised questions about the status of the Strategic Air Command, for the leadership of the Air Force could not ignore the possibility that the question of access might lead to war. Even before Soviet officials sealed off the western sectors of Berlin, General Vandenberg, the Air Force Chief of Staff, asked Atlantic soloist Charles A. Lindbergh, who had been a technical adviser to Army Air Forces units during World War II, to determine the combat readiness of General Kenney's command and to recommend any improvements that might be needed. Lindbergh's report verified concerns that had been growing for months within Air Force headquarters. He found that the attempt to model the Strategic Air Command after the pre-World War II Air Corps was a mistake and had potentially disastrous consequences. Some pilots and crew members, forced to learn several flying and nonflying jobs, failed to master any of them, and the continual programs of individual training left no time to prepare realistically for combat. The remedy, Lindbergh suggested, lay in greater specialization, training that would "simulate probable wartime missions," and a program of pay and benefits that would attract the best officers and men.[13]

Vandenberg agreed that the policies of Kenney and McMullen had not produced a retaliatory force capable of going to war at a moment's notice. To move the command toward preparation for its wartime mission, the Air Force Chief of Staff chose General LeMay, whose command had launched the Berlin airlift. Before going to the U.S. Air Forces in Europe during 1947, LeMay had been Deputy Chief of Staff, Research and Development, working with the Manhattan District and the Atomic Energy Commission on the development and production of nuclear weapons. During World War II, LeMay had fought in Europe and then taken over the XX and XXI Bomber Commands, sending B–29s against

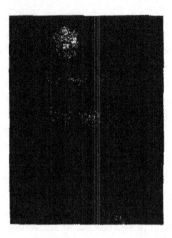

Gen. Curtis E. LeMay,
Commander in Chief,
Strategic Air Command,
October 1948–June 1957.

Japan from China and later the Marianas. His new assignment presented another grave challenge, for the American strategy of nuclear deterrence rested with the Strategic Air Command. When LeMay returned from Europe in October 1948, with the airlift well under way, he launched what proved to be a ten-year campaign to create a command with the greatest possible bombing proficiency and the highest possible morale.

One of LeMay's first command responsibilities was to move the organization's headquarters from Andrews Air Force Base, Maryland, to Offutt Air Force Base, Nebraska. The change, completed in November 1948, reflected concern that airfields along the coasts were more vulnerable to enemy attack than those located farther inland. During his first two years with the Strategic Air Command, LeMay emphasized training and planning. In April 1950, he streamlined the organization of his command, realigning the forces and bases assigned to the three numbered air forces—the Second, Eighth, and Fifteenth—for better balance and flexibility in the strategic mission. Under the realignment, each numbered air force was assigned bombers and reconnaissance aircraft and had command of units and bases in specific geographic regions of the United States.

LeMay also abandoned his predecessor's practice concerning the control of strategic air forces. Formerly, Kenney had seen no need to exercise command over those bombers based outside the United States, so that LeMay, when in command of the U.S. Air Forces in Europe, had received operational control of the conventionally armed B–29s deployed across the Atlantic and operating from bases in Europe. After taking over the Strategic Air Command, however, LeMay insisted on, and received, control over all strategic forces regardless of location. As a result, in April 1949 his command assumed responsibility for the 3d Air Division, the strategic bombardment force based in the United Kingdom. Although the division was assigned to Air Force headquarters, its commander, Leon Johnson, now a major general, reported directly to LeMay on matters affecting the B–29s.

The Berlin crisis also helped persuade the nations of western Europe to rally behind the United States in the North Atlantic Treaty Organization, which involved both diplomatic and military cooperation. The process of drawing together to promote economic recovery and to meet the threat of Soviet aggression had already started when the blockade began. In March 1948, less than a month after the communist coup in Czechoslovakia, the United Kingdom, France, Belgium, the Netherlands, and Luxembourg signed the Brussels Pact, which formed a framework for military cooperation. Although willing to present a united front against a common danger, the five adherents to the Brussels agreement had not yet recovered from the effects of World War II and lacked the resources for so ambitious an undertaking. Consequently, they turned to the United States for help, and as tensions between East and West worsened because of Berlin blockade, American interest increased.

Even before the Soviet Union imposed the blockade of Berlin, Secretary of State George C. Marshall, the wartime Army Chief of Staff, had encouraged European attempts at military cooperation, but he soon became involved in the task of helping persuade a Republican Congress to accept such a plan from a Democratic President. Republican Senator Arthur H. Vandenberg of Michigan, uncle of the Air Force Chief of Staff, proved the decisive individual, sponsoring a resolution, overwhelmingly adopted by his colleagues, that endorsed participation in regional arrangements for collective self-defense. The Vandenberg resolution cleared the way for the United States to negotiate a North Atlantic pact. In April 1949, the United States joined with the United Kingdom, France, Belgium, the Netherlands, Luxembourg, Canada, Denmark, Iceland, Norway, Portugal, and Italy in signing the North Atlantic Treaty, which declared that an armed attack on one signatory would be considered an attack on all.

The North Atlantic pact reflected two imperatives that shaped the military policy of the Truman administration—avoidance of the sort of military expenditures that might so imbalance the federal budget as to endanger the economy, and resistance to Soviet aggression. At that time, however, the North Atlantic Treaty Organization remained a liability rather than an asset; it was not yet an effective mechanism for containing communism, a further reason for the administration to worry about military spending. Member nations would receive about two-thirds of the $1.45 billion voted by Congress for foreign military assistance during fiscal 1950, the equivalent of ten percent of the total amount the President intended to spend on the American armed forces, but this comparatively small amount represented a down payment on the rearmament of western Europe. Further investment and the passage of time would be required if conventionally armed European forces, backed by American retaliatory might, were to present a genuine obstacle to Soviet aggression.

As the North Atlantic Treaty Organization took shape and the Strategic Air Command increased in proficiency, the Truman administration continued to display an ambivalent attitude toward the armed forces. Following the request for a supplemental defense appropriations bill in the spring of 1948, Truman again carefully scrutinized expenditures for the services, even as policy planners urged the containment of an expansionist Soviet Union. The President continued to worry about unbalanced budgets and the possibility of runaway inflation. Although he would respond to the Soviet detonation of an atomic bomb by authorizing work on thermonuclear (hydrogen fusion) weapons, Truman showed an abiding concern about the impact of defense spending on the entire budget and the national economy. He called for a reassessment of national policy and military strategy in the light of the recent behavior of the Soviet Union but, at the same time, remained wary of massive appropriations, which might well result from such a study, since they would prevent his balancing the federal budget. Despite the emphasis on deterrence and the Strategic Air Command, along with a revival of interest in air defense to meet the threat of the Soviet atomic bomb, the authorized strength of the Air Force remained at forty-eight groups, unchanged since the service became independent.

The review of policy and strategy that Truman requested produced a working paper, NSC–68, which was approved in April 1950 by the National Security Council and the President. Aware of the President's preoccupation with the budget, the planners who wrote NSC–68 concentrated on policy rather than costs. The document addressed the Soviet Union's superiority in conventional forces and advances in nuclear technology. Although conceding that direct armed aggression by the Soviet Union seemed improbable in the face of an American nuclear advantage, the statement of policy warned that the United States had to be prepared for such an eventuality. The more likely threat outlined in NSC–68 was "piecemeal aggression," perhaps a limited war begun by one of the satellite nations. As a result, the United States would have to rearm for both general and local wars and remain prepared to meet Soviet aggression at almost any level of violence (a strategy strikingly similar to the one that American policy makers would embrace a decade later as "flexible response"). As the spring of 1950 turned to summer, President Truman and his advisers began addressing the question of paying for the rearmament they had just endorsed, an investment in security that might cost $50 billion annually. Once again, concern for the effect of deficits and higher taxes on the economy had to be weighed against the threat from abroad, and thus far in the Truman years economic issues had imposed constraints on American rearmament.

Money, or its lack, affected every aspect of military policy. The Air Force had established its basic organizational framework, an infrastructure that included the Office of Secretary of the Air Force, an Air Staff, and a network of functional and overseas commands. What the newest of the armed forces lacked was the money to acquire the strength in manpower and equipment to carry out the strategy suggested in NSC–68, a deficiency it shared with the Army and Navy. Weary of the unsuccessful fight for seventy groups, Secretary Symington resigned in the spring of 1950, becoming chairman of the National Security

Resources Board and afterward serving briefly as the administrator of the Reconstruction Finance Corporation. In 1953 he entered politics, was elected to the Senate from Missouri as a Democrat, and functioned for years as a powerful advocate of the Air Force and its programs. Symington's replacement as Secretary of the Air Force was Thomas K. Finletter, former head of the President's Air Policy Commission, whose report had aroused interest in air power and deterrence even though it had not reordered the budgetary priorities of the Truman administration.

Until NSC–68 was backed by appropriations legislation, the armed forces remained ill-prepared for war. The Air Force, like the other components of the military establishment, was short of men and equipment. Although LeMay's reforms were beginning to take hold, the Strategic Air Command was at best a token deterrent. Its strength in Europe had greatly increased, however, as a result of the Berlin crisis, even though the bombers located there were not part of the atomic force. When the Berlin blockade ended, B–29s of the Strategic Air Command were operating from seven airfields in the United Kingdom, and the British government had agreed to share in the cost of rebuilding four Royal Air Force bases to accommodate the new B–36s and the jet-powered B–47s, when they became available for deployment.

Deployment of the Strategic Air Command's B–29s to Europe and the preparations to send bombers more modern than the B–29 were not the only results of the Berlin blockade. As early as August 1948, the Air Force had doubled its tactical air strength in Europe by deploying three squadrons of F–80s from the United States to Fuerstenfeldbruck. The following January, the U.S. Air Forces in Europe formed the 2d Air Division at Landsberg Air Base in Germany and in May began developing a new air defense system composed of six fighter squadrons at Fuerstenfeldbruck and Neubiberg and four radar stations. Spurred by the Berlin crisis, the Air Force had been able to establish at least a foundation for a force structure committed to the North Atlantic Treaty Organization when the military arm of that alliance began taking shape near the end of 1950.

Although the Berlin crisis and the formation of the North Atlantic Treaty Organization occupied the spotlight, Air Force strength had increased in the Pacific during the collapse of Chinese Nationalist resistance to the communists on the Asian mainland, which overlapped the confrontation with the Soviet Union over access to Berlin. Even though some forces were withdrawn from the Pacific after the Berlin blockade ended and the danger of a worldwide conflict seemed to recede, the Air Force still maintained roughly twice the tactical force in the Pacific that it had in Europe, with twenty-one squadrons deployed at bases in Japan, on Okinawa, or in the Philippines. Numbers were deceptive, however, for these squadrons were scattered from the Philippines to Japan, instead of being concentrated in a compact area like western Europe. In Japan, nine F–80 fighter-bomber squadrons operated from Itazuke, Yokota, and Misawa Air Bases. A squadron of RF–80 tactical reconnaissance aircraft and a squadron of F–82

435

History of the United States Air Force

Twin Mustang fighter interceptors flew out of Yokota. (The F–82 Twin Mustang consisted of two P–51 Mustang fuselages connected by a common center wing segment and a common horizontal stabilizer.) On Okinawa, two B–26 light bomber squadrons and another squadron of F–82s operated from airfields at Naha and Kadena. Three F–80 squadrons were based at Clark Air Base in the Philippines. Despite the greater number of combat squadrons in the Pacific, the Far East Air Forces, as the theater command was called, was no better prepared for war than its counterpart in Europe. General Stratemeyer, who in April 1949 had gone from the Continental Air Command to Tokyo as Commanding General, Far East Air Forces, surveyed his organization and expressed doubt that it could do more than provide air defense for American holdings in the Pacific, should an emergency arise. The combat readiness of the Far East Air Forces, indeed of the entire Air Force, would soon be tested when, as the framers of NSC–68 had warned, a local war broke out in the summer of 1950.

Notes

Chapter 1

1. Juliette A. Hennessy, *The United States Army Air Arm, April 1861 to April 1917* (Washington: Office of Air Force History, reprint 1985), p 15.

2. *Ibid.*, Appendix 6, p 225.

3. John F. Shiner, *Foulois and the U.S. Army Air Corps, 1931–1935* (Washington:

Office of Air Force History, 1983), p 2.

4. *Ibid.*, p 3.

5. Thomas M. Coffey, *Hap: The Story of the U.S. Air Force and the Man Who Built it: General Henry H. "Hap" Arnold* (New York: Viking, 1982), p 63.

Chapter 2

1. Russell F. Weigley, *The American Way of War: A History of United States Military Strategy and Policy* (New York: Macmillan, 1973), pp 195–202.

2. John H. Morrow, Jr., *The Great War in the Air, Military Aviation from 1909–1921* (Washington: Smithsonian, 1993), pp 59–70.

3. Raymond H. Fredette, *The Sky on Fire, The First Battle of Britain, 1917–1918* (Washington: Smithsonian, 1976), pp 3–13.

4. Morrow, *The Great War in the Air*, pp 281–348.

5. C.R. Roseberry, *Glenn Curtiss, Pioneer of Flight* (Garden City, New York: Doubleday, 1972), pp 395–98; I.B. Holley, *Ideas and Weapons: Exploitation of the Aerial Weapon by the United States During World War I, A Study in the Relationship of Technological Advance, Military Doctrine, and the Development of Weapons* (Washington: Office of Air Force History, reprint 1983), pp 41–46.

6. Alfred F. Hurley, *Billy Mitchell: Crusader for Air Power* (New York: Franklin Watts, 1964), pp 22–27.

7. Morrow, *The Great War in the Air*, pp 198–200.

8. Richard P. Hallion, *Rise of the*

Fighter Aircraft, 1914–1918, (Baltimore: Nautical & Aviation Publishing, 1988), pp 1–14.

9. Fredette, *The Sky on Fire*, pp 27–33.

10. *Ibid.*, pp 34–101.

11. Morrow, *The Great War in the Air*, pp 81–85; Lee Kennett, *A History of Strategic Bombing* (New York: Scribner, 1982), pp 19–38.

12. Holley, *Ideas and Weapons*, pp 66–81; Henry H. Arnold, *Global Mission* (New York: Harper, 1949), pp 65–79.

13. Arnold, *Global Mission*, pp 50–55.

14. James J. Hudson, *Hostile Skies: A Combat History of the American Air Service in World War I* (Syracuse: Syracuse University Press, 1968), pp 12–22.

15. Holley, *Ideas and Weapons*, pp 39–49.

16. *Ibid*, pp 65–81.

17. Arnold, *Global Mission*, pp 59–68.

18. Holley, *Ideas and Weapons*, pp 103–9.

19. *Ibid*, pp 133–45.

20. Hudson, *Hostile Skies*, pp 24–43.

21. William Mitchell, *Memoirs of World War I: From Start to Finish of Our Greatest War* (Westport, Connecticut: Greenwood Press, reprinted 1975), pp 177–78.

22. James Norman Hall and Charles Bernard Nordhoff, *The Lafayette Flying Corps* (Port Washington, New York: Kennikat, 1920), pp 3–60.

23. Hudson, *Hostile Skies*, pp 46–61.

24. Finis Farr, *Rickenbacker's Luck, An American Life* (Boston: Houghton Mifflin, 1979), pp 40–75.

25. Hudson, *Hostile Skies*, pp 90–117.

26. *Ibid*, pp 119–83; Maurer Maurer, ed., *The U.S. Air Service in World War I, vol III, The Battle of St Mihiel* (Washington: Office of Air Force History, 1979).

27. Hudson, *Hostile Skies*, pp 258–95.

28. Morrow, *The Great War in the Air*, pp 349–78; Harold E. Hartney, *Up and At 'Em*, (Garden City: Doubleday, 1971), pp 287–336; Hudson, *Hostile Skies*, pp 299–304.

Chapter 3

1. U.S. Senate, Committee on Military Affairs, *Hearings on Reorganization of the Army*, 66th Cong, 2d sess, 1919, pp 3–4.

2. Progress Report, Division of Military Aeronautics, Nov 13, 1918, quoted in Ernest L. Jones, "Chronology of Aviation" (MS in AF Historical Research Agency, Maxwell AFB, 168.6501–37).

3. Maurer Maurer, *Aviation in the U.S. Army 1919–1939* (Washington: Office of Air Force History, 1987), pp 44–45.

4. Hurley, *Billy Mitchell*, pp 58–59.

5. *Ibid.*, p 47.

6. William Mitchell, *Winged Defense: The Development and Possibilities of Modern Air Power—Economic and Military* (New York: Putnams, 1925), p 75.

7. Hurley, *Billy Mitchell*, p 92.

8. *Ibid.*, p 97.

9. *Ibid.*, p 98.

10. Robert Frank Futrell, *Ideas, Concepts, Doctrine: Basic Thinking in the United States Air Force 1907–1960* (Maxwell AFB: Air University, reprint 1989) p 49; the exact source is Maj Gen Mason M. Patrick, "The Army Air Service," lecture, Army War College, Carlisle Barracks, Pa., Nov 9, 1925.

11. Hurley, *Billy Mitchell*, p 101.

12. *Ibid.*, p 104.

Chapter 4

1. Shiner, *Foulois*, p 29.

2. Isaac D. Levine, *Mitchell: Power of Air Power* (New York: Duell, Sloan & Pearce, 1943), p 334.

3. Futrell, *Ideas*, p 64.

4. Shiner, *Foulois*, p 58.

5. *Ibid.*, p 69.

6. Norman E. Borden, Jr., *Air Mail Emergency 1934: An account of Seventy-Eight days in the Winter of 1934 when the Army Flew the United States Mail* (Freeport, Maine: Bond Wheelwright, 1968), p 45.

7. Shiner, *Foulois*, p 203.

Chapter 5

1. Futrell, *Ideas*, p 69.

2. *Ibid.*

3. Maurer, *Aviation*, pp 62–63.

4. Futrell, *Ideas*, p 88.

5. *Annual Report of the Chief of Staff for the Fiscal Year Ending June 30 1935*, included in the *Report of the Secretary of War* (Washington: GPO, 1935), p 62.

6. *Ibid.*

7. *Ibid.*

8. Shiner, *Foulois*, p 226.

9. R. J. Overy, *The Air War, 1939–1945* (New York, Stein and Day, 1980), p 11.

10. Arnold, *Global Mission*, p 177.

Chapter 6

1. Joseph P. Lash, *Roosevelt and Churchill, 1939–1941: The Partnership That Saved the West* (New York: W.W. Norton, 1976), p 152.

2. Arnold, *Global Mission*, p 198.

3. Mark Skinner Watson, *United States Army in World War II, The War Department, Chief of Staff: Prewar Plans and Preparations* (Washington: Center of Military History, 1985), p 286.

4. *Ibid.*, p 290.

5. Maurice Matloff and Edwin M. Snell, *United States Army in World War II, The War Department: Strategic Planning For Coalition Warfare, 1941–1942* (Washington: Office of the Chief of Military History, 1953), p 52.

6. Wesley Frank Craven and James Lea Cate, eds, *The Army Air Forces in World War II*. 7 vols, 1948–1958. (Washington: Office of Air Force History, reprint 1983), Vol 1, *Plans and Early Operations, January 1939 to August 1942*, pp 314–16.

7. Samuel Eliot Morison, *History of United States Naval Operations in World War II*. 15 vols. (Boston: Little, Brown, 1959), Vol IV, *Coral Sea, Midway Anglo Submarine Actions, May 1942–August 1942*, p 247, fn 3.

8. Louis Morton, *United States Army in World War II, The War in the Pacific, The Fall of the Philippines* (Washington: Office of the Chief of Military History, 1953), p 17.

9. Arnold, *Global Mission*, p 208.

10. Morton, *Fall of the Philippines*, p 12.

11. Henry L. Stimson and McGeorge Bundy, *On Active Service in Peace and War* (New York: Harper, 1948), p 388.

12. Gordon W. Prange, with Donald M. Goldstein and Katherine V. Dillon, *At Dawn We Slept: The Untold Story of Pearl Harbor* (New York: McGraw-Hill, 1981), pp 94–95.

13. Stimson and Bundy, *On Active Service*, p 391.

Chapter 7

1. Prange, *At Dawn We Slept*, p 524.

2. Stetson Conn, Rose C. Engleman, and Bryon Fairchild, *United States Army in World War II, The Western Hemisphere: Guarding the United States and its Outposts* (Washington: Office of Chief of Military History, 1964), pp 410–11.

3. John L. Frisbee, ed, *United States Air Force Warrior Studies: Makers of the United States Air Force.* (Washington: Office of Air Force History, 1987), p 127.

4. Charles Webster and Noble Frankland, *The Strategic Air Offensive against Germany*, 4 vols. Vol I, *Preparation* (London: Her Majesty's Stationery Office, 1961), p 361.

5. Winston S. Churchill, *Memoirs of the Second World War* (Boston: Houghton Mifflin, 1959), p 653.

Chapter 8

1. Memos, Robert A. Lovett to Lt Gen H. H. Arnold, Commanding Gen, AAF, Oct 14, 1942, and Lt Gen H. H. Arnold to Robert A. Lovett, subj: Aircraft production for 1943, Oct 20, 1942, both in RG 107, File 452.1(7), Production, Item 11a, NA.

2. Haywood S. Hansell, Jr., *The Air Plan That Defeated Hitler* (Atlanta: Higgins–McArthur/Longino & Porter, 1972), p 100.

3. *Ibid.*, pp 61–99.

4. Lash, *Roosevelt and Churchill*, p 81.

5. Craven and Cate, Vol VI, *Men and Planes*, p 284.

6. *Ibid.*, p 219.

7. *Ibid.*

8. Craven and Cate, Vol VII, *Services Around The World*, p 535.

9. Gen Chuck Yeager and Leo Jano, *Yeager: An Autobiography* (New York, Bantam Books, 1985), p 16.

10. *Ibid.*, p 15.

11. Craven and Cate, Vol VI, *Men and Planes*, p 595.

12. Craven and Cate, Vol VII, *Services Around the World*, p 369.

13. *Ibid.*, p 418.

Chapter 9

1. HQ XII ASC, Report on Operations, "Tunisia, 13 January 1943 to 9 April 1943," p 24, Air Force Historical Research Center, Ref No 350.01-2.

2. Daniel R. Mortensen, *A Pattern For Joint Operations: World War II Close Air Support, North Africa* (Washington: Office of Air Force History and U.S. Army Center of Military History, 1987), p 77.

3. Richard G. Davis, *Carl A. Spaatz and the Air War in Europe* (Washington: Office of Air Force History, 1993), pp 203, 205.

4. James Parton, *"Air Force Spoken Here": General Eaker and the Command of the Air* (Bethesda: Adler and Adler, 1986), pp 220-23.

5. Craven and Cate, Vol II, *Europe: Torch To Pointblank, August 1942 to December 1943*, p 305.

6. Craven and Cate, Vol III, *Europe: Argument to V-E Day, January 1944 to May 1945*, p 733.

7. Albert Speer, *Inside the Third Reich*. Translated by Richard Winston and Clara Winston. (New York: Macmillan, 1970), p 339.

8. Craven and Cate, Vol II, *Europe: Torch To Pointblank*, p 704.

9. *Ibid.*, p 524.

10. Ltr, Gen Arnold to Gen Eaker, Feb 10, 1944, Arnold Letters Collection at the Air Force Historical Support Office; Craven and Cate, Vol III, *Europe: Argument to V-E Day January 1944 to May 1945*, pp 373-84.

11. Speer, *Inside the Third Reich*, p 341.

12. Webster and Frankland, Vol III, *Victory Part 5*, pp 117-19.

13. Speer, *Inside the Third Reich*, pp 412-13.

14. Arthur Harris, *Bomber Offensive* (London: Greenhill Books, 1990), p 220.

15. *Ibid.*, p 242; Webster and Frankland, Vol III, *Victory Part 5*, pp 108-9.

16. Webster and Frankland, Vol III, *Victory Part 5*, p 101.

17. *Ibid*, p 105.

18. David MacIsaac, *Strategic Bombing in World War II: The Story of the United States Strategic Bombing Survey* (New York: Garland, 1976), p 41.

19. *Ibid*, pp 141-42.

20. H. M. Cole, *United States Army in World War II, The European Theater of Operations–The Lorraine Campaign* (Washington: Historical Division, Department of the Army, 1950), p 601.

Chapter 10

1. George C. Kenney, *General Kenney Reports: A Personal History of the Pacific War*. 1949. (Washington: Office of Air Force History, reprint 1987), p 44.

2. William H. Tunner, *Over The Hump*. 1964. (Washington: Office of Air Force History, reprint 1985), p 43.

3. Martha Byrd, *Chennault: Giving Wings to the Tiger* (Tuscaloosa, University of Alabama Press, 1987), p 184.

4. M. Hamlin Cannon, *United States Army in World War II, The War in the Pacific, Leyte: The Return to the Philippines* (Washington: Office of the Chief of Military History, 1954), p 4; Morison, Vol XIII, *The Liberation of the Philippines, Luzon, Min-*

danao, the Visayas 1944–1945, p 3.

5. Drainage issue discussed by Gen Casey in Cannon, *War in the Pacific*, pp 35–36, 187–88.

6. Craven and Cate, Vol V, *The Pacific: Matterhorn to Nagasaki, June 1944 to August 1945*, p 567.

7. Herbert Feis, *The Atomic Bomb and the End of World War II* (Princeton: Princeton University Press, 1966), p 123.

8. *Ibid.*, p. 143; Dan Kurzman, *Day of the Bomb: Countdown to Hiroshima* (New York: McGraw-Hill 1986), pp 425–26.

9. MacIsaac, *Strategic Bombing in World War II*, pp 109–33; *United States Strategic Bombing Survey*, Summary Volume for the Pacific (Maxwell AFB, Air University Press, reprint 1987), p 29.

Chapter 11

1. Theodore von Kármán with Lee Edson, *The Wind and Beyond: Theodore von Kármán, Pioneer in Aviation and Pathfinder in Space* (Boston: Little, Brown and Company, 1967), p 225.

2. *Ibid.*, p 271.

3. Henry H. Arnold, *Third Report of the Commanding General of the Army Air Forces to the Secretary of War* (Washington: War Department, Nov 1945).

4. *Ibid.*

5. *Ibid.*

6. *Ibid.*

7. Memo for SECDEF from Gen Dwight D. Eisenhower, subj: Tactical Air Support, Nov 3, 1947, RG 18, AAG, 322, BOX 104, Modern Military Br, NA.

8. Intvw, BG Noel Parish and Alfred Goldberg with Gen Spaatz, Feb 21, 1962.

9. Intvw with Lt Gen Elwood R. Quesada, by Lt Cols Steve Long and Ralph Stephenson, May 12, 1975, Washington, Air Force Oral History Tape, K239, 0512–838.

10. Quesada intvw.

11. Intvw, Arthur K. Marmor with Maj. Gen Leon Johnson, Apr 14, 1954, in Air Force History Support Office.

12. Spaatz Intvw.

13. *Ibid.*

14. John L. Gaddis, *The United States and the Origins of the Cold War, 1941–1947* (New York: Columbia University Press, 1972), p 308.

15. *Ibid.*, p 351.

16. Bernard Brodie, ed., The Absolute Weapon: Atomic Bomb and World Order (New York: Harcourt, Brace, 1946).

17. Memo, Lt Gen Hoyt S. Vandenberg, AC/AS-3, to Gen Eaker, Dep Cmdr, AAF, Jan 2, 1946, subj: The Establishment of a Strategic Striking Force.

18. *Ibid.*

19. Memo for CSA from Gen H. H. Arnold, CG, AAF, subj: Re-Survey of the Troop Basis for the Post-War Army, Mar 31, 1945, in RG 18, AAG, War & Rcrds Div, Decimal File 1945, 381, Box # 189, Postwar File, vol 2, Modern Military Br, NA.

20. Ltr, Robert A. Lovett, Ass S/W for Air, to Gen Carl A. Spaatz, CG, USSAFE, Mar 25, 1945, Spaatz Chron File, Mar 45, Personal, Box 21, Mss. Div, LC.

21. *Hearings before the Committee on Military Affairs, Senate, Departments of Armed Forces and Military Security: Hearing on S. 84 and S. 1482*, p 360, 367.

22. Harry S. Truman, *Memoirs*, Vol II, *Years of Trial and Hope* (Garden City: 1956), p 46.

23. Special message to the Congress recommending the Establishment of a Department of National Defense, Dec 19, 1945, in *Public Papers of the Presidents of the United States: Harry S. Truman, 1945* (Washington: GPO, 1961), p 555.

24. *Ibid.*, p 559.

25. Ltr, James V. Forrestal to Samuel Rosenman, Dec 18, 1945, cited in Richard F. Haynes, *The Awesome Power: Harry S. Truman as Commander-in-Chief* (Baton Rouge: Lousiana State University Press, 1973), p 98.

Chapter 12

1. Interview of Senator Stuart Symington by George M. Watson, Jr., Oct 21, 1981, p 31, on file at the Air Force History Support Office, Washington, file No. K239.0512–1343.

2. Herman S. Wolk, *Planning and Organizing the Postwar Air Force 1943–1947* (Washington: Office of Air Force History, 1984), pp 188–93.

3. von Kármán, *The Wind and Beyond*, p 294.

4. R. D. Specht, *Rand: A Personal View of Its History*, Operations Research, vol 8, no. 6 (Dec 1960), pp 825–39.

5. Michael H. Gorn, *Harnessing the Genie: Science and Technology Forecasting for the Air Force, 1944–1986* (Washington: Office of Air Force History, 1988), p 49; *History of the Air Research and Development Command, 23 January 1950–30 June 1951*, vol I, pp 40, 43, 49; *An Air Force Command for Research and Development, 1949–1976, The History of ARDC/AFSC*, (Air Force Systems Command Historical Office, 1977), p 13.

6. Steven L. Rearden, *History of the Office of the Secretary of Defense*, Vol I, *The Formative Years 1947–1950* (Washington: Office of the Secretary of Defense, 1984), p 281.

7. *Ibid.*, p 321.

8. *Ibid.*, p 403; Walter Millis, ed, *The Forrestal Diaries* (New York: Viking, 1951), pp 513–14.

9. Reardon, *Secretary of Defense*, p 409.

10. *Ibid.*, p 419.

11. *Ibid.*, p 53.

12. *Survival In The Air Age: A Report by the President's Air Policy Commission* (Washington: GPO, 1948), p 23.

13. Rpt, Charles A. Lindbergh to Gen H.S. Vandenberg, CSAF, 14 Sep 48, atch to Memo, Col F. M. Hoisington, Ch Pers & Admin Div, to Maj Gen G.M. Schlatter, Asst DCS/O for AE, "The Lindbergh Report," 19 Oct 48, NA 341, DCS/Ops, Asst/AE, 319.1 Reports AEC, T&T, etc, box 16.

Selected Readings

Books

Acheson, Dean G. *Present at the Creation: My Years in the State Department.* New York: Norton, 1969.

Adkin, Mark. *Urgent Fury: The Battle for Grenada.* Lexington, Massachusetts: Lexington Books, 1989.

Alexander, Charles C. *Holding the Line: The Eisenhower Era, 1952–1961.* Bloomington: Indiana University Press, 1975.

Aliano, Richard A. *American Defense Policy from Eisenhower to Kennedy: The Politics of Changing Military Requirements, 1957–1961.* Athens: Ohio University Press, 1975.

Allen, Thomas B., and Norman Polmar. *Code-Name Downfall: The Secret Plan to Invade Japan and Why Truman Dropped the Bomb.* New York: Simon & Schuster, 1995.

Allison, Graham T. *Essence of Decision: Explaining The Cuban Missile Crisis.* Boston: Little, Brown, 1971.

Anderson, William C. *Bat-21: Based on the True Story of Lt. Col. Iceal E. Hambleton, USAF.* Englewood Cliffs, New Jersey: Prentice Hall, 1980.

Andrews, Allen. *The Air Marshals: The Air War in Western Europe.* New York: Morrow, 1970.

Angelucci, Enzo. *The Rand McNally Encyclopedia of Military Aircraft, 1914–1980.* New York: The Military Press, 1983.

Appleman, Roy. *United States Army in the Korean War: South to the Naktong, North to the Yalu (June–November 1950).* Washington: Office of Chief of Military History, 1961.

Appleman, Roy, James M. Burns, Russell E. Gugeler, and John Stevens. *United States Army in World War II: Okinawa, The Last Battle.* Washington: Center of Military History, 1993.

Arakaki, Leatrice R., and John R. Kuborn. *7 December 1941: The Air Force Story.* Hickam Air Force Base, Hawaii: Pacific Air Forces Office of History, 1991.

Arbon, Lee. *They Also Flew: The Enlisted Pilot Legacy, 1912–1942.* Washington: Smithsonian, 1992.

Armacost, Michael H. *The Politics of Weapons Innovation: The Thor-Jupiter Controversy.* New York: Columbia University Press, 1969.

Arnold, Henry H. *Global Mission.* Blue Ridge Summit, Pennsylvania: Tab Books, 1989.

_____."First Report of the Commanding General of the Army Air Forces to the

Secretary of War." [Also Second Report and Third Report.] In George C. Marshall, H. H. Arnold, and Ernest J. King. *The War Reports of General of the Army George C. Marshall, Chief of Staff, General of the Army H. H. Arnold, Commanding General, Army Air Forces, and Fleet Admiral Ernest J. King, Commander in Chief, United States Fleet, and Chief of Naval Operations.* Philadelphia: Lippincott, 1947.

Baker, James A., III. *The Politics of Diplomacy: Revolution, War, and Peace, 1989–1992.* New York: Putnam, 1995.

Ball, George. *The Past Has Another Pattern.* New York: Norton, 1982.

Ballard, Jack S. *The United States Air Force in Southeast Asia: Development and Employment of Fixed-Wing Gunships, 1962–1973.* Washington: Office of Air Force History, 1982.

Barlow, Jeffrey G. *Revolt of the Admirals: The Fight for Naval Aviation, 1945–1950.* Washington: Naval Historical Center, 1994.

Basel, Gene I. *Pak Six: A Story of the War in the Skies of North Vietnam.* New York: Jove, 1987.

Bates, Charles C., and John F. Fuller. *America's Weather Warriors, 1814–1985.* College Station: Texas A&M University Press, 1986.

Baxter, James Phinney, III. *Scientists Against Time, 1893–1975.* Boston: Little, Brown, 1946.

Beard, Edmund. *Developing the ICBM: A Study in Bureaucratic Politics.* New York: Columbia University Press, 1976.

Bednarek, Janet R., ed. *The Enlisted Experience: A Conversation with the Chief Master Sergeants of the Air Force.* Washington: Air Force History and Museums Program, 1995.

Bell, Kenneth H. *100 Missions North.* Washington: Brassey's, 1993.

Bendiner, Elmer. *The Fall of the Fortresses: A Personal Account of the Most Daring and Deadly American Air Battles of World War II.* New York: Putnam, 1980.

Bennett, Ralph. *Ultra in the West: The Normandy Campaign, 1944–45.* New York: Scribner, 1980.

Berger, Carl. *B–29: The Superfortress.* New York: Ballantine, 1970.

————. *The Korea Knot: A Military-Political History.* Rev. ed. Philadelphia: University of Pennsylvania Press, 1965.

Berger, Carl, ed. *The United States Air Force in Southeast Asia: An Illustrated Account, 1961–1973.* Rev. ed. Washington: Office of Air Force History, 1984.

Beschloss, Michael R. *Mayday: Eisenhower, Khrushchev, and the U–2 Affair.* New York: Harper and Row, 1986.

Biddle, Charles J. *Fighting Airman: The Way of the Eagle.* Garden City, New York: Doubleday, 1968.

Biddle, Wayne. *Barons of the Sky.* New York: Simon & Schuster, 1991.

Biderman, Albert. *March to Calumny: The Story of American POWs in the*

Korean War. New York: Arno, 1979.

Bilstein, Roger E. *Flight in America, 1900–1983: From the Wrights to the Astronauts.* Rev. ed. Baltimore: Johns Hopkins University Press, 1994.

Blesse, Frederick C. *'Check Six': A Fighter Pilot Looks Back.* Mesa, Arizona: Champlin Fighter Museum Press, 1987.

Blumenson, Martin. *U. S. Army in World War II: Salerno to Cassino.* Washington: Office of Chief of Military History, 1969.

Boettcher, Thomas D. *Vietnam: The Valor and the Sorrow, from the Home Front to the Front Lines in Words and Pictures.* Boston: Little Brown, 1985.

Boggs, Charles W., Jr. *Marine Aviation in the Philippines.* Washington: Historical Division, Headquarters, U. S. Marine Corps, 1951.

Bolger, Daniel P. *Americans at War, 1975–1986: An Era of Violent Peace.* Novato, California: Presidio Press, 1988.

Bond, Charles R., and Terry H. Anderson. *A Flying Tiger's Diary.* College Station: Texas A&M University Press, 1984.

Bonds, Ray, ed. *The Vietnam War: The Illustrated History of the Conflict in Southeast Asia.* Rev. ed. New York: Crown, 1983.

Bonney, Walter T. *The Heritage of Kitty Hawk.* New York: Norton, 1962.

Borden, Norman E., Jr. *The Air Mail Emergency, 1934: An Account of Seventy-eight Tense Days in the Winter of 1934 when the Army Flew the United States Mail.* Freeport, Maine: Bond-Wheelwright, 1968.

Borowski, Harry R. *A Hollow Threat: Strategic Air Power and Containment before Korea.* Westport, Connecticut: Greenwood Press, 1982.

Borowski, Harry R., ed. *The Harmon Memorial Lectures in Military History, 1959–1987: A Collection of the First Thirty Harmon Lectures Given at the United States Air Force Academy.* Washington: Office of Air Force History, 1988.

_____. *Military Planning in the Twentieth Century, Proceedings of the Eleventh Military History Symposium, U. S. Air Force Academy, Colorado, 1984.* Washington: U. S. Air Force Academy and Office of Air Force History, 1986.

Bowers, Ray L. *The United States Air Force in Southeast Asia: Tactical Airlift.* Washington: Office of Air Force History, 1983.

Boyne, Walter, J. *The Smithsonian Book of Flight.* New York: Wings, 1994.

Bradin, James W. *From Hot Air to Hellfire: The History of Army Attack Aviation.* Novato, California: Presidio, 1994.

Bright, Charles D., ed. *Historical Dictionary of the U. S. Air Force.* New York: Greenwood, 1992.

Brodie, Bernard, ed. *The Absolute Weapon: Atomic Power and World Order.* Freeport: Books for Library Press, 1972.

_____. *Strategy in the Missile Age.* Princeton: Princeton University Press, 1959.
_____. *War and Politics.* New York: Macmillan, 1973.

Broughton, Jack. *Going Downtown: The War against Hanoi and Washington.* New York: Orion Books, 1988.

445

_____. *Thud Ridge*. Philadelphia: Lippincott, 1969.

Brown, Jerold E. *Where Eagles Land: Planning and Development of U. S. Army Airfields, 1910–1941*. New York: Greenwood, 1990.

Brown, Michael E. *Flying Blind: The Politics of the U. S. Strategic Bomber Program*. Ithaca, New York: Cornell University Press, 1992.

Brown, Seyom. *The Faces of Power: Constancy and Change in United States Foreign Policy from Truman to Clinton*. New York: Columbia University Press, 1994.

Buckingham, William A., Jr. *Operation Ranch Hand: The Air Force and Herbicides in Southeast Asia, 1961–1971*. Washington: Office of Air Force History, 1982.

Builder, Carl H. *The Icarus Syndrome: The Role of Air Power Theory in the Evolution and Fate of the U. S. Air Force*. New Brunswick, New Jersey: Transaction Publishers, 1994.

Bundy, McGeorge. *Danger and Survival: Choices About the Bomb in the First Fifty Years*. New York: Vintage Book, 1990.

Burkard, Dick J. *Military Airlift Command: Historical Handbook, 1941–1984*. Scott Air Force Base, Illinois: Military Airlift Command, 1984.

Burrows, William E. *Deep Black: Space Espionage and National Security*. New York: Random House, 1986.

Butow, Robert J. C. *Japan's Decision to Surrender*. Stanford, California: Stanford University Press, 1967.

Byrd, Martha. *Chennault: Giving Wings to the Tiger*. Tuscaloosa: University of Alabama Press, 1988.

Cable, Larry. *Unholy Grail: The US and the Wars in Vietnam, 1965–68*. London: Routledge, 1991.

Cagle, Malcolm W., and Frank A. Manson. *The Sea War in Korea*. New York: Arno, 1980.

Cannon, M. Hamlin. *U. S. Army in World War II: Leyte, The Return to the Philippines*. Washington: Office of Chief of Military History, 1954.

Carter, Ashton B., and David N. Schwartz, eds. *Ballistic Missile Defense: A Study Jointly Sponsored by the Brookings Institution and the Massachusetts Institute of Technology*. Washington: Brookings, 1984.

Carter, Kit C., and Robert Mueller, eds. *The Army Air Forces in World War II: Combat Chronology, 1941–1945*. Washington: Office of Air Force History, 1991.

Castle, Timothy N. *At War in the Shadow of Vietnam: U. S. Military Aid to the Royal Lao Government, 1955–1975*. New York: Columbia University Press, 1993.

Cave, Hugh B. *Wings Across the World: The Story of the Air Transport Command*. New York: Dodd, 1945.

Chandler, Charles DeForest, and Frank Lahm. *How Our Army Grew Wings: Airmen and Aircraft Before 1914*. New York: Arno, 1979.

Chang, Gordon H. *Friends and Enemies: The United States, China, and the Soviet Union, 1948–1972.* Stanford, California: Stanford University Press, 1990.

Chen, Jian. *China's Road to the Korean War: The Making of the Sino-American Confrontation.* New York: Columbia University Press, 1994.

Chinnery, Philip D. *"Any Time, Any Place": Fifty Years of the USAF Air Commando and Special Operations Forces, 1944–1994.* Annapolis: Naval Institute, 1994.

Cimbala, Stephen J., ed. *Strategic Air Defense.* Wilmington, Delaware: Scholarly Resources, 1989.

Clancy, Tom. *Fighter Wing: A Guided Tour of an Air Force Combat Wing.* New York: Berkley Books, 1995.

Clarke, Jeffrey J. *U. S. Army in Vietnam: Advice and Support, The Final Years.* Washington: Center of Military History, 1988.

Cleveland, Reginald M. *Air Transport at War.* New York: Harper, 1946.

Clifford, Clark. *Counsel to the President.* New York: Random House, 1991.

Cline. Ray S. *U. S. Army in World War II: Washington Command Post, The Operations Division.* Washington: Office of Chief of Military History, 1951.

Clodfelter, Mark. *The Limits of Air Power: The American Bombing of North Vietnam.* New York: Free Press, 1989.

Coffey, Thomas M. *Decision Over Schweinfurt: The U. S. Eighth Air Force Battle for Daylight Bombing.* New York: David McKay, 1977.

_____. *Hap: The Story of the U. S. Air Force and the Man Who Built It, General Henry H. "Hap" Arnold.* New York: Viking, 1982.

_____. *Iron Eagle: The Turbulent Life of General Curtis LeMay.* New York: Crown, 1986.

Coffman, Edward M. *The War to End All Wars: The American Military Experience in World War I.* Madison, Wisconsin: University of Wisconsin Press, 1986.

Cohen, Eliot A., and John Gooch. *Military Misfortunes: The Anatomy of Failure in War.* New York: Free Press, 1990.

Cole, Alice, Alfred Goldberg, Samuel A. Tucker, and Rudolph A. Winnacker, eds. *The Department of Defense: Documents on Establishment and Organization, 1944–1978.* Washington: Historical Office, Office of the Secretary of Defense, 1978.

Cole, Hugh M. *U. S. Army in World War II: The Ardennes, The Battle of the Bulge.* Washington: Center of Military History, 1993.

Cole, Jean Hascall. *Women Pilots of World War II.* Salt Lake City: University of Utah Press, 1992.

Cole, Wayne S. *Charles A. Lindbergh and the Battle Against American Intervention in World War II.* New York: Harcourt Brace Jovanovich, 1974.

Coleman, John M. *The Development of Tactical Services in the Army Air Forces.* New York: Columbia University Press, 1950.

Colgan, Bill. *Fighter Bomber Pilot*. Blue Ridge Summit, Pennsylvania: Tab Books, 1985.

Collier, Basil. *A History of Air Power*. New York: Macmillan, 1974.

Collier, Richard. *Bridge Across the Sky: The Berlin Blockade and Airlift, 1948–1949*. New York: McGraw-Hill, 1978.

Collins, J. Lawton. *War in Peacetime: The History and Lessons of Korea*. Boston: Houghton Mifflin, 1969.

Collins, Michael. *Carrying the Fire: An Astronaut's Journeys*. New York: Farrar, Straus, Giroux, 1989.

Combs, Harry. *Kill Devil Hill: Discovering the Secret of the Wright Brothers*. Boston: Houghton Mifflin, 1979.

Condit, Doris. *History of the Office of Secretary of Defense. Vol. II, The Test of War, 1950–1953*. Washington: Historical Office, Office of the Secretary of Defense, 1988.

Condit, Kenneth W. *History of the Joint Chiefs of Staff: The Joint Chiefs of Staff and National Policy, 1947–1949*. Washington: Joint History Office, 1996.

Conn, Stetson, Rose C. Engleman, and Byron Fairchild. *U. S. Army in World War II: Guarding the United States and its Outposts*. Washington: Office of Chief of Military History, 1964.

Conn, Stetson, and Byron Fairchild. *U. S. Army in World War II: The Framework of Hemisphere Defense*. Washington: Center of Military History, 1989.

Cooling, Benjamin F., ed. *Case Studies in the Achievement of Air Superiority*. Washington: Center for Air Force History, 1994.

_____. *Case Studies in the Development of Close Air Support*. Washington: Office of Air Force History, 1990.

Copp, DeWitt S. *A Few Great Captains: The Men and Events that Shaped the Development of U. S. Air Power*. Garden City, New York: Doubleday, 1980.

_____. *Forged in Fire: Strategy and Decisions in the Air War over Europe, 1940–1945*. Garden City, New York: Doubleday, 1982.

Corn, Joseph J. *The Winged Gospel: America's Romance with Aviation, 1900–1950*. New York: Oxford University Press, 1983.

Cosmas, Graham A., and Terrence P. Murray. *U. S. Marines in Vietnam: Vietnamization and Redeployment, 1970–1971*. Washington: History and Museums Division, Headquarters, U. S. Marine Corps, 1986.

Couffer, Jack. *Bat Bomb: World War II's Other Secret Weapon*. Austin: University of Texas Press, 1992.

Coulam, Robert F. *Illusions of Choice: Robert McNamara, The F–111, and the Problems of Weapons Acquisition Reform*. Princeton: Princeton University Press, 1977.

Coyne, James P. *Airpower in the Gulf*. Arlington, Virginia: Aerospace Education Foundation, 1992.

Crane, Conrad C. *Bombs, Cities, and Civilians: American Airpower Strategy in World War II.* Lawrence: University Press of Kansas, 1993.

Craven, Wesley Frank, and James Lea Cate, eds. *The Army Air Forces in World War II.* 7 vols. Washington: Office of Air Force History, 1983.

Creech, Bill. *The Five Pillars of TQM: How to Make Total Quality Management Work for You.* New York: Truman Talley Books/Dutton, 1994.

Crouch, Tom D. *The Bishop's Boys: A Life of Wilbur and Orville Wright.* New York: Norton, 1989.

_____. *A Dream of Wings: Americans and the Airplane, 1875–1905.* Washington: Smithsonian, 1983.

_____. *The Eagle Aloft: Two Centuries of the Balloon in America.* Washington: Smithsonian, 1983.

Cumings, Bruce. *The Origins of the Korean War, Liberation and the Emergence of Separate Regimes, 1945–1947.* Princeton: Princeton University Press, 1990.

_____. *The Origins of the Korean War: The Roaring of the Cataract, 1947–1950.* Princeton: Princeton University Press, 1990.

Cuneo, John R. *Winged Mars.* 2 vols. Harrisburg, Pennsylvania: Military Service Publishing Co., 1945-1947.

Currey, Cecil B. *Edward Lansdale: The Unquiet American.* Boston: Houghton Mifflin, 1988.

Davidson, Phillip B. *Vietnam at War: The History, 1946–1975.* Novato, California: Presidio Press, 1988.

Davis, Benjamin O., Jr. *Benjamin O. Davis, Jr., American: An Autobiography.* New York: Plume, 1992.

Davis, Richard G. *Carl A. Spaatz and the Air War in Europe.* Washington: Center for Air Force History, 1993.

_____. *The 31 Initiatives: A Study in Air Force-Army Cooperation.* Washington: Office of Air Force History, 1987.

Davison, Walker Philips. *The Berlin Blockade: A Study in Cold War Politics.* London: Hodder & Stoughton, 1988.

Day, George E. *Return With Honor.* Mesa, Arizona: Champlin Museum Press, 1989.

De Seversky, Alexander P. *Victory Through Air Power.* New York: Simon and Schuster, 1962.

Divine, Robert A. *Eisenhower and the Cold War.* New York: Oxford University Press, 1981.

Dixon, Joe C., ed. *The American Military and the Far East, Proceedings of the Ninth Military History Symposium, U. S. Air Force Academy, Colorado, 1980.* Washington: U. S. Air Force Academy and Office of Air Force History, 1982.

Donald, David, ed. *U. S. Air Force Air Power Directory.* Westport, Connecticut: Aerospace Publishing, 1992.

Donnelly, Thomas, Margaret Roth, and Caleb Baker. *Operation Just Cause: The Storming of Panama*. New York: Lexington Books, 1991.

Donovan, Frank B. *Bridge in the Sky*. London: Hale, 1970.

Doolittle, James H., with Carroll V. Glines. *I Could Never Be So Lucky Again: An Autobiography*. Atglen, Pennsylvania: Schiffer Military/Aviation History, 1995.

Dorwart, Jeffrey M. *Eberstadt and Forrestal: A National Security Partnership, 1909–1949*. College Station: Texas A&M University Press, 1991.

Doubler, Michael D. *Closing with the Enemy: How GIs Fought the War in Europe, 1944–45*. Lawrence: University Press of Kansas, 1994.

Douhet, Giulio. *The Command of the Air*. Washington: Office of Air Force History, 1991.

Dramesi, John A. *Code of Honor*. New York: Norton, 1975.

Drury, Richard S. *My Secret War*. Alexandria, Virginia: Time-Life, 1990.

Dugan, James, and Carrol Stewart. *Ploesti: The Great Air-Ground Battle of 1 August 1943*. New York: Random House, 1962.

Dupre, Flint O. *U. S. Air Force Biographical Dictionary*. New York: Franklin Watts, 1965.

Durand, Arthur A. *Stalug Luft III: The Secret Story*. New York: Simon and Schuster, 1989.

Earle, Edward Mead, ed, with the collaboration of Gordon A. Craig and Felix Gilbert. *Makers of Modern Strategy: Military Thought from Machiavelli to Hitler*. Rev. ed. Princeton: Princeton University Press, 1971.

Edmonds, Walter D. *They Fought with What They Had: The Story of the Army Air Forces in the Southwest Pacific, 1941–1942*. Washington: Center for Air Force History, 1992.

Edwards, Lee. *Goldwater: The Man Who Made a Revolution*. Washington: Regnery, 1995.

Eisenhower, Dwight D. *The White House Years: Mandate For Change, 1953–1956*. Garden City, New York: Doubleday, 1963.

_____. *The White House Years: Waging Peace, 1956–1961*. New York: Doubleday, 1965.

Eschmann, Karl J. *Linebacker: The Untold Story of the Air Raids over North Vietnam*. New York: Ivy, 1989.

Ethell, Jeffrey. *Mustang: A Documentary History of the P–51*. London: Jane's, 1981.

Ethell, Jeffrey, and Alfred Price. *One Day in a Long War: May 10, 1972, Air War, North Vietnam*. New York: Random House, 1989.

Evans, Douglas K. *Sabre Jets Over Korea: A Firsthand Account*. Blue Ridge Summit, Pennsylvania: Tab Books, 1984.

Eyles, Allen. *James Stewart*. Thorndike, Maine: Thorndike Press, 1984.

Feis, Herbert. *The Atomic Bomb and the End of World War II*. Princeton: Princeton University Press, 1966.

Feuer, A. B. *General Chennault's Secret Weapon: The B–24 in China.* Westport, Connecticut: Praeger, 1992.

Field, James A., Jr. *History of United States Naval Operations: Korea.* Washington: GPO, 1962.

Finney, Robert T. *History of the Air Corps Tactical School, 1920–1940.* Washington: Center for Air Force History, 1992

Fisher, Ernest F. *U. S. Army in World War II: Cassino to the Alps.* Washington: Center of Military History, 1993.

Fitzgerald, A. Ernest. *The High Priests of Waste.* New York: Norton, 1972.

Flammer, Philip M. *The Vivid Air: The Lafayette Escadrille.* Athens: University of Georgia Press, 1981.

Flanagan, Edward M., Jr. *Battle for Panama: Inside Operation Just Cause.* Washington: Brassey's, 1993.

Flanagan, John F. *Vietnam Above the Treetops: A Forward Air Controller Reports.* New York: Praeger, 1992.

Fletcher, Eugene. *The Lucky Bastard Club: A B–17 Pilot in Training and in Combat, 1943–45.* Seattle: University of Washington Press, 1992.

Fletcher, Harry R. *Air Force Bases. Vol. II, Air Bases Outside the United States of America.* Washington: Center for Air Force History, 1993.

Foot, Rosemary. *The Wrong War: American Policy and the Dimensions of the Korean Conflict, 1950–1953.* Ithaca, New York: Cornell University Press, 1985.

Ford, Daniel. *Flying Tigers: Claire Chennault and The American Volunteer Group.* Washington: Smithsonian, 1991.

Foulois, Benjamin D., and Carroll V. Glines. *From the Wright Brothers to the Astronauts: The Memoirs of Benjamin Foulois.* New York: Arno, 1980.

Fox, Roger P. *Air Base Defense in the Republic of South Vietnam, 1961–1973.* Washington: Office of Air Force History, 1979.

Foxworth, Thomas. *The Speed Seekers.* Rev. ed. Somerset, England: Haynes, 1989.

Francillon, Rene J. *Vietnam: The War in the Air.* New York: Arch Cape Press, 1987.

Frank, Benis M., and Henry I. Shaw, Jr. *History of U. S. Marine Corps Operations in World War II, Vol. V: Victory and Occupation.* Washington: Historical Branch, Headquarters, U. S. Marine Corps, 1968.

Frankland, Noble. *The Bombing Offensive Against Germany: Outlines and Perspectives.* London: Faber, 1965.

Fredette, Raymond H. *The Sky on Fire: The First Battle of Britain, 1917–1918, and the Birth of the Royal Air Force.* Washington: Smithsonian, 1991.

Freeman, Roger A. *The Mighty Eighth: A History of the Units, Men, and Machines of the U. S. 8th Air Force.* Osceola, Wisconsin: Motorbooks, 1991.
———. *Mighty Eighth War Manual.* Osceola, Wisconsin: Motorbooks, 1991.
———. *Zemke's Wolf Pack: The Story of Hub Zemke and the 56th Fighter*

Group in the Skies over Europe. New York: Orion Books, 1989.

Freeman, Roger A., with Alan Crouchman and Vic Maslen. *Mighty Eighth War Diary.* Rev. ed. London: Arms and Armour, 1990.

Frisbee, John L., ed. *Makers of the United States Air Force.* Washington: Air Force History and Museums Program, 1996.

Futrell, Robert Frank. *Ideas, Concepts, Doctrine: Basic Thinking in the United States Air Force, 1907–1984.* 2 vols. Maxwell Air Force Base, Alabama: Air University Press, 1989.

_____. *The United States Air Force in Korea, 1950–1953.* Washington: Air Force History and Museums Program, 1996.

Futrell, Robert Frank, with the assistance of Martin Blumenson. *The United States Air Force in Southeast Asia: The Advisory Years to 1965.* Washington: Office of Air Force History, 1981.

Gaddis, John Lewis. *Strategies of Containment: A Critical Appraisal of Postwar American National Security Policy.* New York: Oxford University Press, 1982.

_____. *The United States and the Origins of the Cold War: 1941–1947.* New York: Columbia University Press, 1972.

Galbraith, John Kenneth. *A Life in Our Times.* Boston: Houghton Mifflin, 1981.

Galland, Adolf. *The First and the Last, The German Fighter Force in World War II.* London: Fontana, 1970.

Gallucci, Robert L. *Neither Peace Nor Honor: The Politics of American Military Policy in Viet-Nam.* Baltimore: Johns Hopkins University Press, 1975.

Garand, George W., and Truman Strobridge. *History of U. S. Marine Corps Operations in World War II, Vol. 4: Western Pacific Operations.* Washington: Historical Division, Headquarters, U. S. Marine Corps, 1971.

Garland, Albert N., and Howard McGaw Smyth, assisted by Martin Blumenson. *U. S. Army in World War II: Sicily and the Surrender of Italy.* Washington: Office of Chief of Military History, 1965.

Garthoff, Raymond L. *Detente and Confrontation: American-Soviet Relations from Nixon to Reagan.* Rev. ed. Washington: Brookings, 1994.

Geffen, William, ed. *Command and Commanders in Modern Warfare, Proceedings of the Second Military History Symposium, U. S. Air Force Academy, Colorado, 1968.* Washington: U. S. Air Force Academy and Office of Air Force History, 1971.

Genet, E. C. C. *An American for Lafayette.* Charlottesville: University Press of Virginia, 1981.

George, Alexander L. *The Chinese Communist Army in Action: The Korean War and Its Aftermath.* New York: Columbia University Press, 1967.

Gibbs-Smith, Charles H. *Aviation: An Historical Survey from its Origins to the End of World War II.* 2d ed. London: Her Majesty's Stationery Office, 1985.

Gilster, Herman L. *The Air War in Southeast Asia: Case Studies of Selected*

Campaigns. Maxwell Air Force Base, Alabama: Air University Press, 1993.

Glines, Carroll V. *Chennault's Forgotten Warriors: The Saga of the 308th Bomb Group in China.* Atglen, Pennsylvania: Schiffer Military/Aviation History, 1995.

———. *Doolittle's Tokyo Raiders.* New York: Arno, 1980.

Goddard, George W., with DeWitt S. Copp. *Overview: A Lifelong Adventure in Aerial Photography.* Garden City, New York: Doubleday, 1969.

Godfrey, John T. *The Look of Eagles.* New York: Random House, 1958.

Goldberg, Alfred. "General Carl A. Spaatz." In Michael Carver, ed. *The Warlords: Military Commanders of the Twentieth Century.* Boston: Little, Brown, 1976.

Goldberg, Alfred, ed. *A History of the United States Air Force, 1907–1957.* New York: Arno, 1972.

Goldberg, Robert Alan. *Barry Goldwater.* New Haven, Connecticut: Yale University Press, 1995.

Goldwater, Barry M., and Jack Casserly. *Goldwater.* New York: St. Martins, 1989.

Golley, John. *The Day of the Typhoon: Flying with the RAF Tankbusters in Normandy.* Wellingborough, England: Patrick Stephens, 1986.

Goncharov, Sergei N., John W. Lewis, and Xue Litai. *Uncertain Partners: Stalin, Mao, and the Korean War.* Stanford, California: Stanford University Press, 1993.

Gordon, Michael R., and Bernard E. Trainor. *The Generals' War: The Inside Story of the Conflict in the Gulf.* Boston: Little, Brown, 1995.

Gorn, Michael H. *Harnessing the Genie: Science and Technology Forecasting for the Air Force, 1944–1986.* Washington: Office of Air Force History, 1988.

———. *The Universal Man: Theodore von Kármán's Life in Aeronautics.* Washington: Smithsonian, 1992.

Gorn, Michael H. , ed. *Prophecy Fulfilled: 'Toward New Horizons' and Its Legacy.* Washington: Air Force History and Museums Program, 1994.

Gorrell, Edgar S. *The Measure of America's World War Aeronautical Effort.* Northfield, Vermont: Norwich University Press, 1940.

Goulden, Joseph C. *Korea: The Untold Story of the War.* New York: McGraw-Hill, 1982.

Greer, Thomas H. *The Development of Air Doctrine in the Army Air Arm, 1917–1941.* Washington: Office of Air Force History, 1985.

Groh, John E. *Air Force Chaplains, 1971–1980.* Washington: Office of Chief of Air Force Chaplains, 1986.

———. *Facilitators of the Free Exercise of Religion: Air Force Chaplains, 1981–1990.* Washington: Office of Chief of Chaplains, USAF, 1991.

Gropman, Alan L. *The Air Force Integrates, 1945–1964.* Washington: Office of Air Force History, 1978.

History of the United States Air Force

_____. "The Air War in Vietnam, 1961-1973." In R. A. Mason, ed. *War in the Third Dimension: Essays in Contemporary Air Power*. London: Brassey's, 1986.

_____. *USAF Southeast Asia Monograph Series, Vol. V, Airpower and the Airlift Evacuation of Kham Duc*. Washington: Office of Air Force History, 1985.

Grossnick, Roy. *Dictionary of American Naval Aviation Squadrons: Attack Squadrons*. Washington: Naval Historical Center, 1995.

Gross, Charles J. *The Air National Guard and the Persian Gulf Crisis: From Shield to Storm*. Washington: Historical Services Division, National Guard Bureau, 1995.

_____. *Militiaman, Volunteer, and Professional: The Air National Guard and the American Military Tradition*. Washington: Historical Services Division, National Guard Bureau, 1995.

_____. *Prelude to the Total Force: The Air National Guard, 1943–1969*. Washington: Office of Air Force History, 1985.

Grow, Malcolm C. *Surgeon Grow: An American in the Russian Fighting*. New York: Frederick A. Stokes, 1918.

Guarino, Larry. *A POW's Story: 2801 Days in Hanoi*. New York: Ivy, 1990.

Gulf War Air Power Survey. Eleven reports in six volumes. Washington: Office of the Secretary of the Air Force, 1993.

Haig, Alexander M., Jr. *Inner Circles*. New York: Warner Books, 1992.

Haldeman, H. R. *The Haldeman Diaries*. New York: Putnam, 1994.

Hall, James Norman, and Charles B. Nordhoff, with Edgar Hamilton, eds. *The Lafayette Flying Corps*. 2 vols. Port Washington, New York: Kennikat Press, 1964.

Hall, R. Cargill, ed. *Lightning over Bougainville: The Yamamoto Mission Reconsidered*. Washington: Smithsonian, 1991.

Hallion, Richard P. *The Legacy of Flight: The Guggenheim Contribution to American Aviation*. Seattle: University of Washington Press, 1977.

_____. *The Naval Air War in Korea*. Annapolis: Nautical & Aviation, 1986.

_____. *On the Frontier: Flight Research at Dryden, 1946–1981*. Washington: Scientific and Technical Information Branch, National Aeronautics and Space Administration, 1984.

_____. *Rise of the Fighter Aircraft, 1914–1918*. Annapolis: Nautical and Aviation, 1984.

_____. *Storm Over Iraq: Air Power and the Gulf War*. Washington: Smithsonian, 1992.

_____. *Strike from the Sky: The History of Battlefield Air Attack, 1911–1945*. Washington: Smithsonian, 1989.

_____. *Test Pilots: The Frontiersmen of Flight*. Washington: Smithsonian, 1988.

Hammond, Paul Y. *The Cold War Years: American Foreign Policy Since 1945*.

454

New York: Harcourt, Brace, and World, 1969.

Hammond, William H. *The U. S. Army in Vietnam: The Military and the Media, 1962–1968.* Washington: Center of Military History, 1988.

Hanak, Walter K., Lawrence J. Paszek, and James N. Eastman, eds. *Aces and Aerial Victories: The United States Air Force in Southeast Asia, 1965–1973.* Washington: Office of Air Force History, 1977.

Hansell, Haywood S., Jr. *The Strategic Air War against Germany and Japan: A Memoir.* Washington: Office of Air Force History, 1986.

Hansen, James R. *Engineer in Charge: A History of the Langley Aeronautical Laboratory, 1917–1958.* Washington: Scientific and Technical Information Branch, National Aeronautics and Space Administration, 1987.

Hardesty, Von. *Red Phoenix: The Rise of Soviet Air Power, 1941–1945.* Washington: Smithsonian, 1982.

Harrison, Marshall. *A Lonely Kind of War: Forward Air Controller, Vietnam.* Novato, California: Presidio, 1989.

Harvey, Frank. *The Air War—Vietnam.* New York: Bantam, 1967.

Hastings, Max. *Bomber Command.* New York: Simon and Schuster, 1989.

Haugland, Vern. *The AAF Against Japan.* New York: Harper, 1948.

Hayes, Grace Person. *The History of the Joint Chiefs of Staff in World War II: The War against Japan.* Annapolis: Naval Institute, 1982.

Haynes, Richard F. *The Awesome Power: Harry S. Truman as Commander in Chief.* Baton Rouge: Louisiana State University Press, 1973.

Head, William. *Every Inch a Soldier: Augustine Warner Robins and the Building of U. S. Airpower.* College Station: Texas A&M University Press, 1995.

Heller, Francis H., ed. *The Korean War: A 25-Year Perspective.* Lawrence: Regents Press of Kansas, 1977.

Hennessy, Juliette A. *The United States Army Air Arm, April 1861 to April 1917.* Washington: Office of Air Force History, 1985.

Herken, Gregg. *Cardinal Choices: Presidential Science Advising from the Atomic Bomb to SDI.* New York: Oxford University Press, 1992.

———. *Counsels of War.* Rev. ed. New York: Oxford University Press, 1987.

———. *The Winning Weapon: The Atomic Bomb in the Cold War, 1945–1950.* Rev. ed. Princeton: Princeton University Press, 1988.

Hermes, Walter G. *U. S. Army in the Korean War: Truce Tent and Fighting Front.* Washington: Center of Military History, 1992.

Herring, George C. *LBJ and Vietnam: A Different Kind of War.* Austin: University of Texas Press, 1994.

Herz, Martin Forian. *The Prestige Press and the Christmas Bombing, 1972: Images and Reality in Vietnam.* Washington: Ethics and Public Policy Center, 1980.

Hewlett, Richard G., and Oscar E. Anderson, Jr. *A History of the United States Atomic Energy Commission. Vol. I, The New World, 1939–1946.* University

Park: Pennsylvania State University Press, 1962.

Hewlett, Richard G., and Francis Duncan. *A History of the United States Atomic Energy Commission. Vol. II, Atomic Shield, 1947–1952*. University Park: Pennsylvania State University Press, 1969.

Higham, Robin. *Air Power: A Concise History*. New York: St Martin's Press, 1972.

Hinton, Harold B. *Air Victory: The Men and the Machines*. New York: Harper, 1948.

Hitchcock, Walter T., ed. *The Intelligence Revolution: A Historical Perspective, Proceedings of the Thirteenth Military History Symposium, U. S. Air Force Academy, Colorado, 1988*. Washington: U. S. Air Force Academy and Office of Air Force History, 1991.

Holley, I. B. *Ideas and Weapons: Exploitation of the Aerial Weapon by the United States during World War I*. Washington: Office of Air Force History, 1983.

_____. *U. S. Army in World War II: Buying Aircraft; Materiel Procurement for the Army Air Forces*. Washington: Center of Military History, 1989.

Hone, Thomas C. *Power and Change: The Administrative History of the Office of the Chief of Naval Operations, 1946–1986*. Washington: Naval Historical Center, 1989.

Hooper, Edwin Bickford. *Mobility, Support, Endurance: A Story of Naval Operational Logistics in the Vietnam War, 1965–1968*. Washington: Naval History Division, 1972.

Hooper, Edwin Bickford, Dean C. Allard, and Oscar P. Fitzgerald. *The United States Navy and the Vietnam Conflict. Vol. I, The Setting of the Stage to 1959*. Washington: Naval History Division, 1976.

Hoopes, Townsend. *The Limits of Intervention*. Rev. ed. New York: McKay, 1973.

Hoopes, Townsend, and Douglas Brinkley. *Driven Patriot: The Life and Times of James Forrestal*. New York: Knopf, 1992.

Hopkins, J. C., and Sheldon A. Goldberg. *The Development of the Strategic Air Command, 1946–1986*. Offutt Air Force Base, Nebraska: Strategic Air Command, 1986.

Hough, Frank O., Verle E. Ludwig, and Henry I. Shaw, Jr. *History of U. S. Marine Corps Operations in World War II, Vol. I: Pearl Harbor to Guadalcanal*. Washington: Historical Branch, Headquarters, U. S. Marine Corps, 1958.

Howard, Frank, and Bill Gunston. *The Conquest of the Air*. New York: Random House, 1972.

Howard, Fred. *Wilbur and Orville: A Biography of the Wright Brothers*. New York: Knopf, 1987.

Howe, George F. *U. S. Army in World War II: Northwest Africa, Seizing the Initiative in the West*. Washington: Office of Chief of Military History, 1957.

Hubbell, John G., with Andrew Jones and Kenneth Y. Tomlinson. *P.O.W.: A Definitive History of the American Prisoner-of-War Experience in Vietnam, 1964–1973*. New York: Reader's Digest Press, 1976.

Hudson, James J. *Hostile Skies: A Combat History of the American Air Service in World War I*. Syracuse, New York: Syracuse University Press, 1968.

Hughes, Thomas Alexander. *Overlord: General Pete Quesada and the Triumph of Tactical Air Power in World War II*. New York: Free Press, 1995.

Huisken, Ronald. *The Origin of the Strategic Cruise Missile*. New York: Praeger, 1981.

Huntington, Samuel P. *The Common Defense: Strategic Programs in National Politics*. New York: Columbia University Press, 1961.

Hurley, Alfred F. *Billy Mitchell: Crusader for Air Power*. New ed. Bloomington: Indiana University Press, 1975.

Hurley, Alfred F., and Robert C. Erhart, eds. *Air Power and Warfare, Proceedings of the Eighth Military History Symposium, U. S. Air Force Academy, Colorado, 1978*. Washington: Office of Air Force History and U. S. Air Force Academy, 1979.

Infield, Glenn. *Big Week: The Classic Story of the Crucial Air Battle of World War II*. Washington: Brassey's, 1993.

_____. *The Poltava Affair: A Russian Warning, An American Tragedy*. New York: Macmillan, 1973.

_____. *Unarmed and Unafraid*. New York: Macmillan 1970.

Ingells, Douglas J. *The Plane that Changed the World: A Biography of the DC–3*. Fallbrook, California: Aero Publishers, 1966.

_____. *They Tamed the Sky: The Triumph of American Aviation*. New York: D. Appleton-Crofts, 1947.

Isaacson, Walter, and Evan Thomas. *The Wise Men, Six Friends and the World they Made: Acheson, Bohlen, Harriman, Kennan, Lovett, McCloy*. New York: Simon and Schuster, 1988.

Jackson, Robert. *Air War Over Korea*. New York: Scribner, 1975.

Jakab, Peter L. *Visions of a Flying Machine: The Wright Brothers and the Process of Invention*. Washington: Smithsonian, 1990.

Jakeman, Robert. *The Divided Skies: Establishing Segregated Flight Training at Tuskegee, Alabama, 1934–1942*. Tuscaloosa: University of Alabama Press, 1992.

James, D. Clayton. *The Years of MacArthur*. 3 vols. Boston: Houghton Mifflin, 1970–1985.

Jensen, Jay R. *Six Years in Hell: A Returned Vietnam POW Views Captivity, Country, and the Future*. Rev. ed. Orcutt, California: P.O.W. (Publications of Worth), 1989.

Johnson, Clarence L. "Kelly," with Maggie Smith. *Kelly: More Than My Share of It All*. Washington: Smithsonian, 1985.

History of the United States Air Force

Johnson, Lyndon Baines. *The Vantage Point: Perspectives of the Presidency, 1963–1969*. New York: Holt, Rinehart and Winston, 1971.

Johnson, Sam, and Jan Winebrenner. *Captive Warriors: A Vietnam POW's Story*. College Station: Texas A&M University Press, 1992.

Joint Chiefs of Staff, Historical Division. *The Joint Chiefs of Staff and the War in Vietnam: History of the Indochina Incident, 1940–1954*. Wilmington: Delaware: Michael Glazier, 1982.

Jones, R. V. *The Wizard War: British Scientific Intelligence, 1939–1945*. New York: Coward, McCann and Geoghegan, 1978.

Jones, Vincent C. *U. S. Army in World War II: Manhattan, the Army and the Atomic Bomb*. Washington: Center of Military History, 1985.

Jorgensen, Daniel B. *Air Force Chaplains, 1947–1960*. Washington: Office of Chief of Air Force Chaplains, 1963.

———. *The Service of Chaplains to the Army Air Units, 1917–1946*. Washington: Office of the Chief of Air Force Chaplains, 1961.

Josephy, Alvin M. Jr., ed. *The American Heritage Book of Flight*. New York: American Heritage, 1962.

Kahn, Herman. *On Thermonuclear War*. Princeton: Princeton University Press, 1960.

Kaplan, Fred. *The Wizards of Armageddon*. New York: Simon and Schuster, 1983.

Kaufman, Burton I. *The Korean War: Challenges in Crisis, Credibility, and Command*. 2d ed. New York: McGraw-Hill, 1997.

Kaufmann, William W. *The McNamara Strategy*. New York: Harper and Row, 1964.

Kelsey, Benjamin S. *The Dragon's Teeth?: The Creation of United States Air Power for World War II*. Washington: Smithsonian, 1982.

Kennan, George F. *Memoirs, 1925–1950*. Boston: Little, Brown, 1967.

Kennedy, Paul. *The Rise and Fall of the Great Powers*. New York: Random House, 1988.

Kennedy, Robert F. *Thirteen Days: A Memoir of the Cuban Missile Crisis*. New York: Norton, 1969.

Kennett, Lee. *The First Air War, 1914–1918*. New York: Free Press, 1991.

———. *A History of Strategic Bombing*. New York: Scribner, 1982.

Kenney, George C. *General Kenney Reports: A Personal History of the Pacific War*. Washington: Office of Air Force History, 1987.

Kinkead, Eugene. *In Every War But One*. Westport, Connecticut: Greenwood Press, 1981.

Kinnard, Douglas. *President Eisenhower and Strategy Management: A Study in Defense Politics*. Washington: Pergamon-Brassey's, 1989.

Kissinger, Henry M. *The Necessity for Choice*. New York: Harper, 1961.

———. *Nuclear Weapons and Foreign Policy*. New York: Harper, 1957.

———. *White House Years*. Boston: Little, Brown, 1979.

_____. *Years of Upheaval.* Boston: Little, Brown, 1982.

Klass, Philip J. *Secret Sentries in Space.* New York: Random House, 1971.

Knaack, Marcelle Size. *Encyclopedia of U. S. Air Force Aircraft and Missile Systems. Vol. I, Post-World War II Fighters.* Washington: Office of Air Force History, 1986.

_____. *Encyclopedia of U. S. Air Force Aircraft and Missile Systems. Vol. II, Post-World War II Bombers, 1945–1973.* Washington: Office of Air Force History, 1988.

Knebel, Fletcher, and Charles W. Bailey, II. *No High Ground.* Westport, Connecticut: Greenwood, 1983.

Kohn, Richard H., and Joseph P. Harahan, eds. *Air Interdiction in World War II, Korea, and Vietnam: An Interview with Gen. Earle E. Partridge, Gen. Jacob E. Smart, and Gen. John W. Vogt, Jr.* Washington: Office of Air Force History, 1986.

_____. *Air Superiority in World War II and Korea: An Interview with Gen. James Ferguson, Gen. Robert M. Lee, Gen. William Momyer, and Lt. Gen. Elwood Quesada.* Washington: Office of Air Force History, 1983.

_____. *Strategic Air Warfare: An Interview with Generals Curtis E. LeMay, Leon W. Johnson, David A. Burchinal, and Jack J. Catton.* Washington: Office of Air Force History, 1988.

Kreis, John F. *Air Warfare and Air Base Defense, 1914–1973.* Washington: Office of Air Force History, 1988.

Kroll, Harry D., ed. *Kelly Field in the Great World War.* 2d ed. San Antonio, Texas: Press of San Antonio, 1919.

Kurzman, Dan. *Day of the Bomb: Countdown to Hiroshima.* New York: McGraw-Hill, 1986.

La Farge, Oliver. *The Eagle in the Egg.* New York: Arno, 1972.

Larrabee, Eric. *Commander in Chief: Franklin Delano Roosevelt, His Lieutenants, and Their War.* New York: Harper and Row, 1987.

Lash, Joseph P. *Roosevelt and Churchill, 1939–1941: The Partnership That Saved the West.* New York: Norton, 1976.

Lavalle, A. J. C., ed. *USAF Southeast Asia Monograph Series. Vol. II, Airpower and the 1972 Spring Invasion,* Washington: Office of Air Force History, 1985.

_____. *USAF Southeast Asia Monograph Series. Vol. IV, Last Flight from Saigon.* Washington: Office of Air Force History, 1985.

_____. *USAF Southeast Asia Monograph Series. Vol. I, The Tale of Two Bridges and the Battle for the Skies over North Vietnam.* Washington: Office of Air Force History, 1985.

_____. *USAF Southeast Asia Monograph Series. Vol. III, The Vietnamese Air Force, 1951–1975: An Analysis of Its Role in Combat, and Fourteen Hours at Koh Tang.* Washington: Office of Air Force History, 1985.

Lee, Ulysses. *U. S. Army in World War II: The Employment of Negro Troops.*

Washington: Center of Military History, 1994.

Leffler, Melvyn P. *A Preponderance of Power: National Security, the Truman Administration, and the Cold War.* Stanford, California: Stanford University Press, 1992.

LeMay, Curtis E., and MacKinlay Kantor. *Mission with LeMay: My Story.* Garden City, New York: Doubleday, 1965.

LeMay, Curtis E., and Bill Yenne. *Superfortress: The Story of the B–29 and American Air Power.* New York: McGraw-Hill, 1988.

Lewin, Ronald. *American Magic: Codes, Ciphers, and the Defeat of Japan.* New York: Farrar, Straus, Giroux, 1982.

_____. *Ultra Goes to War.* New York: McGraw-Hill, 1978.

Lewy, Guenter. *America in Vietnam.* New York: Oxford University Press, 1978.

Lincke, Jack R. *Jenny Was No Lady: The Story of the JN–4D.* New York: Norton, 1970.

Link, Mae Mills, and Hubert A. Coleman. *Medical Support of the Army Air Forces in World War II.* Washington: Office of the Surgeon General, USAF, 1991.

Littauer, Raphael, and Norman Uphoff, eds. *The Air War in Indochina.* Rev. ed. Boston: Beacon Press, 1972.

Lomperis, Timothy J. *The War Everyone Lost—And Won: America's Intervention in Viet Nam's Twin Struggles.* Rev. ed. Washington: CQ Press, 1993.

Lukas, Richard. *Eagles East: The Army Air Forces and the Soviet Union.* Tallahassee: Florida State University, 1970.

MacArthur, Douglas. *Reminiscences.* New York: McGraw-Hill, 1964.

MacDonald, Callum A. *Korea: The War before Vietnam.* New York: Free Press, 1987.

MacDonald, Charles B. *U. S. Army in World War II: The Siegfried Line Campaign.* Washington: Office of Chief of Military History, 1963.

MacGregor, Morris J., Jr. *Integration of the Armed Forces, 1940–1965.* Washington: Center of Military History, 1981.

MacIsaac, David. "The Evolution of Air Power Since 1945: The American Experience." In R. A. Mason, ed. *War in the Third Dimension: Essays in Contemporary Air Power.* London: Brassey's, 1986.

_____. *Strategic Bombing in World War II: The Story of the United States Strategic Bombing Survey.* New York: Garland, 1976.

Mahurin, Walker M. *Honest John: The Autobiography of Walker M. Mahurin.* Alexandria, Virginia: Time-Life, 1993.

Mann, Edward C., III. *Thunder and Lightning: Desert Storm and the Airpower Debates.* Maxwell Air Force Base, Alabama: Air University Press, 1995.

Manning, Thomas A., ed. *History of Air Training Command, 1943–1993.* Randolph Air Force Base, Texas: Air Education and Training Command, 1993.

Mark, Eduard. *Aerial Interdiction: Air Power and the Land Battle in Three American Wars*. Washington: Center for Air Force History, 1992.

Marolda, Edward J. *By Sea, Air, and Land: An Illustrated History of the U. S. Navy and the War in Southeast Asia*. Washington: Naval Historical Center, 1994.

Marolda, Edward J., and Oscar P. Fitzgerald. *The United States Navy and the Vietnam Conflict. Vol. II, From Military Assistance to Combat, 1959–1965*. Washington: Naval Historical Center, 1986.

Marolda, Edward J., ed. *Operation End Sweep: A History of Minesweeping Operations in North Vietnam*. Washington: Naval Historical Center, 1993.

Martin, David C., and John Walcott. *Best Laid Plans: The Inside Story of America's War against Terrorism*. New York: Harper and Row, 1988.

Matloff, Maurice. *U. S. Army in World War II: Strategic Planning for Coalition Warfare, 1943–1944*. Washington: Office of Chief of Military History, 1959.

Matloff, Maurice, and Edwin M Snell. *U. S. Army in World War II: Strategic Planning for Coalition Warfare, 1941–1942*. Washington: Office of Chief of Military History, 1953.

Maurer, Maurer. *Aviation in the U. S. Army, 1919–1939*. Washington: Office of Air Force History, 1987.

Maurer, Maurer, ed. *Air Force Combat Units of World War II*. Washington: Office of Air Force History, 1987.

_____. *Combat Squadrons of the Air Force, World War II*. Washington: Office of Air Force History, 1982.

_____. *The U. S. Air Service in World War I*. 4 vols. Washington: Office of Air Force History, 1978-1979.

May, Ernest. *"Lessons" of the Past: The Use and Misuse of History in American Foreign Policy*. London: Oxford University Press, 1973.

McAulay, Lex. *Battle of the Bismarck Sea*. New York: St. Martin's, 1991.

McCarthy, James R. *USAF Southeast Asia Monograph Series. Vol. VI, Linebacker II: A View from the Rock*. Washington: Office of Air Force History, 1985.

McClendon, R. Earl. *Autonomy of the Air Arm*. Washington: Air Force History and Museums Program, 1996.

_____. *Unification of the Armed Forces: Administrative and Legislative Developments, 1945–1949*. Maxwell Air Force Base, Alabama: Air University Press, 1952.

McConnell, Malcolm. *Just Cause: The Real Story of America's High-Tech Invasion of Panama*. New York: St. Martin's, 1991.

_____. *Into the Mouth of the Cat: The Story of Lance Sijan, Hero of Vietnam*. New York: Norton, 1985.

McDougall, Walter A. *The Heavens and the Earth: A Political History of the Space Age*. New York: Basic Books, 1985.

McFarland, Stephen L. *America's Pursuit of Precision Bombing, 1910–1945*.

Washington: Smithsonian, 1995.

McFarland, Stephen L., and Wesley Phillips Newton. *To Command the Sky: The Battle for Air Superiority over Germany, 1942–1944*. Washington: Smithsonian, 1991.

McGovern, James R. *Black Eagle: General Daniel "Chappie" James, Jr.* Tuscaloosa: University of Alabama Press, 1985.

_____. *Crossbow and Overcast*. New York: Morrow, 1964.

McNamara, Robert S. *In Retrospect: The Tragedy and lessons of Vietnam*. New York: Times Books, 1995.

McNeill, William H. *The Pursuit of Power: Technology, Armed Force, and Society Since A.D. 1000*. Chicago: University of Chicago Press, 1982.

Meid, Pat, and James M. Yingling. *U. S. Marine Operations in Korea, Vol. V: Operations in West Korea*. Washington: Historical Division, Headquarters, U. S. Marine Corps, 1972.

Meilinger, Phillip S. *Hoyt Vandenberg: The Life of a General*. Bloomington: Indiana University Press, 1989.

Melia, Tamara Moser. *"Damn the Torpedoes": A Short History of U. S. Naval Mine Countermeasures, 1777–1991*. Washington: Naval Historical Center, 1991.

Melson, Charles D., and Curtis G. Arnold. *U. S. Marines in Vietnam: The War that Would Not End, 1971–1973*. Washington: History and Museums Division, Headquarters, U. S. Marine Corps, 1991.

Mersky, Peter B., and Norman Polmar. *The Naval Air War in Vietnam*. Annapolis: Nautical and Aviation, 1981.

Mets, David R. *Master of Airpower: General Carl A. Spaatz*. Novato, California: Presidio Press, 1988.

Middlebrook, Martin. *The Schweinfurt-Regensburg Mission*. New York: Scribner, 1983.

Mierzejewski, Alfred C. *The Collapse of the German War Economy, 1944–1945: Allied Air Power and the German National Railway*. Chapel Hill: University of North Carolina Press, 1988.

Mikesh, Robert C. *Japan's World War II Balloon Bomb Attack on North America*. Washington: Smithsonian, 1973.

Miller, John, Jr. *U. S. Army in World War II: Cartwheel, The Reduction of Rabaul*. Washington: Center of Military History, 1984.

_____. *U. S. Army in World War II: Guadalcanal, The First Offensive*. Washington: Historical Division, Department of the Army, 1949.

Miller, Roger G., ed. *Seeing off the Bear: Anglo-American Air Power Cooperation During the Cold War*. Washington: Air Force History and Museums Program, 1995.

Millett, Allan R., and Peter Maslowski. *For the Common Defense: A Military History of the United States of America*. New York: Free Press, 1984.

Millis, Walter. *Arms and Men: A Study in American Military History*. New

York: Putnam. 1956.

Millis, Walter, ed. *The Forrestal Diaries*. New York: Viking, 1951.

Millot, Bernard. *Divine Thunder: The Life and Death of the Kamikazes*. New York: McCall, 1971.

Mitchell, Vance O. *Air Force Officers: Personnel Policy Development, 1944–1974*. Washington: Air Force History and Museums Program, 1997.

Mitchell, William. *Memoirs of World War I: "From Start to Finish of Our Greatest War."* Westport, Connecticut: Greenwood Press, 1975.

_____. *Winged Defense: The Development and Possibilities of Modern Air Power–Economic and Military*. New York: Dover, 1988.

Mixter, George W., and Harold H. Emmons. *United States Army Aircraft Production Facts*. Washington: GPO, 1919.

Molesworth, Carl. *Wing to Wing: Air Combat in China, 1943–45*. New York: Orion Books, 1990.

Momyer, William W. *Air Power in Three Wars*. Washington: Office of Air Force History, 1985.

Montross, Lynn, and Nicholas A. Canzona, based on research by K. Jack Bauer. *U. S. Marine Operations in Korea, Vol. III: The Chosin Reservoir Campaign*. Washington: Historical Branch, Headquarters, U. S. Marine Corps, 1957.

_____. *U. S. Marine Operations in Korea, Vol. II: The Inchon-Seoul Operation*. Washington: Historical Branch, Headquarters, U. S. Marine Corps, 1955.

_____. *U. S. Marine Operations in Korea, Vol. I: The Pusan Perimeter*. Washington: Historical Branch, Headquarters, U. S. Marine Corps, 1954.

Montross, Lynn, Hubard D. Kuokka, and Norman W. Hicks. *U. S. Marine Operations in Korea, Vol. IV: The East-Central Front*. Washington: Historical Branch, Headquarters, U. S. Marine Corps, 1962.

Moody, Walton S. *Building a Strategic Air Force*. Washington: Air Force History and Museums Program, 1996.

Morison, Samuel Eliot. *History of United States Naval Operations in World War II*. 15 vols. Boston: Little, Brown, 1947–1962.

Morrison, Wilbur H. *Point of No Return: The Story of the 20th Air Force*. New York: Times Books, 1979.

Morrow, John H., Jr. *The Great War in the Air: Military Aviation from 1909 to 1921*. Washington: Smithsonian, 1993.

Morse, Stan, ed. *Gulf Air War Debrief*. London: Aerospace Publishing, 1991.

Mortensen, Daniel. *A Pattern for Joint Operations: World War II Close Air Support, North Africa*. Washington: Office of Air Force History and Center of Military History, 1987.

Morton, Louis. *U. S. Army in World War II: The Fall of the Philippines*. Washington: Center of Military History, 1993.

_____. *U. S. Army in World War II: Strategy and Command, The First Two Years*. Washington: Office of Chief of Military History, 1962.

Mossman, Billy C. *U. S. Army in the Korean War: Ebb and Flow, November*

History of the United States Air Force

1950–July 1951. Washington: Center of Military History, 1990.

Mrozek, Donald J. *Air Power and the Ground War in Vietnam*. Washington: Pergamon-Brassey's, 1989.

_____. *The U. S. Air Force After Vietnam Postwar Challenges and Potential for Responses*. Maxwell Air Force Base, Alabama: Air University Press, 1988.

Mueller, Robert. *Air Force Bases. Vol. I, Active Air Force Bases with in the United States of America on 17 September 1982*. Rev. ed. Washington, 1989.

Muirhead, John. *Those Who Fall*. New York: Random House, 1986.

Murray, Williamson. *Strategy for Defeat: The Luftwaffe, 1933–1945*. Washington: Brassey's, 1996.

Murray, Williamson, MacGregor Knox, and Alvin Bernstein. *The Making of Strategy: Rulers, States, and War*. Cambridge: Cambridge University Press, 1994.

Nalty, Bernard C. *Air Power and the Fight for Khe Sanh*. Washington: Office of Air Force History, 1986.

_____. *Strength for the Fight: A History of Black Americans in the Military*. New York: Free Press, 1986.

Nalty, Bernard C., John F. Shiner, and George M. Watson. *With Courage: The U. S. Army Air Forces in World War II*. Washington: Air Force History and Museums Program, 1994.

Nalty, Bernard C. ed. *War in the Pacific: Pearl Harbor to Tokyo Bay*. London: Salamander, 1991.

Neufeld, Jacob. *The Development of Ballistic Missiles in the U. S. Air Force, 1945–1960*. Washington: Office of Air Force History, 1990.

Neufeld, Jacob, and James C. Hasdorff. "The View From The Top: Oral Histories of Chief Master Sergeants of the Air Force." In David R. Segal and H. Wallace Sinaiko, eds. *Life in the Rank and File: Enlisted Men and Women in the Armed Forces of the United States, Australia, Canada, and the United Kingdom*. Washington: Pergamon-Brassey's, 1986.

Neufeld, Jacob, ed. *Reflections on Research and Development in the United States Air Force: An Interview with General Bernard A. Schriever and Generals Samuel C. Phillips, Robert T. Marsh, and James H. Doolittle, and Dr. Ivan A. Getting*. Washington: Center for Air Force History, 1993.

Newhouse, John. *Cold Dawn: The Story of SALT*. Washington: Pergamon-Brassey's, 1989.

_____. *War and Peace in the Nuclear Age*. New York: Knopf, 1989.

Nitze, Paul H., with Ann M. Smith and Steven L. Rearden. *From Hiroshima to Glasnost: At the Center of Decision, a Memoir*. New York: Weidenfeld, 1989.

Nixon, Richard. *RN: The Memoirs of Richard Nixon*. New York: Simon & Schuster, 1990.

Nordeen, Lon O. Jr. *Air Warfare in the Missile Age*. Washington: Smithsonian, 1985.

O'Grady, Scott. *Return with Honor*. New York: Doubleday, 1995.

Osgood, Robert E. *Limited War: The Challenge to American Strategy.* Chicago: University of Chicago Press, 1957.

_____. *Limited War Revisited.* Boulder, Colorado: Westview, 1979.

Osur, Alan. *Blacks in the Army Air Forces during World War II.* Washington: Office of Air Force History, 1977.

Overy, R. J. *The Air War, 1939–1945.* New York: Stein and Day, 1980.

Paige, Glenn D. *The Korean Decision.* New York: Free Press, 1968.

Palmer, Michael A. *Guardians of the Gulf: A History of America's Expanding Role in the Persian Gulf.* New York: Free Press, 1992.

_____. *On Course to Desert Storm: The United States Navy and the Persian Gulf.* Washington: Naval Historical Center, 1992.

_____. *Origins of the Maritime Strategy: American Naval Strategy in the First Postwar Decade.* Washington: Naval Historical Center, 1988.

Paret, Peter, ed. *Makers of Modern Strategy: From Machiavelli to the Nuclear Age.* New York: Oxford University Press, 1986.

Parmet, Herbert S. *Eisenhower and the American Crusades.* New York: Macmillan, 1972.

Parrish, Thomas. *The Ultra Americans: The U. S. Role in Breaking the Nazi Codes.* New York: Stein and Day, 1986.

Parton, James. *"Air Force Spoken Here": General Ira Eaker and the Command of the Air.* Bethesda, Maryland: Adler and Adler, 1986.

Pearson, Henry G. *A Business Man in Uniform: Raynal Cawthorne Bolling.* New York: Duffield, 1923.

Perret, Geoffrey. *Winged Victory: The Army Air Forces in World War II.* New York: Random House, 1993.

Pisano, Dominick. *To Fill the Sky with Pilots: The Civilian Pilot Training Program, 1939–1946.* Champaign: University of Illinois Press, 1993.

Pogue, Forrest C. *George C. Marshall: Ordeal and Hope, 1939–1942.* New York: Viking, 1986.

_____. *George C. Marshall: Organizer of Victory, 1943–1945.* New York: Viking, 1973.

_____. *George C. Marshall: Statesman, 1945–1959.* New York: Viking, 1987.

Poole, Walter S. *History of the Joint Chiefs of Staff: The Joint Chiefs of Staff and National Policy, 1950–1952.* Wilmington, Delaware: Michael Glazier, 1980.

Powell, Colin, with Joseph Persico. *My American Journey.* New York: Random House, 1995.

Prange, Gordon, W. *Miracle at Midway.* New York: McGraw-Hill, 1982.

Prange, Gordon, W., with Donald M. Goldstein and Katherine V. Dillon. *At Dawn We Slept: The Untold Story of Pearl Harbor.* New York: McGraw-Hill, 1981.

Price, Alfred. *Instruments of Darkness: The History of Electronic Warfare.* New York: Scribner, 1978.

History of the United States Air Force

Puryear, Edgar F., Jr. *George S. Brown, General, U. S. Air Force: Destined for Stars*. Novato, California: Presidio, 1983.

_____. *Stars in Flight: A Study in Air Force Character and Leadership*. Novato, California: Presidio, 1981.

Putney, Diane T., ed. *Ultra and the Army Air Forces in World War II: An Interview with Associate Justice of the U. S. Supreme Court Lewis F. Powell, Jr*. Washington: Office of Air Force History, 1987.

Quester, George H. *Deterrence Before Hiroshima: The Airpower Background of Modern Strategy*. New York: Wiley, 1966.

Rae, John B. *Climb to Greatness: The American Aircraft Industry, 1920–1960*. Cambridge, Massachusetts: MIT Press, 1968.

Ravenstein, Charles A. *Air Force Combat Wings: Lineage and Honors Histories, 1947–1977*. Washington: Office of Air Force History, 1984.

_____. *The Organization and Lineage of the United States Air Force*. Washington: Office of Air Force History, 1986.

Rearden, Steven L. *The Evolution of American Strategic Doctrine: Paul H. Nitze and the Soviet Challenge*. Boulder, Colorado: Westview, 1984.

_____. *History of the Office of the Secretary of Defense, Vol. I, The Formative Years, 1947–1950*. Washington: Historical Office, Office of the Secretary of Defense, 1984.

Reddel, Carl W., ed. *Transformation in Russian and Soviet Military History., Proceedings of the Twelfth Military History Symposium, U. S. Air Force Academy, Colorado, 1986*. Washington: U. S. Air Force Academy and the Office of Air Force History.

Rees, David. *Korea: The Limited War*. New York: St Martins, 1964.

Reynolds, Richard T. *Heart of the Storm: The Genesis of the Air Campaign Against Iraq*. Maxwell Air Force Base, Alabama: Air University Press, 1995.

Rhodes, Richard. *The Making of the Atomic Bomb*. New York: Simon & Schuster, 1986.

Rice, Berkeley. *The C–5A Scandal: An Inside Story of the Military-Industrial Complex*. Boston: Houghton Mifflin, 1971.

Rich, Ben, and Leo Janos. *Skunk Works: A Personal Memoir of My Years at Lockheed*. Boston: Little, Brown, 1994.

Richards, Denis. *Royal Air Force, 1939–1945. Vol. I, The Fight at Odds, 1939–1941*. London: Her Majesty's Stationery Office, 1953.

Richards, Denis, and Hilary St. G Saunders. *The Fight Avails, Vol. II, Royal Air Force, 1939–1945*. London: Her Majesty's Stationery Office, 1954.

Rickenbacker, Edward V. *Rickenbacker*. Englewood Cliffs, New Jersey: Prentice-Hall, 1967.

Ridgway, Matthew B. *The Korean War*. Garden City, New York: Doubleday, 1967.

Risner, Robinson. *The Passing of the Night: My Seven Years as a Prisoner of the North Vietnamese*. New York: Random House, 1974.

Robbins, Christopher. *The Ravens: The Men Who Flew in America's Secret War in Laos.* New York: Crown, 1987.

Robinson, Douglas H. *The Dangerous Sky: A History of Aviation Medicine.* Seattle: University of Washington Press, 1973.

Roland, Alex. *Model Research: The National Advisory Committee for Aeronautics, 1915–1958.* 2 vols. Washington: Scientific and Technical Information Branch, National Aeronautics and Space Administration, 1985.

Romanus, Charles F., and Riley Sunderland. *U. S. Army in World War II: Stilwell's Command Problems.* Washington: Center of Military History, 1987.

_____. *U. S. Army in World War II: Stilwell's Mission to China.* Washington: Center of Military History, 1987.

_____. *U. S. Army in World War II: Time Runs Out in the CBI.* Washington: Center of Military History, 1990.

Roseberry, C. R. *Glenn Curtiss: Pioneer of Flight.* Garden City, New York: Doubleday, 1972.

Rostow, W. W. *The Diffusion of Power: An Essay in Recent History.* New York: Macmillan, 1972.

_____. *Pre-Invasion Bombing Strategy: General Eisenhower's Decision of March 25, 1944.* Austin: University of Texas Press, 1981.

Rothgeb, Wayne P. *New Guinea Skies: A Fighter Pilot's View of World War II.* Ames: Iowa State University Press, 1992.

Rowan, Stephan A. *They Wouldn't Let Us Die: The Prisoners of War Tell Their Story.* Middle Village, New York: Jonathan David, 1973.

Rutkowski, Edwin H. *The Politics of Military Aviation Procurement, 1926–1934.* Columbus: Ohio State University Press, 1966.

Ryan, Paul B. *The Iranian Rescue Mission: Why It Failed.* Annapolis: Naval Institute, 1985.

Samson, Jack. *Chennault.* New York: Doubleday, 1987.

Saunders, Hilary St. G. *The Fight Is Won, Vol. III, Royal Air Force, 1939–1945.* London: Her Majesty's Stationery Office, 1954.

_____. *Per Ardua: The Rise of British Air Power, 1911–1939.* New York: Arno, 1972.

Scales, Robert H., Jr. *Certain Victory: the U. S. Arm in the Gulf War.* Washington: Office of the Chief of Staff, U. S. Army, 1993.

Schaffel, Kenneth. *The Emerging Shield: The Air Force and the Evolution of Continental Air Defense, 1945–1960.* Washington: Office of Air Force History, 1991.

Schaffer, Ronald. *Wings of Judgment: American Bombing in World War II.* New York: Oxford University Press, 1985.

Schandler, Herbert Y. *The Unmaking of a President: Lyndon Johnson and Vietnam.* Princeton: Princeton University Press, 1977.

Scharlemann, Martin H. *Air Force Chaplains, 1961–1970.* Washington: Office of Chief of Air Force Chaplains, nd.

Scharr, Adela Rick. *Sisters in the Sky: The WAFS.* Gerald, Missouri: Patrice Press, 1986.

Schemmer, Benjamin F. *The Raid.* New York: Harper and Row, 1976.

Schilling, Warner R., Paul Y. Hammond, and Glenn H. Snyder. *Strategy, Politics, and Defense Budgets.* New York: Columbia University Press, 1962.

Schlight, John. *The United States Air Force in Southeast Asia; The War in South Vietnam: The Years of the Offensive, 1965–1968.* Washington: Office of Air Force History, 1988.

Schnabel, James F. *History of the Joint Chiefs of Staff: The Joint Chiefs of Staff and National Policy, 1945–1947.* Wilmington, Delaware: Michael Glazier, 1979.

_____. *U. S. Army in the Korean War: Policy and Direction, the First Year.* Washington: Center of Military History, 1992.

Schnabel, James F., and Robert J. Watson. *History of the Joint Chiefs of Staff: The Joint Chiefs of Staff and National Policy: The Korean War.* Wilmington, Delaware: Michael Glazier, 1979.

Schneider, Donald K. *USAF Southeast Asia Monograph Series, Vol. VII, Air Force Heroes in Vietnam.* Washington: Office of Air Force History, 1985.

Schratz, Paul R., ed. *Evolution of the American Military Establishment Since World War II.* Lexington, Virginia: George C. Marshall Research Foundation, 1978.

Schubert, Frank N., and Theresa L. Kraus, eds. *The Whirlwind War: The U. S. Army in Operations Desert Shield and Desert Storm.* Washington: Center of Military History, 1995.

Schwarzkopf, H. Norman, with Peter Petre. *It Doesn't Take a Hero: General H. Norman Schwarzkopf, the Autobiography.* New York: Bantam Books, 1992.

Scott, Robert Lee, Jr. *The Day I Owned the Sky.* New York: Bantam, 1988.

Shaller, Michael. *The American Occupation of Japan: The Origins of the Cold War in Asia.* New York: Oxford University Press, 1985.

Shapley, Deborah. *Promise and Power: The Life and Times of Robert McNamara.* Boston: Little, Brown, 1993.

Sharp, U. S. G. *Strategy for Defeat: Vietnam in Retrospect.* San Rafael, California: Presidio, 1978.

Shaw, Henry I, Jr., and Douglas T. Kane. *History of U. S. Marine Corps Operations in World War II, Vol. II: Isolation of Rabaul.* Washington: Historical Branch, Headquarters, U. S. Marine Corps, 1963.

Shaw, Henry I., Jr., Bernard C. Nalty, and Edwin T. Turnbladh. *History of U. S. Marine Corps Operations in World War II, Vol. III: Central Pacific Drive.* Washington: Historical Branch, Headquarters, U. S. Marine Corps, 1966.

Shawcross, William. *Sideshow: Kissinger, Nixon, and the Destruction of Cambodia.* New York: Simon and Schuster, 1979.

Sherrod, Robert L. *History of United States Marine Corps Aviation in World War II.* Baltimore: Nautical and Aviation, 1987.

Sherry, Michael S. *Preparing for the Next War: American Plans for Postwar Defense, 1941–1945.* New Haven, Connecticut: Yale University Press, 1977.
_____. *The Rise of American Air Power: The Creation of Armageddon.* New Haven, Connecticut: Yale University Press, 1987.

Shiner, John F. *Foulois and the U. S. Army Air Corps, 1931–1935.* Washington: Office of Air Force History, 1983.

Showalter, Dennis, and John G. Albert, eds. *An American Dilemma: Vietnam, 1964–73.* Chicago: Imprint Publications, 1993.

Shrader, Charles R. *Communist Logistics in the Korean War.* Westport, Connecticut: Greenwood Press, 1995.

Shulimson, Jack. *U. S. Marines in Vietnam: An Expanding War, 1966.* Washington: History and Museums Division, Headquarters, U. S. Marine Corps, 1982.

Shulimson, Jack, and Charles M. Johnson. *U. S. Marines in Vietnam: The Landing and The Buildup, 1965.* Washington: History and Museums Division, Headquarters, U. S. Marine Corps, 1978.

Slessor, John C. *The Central Blue.* London: Cassell & Co., 1956.

Smallwood, William L. *Strike Eagle: Flying the Strike Eagle in the Gulf War.* Washington: Brassey's, 1994.

Smith, Charles R. *U. S. Marines in Vietnam: High Mobility and Standdown, 1969.* Washington: History and Museums Division, Headquarters, U. S. Marine Corps, 1988.

Smith, Dale O. *U. S. Military Doctrine: A Study and Appraisal.* New York: Duell, Sloan, and Pearce, 1955.

Smith, Felix. *China Pilot: Flying for Chiang and Chennault.* Washington: Brassey's, 1995.

Smith, Perry M. *The Air Force Plans for Peace, 1943–1945.* Baltimore: Johns Hopkins University Press, 1970.

Smith, Peter C. *Dive Bomber.* Annapolis: Naval Institute, 1982.

Smith, Peter C. *Vengeance: The Vultee Vengeance Dive Bomber.* Washington: Smithsonian, 1986.

Smith, Robert Ross. *U. S. Army in World War II: The Approach to the Philippines.* Washington: Center of Military History, 1996.

Snyder, Thomas S., ed. *The Air Force Communications Command: Providing the Reins of Command, 1938–1981, an Illustrated History.* Scott Air Force Base, Illinois: Air Force Communications Command History Office, 1981.

Spaatz, Carl. *Report of the Chief of Staff United States Air Force to the Secretary of the Air Force.* Washington: GPO, 1948.

Spector, Ronald H. *Eagle Against The Sun: The American War with Japan.* New York: Free Press, 1985.
_____. *U. S. Army in Vietnam: Advice and Support, The Early Years, 1941–1960.* Washington: Center of Military History, 1983.

Speer, Albert. *Inside the Third Reich.* New York: Macmillan, 1970.

History of the United States Air Force

Stares, Paul B. *The Militarization of Space: U. S. Policy, 1945–1984*. Ithaca, New York: Cornell University Press, 1985.

Stein, Harold, ed. *American Civil-Military Decisions: A Book of Case Studies*. Tuscaloosa: University of Alabama Press, 1963.

Stephens, Alan, ed. *The War in the Air, 1914–1994: Proceedings of a conference held by the Royal Australian Air Force in Canberra, March 1994*. Fairbairn, Australia: RAAF Air Power Studies Center, 1994.

Stewart, James T., ed. *Airpower: The Decisive Force in Korea*. Princeton: D. Van Nostrand, 1957.

Stimson, Henry L., and McGeorge Bundy. *On Active Service in Peace and War*. New York: Octagon Books, 1971.

Stokesbury, James L. *A Short History of Air Power*. New York: Morrow, 1986.

Stueck, William W.. *The Korean War: An International History*. Princeton: Princeton University Press, 1995.

Sturm, Thomas A. *The USAF Scientific Advisory Board: Its First Twenty Years, 1944–1964*. Washington: Office of Air Force History, 1986.

Suchenwirth, Richard. *Historical Turning Points in the German War Effort*. New York: Arno Press, 1968.

Summers, Harry G. *On Strategy: The Vietnam War in Context*. Carlisle Barracks, Pennsylvania: US Army War College, Strategic Studies Institute, 1981.

Swain, Richard M. *"Lucky War": Third Army in Desert Storm*. Fort Leavenworth, Kansas: U. S. Army Command and General Staff College, 1994.

Swanborough, F. Gordon, and Peter Bowers. *United States Military Aircraft Since 1909*. Third edition. Washington: Smithsonian, 1989.

Sweetser, Arthur. *The American Air Service: A Record of its Problems, Its Difficulties, its Failures, and Its Final Achievement*. New York: D. Appleton, 1919.

Taylor, John W. R., and David Mondey. *Spies in the Sky*. New York: Scribner, 1973.

Taylor, John W. R., and Kenneth Munson. *History of Aviation*. New York: Crown, 1972.

Taylor, Maxwell D. *Swords into Plowshares*. New York: Norton, 1972.

Tedder, Arthur. *With Prejudice: The War Memoirs of Marshal of the Royal Air Force, Lord Tedder*. Boston: Little, Brown, 1966.

Telfer, Gary L., Lane Rogers, and V. Keith Fleming, Jr. *U. S. Marines in Vietnam: Fighting the North Vietnamese, 1967*. Washington: History and Museums Division, Headquarters, U. S. Marine Corps, 1984.

Termena, Bernard J., Layne B. Peiffer, and H. P. Carlin. *Logistics: An Illustrated History of the AFLC and Its Antecedents, 1921–1981*. Wright-Patterson Air Force Base, Ohio: Office of History, Air Force Logistics Command, 1981.

Terraine, John. *A Time for Courage: The Royal Air Force in the European War, 1939–1945*. New York: Macmillan, 1985.

Thayer, Lucien H. *America's First Eagles: The Official History of the U. S. Air Service, A.E.F. (1917–1918)*. Edited by Donald Joseph McGee and Roger James Bender. San Jose, California: R. J. Bender, 1983.

Thies, Wallace J. *When Governments Collide: Coercion and Diplomacy in the Vietnam Conflict, 1964–1968*. Berkeley: University of California Press, 1980.

Thomas, Lowell, and Edward Jablonski. *Doolittle: A Biography*. Garden City, New York: Doubleday, 1976.

Thompson, James Clay. *Rolling Thunder: Understanding Policy and Program Failure*. Chapel Hill: The University of North Carolina Press, 1980.

Thompson, Wayne, ed. *Air Leadership*. Washington: Office of Air Force History, 1986.

Tibbets, Paul. W., with Clair Stebbins and Harry Franken. *The Tibbets Story*. New York: Stein and Day, 1978.

Tilford, Earl H., Jr. *Search and Rescue in Southeast Asia, 1961–1965*. Washington: Office of Air Force History, 1980.

_____. *Setup: What the Air Force Did in Vietnam and Why*. Maxwell Air Force Base, Alabama: Air University Press, 1991.

Tillman, Stephen. *Man Unafraid: History of Military Aviation, 1907–1917*. Washington: Army Times Publishing Company, 1958.

Titus, James, ed. *The Home Front and War in the Twentieth Century: The American Experience in Comparative Perspective, Proceedings of the Tenth Military History Symposium, U. S. Air Force Academy, Colorado, 1982*. Washington: U. S. Air Force Academy and Office of Air Force History, 1984.

Toulmin, Harry A. *Air Service: American Expeditionary Force, 1918*. New York: Van Nostrand, 1927.

Tourison, Sedgwick. *Secret Army, Secret War: Washington's Tragic Spy Operation in North Vietnam*. Annapolis: Naval Institute, 1995.

Trimble, William F. *Wings for the Navy: A History of the Naval Aircraft Factory, 1917–1956*. Annapolis: Naval Institute, 1990.

Truman, Harry S. *Years of Decision*. Garden City, New York: Doubleday, 1955.
_____. *Years of Trial and Hope*. Garden City, New York: Doubleday, 1956.

Tunner, William H. *Over the Hump*. Washington: Office of Air Force History, 1985.

U. S. Army War College Historical Section. *The Signal Corps and Air Service: A Study of Their Expansion in the United States, 1917–1918*. Washington: GPO, 1922.

Ulam, Adam. *The Rivals: America and Russia Since World War II*. New York: Viking, 1971.

Underwood, Jeffery S. *The Wings of Democracy: The Influence of Air Power on the Roosevelt Administration, 1933–1941*. College Station: Texas A&M University Press, 1991.

History of the United States Air Force

Van Dyke, Jon M. *North Vietnam's Strategy for Survival*. Palo Alto, California: Pacific Books, 1972.

Van Staaveren, Jacob. *The United States Air Force in Southeast Asia: Interdiction in Southern Laos, 1960–1968*. Washington: Center for Air Force History, 1993.

VanDeMark, Brian. *Into the Quagmire: Lyndon Johnson and the Escalation of the Vietnam War*. New York: Oxford University Press, 1991.

Vander Meulen, Jacob A. *The Politics of Aircraft: Building an American Military Industry*. Lawrence: University Press of Kansas, 1991.

Venkus, Robert E. *Raid on Qaddafi: The Untold Story of History's Longest Fighter Mission by the Pilot Who Directed It*. New York: St. Martins, 1992.

Verges, Marianne. *On Silver Wings: The Women Airforce Service Pilots in World War II, 1942–1944*. New York: Ballantine, 1991.

Vick, Alan. *Snakes in the Eagle's Nest: A History of Ground Attacks on Air Bases*. Santa Monica, California: Rand, 1995.

Von Kármán, Theodore, with Lee Edson. *The Wind and Beyond: Theodore von Kármán, Pioneer in Aviation and Pathfinder in Space*. Boston: Little, Brown, 1967.

Wagner, Ray. *American Combat Planes*. Garden City, New York: Doubleday, 1968.

_____. *Mustang Designer: Edgar Schmued and the Development of the P–51*. New York: Orion, 1990.

Walker, Lois E., and Shelby E. Wickam. *From Huffman Prairie to the Moon: The History of Wright-Patterson Air Force Base*. Washington: Air Force Logistics Command, 1986.

Warden, John A., III. *The Air Campaign: Planning for Combat*. Washington: National Defense University Press, 1988.

Warnock, A. Timothy. *Air Force Combat Medals, Streamers, and Campaigns*. Washington: Office of Air Force History, 1990.

Watson, George M., Jr. *The Office of the Secretary of the Air Force, 1947–1965*. Washington: Center for Air Force History, 1992.

Watson, Mark Skinner. *U. S. Army in World War II: Prewar Plans and Preparations*. Washington: Center of Military History, 1985.

Watson, Robert J. *History of the Joint Chiefs of Staff: The Joint Chiefs of Staff and National Policy, 1953–1954*. Washington: Historical Division, Joint Chiefs of Staff, 1986.

Watts, Barry. *The Foundations of U. S. Air Doctrine: The Problem of Friction in War*. Maxwell Air Force Base, Alabama: Air University Press, 1984.

Webster, Charles, and Noble Frankland. *The Strategic Air Offensive Against Germany, 1939–1945*. 4 vols. London: Her Majesty's Stationery Office, 1961.

Weigley, Russell F. *The American Way of War: A History of United States Military Strategy and Policy*. New York: Macmillan, 1973.

472

_____. *Eisenhower's Lieutenants: The Campaign of France and Germany, 1944–1945*. Bloomington: Indiana University Press, 1981.

Weinberg, Gerhard L. *A World at Arms: A Global History of World War II*. New York: Cambridge University Press, 1994.

Weintraub, Stanley. *The Last Great Victory: The End of World War II, July–August 1945*. New York: Talley Books/Dutton, 1995.

Weir, Gary E. *Building American Submarines, 1919–1940*. Washington: Naval Historical Center, 1991.

_____. *Forged in War: The Naval Industrial Complex and American Submarine Construction, 1940–1961*. Washington: Naval Historical Center, 1993.

Werrell, Kenneth P. *Archie, Flak, AAA, and SAM: A Short Operational History of Ground-Based Air Defense*. Maxwell Air Force Base, Alabama: Air University Press, 1988.

_____. *The Evolution of the Cruise Missile*. Maxwell Air Force Base, Alabama: Air University Press, 1985.

Westheimer, David. *Sitting it Out: A World War II POW Memoir*. Houston: Rice University Press, 1992.

Wheeler, Gerald E. *Kinkaid of the Seventh Fleet: A Biography of Admiral Thomas C. Kinkaid*. Washington: Naval Historical Center, 1995.

White, William Lindsay. *The Captives of Korea: An Unofficial White Paper on the Treatment of War Prisoners, Our Treatment of Theirs, Their Treatment of Ours*. Westport, Connecticut: Greenwood Press, 1978.

Whiting, Allen S. *China Crosses the Yalu: The Decision to Enter the Korean War*. Stanford, California: Stanford University Press, 1968.

Williams, William J., ed. *A Revolutionary War: Korea and the Transformation of the Postwar World*. Chicago: Imprint Publications, 1993.

Winnefeld, James A., and Dana J. Johnson. *Joint Air Operations: Pursuit of Unity in Command and Control, 1942–1991*. Annapolis: Naval Institute, 1993.

Winnefeld, James A., Preston Niblack, and Dana J. Johnson. *A League of Airmen: U. S. Air Power in the Gulf War*. Santa Monica, California: Rand, 1994.

Winter, Denis. *The First of the Few: Fighter Pilots of the First World War*. Athens: University of Georgia Press, 1983.

Wolf, Richard I., ed. *The United States Air Force: Basic Documents on Roles and Missions*. Washington: Office of Air Force History, 1987.

Wolk, Herman S. "George C. Kenney: MacArthur's Premier Airman." In William Leary, ed. *We Shall Return: MacArthur's Commanders and the Defeat of Japan*. Lexington: University Press of Kentucky, 1988.

_____. "Planning and Organizing the Air Force." *USAF 1947: A Retrospect*. Manhattan, Kansas: Sunflower University Press, 1987.

_____. *The Struggle for Air Force Independence, 1943–1947*. Washington, Air Force History and Museums Program, 1997.

Woodward, Bob. *The Commanders*. New York: Simon & Schuster, 1991.
Wright, Monte D., and Lawrence J. Paszek, eds. *Science, Technology, and Warfare, Proceedings of the Third Military History Symposium, U. S. Air Force Academy, Colorado, 1969*. Washington: U. S. Air Force Academy and Office of Air Force History, 1972.
_____. *Soldiers and Statesmen, Proceedings of the Fourth Military History Symposium, U. S. Air Force Academy, Colorado, 1970*. Washington: Office of Air Force History and U. S. Air Force Academy, 1973.
Yarborough, Tom. *Da Nang Diary: A Forward Air Controller's Year of Combat over Vietnam*. New York: St. Martins, 1990.
Yeager, Chuck and Leo Janos. *Yeager: An Autobiography*. Boston: G. K. Hall, 1986.
Yergin, Daniel. *Shattered Peace: The Origins of the Cold War and the National Security State*. Boston: Houghton Mifflin, 1977.
Zhang, Shu Guang. *Mao's Military Romanticism: China and the Korean War, 1950–1953.* Lawrence, Kansas: University Press of Kansas, 1995.

Articles

Anthis, Rollen H., "Airpower: The Paradox in Vietnam." *Air Force*, L (April 1967).
Barnes, John K. "The Vindication of Squier and Deeds: What Really Happened to the Billion Dollar Aircraft Appropriation." *World's Work*, XLII (July 1921).
Blank, Jonas L. "The Impact of Logistics on Strategy." *Air University Press Review*, XXIV (March–April 1973).
Bonney, Walter T. "Chiefs of the Army Air Force, 1907–1957." *Airpower Historian*, VII (July 1960).
Borowski, Harry R. "Air Force Atomic Capabilities From V–J Day to the Berlin Blockade—Potential or Real." *Military Affairs*, XLIV (October 1980).
_____. "A Narrow Victory: The Berlin Blockade and the American Military Response." *Air University Press Review*, XXXII (July–August 1981).
Bowers, Ray L. "Americans in the Vietnamese Air Force: The Dirty Thirty." *Aerospace Historian*, XIX (Fall 1972).
_____. "USAF Airlift and the Airmobility Idea in Vietnam." *Air University Press Review*, XXVI (November–December 1974).
Boylan, Bernard L. "The Search for a Long-Range Escort Plane." *Military Affairs*, XXX (Summer 1966).
Brands, H. W., Jr. "Testing Massive Retaliation: Credibility and Crisis Management in the Taiwan Strait." *International Security*, (Spring 1988).
Brodie, Bernard. "The Heritage of Douhet." *Air University Press Quarterly Review*, VI (Summer 1953).

Brown, Jerold E. "From The Ground Up: Air Planning in the Office of the Chief Signal Officer, 1917-1918." *Aerospace Historian*, XXXIII (Fall/September 1986).

Buckingham, William A., Jr. "Operation Ranch Hand: Herbicides in Southeast Asia." *Air University Press Review*, XXXIV (July–August 1983).

Chandler, Charles DeF. "General James Allen: Father of Army Aviation." *U. S. Air Services*, XIX (March 1933).

Chang, Gordon H. "To the Nuclear Brink: Eisenhower, Dulles, and the Quemoy-Matsu Crisis." *International Security*, XII (Spring 1988).

Davis, Daniel T. "The Air Role in the War Between the States." *Air University Press Review*, XXVII (July–August 1976).

Davis, Richard G. "Bombing Strategy Shifts, 1944–1945." *Air Power History*, XXXVI (Winter 1989).

_____. "Carl A. Spaatz and Royal Air Force-U. S. Army Air Corps Relationship, 1939–1940." *Journal of Military History*, LIV (October 1990).

Davis, Shadrack E. "U. S. Air Force War Readiness Materiel, 1946–1966." *Air University Press Review*, XVIII (July–August 1967).

Donnini, Frank P. "Douhet, Caproni, and Early Air Power." *Air Power History*, XXXVII (Summer 1990).

Eastman, James N. "The Development of Big Bombers." *Aerospace Historian*, XXV (Winter 1978).

Ennels, Jerome A. "Maxwell Flood Relief." *Air Power History*, XXXVI (Spring 1989).

_____. "Chennault's Trapezers: How One Team Revived and Revolutionized Fighter Tactics." *Air Power Journal*, (Spring 1994).

Falk, Stanley. "General Kenney, the Indirect Approach, and the B-29s." *Aerospace Historian*, XXVII (Fall/September 1981).

Fredette, Raymond H. "Rickenbacker: 'Most Natural Leader I Ever Saw'." *Air Force Magazine*, LVII (April 1974).

_____. "Watch For Burning Balloons." *Air Force Magazine*, LVI (September 1973).

Fritsche, Carl H. "Liberators on the Kwai." *Aerospace Historian*, XXX (Summer/June 1983).

Fuller, John F. "Weather and War." *Aerospace Historian*, XXIII (Spring 1976).

Gardner, Trevor, "How We Fell Behind in Guided Missiles." *Airpower Historian*, V (January 1958).

Gorrell, Edgar S. "Why Riding Boots Sometimes Irritate an Aviator's Feet." *U. S. Air Services*, XVII (October 1932).

Greenwood, John T. "The Air Force Ballistic Missile and Space Program (1954-1974)." *Aerospace Historian*, XXI (Winter 1974).

_____. "The Atomic Bomb—Early Air Force Thinking and the Strategic Air Force, August 1945–March 1946." *Aerospace Historian*, XXXIV (Fall/September 1987).

History of the United States Air Force

Greer, Thomas H. "Air Arm Doctrinal Roots, 1917-1918." *Military Affairs*, XX (Winter 1956).

Gross, Charles J. "The Birth of the Air National Guard, 1943-1946: A Case Study in Institutional Politics." *Military Affairs*, XLIX (April 1985).

———. "George Owen Squier and the Origins of American Military Aviation." *Journal of Military History*, LIV (July 1990).

Gunderson, Brian S. "8th Air Force Newsboys—Cheddington Revisited." *Aerospace Historian*, XXXI (Winter/December 1984).

Hall, R. Cargill, "The B-58 Bomber." *Air University Press Review*, XXXIII (November–December 1981).

Hallion, Richard P. "Battlefield Air Support: A Subjective Assessment." *Airpower Journal*, IV (Spring 1990).

———. "Doctrine, Technology, and Air Warfare: A Late Twentieth Century Perspective." *Airpower Journal*, I (Fall 1987).

———. "A Troubling Past: Air Force Fighter Acquisition since 1956." *Airpower Journal*, IV (Winter 1990).

Harris, J. P. "The Myth of Blitzkrieg." *War in History*, II (November 1995).

Hasdorff, James C. "Jerry Lee, Founding Father of the Philippine Air Force." *Aerospace Historian*, XX (Winter 1973).

———. "Reflections on the Tuskegee Experience: An Interview with Brig. Gen. Noel Parrish, USAF (Ret.)." *Aerospace Historian*, XXIV (Fall 1977).

Herring, George C. "American Strategy in Vietnam: The Postwar Debate." *Military Affairs*, XLVI (April 1982).

Hines, Calvin W. "First Aero Squadron in Mexico." *American Aviation Historical Society Journal*, X (Fall 1965).

Holley, I. B. "Of Saber Charges, Escort Fighters, and Spacecraft." *Air University Press Review*, XXXIV (September–October 1983).

Jacobs, W. A. "Strategic Bombing and American National Strategy." *Military Affairs*, L (July 1986).

———. "Tactical Air Doctrine and AAF Close Air Support in the European Theater, 1944-1945." *Aerospace Historian*, XXVII (Spring 1980).

Keefer, Edward C. "President Dwight D. Eisenhower and the End of the Korean War." *Diplomatic History*, X (Summer 1986).

Kerby, Robert L. "Air Force Transport Operations in Southeast Asia, 1960-1963." *Aerospace Historian*, XXII (Spring 1975).

Kirkendall, Richard S. "Harry S. Truman and the Creation of the Air Force." *Aerospace Historian*, XXXIV (Fall/September 1987).

Kitchens, James H., III. "The Bombing of Auschwitz Re-examined." *Journal of Military History*, LVIII (April 1994).

Kohn, Richard H., and Joseph P. Harahan, eds. "U. S. Strategic Air Power, 1948–1962: Excerpts from an Interview with Generals Curtis E. LeMay, Leon W. Johnson, David A. Burchinal, and Jack Catton." *International Security*, XII (Spring 1988).

Krauskopf, Robert W. "The Army and the Strategic Bomber, 1930-1939." *Military Affairs*, XXII (Summer 1978).

Launius, Roger D. "The Berlin Airlift: Constructive Air Power." *Air Power History*, XXXVI (Spring 1989).

Leary, William M. "The CIA and the 'Secret War' in Laos: The Battle for Skyline Ridge, 1971-1972." *Journal of Military History*, LIX (July 1995).

Leonard, Raymond W. "Learning from History: Linebacker II and U. S. Air Force Doctrine." *Journal of Military History*, LVIII (April 1994).

Lowe, Thomas E. "The 481st TFS in Vietnam: A Personal Account." *American Historical Society Journal*, XX (Summer 1975).

Lytton, Henry D. "Bombing Policy in the Rome and Pre-Normandy Invasion Aerial Campaigns of World War II: Bridge-Bombing Vindicated and Railyard-Bombing Strategy Invalidated." *Military Affairs*, XLVII (April 1983).

Mark, Eduard. "A New Look at Operation Strangle." *Military Affairs*, LII (October 1988).

Maurer, Maurer. "The Constitutional Basis of the United States Air Force." *Air University Press Quarterly Review*, XVI (January–February 1965).

_____. "The 1st Aero Squadron, 1913–1917." *Air Power Historian*, IV (October 1957).

Maurer, Maurer, and Calvin F. Senning. "Billy Mitchell, the Air Service, and the Mingo War." *Airpower Historian*, XII (Spring 1965).

McCarthy, James R. "A Quarter Century of Air Force Maintenance." *Aerospace Historian*, XXIX (March 1982).

Miller, Roger G. "Signal Corps No. 1: Purchasing and Supporting the Army's First Airplane." *Air Power History*, XLI (Fall 1994).

_____. "Wings and Wheels: The 1st Aero Squadron, Truck Transport, and the Punitive Expedition of 1916." *Air Power History*, XLI (Winter 1995).

Mitchell, William. "The Air Service at the Argonne-Meuse." *World's Work*, XXXVIII (no. 5, 1919).

_____. "The Air Service at St. Mihiel." *World's Work*, XXXVIII (no. 4, 1919).

Moody, Walton S. "United States Air Forces in Europe and the Beginning of the Cold War." *Aerospace Historian*, XXIII (June 1976).

Osur, Alan M. "Black-White Relations in the U. S. Military, 1940-1972." *Air University Press Review*, XXXIII (November–December 1981).

Parkinson, Russell. "United States Signal Corps Balloons, 1871-1902." *Military Affairs*, XXIV (Winter 1960-1961).

Parks, W. Hays. "Air War and the Law of War." *Air Force Law Review*, XXXII (1990).

_____. "Linebacker and the Law of War." *Air University Press Review*, XXXIV (January–February 1983).

_____. "Rolling Thunder and the Law of War." *Air University Press Review*, XXXIII (January–February 1982).

Parrish, Noel F. "Vandenberg: Rebuilding the Shoestring Air Force." *Air Force Magazine*, LXIV (August 1981).

Parton, James. "The Thirty-One Year Gestation of the Independent USAF." *Aerospace Historian*, XXXIV (Fall/September 1987).

Paszek, Lawrence J. "Separate But Equal? The Story of the 99th Fighter Squadron." *Aerospace Historian*, XXIV (Fall/September 1977).

Powe, Marc B. "A Great Debate: The American General Staff, 1903–1916." *Military Review*, LV (December 1975).

Putney, Diane T. "From Instant Thunder to Desert Storm." *Air Power History*, XLI (Fall 1994).

Quirk, Richard W. "Pacific Theater in World War II: Challenges to Air Logistics." *Air Force Journal of Logistics*, X (Spring 1986).

Ransom, Harry H. "The Battleship Meets the Airplane." *Military Affairs*, XXIII (Spring 1959).

Rawlings, Edwin W. "The Evolution of Air Logistics." *Air University Press Quarterly Review*, XI (Spring 1959).

Rosenberg, David A. "American Atomic Strategy and the Hydrogen Bomb Decision," *Journal of American History*, LXVI (1979).

_____. "The Origins of Overkill: Nuclear Weapons and American Strategy, 1945-1960." *International Security*, VII (Spring 1983).

_____. "U. S. Nuclear Stockpile 1945-1950." *Bulletin of the Atomic Scientists*, XXXVIII (May 1982).

Schaffel, Kenneth. "A Minority of One: Major General Gordon P. Saville." *American Aviation Historical Society Journal*, XXXII (Summer 1987).

_____. "Muir S. Fairchild: Philosopher of Air Power." *Aerospace Historian*, XXXIII (Fall/September 1986).

Schlight, John. "Civilian Control of the Military in Southeast Asia." *Air University Press Review*, XXXII (November–December 1980).

Shiner, John F. "Birth of GHQ Air Force." *Military Affairs*, XLII (October 1978).

_____. "The General and the Subcommittee: Congress and U. S. Army Air Corps Chief Benjamin Foulois, 1934–1935." *Journal of Military History*, LV (Spring 1991).

Sights, Albert P., Jr. "The Lessons of Lebanon: A Study in Air Strategy." *Air University Press Review*, XVI (July–August 1965).

Smith, Robert P. "Maintenance on the Cheap: Air Force Logistics, 1907–1917." *Air Force Journal of Logistics*, XI (Spring 1987).

Stueck, William. "The Korean War as International History." *Diplomatic History*, X (Fall 1986).

Sturm, Thomas A. "American Air Defense: The Decision to Proceed." *Aerospace Historian*, XIX (Winter 1972).

_____. "Henry Conger Pratt: First Air Corps Permanent General Officer." *Aerospace Historian*, XXII (Summer 1975).

Tilford, Earl H., Jr. "The Development of Search and Rescue: World War II to 1961." *Aerospace Historian*, XXIV (Winter 1977).

Trest, Warren A. "Four Decades of Global Deterrence." *Aerospace Historian*, XXXIV (Fall/September 1987).

_____. "The Legacy of Halfway Unification." *Air University Press Review*, XXXVII (September–October 1986).

_____. "Projects CHECO and Corona Harvest." *Aerospace Historian*, XXXIII (Summer 1986).

_____. "Scores of Pilots, Clouds of Planes." *Air Power Journal*, I (Summer 1987).

_____. "A View from the Gallery: Laying to Rest the Admiral's Revolt of 1949." *Air Power History*, XLII (Spring 1995).

Tuttle, Dwight W. "None But the Fit Shall Fly: The Origins of the Air Force Medical Service." *Air Power History*, XXXVIII (Spring 1991).

Twining, Nathan F. "The Twentieth Air Force." *Military Review*, XXVI (June 1946).

Ullman, Bruce L. "The War Balloon Santiago." *Aerospace Historian*, XXXII (Summer/June 1985).

Watkins, Tarleton H. "Operation New Tape: The Congo Airlift." *Air University Press Quarterly Review*, XIII (Summer 1961).

Watson, George M., Jr. "Cutting the Umbilical Cord: The USAF Medical Service Achieves Independence." *Air Power History*, XXXVIII (Spring 1991).

_____. "A Flight Surgeon's Diary: Malcolm C. Grow's 1934 Alaskan Flight Account." *Air Power History*, XXXIX (Summer 1991).

_____. "Malcolm Grow and the Russian Connection." *USAF Medical Service Digest*, XLII (Spring 1991).

_____. "Man in the Middle: Eugene Zuckert as Secretary of the Air Force." *Air Power History*, XXXVI (Summer 1989).

_____. "Medical Support for Just Cause." *USAF Medical Service Digest*, XLI (Spring 1990).

_____. "The Refugee Children of Operation Babylift, April–May 1975." *USAF Medical Service Digest*, XLI (Summer 1990).

_____. "Stuart Symington—The First Secretary of the Air Force, 18 September 1947-24 April 1950." *Aerospace Historian*, XXXIV (Fall/September 1987).

Weathersby, Kathryn. "Korea, 1949–50: To Attack, or Not to Attack? Stalin, Kim Il Sung, and the Prelude to War." *Cold War International History Project Bulletin*, V (Spring 1995).

_____. "The Soviet Role in the Early Phase of the Korean War: New Documentary Evidence." *Journal of American-East Asian Relations*, II (Winter 1993).

Werrell, Kenneth P. "Linebacker II: The Decisive Use of Air Power." *Air University Press Review*, XXXVIII (January–March 1987).

_____. "The Weapon the Military Did Not Want: The Modern Strategic Cruise Missile." *Journal of Military History*, LIII (October 1989).

Westover, Oscar. "Influence of Air Warfare on Logistics." *The Quartermaster Review*, XIV (January–February 1935).

Wohlstetter, Albert J. "The Delicate Balance of Terror." *Foreign Affairs*, XXXVII (January 1959).

Wolfe, Thomas K. "Truest Sport: Jousting with Sam and Charlie." *Esquire*, LXXXIV (October 1975).

Wolk, Herman S. "The B-29, The A-Bomb, and the Japanese Surrender." *Air Force Magazine*, LVIII (February 1975).

_____. "The Fight for Independence." *Air Force Magazine*, LXXIX (July 1996).

Wolk, Herman S., and Richard P. Hallion. "FDR and Truman: Continuity and Context in the A-Bomb Decision." *Airpower Journal*, IX (Fall 1995).

Zeybel, Henry. "Truck Count." *Air University Press Review*, XXXIV (January–February 1983).

Authors

The authors of this volume, except for Alfred Francis Hurley, were members of the Office of Air Force History, which was renamed the Center for Air Force History in 1992, which became the Air Force History Support Office in 1995.

Bernard C. Nalty (General Editor)

Before retiring in 1994, he was a senior historian at the Office of Air Force History. He earned a B.A. from Creighton University and an M.A. from Catholic University and served as an officer in the U.S. Army from 1953 to 1955. He has written *Air Power and the Fight for Khe Sanh* (1973), an Air Force monograph on the Vietnam War; *Tigers over Asia* (1978), an account of the Flying Tigers during World War II; *Strength for the Fight: A History of Black Americans in the Military* (1986); and two pamphlets dealing with the Marine Corps in World War II—*Cape Gloucester: The Green Inferno* (1994) and *The Right to Fight: African American Marines in World War II* (1995). He is coauthor with Henry I. Shaw Jr. and Edwin T. Turnbladh of *Central Pacific Drive* (1966), a volume in the history of Marine Corps operations in World War II. With Morris J. MacGregor, Jr., he edited the 13-volume *Blacks in the United States Armed Forces: Basic Documents* and its single-volume abridgement: *Blacks in the Military: Essential Documents* (1981).

William C. Heimdahl

Currently the Deputy Air Force Historian at Headquarters U.S. Air Force, he has been a historian with the Air Force history program since 1978. Before assuming his present position, he was the Chief of the Research Division for the Air Force History Support Office. He served in the U.S. Army from 1966 to 1970 and earned a B.A. from the University of Maryland and an M.A. from George Washington University. He was a historian at the Naval Historical Center from 1972 to 1975 and an archivist at the National Archives and Records Administration from 1976 to 1978.

Alfred Francis Hurley

He retired from the Air Force in 1980, as a brigadier general, after a 30-year career, including 19 years as a faculty member of the Department of History at the Air Force Academy, the last 14 as head of the department. He earned a B.A. from St. John's University, New York, and an M.A. and a Ph.D. from Princeton University. Along with writing numerous articles, he is the author of *Billy*

Mitchell: Crusader for Air Power (1964) and co-editor of *Air Power and Warfare* (1978). He currently is Chancellor of the University of North Texas in Denton and the University of North Texas Health Science Center at Fort Worth. He also is President of the Denton campus and a professor of history.

Daniel R. Mortensen
Currently senior civilian historical adviser at the Headquarters U.S. Air Force Historical Branch, he has been part of Air Force history program since 1978. He received a B.A. and an M.A. in history from the University of California, Riverside, and a Ph.D. from the University of Southern California. He taught at several institutions in southern California, including USC, Pepperdine, and Loyola, and at the University of Maryland, College Park. Before coming to the Office of Air Force History in 1981, he served as deputy command historian of the Air Force Communications Command at Scott Air Force Base, Illinois. He specializes in the history of communications, aviation technology, and tactical aviation and has presented papers on all these topics. In 1986 he was temporarily assigned to the U.S. Army Center of Military history, where he wrote *A Pattern for Joint Operations: World War II Close Air Support, North Africa* (1987). He is currently completing two histories of World War II tactical aviation for the Air Force History Support Office.

John F. Shiner (1942–1995)
A career Air Force Officer, retiring as a colonel in 1991, he began his profession as a pilot and flew C–123 cargo planes in Vietnam, where he received the Distinguished Flying Cross. He was an assistant professor of history at the Air Force Academy and served with the Directorate of Plans, Headquarters U.S. Air Force. Besides writing many articles, he is also the author of *Foulois and the U.S. Army Air Corps, 1931–1935* (1983). He received a B.S. from Capital University, an M.A. from the University of Maryland, and a Ph.D. from Ohio State University. Before retiring, Colonel Shiner served as Deputy Chief of the Office of Air Force History.

Warren A. Trest
Before retiring in 1996, he was senior historian with the Air Force Historical Research Agency, Maxwell Air Force Base, Alabama. A Korean War veteran, he joined the Air Force history program in 1962. He headed the history programs at Air Training Command and U.S. Air Forces in Europe, and he was the Histories Division Chief with the Office of Air Force History. While a member of the CHECO team in Vietnam, 1966–1968, he authored or co-authored fifteen special studies on the employment of air power in Southeast Asia. He helped establish and direct Project CORONA HARVEST activities within Headquarters Pacific Air Forces, which produced a series of reports evaluating the Air Force's operations in the Southeast Asian war. His book

about roles and missions is to be published by the Air Force History and Museums Program.

George M. Watson, Jr.

An Air Force historian since 1975, he is now Chief of the Special Projects Team at the Air Force History Support Office and has held various management positions within the Air Force history program, including Chief, Air Staff History Division, and Chief Historian, Office of the Air Force Surgeon General. He has written several books, including *The Office of the Secretary of the Air Force, 1947–1965* (1994); written numerous articles; and conducted many published interviews. He served in the 101st Airborne Division in Vietnam from 1969 to 1970. He earned a B.A. from the University of Maine, an M.A. from Niagara University, and a Ph.D. from The Catholic University of America.

Herman S. Wolk

He is the Senior Historian at the Air Force History Support Office. He served in the U.S. Army from 1953 to 1955. Before joining the Headquarters U.S. Air Force history program, he was a historian at the Strategic Air Command Headquarters (1959–1966). He holds B.A. and M.A. degrees from the American International College, Springfield, Massachusetts, and has studied at the Far Eastern and Russian Institute, University of Washington, under a Ford Foundation Grant. In 1974–1975 he served as a member of the Office of the Secretary of Defense Special Project on the History of the Strategic Arms Competition. He is a Fellow of the Inter-university Seminar on Armed Forces and Society. Among his many publications are *The Struggle for Air Force Independence, 1943–1947* (1997), *Strategic Bombing: The American Experience* (1981), *Evolution of the American Military Establishments Since World War II* (co-authored, 1978), and several essays on the career and contributions of Gen. George C. Kenney. He also authored "General Arnold, the Atomic Bomb, and Surrender of Japan," a chapter in *The Pacific War Revisited* (1997), which is to be published by the Louisiana State University Press.

Photographs

Index

Japan, bombing of: 343, 347, 351, 352, 356, 360
Lend-Lease: 235
maintenance and supply: 246
modernization and expansion: 233, 235
North Africa theater of operations: 270
Officer Candidate School establishment: 250
organization and structure: 132, 183
P-51 Mustang: 242
Pacific theater of operations: 196, 210–11, 216, 217, 222
before Pearl Harbor: 148, 154, 155, 162
pilot training: 255
pursuit aircraft: 141
research and development: 408
rockets: 176
strategy and tactics: 209
training and education: 263
Universal Military Training: 385–87
war production: 173
post-World War I: 71–72, 77, 83, 90, 98, 103, 118, 124, 129, 139
World War II: 201, 234
World War I service: 45, 50, 68
Atomic weapons. *See* Nuclear weapons and warfare.
Attu Island: 220–21
Augusta, Georgia: 23, 61
Australia: 204, 216, 221, 222, 327
Australian air force: 335
Austria: 379
Aviation engineers: 259–50, 272, 311, 348, 350
Aviation equipment development: 87, 139–40, 263–65, 284
Aviation industry, European: 24
Aviation industry, German: 40, 167–68, 170, 232, 300, 301, 302
Aviation industry, Japan: 215
Aviation industry, United Kingdom: 168, 243
Aviation industry, U.S.
automobile industry, mobilization of: 173
competitive bidding: 136–37
fighters: 236
jet aircraft: 243
post-World War I: 78
pre-World War II: 172–74, 231–32
World War I: 43, 44, 45–48, 49–51, 69–70

World War II: 203, 215, 232–33, 234, 235
aircraft development: 240–43
aircraft modification: 244–45
automobile industry participation: 237–38
engine production: 238
procurement process: 237
production: 236–37, 250, 267, 301
profiteering: 237
quantity *vs.* quality issue: 239–40
tax breaks and profit incentives: 237
work force: 238–39

Baker, Addison L.: 294
Baker, George P.: 413
Baker, Newton D.: 44, 50, 51, 74, 75, 126, 127
Baker Board: 126–27, 130, 136, 141, 146, 155, 156
Baldwin, Sgt. Ivy: 6
Baldwin, Thomas S.: 6, 9, 12, 13, 18
Balloon and Airship School: 81
Balloons, aviation
California Arrow: 12
Civil War: 3–5
competitions: 9
Cuba liberation: 6
dirigibles: 8–9, 11–13, 12, 14–15, 36, 37, 40–41, 77
Akron crash: 121
Roma crash: 77
Shenandoah disaster: 98
World War I: 36
disadvantages of: 5, 14–15
General Myer balloon: 6
materials: 4, 6
observation balloon companies: 55
Santiago observation balloon: 6
tethered balloons: 37, 55–56, 77
weather observation: 5–6
zeppelins: 8–9, 11
Barber, Rex: 330
Barbulesco, C. D.: 125
Barksdale Field, Louisiana: 129
Barling, Walter: 92
Barrows, Arthur S.: 400
Barwell, George: 294
Bateson, Charles R.: 307
Batista Field, Cuba: 361
Beck, Paul W.: 18, 19, 20, 27, 28

Made in the USA
Coppell, TX
19 October 2021